H.C.
CHANG

*Chinese
Literature*

FOR MY
WIFE

H.C.
CHANG

*Chinese
Literature*

*Popular
Fiction and
Drama*

COLUMBIA
*University
Press*

Library of Congress Cataloging in Publication Data
Main entry under title:

Chinese literature.

Vol. 1: Reprint. Originally published:
Edinburgh: Edinburgh University Press;
Chicago: Aldine Pub. Co., 1973.
Includes bibliographical references.
Contents: [1] Popular fiction and drama—
[2] Nature poetry.
1. Chinese literature—Translations into
English.   2. English literature—Translations
from Chinese.   I. Chang, H. C. (Hsin-Chang)
PL2658.E1C56   1977   895.1′1′008   81-174030
AACR2
ISBN 0-231-05367-3 (pbk.: v. 1)

Columbia University Press

New York

Foreword

This is a self-contained study and anthology of two related aspects of Chinese literature: fiction in the colloquial language, and the drama. Should the response to it prove favourable, it is hoped to make it the first of a series covering the most important areas of Chinese literary culture.

This book, and such a series, is addressed to the general reading public as well as students of Chinese. It does not offer an assortment of eloquent and moving passages from the whole range of Chinese literature; its aim is to give the Western reader a really close view of certain significant activities on the Chinese literary scene. Thus each volume will be confined to one or two types of writing, and will comprise fresh translations of works or portions of works chosen to illustrate one facet of literary history. A critical survey of its subject will be a feature of each volume.

Projected volumes are:
2. *Nature Poetry*;
3. *Poets and their Creeds*;
4. *Painting and Poetry*;
5. *Autobiography and the Essay*;
and 6. *Tales of the Supernatural*.

Contents

Preface

The purpose of this book is to introduce the English reader to two contiguous realms of Chinese literature, fiction in the colloquial language and the drama, ranging from the thirteenth century to the nineteenth or, in dynastic terms, from the Southern Sung and Yüan down to Ming and Ch'ing. It consists of a dozen interlocking pieces chosen to illustrate the various stages in the development of this literature, the key being supplied in a historical introduction. The picture puzzle that emerges may also be regarded as a panorama of Chinese life of the last seven or eight centuries, though mainly in its humbler aspects.

In my translations, I have sought above all to render fully the meaning I have found in the originals. With the verse, I have tried also to keep to the original lineation and to do justice to the imagery. Some attempt has been made in all cases to reproduce the tone of the original; thus clichés and bathos are rendered as such, and pointless allusions have often been suppressed. In the matter of the age of persons, I have not been consistent. In the translations and in some other instances, I have simply allowed people to be as old as they thought themselves, which — based on the number of calendar years — would usually be a year or so more than their actual age. Where, as in my biographical studies of authors, I have had to supply the age, a more precise reckoning is used.

I wish to thank my friends, Dr M.I.Scott, Professor E.G. Pulleyblank, Dr Joseph Needham, Professor D.Hawkes and Dr G.Dudbridge, and my cousin Mr Yü Ta-kang, for reading over portions of my manuscript and for their kind suggestions. Without the resources of Cambridge University Library and the expert and ungrudging assistance of its officers, especially Dr Scott, the task of preparing such a book would have been far more difficult and vexatious. I am indebted for information about articles in Chinese periodicals to Mr P.K.

Yü of Hong Kong University; and for the supply of photostats or microfilm material, to the officials of the British Museum, to Mrs Frances Wang of the Far Eastern Library, University of Washington, and to Mr C. C. Lan, Librarian of the Institute of History and Philology, Academia Sinica. Finally, in the preparation of the manuscript itself, I have been much aided by the efficient duplicating service provided by the Cambridge Philosophical Library.

For permission to quote from copyright material I am indebted to E. J. Brill, Leiden (Van Gulik, *T'ang-yin pi-shih*, 1956), Cambridge University Press (Needham, *Science and Civilisation in China*, vol. IV, part 3, 1971), and University of London Press (Tregear, *A Geography of China*, 1965).

General Introduction

The Setting

The stories and plays represented in this collection were originally intended for performance before an audience and depended for their full effect on the skill of story-tellers and actors; the longer narrative works, too, which we might call novels and which were meant to be read, continued to adhere to the conventions of story-telling. It would thus seem desirable to sketch the setting in which the earliest performances took place. The growth of cities that followed the expansion of trade, domestic and foreign, throughout the Sung dynasty (960–1279 A.D.) was accompanied by an unprecedented demand for popular entertainment. In the fair-grounds[1] which were a permanent fixture of the Sung capital Pien (i.e. Kaifeng, known as the Eastern Capital) in the eleventh and the first quarter of the twelfth century, story-telling went on the whole year round in booths and wooden sheds, flourishing side by side with comedians' acts; semi-dramatic performances known as 'Melodies in Mixed Modes' (*chu-kung-tiao*), part sung and part narrated; recitals by individual singers; puppet and marionette shows; shadow plays; and a rudimentary drama which included acrobatics. The largest of these sheds were theatres holding several thousand spectators. It was also in the fair-grounds that, during the seven or eight days preceding the Chung-yüan Festival in the seventh month, associated with the pious Mu-lien and his journey through hell in search of his mother, religious plays on the theme, probably relying heavily on spectacle, were staged.[2]

[1] *Tung-ching meng hua lu* (1147), Ku-tien edition, 1956, c. 5, pp. 29–30.
[2] *Ibid.*, c. 8, p. 49; for the story and its Buddhist origins, see Arthur Waley, *Ballads and Stories from Tun-huang*, 1960, chapter 11, 'Mu-lien rescues his mother'. See also Chao Ching-shen, *Yin-tzu chi*, 1946, pp. 149–76, 'On the Changing Forms of the Mu-lien Story'.

Festivals, however, were also held at temples with the attendant variety of entertainments.[1] And during the New Year celebrations, acrobats, conjurers, mountebanks, singers and dancers, and even one determined story-teller who recited the history of the Five Dynasties, gave performances on a high wooden structure erected before the palace gate-tower, watched by the crowds and, from behind yellow curtains, by those in the palace. The festivities culminated in the Lantern Festival, the first full moon of the year, when the streets were adorned with illuminated figures of dragons and gods, the fingers of some deities spouting jets of water at intervals.[2] But the busier parts of the city were lit up at night at all times. Whereas in the T'ang dynasty (618–906), inhabitants of the capital Ch'ang-an (i.e. Sian in Shensi Province) had been confined to their respective wards after sundown, there was no curfew in the Sung capital, only the city gates being locked at night and the bridges closed to river traffic. Food stalls and eating houses with their contingent of singing girls remained open all night, so that feasting and revelry often lasted until dawn. For the ordinary Chinese city-dweller, night-life began under the Sung. In retrospect, the twenty-five-year reign (1101–25) of the pleasure-loving emperor, the too accomplished Hui-tsung, which ended in one of the great disasters of Chinese history,[3] became the golden age of entertainment and patronage.

Thus it was no accident that the long narrative *Shui-hu chuan* —a monument to the story-teller's art—should begin with the rise to fortune of a down-and-out football player whose sidelong kick[4] won the admiration of that same Hui-tsung, then Prince Tuan.[5] Every incident in that glorious and ill-starred reign was stamped on the memory of those who fled south from the Tartar invaders; and when in 1138 Hangchow was fixed upon as the Southern Sung capital and re-named Lin-an (Temporary Refuge), the inhabitants of the city wasted no time in transforming it into another Kaifeng, meticulously comparing each detail in the present with 'what once prevailed

---

[1] *Tung-ching meng hua lu*, c. 8, pp. 47–8.
[2] *Tung-ching meng hua lu*, c. 6, pp. 34–5; the one story-teller, whose voice must have been stentorian, performed regularly in the fairgrounds (c. 5, p. 30).
[3] For the train of events, see Introduction to 'The Twin Mirrors' *infra*.
[4] The ball is kicked with the right foot strategically placed behind the left foot, thus resulting in an elegant posture.
[5] *Shui-hu ch'üan-chuan*, chapter 2.

in *the* capital'.[1] Tea-houses, for instance, were regarded by those who clung to the old ways as something of a novelty and not quite respectable:

> The larger tea-houses [in Hangchow] have pictures and scrolls of calligraphy by famous artists hanging on the wall. In the capital, only restaurants had them, to keep their customers amused while the food was being cooked, but now the tea-houses have adopted the practice.[2]

To the unprejudiced, Hangchow, with its lake surrounded by hills providing an inexhaustible supply of fresh green tea of rare flavouring, its abundance of other produce (endless varieties of silk, of flowers, fruits, herbs, trees including eight types of bamboo, of birds, beasts and fish), and its more varied and elaborate festivals (which included a Flower Festival in the middle of the second month, a Wine Festival at the beginning of April just before the time-honoured Festival of Ch'ing-ming, and the annual exodus in the eighth month to the mouth of the river Che to watch the autumn tidal bores), may seem an altogether more delightful place, far more conducive to leisurely pursuits.[3] Certainly, in the latter half of the twelfth and in the thirteenth century, all the entertainments ever offered in Kaifeng were to be found in similar fair-grounds in Hangchow; only in greater profusion.[4] Story-telling, in particular, grew more specialised, and by the second half of the thirteenth century there was even a guild of writers, some of whose names are recorded,[5] though story-tellers' texts bear no marks of authorship, being often altered in the telling. With the passage of time, certainly by the fifteenth and sixteenth centuries, under the Ming dynasty (1368–1643), the Hangchow story-tellers' pre-occupation with the vanished world of 'former days in the Eastern Capital' gave way to interest in their own city with its

[1] See Jacques Gernet, *Daily Life in China on the eve of the Mongol invasion 1250–1276*, translated H. M. Wright, 1962, chapter 1.
[2] *Tu-ch'eng chi sheng* (1235), in Ku-tien edition of *Tung-ching meng hua lu*, p. 94; the writer could not have been speaking from personal experience.
[3] For variety of produce, see *Meng liang lu* (about 1275), c. 18, in Ku-tien edition of *Tung-ching meng hua lu*, pp. 282–91; for the festivals here mentioned, see *Meng liang lu*, c. 1, p. 145; c. 2, p. 149; c. 4, pp. 162–3; for Hangchow life in the thirteenth century, see Gernet's book mentioned above; for Hangchow in the sixteenth century, see 'Madam White' *infra*.
[4] See *Tu-ch'eng chi sheng*, pp. 95–8; *Meng liang lu*, c. 18, p. 298; c. 20, pp. 308–13; *Wu-lin chiu-shih* (after 1280), in Ku-tien edition of *Tung-ching meng hua lu*, c. 6, pp. 440–1, pp. 453–66.
[5] *Wu-lin chiu-shih*, c. 6, p. 454.

beautiful environs and its clever and charming men and women.

Of the theatre proper, in which literary drama was performed in the thirteenth century in the north, under Tartar and Mongol rule, we possess a description in a poem entitled 'A farmer's visit to the theatre' by Tu Jen-chieh,[1] an older contemporary of the playwright Kuan Han-ch'ing, one of whose early plays was possibly being staged: The harvest had been good and the farmer, satisfied with his lot, entered the city to purchase incense and paper money as his thanksgiving offerings to the local deity. Passing a busy street, he noticed a large crowd gathered near a spot where notices on coloured paper were pasted all over:

'A man stood with his hands raised as if supporting the beam
                                     that served as a doorway,
Shouting aloud: "Pray enter now! Pray enter now!
The place will be full! Late-comers must do without seats!"
He continued: "In the first half we present *The Mock Courtship*[2]
To be followed by *The Story of Liu Shua-ho*!"'[3]

For a fee of two hundred copper cash the farmer gained admittance, and he walked up some sloping boards to find himself on a huge wooden structure with row upon row of seats laid out in circular or semi-circular fashion. Way above, the roof seemed to him like a bell tower; looking down, he saw 'a whirlpool of men'. On a platform in the centre (i.e. the stage) several women were seated and the musicians had begun to play:

'Surely this is not the time of year for a religious procession!

Why, then, all that beating on drums and banging on gongs?' More players entered, and the farmer watched with fascination their strange costumes and made-up faces, one of which was 'daubed with chalk with some black smudges'. They declaimed or sang, ever ready with their tongues and 'knowing such a lot of clever speeches'.

The farmer did not sit through the performance, and such

---

[1] The poem *Chuang-chia pu shih kou-lan* to the tune 'Shua hai-erh' is in Sui Shu-sen (ed.), *Ch'üan Yüan san ch'ü*, Chung-hua 1964, vol. I, pp. 31–2. For Tu Jen-chieh and Kuan Han-ch'ing, see Introduction to 'A Dream of Butterflies' *infra*.
[2] *T'iao feng-yüeh*, specified as a *yüan-pen*, the earlier dramatic form that led to the four-act *tsa-chü* play of the second half of the thirteenth century; initially, however, the terms *yüan-pen* and *tsa-chü* were used rather loosely.
[3] See Hu Chi, *Sung Chin tsa-chü k'ao*, 1957, pp. 221–5, for a discussion of the title of the play and the significance of the line; also Feng Yüan-chün, *Ku-chü shuo-hui*, revised edition 1955, pp. 71–2.

snatches of the action (which he followed imperfectly) that occur in his account seem not to fit Kuan Han-ch'ing's play[1] *Cha ni-tzu t'iao feng-yüeh* ('The Dissembling Girl conducts a Mock Courtship'), the text of which, however, is not preserved in full. 'The Story of Liu Shua-ho' would almost certainly be the play of that name, *Fu-yen Liu Shua-ho*, by Kuan's younger colleague Kao Wen-hsiu,[2] which would date the poem to the 1260's.[3] The locality was Peking, which, as the capital (named Ta-hsing) of the Tartan Chin in 1153–1214[4] and (under the name of Ta-tu) of the Mongol Yüan dynasty (1260–1367), was the centre of dramatic activity in the thirteenth century.

The costumes would seem always to have been sumptuous and the stage itself bare, as may be seen from a coloured wall painting of the period in the Temple of the Dragon King outside Hung-tung (in Shansi Province) depicting a group in a theatrical show.[5] Ten figures in costume, male and female, are shown standing, arranged in three rows, on a tile stage, probably in a temple rather than a regular theatre: the figure in the front centre is a high official in a red robe and a hat with spreading horns, holding before him a memorandum tablet, his symbol of office; the others have in their hands such objects as a sword or fan or flute indicating their respective roles. The entire cast seems to be present, though a half-concealed figure may be seen lifting a corner of the back curtain on one side to peep at the goings-on. The story has not been identified with any certainty. The stage is unfurnished except for two decorative hangings over the back curtain, which, though a short distance apart, form a single picture: an angry dragon on the one appears ready to attack a swordsman taking his stance on the other. From its

[1] In *Kuan Han-ch'ing hsi-ch'ü chi*, pp. 689–703, only the songs and some stage directions being preserved; see Introduction to 'A Dream of Butterflies' *infra*.

[2] The play by Kao Wen-hsiu, now lost, was singled out for special mention by Chia Chung-ming in 1422, and also recorded by Chu Ch'üan in 1398; see *Lu kuei pu*, Ku-tien edition, p. 11; and *Lu-kuei-pu hsin chiao-chu*, pp. 33–4; *T'ai-ho cheng-yin p'u*, in *Lu kuei pu*, p. 140; also Introduction to 'A Dream of Butterflies' *infra*.

[3] As Kuan Han-ch'ing's younger colleague — 'a lesser Han-ch'ing' — Kao could hardly have begun writing for the stage before 1260; the fact that the theatre was a comparative novelty also dates the poem to the 1260's; its author Tu Jen-Chieh survived into the 1270's. See Introduction to 'A Dream of Butterflies' *infra*.

[4] From 1215 Peking was under Mongol occupation.

[5] See Chou I-po, *Chung-kuo hsi-ch'ü lun-chi*, 1960, pp. 393–400: 'A Theatrical Performance in a Yüan Wall Painting'.

name, written large over the valance which overhung the back curtain, the company seems to have been a local one, probably one that had performed at the temple on a particular occasion. The costumed figures in the picture are a valuable source of information to those interested in theatrical tradition, but the picture as a whole suggests that, outwardly at least, the Yüan stage differed little from the Chinese stage of later times.

Story-telling

In the early twelfth century, the two main groups of story-tellers in Kaifeng[1] were: those who recited history, which meant a connected narrative woven round a number of colourful historical characters and presented in the form of a chronicle; and those who related self-contained and relatively short stories with no pretensions to historical accuracy or importance. In Hangchow, in the thirteenth century,[2] they were joined by a third group, those who expounded Buddhist sutras and elaborated religious tales. As their matter differed, so the styles of the three were at variance. To judge by surviving texts from 1321–3,[3] the reciters of history (*chiang shih*) declaimed in debased classical rather than a strictly colloquial language, probably pausing after each sentence to paraphrase and explain like a teacher; their dialogue was deliberately archaic so as to maintain a ponderously lofty tone, but their own claim to neat and elegant phrasing seems justified in many of the narrative passages. These characteristics survive also in sixteenth- and seventeenth-century versions of the long narrative *San-kuo yen-i* ('The Three Kingdoms'; final version in 120 chapters), much amplified from the story-tellers' early text printed in 1321–3.[4]

The sutra reciters (*shuo ching*) offered casuistry as well as all

---

[1] *Tung-ching meng hua lu*, c. 5, p. 30. After 1226, under Tartar rule, many of them doubtless continued to ply their trade in the same fairgrounds.
[2] *Tu-ch'eng chi sheng*, p. 98; *Hsi-hu lao-jen fan-sheng lu* (c. 1253), in Ku-tien edition of *Tung-ching meng hua lu*, p. 123; *Meng liang lu*, c. 20, pp. 312–13; *Wu-lin chiu-shih*, c. 6, pp. 454–6.
[3] Five texts dealing with (a) the rise of Chou (b) the Warring States (c) the rise and fall of Ch'in (d) the Former Han (e) the Three Kingdoms, dating from 1321–3, are reprinted by Ku-tien and Chung-hua (1955–9). I have based my observations on (a), i.e. *Wu-wang fa Chou p'ing-hua* and (d), i.e. *Ch'ien-Han-shu p'ing-hua*.
[4] *San-kuo-chih p'ing-hua*, being (c) in note 2 above. The 120-chapter 'Three Kingdoms' is available in a carefully edited text by Chou Ju-ch'ang, 1959, *San-kuo yen-i* (Jen-min).

the marvels of the Indian imagination. The casuistry conveyed itself in a series of symbolical and enigmatic verses, as surviving, for example, in the stories of the abbot Bright Moon and the girl Liu Ts'ui,[1] and of the two monks Ming-wu and Wu-chieh (in *Ku-chin hsiao-shuo*, c. 29 and c. 30), or in the story of *P'u-sa-man*.[2] The marvellous was represented in the stories grouped round Tripitaka's pilgrimage, surviving in a skeletal version in the thirteenth-century text *Ta-T'ang San-tsang fa-shih ch'ü ching chi*,[3] and in the greatly expanded sixteenth-century narrative *Hsi yu chi* in 100 chapters. But many Buddhist stories have been transmitted in the form of pious recitations (*pao-chüan*), part chant and part recitation, generally regarded as falling outside the story-telling tradition.

The stories pure and simple (*hsiao-shuo*) depended for their interest chiefly on the plot. It is recorded of the history reciters, who included self-styled graduates and higher graduates, that for all their erudition, they dreaded the competition of the tellers of such stories, who were in the habit of covering at a single sitting the events of a whole reign[4] (in other words, making a meal of fare which might have done for six months' rationing). Without the banner of learning or of doctrine, which each had its adherents, or the security of a lengthy, continuous text that could be counted on to draw its share of 'regulars', the tellers of imaginary stories relied on their wits to attract and hold a clientèle. Variety was at a premium with them; their repertory had constantly to be added to, and the very limitations of their medium they exploited to the full. Pauses in the narrative, contrived to coincide with moments of suspense, were filled by singing or the declaiming of verses, the song and verses serving, in turn, as description and illustration, commentary, and mere diversion, while a collection bowl was being handed around. And at the beginning of the performance, the place being not yet filled, the story-teller would come out with a 'preamble' (*ju-hua*), known also as a

[1] The Bright Moon and Liu Ts'ui story was being told in Hangchow in the first half of the sixteenth century; the actual story might not date from much earlier, but it undoubtedly continued the 'sutra recitation' tradition. See Introduction to 'Madam White' *infra*.

[2] In *Ching shih t'ung-yen*, c. 7, but I have taken the title from *Ching-pen t'ung-su hsiao-shuo*, c. 11, where the story is also found. See Introduction to 'The Birthday Gift Convoy' *infra*.

[3] See Introduction to 'The Women's Kingdom' *infra*.

[4] *Tu-ch'eng chi sheng*, p. 98; *Meng liang lu*, c. 20, p. 313.

'lucky preliminary offering' (*te sheng t'ou-hui*). This could be a discourse or a number of songs or a shorter preliminary story, which as a parallel instance of the same situation or predicament, or of the same wisdom or folly, often became wedded to the main story as, for example, in 'The Three Apparitions'.[1] In 'The Twin Mirrors'[2] the preliminary and the main story seem to have been planned by a single writer.

Such devices, available to all, were put to the best use by the tellers of stories pure and simple, who further enlisted the services of a musician, a flautist who accompanied the singing.[3] When the story-teller was a man, a woman singer probably sang the songs; but a female story-teller was expected both to sing and to tell her story. The Yüan man of letters Hu Chih-yü (1227–95), writing in praise of a story-teller of his acquaintance—a Miss Huang, of outstanding talents—who was about to publish a collection of verses, postulates the ideal qualities of an artiste in story-telling, seemingly embodied in that lady, as follows:[4] that she should be of dazzling beauty, elegant and refined in manner and deportment, and of surpassing intelligence with a corresponding insight into men and affairs; that she should possess clarity and fluency of speech, pronouncing each word and phrase distinctly and faultlessly; that her singing voice should be beautifully rounded like lustrous pearls descending in cascades; that she should employ gesture and expression to the full to guide the hearer and facilitate understanding; that her song and recitation should be at a measured pace with careful modulation of the volume and pitch—while knowing her text perfectly, she should never give the impression of monotonous chanting; that she should reveal the joys and sorrows and all other emotions of the protagonists and rehearse the very words and deeds of men of a former age, that they might live again for the hearer, of whose complete absorption in the story she could only then be assured; finally, that she should create new and original effects even in the reciting of old stories, in both plot and diction, so that those already familiar with them might constantly find cause for surprise.

[1] See 'The Clerk's Lady' *infra*.
[2] See 'The Twin Mirrors' *infra*.
[3] See Sun K'ai-ti, *Su-chiang shuo-hua yü pai-hua hsiao-shuo*, 1956, pp. 22–3, on 'yin-tzu-erh'.
[4] 'Preface to Poems by Miss Huang', as quoted in Sun K'ai-ti, pp. 10–11. For Hu Chih-yü, see Introduction to 'A Dream of Butterflies' *infra*.

Thus a star performer of the thirteenth century, a pretty and attractive woman, as seen through the eyes of an undoubted connoisseur who was very likely also a besotted, elderly admirer. (In the seventeenth century the amazing Liu Ching-t'ing, who was middle-aged and ugly and poorly educated, had the audience under his spell day after day while he recited history without sticking closely to any text.)[1] No mention is made of Miss Huang's repertory, which was probably a varied one, consisting of the choicest items from every group. As practised by those who enjoyed no special patronage[2] but earned their livelihood in Hangchow fair-grounds of the time, however, story-telling had diversified to such an extent that stories 'pure and simple' were divided into a number of (unavoidably overlapping) categories, with specialists in each.[3] According to one classification, these were: supernatural stories, involving evil spirits (*ling-kuai*); stories of amorous female ghosts (*yen-fen*); love stories (*ch'uan-ch'i*, i.e. romance); law court stories (*kung-an*); sword fights (*p'u-tao*); cudgel-play (*han-pang*); stories of immortals (*shen-hsien*); stories of magic and magicians (*yao-shu*). The categories 'sword fights' and 'cudgel-play' began as offshoots of, and remained subordinate to, 'law court stories'.

The classification, of the late thirteenth century, is that given in Lo Yeh's *Tsui-weng t'an-lu*,[4] a commonplace-book for story-tellers. It begins with a section entitled 'Industry of the Tongue' consisting of two discourses, one of them on the diversity of human types leading up to a justification of story-telling — 'suitable for use as a Preamble in both history and sutra recitations', and the other on the story-teller's training and repertory. In the second discourse, a little over a hundred titles of stories are listed under the eight above-mentioned categories. Thus under 'sword fights' we find the title 'Green-faced Beast', i.e. Yang Chih, with his heirloom of a sword,

---

[1] See 'The Blood-stained Fan' *infra*.

[2] Many story-tellers, both men and women, were blind, but they were unlikely to have been the most popular or, for our purpose, significant; see Introductions to 'The Lute' and 'Madam White' *infra*.

[3] See *Tu-ch'eng chi sheng*, p. 98; *Meng liang lu*, c. 20, p. 312.

[4] Ku-tien reprint, the opening section being pp. 1–5; see T'an Cheng-pi, *Hua-pen yü ku-chü*, 1957, pp. 13–37, for an analysis of the titles listed by Lo Yeh; also the Catalogue of Works of Fiction by Sun K'ai-ti, *Chung-kuo t'ung-su hsiao-shuo shu-mu*, revised edition 1957, pp. 3–16.

whose story is incorporated in the long narrative *Shui-hu chuan*;[1]
and under 'law court stories', the title 'The Three Apparitions'
probably indicates a much earlier form of the story as printed
in the collection, *Ching shih t'ung-yen*.[2] From the listed titles
also, categories of uncertain meaning have been defined:
ch'uan-ch'i is a love story involving human beings and *yen-fen*
one involving a man and the ghost of a woman.[3] But stories are
quickly told and the list could not have included more than a
selection. A clear omission would seem to be the 'phenomenal
success story' (*fa-chi pien-t'ai*), the Dick Whittington type of
story, mentioned in an earlier account[4] and surviving in such
stories as the sudden rise to fortune of Ma Chou and of Chao
Hsü (*Ku-chin hsiao-shuo*, c. 5 and c. 11).

As stories grew longer in the telling, the original categories
ceased to be valid. Those who kept to the one type of story
strung their tales together into a continuous narrative, as the
history and sutra reciters had done before them. Clusters of
stories about immortals and marvels, about heroes, about
bandits, about crime and justice evolved into cycles or attached
themselves to some existing history or sutra text: thus every
judge's story was potentially a step forword in Judge Pao's
career;[5] every robber worth his salt belonged to the band of a
hundred and eight on Liang-shan-po;[6] and a whole cycle of
marvels infiltrated the campaign of the Chou emperor Wu-
wang against the Shang, originally the matter of a 'history'
text.[7] These were then taken up by editors and revisers
mainly in the sixteenth century, who shaped the longer and
more homogeneous of the narratives into novels, of which more
later.

Stories that remained unattached, ranging in date from
the thirteenth to the sixteenth century, are preserved in
various Ming collections. In the earliest printed collections,
from the Hangchow publishing house Ch'ing-p'ing shan-
t'ang in the mid-sixteenth century, they still retain the form

---

[1] See 'The Birthday Gift Convoy' *infra*.
[2] See 'The Clerk's Lady' *infra*.
[3] See T'an Cheng-pi, pp. 18–26.
[4] *Tu-ch'eng chi sheng*, p. 98, which also supplies the reading for the similar
account, but corrupt, in *Meng liang lu*, c. 20, p. 312.
[5] See 'A Dream of Butterflies' and 'The Clerk's Lady' *infra*.
[6] See 'The Birthday Gift Convoy' *infra*.
[7] The resulting mixture was *Feng shen yen-i* ('Canonization of the Gods')
in 100 chapters, probably late sixteenth century.

of story-tellers' texts (*hua-pen*):[1] the preliminary story or
discourse bears the heading *Ju-hua* (Preamble); one story,
Chien-t'ieh ho-shang ('The Monk's Billet-doux'), has a sub-
title indicating that it is a 'law court' story[2] and ends with the
formula:

'Thus we have told our story
And so break up for the nonce',

found also in the story of the Ape Spirit on Plum-blossom
Peak (*Ch'en hsün-chien Mei-ling shih ch'i chi*); still another,
Loyang san-kuai chi ('The Three Evil Spirits of Loyang'),
concludes with 'And the story is entitled "The Three Evil
Spirits . . ."' etc.[3] Such characteristics are absent in the
manuscript collection *Ching-pen t'ung-su hsiao-shuo*,[4] of uncertain date and provenance,[5] though including undoubtedly early
stories, among them *Hsi-shan i k'u kuei* ('Swarm of Ghosts in
the Western Hills'), whose title was echoed in the name of an
actual tea-house kept by a Mother Wang in one of the thirteenth-century Hangchow fairgrounds—'Swarm of Ghosts
Tea-house.'[6]

In the great corpus of story-tellers' texts, the three collections, each of forty stories, by Feng Meng-lung[7] (1574–
c. 1645), *Ku-chin hsiao-shuo* ('Stories old and new'; c. 1621),
Ching shih t'ung-yen ('Stories to warn the world'; 1624) and
Hsing shih heng-yen ('Stories to awaken the world'; 1627),

[1] For the Ch'ing-p'ing shan-t'ang texts, see Introduction to 'The Shrew'
infra. 'The Monk's Billet-doux' is in T'an Cheng-pi (ed.), *Ch'ing-p'ing
shan-t'ang hua-pen*, pp.6–19; the story of the Ape Spirit is found on pp.
121–34; 'The Three Evil Spirits of Loyang' on pp. 67–77. See also P.
Hanan, 'The Early Chinese Short Story: A Critical Theory in Outline',
Harvard Journal of Asiatic Studies vol.xxvii (1967), pp. 168–207.
[2] *Kung-an ch'uan-ch'i*, presumably *kung-an* story.
[3] See 'The Birthday Gift Convoy' for parallel examples embedded in the
Shui-hu chuan narrative.
[4] Ku-tien reprint of 1954 containing seven stories, being cc.10–16;
'Swarm of Ghosts' is on pp.29–42.
[5] See Cheng Chen-to, *Chung-kuo wen-hsüeh yen-chiu*, 1957, vol.i, pp.
372–8; and Y.W.Ma and T.L.Ma, 'On the Periods of the Stories of
Ching-pen t'ung-su hsiao-shuo and the authenticity of the Collection',
Tsing Hua Journal of Chinese Studies, New Series v (1965), pp. 14–32.
[6] See *Meng liang lu*, c. 16, p. 262; this is also pointed out in J. Průšek,
'Researches into the Beginnings of the Popular Chinese Novel, Part I,
(Continuation)', *Archiv Orientální*, vol. xxiii (1955), pp. 651–2. One of
the ghosts in the story was the matchmaker Grandmother Wang.
[7] See C. Birch, 'Feng Meng-lung and the *Ku-chin hsiao-shuo*', *Bulletin of
School of Oriental and African Studies*, vol. xviii (1956), pp. 64–83. The
three collections are available in reprints by Jen-min wen-hsüeh ch'u-pan-
she, 1958.

the texts have been edited for reading and diverge somewhat
from those found also in the earlier collections.[1] And in his
Preface to *Ku-chin hsiao-shuo* Feng states the case for all time of
a Chinese literature written in colloquial speech[2]—resorted to
by those who told stories pure and simple from the beginning
—and appealing to a wide reading public. He compares the
colloquial story in the manner of the Sung story-tellers with
the *ch'uan-ch'i* tale written in the classical language after
T'ang models:

> For in general the narrative writer in the T'ang manner
> carefully selected his language so as to appeal to the literary
> mind; but the writer of stories in the Sung manner fell
> back upon vulgar speech, addressing himself to the village
> ear. Since, in the world, literary minds are few and far be-
> tween, but vulgar ears legion, stories depend perforce less
> on choice diction than on ordinary speech. Thus we see
> the story-tellers of the day at their performances, how their
> graphic descriptions of persons and events awaken, in turn,
> merriment and astonishment, sorrow and tears; and how,
> being roused, some in the audience almost dance and sing,
> and further express themselves ready to participate in the
> events being unfolded—such as wanting to clutch at the
> sword of some hero or villain, or to fall on their knees before
> some magnanimous character, or to rush into a duel on
> behalf of the weak, or to offer gifts of money to those in
> distress, in which process, the cowardly grow brave, the
> lecherous chaste, the frivolous sober, the dumb and stupid
> suddenly ashamed of themselves. Daily[2] reading of The
> Analects and the Classic of Filial Piety could not have so
> wrought upon anyone—neither effecting so swift a
> transformation nor leaving an impression so deep. Without
> recourse to vulgar speech, could this have been achieved?

The role of performer the story-tellers retained down to the
present; the privileged position of keeper, transmitter and

---

[1] The story of the two monks Ming-wu and Wu-chieh (in *Ku-chin hsiao-shuo*, c.30) diverges greatly from the Ch'ing p'ing-shan-t'ang version (*Ch'ing-p'ing shan-t'ang hua-pen*, pp. 136–45), but may have been derived from a different text. For the most part, Feng's changes are those of an editor.

[2] *Ku-chin hsiao-shuo*, Jen-min edition: a misprint—'small' for 'daily'—being corrected by the reading (blurred) in the facsimile edition by Li T'ien-i, 1958: 'daily reading of The Analects', etc.

creator of stories they lost with the successive publication of
their texts.

Drama

The political division of China during the Tartar and Mongol
occupation of the north gave rise to two separate dramatic
traditions, each deriving in part from the kind of dramatic
performance with much spectacle and little text held in
Kaifeng fairgrounds, early in the twelfth century. The
invaders brought with them their own music, including a
variety of string instruments and a large repertory of tunes,
which gradually transformed the Chinese stage. The song had,
as a medium, always been accessible to both the learned and
the populace. The *tz'u* poem or song, and adaptations of it
for performances with dancing, which had hitherto prevailed,
relied much on poetic diction; the practice now began of
writing songs (*ch'ü*) to the tunes of the new music with the
prosodic rules relaxed to accommodate a language really close
to colloquial speech in which the words were accorded the
actual pronunciation of the time. This meant, in terms of
prosody, abolition of the short and abrupt *ju-sheng*, the so-called
fifth tone, already obsolete in northern dialects. (In the south,
the fifth tone persists even today.) Adaptation of the new kind
of song to a dramatic context—to some extent anticipated by
the song and narrative performance known as 'Melodies in
Mixed Modes' (*chu-kung-tiao*) in Kaifeng—and the grafting
of a whole set of new musical conventions into the traditional
type of stage performance resulted eventually in the Northern
Drama.

Chief of the conventions was the dominance of the 'mode',
nine of which were used in song. Each act (*che*) of a play had
all its songs, ranging from seven or eight to over twenty,
based on the tunes in a particular mode and arranged in a fixed
sequence. Thus the tone or mood of each act would be set by the
mode chosen, and the act might also be regarded as a musical
division. The four-act *tsa-chü* play, therefore, the norm of the
Northern Drama, was also a musical performance divided
neatly into four parts, with the unity maintained by this rather
austere construction further strengthened by another convention: the use of a single singer throughout. The other
characters in the play, who could declaim verse but not sing,

would thus be completely overshadowed by the hero or
heroine, impersonated by the singer, whose outpourings
constituted the substance of the drama. The unity of mood was
inimical to dramatic progression, and a short Prelude (*hsieh-
tzu*) generally laid the scene or introduced the action, after
which a simple plot, often already known to the audience,
threaded its way through the four long song sequences.

The music has not survived, and the songs may only be read
as verse, the names of tunes indicating no more than prosodic
patterns. Other limitations of the form, too, are obvious. Its
appellation *tsa-chü* ('variety play') was inherited from the
earlier (i.e. Sung) performances of that name, and it remained
hospitable to miming, horseplay and low comedy, usually left
to the actors' own devices, the stage directions being sketchy.
The principal characters including the singer had to fit into
types, and every other minor character verged on the role of
clown. The prose dialogue was repetitive and, coming after
the high-flown verse, at times complete bathos; it also lent
itself to constant improvisation, which accounts for the interminable textual variants that are the nightmare of editors.
Nevertheless the Yüan *tsa-chü* play opened up a whole
realm of experience not previously explored in Chinese
literature—the secrets of the heart without the sanction of
custom or the rationalization of orthodox doctrine. It was,
moreover, deeply rooted in common life, and its lines pulsate
with the heartbeat of the aged and helpless, the defeated and
downtrodden, the widow and orphan, in moments of agony or
acute distress. In its sustained eloquence it undoubtedly merits
the title of 'lyrical drama'.

The beginning of the four-act *tsa-chü* play, in Ta-tu (i.e.
Peking), probably very nearly coincided with the formal inauguration of the Yüan dynasty in 1260. (If, as tradition has
it, Kuan Han-ch'ing was its first playwright, then the form could
not have begun more than a few years previously.)[1] But it was
preceded by perhaps a century of dramatic development
during the period of the Chin, culminating in the *yüan-pen*
('entertainment text') play,[2] which approximated the *tsa-chü*

[1] See Introduction to 'A Dream of Butterflies' *infra*.
[2] See T'ao Tsung-i, *Nan-ts'un cho keng lu* (1366), c. 25, Chung-hua ed.,
1959, p. 306, on the difference between the two forms, *yüan-pen* and *tsa-
chü*. No early *yüan-pen* texts survive; presumably the more promising
among them were all absorbed into the *tsa-chü* repertory.

proper and survived into the Yüan. With the extension of Mongol rule to the whole of China in 1280, the *tsa-chü*, the Northern Drama, gradually moved south, to Hangchow, where a large and discriminating audience had its effect on the theme and plot of new plays. For over a century, the Northern Drama held sway, its playwrights numbering over a hundred for the Yüan dynasty alone. Early in the Ming (1368 onwards), however, its supremacy was challenged by plays of the Southern repertory—among them, Kao Ming's *P'i-p'a chi* ('The Lute')[1]—with a different set of conventions, musical and dramatic. But the removal of the Ming capital from Nanking to Peking in 1421 ensured the continued reign of the Northern Drama, now showing traces of Southern influence, until the latter half of the sixteenth century.

The Southern Drama originated in the seaport of Wenchow (in Chekiang Province), probably soon after the Sung court had moved to Hangchow, in the twelfth century. By the second half of the thirteenth century, it was ready to invade Hangchow, where in 1268–9 one of its plays 'The Beau Wang Huan'[2] had a successful season. After 1280 it continued to flourish in Wenchow, making rapid advances in the next few decades. Certainly a local guild of writers[3] supplied the stage with texts, and when, in the 1320's and 1330's, Kao Ming as a young man saw the plays upon which he later based his own *P'i-p'a chi*, the form of the Southern Drama would already be fixed. Known initially as *hsi-wen* ('play text') and later as *ch'uan-ch'i* ('romance'), the Southern play set out, above all, to tell and enact a story. Like the Northern Drama, it relied heavily on music, but the underlying aim was a dramatic, not a musical, performance: its unity resided in the structure of the plot; its music was a conglomeration of every available tune.

The dramatic conventions differ little from those of other lands, and Indian influence has been suspected,[4] especially in the form of the Prologue (*k'ai ch'ang*), in which, after a short

---

[1] For Kao Ming and 'The Lute', see *infra*.
[2] *Wang Huan* or *Feng-liu Wang Huan Ho Lien-lien*; see Cheng Chen-to, *Chung-kuo wen-hsüeh shih* (Illustrated edition, Jen-min 1959), chapter 40, 'The Rise of *hsi-wen*', p. 574.
[3] The guild was 'Chiu-shan shu-hui', responsible for the text of *Chang Hsieh chuang-yüan* (see Introduction to 'The Lute' *infra*). Chiu-shan is a hill in Wenchow; see Tung Mei-k'an, *P'i-p'a-chi chien-shuo*, 1957, p. 3.
[4] Cheng Chen-to, chapter 40.

parley with an invisible company, the author or producer announces the title of the play and gives a summary of the action, which itself follows in two or three dozen or more scenes (*ch'ü*). Almost every incident is represented on the stage, and each character given the chance to explain himself and tell his own version of the story. All may sing in any or every scene (and must therefore fit into types or voice parts), or declaim verse or speak prose a shade too fine, necessarily all in a southern dialect for prosodic considerations (including the fifth tone) and for the sake of the puns, witticisms and, at times, bawdy, which take the place of coarse comedy. The tunes are chosen at random from any mode, indeed any repertory including later the Northern, and the verse forms, too, range from pure *tz'u* to popular rhymes. The Southern Drama, which we may call 'dramatic romance', lacks the power and concentration of the Northern, but its approach to life is altogether more human — its characters do not brood in isolation, and even their soliloquies are directed to the audience, not monologues. Its special triumph is in the use of chorus and refrain, by means of which a whole stanza, or two or three significant lines, could be echoed or repeated emphatically or playfully, jubilantly or grudgingly, accusingly or ironically, or simply in harmonious approval. The lone voice in the wilderness on the Northern stage is here silent, and man has returned to the fold of society.

The Southern Drama prevailed in various local centres in Kiangsu, Chekiang and Kiangsi in the fifteenth century. Towards the middle of the next century, one of these centres, K'unshan (in Kiangsu Province), startled the theatrical world with a new style of performance, perfected after a lifetime of study and experiment by the singer and musician Wei Liang-fu (dates uncertain): its meticulous singing style combined various Northern and Southern styles and it had for accompaniment a sizeable orchestra of woodwind and strings, thus ensuring that, musically, the Southern Drama need never be despised again. From the second half of the sixteenth century onwards literary men vied with professionals in writing plays for the K'un-shan School,[1] and the Southern Drama became

---

[1] T'ang Hsien-tsu (1550–1616), the greatest dramatist of his time, chose not to write for the K'un-shan School but for the I-huang School of his home district; see 'The Peony Pavilion' *infra*.

the dominant form, dethroning the Northern Drama even in Peking. In the eighteenth century, however, literary drama generally declined, giving way under the patronage of the Manchu emperors [1] to the kind of mixed repertory always popular with actors and audiences. Acrobatics and spectacle ousted the text on a three-tiered stage representing heaven, earth and hell. The Peking Opera of today, itself dating back a century or more and deriving mainly from the Anhwei School of much earlier origin, continues a traditional style of singing: it is a salutary reminder that the Chinese theatrical tradition and, above all, the Chinese language being what they are, singing comes to performer and audience alike more naturally than declamation, and song and dance will continue to form part of the actor's equipment.

The Novel

The language of story-telling, whether plain colloquial or a mixture of stilted colloquial and diluted classical, offered no outlet for the talents of the learned, who were slow to see its possibilities. In contrast, the stage attracted men of letters almost from the start, providing as it did the opportunity of composing lyrics by the score for the Northern and by the hundred for the Southern Drama. Of the story-writers of the fourteenth and fifteenth centuries, presumably all members of writers' guilds, whose collaborate efforts appeared in a blaze of glory in sixteenth-century printed versions, little is known. The patchy and meagre 'history' texts of 1321–3 and some others [2] were a definite starting point for their activities, but the slow process of accumulation and accretion, of innovation and excision, that resulted in the long continuous narrative may only be inferred. The clearest example of the coalescing of diverse elements under the hands of successive library craftsman is the narrative about the Liang-shan-po bandits, [3] *Shui-hu chuan* ('Water Margin'), with which two names are associated: Shih Nai-an and Lo Kuan-chung. Lo was a mid-

---

[1] See Chou I-po, *Chung-kuo hsi-chü-shih chiang-tso*, 1958, chapters 9 and 10.
[2] Notably *Hsüan-ho i-shih* of about the end of the thirteenth century, a miscellaneous compilation rather than a story-tellers' text; see 'The Birthday Gift Convoy' *infra*. The 'history' texts of 1321 have been mentioned in the section on story-telling above.
[3] See 'The Birthday Gift Convoy' *infra* for Liang-shan-po and *Shui-hu chuan*, and for an example of how *one* story evolved.

fourteenth-century professional writer in Hangchow.[1] He wrote three *tsa-chü* plays, one of which survives; he also edited and revised many story-tellers' narratives, in particular, *San-kuo yen-i* ('The Three Kingdoms') and *Shui-hu chuan*, the two most substantial narrative texts printed in the sixteenth century. Shih, whose name Nai-an (Patience Temple) resembles those of the thirteenth-century Hangchow sutra-reciters[2], would be a generation or two before Lo and might well have been both story-teller and writer in that city; but he remains a shadowy figure.

Shih and Lo probably laid down the over-all scheme, itself a considerable achievement, of men fleeing from the law converging in twos and threes or in small bands upon the stronghold of Liang-shan-po, where they readily fitted into a hierarchy, each being allotted his place at table and in battle formation. It thus followed that incidents and characters—the number of bandits grew from thirty-six to a hundred and eight in the course of the fourteenth and fifteenth centuries—in stories then already existing, would be re-arranged to fall in with it: adventures otherwise unrelated could be grouped together round some central event, so that the whole should present an impression of divinely ordained symmetry. Such a scheme invited further development, which no doubt went on all through the fifteenth century, as indeed even after the printing of the first full version of the sixteenth century. For the first full version, however, known to us through the edition of 1589 though dating back to the mid-century or before, a further thorough revision took place:[3] the result revealed the touch of a master, who commanded a colloquial prose style more assured than any before and who removed irrelevancies and excrescences in his original or originals without detracting from the zest of story-telling. The reviser remains unknown, but the sudden advance in prose style paved the way for original creation in the form of the novel.

[1] According to *Lu-kuei-pu hsü-pien* (c. 1425), whose author in his youth 'met Lo for the second time' in 1364; in Ku-tien edition of *Lu kuei pu*, p.102.
[2] As noted in Yen Tun-i, *Shui-hu-chuan ti yen-pien*, 1957, p. 227; see pp. 206–38 for a thorough but somewhat involved discussion of the precise roles of Shih and Lo and their identity.
[3] According to the Preface of Wang Tao-k'un to the edition of 1589, re-printed in *Shui-hu ch'üan-chuan*, pp. 1825–7; see also Introduction to 'The Birthday Gift Convoy' *infra*.

The more obvious success of *Shui-hu chuan*, however, was its structure. While alluding to historical dates and events now and then, it broke away from the framework of the 'history' text, i.e. chronicle, which saddled one with a cast-iron time scheme, fatal to digression. The symmetry of the seating plan in *Shui-hu chuan*, which we might call the 'banquet pattern' in fiction, had a logic immediately comprehended by the Chinese reader or audience, who seldom tired of waiting to discover whether some character or other had taken his place at the gathering. At the same time, it encumbered and retarded the narrative. To bring together ten or a dozen from all over the empire meant at least so many exciting adventures — collecting a hundred and eight entailed considerable duplication of types and incidents — but once the company were assembled, the account read like a society column; battle scenes became catalogues of faces, armours, weapons; victory brought more celebrations, at which all again presented themselves, etc. Nevertheless, no better structural device has been found — as an almost sacramental act of rejoicing in good fellowship, in re-union, in everyday blessings, the banquet was part of every Chinese occasion — and later novelists, with far greater literary resources, have still returned to the 'banquet pattern'. Thus in the eighteenth-century *Hung-lou meng* ('Red Chamber Dream'),[1] the cousins have parties and gatherings day after day in the garden, in which they are all housed; and in the still later *Ching hua yüan* ('Flowers in the Mirror')[2] — the first part of which follows an alternative pattern, the journey, exemplified in *Hsi yu chi* ('Tripitaka's Pilgrimage') — the hundred 'Flowers' are united at their Examination and make one another's aquaintance during the ensuing feasting and celebrations.

The paraphernalia of story-telling, present throughout *Shui-hu chuan*, were retained by novelists of the Ch'ing (Manchu) dynasty (1644–1910). Breaks in the narrative, marked by suspense and filled by two or four lines of verse, became the chapter ending, often with a contrived crisis. Verse passages were convenient in days when the exchange of verses was still part of gracious living: hero and heroine composed the author's own best poems; his worst were

[1] See 'A Burial Mound for Flowers' *infra*.
[2] See 'The Women's Kingdom' *infra*.

attributed to some clown or villainess, who could also be illiterate. Even the digressions, so much a feature of short story-tellers' texts, were put to good use: pieces of traditional lore, a crux in one of the better-known classics, the rules of a game no longer correctly played, some herbalist's recipe, these could be explained in the appropriate setting by one or other of the characters. The most important convention of all was the simple beginning: 'The story went . . .', with which the literary man unobtrusively steps into the shoes of the story-teller and, concealing his omniscience and cunning, recounts everything in a factual tone that lends authority to his account.

For in the Chinese literary tradition narrative was merely the instrument of history, and fiction had constantly to masquerade—as in *ch'uan-ch'i* tales in classical prose of the T'ang dynasty and since—as the record of some actual occurrence. And the accepted view of history, based on the Annals of Spring and Autumn, had always been a succinct account of events with judgement implied in the choice of wording, i.e. a purportedly factual account coloured by the (presumably ortho-dox) outlook of the historian. The story-tellers, who set out to entertain, successfully defied the claims of history, but the learned—and the Ch'ing novelists were learned—pretended to conform to the conventions of historical narrative while subtly undermining them. Such stylistic qualities as brevity, restraint, a tone of studied detachment and a solemn diction might be enlisted in the narrating of some 'true story' or even history of sorts, though without an orthodox outlook—it being impossible for any novelist to possess the outlook of an orthodox Confucian, whose gaze strayed no further than was directed by ritual—thus producing not history, but satire; straightforward satire tempered by instruction as in *Ching hua yüan*, and deadly satire, restrained and detached, as in the eighteenth century *Ju-lin wai-shih* ('Unofficial History of the World of Learning').[1]

Ju-lin wai-shih adopts a historical framework and certain firm historical dates, but adjusts its time scheme to the life cycles of individuals. Its waves of characters and events reflect the ebb and flow of the Chinese universe, in which days and months may be carefully noted but the true measure of time is the generation. Its unity is the unity of the handscroll, a suc-

[1] See 'Young Master Bountiful' *infra*.

cession of durations, varied and full of pleasant surprises, and seemingly unending, with neither climax nor anticlimax. Its subjective time, which gives the work cohesion, must be regarded as a greater technical achievement than even its satire and parody. In contrast, Ts'ao Chan (died 1764), author of *Hung-lou meng*, scatters history to the winds:

> The Taoist of the Void objected: 'But, Brother Stone, this story of yours, which you claim to be of sufficient interest for publication to the world, falls short, in my opinion, on two counts. First, it would seem to be set in no particular dynasty or reign. Second, its pages are graced by no example of good government by the loyal and sagacious . . .'[1]

and professes to be writing only about a few women he had known all his life. As against the reality of events, he opposes the reality of the inner world, mirrored in a symbolic scheme embracing truth and fiction, existence and non-existence. The work was unfinished and later completed by another hand; but its knowledge of the heart and soul marks the highest point in Chinese fiction.

[1] *Hung-lou meng*, Yü edition, chapter I, p.3; see 'A Burial Mound for Flowers' *infra*.

The Shrew

Of all the pieces included in the present anthology of Chinese colloquial literature, this is the one in which the living voice breaks loud and clear through the barrier of the printed page. For the voice is that of the shrew Ts'ui-lien, whose story is entitled in the original *K'uai-tsui Li Ts'ui-lien chi* ('Story of the sharp-tongued Li Ts'ui-lien'). It was one of sixty stories in six collections from the publishing house of Ch'ing-p'ing shan-t'ang in Hangchow in the mid-sixteenth century, of which twenty-seven surviving stories and fragments—mostly story-tellers' texts (*hua-pen*)—are edited with scrupulous care by T'an Cheng-pi in *Ch'ing-p'ing shan-t'ang hua-pen*, 1957, 'Sharp-tongued Ts'ui-lien' being found on pp. 52–66. But, whereas the usual story-teller's text is mainly prose narrative with a sprinkling of descriptive or lyrical poems, our heroine tells her own story by singing or declaiming a whole succession of speeches in verse, held together by the barest thread of a plot. 'The Shrew' thus contains within itself the two basic ingredients that make up this book: story-telling and dramatic performance.

In this, our story harks back to the T'ang monastery chants and recitations (*pien-wen*) as preserved in tenth century manuscripts at Tun-huang, in which verse and prose alternate in both narrative and dialogue.[1] The form of its verse, in which seven-syllabled lines predominate, interspersed with three-syllabled lines and punctuated by a rough and ready rhyme (not reproduced in the translation), is similar to that in Tun-huang stories, which it moreover resembles in its mixing of the serious with the grotesque, in its naive tone and incoherence, and in its homeliness of language and infelicitous allusions. And

---

[1] As collected in Wang Chung-ming, *Tun-huang pien-wen chi*, 2 vols., 1957; and translated in Arthur Waley, *Ballads and Stories from Tun-huang*, 1960, which includes valuable appendices.

when it is further remembered that the heroine ends up as a nun, the monastic origins of the story would seem beyond doubt. Monastery performances were forbidden early in the eleventh century and soon gave way to story-telling in fairgrounds, in which the Buddhists managed nevertheless to hold their own, certainly in the thirteenth century in Hangchow. Thus our story of the chanting or declaiming Ts'ui-lien, which is set in the Northern Sung capital (Kaifeng), could be among the first Buddhist recitations in the fair-ground booths, though the text we possess is probably no earlier than the first reigns of Ming (late fourteenth and early fifteenth century). Whatever its actual date,[1] as a representative of the earlier oral tradition dating back to T'ang, it is placed at the head of this collection.

As to the wedding customs described in our story, they are paralleled in accounts of Kaifeng in the early twelfth and of Hangchow in the next century. Thus in Kaifeng:[2]

'On the wedding day, the bridegroom's family send a carriage or decorated sedan-chair led by a procession to the bride's home. The bride's family entertain those in the procession and present them with coloured silks, after which the bride ascends the sedan to the sound of music. But the attendants and bearers refuse to move until they have received generous tips on this auspicious occasion, which haggling is known as "raising the sedan"....

'When the bride descends from the sedan [outside the groom's house], an astrologer holding a peck filled with grain, beans, copper coins, fruits and grass, chants his prayers and scatters the contents of the vessel in the direction of the gate, while street urchins rush about picking them up; this being known as "scattering grain and beans", which is said to propitiate the evil spirits. The bride treads on a long strip of green cloth or on a carpet or mat without letting her feet touch the ground. She is led by someone holding

---

[1] See discussion below.

[2] *Tung-ching meng-hua lu* (1147), c. 5, Ku-tien reprint of 1956, p. 30, the customs described being those of the first quarter of the twelfth century in the Northern Sung capital. The sentences about climbing over the saddle and the entwining of the hair make difficult reading, and in these two instances elucidation has been sought in *Meng-liang lu*, c. 20, which records customs prevailing in thirteenth-century Hangchow (pp. 306–7 of the same Ku-tien volume).

a mirror and walking backwards; she is helped on to a saddle, which she must bestride and climb down from the other side, stepping over a pair of scales.

'On entering the house, she is taken into a room with bed-curtains hanging in the middle; this is known as "sitting within false bed-curtains" [i.e. so as to mislead the evil spirits]. But she may also be led straight to the bridal chamber, where she will sit on the bed, which is called "sitting on her future welfare and happiness". . . . [When the bridal pair have worshipped the ancestors and met the relatives, they return to the bridal chamber,] where they sit on the bed, the bride turning towards her left and the groom towards his right, thus facing each other. While they remain thus seated, the women throw golden coins (amulets?) and fruits tied with coloured silk thread at them, and this is known as "strewing the bed-curtains". With the groom still seated on the left and the bride on the right, some of his hair and some of hers are entwined and fastened together, where-upon members of both their families offer them gifts of rolls of silk, hair-pins, combs, hair-cord, etc.; this being called the "fastening of the hair". They are then brought two cups of wine tied together with a ribbon, from one of which each of them would drink, then offering it to the spouse; which is known as "drinking the nuptial cup".'

The same customs were found in the Southern Sung capital, Hangchow, often in a more elaborate form. A thirteenth-century account[1] refers to the lifting of the bridal veil, and also describes a chorus of verses being intoned outside the houses of bride and groom—a survival from T'ang times, as may be seen from the elaborate wedding chorus preserved at Tun-huang.[2] But the astrologer's chant as he strews the bed-curtains in our story finds an exact parallel in the *ch'uan-ch'i* tale, *Tung-t'ien hua-chu chi* ('A Wedding among the Gods') in Li Chen's *Chien-teng yü-hua* (1420), in which a student is invited by some dull-witted gods to compose all the epistles, orations and songs for one of their weddings, which he does without a moment's hesi-

---

[1] *Meng-liang lu*, c. 20, pp. 306–7. The author Wu Tzu-mu's own Preface is dated 1274, but some of the material would be later; see Editor's note, pp. 4–5, *Tung-ching meng-hua lu*, Ku-tien reprint.
[2] 'Hsia nü-fu tz'u' in *Tun-huang pien-wen chi*, c. 3, pp. 273–7; Waley, *Ballads and Stories from Tun-huang*, pp. 189–201, 'Marriage Songs'.

tation, obviously following the best models.[1] As in our story, in Li's first stanza, the set phrase 'Scatter the grain east of the bed-curtains' (literally, 'Strew bed-curtains east'), a three-syllabled line, is followed by three seven-syllabled lines. The other stanzas begin with the same formula: west, south, north, above, below, etc., each followed also by three seven-syllabled lines. However, the total effect is one of greater elegance and artificiality, all the seven-syllabled lines in Li's poem being quotations from earlier poets. But clearly the form was a current one in the early fifteenth century. And indeed a much shortened form consisting of 'Scatter the grain . . . bed-curtains' followed by a line of seven or five syllables survives in wedding chants of today.[2]

Many of the ceremonies themselves pre-date Sung and continue down to the present, their purpose being to promote fecundity and ward off evil. The shrew Ts'ui-lien offends principally against two: strict avoidance of all mention of misfortune, and especially death, on joyful occasions; and complete passivity and silence on the part of the bride. Her contempt for the world with its conventions and human ties is essentially Buddhist, and once the direction of her progress becomes clear, her behaviour is easily accounted for and her defiance of the proprieties suddenly seems venial. The scolding and cursing Ts'ui-lien with her ready fist, the militant female proselyte, is the counterpart of a type common in Chinese fiction, the drinking, swearing and fighting bandit-monk.[3] In the light of her creed, however, her story must be regarded as another version of the martyrdom of the quick-tempered Li Ts'ui-lien and the descent into the nether world of her husband Liu Ch'üan, which is incorporated in the sixteenth-century narrative about Tripitaka

[1] Li's facility in composing set pieces in verse and florid prose is shown to advantage in all his tales, which are in the manner of the T'ang and Sung classical *ch'uan-ch'i*; *Chien-teng yü-hua* is included with the Ku-tien reprint of Ch'ü Yu's *Chien-teng hsin-hua*, 1957, of which 'A Wedding among the Gods' forms pp. 243–7.
[2] See Chu Tzu-ch'ing, *Chung-kuo ko-yao*, 1957, pp. 160–1.
[3] For example, in *Shui-hu chuan*, Lu Ta (*Shui-hu ch'üan-chuan*, ed. of 1954, chapters 4, 5, 6, etc.), Wu Sung and the ferocious monk whose rosary of human skulls he inherits (chapter 27, p. 430; chapter 31, pp. 483–4); and, in their own fashion, Tripitaka's three disciples in *Hsi yu chi*; and the monk Fa-ts'ung in the semi-dramatic chu-kung-tiao *Hsi-hsiang chi* (Wen-hsüeh ku-chi reprint of 1955, I, p. 22ᵃ–p. 23ᵇ, etc.) as well as the monk Hui-ming in 'The West Chamber' plays (*Hsi-hsiang chi*, ed. Wang Chi-ssu, 1954, II, hsieh-tzu).

and his monkey disciple, *Hsi yu chi*, chapters 11–12.[1]

The story of Liu Ch'üan and Li Ts'ui-lien is found in religious and secular recitations (*pao-chüan* and *ku-tz'u*) all over China[2] and is the subject of a Yüan (thirteenth-century) play, *Liu Ch'üan chin kua* ('Liu Ch'üan presents the pumpkins'), now lost,[3] as well as the drama of various localities in the present.[4] In the *Hsi yu chi* account, the pious Ts'ui-lien is reproved by her wealthy husband Liu Ch'üan for being too forward in her attentions to a monk at the gate, so much so as to pluck a gold hair-pin from her own head and hand it to him as her offering. The rebuke so incenses Li Ts'ui-lien that she hangs herself, leaving her family, including a son and daughter, disconsolate. At the intervention of the king of hell, however, she is restored (albeit in a borrowed body) to her husband when, three months later, he visits the infernal regions to bring some pumpkins from the T'ang emperor T'ai-tsung to the rulers of the underworld. (The story thus ties up with the Tun-huang story about T'ai-tsung visiting hell,[5] from which it may well be derived.) Thereafter Li Ts'ui-lien and Liu Ch'üan spend their days expounding the dharma. The charge of unseemly conduct, the repeated threats of *our* shrew to take her own life, her pointed references to Yama, King of Hell, and, earlier, her expectation of a rich husband bear out the relation of the two stories.

The essential Ts'ui-lien, the Shrew, would seem to have been derived from another character, also preserved in a Tun-huang chant and recitation text, *Ya-ch'ia shu* ('Book of the

[1] *Hsi yu chi*, Tso-chia reprint of 1954 (based on edition of 1592), pp. 125–129, where Li Ts'ui-lien and her husband are both natives of Chün-chou (in Hupeh Province); for pumpkins, see p. 118.
[2] The texts of these recitations, which would be of comparatively recent date, are not available to me, and I rely on Ma Lien's Prefatory Note of 1929 incorporated in T'an Cheng-pi's *Ch'ing-p'ing shan-t'ang hua-pen*, p. 188, and Fu Hsi-hua's Introduction to *Sung Yüan hua-pen chi*, 1955, p. 16. The title 'Li Ts'ui-lien' is listed among *ku-tz'u* texts in Chao Ching-shen's own collection in his Preface to *Ku-tz'u hsüan*, 1957, p. 10.
[3] *Liu Ch'üan chin kua* by Yang Hsien-chih, who was contemporaneous with Kuan Han-ch'ing (discussed in 'A Dream of Butterflies' *infra*); see Fu Hsi-hua, *Yüan-tai tsa-chü ch'üan-mu*, 1957, p. 80.
[4] A Shansi play entitled 'A Hundred Thousand Taels, or Li Ts'ui-lien hangs herself' is reported by Ma Lien in the same Prefatory Note.
[5] 'T'ang T'ai-tsung ju ming chi', in *Tun-huang pien-wen chi*, c. 2, pp. 209–214; 'T'ai-tsung in Hell', Waley, *Ballads and Stories from Tun-huang*, pp. 165–74.

Quarrelsome Bride'),[1] which begins:

> The quarrelsome bride in our tale
> Was one so made by nature.
> She engaged in duels of the tongue;
> To argue was her chief concern.

Being too audible, she fails to please her new relations:

> If annoyed, she bellowed like a wounded buffalo;
> And when she laughed, you heard a creaking windlass.

The bride is described as maltreating her husband whom she
loudly abuses, disrespectful and disobedient to her parents-in-
law whom she contradicts, and boisterous and clumsy in the
kitchen, where pots clang, bowls crack and the porridge flies.
She is, moreover, lazy and, when given a rebuke, keeps to her
bed all day. A quarrel with the mother-in-law leads to instant
divorce, suggested by the bride herself to the relief of the
family. Forthwith the deed of renunciation is drawn up with
such clauses as the return of the dowry and the declared wish of
both parties never to meet again. The bride makes a summary
departure, not without curses and imprecations, and returns to
her village to enjoy a life of leisure, never to be molested by her
forsworn relatives:

> For such indeed was her nature—
> If you beat her to death, she would not therefore change.

The narrative portion concludes with a moral for the
parents-in-law, that they were on no account to leave the choice
of another wife for their son to a matchmaker. And the bride's
chant, a mixture of homily and protestation, begins thus:

> 'It's known to all, how I am quarrelsome by nature.
> Why, then, mother-in-law, will you carp at each trivial thing?
> If you must have me mince words to comply with etiquette,
> First change my skin, not once but a hundred times over!'

Even allowing for the continuity of customs and prescribed
usage, the similarity to our story remains striking. Close verbal
parallels are not to be found, and we may assume that our
Shrew is derived in part from a version of the story of the unnamed 'quarrelsome bride'. In turn, our story of 'The Sharp-
tongued Ts'ui-lien', printed in the mid-sixteenth century, seems
to have suggested a number of features in the account of the

---

[1] In *Tun-huang pien-wen chi*, c. 7, pp. 858–61; collation, pp. 861–4. See also
Cheng Chen-to, *Chung-kuo su-wen-hsüeh shih*, Wen-hsüeh ku-chi ed. 1959,
pp. 177–8.

wedding of Su-chieh, a more persistent and violent shrew, in chapter 44 of the novel *Hsing shih yin-yüan*[1] by P'u Sung-ling (1640–1715): the bride's admonishing parents, the ceremony itself including the scattering of the grain as well as the chanting of verses, the infuriated bride and the fleeing Master of Ceremonies, and the bridegroom kept out of the nuptial chamber.

The nostalgia played upon by story-tellers in Hangchow when referring to 'former days in the Eastern Capital'[2] (i.e. Kaifeng or Pien, the Sung capital until 1125 when it fell to the Chin Tartars) is absent in 'Sharp-tongued Ts'ui-lien'. Its atmosphere of rude simplicity, the almost ostentatious display of hardiness and thrift, the special mention of olives from 'south of the Yangtze' and the apparent scarcity of tea in the house (unthinkable in or near Hangchow) all point to a northern origin. Such savage names as Tiger and Wolf find the occasional parallel in the northern drama of the Yüan, e.g. the father Ch'en Tiger and step-son Ch'en Leopard in *Ho han-shan*[3] ('The Divided Shirt'). Under the Yüan also, in the north, life was simple and manners crude, at least as reflected on the stage. Moreover, in our story, banknotes are called *ch'ao* (i.e. *chiao-ch'ao*, exchange note), the term used under the Tartars and the Mongols; in the south, under the Sung, the name was *hui-tzu* (check medium).[4] Banknotes were issued by both the Sung government and the invaders from the middle of the twelfth century onwards, but it was only after the accession of Qubilai in 1260 that they effectively replaced silver and copper cash, remaining in circulation until 1350, when copper coins were revived.[5] By 1283, however, inflation had reduced the notes first issued in 1260 to a fifth of their face value; new notes were accordingly issued, which in turn had depreciated to a fifth of their value by 1309,[6] so that for over a year, in 1310–11, copper coins had again to be used.[7] In our story, the

[1] Shih-chieh shu-chü ed., Taipei 1953, pp. 363–72; and chapter 45, pp. 372–80.

[2] See General Introduction.

[3] By Chang Kuo-pin, in *Yüan-ch'ü hsüan*, Wen-hsüeh ku-chi reprint of 1955, pp. 118–40. The play is probably late thirteenth century.

[4] See L. S. Yang, *Money and Credit in China*, 1952, chapters 6 and 7, §§ 6.13, 6.27, 7.7, etc.

[5] L. S. Yang, chapters 6 and 7, especially §§ 7.7–7.16.

[6] *Yüan shih*, c. 93, pp. 11ᵇ–12ᵇ. References to the Dynastic Histories are to the punctuated edition of Chung-hua Book Co. for the first four, and the Ssu-pu pei-yao edition for the rest.

[7] *Yüan shih*, c. 93, p. 12ᵇ; c. 23, p. 8ᵇ, p. 11ᵇ; c. 24, p. 5ᵃ.

banknotes seem worth little: a note with a face value of one string, i.e. a thousand copper cash, is thrown in as an extra for the match-maker to buy a cake with. Thus I would date the substantial part of our story to the Yüan, about the end of the thirteenth century.

It is the bride Ts'ui-lien herself who distributes the banknotes among the chair-bearers and attendants, and one wonders, therefore, if she could be wearing a veil. (The account of life in Northern Sung Kaifeng makes no mention of a bridal veil.)[1] One line in the astrologer's chant in our story refers unmistakably to the veil without actually using the word: it reads literally—'Lift up and you will see moon goddess face'. From the parallel of Li Chen's lines in 'A Wedding among the Gods', however, the elaborate chant seems likely to be a later addition. Another significant detail is the bridegroom's hairnet,[2] an article of the male head-dress which began under the first Ming emperor, T'ai-tsu (reigned 1368–98), who is said to have instituted it.[3]

We may thus conjecture that, deriving from Buddhist recitations of still earlier date, our story was recited under the Mongols in the north and assumed more or less its present shape about the end of the thirteenth century but that some time later, probably early in the fifteenth century, it found its way to Hangchow, where it was adapted for some story-teller's repertory. Changes of detail were made as required, the astrologer's chant added or revised, and the introductory and concluding verses inserted; certainly the introductory verses bear the heading *ju-hua*, which we may translate as 'The Story-teller's Preamble'.

[1] The expression *kai-t'ou* (literally, head cover) seems not to have acquired the specialized meaning of 'bridal veil' until the thirteenth century in Hangchow (in *Meng-liang lu*, c. 20, already referred to). In the twelfth century *Tung-ching meng-hua lu*, c. 5, it is used merely in the sense of head-scarf, worn, for example, by high-class matchmakers (p. 30). In our story, also, *kai-t'ou* means headscarf, pictured as worn by the sister-in-law and younger sister in mourning.

[2] This is pointed out in Yeh Teh-chün, *Sung Yüan Ming chiang-ch'ang wen-hsüeh*, 1957, p. 58.

[3] See Lang Ying (1487–after 1566), *Ch'i-hsiu lei-kao*, c. 14, Chung-hua reprint of 1959, p. 210.

The text of *K'uai-tsui Li Ts'ui-lien chi* used is that in T'an
Cheng-pi, *Ch'ing-p'ing shan-t'ang hua-pen*, Ku-tien wen-hsüeh
ch'u-pan-she, 1957; I have also consulted the notes in Fu Hsi-
hua, *Sung Yüan hua-pen chi*, 1955, pp. 178–81, and in Wu Hsiao-
ling, Fan Ning and Chou Miao-chung, *Hua-pen hsüan*, 1959,
pp. 59–61.

The Shrew

She declaims whole chapters extempore—
                              let no one despise her gift!
Each speech brings her fresh enemies;
                          her fate moves men to pity.
Though she lacks the persuasion of the wise Tzu-lu[1]
May her tale yet win a laugh from you.[2]

These lines refer to former days in the Eastern Capital,[3] where dwelt a gentleman by the name of Chang Eminent, who had in his house much gold and silver. Of his two grown-up sons,[4] the older was called Tiger, the younger Wolf. The older son had already taken a wife, the younger was not yet married. In the same city was another gentleman, Li Lucky, who had a daughter named Ts'ui-lien,[5] aged sixteen and uncommonly pretty, accomplished in the art of the needle and conversant even with the Classics, Histories and Hundred Philosophers. She was, however, somewhat too ready with her tongue. In speaking to others, she composed whole essays, and the flow of her speech became a flood. Questioned about one matter, she answered about ten, and when questioned about ten, she answered about a hundred. There is a poem to prove it:

Asked about one thing, she tells about ten—indeed a feat!
Ask her ten things, she'll tell you a hundred—rare talent!
Her speech is ready, her words come swift—truly a marvel!
Regard her not as common; she is no ordinary maid.

The story went that in the same city was a Madam Wang who

[1] The disciple of Confucius noted more for fortitude than wisdom or eloquence.
[2] These verses are preceded by the words *ju-hua* (preamble), here omitted; see Introduction.
[3] i.e. the Northern Sun capital Pien; or Kaifeng; see Introduction.
[4] The original merely says 'two sons', but Wolf's younger brother is later mentioned.
[5] The name means 'Blue Lotus', and thus has Buddhist associations; see Introduction.

went to and fro between the two families to arrange about a marriage. The family stations corresponding, a match was agreed upon, and a propitious day and hour chosen for the wedding. Three days before the event, Li Lucky said to his wife, 'Our daughter is faultless in most respects; only her tongue is quick and you and I cannot be easy about it. Should her father-in-law prove hard to please, it were no trifling matter. Besides, the mother-in-law is certain to be fussy, and they are a large family with older brother, sister-in-law, and numerous others. What shall we do?' And his wife said, 'You and I will need to caution her against it.' With this, they saw Ts'ui-lien come before them, and when she found that the faces of both her parents were clouded with grief, and their eyebrows closely knit, she said:

'Dad as bounteous as heaven, Ma as bounteous as earth,
To arrange this match for me today!
The man finds a wife, the maid a mate,
It's a time for rejoicing: be gay for luck!
A fine husband, people all say,
Possessed of riches and many precious things, and well connected,
Clever and nimble,
Good at the Double-Six,[1] chess and all the gentle arts.
He composes verse, and antithetical couplets[2] on demand;
He even knows trade and commerce, selling and buying.
How do you like him for a son-in-law
That bitter tears should fall in drops?'

When Li Lucky and his wife had heard her to the end, they were exceedingly angry. They said, 'We were grieving even because your tongue is as sharp as a blade. We feared that when you entered your husband's house you might talk too much and offend against the proprieties, and thus incur the displeasure of your parents-in-law and everyone else, and become a laughing stock. So we called you, to caution you to talk as little as possible. But higgledy-piggledy, you come out again

[1] A dice game, the finer points of which are discussed in *Ching hua yüan* (early nineteenth century), chapter 74. Skill in the game was rated an accomplishment, certainly in the Yüan and Ming. In *Chin P'ing Mei* (late sixteenth century), go-betweens cataloguing the virtues of prospective lovers and bridegrooms invariably mention a knowledge of chess and Double-Six (*Chin P'ing Mei tz'u-hua*, ed. of 1935, chapter 2, p. 24; chapter 3, p. 30; chapter 69, p. 848; etc.).
[2] Making up such couplets was part of the schoolboy's exercise in composition.

with a long discourse! What a bitter lot is ours!' Ts'ui-lien, however, said in reply:

'Dad, ease your mind; Ma, be consoled;
Brother, rest assured; sister-in-law, stop worrying;
It is not that your daughter would boast of her cleverness
But from childhood she has been on her mettle:
She can spin, she can weave,
She makes dresses, does patching and embroidery;
Light chars and heavy duties she takes in her stride,
Has ready the teas and meals in a trice;
She can work the hand-mill and pound with the pestle;
She endures hardship gladly, she is not easily tired,
Thinks nothing of making dumplings and cookies,
Prepares any soup or broth, does to a turn some cutlet or chop.
At night she is vigilant,
Fastens the backdoor and bolts the gate,
Scrubs the frying pan, shuts the cupboard,
Tidies up the rooms both in front and behind,
Makes ready the beds, unrolls the quilts,
Lights the lamp, asks the mother-in-law to retire,
Then calls out "Rest well" and returns to her room:
Thus shall I serve my parents-in-law,
And would they be dissatisfied?
Dear Dad and Ma, let your minds be at rest—
Besides these set tasks, nought matters more than a fart.'

When Ts'ui-lien had finished, her father rose from his chair to beat her. But the mother pleaded with him, and loudly reproved her, saying, 'Child, your father and I were worried just because of your sharp tongue. From now on, talk less. The ancients say, "Loquacity earns the hatred of many". When you enter your husband's house, be wary of speaking. A thousand times remember this!' Ts'ui-lien thereupon said, 'I know now. From this time onwards I will keep my mouth shut'.

On the eve of the wedding,[1] Mrs Li said to Ts'ui-lien, 'Old grandfather Chang next door is a neighbour of long standing, and you grew up, as it were, under his very eyes. You should go over and bid him farewell.' And Mr Li also said, 'That would be right.' Ts'ui-lien then went over to the neighbours', crossed their threshold, and spoke in a loud voice:

[1] The time is not mentioned in the original, and these words are inserted by the translator.

'Grandpa Chang, hearken; grandma Chang, hearken;
Hearken to my speech, you two old ones.
Tomorrow at dawn I mount my bridal sedan;
Today I am come to make the announcement.
My parents are frail, they have no support;
Pray keep an eye on them morning and night.
If my brother and his wife offend you in any way,
Forgive them for my parents' sake.
When I return a month after the event,
I shall myself come to ask your pardon.'
Grandfather Chang replied: 'Little lady, set your mind at rest.
Your father and I are dear old friends. I shall certainly look
after him morning and evening. And I shall ask my aged
spouse to keep your mother company. On no account let it
trouble you.'

When Ts'ui-lien returned from bidding grandfather Chang
farewell, Li Lucky and his wife said to her: 'Child, you should
now tidy up and go to bed early. Tomorrow you have to rise
before daybreak to attend to things.' Ts'ui-lien then said:

'Dad, retire first; Ma, retire first;
You are not like us young ones.
Sister-in-law and brother can keep me company
While each part of the house I tidy up.
The young can watch all through the night;
Older folk, when they try it, fall a-dozing.'
When Ts'ui-lien had spoken, the father and mother were
greatly vexed. They cried, 'Have done! Have done! As we
were saying, you would never change. We will now retire.
You can tidy up with your brother and sister-in-law, and then
"Early to bed and early to rise".'

When Ts'ui-lien saw that her parents had gone to rest, she
hurriedly went to the door of her brother's room and shouted
aloud:

'Do not pretend to be drunk, sister-in-law and brother,—
How distressing even to think of you two!
I am your own dear little sister
And shall be home just one more night.
However could you two act in this way,
Leaving all the chores to me,
Shutting your door, ready to fall asleep?
Sister-in-law, how ungracious of you!

I am at home but this short while—
Would it matter so much if you lent a hand?
You cannot wait to send me away
That the two of you may be free and easy.'
Ts'ui-lien finished speaking, and the brother remonstrated with
her, saying, 'How could you still behave like this? With Dad
and Ma there, I am not in a position to scold you. Go and rest
now, and get up early tomorrow. Your sister-in-law and I
will attend to whatever has to be done.' So Ts'ui-lien went back
to her room to sleep. In a little while the brother and sister-in-
law had tidied up each part of the house, and the entire family
retired for the night.

Li Lucky and his wife woke up after a good sleep. They
called out to Ts'ui-lien, saying, 'Child, what time is it now?
Is it fine or rainy?' Then Ts'ui-lien broke into speech:

'Dad, do not rise yet; Ma, do not rise yet;
I do not know if it be rainy or fine;
I do not hear the watch being sounded—nor the cock crow.
The streets are quiet, none are conversing;
I only hear Mrs Pai next door
                              making ready to grind her bean-curd,
And old father Huang opposite pounding his sticky rice.
If not still the fourth watch,
Certainly it would be the fifth.
Let me rise first,
Start the fire, chop the wood and fetch the water.
Next let me scrub the pot,
Boil water with which to wash my face,
And comb my hair till it is smooth and shining.
Let everyone else rise early too
Lest the bridal procession find us all in a flurry.'

Then father, mother, brother and sister-in-law all rose from
their beds. And the father and mother said in an outburst of
rage, 'All too soon it will be bright in the east. Yet instead of
attending to your toilet, you are busy wagging your tongue.'
But Ts'ui-lien said in reply:

'Dad, do not scold; Ma, do not scold;
See how cleverly I adorn myself in my room.
My raven black hair I flatten around each temple,
Mix powder and rouge and rub them on my cheeks,
Then paint my red lips and pencil my eyebrows.

A golden ear-ring I wear in each lobe;
Silver and gold, jade and pearl I pin all over my head;
Pendants of gems and tinkling bells I attach to my sides.
You are marrying me off today,
But, oh! my Dad and Ma, how could I leave you?
I bethink me of the favours of giving suck and rearing
And teardrops wet through my scented silk handkerchief.
Hark, I hear voices outside the house—
Despite myself I grow alarmed.
But today is my lucky day:
Why go on tattling and prattling like this?'
Ts'ui-lien stopped. However, when her toilet was done, she
went straight into her parents' presence and said:
'Dad, hear my report; Ma, hear my report;
The dumplings are steamed, the noodles are cut,
The viands and box of delicacies are laid out.
I have them all ready, and now wait patiently
Even while the drum-beats give out the fifth watch.
Mark how our own rooster crows right on the hour!
We must send for the relatives who planned to see me off.
It would matter little if Ma's sister and Uncle's wife stayed away,
But how wicked of Dad's own sister!
She sets no store by her words.
She promised to be here by the fifth watch only yesterday;
The cock has crowed, yet there is no trace of her.
When, later, she enters our gate, I must just—
Instead of a final invitation—
Offer her a resounding slap with all five fingers outstretched.'[1]
Angry though they were at her words, Li Lucky and his wife
forbore to speak out. Mrs Li said, 'Child, go and ask your
brother and sister-in-law to rise now and attend to things. The
bridal procession will soon be here.' When Ts'ui-lien heard
her mother say this, she hurriedly went to the door of the
brother and sister-in-law, and shouted aloud:
'Dear sister-in-law, dear brother, you are no longer children.
From now on I shall seldom be home;
You could at least have risen early today—
Will you sleep until broad daylight?
It's time to unbolt the gate and open the windows;

[1] Presumably to give a harder smack; demonstrated by Wu Sung in
Shui-hu ch'üan-chuan, c. 32, p. 495.

Next, you might light the candles and aromatic incense;
Then give the ground, within and without, a sweeping:
The bridal sedan is expected any moment,
And if the hour[1] be missed and my parents-in-law annoyed,
The pair of you shall hear from me!'

The brother and sister-in-law swallowed the affront and kept silent, and they attended to various tasks in the house. Then Li Lucky said to Ts'ui-lien, 'Child, you should go before the family shrine, make obeisance to your ancestors and bid them farewell. I have already lit the candles and incense; so do it while we wait for the bridal procession. May the ancestors protect you and you be at peace in your husband's home.' Thus instructed, Ts'ui-lien took a bunch of lighted incense sticks and went before the shrine, and even as she made obeisance, she prayed aloud:

'Shrine that guides the household,
Your sages that were our ancestors,
This day I take a husband,
Yet shall not dare keep my own counsel:
At the solstices and equinoxes, and the beginning of each season,
I still will offer up the smoke of incense.
I pray to your divine wisdom
Ten thousand times that you pity and hearken!
The man takes a wife, the maid a mate—
This is in the nature of things—
May there be good fortune and rejoicing!
May husband and wife both remain sound and whole,
Without hardship, without calamity,
Even for a hundred years!
May they be merry as fish in water
And their union prove sweeter than honey,
Blessed with five sons and two daughters—
A complete family of seven children—
Matched with two worthy sons-in-law,
Wise and versed in etiquette,
And five daughters-in-law too,
Paragons of filial piety.
May there be grandsons and grand-daughters numerous
To flourish generation after generation.

---

[1] The lucky hour fixed upon by the astrologer for the wedding ceremony.

May there be gold and pearls in heaps
And rice and wheat to fill a granary,
Abundance of silkworms and mulberry trees,
And cattle and horses drawn up neck to neck,
Chickens, geese, duck and other fowl,
And a pond teeming with fish.
May my husband obey me,
Yet his parents love and pity me;
May the sister-in-law and I live in harmony
And the older and the younger brother be both easy to please;
May the servants show full respect,
And the younger sister take a fancy to me.
And, within a space of three years,
Let them die, the whole lot,
And all the property be left in my hands:
Then Ts'ui-lien would be happy for some years!'
When Ts'ui-lien had finished her prayer, there was a din
outside the gate. It was a confused noise of many musical in-
struments, above which rose the shrill notes of pipes and sing-
ing. The procession from the bridegroom's family, carriage,
horsemen and all, was at the gate. And the astrologer accompanying the procession chanted in verse:

'Roll up your bead curtain and fasten it with jade hooks;
A perfumed carriage, followed by noble horses,

has reached your gate.

Be liberal in your happy-omened tips on this auspicious occasion
And in wealth, honour and splendour pass a hundred autumns.'

Li Lucky then asked his wife to fetch money to reward the
astrologer, the match-maker, the grooms and other attendants.
But when Mrs Li came out with the banknotes,[1] Ts'ui-lien
snatched them from her, saying, 'Let me distribute these notes —

Dad, you are not used to this; Ma, you are not used to this;
Brother and sister-in-law, you too are not used to this dealing.
Hey, all of you there, come and stand before me!
Be it less or more, it is as I shall apportion.
To the sedan-bearers, five thousand copper cash;
Mr Astrologer and the match-maker each get two and a half.
Keep your money well, do not start a row;
If any of you lose it, you have but yourself to blame.
Look, there's another thousand cash note remaining—

[1] See Introduction.

Take it, match-maker, and buy a cake

To comfort your dotard of a husband at home.'

The astrologer, the sedan-bearers and the others were all aghast when they heard this. They said, 'We have seen thousands of brides but never one so quick in speech.' They gaped and put their tongues out and, swallowing their anger, crowded around Ts'ui-lien and helped her on to the bridal sedan.

While they were on their way, the match-maker kept on admonishing Ts'ui-lien, 'Little lady, when you reach the gate of the house of your parents-in-law, on no account open your mouth.' Before long, the procession reached the gate of the Chang home and the sedan-chair was let down. The astrologer chanted:

'The sound of nuptial music is heard all over the capital;

The Weaving Maid this day weds the Divine Cowherd.[1]

The relatives of this house come forth to receive the treasure;

The bride in her finery accepts her mouthful of rice—

a custom from time immemorial.'

To go on with the story, the match-maker held up a bowl of rice and shouted aloud: 'Little lady, open your mouth to receive the rice.'[2] Upon this, Ts'ui-lien in her bridal sedan burst out in rage:

'Shameless old bitch! Shameless old bitch!

One moment you tell me to shut my mouth,

and the next you ask me to *open* it!

Oh! the unfathomable glibness of match-makers!

However could you change your 'don't's at once into 'do's?

Are you drunk already so early in the day

That foolishly you open *your* mouth,

lying and wagging your tongue?

Just then while you walked by my sedan

You warned me on no account to open my mouth.

I have only now been set down before the gate—

Why then do you ask me to open my mouth?

Blame me not for calling you names—

Really you are but a painted old bitch.'

The astrologer then said, 'Bride, cease your anger. She is the

---

[1] Weaving Maid and Divine Cowherd: the lovers who were transformed into two stars separated by the Milky Way, to meet only on the night of the seventh of the seventh moon each year.

[2] The custom is not recorded in the accounts of Sung city life.

match-maker. You go too far in your words. There is no precedent for such behaviour in a bride.' But Ts'ui-lien replied:

'Mr Astrologer, you are a man of learning;
How then could you be so dull of apprehension?
Not to speak when one ought to is, by definition, slow-witted.[1]
This bawd of a matchmaker will be the death of me!
She says the bridegroom's family is wealthy and high-ranking,
Possessed of riches and precious things, much silver and gold;
A calf or horse they would kill for their table;
Their gate is made of sandal and sapanwood;
They have silks, gauzes, brocades in numberless rolls
And pigs, goats, cattle and horses all in droves.
Yet even before I enter the house, they dish up this cold rice:
Better be poor than wealthy and high-ranking in *this* fashion.
Hard indeed to endure a family so uncouth
As would serve up cold rice and expect me to swallow it!
Had I no regard for the faces of both parents-in-law,
I could beat you till you saw stars!'

Ts'ui-lien having had her say, the match-maker was so incensed
that she tasted not a drop of wine but, like a whiff of smoke,
vanished into the house, neither minding Ts'ui-lien's descent
from the bridal sedan[2] nor the ensuing ceremony at the altar.

But the relatives of the bridegroom's family crowded around
Ts'ui-lien and escorted her into the ceremonial hall, where they
made her stand with her face to the west.[3] The astrologer,
however, announced: 'The bride will turn and face the east.
The stars of good luck are all in the east today.' At this, Ts'ui-
lien again burst out:

'Just then it was west, and now I must face east.
Will you drag the bride about as you would lead a beast?
Having turned round and round, tending in no fixed direction,
I am so vexed, my heart is afire:
I cannot tell who my mother-in-law
Nor who my father-in-law is
Amidst this noisy crowd of relatives even to the ninth degree,
With the younger brother and sister adding to the confusion.

---

[1] In *Chin P'ing Mei tz'u-hua*, chapter 7, this is given as: 'Not to speak
when one ought to is, by definition, timidity' (p.63).
[2] This involved much ceremony; see Introduction.
[3] This is the customary position. The altar is in the north, and as seen by
the guests, the bride would be on the right, the groom on the left. See
Teng Chih-ch'eng (ed.), *Tung ching meng-hua lu chu*, 1959, p.159, n.17.

The red paper tablet is placed in the centre
And red silken lanterns, several pairs of them, are lit.
But, wait, my father-in-law and mother-in-law

are not yet deceased.
Why then should there be a lamp for the dead?'
Old Chang Eminent and his wife were furious when they heard
this. They exclaimed: 'It was earlier agreed that our son would
marry the daughter of a respectable family. Who would have
known it would turn out to be this ill-mannered, ill-bred, long-
tongued wayward peasant girl?' And all the relatives of the
nine degrees gaped, utterly confounded.

Finally the astrologer said, 'This child has been spoilt at
home. She has only just arrived today. You will need to train
her gradually. Let us proceed with the ceremony of bowing before the altar, to be followed by the bowing to the relatives.'
And when the ceremony was over and all the relatives, old and
young, had been introduced, the astrologer, chanting in verse,
requested the bride and groom to enter the nuptial chamber for
the strewing of the bed-curtains:[1]

'The newly wed move their steps across the lofty hall;
Nymph and god together enter the nuptial chamber.
Be liberal in your happy-omened tips

on this auspicious occasion—
Scatter the grain in all directions,

that *yin* and *yang* mingling may increase.'
Wolf went in front, with Ts'ui-lien behind him. The astrologer,
holding before him a peck containing a mixture of the five
grains, followed them into the nuptial chamber.

The newly wedded couple sat on the bed while the astrologer
chanted with the grain in his hand:

'Scatter the grain east of the bed curtains—
Red candles cast their shadows where thick screens enfold.
Long may youthful charms bloom, not fade;
Eternal spring prevail in the painted hall!

Scatter the grain west of the bed curtains—
Pennants and ribbons stream down the corners of the bed.

---

[1] Sedan-chair, saddle, veil and the strewing of the bed-curtains are mentioned or form part of the action in the mock wedding in Chu Yu-tun's play
about Li K'uei, *Hei-hsüan-feng chang-i su-ts'ai* ('The Generous Acts of the
"Black Whirlwind"'; about 1430); see *Ming-jen tsa-chü hsüan*, Jen-min
wen-hsüeh ch'u-pan-she, 1958, pp. 202–5.

Anonymous   43

Lift the veil and you will see the goddess's face;
The godlike bridegroom attains his laurel branch.[1]

Scatter the grains south of the bed curtains —
Nuptial bliss long to linger over!
A gentle breeze in moonlight cools hall and bower,
Flapping two belts adorned with the "heir bearing" plant.[2]

Scatter the grain north of the bed curtains —
That overflowing beauty between her eye-brows!
In the warmth of the embroidered curtains on a night in spring
The moon goddess detains her favoured guest.

Scatter the grain above the bed curtains —
A pair of intertwining mandarin ducks!
May you dream tonight of the bear[3]
And the pearl-oyster falling on to your palm!

Scatter the grain within the bed curtains —
A pair of jade hibiscus under the moon!
It's as if one encountered a fair immortal,
Wrapped in crimson clouds, alighting from Mount Wu.[4]

Scatter the grain under the bed curtains —
Some say a golden light will shine in the room.
Share now the lucky dreams of this night:
Bring forth next year a man child and win enhanced standing.

[1] For veil, see Introduction. The goddess Ch'ang-o dwells alone with a white rabbit and a laurel tree in the moon, where her earth-bound husband, Yih, eventually joins her; see *Li-tai shen-hsien t'ung-chien*, I, c.3, iii. In other versions, she is visited by the woodcutter Wu Kang, who is, however, condemned to hack eternally at the laurel branches, which heal at once; see Yüan K'o, *Chung-kuo ku-tai shen-hua*, 1950, pp. 88–9 and notes. Thus mythology. T'ang examination candidates spoke of 'breaking off a laurel branch' when they were successful. Since successful examination candidates were readily accepted as bridegrooms, 'attainer of the laurel branch' and 'moon goddess's guest' came to be applied to both successful examinees and bridegrooms.   [2] The day lily.
[3] Omen of the birth of a son in *Shih ching*, Hsiao-ya, 'Ssu kan':
'The diviner thus interprets it:
  "Black bears and brown
  Mean men-children.
  Snakes and serpents
  Mean girl-children."' Arthur Waley, *The Book of Songs*, 1954, p. 283.
The pearl-oyster is the symbol of pregnancy.
[4] Mount Wu, whose goddess came to the Ch'u king, Huai-wang, in a dream. Her presence, she told him, was to be felt in the morning clouds and evening rain: hence the expression 'clouds and rain' for a love encounter. See Sung Yü, 'Kao-t'ang fu', *Wen-hsüan*, c. 19.

Scatter the grain in front of the bed-curtains—
Hovering in the air is neither mist nor smoke,
It is the coiled-dragon-incense fume:
The student at last meets his fairy bride.[1]

Scatter the grain behind the bed curtains—
Man and wife agreeing, long cherish each other.
From of old "Wife chimes in when husband sings";
Do not then roar like the proverbial lioness.'[2]

To go on with the story, the astrologer had not yet completed the ceremony of strewing the bed-curtains, when Ts'ui-lien sprang up and, groping about, found a rolling-pin, with which she dealt him two smart blows in the sides, and roundly abused him: 'You skunk of a windbag. It's your own wife who would be the lioness.' And without further ado she drove him out of the bridal chamber, shouting after him:

'Scatter the grain indeed! I ask you, to what purpose?
Having littered that way, again to litter this way,—
Beans, rice, wheat, barley all over the bed.
Just pause to think: Ain't it a pretty sight?
The parents-in-law are rude and rash,
The bride's untidy and careless, they'll say.
And if the husband should pretend to be vexed
He would say the wife was slatternly.
Off with you at once—out of the gate.
And spare yourself more blows from my rolling-pin.'

The astrologer took his beating and went out through the gate. The bridegroom, Wolf, was now roused and exclaimed: 'Of the thousands of misfortunes, to have married this peasant woman! Strewing the bed-curtains is an ancient ceremony.' To this, Ts'ui-lien said in reply:

'Husband, husband, be not angry,
Hear me and judge the right and wrong for yourself.
The mere thought of that man tries my patience,
Littering beans and barley all over the place.
Yet you ask no one to sweep them away;
Instead you say, I lack womanly obedience.
If you vex me any further,
You too I will drive out with him,

[1] The student Wen Hsiao met his fairy bride Wu Ts'ai-luan in the mountains; see *Li-tai shen-hsien t'ung-chien*, iii, c. 17, v.
[2] Euphemism for wife's scolding.

Shut my door, sleep by myself.
"Early to bed and early to rise" as I please.
And "Amitabha" chant my prayers
With my ears undisturbed in careless solitude.'
And Wolf, at a loss what to do with her, went out to join in the
feasting and toast his guests.

By nightfall the feast broke up and the relatives all went
home. Sitting alone in the nuptial chamber, Ts'ui-lien thought
to herself: 'Soon my husband will come into the room and his
hands are certain to rove in some wild ecstatic dance. I have to
be prepared.' So she stood up, removed her jewellery, un-
dressed and, getting into bed, rolled herself tightly in a quilt
and slept. Now, to go on with the story, Wolf came in and un-
dressed, and was about to go to bed, when Ts'ui-lien stunned
him with a thundering cry:

'Wretch, how ridiculously mistaken in your designs!
Of a truth, what an uncouth rustic!
You are a man, I a woman;
You go your way, I go mine.
You say I am your own bride—
Well, do not call me your old woman yet.
Who was the match-maker? Who the chief witness?
What were the betrothal presents? How was the gift of tea?
How many pigs, sheep, fowl and geese? How many vats of wine?
What floral decorations embellished the gifts?
How many gems? How many golden head ornaments?
How many rolls of silk gauze, thick and thin?
How many pairs of bracelets, hat pins, hair pins?
With what should I adorn myself?
At the third watch late at night,
What mean you to come before my bed?
At once depart, and hurry away,
Lest you annoy my folk at home.
But if you provoke my fiery temper,
I will seize you by the ears and pull your hair,
Tear your clothes and scratch your face;
My heavy hand with outstretched fingers
                                shall fall pat on your cheek.
If I rip your hair-net,[1] don't say I did not warn you,
Nor complain if your neatly coiled hair gets dishevelled.
[1] See Introduction.

This is no bawd's lane.

Nor the dwelling of some servile courtesan.

What do I care about silly rules like "Two and two make four"

With a sudden laying about of my fist

I'll send you sprawling all over the room.'

When Wolf heard his bride declaim this chapter, he dared not approach her, nor uttered even a groan, but sat in a far-off corner of the room.

To go on with the story, soon it was indeed almost the third watch, and Ts'ui-lien thought to herself: 'I have now married into his family. Alive, I shall remain one of their household; dead, I shall dwell among their ghosts. If we do not sleep in the same bed tonight, when tomorrow my parents-in-law learn about it, they will certainly blame me. Let it be, then! I will ask him to come to bed.' So she said to Wolf:

'Dumb wretch, do not say you are drunk!

Come over, I will share the bed with you.

Draw near me and hear my command:

Fold your hands respectfully before you;

                                        tread on your toes; do not chatter.

Remove your hair-net and off with your cap;

Gather up your garments, socks and boots;

Shut the door, lower the curtain,

And add some oil to the lamp grown dim.

Come to bed, and ever so softly

We'll pretend to be mandarin ducks or intertwining trees.

Make no noise, be careful of what you say;

When our conjugal rites are completed,

                                        you'll curl up next my feet,

Crooking your knee-joints, drawing in your heels.

If by chance you give even one kick,

Then know it's *death* for you!'

And the story went that the whole night through Wolf indeed dared not make the least noise. They slept until dawn, when the mother-in-law called out: 'Wolf, you should ask your bride to rise early, finish her toilet, and come out to tidy up.' So Ts'ui-lien spoke out:

'Do not hurry, do not rush;

Wait till I have donned my everyday clothes.

Now—vegetables with vegetables, ginger with ginger,

Each variety of nuts into a separate pack.

Pork on one side, mutton on the other;
We'll sort out the fresh fish from boiled tripe.
Wine by itself, away from the broth;
Salt chicken and smoked venison should not be mixed.
In the cool of this time of year
They will keep yet a good five days.
Let me set apart some neat slices
To serve on the third morn with tea for the aunts.
And if the relatives do not eat them all,
The parents-in-law can have the left-overs as a treat.'
When the mother-in-law had heard this, she was a long
while speechless. She wanted to scold Ts'ui-lien but was afraid
she would only make herself a laughing stock. So she swallowed her anger and endured in silence until the third morn,[1]
when the bride's mother called in to present her gifts. And
when the two mothers-in-law had met, Mrs Chang could no
longer contain herself: she recounted from beginning to end
how Ts'ui-lien had inflicted blows on the astrologer and how
she had abused the match-maker, how she had insulted her
husband and how she had slighted her parents-in-law. Upon
hearing this account, Mrs Li grew exceedingly ashamed. She
went straight to her daughter's room and said to Ts'ui-lien,
'What did I warn you against when you were still at home? I
told you not to jabber and chatter when you entered your
husband's house, but you never listened to me. It is only the
third day, yet your mother-in-law made many complaints
about you just then, causing me to be in fear and trepidation,
and unable to utter a word in reply.' Ts'ui-lien, however, said:
'Mother, don't start a row yet;
Listen while I relate it in each particular.
Your daughter is no untaught peasant woman;
There are some matters you little know about.
On the third morn the new daughter-in-law enters the kitchen[2]
(Ha ha, to relate this would but earn me ridicule)
Two bowls of thin rice porridge with salt was all they provided
And, to serve with the meal, not even tea but plain boiling water!
Now you, their new relation, make your first call,

[1] 'On the third day, the bride's family send gifts of coloured silks and
honey cake; or they themselves call, which is known as "comforting the
daughter".' (*Tung-ching meng-hua lu*, c.5, p.32.)
[2] In accordance with custom, to prepare her first meal for the family.

At once they start their tittle-tattle:
Regardless of white or black, true or false,
Harassing me is all they are bent on.
My mother-in-law is by nature too impetuous,
The things she says are none too proper.
Let her beware—lest driven to my last resource,
With a bit of cord and a swing from the noose
I leave her to answer for my corpse.'

When the mother found Ts'ui-lien talking in this way, she could not very well scold her. And without drinking her tea or tasting the wine, Mrs Li instantly took leave of her new relations, mounted her sedan-chair and returned home.

To go on with the story, Wolf's older brother, Tiger, now began to shout in the house: 'What kind of a family are we now? It was said at first that brother would be marrying a well-behaved young woman. Who would have expected it to be this tavern waitress who chatters the whole day, wagging her tongue and declaiming sentences and maxims? It is quite outrageous!' Ts'ui-lien heard him and said in reply:

'Brother-in-law, you err against ritual;
I did not in the least provoke you.
A full-grown, manly pillar of society
To call his sister-in-law a glib tavern waitress!'

Tiger then called to Wolf and said, 'Haven't you heard the old saying: "Teach a wife when she first comes to you"? Though you need not go so far as to beat her, you might at least lecture her now and then; or else go and tell her old bawd of a mother.' At this, Ts'ui-lien exclaimed:

'Busy-body of a brother-in-law!
I did not dip my fingers in your bowl of rice.
Though I may be a bit loquacious,
There's husband, and mother-in-law, to keep me in order.
Your new relations did not provoke you—
Why then do you call my mother a bawd?
Wait till I go back when the month is over;[1]
I will tell my own dear brother at home.
My brother is a hotheaded firebrand;
You will perhaps know me better
When his fist and hand shall both at once hit out,
And like a tortoise in a drought you'll crawl in vain for shelter.'

[1] A month after the wedding, the bride visits her own home.

Tiger was enraged by her speech and, laying hands upon Wolf, thought to give the brother a thrashing. But his wife, Mistress Ssu, ran out from her room and said, 'To each his own; how should brother's wife concern you? It was said of old: "Don't wear your clean shoes to tread on a dunghill".' At once Ts'ui-lien burst out again:

'Sister-in-law, don't start trouble;
This kind of conduct would never do.
Was it not enough for brother-in-law to shout at me
But you must step forward to scold some more?
It ever has been: when the wife is dutiful, the man shuns all ills
And succeeds in the highest enterprise.
Go off then quickly, back to your room,
And sit in hiding in some secure corner.
Sister-in-law, I did not provoke you—
Why then do you liken me to dung?
Since we must die even if we lived to a hundred,
Shall you and I now fight it out?
And if any mishap befell me,
Before Yama, King of the Underworld,[1] I would not let you off.'

The daughter of the house, Wolf's younger sister, heard this. She went into her mother's room and said, 'You are her mother-in-law. Why don't you keep her under control? How very unseemly it would be if she carried on like this unchecked! People would only laugh at us.' But when Ts'ui-lien saw the younger sister thus engaged, she called out after her:

'Younger sister, how wicked of you
To sneak within to incite your mother!
If my mother-in-law should beat me to death,
I would carry you off with me to the king of hell.
My father is by nature pugnacious—
He's not one to endure wrongs meekly—
He would insist on a hundred priests, Taoist and Buddhist,
To conduct services seven nights and seven days,
And a pine-wood coffin with a solid block for base,
And mother-in-law and father-in-law to burn paper-money for me.
You, younger sister, and sister-in-law,
                          would wear mourning headscarves,[2]
And brother-in-law could prostrate himself as my heir,

---

[1] See Introduction.   [2] i.e. *kai-t'ou*; see Introduction.

And the relatives of the nine degrees would carry the bier.
The funeral ended, your troubles would start afresh:
Accusations would have sped to the local and high courts,
Whose judges with all your silver you would bribe in vain.
Even had you millions upon millions of strings of cash,
You would spend them all and still forfeit your lives.'
The mother-in-law now came out and said to Ts'ui-lien,
'Luckily you have been my daughter-in-law only these three
days; had you been these three years, would any of us in this
family, old ones and young ones, ever get to speak at all?'
Ts'ui-lien replied:
'You are too easily swayed, my mother-in-law;
When older folk grow slack, they lose the respect of the young.
Dear younger sister, do not tempt fortune too far;
Must you splutter all before your mama,
Exaggerating heavily the lightest rumours?
To which the old fool listening and readily believing,
Stings me to the quick with this remark or that
In words unfit for the ear.
If any mishap befell me,
Rest assured the old one would pay with her life.'
When the mother-in-law heard this, she went straight back to
her room. And she said to the old gentleman. 'Just look at that
new daughter-in-law of ours. Her tongue is as sharp as a blade,
and she has insulted each member of the family in turn. You are
her father-in-law. Don't be afraid to summon and reprimand
her.' The old gentleman said, 'I am the father-in-law, and so
hardly in a position to reprimand her. However, let me ask her
for some tea to drink, and we can then see what happens.' His
wife then said, 'When she sees you, she will not dare wag her
tongue.'

Thereupon Mr Chang gave the order: 'Ask Wolf's wife to
brew some mid-day tea.' When Ts'ui-lien heard the father-in-
law calling for tea, she hurriedly went into the kitchen, scrubbed the pot and boiled the water. She then went to her own
room and took out a variety of nuts, and returning to the
kitchen, made bowls of tea, which she placed on a tray. Holding
the tray before her, she went into the ceremonial hall, where
she arranged the chairs. She then went before her parents-in-
law, saying 'Pa and Ma will please have their tea in the hall.'
And she also went to the sister-in-law's room and said:

'Brother and sister-in-law will please have tea in the hall.' Mr
Chang then remarked: 'You were all saying the new daughter-
in-law had a sharp tongue. Now when I order her to do something, she dare not raise her voice.' His wife rejoined: 'Since
this is so, you shall give her all the orders.'

In a little while the entire family were gathered in the ceremonial hall, and sat down in order of seniority. And they saw
Ts'ui-lien come forward with her tray to address them:

'Pa, have tea; Ma, have tea;
Brother and sister-in-law, come and have your tea.
If younger sister and younger brother would like tea,
They can help themselves to the two bowls on the oven.
But hold your bowls well, the pair of you, and tread with care
Lest the hot tea scald your hands and you cry "Oh! oh!"
This tea we call Granny's Tea;
The name is homely, the taste delicious.
Here are two chestnuts freshly roasted brown,
Half a pinch of fried white sesame seeds,
Olives from south of the Yangtze,[1] and mixed nut kernels,
And walnuts from beyond the Great Wall, and shelled haws.
You two venerable ones will eat them slowly
Lest all unwares you lose a tooth or two.'

When the father-in-law found her speaking in this manner,
he said in a rage: 'A female person should be gentle and staid,
and sober in speech: only then is she fit to be a daughter-in-law.
Was there ever a long-tongued woman like this one!' But
Ts'ui-lien again spoke out:

'Venerable Pa, venerable Ma,
And brother and sister-in-law too, sit you down,
You two old ones, do not scold me
But listen to your daughter-in-law's account:
She is not stupid nor is she sly;
From childhood on, she was straight and blunt,
And unkind words, once uttered, slip clean out of her mind.
Pa and Ma, do not detest her overmuch;
But if you really disapprove, then—repudiate her:
She will not grieve nor be afraid;
She will mount her sedan and return home.
No new husband shall she think of—
                    neither one who would dwell with her parents

[1] See Introduction.

Nor one who would take her to his own house.
She will not put on powder and rouge, nor adorn herself,
But, as in mourning, wear white from top to toe,
And so wait on her parents and end her days.
I remember many ancient men of wisdom:
Chang Liang[1] and K'uai Ch'e were skilled in argumentation,
Lu Chia and Hsiao Ho ever ready with some learned allusion;
Ts'ao Chih and Yang Hsiu were no less ready in wit;
The eloquence of Chang I and Su Ch'in
                                        swayed the Warring States,
And Yen-tzu and Kuan Chung overcame mighty princes
                                        through persuasion;
And there were Ch'en P'ing with his six stratagems,
                                        and Li Tso-chü,
And the twelve-year-old official Kan Lo,
                                        and the disciple Tzu-hsia himself:
These ancients all excelled in making speeches;
They regulated their households, governed their kingdoms,
                                        and pacified the Empire.

  If Pa would stop me from speaking,
  Then you must stitch up my mouth.'
Mr Chang cried, 'Have done! Have done! Such a daughter-
in-law would one day bring down the family name and be a reproach to the ancestors.' And he called Wolf before him and
said, 'Son, put your wife away. I will find you another, a better
wife.' Though Wolf assented to this, he could not find it in his
heart to cast her off. And Tiger and his wife both pleaded with
the father, saying, 'Let her be taught gradually.' But Ts'ui-lien,
having heard them, once more spoke up:

  'Pa, do not complain; Ma, do not complain;
  Brother and sister-in-law, do you not complain.
  Husband, you need not persist in clinging to me;
  From now on, each will do as he pleases.
  At once bring paper, ink, slab and brush,
  Write out the certificate of repudiation and set me free.

[1] Chang Liang, etc. All were eloquent and persuasive speakers, including
the twelve-year-old Kan Lo, who belonged to the Warring States period,
as also Chang I and Su Ch'in; still earlier, Yen-tzu and Kuan Chung were
ministers of the Ch'i state, and Tzu-hsia, the disciple of Confucius.
Chang Liang, K'uai Ch'e, Lu Chia, Hsiao Ho, Ch'en P'ing and Li Tso-
chü were early Han; and Ts'ao Chih and Yang Hsiu were of the Three
Kingdoms period.

But[1] note: I did not strike my parents-in-law
                                nor abuse the relatives;
I did not deceive my husband nor beat the humble and meek;
I did not go visiting neighbours, west or east;
I did not steal nor was I cozened;
I did not gossip about this person nor start trouble with that one;
I was not thievish nor jealous nor lewd;
I suffer from no foul disease; I can write and reckon;
I fetched the water from the well, hulled the rice
                                and minded the cooking;
I spun and wove and sewed.
Today, then, draw up the certificate as you please,
And when I carry away my dowry, do you not resent it.
In between our thumb-prints add these words:
"Never to meet again, never to see each other".[2]
Conjugal affection is ended,
All feelings dead;
Set down on paper many binding oaths:
If we chance upon each other at the gate of hell,
We shall turn our heads away and not meet.'

Wolf, because his parents had decided for him, wrote out the document with tears in his eyes, and the two of them affixed their thumb-prints. The family called for a sedan-chair, loaded the trousseau on it, and sent Ts'ui-lien home with the certificate of repudiation.

In the Li family, Ts'ui-lien's father, mother, brother and sister-in-law all blamed her for her sharp tongue. But she said to them:

'Dad, do not shout; Ma, do not shout;
Brother and sister-in-law, do you not shout.

[1] According to *Ta Tai li-chi*, c. 13, a wife may be repudiated on any one of seven grounds: if she refused to obey her parents-in-law; if she produced no heir; if she was lewd; if she was jealous; if she suffered from foul disease; if she talked too much; if she thieved or robbed. A wife may not, however, be repudiated if she no longer had her own family to return to; or if she had mourned her parents-in-law for three years; or if her husband had been poor at the time of their marriage but since grown rich and important. See *Ta Tai li-chi pu-chu*, Kuo-hsüeh chi-pen ts'ung-shu ed., vol. I, p. 156. In Ts'ui-lien's list of faults of which she is innocent occurs one important omission.

[2] Such bitter oaths were common, e.g. *Chin P'ing Mei tz'u-hua*, chapter 21, where Yüeh-niang swears repeatedly that she would have nothing to do with her husband for a hundred, a thousand, years, etc. (pp. 209, 218, 219), but few held them as binding.

It is not that your lassie would sing her own praises,
But from childhood she has been of high mettle.
This day I left their household,
And the rights and wrongs of the affair I will leave off.
It is not that my teeth are itching to speak,
But tracing patterns and embroidering, spinning and weaving,
Cutting and trimming garments, in all these I am skilled.
True it is, moreover, I can wash and starch, stitch and sew,
Chop wood, carry water, and prepare choice dishes;
And if there are silkworms, I can keep them too.
Now I am young and in my prime,
My eyes are quick, my hand steady, my spirits bold;
Should idlers come to peep at me,
I would give them a hearty, resounding slap.'

Mr Li and his wife cried: 'Have done! Have done! The two
of us are now old; we can no longer keep you under our control.
What we are afraid of is that some indiscretion or other would
make you simply an object of ridicule. Poor, pitiful one!' But
Ts'ui-lien went on:

'Your daughter was destined at birth to a lonely, wretched life
She married an ignorant, foolish husband!
Though I might have endured the severity of his
                                        father and mother,
How could I have borne those sisters-in-law?
If I but moved my lips,
Off they went and stirred up the old ones.
Besides, such venom lay behind their scolding,
It soon led to blows and kicks,
From which began an incessant to-do;
Then all at once they wrote the certificate of dissolution.
My one hope was to find contentment and peace at home—
How should I expect even Dad and Ma would blame me?
Abandoned by the husband's family and my own,
I will cut off my hair and become a nun,
Wear a straight-seamed gown and dangle a gourd from a pole
And carry in my hands a huge "wooden fish".[1]
In the daytime from door to door I shall beg for alms;
By night within the temple I shall praise the Buddha,

[1] Skull-shaped block on which Buddhist priests beat time when chanting.
As a religious recitation, 'Sharp-tongued Ts'ui lien' was probably accompanied by the 'wooden fish' in the first instance.

Chant my "Namah",
Observe my fasts and attend to my exercises.
My head will be shaven and quite, quite bald;
Who then will not hail the little priestess?'

And having spoken, she removed her ornaments and changed out of her gay garments into a suit of cotton clothes. She then went before her parents, joined the palms of her hands to perform a Buddhist salute, and bade them farewell. And she turned and bade her brother and sister-in-law farewell. And the brother and sister-in-law said to her: 'Since you have chosen to take the vows, let us accompany you to the Clear Voice Temple in the street in front.' Ts'ui-lien however, replied:

'Brother and sister-in-law, do not accompany me,
                                        I will go by myself;
And when I am gone, you can be easy and free.
As the ancients put it well:
"Though here not welcome, elsewhere I shall be".[1]
Since I am renouncing the world
And shall have my head shaven,
All places may be my home—
Why only the Clear Voice Temple?
Unencumbered and without a care,
I too shall be free and easy.'

She would not cling to wealth and rank;
Wholeheartedly she embraced her vows.
She donned her nun's brocade robes
And constantly fingered her beads.
Each month she kept her fasts;
Daily she offered up fresh flowers,
A Bodhisatva she might not become:
To be Buddha's least handmaid would still content her!

[1] A fairly common saying, e.g. *Shui-hu ch'üan chuan*, c. 19, p. 286, n. 66; also 'The Clerk's Lady' *infra*.

A Dream of Butterflies

'A Dream of Butterflies'—the full title of which reads 'Judge Pao thrice investigates his dream of butterflies' (*Pao tai-chih san k'an hu-tieh meng*)—is a fairly typical example of the Northern Drama (*tsa-chü*) of the Yüan period, with its prelude and four acts, the extract here being act II. About its author, Kuan Han-ch'ing, who was not a scholar-official nor noted for filial piety and virtue, the usual documentary details are missing.[1] His name is linked with that of his fellow dramatist Po P'u (1226–after 1306), who takes precedence over him in age;[2] as does, also, the poet and official Hu Chih-yü (1227–95), from one of whose poems Kuan lifted two lines for a song in an early play, 'The Dissembling Girl'.[3] We may presume him to be perhaps five or six years younger than these men, and place the year of his birth at about 1232. Kuan's birthplace was, according to local tradition, Ch'i-chou (i.e. Ankwo in Hopei Province), a little over a hundred miles to the

[1] Of the many articles on Kuan Han-ch'ing's life conveniently assembled in *Kuan Han-ch'ing yen-chiu lun-wen chi*, 1958, I have found the one by Wang Chi-ssu on pp. 47–66 the most convincing, but have also profited from the discussions of Sun K'ai-ti, Su I, Ts'ai Mei-piao, Sui Shu-sen and Chao Wan-li.

[2] In Chung Ssu-ch'eng's Catalogue (1330), Po P'u's name occurs immediately after Kuan's; but in Chu Ching's Preface of 1364 to Hsia T'ing-chih's *Ch'ing-lou chi* ('Biography of Female Singers and Entertainers'), Tu Jen-chieh (c. 1196–c. 1275), Po P'u (b. 1226) and Kuan are named as song-writers early in the Yüan who could have accepted office but chose not to. See *Ch'ing-lou chi*, in *Chung-kuo ku-tien hsi-ch'ü lun-chu chi-ch'eng*, vol. II, pp. 15–16; and Sun K'ai-ti's article noted above.

[3] The lines occur in act II of *Cha ni-tzu t'iao feng-yüeh*, in the song 'Wu-sha':

Fading flowers surrender their nectar to the honey-bee;
Fine rain softens the mud for nesting swallows.

(*Kuan Han-ch'ing hsi-ch'ü chi*, p. 696.)

They are taken from Hu Chih-yü's 'Yang-ch'un ch'ü' (in *Ch'üan Yüan san-ch'ü*, p. 68); see Wang Chi-ssu's article mentioned above. The play, which survives in a text without prose dialogue, could be Kuan's earliest extant work; see note on p. 61.

south of the Yüan capital Ta-tu (i.e. Peking) where he actually lived. In its day the family had probably been one of prominence, but after several generations of Tartar, followed by Mongol, rule, Kuan himself was registered—at least for purposes of taxation and corvée—as a physician, which profession he might well have practised.

His chief reputation, both among his contemporaries and later, was as a resourceful, prolific and moving playwright, the moulder of the *tsa-chü* form. In Chung Ssu-ch'éng's catalogue of the works of dramatists, entitled *Lu kuei pu* ('Ghosts of the Playhouse'), 1330, Kuan Han-ch'ing heads the list of writers of an earlier generation, with threescore or so titles of plays to his credit.[1] In the same list, as revised by Chia Chung-ming (1343–after 1422), we find it stated that the versatile Kao Wen-hsiu, who wrote about thirty plays in a short life, had the reputation of being 'a lesser Han-ch'ing'.[2] The Ming prince, Chu Ch'üan, ranks Kuan lower than a number of other song-writers in his treatise *T'ai-ho cheng-yin p'u* (1398) and declares Kuan's style to be uneven, while conceding that he was the first to write *tsa-chü* plays.[3] But the theatrical tradition of late Yüan and early Ming is probably best represented by the aforementioned octogenarian Chia Chung-ming, himself author of some seventeen *tsa-chü* plays, in his revised version of Chung's Catalogue, 1422, in which Kuan's plays are praised[4] for the natural flow of the speech and the sparkling words and phrases, for insight into the recesses of the heart and for familiarity with the whole range of love's sentiments. As regards the man's influence, his name was known all over the empire—'as a leader leader among leaders of the stage, as head of all the masters of play-writing, as patron of all acting companies'.

---

[1] The text of Chung's catalogue survives in three divergent versions, none of them earlier than the Ming. Rather than resort to a whole series of conjectures about the 'real' Kuan of the thirteenth century, I have relied on the version revised by Chia, the fullest of the three, as the attested evidence of a veteran of the fourteenth-century theatre. See *Lu kuei pu* (wai ssu-chung), Ku-tien edition of 1957, Editors' Introduction; for Kuan Han-ch'ing, see pp. 8–10; 'The Dissembling Girl' and 'A Dream of Butterflies' are both found on p. 8; Po P'u is on p. 10.
[2] *Ibid.*, p. 11.
[3] See *T'ai-ho cheng-yin p'u*, included with the Ku-tien edition of *Lu kuei pu*, p. 125.
[4] *Lu kuei pu*, p. 8; for Chia Chung-ming's plays, see Fu Hsi-hua, *Ming-tai tsa-chü ch'üan-mu*, 1958, pp. 39–45.

There seems little doubt that Kuan was producer and actor as well as playwright. The painter and Minister Chao Meng-fu (1254–1222), who would be his younger contemporary, reports a conversation of Kuan's to the effect that the theatre, acting included, was for him and his family both art and livelihood;[1] and this, or a similar account, would be alluded to by the editor Tsang Mou-hsün in the Preface[2] to his great collection of Yüan drama, *Yüan-ch'ü hsüan* (1616), in which Kuan is described as eagerly treading the boards with his face painted. As a theatrical man, Kuan spent much of his time with actresses and entertainers, and his lively courtesan-heroines have been noticed by critics. Of his gay life he was proud, and he pictures himself as a gallant and voluptuary in a poem entitled 'Not old—but a veteran',[3] 'old' being presumably the jibe of younger rivals. He begins with a stanza about the sweet flowers and graceful willows—the fluffy, scented creatures that sang songs of his composing—how he sought them, how they lured him, how he now plucked a bud and now broke a branch, sleeping and waking among them for the best part of his life. For, the poet continues, he is

Captain of the libertines of the world
And chief of the tribe of profligates,

whose only delight is in the company of the ladies of the town, drinking, music-making, playing games. Then, in reply to the jeering of young bucks unconversant with the thousand wiles and snares of the bawdy-house, he enlarges upon the image of 'a dried pea, hard as brass'—slang in Kuan's day for a rake—and declares:

I am a hard, dried pea,
Uncrushed by all the pounding,
Not bloated with the repeated steaming
Nor melted by prolonged stewing
Nor scorched with the occasional frying,
From all which I emerge sound, whole, bouncy,
And noisy as brass.

He would taste of all the pleasures of life:

---

[1] In Chao Meng-fu, *Lun ch'ü*, quoted in *T'ai ho cheng-yin p'u*, p. 135, and in Wang Chi-ssu's article, p. 52.
[2] In the Second Preface (1616).
[3] The poem *Pu fu lao*, to the tune of *I-chih hua* in the *nan-lü* mode, is undated and may be found in *Kuan Han-ch'ing hsi-ch'ü chi*, pp. 949–51.

I choose for my enjoyment the moon of Prince Liang's garden,[1]
And sipping wine in the Eastern Capital,
And contemplating the peonies of Loyang,[2]
And threading the maze of willows along Chang Terrace,
(the Chang Terrace willow being a talented mistress after the
T'ang tale 'Miss Willow'[3] by Hsü Tso-yao). He is versed in
every accomplishment of the man of fashion,

In board games and in football,
In hunting, in jesting and witticism,
In song and dance, in woodwind and strings,
In presiding over banquets and tossing off verses,
Not to speak of the Double Six.

And he is already so confirmed in his ways that:

Though you knocked out my front teeth,
And twisted my mouth,
Crippled my leg
And broke my arm,
Yet, born as I was with such cursed cravings,
Indulge them I would none the less.

And he concludes that he will still be found with the ladies until
death itself summons him.

Kuan would thus seem to have visited Loyang as well as
Kaifeng, which, after a century of Chin Tartar occupation, had
passed into Mongol hands in 1233. In his later years, he
visited the Southern Sung capital Lin-an (i.e. Hangchow) —
like Marco Polo — in the wake of the Yüan conquering army,
almost certainly in 1278. For in his song entitled 'Hangchow
Scenes' Kuan refers to the newly defeated Sung:[4] singers
expected song-writers to be topical, and it was at the end of
1277 that the city reverted to its earlier name of Hangchow.[5]
In similar fashion, ten songs of his, probably among his last,
were entitled 'Songs of Ta-te',[6] Ta-te being a new reign which

[1] Liang-yüan, garden of Liang-hsiao-wang of Han, situated outside
Kaifeng and celebrated by Li Po and others.
[2] The best peonies came from Loyang, a T'ang capital, where, according
to tradition, they flourished after they were banished from the T'ang
capital proper, Ch'ang-an, by the Empress Wu; see H. L. Li, *The Garden
Flowers of China*, 1959, pp. 22–30, and Introduction to 'The Women's
Kingdom' *infra*.
[3] *Liu-shih chuan*, included in Lu Hsün, *T'ang Sung ch'uan-ch'i chi*, ed. of
1956, pp. 47–50.
[4] In *Kuan Han-ch'ing hsi-ch'ü chi*, p. 948.
[5] See *Yüan shih*, c. 9, p. 12ª.
[6] In *Kuan Han-ch'ing hsi-ch'ü chi*, pp. 993–6.

began in 1297 and lasted until 1307, during which decade we may presume Kuan's life to have come to an end.

Of Kuan's sixty-odd plays listed in the Chung-Chia Catalogue, fifteen survive. 'A Dream of Butterflies', which was very likely an adaptation of an older play of the form known as *yüan-pen*, performed under the Chin in the first half of the thirteenth century, would seem to be one of Kuan's earlier efforts.[1] The *yüan-pen* repertoire surviving from the Chin into the Yüan, transcribed in Tʻao Tsung-i's *Cho keng lu* (1366), includes two titles about dreams and butterflies:[2] 'The Dream of Chuang-tzu' and 'A Dream of Butterflies (or, a Butterfly)',[3] the latter of which, as distinct from Chuang-tzu's butterfly dream, would seem to be our play. Indeed, as the creator, or one of the creators, of the four-act *tsa-chü* play, Kuan must have drawn upon earlier elements in the theatre. But of the old 'Dream of Butterflies' nothing is known beyond the title: it need hardly be responsible for the crudity of the action, which in our play merely reflects the manners of a society dominated by the Mongol ruling class, of which the 'royal kinsman'—the villain of the piece—may be regarded as representative.

Judge Pao is a historical person claimed by legend. According to the official Sung history, Pao Cheng (999–1062), a native of Hofei in Lu-chou (in Anhwei Province), served during the reign (1023–63) of the emperor Jen-tsung.[4] Being noted for his forthright views and absolute incorruptibility, he occupied successively the ranks of Scholar (*tai-chih*) of Tʻien-chang Library and Senior Scholar (*chih-hsüeh-shih*) of Lung-tʻu Library, and was appointed Prefect of Kaifeng. As

---

[1] It seems reasonable to infer that Chia Chung-ming, like all conscientious editors, was aiming at a broadly chronological arrangement of the titles of plays by each dramatist. 'A Dream of Butterflies' is the seventeenth title under Kuan; 'The Dissembling Girl'—see discussion above—is the seventh.

[2] *Nan-tsʻun cho keng lu*, Chung-hua reprint of 1959, c. 25, pp. 306–15; the two titles are on p. 308.

[3] The title of the *yüan-pen* play is *Hu-tieh meng*, which is identical with the short title of Kuan's play as it appears in *Lu kuei pu* and other early accounts. Chuang-tzu's dream is the subject of a play by Shih Chang, who was of the same generation as Po Pʻu and Kuan; see Fu Hsi-hua, *Yüan-tai tsa-chü chʻüan-mu*, p. 11, and *Lu kuei pu*, pp. 25–6.

[4] *Sung shih*, c. 316, pp. 1ᵃ–2ᵇ; see also R. H. van Gulik, *Tʻang-yin-pi-shih*, Parallel Cases from under the Pear-tree; A Thirteenth Century Manual of Jurisprudence and Detection, 1956, pp. 108, 143.

Prefect and, earlier, as County Magistrate of T'ien-ch'ang,[1] Pao showed himself a shrewd but severe judge with an uncanny insight into doubtful cases; and he broke with tradition in permitting litigants to approach and directly address the Prefect seated at his high bench. Thus when Kaifeng itself became part of legend after the Northern Sung, Pao the Scholar of Lung-t'u Library sitting in judgment in the prefectural court of the former Eastern Capital was held up in play after play,[2] and story after story,[3] as the shining example of justice.

Chinese court proceedings were in the nature of a spectacle and the methods of interrogation harsh:

> In the local tribunals, court room and court procedure were primarily intended to impress everyone with the majesty of the law, and with the dreadful consequences of becoming involved with it. . . When the court was in session the magistrate, decked out with the full regalia of his office, sat behind a high bench covered with red cloth and standing on an elevated dais; he was a forbidding figure, enthroned high above all that happened in the court below.[4]

While the magistrate was supported by all the pomp and circumstance of his office, court procedure placed everyone who appeared before him in a most disadvantageous and humiliating position. The accused had to kneel on the bare floor, far below the judge, and remain thus throughout the proceedings. Close by stood the *li*, the constables, carrying their awe-inspiring paraphernalia, traditionally called *san-mu*, the 'three wooden instruments'; these were the cangue (*chia*), manacles (*ch'ou*) and fetters (*lao*). The constables also carried flat bamboo staves used for meting out the punishment of bambooing (*chang*) and whips of leather thongs (*pien*) or rattan (*ch'ih*). Bamboo and whips were

---

[1] T'ien-ch'ang, the county town, is the home of Tu Shao-ch'ing in 'Young Master Bountiful' *infra*.

[2] Judge Pao figures in ten Yüan plays, of which 'A Dream of Butterflies' seems to be the earliest; titles are preserved of at least three other plays in which Pao was a chief character. See Yen Tun-i, *Yüan-chü chen-i*, 1960, pp. 340–1; p. 349, n. 3.

[3] Most of the stories are preserved in *Pao-kung an* and *Lung-t'u kung-an*, both compilations dating from the Ming (see Sun K'ai-ti's Catalogue, pp. 110–11), and further developed in the late nineteenth century *San-hsia wu-i* and *Ch'i-hsia wu-i*; see Hu Shih's Preface to *San-hsia wu-i* in *Hu Shih wen-ts'un*, ed. of 1953, vol. 3, pp. 441–72. 'The Clerk's Lady' *infra* is another story about Judge Pao.

[4] R. H. van Gulik, *T'ang-yin pi-shih*, p. 52.

used freely during the interrogation in order to urge an accused to confess, and further [if] the accused, accuser or one of the witnesses said or did something that displeased the judge. The constables were both feared and despised by the people in general. Few decent persons would take this office, the constables were mostly rogues ready to abuse their power and to extort money from everyone who came to the tribunal.[1]

Seated behind his high bench, the judge could not see or hear clearly the persons kneeling on the floor below. This was no mean handicap since the judge in order to form an opinion on a person's character relied to a large degree on his facial expression and his voice.[2]

The principle of assuming *a priori* the guilt of an accused is one of the factors that brought into being the fixed custom of beating an accused—and often beating him cruelly—as soon as he denied his guilt . . . Another fact that gave occasion to beatings and other tortures in court was the old-established rule that no criminal could be convicted unless he admitted his guilt . . .[3]

As for prisons and prisoners:

As a rule the court formed part of the compound that housed the offices of the district administration, the private residence of the magistrate, and also the prison; ordinarily the prison adjoined the courtroom. These prisons were dismal places, the inmates were kept in chains all the time, and for their food had to depend largely on what was sent them by relatives and friends outside; as a consequence, the rate of mortality among the prisoners was high.[4]

But much of the sound and fury in our play is simply good theatre, supported by the voice of Mother Wang, who is the singer in 'A Dream of Butterflies', and by the miming of the judge, whose dream we would expect to be enacted to perfection, and by the clowning of the attendant Chang and the three Wang boys. A synopsis of the plot will here be in place. The prelude (which contains two songs) shows Father and Mother Wang rejoicing in their three studious young sons. In act I (13 songs), Father Wang going to the market to buy paper and writing brushes for his boys, knocks against the horse ridden

[1] van Gulik, p. 55.   [2] van Gulik, p. 58.   [3] van Gulik, p. 56.
[4] van Gulik, p. 54.

by a nobleman Ko Piao, who thereupon strikes Wang repeatedly and tramples him to death. While Mother Wang cries over the corpse, the sons find Ko in the street, reeling and drunk. They fight with him and soon discover that they have killed him. Mother Wang laments their ill luck and the futility of all their learning.

In act II, the three brothers are sent up from their county, Chung-mou, to Kaifeng for trial. Mother Wang, who seems to have been detained but later released, accompanies them. She relates their story, and in twelve songs describes her sad predicament. After committing all three boys unaccountably to the condemned cell, Judge Pao (in act III) has the two older brothers secretly released, as if acceding to her wish that they be spared in preference to their youngest brother. But it turns out (in act IV) that he meant to save the whole family, and that under the guise of executing the youngest brother as demanded by the law, he has instead put to death a condemned criminal.

The story itself may have been derived from the account in *Lieh-nü chuan* ('Lives of Women') of the woman whose two sons were involved in a case of manslaughter in the time of King Hsüan of Ch'i (fourth century B.C.).[1] The mother asked that her own son be executed so that the older brother, the step-son, might live. Eventually both sons were pardoned by the King. But similar stories were doubtless found in other ages. The official Yüan history records a comparable example from the years 1358–64, also of a mother and her son and step-son.[2] The devoted mother who by wise teaching, or through inordinate self-sacrifice, inspires her children to noble deeds is a common theme in the drama, as, for instance, the story of Mother Ch'en (apparently of Sung Dynasty) whose three sons attain, in turn, the highest examination success. Mother Ch'en is alluded to in our extract, and in the ensuing act (act III) Mother Wang compares her former self with that fortunate lady in a song:[3]

---

[1] *Lieh-nü chuan chiao-chu*, Ssu-pu pei-yao edition, c. 5, pp. 6ᵃ–6ᵇ, 'The good step-mother of Ch'i'. This is pointed out in *Ch'ü-hai tsung-mu t'i-yao*, revised edition of 1959, c. 1, pp. 24–5.

[2] *Yüan shih*, c. 201, pp. 4ᵃ–4ᵇ, Life of Ch'in Jun-fu's wife, née Ch'ai. The parallel is noted by Chu Tung-jun; see Yen Tun-i, *Yüan-chü chen-i*, pp. 337–8.

[3] Tune: 'kun-hsiu-ch'iu', *Kuan Han-ch'ing hsi-ch'ü chi*, p. 462; 'Selected Works', pp. 96–7.

I was even as Mother Ch'en, who—as said of old—
Desired not gold and precious jade in abundance
But only that her sons and grandsons all be worthy.
Mother Ch'en is the subject of a play by Kuan himself, *Chuang-yüan-t'ang Ch'en-mu chiao tzu*, the last in the list of Kuan's plays in the Chung-Chia catalogue;[1] and in act I of that play, she declaims two lines similar to the last two quoted:

I desire not gold and precious jade in abundance
But only that my sons and grandsons all be worthy.[2]
The parallel has caused some speculation about the relative dates of these two plays,[3] but from the words 'as said of old' Kuan would seem to be quoting, in both plays, from some familiar common source.

'A Dream of Butterflies' survives in two main versions: a relatively little edited version in the series *Ku ming-chia tsa-chü*[4] (1588) and a more carefully edited one in Tsang Mou-hsün's collection *Yüan-ch'ü hsüan* (1616). The differences between the two are, however, in most instances immaterial. I have availed myself of the detailed collation in the Collected Works edited by Wu Hsiao-ling, Shan Yao-hai, Li Kuo-yen and Liu Chien, *Kuan Han-ch'ing hsi-ch'ü chi*, Chung-kuo hsi-chü ch'u-pan-she, 1958, pp. 447–98 (and bibliographical note, pp. 1012–4), but have followed the text in the Selected Works from the same press edited by Wu, Li, Liu and Huang P'in-lan, *Ta hsi-chü-chia Kuan Han-ch'ing chieh-tso chi*, 1958, pp. 83–103 (act II being pp. 87–96), with its valuable Glossary.

In the translation, the songs are rendered in verse, each line corresponding to a line in the original; but no attempt is made to reproduce the rhyme in the original, and the names of the tunes have been omitted. Speeches in verse also are rendered in verse. Both in the songs and dialogue I have sought, above all, to recapture something of Kuan's verve and eloquence.

---

[1] *Lu kuei pu*, p. 10.
[2] *Kuan Han-ch'ing hsi-ch'ü chi*, p. 345.
[3] Yen Tun-i, pp. 339–40.
[4] Reprinted in facsimile in *Ku-pen hsi-ch'ü ts'ung-k'an*, Series IV.

A Dream of Butterflies

[*The judge's attendant, Chang,*[1] *leading the various court officers in procession, enters to arrange the court and open proceedings.*]

ATTENDANT CHANG: Peace reigns over the court! Salute!

JUDGE PAO[2] [*enters and declaims*][3]

> Tum, tum goes the Prefectural Court drum,
>
> Officers and runners stand on either side,
>
> The terror of the King of Hell's judgement hall
>
> Or the tower where departed souls are consigned!

My surname is Pao; name, Cheng; style, Hsi-wen. I am from Chin-tou[4] Sub-prefecture in Lu-chou, from Old Boy Village of Outlook District. I was made a Scholar of Lung-t'u Library, and formally appointed Prefect of Kaifeng. Today I hold court, and open the morning session. Chang, if there are documents to sign, bring them for me to sign.

CHANG: Clerks of the offices, are there any documents to sign?

[*Voice answers from within*]

CHANG: Why didn't you report this earlier? It was a good

---

[1] Chang Ch'ien, a stock character in *tsa-chü* plays.

[2] The role of Judge Pao is assigned to an actor who specializes in impersonating officials, a *ku*, who would be suitably made up and costumed.

[3] At their first entrance, the more important characters declaim four lines of verse and then introduce themselves. Pao's opening verses and speech 'Tum, tum ... appointed Prefect of Kaifeng' are duplicated in the (probably later) play *Lu Chai-lang* (full title: *Pao tai-chih chih chan Lu Chai-lang*, 'The Execution of Lu Chai-lang'), attributed also to Kuan. Since in *Lu Chai-lang* the action does not take place in Kaifeng but in Hsü-chou, Pao is obliged to add: 'But now at the Emperor's command I go on a tour of inspection of the southern regions . . .' (Act IV; *Kuan Han-ch'ing hsi-ch'ü chi*, p. 402). In the still later anonymous play *Ch'en-chou t'iao-mi* ('Rice Rationing at Ch'en-chou'), Pao introduces himself in the same words as here, though without the verses, and then adds: 'At the Emperor's command I went on a tour of inspection of the southern regions, from which I have now returned . . .' (Act II; *Yüan-ch'ü hsüan*, p. 41). Thus the legend grew.

[4] Chin-tou: this could be read as 'hot box-iron', which Pao indeed was in his redress of wrongs and grievances. 'Old Boy Village' would also seem a popular touch.

thing I asked you. Saluting Your Honour! A horse-thief, Chao Stubborn Mule, has been delivered over from Sour Jujube County.[1]

P A O: Bring him forward.

[*Officer escorts prisoner in; prisoner kneels*]

P A O: Remove the cangue. You, fellow there. Are you Chao Stubborn Mule? Was it you who stole the horse?

P R I S O N E R: It was I who stole the horse.

P A O: Chang, put him in a heavy cangue, and commit him to the condemned cell.[2]

[*The prisoner is escorted away*]

P A O: I feel tired just now. Chang, don't you and the clerks of the offices start a row. I shall have a short rest.

C H A N G: Clerks and all officers of this court. Don't you start a row. His Honour will have a short rest.

P A O [*falls asleep at his desk; then rises and enacts his dream*]

Burdened with affairs as I am, how could I go to sleep? I shall take a stroll. At the back of this hall I find a side-door. I will open it and look out. Ah, it is a lovely garden! See the many flowers all in full bloom, and the beauty and warmth of this spring scene. Behind that flower bush is a pavilion with up-turned eaves, and in the pavilion, a spider's web. Lo, a butterfly fluttering among the flowers is entangled in the web. I, Pao Cheng, am secretly sorry for the butterfly, that it should have flown this way.

    The untoward befalls even insects;

    Is man, then, master of his own fate?

Ah, the lowest creatures yet emit a spark of the divine! A large butterfly appears and frees the butterfly that was caught. (Oh, another butterfly is entangled, and again the large butterfly rescues it!)[3] Oh, yet another small butterfly comes along and is caught in the net. The large butterfly will surely rescue *it* also! How strange! the large butterfly flutters again and again near the flower bush without trying to rescue the small one, and now unconcernedly it flies off. As the sage expressed it, the feeling of commiseration is inherent in

---

[1] Sour Jujube County—Suan-tsao, i.e. Yentsing in Honan Province), about twenty-five miles north of Kaifeng across the Yellow River.

[2] Under Mongol rule, the theft of a government post-horse was punishable by death; see *Yüan shih*, c. 104, p. 10[b].

[3] The sentence in brackets is supplied by the translator.

men.[1] If you would not rescue it, I will.

[*Releases the butterfly and returns to his desk*]

CHANG: Saluting Your Honour! It is the noon hour.

PAO [*awakes; then declaims*]

> The lives of insects and butterflies
>
> May hang by a silk thread!
>
> Suddenly I wake from my dream—
>
> My attendant gives out the noon hour.

Chang, are there any prisoners to be tried? Bring them forward for trial.

CHANG: Clerks of the offices, are there any prisoners to be tried? Bring them forward for trial.

[*Voice answers from within*]

CHANG: Saluting Your Honour! The prisoners from Chungmou County,[2] three brothers accused of killing an innocent man, Ko Piao, are sent up for trial.

PAO: Killing an innocent man? People of a tiny county like that? Are they here?

CHANG: They have been delivered over.

PAO: Bring them forward and give a stroke for each step they take.

[*Runners escorting the three Wang brothers enter*]

MOTHER WANG [*enters and sings*][3]

> Delivered over to the impartial Censorate,
>
> To Kaifeng Prefecture with its High Judge,
>
> These three as yet unknown young scholars
>
> Are beaten like felons sentenced to death,
>
> Causing me to waver in my resolution
>
> Shaken by my heart's palpitations.
>
> True it is, fear ever haunts the thief[4]—
>
> I am now disposed to confess their crime:
>
> For these are not the simple clerks of our county.
>
> In this great prefecture the law's course is clear and upright
>
> Unlike the muddled ways of Chung-mou's magistrate.

[1] See Legge, *Mencius*, II.i.VI.4.

[2] Chung-mou (i.e. Chungmow in Honan Province) is less than twenty miles west of Kaifeng; the prisoners and Mother Wang have walked all the way.

[3] The role of Mother Wang is taken by the female lead, who sings throughout the four acts. The tunes in act II are in the *nan-lü* mode; the names of the tunes have been here omitted.

[4] The thief, i.e. the guilty.

Bum-tum-tum proclaims the drum, the court renews its sitting —
It so stuns me that hands and feet lose coordination,
And I no longer dare act as brave and reckless;
It so alarms me my soul is fled its seat,
Even if walking had not spent my strength and sinews.
The trial will be no ordinary judgment:
It may entail the harshest, severest punishment.
Ah, ah, ah, first their father, my husband, newly dead,
                                    his body not yet interred!
Then, then, then, almost at once, sons and mother
                                    in the misery of incarceration!
Oh, oh, oh, soon these brothers confront the risk of death
                                    by sword or rope!

How fearful!
By this wall here I spy with my eyes and prick up my ears:
What an awesome hall of justice!
The verdict today will decide for us weal or woe,
And sift the false from the true.

[*Mother Wang and the others kneel before the Judge*]

CHANG: Prisoners, face the court.

PAO: Chang, undo their cangues, and dismiss the prisoners' escort with a form of acknowledgement.

[*Chang removes the cangues*]

WANG THIRD: Mother, brothers, I am going home.

PAO: Where are you going? Do you think you're still in Chung-mou and free to go about? Chang, these three are the boys who have killed a man. Who is the woman? Would she be a witness? Or would she be a relative of the boys? You, woman there. What relation are these two to you?

MOTHER WANG: They are my elder sons.

PAO: And the wee one?

MOTHER WANG: Is my third son.

PAO: Silence! A fine way you have brought up your family! In former days, the mother of Mencius chose her neighbourhood with the utmost care for the sake of her son;[1] and the mother of T'ao K'an sold her own hair so as to provide adequate

[1] The mother of Mencius first found an abode near the graveyard, then moved to the vicinity of the market, and finally settled in the neighbourhood of a school for the sake of her impressionable young son; see *Lieh-nü chuan*, c. 1, pp. 10ᵃ–11ᵇ. The story is dramatised in the anonymous play, *Meng-mu san-i* (probably second half of fourteenth century), in *Ku-pen Yüan Ming tsa-chü*, original vol. 13.

hospitality for her son's friend;[1] and the mother of the three
Ch'en brothers taught them all so well that each in his turn
won top place at the palace examination.[2] You, village woman,
taught your sons so well that they went and killed an innocent
man. Confess your guilt!

MOTHER WANG [*sings*]

My sons have committed a crime deserving of the forfeit
                                                    of their lives;
Yet that wretch himself had so outrageously transgressed
                                                    against us
That their killing of him must even seem pardonable.
We are pitifully poor, and the humblest of common people;
I appeal to Your Honour, and beg you will take up our cause.
These three from childhood plied at their books.
They followed the teachings of the classics,
                                    learnt ritual and right behaviour—
What could they know of scheming,
                                    or plotting to do grievous harm?
But with the hundredfold tortures it was hard to prove our case.
For is it not said: 'Three spoil a conspiracy;
Six ears do not favour an intrigue'?

PAO: No confession without flogging. Chang, flog her soundly.

MOTHER WANG [*sings*]

My boys have broken the law of the land, are liable to be
                            imprisoned or banished, strangled or beheaded.
In vain have they read the sacred writings of the reverent,
                            temperate, gentle and good Confucius.
Flogged until their bodies became unsightly,
So beaten that tendons and bones were displaced—
How far removed from the self-inflicted pinpricks
                            and hair-pulling of dozing students!
Sheltered by parental indulgence, have they ever suffered so?

PAO: There must have been a leader among the three. Who
was it that dealt the fatal blow?

WANG ELDEST: It neither concerns mother nor my two
younger brothers; it was I who killed the man.

---

[1] T'ao K'an's mother, née Chan, is usually cited as the example of self-
sacrifice for the sake of the son's career; T'ao K'an became a great general.
See *Chin shu*, c. 96, p. 3ᵇ. Their story is the subject of Ch'in Chien-fu's play
Chien-fa tai-pin (first half of fourteenth century), in *Ku-pen Yüan Ming
tsa-chü*, original vol. 6.
[2] For the Ch'en brothers and their mother, see Introduction.

WANG SECOND: Your Honour, it neither concerns my mother nor my elder and younger brother; it was I who killed the man.

WANG THIRD: Your Honour, it neither concerns my mother nor my two older brothers; nor does it concern me.

MOTHER WANG: It does not concern the three boys. When the royal kinsman Ko Piao had killed my husband, I found it hard to endure and in a fit of rage fought with the man and killed him. It was really I who did it.

PAO: Nonsense! This one is owning up! That one is owning up! Clearly a case of collusion. We must have *one* to pay with his life. Chang, flog them hard.

MOTHER WANG [*sings*]

It is ever so still here, with no voice raised in protest!
Under my very eyes they receive their flogging.
Boys, you had better just confess as required of you,
But before the Judge let me respectfully speak up:
That wretch with his overbearing manner
Wantonly killed my dear husband,
Yet the magistrate then had me confined,
While the runners were as tigers and wolves.
Your Honour will please be patient with us.
Not to speak of the whip-lash and head–compressor,
The interrogations under the criminal code
And the numberless prolonged cross-examinations,
They now are flogged until the body is bloody and grimy.
The eldest cries out 'Grave injustice!'
But the Judge will allow no explanation.
The second suffers the tortures of Hell;
However will he survive the pain?
The third is yet more cruelly beaten,
Poor old me, whose bowels are stabbed with the sight,
Turning now towards this one, now towards that one,
Bewildered and all at sea,
My eyes answering their dumb stare;
Hither and thither I hobble,
Now weeping, now wailing.
You will simply kill them with this flogging,
                              you Scholar of Lung-t'u Library!
Why did their father in the beginning
Ever scheme for the children's happiness?

Hard indeed to relate it all—
I gulp and choke—
A deep sigh relieves the low moaning;
My tormented entrails are afire
But my tears fall like pearl-sized raindrops.

P A O: Let me read over the indictment. [*holds up document*] What a dunce the County Magistrate of Chung-mou is! Why, it is written in the indictment 'Wang Eldest, Wang Second, Wang Third killed an innocent man, Ko Piao'. Have they no clerk in their offices? These three boys must have their own names, or at least nicknames. You, woman there. What is your eldest son called?

M O T H E R W A N G: He is called Gold Accord.

P A O: What is your second son called?

M O T H E R W A N G: He is called Iron Accord.

P A O: And the third one?

M O T H E R W A N G: He is called Stone Accord.

W A N G T H I R D: Light.

P A O: What light?

W A N G T H I R D: Stone Aco-lyte.[1]

P A O: Hey? No wonder you knock people down dead. Why should an ordinary family pick such hard and inflexible names for the sons? Was it Gold Accord who killed the man?

M O T H E R W A N G [*sings*]

This one is only Gold.

Is he then beyond melting?

P A O: Was it Stone Accord who killed the man?

M O T H E R W A N G [*sings*]

This one is only Stone.

Would he be hollow within?

P A O: Was it Iron Accord who killed the man?

M O T H E R W A N G [*sings*]

This one is only Iron.

Could he withstand the blast-furnace of the law?

P A O: Chang, give these thick-skinned brutes more.

M O T H E R W A N G [*sings*]

Though indeed they are not thick-skinned beasts,

[1] Stone Aco-lyte. 'Stone Novice', suggesting a stubborn character, seems to be the nickname of Stone Accord, who flaunts it almost in defiance of the severe Pao. I have done the best I could with the pun. In act III, Wang Third is addressed as 'Stone Novice' in the song 'hsiao-ho-shang' (*Kuan Han-ch'ing hsi-ch'ü chi*, p. 463; 'Selected Works', p. 98).

They have truly been saddled with injury,
                    the bit of injustice between their teeth.
PAO: It is said, 'The killer forfeits his life and borrower
repays the loan'. Chang, remove the oldest boy. His life shall
be the forfeit of the crime.
MOTHER WANG [*sings*]
    Alas, my eyeballs bulge with staring, yet I may not save him,
    Escorted down these steps, to march soon out of sight
    So that I tremble both for him and us left behind,
    A hundred times bemoaning my sad perplexity.
The great judge Pao? Fiddle-de-dee!
PAO: I ordered that the oldest son forfeit his life. What did
the woman say?
CHANG: She clutched at his cangue and said, 'The great judge
Pao! Fiddle-de-dee!'[1]
PAO: Did the woman cry 'Fiddle-de-dee'? Bring her forward.
[*Mother Wang kneels*] I ordered that your eldest son forfeit his
life. Why did you cry 'Fiddle-de-dee'?
MOTHER WANG: How dare this poor woman cry 'Fiddle-de-
dee'? But my boy shows such filial devotion, and if he were put
to death, who would look after me?
PAO: Since his mother affirms that the eldest boy is filial and
the neighbours guarantee his good conduct, I must have been
mistaken. I will spare the eldest, to allow him to look after her.
Chang, let the second boy forfeit his life!
MOTHER WANG [*sings*]
    On one side, the eldest brother to whom my entrails are tied!
    On the other side, the second brother
                        whose least wheeze chokes my lungs!
    If you want a life forfeited, spare the boys:
    Rather seize me poor woman.
    Oh, such unfeeling cruelty!
    Yet there seems no appeal—
    So I clutch at the cangue and cry 'Grave injustice'.
The great judge Pao? Fiddle-de-dee!
PAO: What is she clamouring about now?
CHANG: Again she said, 'The great judge Pao! Fiddle-de-dee!'
PAO: Bring her forward. [*Mother Wang kneels*] You, woman
there. I ordered that your second son forfeit his life. Why did

[1] The attendant Chang, a clownish character, may be relied upon to make
the most of this business and get his own back on his master.

you again cry 'Fiddle-de-dee'?

MOTHER WANG: How dare I cry 'Fiddle-de-dee'? But this second boy is good at commerce. If his life were forfeit, who would support me?

PAO: I ordered the eldest to be put to death, and you objected on the ground of his filial piety; I ordered the second to be put to death, and you rejoined that he was good at commerce. Whose life shall be forfeit then? [*Wang Third places his own cangue on his neck*] What is the fellow there doing?

WANG THIRD: Eldest brother's life is not forfeit; second brother's life is not forfeit. Clearly it will be my turn next. Why not do it handsomely by offering myself?

PAO: So be it then. Chang, remove the wee one and let him forfeit his life. [*the brothers are shuffled back and forth*] You, woman there. What do you say to having the third boy put to death?

MOTHER WANG: That would be right. Is it not said, 'When three travel together, the youngest fares ill'? It is right that he should forfeit his life.

PAO: And the judge. . . . 'Fiddle-de-dee'?

MOTHER WANG: The great judge Pao—no fiddle-de-dee!

PAO: Silence! Chang, bring him back. I was nearly imposed upon by the woman. See before us a partial step-dame: these two boys must be your own, and the wee one, an adopted son, not rooted in your affection, and therefore you have allowed him to forfeit his life! Speak, woman, and if you answer rightly, I have a plan. But if you answer wrongly, do not expect me to show mercy.

MOTHER WANG: All three are my children. What do you want me to say?

PAO: If you do not tell the truth—Chang, be ready with the bamboo.

MOTHER WANG: Eldest, second, third, my children. I have to tell, but do not feel estranged among yourselves.

PAO: Is the big fellow your own son?

MOTHER WANG [*sings*]

Though this boy was not born of me

Yet I fed him from earliest childhood.

PAO: And the second?

MOTHER WANG [*sings*]

The middle-sized one too was reared by me.

PAO: And the wee one?

MOTHER WANG [*sings sorrowfully*]

>   This one is my own;
>   Of the other two I am but the step-dame.

PAO: You, woman there. Come near. You are surely mistaken. Would it not be better to let one of your step-sons forfeit his life and have your own son living to look after you?

MOTHER WANG: It is Your Honour that is mistaken. [*sings*]

>   If I made a step-son forfeit his life,
>   It would show the step-mother to be spiteful indeed.
>   If I followed after the ignoble widow Sang,[1]
>   Could I face up to the magnanimous aunt of Lu?[2]

PAO: Woman, you must cause them to be content with this arrangement. Who was it really that killed the man?

MOTHER WANG [*sings*]

>   Even had they mouths all over, they could not plead,
>   Being stopped up like bottle-gourds
>   By beating until the skin cracked and the body was furrowed.
>   The blood and mangled flesh
>   Re-enacted the torture chambers of the nether world:
>   All three boys swooned with pain.
>   You officials are leagued together, swayed by mighty relatives,
>   Not to speak of royal kinsmen.

[*sings mournfully*]

>   The eldest, found guilty, was due for execution;
>   The second stood at the fork of life and death;
>   The third is doomed to enter the world of shades,
>   Leaving accursed me, old useless body.
>   The eldest is filial and knows the human relationships;
>   The second I must keep to oversee the household;
>   The third, alas, had best be silent—

---

[1] Widow Sang (or possibly, the widow of Sang), whom Chuang-tzu found at her husband's tomb waiting for the earth to dry in order to be in a position to marry again. She figures in the story about Chuang-tzu in *Ching-shih t'ung-yen*, c. 2, where she is unnamed. Li Shou-ch'ing's play *Ku p'en ko Chuang-tzu t'an k'u-lou* ('Chuang-tzu and the Skeleton'), noted in *Lu kuei pu*, pp. 14–15, deals with the same story but is now lost. A later stage version is preserved in *Chui pai ch'iu* vol. VI (1770), Chung-hua reprint, pp. 131–68.

[2] The magnanimous aunt of Lu, who, in her flight from the invading Ch'i army, abandoned her own toddler son in order to save her small nephew; see *Lieh-nü chuan*, c. 5, pp. 5ᵃ–5ᵇ. She is the heroine of Wu Han-ch'en's play *Ch'i tzu ch'üan chih Lu i-ku*, noted in *Lu kuei pu*, p. 17, now lost.

It is right that you forfeit your life.
Was it not said: 'When three travel together,

the youngest fares ill'?—

The blood-thirsty runners now raise a hue and cry.[1]

PAO [*aside*] After hearing what she had to say, I can now believe that

'The shrewd merchant parades his empty bag

and so hides his treasure,

While the man of consummate wisdom too often acts the fool.'[2]
It seems to me in this case that the mother is of the highest character and the sons exceedingly filial, that the mother is the equal of the mothers of Mencius and T'ao K'an and the sons no different from the disciples Tseng and Min.[3] Just then, when I had my nap, I dreamt that a butterfly got entangled in a spider's web and was rescued by a much larger butterfly; that another butterfly was similarly rescued; that, when a third fell into the net, the large butterfly would not rescue it, but flew off. I took pity on the small butterfly and released it from the web. Heaven sent me this premonition so that I might save the life of the youngest one. [*declaims aside*]

I had nearly given judgement under the penal code,
Not sensing the secret anguish behind these proceedings.
The offence was homicide, not to be lightly passed over—
Let no man think to flout the law with impunity!
At first I ordered the eldest to undergo decapitation;
She pleaded: he was filial, thus necessary for her support.
I commanded that the second be put to the sword instead;
She objected: he was practical, upheld the domestic establishment.
I came down upon the youngest, her own son,

for the capital punishment;

She willingly, nay with alacrity, agreed to his dispatch,
Entreating for mercy for the sons of a previous wife
While her own child went unlamented.
A woman of such virtues merits a decoration
And a state pension too, for her rare example.

---

[1] The alternative reading of this line, as given in *Yüan-ch'ü hsüan*, is: 'Therefore cease from your shouting and wailing!', which would be directed to the youngest boy.

[2] 'The shrewd merchant ...', attributed to Lao-tzu, being the advice he gave to the inquiring Confucius; see *Shih chi*, c. 63, p. 2140.

[3] Tseng-tzu and Min Tzu-ch'ien, the two disciples of Confucius especially noted for filial piety.

Suddenly I see it clear and distinct:
The spirits, moved by her, sent me an omen.
The three little insects caught unsuspectingly in the web
But foreshadow mother and sons caught in the law's meshes.
Once and again the step-mother abandoned her own child
As forewarned in my noonday dream of butterflies.
Chang, have all the prisoners committed to the condemned cell.
MOTHER WANG [*in alarm hurries forward and clings to the boys; sings*]

See how forcibly they lay hands on them, tugging and pushing,
I will hold on to your cangues and shout aloud 'Injustice!'
Before my eyes they head for an exit
                            from which there's no re-entrance,
While I bemoan a hundred times my sad perplexity.
We may as well all die together—would it matter?
Willy-nilly they must away with the runners:
But dead or alive I will bar their way
And here clutch tightly at their clothes.
[*Chang pushes her away and marches the three brothers out of the court*]
MOTHER WANG [*sings*]

Prefect Pao's past judgements were known as unerring
But today he is muddled and fuddled.
All in vain do you sit in the Prefectural Court
                            and wear your badge of authority,
Occupy your high rank and draw your salary—
You have gravely wronged my children,
Condemning them without a hearing to the cell for the dead.
I could risk all and go through fire and water,
Appeal to the Privy Council, to every Minister,
Walk up to the Palace gate, sound the Drum of the Aggrieved,[1]
And complain in the Emperor's presence,
                            braving the Dragon's wrath.
But, oh, silly woman with her tale of woes!
Since there is no one to take up our cause,

[1] Drum of the Aggrieved (*teng-wen ku*), drum outside the Emperor's audience chamber to be sounded by those of his subjects with a particular grievance. The institution was already in existence in A.D. 269 in the Tsin capital, Loyang (see *Chin shu*, c. 3, p. 6ᵃ); it continued all through the T'ang. In the Sung, a government bureau known as 'Bureau of the Drum of the Aggrieved' (teng-wen-ku yüan) was set up to deal with people's complaints about their grievances; see *Li-tai chih-kuan chien-shih*, p. 144, in *Li-tai chih-kuan piao*, edition of 1965.

Would it not be better to seek a place to die
And never again know the plight of widow and orphans
Than drag on, unattached and drifting,
Writhing with pain, weeping and wailing, alive but suffering?
[She goes off
PAO: Chang, come forward. Your orders are . . . [*whispers*]
CHANG: But will it work?
PAO: Idiot, will what I say work? [*declaims*]
Under the benevolent rule of our present Emperor,
I mean to establish for all time incorruptible justice.
If elementary cases like this one escaped my discernment,
Could I have held the Prefect of Kaifeng's high office?
[Exeunt

The Lute

Among the stories and plays represented in this book, *P'i-p'a chi* ('The Tale of the Lute') is undoubtedly the most Chinese in sentiment. For its theme is the family with its unending ties; its setting alternates between the famine-stricken countryside and the Emperor's capital with its Palace and Ministerial residences, which have always been the reality and the dream of Chinese existence; its characters run true to type, and even the courageous and resourceful heroine, Miss Chao, is wonderfully ordinary, a miracle of conventional womanly virtue. Its author was Kao Ming (c. 1305–c. 1369), better known as Kao Tse-ch'eng, who had an unremarkable career as a scholar-official.[1] He came from a family who had retreated to their home in Jui-an, about fifteen miles south of Wenchow on the Chekiang coast, after the overthrow of the Southern Sung. Himself by inclination a recluse, Kao was devoted to his mother—his father seems to have died early—and might have led the same contemplative life as his grandfather and uncle and his wife's relations, composing verse at leisure after T'ang and Sung models.[2] But the family fortune had decayed and Kao eventually gave way to his own desire (or was persuaded by others) to seek recognition and the rewards of office under the

[1] In the official Ming history, Kao Ming receives a brief mention of three or four lines in the 'Biography of Literary Men' (*Ming shih*, c. 285, p. 11a); a somewhat fuller account appears in the local history of Jui-an. Other sources of Kao's life are: a farewell adress by Chao P'ang (1319–69) on the occasion of Kao's departure for home, about 1352; poems addressed to Kao by Liu Chi and others; Kao's own prose and verse compositions. Most of the relevant material may be found in *P'i-p'a-chi t'ao-lun chuan-k'an* (Jen-min, 1956), pp. 334–53; the valuable biographical studies by Ch'ien Nan-yang and Tai Pu-fan are in the same volume, pp. 316–24 and pp. 325–333 respectively; some additional information is provided in Tai's *Lun ku-tien ming-chü P'i-p'a-chi*, 1957.

[2] Kao's grandfather Kao T'ien-hsi and uncle Kao Yen were both poets. Kao married his cousin of the Ch'en family: her grandfather Ch'en Tse-weng and her uncle Ch'en Yü-shih were also poets.

Mongols. Sadly recoiling from this experience some ten years later, by which time, too, his mother was probably dead, he took up the form of drama of his native Wenchow known as *hsi-wen* ('play text') or, more aptly, *ch'uan-ch'i* ('romance') — the dramatic romance that rambles on in dozens of unhurried scenes — and infusing his own feelings into the plot of an existing play about a poor scholar who sought advancement in the world and the faithful wife and aged parents he left behind, wrote *P'i-p'a chi*, the first great work in the southern repertory.

Kao himself did not leave his home until 1345, when at the age of forty or so he set out for the Yüan capital, Peking. He had passed his provincial examination[1] only the year before: it was a late start for a man so gifted, but his hopes were high[2] and he duly obtained his *chin-shih* degree in that year. He was appointed District Judicial Officer at Ch'u-chou (i.e. Lishui in his own province, Chekiang) and discharged his duties with such benevolent care that at the end of his term the local inhabitants erected a stone tablet in his honour with a commemorative address by his younger contemporary Liu Chi (1311–75), a fellow Chekiang man. Kao's talents attracted notice and he was appointed to a post at Hangchow. Then, in the spring of 1349, on the strength of his familiarity with local conditions, Kao was transferred to the Chekiang High Command in its campaign against Fang Kuo-chen, the salt trader and pirate who had broken out in open rebellion along the Chekiang coast.[3] Disillusion now set in: the army camp did not suit Kao, and he and Liu Chi, who was a fellow adjutant or superior officer, both chafed under their stiff Mongol commander. After three years, the campaign was called off when Fang Kuo-chen agreed to accept office under the Yüan. Kao departed for Jui-an but was recalled to other posts, and doggedly held on while the Yüan empire slowly disintegrated.

In 1355, while journeying through Ningpo on his way to yet another post in Fukien Province, Kao was confronted with a

[1] The Mongols revived the civil service examinations in 1314–15 (see *Yüan shih*, c. 81, pp. 2^b–3^a; c. 24, p. 15^a; c. 25, p. 4^a); for examinations, see also 'Young Master Bountiful' *infra*.
[2] See Ch'en Yü-shih's poem addressed to Kao, quoted in *P'i-p'a-chi t'ao-lun chuan-k'an*, p. 353.
[3] Fang Kuo-chen's biography is in *Ming shih*, c. 123, pp. 6^b–8^b.

personal invitation from the former rebel Fang Kuo-chen, now a local war-lord, to join his staff. It was the last straw. Kao threw up his Fukien post and hid in a little place named Li-she a few miles outside Ningpo, shutting himself up in an upstairs room in a lodging house. According to tradition as it was known to the painter and dramatist Hsü Wei (1521–93) writing in *Nan-tzʻu hsü-lu*:

> Kao remained in a tiny upstairs room for three years and finished *Pʻi-pʻa chi*. He was in the habit of tapping his foot to beat time as he wrote his songs, and in the end the floor boards were full of holes. On one occasion he sat up late at night singing to himself, and the flames from two candles suddenly joined together to give out a brilliant light which lasted a long while. It was thought that the very spirits had been moved by his song.[1]

In his younger days Kao seems already to have begun a draft of *Pʻi-pʻa chi*. There is a tradition in Chin-hua (i.e. Kinhwa, a hundred miles north west of Wenchow, also in Chekiang Province) that Kao had studied for a time under the celebrated local Neo-Confucian scholar Huang Chin (1277–1357), who had thought his pupil rather idle until visiting Kao one day in his lodgings outside town, the master came upon a draft of *Pʻi-pʻa chi* in a room on the upper floor and read it with surprise and admiration.[2] The visit is associated with a pavilion behind a cliff to the south of Chin-hua, where master and disciple thrice pledged each other at their parting. The event would have taken place before Kao's examinations in 1344–5, which appears entirely plausible. Kao must indeed have developed an interest in the drama of his home district before he embarked upon his official career. And the upstairs room, which meant a quiet room with a view often to be had at a lower rent, is a link with the retreat at Li-she.

It would be to Li-she that on an autumn's day in 1355 or 1356 Liu Chi came in a tiny boat with a rush awning. The friends exchanged poems on the subject 'In the Rain': Kao's is no longer preserved, but Liu Chi's three stanzas lament the troubled state

---

[1] *Nan-tzʻu hsü-lu*, in *Chung-kuo ku-tien hsi-chʻü lun-chu chi-chʻeng*, vol. III, pp. 239–40. Hsü Wei was also a Chekiang man (from Shao-hsing) and as good an authority as any on the Southern Drama.
[2] *Che-chiang tʻung-chih*, c. 47, 1934 Reprint of edition of 1899, p. 1036; see also *Pʻi-pʻa-chi tʻao-lun chuan-kʻan*, pp. 318, 349.

of the empire.[1] Liu Chi, who was then stationed in Shao-hsing, retired within a year or two to his native Tsingtien, to re-emerge in 1360 as one of the leaders of the advancing Ming army. Kao remained at Li-she, but his voluntary seclusion ended in the second month (i.e. March) of 1357 when, as we learn from one of his own dated poems, he actually went on a visit to three brothers living in a village in the Shao-hsing area.[2] In so far as one may conjecture at all, 'The Lute' had been finished: it was the third calendar year of his stay at Li-she.

While allowing himself somewhat greater freedom of movement, Kao continued his dramatic compositions. The title of a second play — on the paragon of filial piety Min Tzu-Ch'ien — is recorded, though the text has not survived.[3] In the meantime, 'The Lute' circulated in manuscript and won enthusiastic praise from the founding emperor of Ming, T'ai-tsu, who was reported to have said:

> 'The Five Classics and the Four Books are but daily fare like beans and millet, to be found in every family; they are common as homespun cloth. But *P'i-p'a chi* is a real delicacy, hard to come by; and therefore no great household should be without it.'[4]

No doubt there was a reference to the difficulty of obtaining manuscript copies of the new play text (some forty-two scenes of it), which would suggest the scarcity of the army camp rather than the sumptuous palace; but equally certainly T'ai-tsu, himself of humble origins and then perhaps not yet emperor, was expressing his predilection for this dramatized version of the simple lessons of duty and filial observance, sweetened by kind fortune or embittered by grievous calamity, which seemed not just more palatable but a veritable feast of wisdom and good counsel when compared with the dry precepts and rigid rules laid down by the sages. And actors and singers

[1] In Liu Chi's Collected Works, *Ch'eng-i-po wen-chi*, Ssu-pu ts'ung-k'an edition, c. 16, pp. 43ᵃ–43ᵇ; see *P'i-p'a-chi t'ao-lun chuan-k'an*, p. 353, where the stanzas are quoted, and Tai's note 15 on p. 333. Liu Chi's life is in *Ming shih*, c. 128.

[2] In *P'i-p'a-chi t'ao-lun chuan-k'an*, p. 343.

[3] In Hsü Wei's *Nan-tz'u hsü-lu*, p. 252.

[4] *Nan-tz'u hsü-lu*, p. 240. The words are variously reported, though generally supposed to have been pronounced from the throne after Kao's death; but T'ai-tsu's admiration would date from earlier, as, for example, in T'ien I-heng's account in *Liu ch'ing jih-cha* (sixteenth century), quoted in Ch'ien's biographical study, p. 321, and the tribute itself might well be earlier.

were later trained in the southern tunes and style of acting in
order to perform the play in the palace.[1] But indeed at any time
in the 1360's patronage was more than assured for Kao, firmly
anchored to his hermit's ways; he had only to cross over to the
Ming camp to find his friend Liu Chi next in authority to the
future emperor. An actual summons from the throne came in
1368 with the inauguration of the Ming dynasty: Kao was too
ill to appear at court and probably died soon afterwards.

The hero of 'The Lute', Ts'ai Po-chieh, was an actual person
of the Later Han, the famous scholar Ts'ai Yung (A.D. 133 –
192), styled Po-chieh, from Ch'en-liu (in Honan Province),
who had occupied the position of First Lieutenant-Colonel of
the Palace Guards (*tso chung-lang-chiang*, shortened form
chung-lang). Ts'ai played the guitar well and was especially
noted for his deep filial piety.[2] But the identification is almost
irrelevant. For the plot derives from the popular tradition of
the Sung and Yüan, in which Ts'ai Po-chieh appears as a black-
hearted villain, monstrously selfish and unfilial, who abandons
his parents and his wife in a year of famine. It would seem that
the name of Ts'ai Po-chieh, who was Ts'ai the *chung-lang*, got
somehow attached to a story of the time about an ambitious and
reprehensible young man known as Ts'ai Second (Ts'ai erh-
lang).[3] Already in the twelfth century the poet Lu Yu (1125 –
1210), a Shao-hsing man, was deploring the stories told in
towns and villages about the unfortunate Ts'ai Po-chieh:

In the Chao hamlet, under tall willows bathed in the evening sun,
A blind old man taps his drum and begins his recitation.
How indeed does one forecast
                    the posthumous reputations of men!
A whole village now drinks in poor Ts'ai's unfilial deeds.[4]
On the stage also, the unfilial Ts'ai may be traced back to the
twelfth century. Both Chu Yün-ming[5] (1460 – 1526), who

[1] *Nan-tz'u hsü-lu*, p. 240.
[2] Ts'ai Yung's biography is in *Hou-Han shu*, c. 60b, pp. 1979–2008.
[3] See Tung Mei-k'an, *P'i-p'a-chi chien-shuo*, 1957, chapter I, esp. pp. 19–20,
for some sensible observations. For 'chung-lang' to mean 'second son' (i.e.
middle son) and thus be interchangeable with 'erh-lang' would pre-sup-
pose three sons in the story, but such vagaries are not usually governed by
logic.
[4] In *Lu Fang-weng shih-chi*, Ssu-pu ts'ung-k'an edition, vol. I, c. 9, p. 60a:
'My boat approaches a village', third stanza; see also Shen Te-fu (1578–
1642), *Ku ch'ü tsa-yen*, in *Chung-kuo ku-tien hsi-ch'ü lun-chu chi-ch'eng*, vol.
IV, p. 201; Tung Mei-k'an, pp. 13–14; Tai Pu-fan's book, pp. 10–12.
[5] In *Wei-t'an*, quoted in Tung Mei-k'an, p. 2.

claims the authority of an old proclamation prohibiting the performance of certain plays, and Hsü Wei[1] put 'Ts'ai Second' among the earliest plays of the Wenchow drama, which dates back to the early Southern Sung. In the list of Sung and Yüan titles of the southern repertory in Hsü Wei's *Nan-tz'u hsü-lu*, the first item is 'The Chaste Chao Daughter and Ts'ai Second', accompanied by this note: 'being the old play about Po-chieh who abandoned his parents and betrayed his wife and eventually met his death when struck by lightning; an absurd work by some vulgar hand, it marked the beginning of the Southern Drama (*hsi-wen*)'.[2] Kao's two plays occur towards the end of the same list.[3] Thus in Hsü Wei's day 'The Lute' and the old play about Ts'ai Second existed side by side, appealing to two levels of audience. The earlier play, which no longer survives except perhaps in its ending, itself probably underwent changes independently of Kao's version: its denouement of divine vengeance in the form of electrocution by lightning and thunder is still adopted in certain parts of China;[4] and, according to theatrical tradition,[5] it includes a scene in which Ts'ai's wife, 'the chaste Chao daughter', was trampled to death by a horse in the streets of the capital after his rejection of her, an obvious borrowing from the much feared Mongol horses of the Northern Drama of the thirteenth and early fourteenth centuries.[6] And in the northern repertory itself, 'Ts'ai Po-chieh' is found in the list of Chin and early Yüan *yüan-pen* titles transcribed by T'ao Tsung-i in 1366.[7]

As Hsü Wei's list makes clear, Kao's *P'i-p'a chi* was a new play, not a mere revision of the Wenchow text. He inherited the plot, and probably based many of his scenes on the old stage version. (In Yo Po-ch'uan's *tsa-chü* play of the late thirteenth or early fourteenth century, '*T'ieh-kuai' Li*, there is a reference to the chaste Chao daughter who with her own skirt carried earth to build the tomb, i.e. of her parents-in-law, but this

---

[1] *Nan-tz'u hsü-lu*, p. 239.

[2] *Nan-tz'u hsü-lu*, p. 250.   [3] *Nan-tz'u hsü-lu*, p. 252.

[4] In the theatre of Hunan; see *P'i-p'a-chi t'ao-lun chuan-k'an*, pp. 17, 20–21, 247–8.

[5] See Tung Mei-k'an, p. 37 and *P'i-p'a-chi t'ao-lun chuan-k'an*, pp. 17, 20–21; attempts at reviving this scene have met with but poor response from an audience ready enough to see the wicked Ts'ai struck by lightning.

[6] See 'A Dream of Butterflies' *supra*.

[7] See Introduction to 'A Dream of Butterflies' *supra*; *Nan-ts'un cho-keng lu*, c. 25, p. 310.

would seem a reference to the old *yüan-pen*, rather than the Wenchow, play.)[1] The songs and most of the dialogue, however, would be his own, and he was concerned to exonerate, indeed to rehabilitate, the Han scholar Ts'ai Yung, adding the occasional touch for the sake of historical veracity, e.g. in scene 21, in which Ts'ai plays on his guitar (*ch'in*), known as 'Charred Tail', being made from a board rescued from a pile of burning wood and mentioned by name in *Hou-Han shu* (p. 2004). Above all, his aim was to portray Ts'ai and his wife—or his two wives—as patterns of filial piety and virtue.

Filial piety is, to be sure, a matter of definition. For Father Ts'ai, it consists in honouring one's parents, in serving one's sovereign, in being true to oneself (scene 4, p. 27). And honouring one's parents means serving them in their lifetime, burying them at their death, and sacrificing to them after their burial. Hence the charge of 'thrice unfilial' made against Ts'ai by Squire Chang in scene 37 (p. 209) and in other versions of the story,[2] being probably an original feature of the old Wenchow play: to which Kao opposes the phrase 'thrice frustrated' (p. 210). The plea is incapacity. Ts'ai begged to remain at home, but his father compelled him to enter for the examinations; he declined the marriage proposal from the powerful Niu family, but the Emperor commanded him to marry the Minister's daughter; he tried to resign from his office and return to the village, but was repeatedly foiled by his crafty and domineering father-in-law. On the positive side, since obedience is part of loyalty to the throne as well as of filial piety, Ts'ai, who did but obey his father in the beginning and, afterwards, his Emperor, is found not guilty:

'Completely loyal, and thus completely filial,

remained Ts'ai Po-chieh!'

Thus ends the Prologue,[3] in which a synopsis of the story is provided and—for purposes of performance—the title of the play declared to be

'The thrice thwarted Ts'ai Po-chieh and the story of the Lute'.[4]

---

[1] Act II, final song 'sha-wei', in *Yüan-ch'ü hsüan*, Wen-hsüeh ku-chi ed. 1955, p. 501. This is pointed out in Tai Pu-fan's book, p. 11.

[2] For example, in the theatre of Hunan, in the scene quoted in Tung Mei-k'an, pp. 42–4; see also *P'i-p'a-chi t'ao-lun chuan-k'an*, pp. 18–19.

[3] See discussion below.

[4] For this precise title Kao himself seems not to have been responsible; see discussion below.

We may additionally note that the hero was surely aged forty or so at the time of his departure from home, his parents being almost eighty; that journeys were difficult and uncertain, and that Ch'en-liu, but a short distance from Loyang, could be effectively cut off while a famine raged unchecked for several years, even as Kao himself managed to move from post to post in his native Chekiang and yet seemed a long, long way from home; and that the lute ($p'i$-$p'a$) itself did not play a really prominent part in the action. The Prologue is, in fact, one of the documents of literary history and deserves a fuller study. In brief, it is addressed to an audience accustomed to the Northern Drama (which, after the fall of Hangchow, migrated south) with its four-act structure and its rigid sequence of tunes governed by a single mode in each act, but also with its clowns and buffoonery and its often lamentable improvisation. Thus the Prologue may be regarded as an apology for the Southern Drama with its indiscriminate use of tunes in a variety of modes (which repelled purists but permitted a far wider range of expression), its refinement of language and its stress on sentiment. In his discourse, Kao also brings to the fore his own particular contribution to the stage—the idea of characters as guiding examples, patterns of behaviour in the midst of trials and tribulations.

But 'The Lute' requires no detailed commentary or annotation. Allowing for the universal conventions of the stage, it may be trusted to speak to any reader, even in an extract. The whereabouts of Ch'en-liu and Loyang do not matter: they are synonymous with 'native village' and 'metropolis'. For distance and time are mere accidents in this morality play about a Chinese Everyman who found his Good Angel in a Chinese Everywoman.

P'i-p'a chi survives in a number of Ming and Ch'ing printed editions from the sixteenth century onwards,[1] but also in a Ch'ing manuscript[2] which claims to be derived from a Yüan text and embodies certain archaic features. The scene divisions are unmarked, and the scenes therefore are unnumbered and

---

[1] See Introduction, pp. 4–6, in Ch'ien Nan-yang's edition.
[2] A facsimile of which is in *Ku-pen hsi-ch'ü ts'ung-k'an*, series I: *Yüan-pen Ts'ai Po-chieh p'i-p'a chi*.

have no titles;[1] and the Prologue, in which the four lines that constitute the play's formal and complete title are placed at the beginning rather than at the very end,[1] is probably as the author wrote it and not the stage version found in the printed editions. For the translation I have followed in the main the text of Ch'ien Nan-yang in his annotated edition based on the manuscript (Chung-hua, 1960), and my scene and page references are to that edition. I have known and liked the play best, however, in the edition of the Ming painter and connoisseur Ch'en Chi-ju (1558–1639),[2] whose succinct comments are a reminder of the traditional view and whose readings I have now and then adopted by preference or out of expediency. For the Prologue, I have departed from the manuscript and adopted the stage version (of the Ch'en Chi-ju edition), which includes a short dialogue between the declaimer of the lines and a voice (or voices) backstage announcing the one-line title of the play, a piece of business usually left to the company.[3]

In the translation, the songs are rendered line by line, with the names of the tunes omitted; no attempt is made to reproduce the rhyme of the original. Where the song is interrupted by speech, the speech is rendered as prose, but an interruption consisting only of the name of the person addressed, or of a vocative or exclamation, is simply incorporated in the verse. Similarly, speeches in verse are rendered line by line. The songs and speeches in the original are an easy blend of sublimity and mawkish sentimentality, which I have sought to reproduce, though in the process some of the sparkle and effervescence has inevitably given way to artificial flavouring and sediment.

---

[1] As in the three early *hsi-wen* texts preserved in *Yung-lo ta-tien* (1407), c. 13991: *Hsiao Sun t'u, Chang Hsieh chuang-yüan* and *Huan-men tzu-ti ts'o li shen* which are probably the earliest extant southern plays (facsimile of the three texts in *Ku-pen hsi-ch'ü ts'ung-k'an*, series 1).

[2] Reprinted Wen-hsüeh ku-chi, 1954.

[3] A similar dialogue is found in the early *hsi-wen* text *Hsiao Sun t'u* (see n. 1 above); but in such late Yüan and early Ming southern plays as *Ching-ch'ai chi* (Chung-hua edition, 1959) and *Sha kou chi* (Chung-hua edition, 1960) one finds, at this point in the Prologue, the stage direction: 'Usual question and answer'.

The Lute

PROLOGUE[1]

The lamp in autumn lights up the emerald curtain,
At my desk by night I browse among rue-scented volumes.[2]
Of times past and present
How many are the stories recorded!
No lack of tales of fair ladies and men of talent
Nor of the gods and spirits,
But all so paltry as would not bear reading.
Thus is seen: where the subject concerns not moral example,
Though good the tale, yet is it told in vain.

In drama, to seek to please is easy, to move men difficult.
True patrons of our art,
View it this time with different eyes:
Have no regard to the clowns' buffoonery
Nor ascertain the key nor trace the tune—
Mark only filial piety in a son, womanly virtue in a wife,
A pair such as the twin steeds Hua and Liu[3] that,

                                       rushing headlong,
Defy a myriad horses to take the lead.

[*asks within*] Children of the Pear Garden, I ask you, whose story do you enact today? What is the play?
[*voice from within*]
'The thrice thwarted Ts'ai Po-chieh and the Story of the Lute'.
I see it is *this* play. Let me set forth the argument in brief that

[1] The Prologue is spoken by a secondary male singer, a *fu-mo*, presumably impersonating the playwright; in printed editions, it constitutes scene 1. Regarding text and significance, see Introduction.
[2] Leaves of the bitter scented rue were scattered among books to keep away silver-fish and other insects.
[3] Hua and Liu, originally the name of a single horse, Hua-liu, in the stable of the Chou emperor, Mu-wang; see *Shih chi*, c. 5, p. 175. The name Hua-liu figures in the catalogue of horses in the Imperial stables at Loyang in scene 9 (in most editions, scene 10), p. 56.

you may learn the purport of the action.[1]

The Chao daughter was beautiful
And Ts'ai Po-chieh accomplished in scholarship.
They were but two months married,
When, alas, the Examinations were proclaimed
And men of learning sought all over the Empire.
By stern paternal command
Compelled to enrol himself among the candidates,
Po-chieh with one attempt won top place at the Palace,
And married again the daughter of Prime Minister Niu.
Ensnared by advancement and honour, he failed to return.
In a year of famine his parents both perished with hunger,
A conjuncture truly deserving pity!
Deserving of pity,
The Chao daughter still bore up,
Cut and sold her hair to bury the parents-in-law.
With her sackcloth skirt she carried earth
And heaped it up in a mound;
Then with her lute she recounted her many sorrows
As she made her way to the capital.
Oh, filial Po-chieh! Oh, virtuous daughter of Niu!
Too, too grievous the reunion in the library!
They all returned to dwell in huts by the grave,
The man and his two wives,
Upon whose house the Emperor conferred distinction.

Richest and most exalted was Prime Minister Niu;
In charity and benevolence excelled Squire Chang.
With virtue and courage behaved the daughter of Chao;
Completely loyal, and thus completely filial,
                                    remained Ts'ai Po-chieh![2]

---

[1] [*asks within*] . . . purport of the action: a stage convention, not part of
the author's text. The lines before, about 'filial piety in a son, womanly
virtue in a wife', clearly show that this is an interpolation; see Introduction. Children of the Pear Garden: members of the theatrical profession,
the T'ang emperor Hsüan-tsung having trained his three hundred
musicians in a pear garden.
[2] The four lines constitute the play's full title and occur originally at the
beginning of the Prologue; see Introduction.

Scene 19   Feeding the Parents-in-law[1]
CHAO[2] [*enters and sings*]

The fields are barren, the plains bare,
The man is far off, the farm in ruins.
With heart and soul I carry out a daughter-in-law's duty,
Drooping, worn out with fatigue:
Fortunately father and mother still seem hale.
It is too piteous
To see the hungry howling all along the road.
I scan the horizon, whispering:
On whom may I depend for succour?

[*declaims*]

No smoke of cooking rises from the desolate wastes;
The dim sun casts its sad rays on the village.
A widow bewails her husband, perished in the plains;
Setting out for distant parts, a mother clings to her son.
Gazing upon this grievous sight,
I recall my own sad plight.
The parents are old, their days fraught with risk;
The husband in search of honours neglects to return;
Strength sapped, wits spent, tears dried up—
Who knows when I too shall breathe my last?
The yellow earth in the plains abounds in heaps—
Would someone, then, with a shovelful bury poor me?

Ever since my husband left home, famine has visited us year after year. My clothes and jewellery have been sold or pawned, and of other means of sustenance there is none. And the aged

---

[1] The usual title, being scene 20 in most editions. The scene is the village home in Ch'en-liu County, where in scene 2 Father and Mother Ts'ai rejoice, as Chinese people do, in their great age and in their happiness but where in scene 4 Father Ts'ai sends our reluctant hero Ts'ai Po-chieh to the examinations. Ts'ai has been away from home since scene 5, the parting scene between him and his wife, Chao the fifth daughter. In scenes 9, 11, 12, 13, 14 and 15, Ts'ai passes his examinations in the capital, resists the alliance proposed by the Niu family and asks to resign from office. (A burlesque examination scene, which is scene 8 in most editions, does not occur in the manuscript version.) The effects of the famine begin to be felt in scene 10, in which Mother Ts'ai upbraids Father Ts'ai for sending their son away. In scene 16 the government granaries are opened and Chao claims her rations, but the village headman waylays her and robs her of all the rice she obtained. In scenes 17 and 18, in the capital, Ts'ai marries Miss Niu.
[2] The role of the heroine Chao, known as Chao wu-niang, i.e. fifth daughter of Chao, is assigned to the leading female singer, the *tan*.

parents surely need care, yet I have no delicacies to lay before them morning and evening. Thus I have only dished up a few mouthfuls of plain rice. And I myself will make a meal of the chaff, to keep body and soul together. Of this I dare not tell them, for fear of vexing them further. So when I eat, I must stay away from them. [*she serves up the rice*] Pa and Ma have already come!

FATHER AND MOTHER TS'AI[1] [*enter and sing*]

How much longer

Must we put up with this hunger?

CHAO: The meal is ready.

MOTHER TS'AI [*showing disgust*] It may be a year of famine, but is this what you expect me to have?

FATHER TS'AI: Gulp it down somehow. In times like these you should not be so particular.

MOTHER TS'AI [*sings*]

I have been famished all morning.

The rice you have brought—can one eat *that?*

At once remove it,

Or do you mean to take me for a glutton?

FATHER TS'AI [*sings*]

See, all her garments are disposed of.

With what then could she buy good food?

Ma, this is a natural calamity;

The daughter-in-law is hard put to it to make provision.

CHAO [*sings*]

Mother, calm yourself; do not upbraid me.

I will prepare something in a twinkling.

[*chorus*]

When I pause to reflect,

Rounded tears course down my face.

We shall all likely be dead—

Our corpses piled up in trenches—

And even if alive, yet in unbearable misery!

Oh, the hateful Ts'ai Po-chieh!

MOTHER TS'AI [*sings*]

Let me try and discover the cause:

Perhaps you are plagued with a fit of private gormandise?

Perhaps you have purveyed for yourself some favourite dish?—

[1] Father and Mother Ts'ai are played by secondary singers, a *wai* and a *ching* respectively.

Why is it, when we sit down to table, she is absent?

Her actions pronounce her guilty.

FATHER TS'AI [*sings*]

Ma, she is devoted to you.

Too perversely you now turn against her.

CHAO [*sings*]

What hardships have I shirked?

Could there be grounds for suspicion?

[*chorus*]

When I pause to reflect,

Rounded tears course down my face.

We shall all likely be dead—

Our corpses piled up in trenches—

And even if alive, yet in unbearable misery!

Oh, the hateful Ts'ai Po-chieh!

MOTHER TS'AI: Remove it! Remove it!

FATHER TS'AI: Daughter, take it away then.

CHAO [*clearing away the rice*] Let me go and buy something, and then prepare another meal.

MOTHER TS'AI: Very well, go!

CHAO: I see then:

  'The dumb when they are prescribed the gentian-root

  May not reveal the taste of the bitter cup.'   [*She goes off*

MOTHER TS'AI: Daddy, there's nothing like one's own flesh and blood. You wouldn't keep our own son at home, so now you have this daughter-in-law to provide for you! A time was when she still served fish and vegetables, but these last few meals there was just rice alone. How could I endure it? Perhaps a few days from now even rice would not be served! Did you notice how at meal times she hid herself from me in a hundred ways. I dare say she has really bought some dish or other for her own enjoyment.

FATHER TS'AI: Ma, you could be mistaken in this. The daughter-in-law seems to me to be suffering greatly. She is not that sort of person.

MOTHER TS'AI: If that's what you think, we'll wait till she is having her meal, and go and spy on her to find out the truth.

FATHER TS'AI: Rightly said.

BOTH [*declaim*]

In troubled water one cannot tell carp from bream;

They each grow distinct as mud settles in the stream.

Scene 20   Eating chaff[1]

CHAO [*enters and sings*]

In tumult and disorder, the year of dearth;
Far, far distant, the unreturned husband;
Seething with resentment, the impatient parents;
Timid and weak, inadequate, lonely me!
My dresses are pawned, I am draped with no inch of silk;
Many a time I was ready to sell myself as a slave,
Yet to whom could I leave the helpless parents-in-law?

[*refrain*]

To contemplate—mysterious are the ways of fate,
                                        hard indeed to fathom;
But to bear—too, too real the calamities that scourge!

Drop by drop, my inexhaustible tears;
A confused tangle, sorrow's strands slow to unknit;
Bones sticking out of their decrepit, thin bodies;
Quaking and trembling, we in this interminable hour and year!
Alas, this chaff—if I do not feed on it,
Could I endure the hunger?
Yet how could I swallow it?
Woe! now I consider the matter—better to die myself
Than live to see *his* parents die!

[*refrain*]

To contemplate—mysterious are the ways of fate,
                                        hard indeed to fathom;
But to bear—too, too real the calamities that scourge!

In the morning I prepared some rice for the father and mother.
It is not that I would not buy fish and vegetables, but, alas, there
is no money for it. I hardly expected that the mother-in-law
would complain so bitterly, thinking that I had something to
eat behind their backs. She little knew that I had been eating
chaff and, not wishing for them to know this, could only hide
myself while I fed. But even if her grumbling drives me to distraction, I dare not explain. Oh, misery! how indeed can one
swallow these husks? [*she eats, then vomits; sings*]

This vomiting convulses my very entrails
While tears of pain gush forth;
My throat is choked, my voice turns hoarse.

[1] The usual title, being scene 21 in most editions.

Oh husks, you were put through the mill, pounded by the pestle
Sifted and winnowed,
Underwent all manner of rough handling:
You are as wretched as wretched me,
Who have known a thousand bitter hardships.
Bitter food for one too well acquainted with bitterness—
Like wormwood to gall—
Only, alas! down it will not go.

[*she again eats and vomits; then sings*]

Rice and husk
Which cling together as a cohering whole
Are sent flying asunder by the winnowing fan—
One prized, and one despised,
Like my husband and me,
Forever severed.
Oh, husband, you are the rice
Scattered abroad, nowhere to be found,
And I am even as the husk.
Yet how may the husk serve to relieve hunger?
Thus, too, the husband being away,
How could the poor wife provide suitable delicacies
                                    for the parents-in-law?

[*she puts down her bowl; then sings*]

I live to little purpose;
My death would cause no stir.
Better to starve, then, with a will!
Yet the parents are old;
They completely rely on me,
And for their sakes I must linger on in life.
Lingering on alive is easily said:
What hope is there of eventual re-union with him?
Figure myself as the chaff?
Even *it* is still eaten and absorbed,
But where would *my* bones find their resting place?

FATHER AND MOTHER TS'AI [*enter to spy on her*] Daughter-in-law, what are you muttering there?

[*Chao hides her bowl of chaff*]

MOTHER TS'AI [*searches out the bowl and strikes Ch'ao*]
Daddy, do you see there? She really has food prepared for herself to eat behind our backs. The hussy deserves a beating!

FATHER TS'AI: You eat it up then and see what it is.

[*Mother Ts'ai eats the chaff ravenously, then spits it out.*]

FATHER TS'AI: Daughter-in-law, what have you prepared there?

CHAO [*sings*]

It is the rind of the corn,

The hull of the rice,

Served up to allay my hunger.

FATHER AND MOTHER TS'AI: This is chaff! How could you eat it?

CHAO [*sings*]

I hear it said in ancient scriptures:

'What the dogs ate, men ate'.[1]

This at least is better than roots of grass

or bark stripped off trees.

FATHER AND MOTHER TS'AI: Did it not choke you?

CHAO [*sings*]

Famished in his freezing dungeon, Su Wu chewed felt with ice:[2]

His remained a sound body.

Hermits existing on seeds of fir and pine

Are known to have gained the company of immortals.

What harm could there be in feeding on chaff?

Father and mother, though others might not find it palatable, I can eat it.

FATHER AND MOTHER TS'AI: Nonsense! How should you alone be capable of eating chaff?

CHAO [*sings*]

Pa and Ma, pray, do not be mystified:

For I am but the lowly wife[3] of your own son.

FATHER AND MOTHER TS'AI [*wailing*] Wrongly we accused her! Oh, we die of very shame! [*they swoon*]

CHAO [*stoops and calls them; then sings*]

Heavily they sink into unbreaking sleep:

In vain do I call at their ear.

Father, Mother, I fear I have not served you with all my heart;

Instead I have caused you now to enter your grave!

[1] A misreading of Mencius I.i.III.5: 'Your dogs and swine eat the food of men, and you do not know to make any restrictive arrangements' (Legge).

[2] Su Wu, denied food by Hsiung-nu tribesmen who imprisoned him in a dungeon, survived by chewing felt and ice, thus winning for himself the admiration of his captors; see *Han shu*, c. 54, pp. 2462–3.

[3] Literally, wife who shared his days of chaff (i.e. adversity), which indeed she is.

Father, Mother, people will wonder

> why you have met your deaths;

Father, Mother, how is it you have left me behind?

Father! Mother!

FATHER TS'AI [*wakes from his swoon; sings*]

Daughter, you endured hunger, to serve your parents-in-law;

Daughter, you endured hunger, at what cost!

Unjustly blamed, you yet would not leave off!

At last I know who is a lowly, devoted wife.

Daughter, too soon, alas, I shall go down to the shades;

Daughter, do not on account of the dead

> further torment yourself, the living!

CHAO [*calls Mother Ts'ai; sings*]

Mother, if you die, how shall I answer for you?

Mother, if you die, how shall I pull through?

Amidst a thousand hardships I have tried to protect her,

But now, oh husband! protect her I can no longer.

My great worry is, with mother dead,

> father too seems doomed—

Not to speak of the purse spent and clothes all pawned.

FATHER TS'AI [*calls Mother Ts'ai; sings*]

Mother, I too rashly at first

Ordered our son to the capital,

Leaving the daughter-in-law in misery and alone.

And now I send you journeying to the nether springs!

Lay all the blame on me!

Alas, where would my bones find a resting place?[1]

Scene 24   Parting with her Hair to bury her Parents-in-law[2]

CHAO [*enters and sings*]

First, the famine brought distress;

Then, woe upon woe, both parents died.

All by myself, how may I hope to fare?

My clothes are sold and gone,

Not a pennyworth of jewellery remains.

At my wits' end I can but clip my tresses.

[1] Mother Ts'ai dies and Squire Chang, an elderly neighbour, provides the money for her coffin in the rest of this scene. Father Ts'ai dies in scene 22 (in most editions, scene 23).
[2] The usual title, being scene 25 in most editions.

[*declaims*]

How might one brush aside a thousand trials and hardships?
My strength exhausted, my mind forspent,

in vain I weep tears of blood.
My housewife's coarse garments are worn out,

my station has come to an end:
The father-like *cedrela* is hewn down,

the matriarchal day-lily uprooted.[1]

The metal of the scissors gleams like snow
Against black clouds that weigh upon
A faint crescent of two sad eyebrows.
My pious thoughts—could I express them in full!
My thoughts, then, I leave to these silken hairs.
When, earlier, my mother-in-law was no more, it was Squire
Chang who gave me succour. And now my father-in-law is also
dead, and there is no money for the burial, it would not do to
ask for his help again. I have thought it over, and there is no
other way, but I must cut off my hair and sell it for a few strings
of cash to provide for the last rites. Yet this hair is worth little,
it can but serve as a token, and this is no different from begging.

[*declaims*]

Alas, that I should lose both parents!
If you seek help, twice can be too often.
Perhaps with my own black tresses
I could bury the hoary-headed old ones.

[*sings*]

Ever since the phoenix left its mate
Who has to her curls attended?
On the idle dressing table, dust has settled.
Besides, have not hairpins and comb

and head ornaments all been pawned?
Black hair, I have wasted your youth
And now I clip you that I might inter the aged parents.

---

[1] *Cedrela* and day-lily. The day-lily 'was called in ancient times Hsüan . . .
also known by the name I Nan Ts'ao (Boy-favoring Herb) because it was
believed to favor the birth of sons when worn in women's girdles . . .
Hsüan is also traditionally the literary figure of speech for mother, while
Ch'ün, the Chinese mahogany tree, *Cedrela sinensis*, a long-lived tree of
high quality, is the metaphor for father.' (H.L.Li, *The Garden Flowers of
China*, 1959, p. 110).

To cut my hair, how it wounds my feelings!
If I complain though, it is only of the faithless man
                            with whose hair mine was entwined.[1]
[*she lifts her scissors to her hair, but pauses and drops her hand; sings*]
To think this faithless man
Should betray me all my life!
Before I have shorn one lock
Tears drip all around me.
If formerly I had shaven my pate.
And taken the vows of a nun,
Of this grief I should be spared today.
Alas, my head of hair! Was it ever, like the bejewelled heads of
beautiful ladies, [*sings*]
Surrounded with pearls, studded with jade, scented with musk?
But in such straits, [*sings*]
If I die myself, would I so much as earn a burial?
Why grieve, then, over the shedding of your hairs, silly woman?
Pity the silly woman, destitute and all alone!
Hair, if I do not cut you so as to part with you, [*sings*]
How unbearable the shame of openly begging!
And if I do cut you, [*sings*]
Where the blade grazes, the heart will feel the pain.
My raven coils, then, let me unwind,
With the waves breaking over each temple:
Thus like a grateful crow I requite those white cranes,
                                            the parents,[2]
That men may say
A girl lost her luxuriant crown of black cloudlike curls
And thus buried father and mother with the frosty temples.
[*she cuts her hair; then, as she weeps, sings*]
Without a plan, both parents being dead,
I have cut off these tresses.
This is no desperate bid for lasting fame:
For easier it is to brave a savage beast
Than confide in others our hidden sorrows.
Since it is done, I must now take it into the street to sell it.

---

[1] The tying together of the bride's hair and the groom's was part of the
wedding ceremony, the recollection of which saddens her the more now
that she has to clip her own hair; see Introduction to 'The Shrew' *supra*.
[2] It was believed that the young crow fed its parents in gratitude; the white
cranes are an extension of the simile.

Down the main street, along the short alleys, I will cry 'Hair
for sale!' [*She makes a vendor's cry; then sings*]

Hair for sale!
You who would buy it, do not grudge the price!
Have pity on one hit by the famine
Whose money-bag has quite run out.
While my husband is away from home,
The parents-in-law died, one after the other.
What could I do—
But sell my hair
To bury them?

How now? Will no one even make an offer?
[*she repeats her cry; then sings*]

Pray, look at this black silk hair
Glorious even when clipped:
But, though I would sell, none would buy it!
Famine and these afflicting deaths—
Could I, a mere daughter-in-law,
Withstand alone such misfortunes?
Besides, for days I have not fed;
I can scarce lift my feet.
Alas, hard indeed to bear!

[*she falls; then, struggling up, sings*]

I search the back street and the front:
No one is there.

I should cry out again, but—[*sings*]

My breath is choked—
I can no more!
Ah, woe! should I die now
My bones might lie exposed;
For who would cover them?

Heaven above, at worst it is but death for me, [*sings*]

So let me endeavour to sell this,
And having sold it, bury the mother and father,
That dying, I leave no regrets.

SQUIRE CHANG[1] [*enters and declaims*]

Mercy alone outweighs a thousand prayers;
Evil-doing renders void ten thousand incense offerings.

Ah, is this not young Mistress Ts'ai? Why is she lying helpless
in the street?

---

[1] Squire Chang is played by a secondary male singer, a *mo* or *fu-mo*.

CHAO: Squire, save me.

SQUIRE [*helping her up*] Young mistress, what were you doing with that hair in your hand?

CHAO: My father-in-law is no more; I had hoped to provide for his funeral by selling this hair.

SQUIRE [*weeping*] And so your father-in-law too is dead. Why did you not come to me for counsel? What was the good of cutting off your hair?

CHAO: I had already troubled you many times. I could not venture to come again.

SQUIRE: What nonsense! [*sings*]

Your husband had entrusted me:

Could I deny my word?

Since you are short of cash

I must supply it.

That you should have shorn off your curls

And lain helpless even now in the street—

The fault was mine alone.

[*chorus*]

I lament a family wrecked!

The darkest hour is here—yet where is dawn?

Weep, weep us both!

CHAO [*sings*]

For your pity, Squire, I thank you

And for your freely proffered loan.

My parents-in-law even in their last resting place will be grateful.

I fear, though, that poor me

May die unmourned too soon;

And then, Squire, who will repay your repeated kindnesses?

[*chorus*]

We lament a family wrecked!

The darkest hour is here—yet where is dawn?

Weep, weep us both!

SQUIRE: Young mistress, return home first. I will ask my man to send you some cloth, money and food.

CHAO: Pray, keep the hair, Squire.

SQUIRE: What should I do with this hair?

CHAO: Accept it as a token of thanks for your rescue of a poor woman.

SQUIRE: Even though her husband had counted on me, his own neighbour?

Both: Thus it seems—

A providential hand reaches down from the very skies
To release from fate's cobweb the innocent, trapped mortal.
[*Both leave the stage*

Scene 28   In Search of her Husband she sets out begging[1]

Chao [*enters and sings*]

Back again to the bare tomb
For the ceremony of leave-taking!
Troubled by the future, anguished in the present,
Their portrait I will now paint, to show all whom I meet;
Dumbly eloquent in their sorrow, they will plead for me.

Though the ways of spirits are dark, yet one must believe that they do respond to our distress. Yesterday I was alone in the hills, trying to make the grave; wearied by the toil, I fell asleep, and in my sleep a god appeared who called himself a mountain deity and led a troop of spirits to build the grave. He also commanded me to disguise myself and seek my husband in Ch'ang-an. When I awoke, I found a tomb complete even with a terrace;[2] clearly the gods came to my aid. As is said, it would be safer to believe in spirits than to doubt they exist. And so, now that the parents are buried, I must adopt the guise of a nun and go begging in the streets by singing some ballads about filial piety, with the lute as accompaniment. There is just one thing. These several years my parents-in-law and I have lived together. How could I bear to leave them behind? I have always known how to paint. Why not recall their likeness and do their portrait? I could carry it on my back and it would be as if I was still with them. And at anniversaries I would unroll the portrait, burn incense and offer up thin gruel or rice. This would at least enable me to express my deeper feelings. So now I will paint the portrait. [*sings*]

Ever since their death—
Could one still hope to meet them
Except in dreams when fleetingly we are again together?
Though I mean to paint them, yet paint them I cannot.

[1] The usual title, being scene 29 in most editions.
[2] 'Yesterday . . . even with a terrace': the action took place in scene 26 (27 in most editions). For 'Ch'ang-an', Loyang is intended; Ch'ang-an (capital of the Former Han and of T'ang) being in popular parlance the equivalent of 'capital'.

I imagine them as they were
And before I have begun to paint, tears well up.
Their sorrowful minds I am unable to portray;
The disease called hunger I am unable to portray;
The wide, staring eyes longing for their son
                                    I am unable to portray;
I can only portray them with their thin white hair
And their dirty, ragged garments.
Alack! alack! If I show them to be of fine appearance,
They would not be the parents-in-law of the Chao daughter.

I could paint your cheeks as fleshy—
But, then, you were famished and starving;
I could paint your cheeks as smiling—
But, then, your faces always were furrowed:
Portrayed, you cannot but be ugly.
Besides, so grieved I am,
    I will not paint a cheerful countenance.
It is not that I am incapable of presenting them better, but from
the time I married into this family
    For two months only I found them somewhat carefree;
    The rest was one long misery.
And the two months when they were carefree I can no longer
recall. These three or four years I remember them only as
shrunk and shrivelled. Alas, in this portrait,
    Even their own son, I fear, would not know his father and mother.
    Alack! Alack! Even if he would not know them to be
                        Ts'ai Po-chieh's former pa and ma.
    He shall know them as the Chao daughter's late parents-in-law.
Since the portrait is finished, I will burn incense and paper ingots, offer up food and water, and take my leave of them before
setting out.
[*sings*]
    Papa and Mama,
    It is not just longing for my husband that makes me wander far—
    It is even more concern for your son and heir.
    As soon as I find him, I will return
    Nor delay on the way.
    Wretched me, how may I hope to accomplish the journey?
    Dear parents-in-law, I pray that you protect me
    While I travel in distant parts.

[*she does obeisance before the portrait*]

Alas, there would be none left even to mourn them!

How then could *they* protect me?

This tomb, when I am away,

Will be cheerless, with none to sweep it or tender respect.

At the customary times in spring and autumn

Whence would come the paper-money offering?

Alack! Alack! Alive, you were but cold and starving parents;

And dead—forlorn spirits, to whom none sacrifice.

I have made obeisance and taken leave of the parents; I must now go to bid Squire Chang farewell. But, how is this? Squire Chang has in fact come!

SQUIRE [*enters and declaims*]

A late cicada in the faded willows,

                      its chirping too sad for the ear—

Dead leaves fluttering before the wild west wind—

On the ancient Ch'ang-an road do not turn your head to linger:

West of the Yang-kuan Pass there will be no familiar faces.[1]

CHAO: I was just about to call on you, Squire.

SQUIRE: Are you leaving now?

CHAO: I am.

SQUIRE: What's that you have painted?

CHAO: It is a portrait of my parents-in-law, and on my journey I shall carry it as something to show people while I beg; but in the morning and evening I will burn incense and paper-money before it.

SQUIRE [*looks at portrait and declaims*] Young mistress,

When death parts dear ones, do they not meet in dreams?

Must a daughter-in-law, though filial,

                      even paint the parents' portrait?

A pity they could not be shown in the midst

                  of some family celebration—

The colours are wasted, the painter but brings herself grief.

Their clothes are tattered, their hair loosened;

A thousand sorrows sit on their brows.

Master Ts'ai would not know these altered faces—

Daughter Chao has portrayed their last, sad features,

                      to no purpose.

[1] The T'ang poet Wang Wei's famous line from his 'Wei-ch'eng ch'ü', sung or quoted at almost every leave-taking in the succeeding centuries.

I heard about the long journey you were taking, and have a few strings of cash here to help you out with expenses.

CHAO: I have already burdened you too much. How could I trouble you again? There is just this, though; I have a further request, which may seem unreasonable. When I am gone, out of regard for your old friends, my parents-in-law, will you look after their tomb for me?

SQUIRE: Do not worry on that score. But before you go, I still have a few words of advice for you. Young mistress, you were brought up in the inner apartments; little do you know the way of the world. When, formerly, Master Ts'ai was not yet away, you were in the prime of youth. Now you have gone through famine and hunger, and are plain and care-worn. As it is said,

> 'Each spring brings the same peach blossoms
>
> But a woman's face changes from year to year.'

At the time of Master Ts'ai's departure, did he not promise that if he made the least headway he would at once return? Thus it is: [*declaims*]

> 'Paint a tiger, show its stripes; how will you show its bones?
> Know a man, ken the face; who may ken the heart?'[1]
> Ah, a learned man was Master Ts'ai,
> Certain of immediate success and fame.
> Long he tarries, one wonders why;
> Famine and bereavement cannot recall him.
> Young mistress, when you reach the capital, tread with care,
> Meekly inquire the truth of all you meet,
> And when you find him, restrain your tale of woe:
> Unfold it by degrees through songs sustained by the lute.
> Do not reveal too soon you are his wife;
> Do not tell at once both parents are dead.
> And if Master Ts'ai should long for home,
> A kind thought he might spare for old neighbour Chang.
> Three score and ten I am this year
> But ten years less than your pa and ma;
> Before you start, old Chang is here to bid farewell—
> When you return, alas, will he yet be there?

This parting is a case of

> Tear-stained cheeks meet the gaze of streaming eyes

---

[1] 'Paint a tiger' etc: a common saying, then as now. Among the author's poems is one inscribed on someone's picture of a tiger, quoted in *P'i-p'a-chi t'ao-lun chuan-k'an*, p. 340.

While one broken heart sends off another.

CHAO [*sings*]

Their departed souls are shrouded in mystery;
What may I yet lean on?
A myriad *li* journey before me—
My thoughts pre-occupied with death![1]
When I am away, the lonely tomb
I beg you will watch over.

[*refrain*]

Desolate wherever I raise my eyes!
Tears well up and descend in showers.

SQUIRE [*sings*]

Since you have entrusted me,
I will do my part.
The lonely tomb I will watch over;
My promise I mean to keep.
I only pray that on the journey
Good health still be yours.

[*refrain*]

Desolate wherever I raise my eyes!
Tears well up and descend in showers.

CHAO [*sings*]

I deeply thank you, Squire,
For readily consenting.
Dare I ever forget
This debt of gratitude?
I only fear the way too long
And the body weak—
Illness might harass me,
Exhausting my strength, wearing out my feet.

[*refrain*]

The lonely, deserted tomb,
The bitter hardships of the journey,
Wretched indeed, both there and here!
With ten thousand griefs, where does one start probing?

SQUIRE [*sings*]

Your husband would likeliest be
High in rank and office.
When you come to his house,

[1] The original is obscure and may be corrupt. I have not tried to emend the text, but simply to fill up with a line that would make sense here.

Of his intentions you really must be wary.

The way you have disguised yourself,

Do you expect him to discover you?

The one rich, the other poor,

I fear he might persist in denying all knowledge of you.

[*refrain*]

The lonely, deserted tomb,

The bitter hardships of the journey,

Wretched indeed, both there and here!

With ten thousand griefs, where does one start probing?

CHAO [*declaims*]

In search of my husband I forsake the lonely tomb.

SQUIRE [*declaims*]

Your husband, I fear, his true wife might deny.

BOTH [*declaim*]

Tear-stained cheeks meet the gaze of streaming eyes

While one broken heart sends off another.   [*Both go off*

Scene 34   The Rivals brought Face to Face[1]

MISS NIU[2] [*enters and sings*]

My cares which I may confide in none

Have turned the last few days to torment.

Father has now relented;

Husband's griefs are half consoled;

But about those who will be on their way here

Can I help being anxious?

[*declaims*]

Eight or nine times out of ten, one's hopes are disappointed:

Not even two or three persons there are,

                              whom I could tell in confidence.

---

[1] The usual title, being scene 35 in most editions. The scene is Prime Minister Niu's residence in Loyang, the later Han capital, where Ts'ai plays sadly on his guitar in scene 21, confides in the house-steward in scene 23, receives a letter from Ch'en-liu forged by a spurious messenger in scene 25, and at last reveals his griefs to his new wife, Miss Niu, in scene 29. In scene 32 old Minister Niu relents and agrees to send for Ts'ai's parents and first wife. In the meantime Chao has reached the capital, disguised as a nun. In scene 33 she plays on the lute at a temple and unrolls her picture of Ts'ai's parents, but when an important official is announced, she is chased off by the temple attendant. The 'important official' turns out to be Ts'ai, who picks up the picture she dropped in her haste and decides to keep it.

[2] Miss Niu's role is assigned to a secondary female singer, a *t'ieh-tan*.

Ever since I married Ts'ai Po-chieh, the man has been sad and dejected. I tried all manner of tricks to wrest the truth from him, and when at last I got him to speak, I went and told my father I would go back with Po-chieh, but this, father would not allow. Finally, father yielded so far as to send a servant to fetch his parents and his wife. But how will they fare on the journey? How I have worried on his behalf! What's more, the few younger maidservants are all away; though there are still some others, what use are they? If only I could get a capable maid, then, when my parents-in-law arrive, they would at least have her to wait upon them. I will call the steward and ask him about it.

STEWARD [*enters and declaims*]

A good book, read by one in the mood, is finished too soon;
Often the agreeable guest is prevented from coming at all.
How few in this world really have things their own way—
Not to mention time with its cruel mutations!

What is my mistress' command?

NIU: Look about in the streets for me, and find a capable serving woman.

STEWARD: That is easy. I see a woman coming from yonder; I wonder what she would be.

CHAO [*enters and sings*]

Fed by the winds, finding shelter on the river,
When shall I be secure?
Ask Heaven,
How will Heaven end it all?

NIU [*sings*]

Unadorned and plainly attired—
Her manner and bearing are worth sketching,
Worth painting.
Who has sent her to seek me out?

STEWARD [*to Chao*] Priestess, my mistress asks you to come forward.

CHAO [*saluting*] Countless blessings to the lady!

NIU: Priestess, what are you doing here?

CHAO: The poor nun is begging and entreats the lady to give alms.

STEWARD: My mistress, would not this woman do? If indeed she has to beg, why not retain her?

NIU: Priestess, have you any accomplishments?

CHAO: In great matters, the guitar, chess, calligraphy, painting; in lesser matters, the art of the needle; in lowly matters, food and drink, and choice viands—in all these I am accomplished, all these I know.

STEWARD: Mistress, keep her here then.

NIU: Priestess, begging all over the country is very hard. What do you say to remaining in my hall and having all your needs provided for?

CHAO: The lady is kind to accept me as a servant, yet I fear I may not please the lady.

STEWARD: That is truly said.

NIU: Priestess, was it in your childhood that you renounced the world? Or was it after you had taken a husband?

CHAO: Lady, I will not conceal it. My husband left home long ago for the capital. His parents died at home one after the other, and it fell to me to bury them both. The property was ruined, I had no one to depend upon, and I came in search of my husband. With my lute I begged all the way, yet have not found my husband.

NIU: I had almost blundered!

STEWARD: Yet ask who her husband is.

CHAO [*aside*] What shall I do?

NIU: Priestess, what is your husband's name?

CHAO: So that the lady may know, my husband's name is Ts'ai Po-chieh.[1]

NIU AND STEWARD: Priestess, where did you live?

CHAO: We lived in the county of Ch'en-liu. Perhaps the lady might know him?

NIU: How should I know him? Steward, since she has a husband, it would be difficult to have her. Give her some money and rice, and tell her to go.

STEWARD: Priestess, my mistress is giving you some money and rice, and asks you to go.

CHAO [*aside*] Alack! I should not have said I had a husband. What shall I do now? [*aloud*] I sought my husband all the way here, and everyone told me that he was living in one of the courts in Prime Minister Niu's residence. How should the lady not know him? The lady must be mocking me.

---

[1] In later versions, Chao gives Ts'ai's name in the form of an anagram. Here, it would seem that Niu and the steward are struck by the name but inclined to dismiss it as mere coincidence.

NIU: Why should I mock you? Steward, is there such a person?

STEWARD: There is no such person.

CHAO: Everyone said he lived in a court in Prime Minister Niu's residence. If he is not here, he must be dead. Alas, husband, if you should be dead, on whom could I depend? [*weeps*]

NIU: How pitiable this woman is! Have done, have done! Priestess, supposing you stayed in my house and in the meantime I had people to search for your husband?

STEWARD: My mistress says well.

CHAO: I thank the lady.

NIU: But in my house, priestess, you shall not dress like this. I will have your clothes changed. Steward, bring some clothes and ornaments.

STEWARD: I obey. [*exit and re-enters*] The clothes and ornaments are here. Thus it is:

> Give a good sword to the warrior
> But powder and rouge to the fair.   [*Exit*

CHAO: I have six years of mourning to observe for the parents-in-law,[1] and a further six on my husband's behalf. How could I remove these mourning clothes?

NIU: No matter. The old master my father cannot bear this style of dress.

CHAO: Alas, how could this be?

[*Chao holds up a mirror and is filled with self-pity. She looks at the gorgeous clothes and ornaments but refuses to put them on. Niu is moved by her story and tells how her own husband too left wife and parents behind, being detained in the capital against his will, and how at last he has sent for them*][2]

CHAO [*sings*]

> Hearing her part of the story
> Leaves me sadder still.

[*aside*]

She seems not given to jealousy.

[*aloud*]

> Lady, since he has a wife at home—
> Should she be sent for, you two might not agree.

NIU [*sings*]

> If she be as long-suffering as you,

---

[1] Three years for each parent.
[2] [*Chao . . . sent for them.*] Four songs interspersed with dialogue on pp. 192–3 are here summarized.

I would gladly attend on her and be her subordinate.
But the hardships of the journey
Make one await their coming with trepidation.

CHAO [*sings*]

Error upon error,
Dissembling upon dissembling,
As in the land of moonshine we speak in riddles.
Lady, if you would know the wife of Ts'ai Po-chieh,

NIU: Where might she be?

CHAO [*sings*] I am even she.

NIU [*sings*]

If you be truly she without deception,
For my sake you suffered fortune's buffetings
For my sake you underwent terrible vicissitudes;
You must hate me, even as I hate my father!

Alike in being his wife,
I safe from harm and you disaster's victim!
You are the filial young woman; I am loathed and scorned.
Since his father died because of me
And his mother died because of me,
I would gladly exchange my ornaments
                                for your mourning garments.

[*refrain*]

Lovers *will* be tormented!
My undoer came this way—
There was no escaping the embroilment.

CHAO [*sings*]

At the beginning, he had no alternative:
Chosen and compelled to take part in the examinations,
He excused himself, but the father would not hear his plea;

NIU [*sings*]

Nor was he later permitted to resign from office
Nor to back out of marriage with—me.

BOTH [*sing*]

His pleas thrice rejected led to a calamity
                                of cosmic proportions!

[*refrain*]

Lovers *will* be tormented!
My undoer came this way—
There was no escaping the embroilment.

N I U : Elder sister, do not blame me for saying this. I asked you
to change your clothes, and you wouldn't. Yet, being ragged,
you are afraid that Po-chieh would be ashamed to acknowledge
you. Elder sister, Po-chieh is addicted to literary compositions. Why don't you go into the study and write a few lines to
arouse his curiosity? And when he has read them, I will so contrive matters as to bring about your reunion with him.

C H A O : I had better agree, and even if I write wretchedly, it
cannot be helped. I thank you, lady, and throw myself upon
your mercy.

N I U : Elder sister, do not talk in this way. [*declaims*]

    Slimy depths of misery clogging the heart

    Are swept clean away by a gust of plain speaking.

C H A O [*declaims*]

    Like a single duckweed floating out to sea

    I was adrift, and yet we chanced to meet!   [*Exeunt*

Scene 36   The Reunion in the Library[1]

T s ' A I [2] [*enters and sings*]

    Having, at the P'i-hsiang Hall,[3] attended the Emperor's banquet

    And sauntered thereafter in the Shang-lin Park,

    A groom helping me intoxicated to mount my horse,

    I amble back to these cloisters alight with torches

    And the moon perched on the plum tree in the forecourt.

[*declaims*]

    Towards sunset I leave the Palace gates;

    By dawn I attend at the presence-chamber.

    How much better to sit at one's own desk

    Taking one's ease like the ordinary man!

I attend the morning audiences in the Ch'ang-lo Palace, or am
on night duty there. I am consulted with marked condescension
by the Emperor on learned matters, but also spend solitary
hours in the Imperial library. Under the stars, braving the

---

[1] The usual title, being scene 37 in most editions.
[2] The hero, Ts'ai Po-chieh, is played by the leading male singer, the
sheng.
[3] P'i-hsiang Hall was part of a Han palace; Shang-lin was the hunting
park celebrated by the Han *fu*-writer Ssu-ma Hsiang-ju; Ch'ang-lo was a
Han palace: all three are named by the eunuch who in scene 15 (in most
editions, scene 16) watches dawn break over the capital.

dark, I have rushed in and out of the palace grounds, but I have not written in my *Classics* marginal notes in red ink prepared with the morning's dew.¹ Fortunately the last few days' affairs of State have not proved harassing, and most officials are at leisure. This should enable me, then, to pursue my literary studies or to perfect my calligraphy. It was truly said,

> To accomplish great deeds one must read many books;
> So treasure your time each moment of your life.

[*opens a book*] What volume is this? It is the Canon of Yao, the first chapter of the *Book of History*. [*reads aloud, then puts the book aside*] It says in this Canon of Yao: 'Shun's father was obstinately unprincipled; his step-mother was insincere; his half brother Hsiang was arrogant. He was able, however, by his filial piety to live in harmony with them . . .'² There! His parents treated him ill, yet through filial devotion he was able to live in harmony with them. In what way have my parents wronged me that I should keep out of their sight? I had better not read the *Book of History*. Let me look at the *Spring and Autumn Annals*. [*reads*] '. . . I have a mother who always shares in what I eat. But she has not eaten of this meat which you, my ruler, have given, and I beg to be allowed to leave this piece for her.'³ There! This worthy tasted a bit of broth and remembered his mother. I am now a high official, enjoying riches and honour. Why have I abandoned *my* parents? Ah, to read these books and not be able to practise what one reads — what good is it? Just see, on which page does one not find some mention of filial piety? In the beginning my parents had made me study, the better to know the meaning of filial piety. Who would have thought that a scholar's career would lead me astray? Alas, how could I call myself a filial son? [*sings*]

> I lament my parents' fond hope in their son
> In exhorting him to read the sages' discourse.
> That I who am learned should cast my parents aside
> While some illiterate serves his all through their days!
> A golden mansion vainly I sought in books,⁴

---

¹ An allusion to Kao P'ien's poem 'Pu hsü tz 'u', the last line of which reads: 'Writing notes in his Book of Changes in red ink prepared with dew.' The poem is in *Ch'üan T'ang shih*, Chung-hua edition of 1960, c. 598, p. 6920.
² See Legge, *The Chinese Classics*, vol. III, part I, p. 26.
³ See Legge, *The Chinese Classics*, vol. V, part I, p. 6.
⁴ In 'Exhortation to Study', attributed to the Sung emperor Chen-tsung,

Forsaking the hall of the day-lily and *cedrela*.
Reflecting on it now—
Learning has deluded me,
And my parents I too have deluded.

Instead of this ungrateful wretch of lofty rank
I'd sooner be a peasant whose truth has been tried.
'The Forlorn Wife's Complaint'[1] I know by heart
Yet leave behind the raven-haired poor woman!
A jade-like beauty vainly I sought in books.[2]
Forsaking my lowly devoted wife and home.
Reflecting on it now—
Learning has deluded me
And my wife I too have deluded.

Since I cannot face these books, I will look at the landscape and other old pictures on the wall. That portrait-scroll was the one the servant picked up yesterday when I went to the temple to offer up incense; what is it doing on this wall? I wonder if it contains a story. [*sings*]

Intently I look:

Whose brushwork can this be?

Gazing on it, I feel a strange sorrow.
[*examines the picture closely*]

They are like my parents.

But, no, is not my wife a good needlewoman? Even if they were my parents,

Why would they be in rags?

In their letter not long ago,[3] they had said

'Our countenance is but little altered'.

Why then such a mournful expression?

---

are found the lines:

Remember, when you dream of palatial splendour,
A golden mansion in books awaits possession;
Remember, when you despair of finding a wife,
A jade-like beauty attends you in the realm of books;

which, taken literally, encouraged the worst type of examination mentality. See Ch'ien's note 10 to scene 18, on p. 112.
[1] 'The Forlorn Wife's Complaint' (*Pai-tou yin*) by Cho wen-chün was addressed to her husband Ssu-ma Hsiang-ju when he was on the point of taking another wife; the poem is in *Ku shih yüan*, c. 2.
[2] See note on 'golden mansion' above.
[3] The letter, allegedly from Ts'ai's parents, was forged by a trickster, to whom Ts'ai thereupon entrusted gold and valuables for his family; see scene 25 (in most editions, scene 26).

Considering what difficulty even I had had in sending a letter
home,

    Who would come to the capital just to bring a portrait?
There's no lack of likenesses in the world;

    Was not Confucius mistaken for the villainous Yang Hu?[1]
I see it now—

    It is some scurrilous street artisan

    Mocking the sallow faces of starving peasants.
Alas, my father and mother,

    Had they no prop in a good daughter-in-law

    Could be reduced to the same desolation.
[*as if struck by a new thought*]

    Might this not be an icon of two gods?
If not, then, as I was looking,

    Why did my heart bounce like a frisking roe?
And yet they do not appear to be gods or Bodhisatvas though
the fault may lie with the painter;

    For the artist will impose his own image on the picture,

    And the beauty, Wang Ch'iang, was ruined by her painter Mao
Wait! If they are gods or Bodhisatvas, there should be an inscription at the back. [*suddenly sees the verses*][3] Ah, these verses
weren't there before. The ink is not even dry. Someone must
have inscribed them just now. [*guessing*] Who could have entered my study? and with what intention? [*calls aloud*]
Niu [*enters and sings*]

    For fear that his thoughts might not tend that way

    I have caused her to inscribe the verses as a dark indication.

    The calligraphic strokes piercing his heart

    And the colours of the portrait captivating his eyes

    Speak better far than so many words.
Ts'ai [*angrily*] How extraordinary!
Niu: What is extraordinary?

[1] Confucius was mistaken for Yang Hu at K'uang, where the sage was
detained for five days; see *Shih chi*, c. 47, p. 1919.
[2] The beauty Wang Ch'iang in the harem of the Han emperor Yüan-ti
refused to bribe her portrait painter, who therefore sent up such a wretched
likeness of her that the Emperor decided to marry her off to the Hsiung-nu
chieftain; see *Hsi-ching tsa-chi*, c. 2 (*Han Wei ts'ung-shu*, Hsin-hsing
reprint of 1966, p. 669). The story is dramatized by Ma Chih-yüan (died
c. 1322) in the *tsa-chü* play *Han-kung ch'iu* ('Autumn in the Han palace'),
in which the painter Mao Yen-shou becomes an arch-villain: it is the first
play in *Yüan-ch'ü hsüan*.
[3] Inscribed by Chao in scene 35 (in most editions, scene 36).

Ts'AI: Who has been in my study?

NIU: No one.

Ts'AI: At the temple yesterday where I went to offer up incense, I picked up a picture, which is now hanging there. Who was it that came and wrote some verses at the back?

NIU: Would it not be done by the person who painted the picture?

Ts'AI: How could that be? The ink is not dry yet; the verses have been inscribed just now.

NIU: Oh, I see! Husband, read the verses aloud for me.

Ts'AI [*reading aloud*]

On Mount Kun-lun was a sparkling jade,
Lustrous as lustrous can be;
Alas, that one small blemish
Should mar a priceless gem!
Men are not born like Yen Hui[1] or Confucius—
They fall short in conduct and reputation.
What a fool was the Prefect of Hsi-ho,
How unlike the remorseful Kao Yü!
But Sung Hung, who remained faithful to his spouse,
Shames forever the climbing Huang Yün.
'Too late' cries the falling leaf
               when the restless wind grows still;[2]
Entwining trees submit to no fresh grafting.[3]
Thus to the highflying gentleman I send a message:
Pray remember kindly your own kin.

NIU: Explain them to me so that I may understand their meaning.

Ts'AI: Quite a few old stories are alluded to.

NIU: How did the stories go?

Ts'AI: The Prefect of Hsi-ho was Wu Ch'i of the time of the Warring Kingdoms. Duke Wen of Wei made him Prefect of Hsi-ho, and when his mother died, he would not return home for the funeral.[4] Kao Yü was of the *Spring and Autumn Annals* era; he went on his wanderings all over the land and when he came back, he found both his parents dead, upon which, over-

[1] The most gifted disciple of Confucius and the Master's favourite.
[2] See note on Kao Yü below.
[3] Loving couples do not seek other attachments.
[4] In the account in *Shih chi*, c. 65, Wu Ch'i vowed that he would not return home until he had attained high office and stayed away even from his mother's funeral, to the horror of his teacher, the great Tseng-tzu (p. 2165).

come with remorse, he slit his own throat and died.[1]

NIU: What other stories are alluded to?

TS'AI: Sung Hung[2] served under Emperor Kuang-wu, who offered to marry his own sister, the Princess Hu-yang, to Sung Hung, but Sung Hung declined the honour, saying:

Remember the friends of your humble days;
Cherish always your lowly wife.

Huang Yün[3] lived in the time of Emperor Huan. The minister Yüan Wei looking about for a husband for his niece, found Huang very eligible. Thereupon Huang put away his own wife and married Miss Yüan.

NIU: Husband, as between him who stayed away from his mother's funeral and him who slit his own throat upon return, which was the filial one?

TS'AI: The one who stayed away from his mother's funeral was *unnatural*.

NIU: As between him who remained true to his wife and him who repudiated his wife to seek a better match, which was the upright one?

TS'AI: The one who repudiated his wife to seek a better match was *unnatural*.

NIU: Whose example would you follow?

TS'AI: I cannot know for certain whether my parents are still living, but I will not follow in the steps of the man who put away his wife to seek a better match.

NIU: Though you may not wish to follow in his steps, yet rich and exalted as you are, would not a wife of humble condition, ugly and in tatters, disgrace you? Had you not better repudiate her?

TS'AI: However ugly and tattered she might be, she would remain my wife. I would not forswear her.

[greatly offended, sings]

---

[1] Kao Yü, who mourned his neglected parents inconsolably; his dying confession to Confucius included the sentences: 'When the tree would be still, yet the restless wind blows on. And when the wandering son returned to his parents, alas, they were no longer there to wait for him.' The disciples were so moved that many of them at once took leave of the Master to return to their parents. See *Han shih wai-chuan*, c. 9 (*Han Wei ts'ung shu*, reprint of 1966, p. 136). Hence the line ' "Too late" cries the falling leaf' etc. in the verses inscribed by Chao, 'falling leaf' being the translator's substitute for 'tree'.

[2] Sung Hung, of the Later Han; see *Hou-Han shu*, c. 26, pp. 904–5.

[3] Huang Yün, of the Later Han; see *Hou-Han shu*, c. 68, p. 2230.

Your speech is all too laughable
And betrays an ungenerous mind!
Never would I follow in the steps of that Huang Yün,
Causelessly throwing away the plum in his hand
To seek the fleshier peach.
The ancients say: For seven offences may a woman be sent home.[1]
But she is not jealous nor lewd nor thievish;
Under what clause would she stand condemned?
Besides, those who abandon their wives
Are loathed by all
While those who cherish their wives
Are universally praised.
Even though she might be uncouth,
How could I even think of putting her away?

N I U [*sings*]

This might be so, and yet—
You are noble and rich
And, moreover, still in your youth.
See how well the purple robe sits on you,
And the golden belt hanging loose at your waist.
Your wife, then,
Should be a titled lady
By letters patent with the Emperor's seal.
She must be elegant;
She must be winsome,
If then her appearance be uncouth,
Husband, why scruple to put her away?

T s' A I [*sings*]

Your words so strangely inconsistent
Only add to my vexation.
Ah, ha! Can it be you are mocking me
And deliberately acting a part?
You have caused my tears to roll as if chasing one another,
Their furrows crossing and re-crossing.
Mistress, who was it that inscribed the verses?

N I U : Why do you want to know?

---

[1] According to *Ta-Tai li-chi* the seven offences are: disobedience to the parents-in-law, barrenness, lewdness, jealousy, foul disease, talkativeness, thievery (see 'The Shrew' *supra*). The same authority however, states expressly that no man who has since risen in the world may put away the wife who shared his humble life.

Ts'AI: [*sings*]
  The writer made fun of me:
  It was utterly unpardonable!
  Let me know now—
  Indeed I am determined to pursue this matter.
NIU [*sings*]
  I knew in my heart
  The story ought not to have a callous ending.
  It is certain, then, I have contrived their reunion
  For this very day.
Husband, can you tell who it was that wrote the verses?
Ts'AI: I cannot tell.
NIU [*sings*]
  Then you have worried in vain;
  Your eyes have not perceived—
The writer of the verses was
  None other than your wife,
  The Chao daughter.
  I was waiting to tell you all about it—
  I am no less determined to pursue this matter.
CHAO [*enters and sings*]
  I hear squabbling voices;
  Can that be my husband shouting upon seeing the verses?
NIU: Elder Sister, come out.
CHAO [*sings*]
  Who is that calling for 'elder sister'?
  I suppose it is the lady of the house summoning me.
  A resolution must be in sight!
NIU [*sings*] It was she who inscribed the verses: do you know her
Ts'AI: Mistress, where is she from?
NIU [*sings*] She came all the way from Ch'en-liu looking for you
Ts'AI [*recognizing Chao, sings*]
  It is you! Why, then, this torn jacket?
  And why are all your garments an ominous white?
  Ah, can it be that my
  Parents are dead?
CHAO [*sings*]
  Since you left,
  Flood was followed by drought.
Ts'AI: Oh, so there was flood as well as drought.

CHAO [*sings*] The three of us thought we would starve
                                        to death together.
Ts'AI: Did not Squire Chang help you?
CHAO [*sings*]
  Only Squire Chang took pity on us.
  Alas, the poor parents had no other succour.
Ts'AI: What then?
CHAO [*sings*]
  They died one after the other:
  I cut and sold my hair to provide the last rites
                                        for your late father and mother.
Ts'AI: They have been buried then?
CHAO [*sings*]
  I built the tomb myself,
  Holding up my sackcloth skirt to carry the earth.
Ts'AI:
  This woeful account has brought such anguish,
  I swoon with agony!
[*He swoons. Chao revives him. He gets up and does obeisance before the portrait, weeping; then sings*]
  I, Ts'ai Po-chieh, have been unfilial
  And cast aside my own parents!
  Father, Mother, when I left you, you were not like this!
  Had I visualized your shrivelled, ailing frames,
  I could not have remained at the Emperor's court.
  Wife, what distress and hardships you suffered on my behalf!
  I thank you now for attending to my father
  And to my mother too, at their last extremity.
  Could I ever requite you for your sacrifice?
  People say 'For support in one's old age, bring up a son':
[*chorus*]
  But all the travail and grief!
  And the remorse that knows no atonement!
  When heaven rains affliction, can man escape?
CHAO [*sings*]
  This true likeness of your parents
  I myself painted.
  All the way here I begged, fingering my lute,
  Undaunted by the distance.
  Husband, need one dwell on distress and hardships?

If still in doubt, look at your father there
And at your mother too, in that portrait:
Dried and wizened even more than when you left them.
It was indeed hard for me alone to bear

[*chorus*]

All the travail and grief!
And the remorse that knows no atonement!
When heaven rains affliction, can man escape?

Niu [*sings*]

But I will dwell on the trick
Played by my father to detain him here.
Forced into the role of ministerial son-in-law,
How could he carry out his filial duties?
Sister, through me you endured misfortunes
                              and a fearful journey!
Husband, it was I who cheated your father
And your mother too, out of all their hopes;
And I have given you an odious name – unfilial.
Alas, I am not 'the wise spouse that saves her man from folly'.

[*chorus*]

Oh, all the travail and grief!
And the remorse that knows no atonement!
When heaven rains affliction, can man escape?

Ts'ai [*sings*]

I will remove my official's cap
And hang up my ceremonial robes;

Chao [*sings*]

And supplicate for your resignation
At the Emperor's very next audience!

Niu [*sings*]

Husband, how dare I shirk the distress and hardships?
I will go with you to pay my respects to your father
And to your mother too, at their burial place,
And myself sweep their tomb,
That honour and distinction may yet accrue to the dead.

[*chorus*]

Oh, all the travail and grief!
And the remorse that knows no atonement!
When heaven rains affliction, can man escape?

ALL [*sing*]

　　Severed for years, cut off from all news of each other,

　　Divided by a thousand mountains and rivers—

　　His efforts to rejoin them thrice thwarted,

　　　　　　　　　　　　　　disaster's seed was sown.

TS'AI: Tomorrow I return with her to watch by the parents'
tomb,[1] to show in some measure my filial devotion. Will you
come too?

CHAO: I fear her father would not consent.

NIU: When he learns about *your* filial devotion, even he will
consent.

TS'AI [*declaims*]

　　The Emperor and both fathers thrice refused my pleas,

　　Thus cleaving forever clinging flesh and bone.

ALL:

　　Tonight let's have all lamp-flames burning high

　　To re-assure ourselves the reunion was no dream.[2]

---

[1] Which they do in scenes 38 and 40, whereupon at the Emperor's command Minister Niu himself follows in scenes 41 and 42 to confer honours
on all three, and on the dead parents as well.

[2] The two concluding lines are taken from the *tz'u* poem to the pattern of
'Che-ku-t'ien' by Yen Chi-tao (born c. 1031), in *Ch'üan Sung tz'u*,
Chung-hua 1965, vol. I, p. 225.

Anonymous

The Twin Mirrors

The story is taken from Feng Meng-lung's printed collection *Ching shih t'ung-yen*[1] (1624), *chüan* 12, where it bears the title *Fan Ch'iu-erh shuang-ching ch'ung yüan* ('Fan the Loach and the Re-joining of the Twin Mirrors'). It is also found in the manuscript collection *Ching-pen t'ung-su hsiao-shuo*, *chüan* 16, with a different title, *Feng Yü-mei t'uan-yüan* ('Feng Jade Plum Reunited with Her Husband') and some other slight divergences — notably in the names of the heroine and her father in the main story, and in a deliberate piece of archaism in a pointed reference to 'our Sung' instead of 'the Southern Sung'. Since, however, *Ching-pen t'ung-su hsiao-shuo* seems unlikely to predate Feng's printed collections, the *Ching shih t'ung-yen* version is here adopted.[2]

The sources of the story are known.[3] The preliminary story about the missing wives is derived from the supplementary volume to *I-chien-chih* by Hung Mai (1123–1202), recommended as a stand-by for story-tellers' plots in Lo Yeh's *Commonplace Book*.[4] The rather short account in classical prose entitled 'Hsü Hsin's Wife' in *I-chien-chih pu* (Han-fen-lou edition 1927, c. 11, pp. 5ᵇ–6ᵃ) begins with the visit to the teahouse in Chien-k'ang (i.e. Nanking) and ends with the reunion of the two couples. Earlier events are only briefly recalled, and

[1] Jen-min edition 1958, pp. 158–68. The punctuation in the Ku-tien edition of *Ching-pen t'ung-su hsiao-shuo*, 1954, pp. 93–104, is, however, much to be preferred. For Feng Meng-lung and *Ching shih t'ung-yen*, see General Introduction.
[2] The case against *Ching-pen t'ung-su hsiao-shou* as an early manuscript independent of the printed collections is stated fully in Y. W. Ma and T. L. Ma, 'On the Periods of the Stories of *Ching-pen t'ung-su hsiao-shuo* and the Authenticity of the Collection', *Tsing Hua Journal of Chinese Studies*, New Series, vol. v (1965), no. 1, pp. 14–32. I am indebted to my friend Professor C. T. Hsia for drawing my attention to this article.
[3] See the article mentioned in the previous note, pp. 18–19; and Fu Hsi-hua, *Sung Yüan hua-pen chi*, 1955, Introduction, pp. 3–4.
[4] *Tsui-weng t'an-lu*, Ku-tien edition 1957, p. 3; see General Introduction.

of the four persons in the story, the army officer Hsü Hsin alone is named. Their home towns in the north, Ch'en-chou and Cheng-chou, are as in our story, though there is no mention of their route to the south. But the derivation is unmistakable, both in the similarity of numerous details—the staring stranger at the adjoining table, the surreptitious pursuit to the house, the uneasy walk to the deserted lane, fear of the gossiping neighbours—and in a number of verbal parallels, especially in the conversation of the two men.

The main story is likewise based on a twelfth-century account, apparently also of an actual occurrence,[1] written by Wang Ming-ch'ing (b. 1127) in his *Chih ch'ing tsa-shuo* (Ts'ung-shu chi-ch'eng ed., pp. 2–4). The account is in classical prose and without a title, but it gives a full relation of the events, which our story follows closely: the rebel leader whose whistle mustered a crowd of over a hundred thousand; the newly appointed Controller of Taxes journeying from the north-west to Fukien; the young clansman and the fair captive; the beleaguered city; the mysterious army captain; the final reunion. Parts of our story read like paraphrases of the earlier account with a thick residue of the original words and phrases. But there is also much embroidering. The hero Fan Hsi-chou's nickname 'the Loach' would be a popular touch, as also the heroine's name Shun-ko ('the fortunate child'), here rendered as Lucky Maid. Lucky Maid is aged sixteen at the beginning of the story; in the original account, the heroine—described simply as Miss Lü—is already seventeen or eighteen. And the age of young Fan is reduced from twenty-five or twenty-six in the original to twenty-three. The detail of the twin mirrors, a distinguishing feature of our story, is a further addition.

The proverbial expression 'a broken mirror re-joined', i.e. a broken marriage mended, dates back to the story of the courtier Hsü Te-yen, who anticipating the collapse of the Ch'en (A.D. 557–89), one of the precarious Southern dynasties, broke a

---

[1] Wang had heard the story from a certain army officer of Canton. A later version of this story, based substantially on Wang's and in classical prose, was translated into English by Sir George Staunton (1781–1859) and published in 1814 under the title of *Fan-hy-cheu: A Tale in Chinese and English*, accompanied by some grammatical notes by Stephen Weston, B.D.,F.R.S.S.A., and also Weston's word for word translation of the Chinese text, a page of which was reproduced.

mirror into two halves and handed one of them over to his wife, the Princess Lo-ch'ang, as a token for mutual recognition should they be separated. The dynasty came to an end, and the Princess was sent up to the Sui capital, Ch'ang-an, where she was assigned to the household of the Minister Yang Su. On a pre-arranged day—the first full moon of the year—she ordered the steward to go to the market with *her* half of the mirror and offer it for sale at a fantastic price. Hsü, who in the meantime had made his way to the capital, approached and produced *his* half of the mirror, and the couple were eventually reunited. The story, which is recorded in the T'ang writer Meng Ch'i's *Pen-shih shih* (886) (pp. 1ᵃ–1ᵇ, in *Ku-shih wen-fang hsiao-shuo*, Ssu-pu ts'ung-k'an ed.), would be part of popular tradition. At the same time, it may be allowed that the writer of our story was capable of *some* invention. Certainly the welding, in accordance with the demands of story-telling,[1] of two such disparate components as our preliminary and the main story calls for more than a modicum of skill, and 'The Twin Mirrors' would seem a clear example of the work of a single story-writer, who went direct to two or more literary sources and fashioned out of the diverse elements something pleasing and homogeneous.

Underlying the main theme of 'The Twin Mirrors', enforced separation and unexpected reunion in times of war, famine, banditry, uprisings, migration and upheaval, a recurrent one in Chinese literature and life, is another theme, the past glory of the Northern Sung and the revival and emulation of that glory by the Southern Sung, which constitutes the special province of Chinese colloquial fiction.[2] In our story, the glory is ephemeral enough; the suffering only too real. But the account of the flight before the invading Tartars in the preliminary story rings true, and the story as a whole is surely memorable for demonstrating that the route from the one earthly paradise to the other lay along a succession of unknown muddy roads, of tiny inn rooms packed with squatting fugitives, of cruel and rapacious soldiers, brigands, rebels, of biting hunger and the sharpened taste for the plainest and coarsest food, of acts of self-preservation and selfless sacrifice. For the characters in the preliminary story, the course led from the certain loss of their homes in the north to the conquering Tartars, to the

[1] See General Introduction.   [2] See General Introduction.

uncertain search for a haven in the south in the wake of their fleeing Emperor. For the official and his family in the main story, the promised sanctuary in remote Fukien turned out, after weary months of travelling, to be a nest of rebels. But it is coincidence in both the stories that the story-writer himself tends to stress. For where uncertainty is so great, coincidence becomes part of the scheme of things. And indeed coincidence is not a clumsy contrivance in Chinese literature; it is of the stuff of Chinese life.

A chronology of the historical events referred to in the story may be helpful: The Northern Sung Emperor Hui-tsung reigned 1101–25. His capital was Pien (i.e. Kaifeng in Honan Province), known also as the Eastern Capital. An accomplished painter himself and a great connoisseur, Hui-tsung indulged his passion for collecting as no other Emperor before or since. The tax-gathering machinery devised in an earlier reign by Wang An-shih (1021–86) was used by Hui-tsung's minister Ts'ai Ching to satisfy the Emperor's extravagant tastes. Of the Emperor's many excesses, the most widely resented was the 'rock convoys' (*hua-shih-kang*) which lasted the greater part of his reign. These began with the quarrying of rocks in Chekiang which were then arduously transported by boat along rivers and canals to the new Imperial park, Ken-yüeh. But the boats soon became a fleet, and an army of agents scoured the southern regions, robbing private houses and gardens of curious stones, plants and trees, and conscripting labour for their removal to the capital.

The exchequer was also drained annually by the enormous sums exacted as tribute or indemnity by the militant barbarian tribesmen in the north—the Liao (or Ch'i-tan) who had demanded such payments from the early eleventh century; the Hsi Hsia, from the middle of the eleventh century; and the newly risen Chin Tartars—against all of whom the Chinese were helpless. Disaster fell in the last period of Hui-tsung's reign (the reign title was Hsüan-ho, lasting from 1119 to 1125), when the Chin Tartars, having conquered the Liao, turned upon the Chinese, with whom they had been in alliance. Hui-tsung abdicated in disgrace. Early in 1126, the crown prince became the Emperor Ch'in-tsung and for a brief twelve months he fought and parleyed with the Tartars. The capital fell at the end of the year, and in the following year, 1127, the

Tartars took both Emperors captive and moved them to the northern desert plains, where Hui-tsung died in 1135 and Ch'in-tsung in 1161. Ch'in-tsung's reign title, Ching-k'ang, was later associated with one word — 'shame'.

Also in 1127, Prince K'ang, next in line of succession, rallied the remaining Chinese army and was enthroned at Ying-t'ien (today, Kuei-te in Honan Province), thus becoming the Emperor Kao-tsung. Retreating by stages before the Tartar advance, he left for Yangchow and, in 1129, crossed the Yangtze. According to legend, after a narrow escape from the pursuing Tartars, Kao-tsung was borne across the river by a clay horse — a delightful, if unintended, compliment to Sung statuary art. From Chinkiang he moved to Hangchow and then, still pressed by the invaders, as far south as Wenchow. Finally, in 1138, he fixed upon Hangchow, which he called Lin-an, as his capital.

Kao-tsung was on the throne 1127–65, and was the first Emperor of the Southern Sung. His first reign title was Chien-yen, 1127–30; he then adopted the reign title Shao-hsing (Revival), 1131–65. In the earlier years of his reign his generals, most notably Han Shih-chung (1089–1151) and Yo Fei (1103–41), fought with great courage and daring against the Tartars, pushing them back well north of the Yangtze to the river Huai. But the northern half of the Empire was not to be recovered. And the southern half was infested with bandits and with rebels, two of the most formidable being Fan Ju-wei, who from the commanding position of Chien-chou (today, Chien-ou in Fukien Province) made inroads on towns near and far in the years 1130–2, and Yang Yao, who, with his island stronghold in the vast Tungting Lake and a flotilla of paddle-wheel boats, was a still greater threat in the years 1132–5. In 1132, moving with surprising swiftness with an army of thirty thousand, Han Shih-chung (in our story, the Grand Duke Han) occupied Phoenix Hill overlooking Chien-chou and, with the aid of towers and scaling-ladders, took the city by storm after a siege lasting five days. The rebel chief Fan burned himself to death and over five hundred leaders were captured, though many of them were later pardoned. And in 1135, Yo Fei (in our story, Junior Guardian of the Heir Apparent, General Yo) crushed the Tungting Lake rebels.

Our story-writer is at some pains to verify his history, and the sequence of events in our story, being based on contemporary sources, corresponds in the main to that in historical accounts.[1] He inserts—correctly—the year and month of the subjugation of Chien-chou: 'first month, in the spring of the second year of Shao-hsing' (i.e. 1132) following upon the exchange of vows by hero and heroine in the twelfth month, in the winter of the first year of that reign (corresponding to 1131). The original account places these events in 'that winter' (i.e. of 1131). It may also be noted that the description of the Yo army as consisting of men from the north-west unaccustomed to fighting on water is paralleled in the 'Life of Yo Fei' in the official Sung history, compiled rather late in the Yüan dynasty, in 1343–5, from older records:[2] 'The men under Yo Fei's command were all from the north-west, not accustomed to fighting on water.' (*Sung shih*, c. 365). The story-writer no doubt had access to this or some similar historical source. It seems at least likely that he drew upon other early accounts for further details in his narrative.

The story itself is, however, dated by the introductory poem with the concluding line,

The crescent moon shines alike upon each province.

The poem is quoted[3] in T'ien Ju-ch'eng's *Supplement to A Guide to the West Lake*, 1547, and is there stated to have been composed by Ch'ü Yu (1341–1427) under the inspiration of a folk-song in the Soochow manner sung by an ex-courtesan in Kashing. The folk-song, which T'ien also quotes, differs somewhat from the one in our story. It runs:

[1] Most of the events outlined above are well known. The rock convoys are described in the 'Life of Chu Mien' (*Sung shih*, c. 470); they were terminated only a few days before Hui-tsung's abdication (*Sung shih*, c. 22). Kao-tsung's movements are clearly summarized in A. C. Moule, *The Rulers of China*, 1957, p. 88. The campaigns of Han Shih-chung and Yo Fei against the rebels are recorded in their 'Lives' in *Sung shih*, cc. 364, 365.

[2] For the dates of the compilation of *Sung shih*, see *Yüan shih*, c. 41.

[3] T'ien Ju-ch'eng, *Hsi-hu yu-lan chih yü*, c. 25, Chung-hua edition 1958, p. 447. T'ien's quotation was noted by J. Průšek in 'Popular Novels in the Collection of Ch'ien Tseng', *Archiv Orientální*, vol. x (1938) pp. 292–3. It should also be noted, however, that the first two lines already occur in 'Chu-chih ko' by Yang Wan-li (1127–1206), who was inspired by the song of a boatman on a river journey to Tan-yang, the first line being part of the boatman's song actually heard by Yang; see Chou Ju-ch'ang (ed.), *Yang Wan-li hsüan-chi*, 1962, pp. 180–1. For Ch'ü Yu, see the Introduction and Prefaces to his collection of tales, *Chien teng hsin-hua*, Ku-tien edition 1957. Kashing, standing on the Grand Canal, is mid-way between Soochow and Hangchow.

The crescent moon shines alike upon each province:
How many in the world rejoice, how many are sorrowing?
How many carouse merrily on a high balcony?
How many are wandering far from their homes?

Ch'ü was born under the Yüan, but most of his rather gay, but unsuccessful, life was spent under the Ming. At the age of fourteen, he was already known as a song-writer. His poem could thus have been written at almost any time in the latter half of the fourteenth century, and would be current then and early in the fifteenth century.

It is to the early Ming also, to the second half of the fourteenth century representing still a relatively early phase of story-telling, that I would assign our story. Above all, 'The Twin Mirrors' *reads* like an early story. The simple, engaging manner, suggestive of a story-writer not yet overburdened with clichés or hardened by stock responses, nor feeling the need to startle or coax his audience, in short, not cynical, is the certain sign of its early date and its best recommendation.

The Twin Mirrors

The curtain is rolled up at the riverside balcony;[1]
To a new tune we fit doggerel verses
About the dreams of pleasure-seeking youth.
Stay! Do not sing
But quaff a jar of wine ere we die!

Tomorrow I board my boat again:
Tonight I revisit these old haunts.
Like you, I have wandered far from my native place.
Stay! Do not grieve—
The crescent moon shines alike upon each province.

The last line of this *tz'u* poem was taken from a Soochow folk-song.[2] The song went:

The crescent moon shines alike upon each province[3]—
How many families are rejoicing, how many in grief?
How many wedded couples are at home and abed,
How many scattered over strange provinces and divided?

This song originated in the Chien-yen reign[4] of the Southern Sung dynasty and described the sorrows of separation among the people caused by the wars. For in the Hsüan-ho reign[5] misrule led to the seizing of power by a pack of rogues so that subsequently, in the Ching-k'ang reign, the Tartar tribesmen

[1] The riverside balcony (or perhaps, The Riverside Balcony) would be an eating house, where, it being early evening and the sun no longer oppressive, the bamboo curtain was rolled up.

[2] For the date of the poem and also of the folk-song, see Introduction.

[3] In the original, the line reads: 'The crescent moon shines upon how many provinces?', which presents greater structural unity with the other three lines. The slight change here made would seem to bring out better the sentiment of the whole song and also to fit more easily into the preceding poem.

[4] Chien-yen reign, 1127–31, the first reign title after the migration of the Sung court to the south.

[5] Hsüan-ho reign, 1119–25; Ching-k'ang reign, 1126. For these events and Prince K'ang's flight, see Introduction.

entered the capital and brought the two Emperors, Hui-tsung and Ch'in-tsung, as captives with them to the north. Mounted on a clay horse, Prince K'ang crossed the Yangtze; thus abandoning the Sung Eastern Capital, he asserted his sovereignty in a corner of the Empire and changed the reign title to Chien-yen. In mortal fear of the Tartars, the inhabitants of the entire region of the Eastern Capital followed the new Emperor in an exodus to the south. But they were hotly pursued by Tartar horsemen and, what with battles and skirmishes, hurried flights and narrow escapes, how many families were broken up! All too often, parents and children were severed, husband and wife torn apart, never to meet in their lifetime. Nevertheless, some that had been separated were eventually joined together again, and the strange manner in which this was brought about made such re-unions the talk of the people. True it is,

Released from bondage to two separate masters,
> the twin swords sought the same river bed;[1]
On a lotus leaf, the pearly dew-drop tumbles and scatters,
> then rolls into a rounded whole.[2]
In a myriad occurrences, look still for the hand of fate—
Not one iota of our lot but is decreed by heaven.

The story goes that in Ch'en-chou[3] there was a man named Hsü Hsin, who even as a lad excelled in feats of arms. He took to wife a Miss Ts'ui, a pretty young woman. The couple had ample means and led a comfortable life. When, however, the Tartar army invaded the Empire and took the two Emperors captive, Hsü Hsin and his wife decided between themselves that it was no longer safe to remain where they were. They

[1] Chang Hua (232–300), attracted by a purple glint in the night sky between the constellations of Sagittarius and Capricorn, enlists the services of the astrologer Lei Huan to make an excavation at Feng-ch'eng (south of Nanchang in Kiangsi Province). A stone vessel was found, containing two swords, supposedly the male and the female sword forged by the sword-making couple, Kan Chiang and his wife Mo Yeh, of the ancient Kingdom of Wu, and named after themselves. Lei Huan kept one of the swords, giving the other to Chang Hua, for whom he then predicted a bad end. When, later, Chang was killed, his sword unaccountably vanished. Lei himself dying soon afterwards, his son went on a journey wearing the remaining sword, which leapt out of its scabbard at the Yenping Ford and plunged into the river. A diver who tried to recover the sword found only two huge dragons splashing in the waves. See *Chin shu*, c. 36; *Wu Yüeh ch'un-ch'iu*, c. 2.

[2] Like the previous line, an image of reunion.

[3] Ch'en-chou (i.e. Huai-yang in Honan Province) is about eighty miles south of Kaifeng, the Sung capital.

packed their valuables and money in two bundles and each
shouldering one of them, joined the fleeing masses, journeying
night and day. When they reached the City of Yü,[1] behind them
was raised a thundering war-cry. They at once thought that the
Tartars had caught up with them, but it turned out only to be
scattered Chinese troops. For the army having long been neglected and discipline grown slack, these men, every one of them,
when confronted with the enemy, grew faint-hearted and panic-
stricken, and without staying to fight, took to their heels.
But when they met the common people, they were again full of
bravado and prowess, robbing them of their possessions and
carrying off their women. Though Hsü Hsin was skilled in
combat, the soldiers were a thick crowd so that single-handed
he could not repel their vast numbers. Thus abandoning the
fray, he saved himself in flight. As he rushed headlong towards
the open country, he heard bitter weeping and wailing all
round him. He looked behind, only to discover that his wife,
Mistress Ts'ui, had disappeared. In the tumult, there was nowhere to look for her, and he could only press forward. After
walking on for several more days, he heaved a sigh and gave up
hope of ever finding her.

When he reached Sui-yang,[2] feeling great hunger and thirst,
he entered a wayside inn to buy some food and drink. For in
times of such commotion, the inns no longer served wine as in
former, happier days, and even the meals consisted of only the
plainest fare. And for fear of the mob running away with the
food, every item had to be paid for before it was dished out to
allay your hunger. As Hsü Hsin counted out his money, he
suddenly heard a woman sobbing. It is said:

'Let nothing move you!

Lest—no sooner moved than hooked.'

Hsü Hsin left off counting out the money and rushed out of the
inn. There was indeed a woman, dressed in thin undergarments
and dishevelled, seated on the ground, exposed to the elements.
It was not his wife; yet in age and appearance, she was not
dissimilar. Hsü Hsin was moved by pity and, taught by his own
bitter experience, said to himself: 'This woman would certainly

[1] To the north east of Ch'en-chou, in that part of Honan Province which
borders Kiangsu Province.
[2] The route requires Sui-ling (Sui-ning of today), in Kiangsu Province.
Sui-yang (in Honan Province) would have meant turning back towards
Ch'en-chou.

be a fellow victim.' He needs must step forward to ask where
she hailed from. The woman gave an account of her afflictions:
'I am a daughter of the Wang family of Chengchow;[1] my
name is Winning.[2] With my husband, I fled from the wars. But
we lost each other half-way, and I alone was captured by some
stray soldiers and marched with them for two days and a night.
When we got here, my feet were so swollen I could not move
an inch further. The villains then left me after stripping me of
my outer garments. Shivering with cold and starving in a
strange place away from all my kin, I see no other future but
death for me. That is why I was weeping.'

Hsü Hsin said: 'I, too, lost my wife in the rout. Our common
ills bring us the closer. Fortunately I still have some money
with me. You might as well stay at this inn for a few days to
recuperate, while I seek news of my wife and, at the same
time, of your husband. What do you think, Madam?' The
woman dried her tears and thanked him, saying, 'That would
be best.' Hsü Hsin undid his bundle and took out some of his
wife's clothes for the woman to wear. He then brought her into
the inn, where they had some food and drink, after which he
paid his rent for part of a room, into which they both crowded.
Hsü Hsin was exceedingly attentive to the woman, and every
day he brought in the tea and the meals. And the woman in her
gratitude considered that the search for the missing wife and
husband was but a vain undertaking, whereas the throwing
together of a man and a woman each bereft of a spouse was a
heaven-sent boon—like victuals fed to the hungry—and she
was not inclined to repulse him.

A few days later, her feet no longer troubled her and they
travelled together as husband and wife until they reached
Chien-k'ang.[3] At this time, Prince K'ang, later known as the
Emperor Kao-tsung, having crossed the Yangtze and ascended
the throne, altered the reign title to Chien-yen and had placards
posted up everywhere for recruitment to the Imperial Army.
Hsü Hsin went forward and was enlisted as an officer, and thus
made his home in the city of Chien-k'ang.

Days and months streamed by. It was soon the third year of

[1] Chengchow, in Honan Province, forty odd miles to the west of Kaifeng.
[2] The original is: Chin-nu, Girl of Advancement. 'Winning' thus seems
to me a justifiable rendering.
[3] Chien-k'ang, i.e. Nanking.

the Chien-yen reign.[1] One day, Hsü Hsin and his wife were on their way home after visiting a relative outside the city. It was late in the afternoon, and the woman felt thirsty. So Hsü Hsin led her into a tea-house to drink tea. A man sitting at a table within got up when he saw the woman enter, and from where he stood, stared fixedly at her. But the woman, who demurely bowed her head, paid no attention to the man. And Hsü Hsin thought it an odd thing.

In a little while, they had finished their tea. They paid the reckoning and left the tea-house, but the man came after them, though keeping his distance. When they reached home, the man lingered at the gate and would not depart. Hsü Hsin now flared up. He shouted to the man: 'Who are you that dare thus spy upon another's womenfolk?' The man folded his hands in salute and made his apology: 'Pray desist from anger, Sir. I have a question to put to you.' Hsü Hsin's anger was not yet appeased and he cried: 'Out with it, then!' The man said, 'If you can bear with me, Sir, let us walk a few steps further. I have something to tell in confidence. But if you are still angry, I dare not speak.' So Hsü Hsin followed the man into a secluded lane. The man now made ready to begin his story, yet somehow he was held back from speaking. Hsü Hsin declared: 'I, Hsü Hsin, am a man of honour. Speak your mind freely.' Only then did the man ask: 'Who was that woman just then?' Hsü Hsin said, 'She is my wife.' The man again asked: 'How long has she been married to you?' Hsü Hsin replied: 'Three years.' The man continued: 'Would she be from Chengchow? A daughter of the Wang family, her name Winning?' Amazed, Hsü Hsin exclaimed: 'How did you know it, Sir?' The man at last said: 'She was *my* wife. I lost her as we fled from the invaders. But how could I know she would fall into your hands?'

When Hsü Hsin heard this, he was exceedingly embarrassed. He recounted in detail how he himself had lost his wife outside the City of Yü, and how at the inn in Sui-yang he had found the woman, adding: 'It was really because I took pity on her, seeing her all alone and without support. But I could not know that she was *your* wife. And now the harm is done.' The man said, 'You have nothing to fear from me, Sir. I, too, have re-married, and it is useless to dwell upon vows of the past. But

[1] *Ching-pen t'ung-su hsiao-shuo* has 'second year', erroneously, as is clear from a later reference in the text.

we were separated in the stampede without so much as bidding each other farewell. If I may meet her but once and talk of our sorrows, I shall die content.' Hsü Hsin was deeply affected and felt a twinge in his own heart. He said: 'Speaking as man to man, I trust you and willingly grant your request. Tomorrow I shall expect you in my home. Since, however, you have taken another wife, please bring her too. We shall pretend to be relatives so as not to start any gossip among the neighbours.' Overjoyed, the man bowed his thanks. Before they parted, Hsü Hsin asked his name. The man said, 'I am Lieh Chün-ch'ing[1] of Chengchow.'

That night, Hsü Hsin told his wife Winning what had happened. Winning remembered the conjugal affection of her former husband and, lying awake all night, secretly shed many tears. They rose at dawn, and as soon as they had tidied themselves, Lieh Chün-ch'ing and his wife arrived. Hsü Hsin came out of the gate to welcome them; but when he and Lieh's wife saw each other, they were both astounded and wept aloud. For the woman was no other than Hsü Hsin's former wife, Mistress Ts'ui. After searching in vain for him near the City of Yü, where they had been separated, she travelled in the company of an old woman to Chien-k'ang; there, disposing of some of her jewellery, with the proceeds she rented a house. Three months passed and there was still no news of her husband. The old woman concluded that living alone in a strange place in times of war was no proper ending for a young woman; thus, acting as go-between, she arranged for Mistress Ts'ui to marry Lieh Chün-ch'ing. And, indeed, who would have thought that on this day those two couples would suddenly be brought face to face? It was such a coincidence as could only have been contrived by heaven! They each sought out their former wives or husbands, whom, crying, they embraced. Hsü Hsin and Lieh Chün-ch'ing then knelt and kowtowed eight times to each other and called themselves brothers. At night, they each restored to the other his original wife, in fair exchange. And from then on, they were as one family. There is a poem to prove it:

> The man took a new wife, the woman a new husband
> In a curious change of partners in a marriage game.
> Thanks to their stars, all were again joined together,
> Each grinning under the lamplight to discover an old spouse.

[1] *Ching-pen t'ung-su hsiao-shuo* has 'Liu Chün-ch'ing'.

The story just told was entitled 'The Exchanged Wives';
the incident occurred in the third year of the Chien-yen reign in
Chien-k'ang. There was another series of events from that
time known as 'The Twin Mirrors Re-joined'; though, in the
telling, it seems not so very remarkable for coincidence, it
excels this one by far in respect of marital fidelity and wifely
devotion, and of moral conduct. For indeed:

To spread far and wide, a story must appeal to the populace;
To move men's hearts, let words illustrate moral teaching.
The story goes that in the fourth year of the Chien-yen reign
of the Southern Sung an official from west of Han-ku Pass
named Lü Chung-i[1] was appointed Controller of Taxes in
Foochow. At the time, the Fukien region was still at the height
of prosperity. And because Foochow was a great city of the
south east, a rich and populous centre sheltered by the mountains and overlooking the sea, a haven from the wars of the
middle provinces, Lü brought his family with him to take up his
post. He set out that same year and in the spring of the following
year was travelling towards Chien-chou.[2] Now, according to
the Topographical Gazetteer, Chien-chou with its blue-green
rivers and red hills was one of the most beautiful places in
Fukien. However, on this occasion, it proved not so, as was well
expressed in the old saying,

'They tell me, in Loyang in the third month,

                                    the flowers are like brocade;

Accordingly I timed my visit there, yet I saw no sign of spring.'
For, from of old, famine joined hands with war. The Tartar
tribesmen crossed the river[3] and wrought havoc even in the
province of Chekiang. Though Fukien was not ravaged by
invaders, it had been a year of dearth. Such, alas, seemed the
will of heaven.

The story continues that in Chien-chou there was a great
famine, a peck of rice fetching as much as a thousand copper
cash, so that the people were hardly able to scrape a living.
However, it being a time of national emergency in the wars
against the invaders, rations for the troops came before all
else, and the local authorities were more concerned with collec-

---

[1] In *Ching-pen t'ung-su hsiao-shuo*, his name is given as 'Feng Chung-i'.
West of Han-ku Pass lie the Provinces of Shensi and Kansu in the north
west.
[2] Chien-chou is today Chien-ou, in Fukien Province.   [3] The Yangtze.

ting the taxes to fill their quotas than with the plight of the impoverished people with their empty coffers. As is often said,

Even granny herself never made gruel without rice.

Since the people had neither money nor grain with which to pay their taxes, they were flogged with the whip or bamboo, until unable to endure it any longer, they escaped in twos and threes into the hills, where they banded together as robbers. There never is a snake without its head, and a dunghill emperor emerged, one Fan Ju-wei, who raised his voice in righteousness to save the people from the torments of oppressive government.[1] The robbers flocked after him like water rushing down a valley until at last his whistle could muster a gang a hundred thousand odd strong. And what did they do?

They set fire to houses when the wind rose,

And killed off their prey while the moon was darkened.

As food grew scarce, each and all went hungry;

When meat came their way, it was share and share alike.

The government troops could not withstand these bandits, and lost several battles in a row. Fan Ju-wei thereupon occupied the city of Chien-chou and, styling himself Field-Marshal, sent out his men in all directions to plunder the neighbouring towns. And he gave all his clansmen rebel titles and made them officers in the rebel army. Among the clansmen was a young cousin named Fan Hsi-chou, aged twenty-three, who from childhood onwards had been an unusually agile swimmer. He could stay under water for three or four days and nights at a stretch, and thus won the nickname, Fan the Loach.[2] He was a student who had not yet passed the examinations but, being compelled by Fan Ju-wei, who threatened to behead publicly those of his clansmen who would not make common cause with him, and anxious to preserve his own life, could not but join in the rebellion. Though Hsi-chou was among the rebels, he took it upon himself to help those in difficulties and had no part in the

[1] Fan Ju-wei's rebellion began in the fourth year of Chien-yen (1130), in the seventh month. At the end of the year, he surrendered to government forces. It was not until the tenth month of the following year (1131, first year of Shao-hsing) that he actually occupied Chien-chou in renewed rebellion, and sent his men to attack other towns. In the first month of the second year of Shao-hsing (1132), Han Shih-chung recaptured Chien-chou after a siege of five days. See *Sung shih*, c. 26; and c. 364 (Life of Han Shih-chung).
[2] The loach (*ch'iu*), which would be a local fish, would seem to be a pun on his name, Hsi-chou.

plundering and looting. When the rebels found him so timid, as they thought, in all he did, they changed his nickname to Fan, the Blind Loach, thus mocking his inactivity.

To return to Controller of Taxes Lü—he had a daughter named Lucky Maid,[1] aged sixteen, who was of resplendent beauty and exceedingly meek and gentle; and she was travelling with her parents on their way to Foochow. When they reached the neighbourhood of Chien-chou, they were intercepted by a foraging party of rebels, who robbed them of their baggage and money, and chased them and their servants and attendants all over the countryside. Thus Controller of Taxes Lü lost sight of his daughter, whom having sought in vain, he at last with a deep sigh resumed his journey with his wife in order to take up his post.

To go on with Lucky Maid, who was unsteady on her small, bound feet and could not run very far. The rebels captured her and took her with them into Chien-chou city. Lucky Maid cried all the way and was presently seen by young Hsi-chou, who taking pity on her, asked her who she was. Lucky Maid described herself as the daughter of an official. Hsi-chou thereupon ordered the men to leave her alone, and himself untied her and brought her to his home, where he comforted her with fair words and wooed her with a true heart: 'I was no rebel, but compelled to join in by my clansmen. One day we shall receive the Emperor's pardon and I can be His good subject again. If you, lady, do not disdain my humble station and are willing to marry me, then indeed I shall consider myself thrice blessed.' Lucky Maid was not really willing to marry the man but, being in his power and utterly helpless, she gave her consent.

The next day, Hsi-chou notified the rebel leader Fan Ju-wei of the happy event, at which the leader himself expressed his great delight. Hsi-chou then arranged for Lucky Maid to stay at the official residence while an auspicious day was being chosen and the gifts prepared. Now Hsi-chou possessed an heirloom, a pair of bronze mirrors which together formed a rounded whole; their brilliance was piercing and they could be taken apart or re-joined. They bore the inscription 'Mandarin Ducks'[2]

[1] Lucky Maid, i.e. Shun-ko; see Introduction. *Ching-pen t'ung-su hsiao-shuo* gives her name as Yü-mei, Jade Plum.
[2] 'Mandarin Ducks'—*yüan-yang*, with one character on each mirror. The inscription, and most likely also the figure of a bird, would be on the reverse side of each mirror.

and were thus called Mandarin Duck Twin Mirrors. He made
these mirrors his betrothal gift and, inviting all the Fan clan,
celebrated his wedding with due pomp. For indeed:

The one was scion of an old family;
The other, a beauty of distinguished parentage.
The one was handsome and of noble presence;
The other, tender-hearted and gentle in disposition.
The one, though living among thieves,
Had still the air of a conqueror;
The other, even while a prisoner of war,
Retained the manner of a great lady.
That day the brigands toasted bride and groom;
That night a lovely maiden gained a husband.

From that time on, the couple lived in complete harmony, and
in mutual respect as between two friends. It was said of old:

There's never an earthenware pitcher but ends up

in pieces on the well-curb.

The rebel leader Fan Ju-wei started his rebellion at a time when
the Emperor's court was pre-occupied with the Tartar invasion
and had no troops to patrol the area. But he had hardly reckoned
with the famous generals, Chang Chün, Yo Fei, Chang Chün,
Chang Yung, Wu Chieh and Wu Lin, who defeated the invaders in successive battles and re-established the authority of
the Sung ruling house.[1] Thereafter, the Emperor Kao-tsung
transferred his capital to Lin-an[2] and changed the reign title to
Shao-hsing.[3] In the winter of that year, the Emperor commanded the Grand Duke Han[4] to lead an army of a hundred
thousand against the Fan rebels. Now would the rebel leader
Fan Ju-wei be a match for the Grand Duke Han? Fan therefore

[1] 'Chang Yung' should perhaps be Chang So, as in *Ching-pen t'ung-su
hsiao-shuo*. For the exploits of these generals, see their lives in *Sung shih*,
c. 361 (Chang Chün); c. 363 (Chang So); c. 365 (Yo Fei); c. 366 (the
Wu brothers, Chieh and Lin); c. 369 (Chang Chün). Yo Fei was a great
hero of fiction as well as history. However, in the struggle against the
Tartars, the tide turned only with the river battles waged by Han Shih-
chung (here, Grand Duke Han) against the retreating Tartar Prince,
Wu-chu, who for a time was cut off from the north by the sea-faring junks
which Han had anchored off Golden Mountain Island in the Yangtze. The
river battles took place in the third and fourth months of the fourth year
of Chien-yen (1130). See *Sung shih*, c. 26; c. 364.
[2] Lin-an (Temporary Refuge), i.e. Hangchow.
[3] Shao-hsing (Revival), 1131–62.
[4] The posthumous title conferred by the grateful Emperor upon the
courageous Han Shih-chung (and used in the original) was 'Prince of
Ch'i'; in English, however, 'Grand Duke' is less misleading.

barred Chien-chou's city gates and prepared to stand a long siege, while the Grand Duke Han built a parapet which hemmed in the city.

It turned out that the Grand Duke Han and Controller of Taxes Lü had been friends in the old days in the Eastern Capital, and when the Grand Duke set out on his campaign against the Fan rebels, he learned that Lü was at his post in Foochow and concluded that he would be well acquainted with the manners and customs of Fukien. At that time, marshals and generals who were sent on expeditions usually carried with them blank commissions, which at their discretion they filled locally. The Grand Duke Han, therefore, made Controller of Taxes Lü a Deputy Commander in his own army, and stationed him outside Chien-chou city to assist in the conduct of the siege.

Within the beleaguered city, day and night, the noise of weeping and wailing filled the streets. The rebel leader Fan Ju-wei now tried to break through the besieging army by making repeated sallies from the city-gates, but he was beaten back each time, and the situation grew desparate. Lucky Maid said to her husband: 'I have heard the saying—"The loyal vassal serves only one prince; the chaste wife, one husband." When I was taken captive by your men, death was all I expected. But you rescued me, and I became your wife. And to you I now belong. The army is at every gate; the city is doomed. When the city falls, you—who are of the rebels' clan—will meet with no mercy. Let me, therefore, die before you do; for I cannot bear to see you killed.' And she reached for the two-edged sword hanging at the head of the bed, and tried to stab herself with it. Hsi-chou hastily put his arms round her; and depriving her of the weapon, he comforted her by saying: 'That I should have cast in my lot thus with the rebels was far from my original intention. And now that I have no means of clearing myself— the innocent suffering with the guilty[1]—I commend my life wholly to fate. But you are the daughter of a government official; you were captured by rebels and could not be in any way guilty. What is more, the officers serving under Field Marshal Han are all northerners. You yourself are a northerner; you speak as they do, and will find other ties with them. You might even come across relatives or friends of your family, and

[1] Innocent . . . guilty: in the original, 'jade and stone alike must perish in the flames'.

through them gain contact with your father—for there still
seems hope of your being reunited with him. Life is precious.
Do not fling yours away needlessly.'

Lucky Maid said: 'If I should indeed survive this, I solemnly
swear never to marry again. But I fear that some army officer or
other might lay hold of me, and his sword must then be the instrument of my death; for I would not for anything submit to
shame.' Hsi-chou replied: 'Your vows of chastity are more
than I could ask for, and I shall die content. And in return for
your loving devotion—if yet I chance to slip through the net to
drag out my miserable existence, I, too, swear never to marry
again all my life.' Lucky Maid then said: 'The Mandarin
Duck Mirrors were your betrothal gift to me. The pair must
now part company. I will carry one on me; you shall wear the
other on your person, securely hidden. One day, if these mirrors
come together again to form a rounded whole, husband and
wife, too, shall be reunited.' Thus they spoke to each other,
and their words were followed by much weeping. It was then
the twelfth month, in the winter of the first year of the Shao-
hsing reign.

In the first month, in the spring of the second year of Shao-
hsing, the Grand Duke Han breached the city wall. In his desperation, the rebel leader Fan Ju-wei started a fire and burned
himself to death. The Grand Duke Han then flew the yellow
Imperial flag over the city and accepted the surrender of the
other rebels, all of whom he pardoned saving only the Fan clan.
About half of the Fan clansmen had died in the street-fighting;
the rest were caught and sent up as prisoners to Lin-an. When
Lucky Maid saw the end suddenly approaching, she thought
that Hsi-chou would certainly be killed. So she ran into a deserted house, where, removing her silk scarf and tying its ends
to a beam, she hung from the loop by the neck. Thus,

    Rather remain an unsullied ghost

    Than survive, a defiled woman!

But her hour was not yet. For it happened that Deputy Commander Lü was leading his men past the place, and when he
saw in the deserted house a woman trying to hang herself, he at
once ordered an officer to enter and untie her. He himself then
drew near, and when he looked, it was no other than his own
daughter, Lucky Maid. She appeared to be dead, but soon
revived, though it was a long while before she regained her

speech. Joy and grief intermingled in this reunion of father and daughter. Lucky Maid then told her father how she had fallen into the hands of the rebels but had been rescued by Fan Hsi-chou, whom she had later married. And Deputy Commander Lü heard it in silence.

The story goes that when the Grand Duke Han had pacified Chien-chou and calmed the people, he brought Deputy Commander Lü back with him to Lin-an, where he reported the victory in person to the Emperor. And the Emperor distributed rewards and made promotions according to merit and service, which we need not relate. One day, Deputy Commander Lü spoke with his wife about their daughter, how that she was young and without a husband, which seemed not proper. And they both came to her room to urge her to re-marry. Lucky Maid firmly refused her parents' suggestion and repeated the vows she and her husband had exchanged. Deputy Commander Lü exclaimed: 'Under duress, the daughter of a good family marries a rebel, there being no other way of saving herself. Heaven be praised!—he dies and sets her free. And must she still be thinking of him?' Lucky Maid then said with tears in her eyes: 'He was a student and a gentleman, and was compelled to join in by his clansmen, who had left him with no alternative. Rebel he might be, but he constantly helped others and never harmed a soul. If heaven protect the just, that man would surely have escaped death. Who knows but that—both of us perhaps now adrift in the sea of this world—we might even meet again? Until which time, I will stay in my parents' house, dutifully attending upon them, while with fasting and prayers I lead a nun's existence. And even if I remain thus a widow all my life, I shall never complain. But if you must have me marry again, then I beg of you—let me end my life now, so that at least I die a chaste and devoted wife!' Her father heard her out and did not again plead with her.

Time sped like an arrow. Soon it was the twelfth year of the Shao-hsing reign. After successive appointments, Deputy Commander Lü became a Regional Commander-in-Chief, and was stationed with his army at Feng-chou.[1] One day, the commanding officer at Canton sent a certain Captain Ho Ch'eng-hsin with an official dispatch for the Regional High Command at Feng-chou. Commander Lü invited the Captain into the hall

[1] Feng-chou is today Feng-ch'uan, in Kwangtung Province.

and asked him various questions about local affairs at Canton;
and they had a long conversation before the Captain ventured to
withdraw. In the inner hall, Lucky Maid stood behind a screen
and took a peep at the visitor. And when Commander Lü
stepped behind into the residence, she asked her father: 'Who
was the man that came with the official dispatch?' Commander
Lü said: 'One Ho Ch'eng-hsin, a Captain from Canton.'
Lucky Maid cried: 'But how strange! In his manner of speaking
and in his gait, he was so very like my husband of the Fan
family.' Commander Lü burst into laughter and said: 'But the
Fan clan were all rounded up when we took Chien-chou! Some
might have been unjustly killed—none certainly were spared.
The messenger from Canton is surnamed Ho, and a regular
officer of the Imperial army. How could he have anything to do
with you? Mere wishful thinking, my child! And, mind, don't
let the servants hear of it.' After this derision from her father,
Lucky Maid flushed with shame and said no more. Indeed it
was:

For that conjugal devotion still weighed most with her,

Thus daughter provoked father to his first unkind teasing.
Half a year later, Captain Ho returned to deliver another dispatch to Commander-in-Chief Lü. Again Lucky Maid peeped
at him from behind the screen, and her curiosity was roused
beyond measure. She said to her father: 'You know that I have
all but taken the veil and that thoughts of love are far from my
mind. Nevertheless, I have carefully sifted my impressions and
recollections, and the man named Ho from Canton is the exact
likeness of my husband, Master Fan. Father, why don't you
invite him to a meal in the inner hall and, while you entertain
him, find out more about him? He was nicknamed "the Loach".
Before the rebels' final defeat—while we were still in that be-
sieged city—we each kept one of a pair of Mandarin Duck
Mirrors as a token for future recognition. Call him by his nickname, and then try the mirror on him—surely he would come
out with the truth!' So her father promised to do this.
The following day, Captain Ho again called to collect the
dispatch in reply. Commander Lü invited him into the inner
hall, where wine and food were laid out. As they drank, Commander Lü asked the Captain about his place of origin and his
family history. The Captain tried to evade the questions and
seemed much ashamed of himself. Commander Lü then said:

'Was not your nickname "the Loach"? I know all about you. Have no fear, but speak freely.' Captain Ho requested that the servants be dismissed, after which, going down on his knees before the Commander, he cried: 'A prisoner entreating your mercy, Sir.' Commander Lü helped him up and said: 'This is uncalled for. Proceed to the matter.' It was only then that the Captain told his story, in doing which he poured out his heart: 'I am from Chien-chou, my real surname Fan. In the fourth year of the Chien-yen reign, my clansman Fan Ju-wei fanned the flame of discontent among the hungry and started a rebellion, using Chien-chou as his base. I was trapped there and, against my wish, made to join the rebel cause. But when the Imperial army marched against Chien-chou, the city fell and my clansmen were all executed save only me, who, being in the habit of helping others in difficulties, was myself on that occasion shielded by a friend. Thereafter I altered my name to Ho Ch'eng-hsin, and gave myself up as a common rebel; and thus I was enlisted as a private in the Imperial army. In the fifth year of the Shao-hsing reign, my unit was detached to serve under the Junior Guardian of the Heir Apparent, General Yo,[1] in his campaign against the rebel of Tungting Lake, Yang Yao. General Yo's army consisted mostly of men from the north west not accustomed to fighting on water,[2] whereas I, being a southerner, had learned swimming in my childhood and could stay under water for three days and nights: hence my nickname, Fan the Loach. General Yo, therefore, singled me out to lead every attack and, when eventually the rebellion was crushed, upon the General's recommendation I was made a regular officer. After several promotions, I am now a Captain attached to the Canton Command. I have kept my secret these ten years, but since it was your pleasure, Sir, to know it, I have not dared withhold the least part.'

Commander Lü then asked: 'What is your wife's maiden name?—for surely you are married, Sir. Is she your first wife? or one by a later marriage?' The Captain replied: 'When I was among the rebels, I came upon a captive, the daughter of an

---

[1] Yo Fei, whose campaign against the Tungting Lake rebels in the fifth year of Shao-hsing (1135) was a triumph of strategy. See *Sung shih*, c. 365; c. 28. The rebel Yang Yao was also known as Yang T'ai.

[2] See *Sung shih*, c. 365: 'The men under Yo Fei's command were all from the north west, not accustomed to fighting on water.'

official, whom I took as my wife. The following year, the city fell and we have not seen each other since. Yet we had vowed, should either of us remain alive, I would take no other wife, and she no other husband. Later, in Hsin-chou, I found my aged mother, who lives with me even now. A woman servant does the cooking: I have not re-married.' Commander Lü continued: 'When you and your wife made your parting vows, did you exchange tokens?' The Captain said: 'We had a pair of Mandarin Duck Mirrors, which joined together formed one, but taken apart were two separate mirrors. We each kept one of them.' Commander Lü asked: 'And where is the mirror now? The Captain replied: 'My half is with me day and night—I would not be parted from it even for a moment.' Commander Lü said, 'May I see it?' The Captain lifted the tail of his coat and untied from the silk cord round his waist an embroidered case, from which he took out a mirror. Commander Lü held the mirror in his hand and examined it and, producing the other one from his sleeve, joined the two mirrors together, and it was as if they were one. When the Captain found the two mirrors tallying, he burst out sobbing. Touched by his true devotion, Commander Lü felt the tears flowing down his own cheeks as he said: 'Your wife was my own daughter, who is with me in the residence here.' And he led the younger man behind into the parlour, where the severed couple were reunited, both crying aloud. Commander Lü, however, exhorted them to calm down and join in a feast of celebration; and that night he kept his son-in-law in the residence.

After a few days, Commander Lü produced his reply to the dispatch and sent his son-in-law on his way together with his daughter Lucky Maid, whom he ordered to accompany her husband to his post in Canton. A year later, his term of office completed, Captain Ho was recalled to Lin-an, and he and his wife stopped on their way at Feng-chou to bid her parents farewell. Commander Lü provided for his daughter a handsome dowry and an elaborate trousseau, and sent one of his own couriers to escort them. When Captain Ho reached Lin-an, he considered that the rebellion at Chien-chou was past history and unlikely to attract notice but that it would be wrong if there was no one left to bear the name of the Fan clan: he therefore made application to the Board of Rites for permission to revert to his original surname Fan, while retaining his present name

Ch'eng-hsin, and thus called himself Fan Ch'eng-hsin. Afterwards, he was promoted repeatedly and became Commissioner of the Huai Region,[1] and he and his wife Lucky Maid together attained a ripe old age. And the Mandarin Duck Twin Mirrors were treasured for generations by their children and grandchildren.

Men of later times have commented thus on Fan the Loach's sojourn among the rebels: that the man was dipped in ink, yet not blackened;[2] that, being fond of helping those in difficulty, he saved many lives; and that his escape from death and reunion with his wife were heaven's reward for his secret good deeds, as is proved by a poem:

A pair of mandarin ducks torn asunder ten long years
Find their images reunited in a now re-joined mirror.
Impute not to chance such strange partings and reunions:
The heavens on high *do* reward men's secret good deeds.

[1] *Liang Huai liu-shou*, a fictitious post.
[2] 'Is it not said, that, if a thing be really white, it may be steeped in a dark fluid without being made black?' (*The Analects*, Legge, XVII. vii. 3).

The Birthday Gift Convoy

Of the group of bandit stories in circulation during the three or four preceding centuries which were absorbed into the six-teenth- and seventeenth-century versions of the long narrative work *Shui-hu chuan*, the 'Birthday Gift Convoy' was among the earliest. It belonged to the core of the tradition; for it was about the one robbery that led to a hundred other crimes. Being engineered with diabolical cunning and rewarded with a glittering prize of gold, silver and jewellery to the tune of a hundred thousand strings of cash, the exploit was outlawry at its most daring, with the gravity of the offence diminished by such circumstances as that the gifts were from one corrupt Minister to another, both enemies of the common weal, and that the immediate victims were the Ministers' lackeys and atten-dants, who nevertheless escaped physical injury. The eight who carried it through emerged as heroes and, finding refuge in a thieves' hide-out in the marsh of Liang-shan-po, trans-formed it into a flourishing colony of fugitives. Moreover, an officer of law, Sung Chiang, a man of unswerving devotion to the bonds of brotherhood, being implicated in the venture, was compelled to join forces with them, eventually assuming the role of chieftain. Thus the raid on the Birthday Gift Convoy marked the real beginning of the stout fellows of Liang-shan-po.

Bandits and corrupt officials were, of course, part of the scene in the last days of the Northern Sung.[1] Sung Chiang and his men are recorded several times in the official Sung history.[2] The band numbered thirty-six and their prowess had never been in doubt. Thus in the winter of 1120–21, at the height of

[1] See Introduction to 'The Twin Mirrors' *supra*; also R.G. Irwin, *The Evolution of a Chinese Novel: Shui-hu-chuan*, 1953, chapter II 'Historical Foundations', pp. 9–22.
[2] *Sung shih*, c. 22 (p. 3ᵃ); c. 351 (p. 11ᵇ); c. 353 (p. 4ᵃ).

the rebellion of Fang La, who had owed his success to popular discontent with the intrusion into private houses and confiscation of prized possessions in the name of the 'rock convoys',[1] a memorial addressed to the throne recommended the enlistment of Sung Chiang and his followers in the government army in its campaign against Fang La:

> With his band of thirty-six, Sung Chiang ravages Ch'i and Wei [i.e. Shantung and parts of Honan and Shansi Provinces], unchecked by the several tens of thousands of government troops, who dare not oppose them: which is clear evidence of outstanding ability. . . .[2]

In the end Sung Chiang surrendered or was taken prisoner, though not before the capture of Fang La in 1121.[3] Nevertheless, tradition has it that he received his pardon at the hands of the District Magistrate Chang Shu-yeh, after which he and his followers fought with valour against Fang La and helped to bring the rebellion to an end.[4]

By the thirteenth century, Sung Chiang's band had become legendary heroes. Claiming the example of even such a great artist as Li Sung (active 1190–1230), the painter Kung K'ai (1222–1304 or later) did a series of illustrations of the thirty-six men with short inscriptions in praise of each and a brief prefatory essay, in which he states that in his youth he had been inspired by stories told about them in the city streets and lanes.[5] Of these early stories, a skeletal version is preserved in the miscellaneous compilation *Hsüan-ho i-shih*, a nostalgic and somewhat confused account of events and personalities connected with the Hsüan-ho reign, the last of the Northern Sung. The Emperor Hui-tsung himself; his chief financial adviser and tax-

[1] For rock convoys, see Introduction to 'The Twin Mirrors' *supra*; for Fang La, see Irwin, pp. 10–13 and *Sung shih*, c. 468, pp. 6ᵃ–7ᵇ.

[2] The memorial was written by Hou Meng; see *Sung shih*, c. 351 (p. 11ᵇ).

[3] See Yen Tun-i, *Shui-hu-chuan ti yen pien*, 1957, 'The Historical Sung Chiang', pp. 1–25, esp. pp. 7–8. It is recorded in *Sung shih* c. 353 (p. 4ᵃ) that Sung Chiang surrendered to Chang Shu-yeh, District Magistrate of Hai-chou. The time of Fang La's capture is itself variously given as the seventh month (*Sung shih*, c. 22, p. 3ᵇ) and the fourth month (c. 468, p. 7ᵃ) of 1121.

[4] See Yü Chia-hsi, *Sung Chiang san-shih-liu jen k'ao shih*, 1955, pp. 13–29; Irwin, pp. 13–14.

[5] The inscriptions and prefatory essay are found in *Kuei-hsin tsa-shih*, hsü chi (1296), by Chou Mi (1232–1298), and quoted in full in K'ung Ling-ching, *Chung-kuo hsiao-shuo shih-liao*, edition of 1957, pp. 11–14. Kung K'ai was noted for his inscriptions; see T'ang Hou, *Ku-chin hua-chien*, Ts'ung-chu chi-ch'eng ed., p. 18.

gatherer Ts'ai Ching; his master of the revels, the Minister
Kao Ch'iu; the courtesan Li Shih-shih; the rebel Fang La;
Sung Chiang *and* his thirty-six:[1] these all figure in *Hsüan-ho
i-shih*, which dates from after the Yüan conquest of 1279,
probably from the end of the century.[2] The 'Birthday Gift Convoy' is one of the stories already found in this compilation.

In this early version,[3] the hero of our story, Yang Chih,
known even then as the Green-faced Beast, had nothing to do
with the forwarding of the birthday presents. He was in charge
of a regular rock convoy and received his commission as
escorting officer at the same time as eleven others, the twelve
thereupon entering into a bond of brotherhood, swearing to
come to one another's aid in times of distress and danger.
While waiting at Ying-chou (i.e. Fowyang in Anhwei Province) for his companion Sun Li, who had been unaccountably
delayed further south, Yang Chih was snow-bound and reduced
to extreme want. He stood all day at the market, trying to sell
his precious sword; but this led only to a brawl with a young
ruffian, whom Yang Chih beheaded with a single blow. Yang
Chih was then deprived of his rank and sentenced to banishment to Wei-chou (i.e. Chihsien in Honan Province). His
companion Sun Li arriving immediately after, learned all that
had happened, and hastened to the capital to tell the ten
others, who in the meantime had successfully brought their convoys in. The eleven sworn brothers remained true to their bond
and decided to rescue Yang Chih. They waited on the north
bank of the Yellow River until Yang Chih and the two soldiers
guarding him had been ferried across, killed the soldiers, and
took him with them into the Taihang Mountains further
north, where they all became bandits.

To continue the early account—that same year [1120], the
second year of Hsüan-ho, the Regent of the Northern Capital,
Liang Shih-pao, sent off a team of porters bearing gifts of gold,

[1] 'Sung Chiang and his thirty-six' or 'Sung Chiang among the thirty-six'
was a nice point which taxed the ingenuity of story-tellers and others.
For Kung K'ai, the thirty-six included Sung Chiang; in *Hsüan-ho i-shih*,
they were subordinate to Sung Chiang.
[2] The arguments for dating the work to the end of the thirteenth century
are well summarized in Irwin, pp. 25–6. Some of its material may well be
earlier.
[3] What follows is part paraphrase and part summary of the account in
Hsüan-ho i-shih, yüan chi, Reprint of 1954, pp. 36–9, the original being
also sketchy. Irwin, pp. 26–8, provides a translation of the whole passage.

pearls and gems, silks and brocades of the most curious patterns, worth in all a hundred thousand strings of cash, to Kaifeng, the capital proper. The gifts were for the Grand Tutor Ts'ai Ching, whose birthday was on the first of the sixth month. The porters with their pole loads set out in the fifth month, escorted by Chief Constable Ma An-kuo. On reaching the river embankment at Wu-hua-ying (Five Camps)—which was but half a day's march from Taming, the Northern Capital—they stopped under the willow trees and bamboos by the fields in order to cool themselves. It happened that eight hefty fellows, one of whom seemed a pedlar with a load of two buckets of wine, also came to rest in the shade along the embankment. Chief Constable Ma, being much fatigued and thirsting for a drink, expressed an interest in the wine, which, the pedlar claimed, was sweet-smelling yet pungent and peppery, thus possessing excellent cooling properties. Chief Constable Ma then bought two bottles of the beverage, which he and his party drank, but they immediately felt giddy and dropped senseless, upon which the eight men carried off the loads of gold, pearls and gems, silks and brocades, leaving only the buckets.

The Chief Constable and the porters reviving at midnight, saw that their treasure had disappeared, and hurried forward to the nearest County, Nanlo (in Hopei Province), taking the buckets with them. The Magistrate of Nanlo examined the buckets and located the vintner, who identified the eight men who had bought the wine from him as: Ch'ao Kai of Stone Tablet Village in Yün-ch'eng County, known as the 'Iron Demon'; Wu Chia-liang, otherwise known as 'Star of Intelligence';[1] Liu T'ang, the 'Red-haired Devil'; Ch'in Ming; the three Yüan brothers; and Yen Ch'ing, the 'Prodigal Son'. A writ for the arrest of the men being delivered to Yün-ch'eng County (some sixty miles away, in Shantung Province), the Magistrate's Clerk there, who was named Sung Chiang, received it and, under cover of the dark, rushed to Stone Tablet Village to give the alarm. Thus Ch'ao Kai and his accomplices fled the same night. The next morning Sung Chiang handed up the writ, and thirty runners were dispatched to Stone Tablet Village to apprehend the outlaws, by which time the birds had flown. When, therefore, Ch'ao Kai and his seven followers had suc-

[1] This and the following nicknames are taken from the continuation of the story in the same compilation, *Hsüan-ho i-shih*, heng chi, p. 42.

ceeded in robbing the Grand Tutor Ts'ai of his birthday
presents, they realized that they would be charged with no
ordinary crime; so they entered into a bond of brotherhood
with Yang Chih's band of twelve, and all twenty became
bandits at Liang-shan-po in the Taihang Mountains.

The scribe or perhaps the story-teller himself has misplaced
Liang-shan-po.[1] The hills of Liang-shan, now surrounded by
low-lying country, are only fifteen or sixteen miles from the
present town of Yün-ch'eng, but in the eleventh and twelfth
centuries there was a wide expanse of water:

> When the Yellow River changed its course in July, 944,
> debouching thereafter to the south of the Shantung penin-
> sula, the entire area about Liang-shan was inundated. In
> 1019 and again in 1077 similar floods occurred; in each case
> this region remained submerged after the waters had
> receded. The *Old History of the Five Dynasties* describes the
> first inundation as extending over several hundred *li*. In the
> *Sung History*, which equates Liang-shan-po with the famous
> Chü-yeh Marsh, it is reported as several hundred *li* in
> circumference.[2]

And the site of Stone Tablet Village near by was still being
pointed out to visitors in the fourteenth century.[3] It was natural
for anyone from Yün-ch'eng county in trouble with the
authorities to flee to the marsh of Liang-shan-po. The Taihang
Mountains, on the other hand, were far off (in Shansi Province)
and have clearly been transposed from the Yang Chih story.

The transposition may not have been fortuitous. Whatever
the relation in which the Yang Chih (or rock convoy) story
and the birthday presents story originally stood, in the *Hsüan-
ho i-shih* version they are already connected in that the two
groups of fugitives finally merge. Moreover, the two stories
are juxtaposed and placed in the same year; and the confusion
of Liang-shan-po with the Taihang Mountains would seem
further to indicate a tendency to knit the stories even closer

[1] The anomaly is pointed out in an essay on *Shui-hu chuan* by Li Hsüan-
po, who postulates two cycles of stories—a Liang-shan-po cycle and a
Taihang Mountains cycle; see Hu Shih's Preface (1929) to the Reprint
of the 120-chapter *Shui-hu chuan* in *Hu Shih wen-ts'un*, III, pp. 413–16, and
Irwin pp. 31–2.
[2] Irwin, p. 17.
[3] See poem by Lu Yu on Sung Chiang's band, quoted in Yü Chia-hsi, p. 24;
also Yen Tun-i, pp. 102–3.

together. If there was such a tendency, it could lead to two developments:

(a) the shifting of the scene of the robbery from the somewhat drab river embankment at Wu-hua-ying to the Taihang Mountains, whose fearful rocks and ravines recalled battles and massacres of long ago;[1]

(b) Yang Chih, the unlucky courier, being made the victim of the robbery—memories of the early twelfth-century rock convoys having with the passage of time grown dim, an officer in charge of one cut but a poor figure, whereas escorting a consignment of gifts of fabulous value remained a dangerous and challenging task.

These developments one in fact finds in the version of the stories embedded in the sixteenth century *Shui-hu chuan* ('Water Margin') in a hundred chapters, of which our story 'The Birthday Gift Convoy' forms nearly the whole of chapter 16. The earliest surviving 100-chapter edition of *Shui-hu chuan* is that of 1589,[2] itself a reprint of an edition dating from before the mid-century.[3] There would seem to have been still earlier editions, embodying a version even closer to the story-tellers' texts with their familiar digressions and parallel instances;[4] but of these we have no direct knowledge, and for the purpose of this discussion we may regard the version of the Yang Chih and the birthday presents stories in the 100-chapter *Shui-hu chuan* as of the mid-sixteenth century or shortly before. As regards later versions, the account is left unchanged in the 120-chapter edition of 1614; and in the 70-chapter edition of 1644 revised and excised by Chin Sheng-t'an, the narrative remains substantially the same but the verse passages are cut out.[5]

---

[1] Taihang Mountains—see p.167, nn.1, 2.

[2] A fragment of five chapters (chapters 51–55) from an earlier (probably mid-century) edition survives; its text is almost identical with that of the same chapters in the edition of 1589. A brief summary of the various *Shui-hu chuan* editions is given in Cheng Chen-to's Preface (1953) to *Shui-hu ch'üan chuan*. Irwin's extended study in his chapter IV 'Evolution of the Novel, part II' remains valuable but was written before early editions became accessible through reprints and facsimiles.

[3] Known as the Kuo Hsün edition, now lost. Cheng Chen-to's claim that the fragment mentioned in the previous note is of the Kuo Hsün edition is unproven.

[4] See the evidence in Wang Tao-k'un's Preface to the edition of 1589, reprinted in *Shui-hu ch'üan-chuan*, pp. 1825–7; and Yen Tun-i, pp. 169ff. In his Preface, Wang states that in the Chia-ching period Kuo Hsün reprinted' (*ch'ung k'o*), i.e. made a new edition of, the book.

[5] I have used the Jen-min wen-hsüeh ch'u-pan-she edition in 120 chapters,

In the *Shui-hu chuan* account, Yang Chih is not only an army officer but also a grandson of the famous (tenth century) general, Yang Yeh.[1] He had lost his rock convoy through shipwreck and had remained in hiding until he was pardoned. When he first appears, in chapters 11–12, he is on his way to the capital, where he hopes to be reinstated. But he is summarily dismissed by the notorious Chief of the Army, Kao Ch'iu ('Football' Kao, being, in the story, an ex-professional football player). Jobless and destitute, Yang Chih tries to sell his sword, an heirloom, in the streets of the capital. His only customer turns out to be a local bully and, provoked beyond measure by the man, Yang Chih kills him. Yang Chih's sword is confiscated and, with a stroke of the pen, the Prefect of Kaifeng banishes him to—Ta-ming, the Northern Capital! Yang Chih reaches Ta-ming early in the second month, and is recognized by the Regent of the Northern Capital, Secretary of State Liang, as a former acquaintance. The Regent—who is now son-in-law of the Grand Tutor Ts'ai and whose name has been changed from Liang Shih-pao to Liang Shih-chieh[2]— stages, in chapter 13, a contest of arms, in which Yang Chih distinguishes himself and, as a result, is made a Captain of the Militia.[3]

Some three months later, on the occasion of the Dragon Boat Festival, which is the fifth of the fifth month, the Regent and his wife Lady Ts'ai being seated at a private banquet in the inner hall, Lady Ts'ai suddenly asks a question—'My lord, since your student days you have risen to the weighty and responsible position of Regent and Commander of the Army

Shui-hu ch'üan-chuan (1954), the text of which is based on the 100-chapter edition of 1589 with the twenty additional chapters taken from the 120-chapter edition of 1614, and in which all variant readings are recorded. The edition was reprinted by Chung-hua Book Company in Hong Kong in 1958.

[1] 'Yang ling-kung' (i.e. Yang Yeh) and 'Green-faced Beast' (i.e. almost certainly Yang Chih) are two titles under the category 'sword fights' in Lo Yeh's repertory of stories in *Tsui-weng t'an-lu* (late thirteenth century). As a family of warriors, Yang Yeh, his wife, their children and grandchildren are celebrated on the stage and in fiction, but Yang Chih does not come into their story.

[2] The original name Liang Shih-pao suggests a connection with the powerful eunuch, Liang Shih-ch'eng, at Hui-tsung's court (*Sung shih*, c. 468, pp. 7b–8b); the change to Liang Shih-chieh is perhaps intended to show that the man had no influential kinsmen but owed his rise to his father-in-law alone.

[3] Captain of the Militia—see note on p.159.

of the Northern Capital. To whom have you owed your rank and honours?' The Secretary of State protests earnestly: 'I, who was brought up on the pious lessons of the classics and history, am all the more sensible of the magnificent favours of my gracious father-in-law, for whose continuing patronage I shall ever be grateful.' Her ladyship then says, 'If indeed you remember my father's favours kindly, how have you forgotten even his birthday?' The Secretary of State cries: 'Forgotten? That date, the fifteenth of the sixth month, is constantly on my mind. Already a month ago I set aside a hundred thousand strings of cash and entrusted the purchase of gifts to various members of my retinue. Nine-tenths of the presents are ready and the remaining items being completed, I could dispatch them to the capital in the next few days.'

News of the projected birthday gift convoy—for convoy it had to be, Yang Chih being immediately associated with convoys by the audience, who had heard of his delay and shipwreck—having spread, Liu T'ang, a dark-visaged tramp with a disfiguring birthmark, known as the Red-haired Devil, brings word of it, in chapter 14, to the far-famed Ch'ao Kai, squire and headman of East Brook Village in Yün-ch'eng County (in Shantung Province). They take into their confidence the schoolmaster Wu Yung, still also known as Wu Chia-liang and having the same luminous nickname, who suggests that they rope in also the three Yüan brothers of Stone Tablet Village adjoining Liang-shan-po. The Yüan brothers are seen, in chapter 15, to be hairy-chested, brawny-armed, bare-footed fishermen, all three strong swimmers and excellent fighters. Finally, a Taoist priest Kung-sun sheng joins them, having, at the beginning of chapter 16, ascertained the convoy's route. Yellow Mud Bank along the route is chosen as the spot, and Po Sheng, a gambler, whose house in An-lo Village is a convenient ten *li* from it, made the eighth of the band. Two of the original eight in *Hsüan-ho i-shih*, Ch'in Ming and Yen Ch'ing the 'Prodigal Son', having dropped out, the Taoist priest and the gambler Po Sheng now take their place, the re-shuffle involving other stories and characters in later chapters of *Shui-hu chuan*, in which the number of the Liang-shan-po band has finally grown to a hundred and eight.

Having been planned with military precision, the raid itself follows in the rest of chapter 16. After the robbery, Yang

Chih plunges down Yellow Mud Bank in one of those contrived, end-of-chapter climaxes. At the beginning of chapter 17, however, he has already had second thoughts and rushes down the slope unhurt. He comes across the redoubtable Lu Ta, who too had once been an army officer but who, after killing a butcher in a brawl, had sought sanctuary in a monastery and become a monk. Together Yang and Lu seize a bandit stronghold, Twin Dragon Mountain (a mountain along the convoy's route, but now placed in Ch'ing-chou, part of Shantung Province), where they remain.

The confusion of Liang-shan-po with the Taihang Mountains persists. Yellow Mud Bank, topographically part of the dreadful and deserted Taihang Mountains — being specifically thus described in a verse passage — is geographically and administratively part of busy and populous Chi-chou (i.e. Kuyeh in Shantung Province), whose Prefect has jurisdiction also over Yün-ch'eng County. And it is to the Prefect of Chi-chou that the old steward Hsieh and his companions, on recovering from their sleep, report the theft. Yang Chih is now accused of complicity and betrayal. Missives from both the Regent and the Grand Tutor descend upon Chi-chou, where efficient inquiries lead, in chapter 18, to the arrest of the gambler Po Sheng. A Police Superintendent is then dispatched to Yün-ch'eng County to apprehend the robber Ch'ao Kai and six others. But warned by the exemplary Sung Chiang (known among all good fellows over the Empire as 'Protector of Justice'), Ch'ao Kai and his accomplices flee with their loot to Stone Tablet Village, whence, after a battle on water (in chapter 19) in which the police are worsted, all seven escape to Liang-shan-po, where Ch'ao Kai is made bandit chief in chapter 20.

In *Shui-hu chuan*, the all important birthday has been moved from the first to the fifteenth of the sixth month, the effect being to keep the men longer on the road under the scorching July sun. The change has enabled the story-teller to draw upon a fund of verse compositions about the heat of summer and weave them into the narrative. Of these, the poem about the noble lord in his water pavilion is attributed to Wu I,[1] who under his title 'the Seventh Prince Wu' is quite a favourite with the

[1] Wu I (1124–71), brother-in-law to Emperor Kao-tsung of the Southern Sung; see Wang Li-ch'i, '*Hua-pen* Material in *Shui-hu chuan*' in *Shui-hu yen-chiu lun-wen-chi*, 1957, pp. 312–13 and *Sung shih*, c. 465, pp. 3ᵇ–4ᵃ.

story-tellers. Thus in the story *P'u-sa-man*,[1] the Seventh
Prince Wu is the patron of the monk poet K'o-cha'ng, whose
succession of *tz'u* poems in the *P'u-sa-man* pattern leads him
from favour to disgrace. Wu I, however, was a dilettante of
limited attainments, and the lines in question were written,
or at least begun, by Chao K'uei (1186–1266), about whom
this anecdote is recorded:[2]

> The Sung Prime Minister Chao K'uei had two houses in the
> County [of Li-yang], one in the north and one in the south,
> about a *li* apart. For relief from the heat, however, he would
> repair to a water pavilion, where on one occasion he began a
> poem:

'In a dreamy water pavilion enclosed by vermilion balustrades,
Round which goldfish frisk merrily in the duckweed-shaded pond,
While the Six Dragons of the Ocean are in hiding from the heat
And the sea off P'eng-lai Island has grown a seething cauldron,
On a milk-white sharkskin mat reclines an illustrious lord,
His noble head supported by a blood-red amber pillow.'

> When he had completed six lines, he fell asleep; upon which
> an attendant maidservant finished the poem thus:

'Languidly my lord complains of his handmaid's fan too sluggish,
While on sun-parched, dusty roads, travellers trudge their way.[3]'

To connect the anecdote with the Seventh Prince Wu, already
familiar as a patron of poetical talent in one story, would be
typical of the story-tellers, and there was indeed a story with
the title 'Prince Wu enjoying the cool in his summer pavilion'.[4]
The story is now lost, but one would expect it to revolve, like
the story of *P'u-sa-man*, round a series of verses, of which the
poem quoted was the highlight.

The transference of this poem from another story, and very
likely of the words of explanation about the noble lord cooling
himself with the aid of iced melon and lotus-root also,[5] affords

---

[1] In *Ching Shih t'ung-yen*, c. 7, and *Ching-pen t'ung-su hsiao-shuo*, c. 11;
I have taken the title from the latter.
[2] *T'u-shu chi-ch'eng*, 11, c. 100, p. 22ª, quoting from the local history of
Li-yang; see the article by Wang Li-ch'i, who quotes from the shorter
version of the anecdote in Chu Jen-huo, *Chien-hu chi*, IV, c. 4 (1965).
[3] In the version of the poem quoted in our story, the order of the lines has
been changed; the first line reads differently, and there are other small
divergences: I have therefore given two slightly different renderings.
[4] The title, probably of a manuscript, is recorded in the mid-sixteenth
century catalogue of the bibliophile Ch'ao Li's collection, *Pao-wen-t'ang
shu-mu*, Reprint of 1957, p. 117.   [5] See p. 163.

some insight into the methods of composition of the story-teller and the anonymous story-writer. For *Shui-hu chuan* stands halfway between the improvisations of the market booths and the conscious artistry of the novelist;[1] and the consummate skill of its successive editors and revisers has not obscured its story-telling origins, which show through such tags as:

> 'Alack! If your story-teller had been born at the same time as our hero, and grew up with him, then I would have held him round the waist and pulled him back [from his rash and dangerous enterprise].' (Chapter 32, p. 507.)
>
> 'We need not dwell on the dumb horror of those two servant girls—if your story-teller himself had seen those corpses, he too would have been terror-stricken and tongue-tied.' (Chapter 31, p. 476.)

And the ending of our story provides a further example:

> 'And the story is entitled
> "The Perfect Trap for the Birthday Gift Convoy".'

Above all, it is the verse passages that lead back to the performer, who, through them, added variety and zest to the story. Existing translations of *Shui-hu chuan*—'All Men are Brothers' by Pearl Buck and 'Water Margin' by J. H. Jackson (both 1937)—are based on the somewhat artificial 70-chapter version of Chin Sheng-t'an, which is admirably suited to reading, with the more obvious inconsistences corrected and the later (often tedious) chapters omitted, but with the verse also removed. Our excerpt from the fuller version of a hundred chapters may in that way be regarded as a truer sample of *Shui-hu chuan*.[2]

[1] See General Introduction.
[2] In 'The Prime Minister's Birthday Present' in *The Peach Blossom Forest and Other Chinese Legends*, 1951, by Robert Gittings and Jo Manton, our story is charmingly retold.

The Birthday Gift Convoy

To turn to Secretary of State Liang,[1] now Regent of the
Northern Capital, Ta-ming-fu[2]—when he had expended a
hundred thousand strings of cash on gifts in honour of the
birthday of his father-in-law, the Grand Tutor Ts'ai,[3] he
waited but for an auspicious day on which to dispatch his
carriers. One day, as he sat in the inner hall, his wife, Lady
Ts'ai, asked: 'My lord, when does the birthday gift convoy[4]
start?' The Secretary of State paused before replying, 'The
presents are ready and could go off tomorrow or the day
after; and yet one thing has been on my mind, causing me
much hesitation and debate.' Lady Ts'ai said, 'And what may
cause my lord to hesitate?' Secretary of State Liang sighed:
'Last year I paid out a hundred thousand strings, collected
together curios and antiques,[5] gold ornaments, pearls and

[1] The story begins near the beginning of chapter 16 of *Shui-hu ch'üan-chuan*,
on p. 226, the chapter title being:
  'Yang Chih escorts great loads of gold and silver:
   Wu Yang sets a trap for the Birthday Gift Convoy.'
Secretary of State Liang, i.e. Liang *chung-shu*, is previously mentioned in
chapter 13 (p. 194) and first introduced in chapter 12 (p. 182), where he is
already Regent. His connection with the powerful Ts'ai Ching, for whom
the fabulous gifts are intended, is a poor recommendation to the reader
after the spiteful and vindictive Kao Ch'iu, chief of the army and the Emperor's favourite, of chapters 2–12. Later in the book, the Regent has the
unenviable task of defending the Northern Capital against the repeated
assaults of the bandits (chapters 61–7).
[2] The Northern Capital, Ta-ming (in Hopei Province), was one of the four
Sung capitals. The Emperor dwelt in Pien, the capital proper, but a
Regent (*liu shou*) was resident in each of the other three capitals; see
Li-tai chih-kuan chien-shih, p. 114, in *Li-tai chih-kuan piao*, 1965.
[3] Ts'ai Ching (1047–1126), who dominated Emperor Hui-tsung's
court, was popularly regarded as 'the wickedest of the six villains who
ruined the Sung empire'; see *Sung shih*, c. 472.   [4] See Introduction.
[5] The detail is inserted from chapter 13 (p. 194); there is no mention of
curios and antiques in the text here. One would presume the inclusion of
jade and bronze objects among the gifts of the previous year. For the
present convoy, however, antiques and curios are not mentioned at all,
probably to make packing in basket-loads a feasible proposition.

jewels, the best to be had, and sent off the gifts to the Eastern Capital.[1] But my man failed me—bandits attacked the convoy midway, and made off with the treasure. Even now the thieves are at large! And this year I see not one officer under my command capable and discreet enough to be put in charge of the convoy. The fear of another disaster has left me undecided.'

Lady Ts'ai pointed a finger at the courtyard steps and said, 'You have always declared that *that* person could perform wonders. Why don't you send *him* along with the appropriate form of authority? All should go well then.' The Regent then noticed that it was the Captain of the Militia, Yang Chih,[2] nicknamed the Green-faced Beast, who stood at attention below the courtyard steps. Overjoyed, he at once summoned the Captain into the main hall and spoke thus to him: 'We had almost forgotten you! If you will escort the birthday gift convoy to the capital for us, you may be certain of our continued interest in your elevation.' Stepping forward with his hands folded before him in salute, Yang Chih cried: 'There could be no mission of Your Excellency's that I would not venture upon! But might I ask about the arrangements for the convoy and the date of departure?' The Regent replied, 'We shall direct the Prefect of Ta-ming-fu to have ready ten wagons, and shall ourselves dispatch ten of our militiamen to guard the wagons, each of which will fly a yellow banner proclaiming— "Convoy of Birthday Gifts for the Imperial Grand Tutor". In addition, a militiaman is to follow each wagon on foot. The Convoy must start within three days.'

Yang Chih now pleaded—'Your Excellency! Let it not be said that I, Yang Chih, wished to withdraw from the undertaking; but really it could not be accomplished! I beg of Your Excellency, send another, someone of greater valour and

[1] Pien (Kaifeng), the Sung capital proper. Ta-ming is over a hundred miles north of Kaifeng.
[2] Yang Chih is first introduced in chapters 11–12 (pp. 171, 176–7) as a third generation military officer, a tall man with a greenish scar on his face and a faintly reddish brown beard. He has lost a convoy of rocks and, after further misadventures, is kindly received by Secretary of State Liang, who offers him a new start as a *kuan-chün-t'i-hsia-shih* (chapters 12–13). The post is fictitious, not corresponding to *t'i-hsia* (Prefect's or Governor's Military Deputy) by which he is also addressed, and I have simply translated it as 'Captain of the Militia'. The nickname 'Green-faced Beast' is derived from the scar on Yang's face. See Introduction.

discretion than your servant.' Secretary of State Liang, however, exclaimed with impatience: 'But we intend this as an
advancement for you! A letter will be enclosed with the congratulatory epistle and inventory of gifts, a letter recommen-
ding you highly to the Grand Tutor, ensuring that you return
with an imperial appointment. And do you really expect us to
accept your silly excuse?' Yang Chih then said: 'I have heard
it told, Your Excellency, how last year's convoy was intercepted by bandits, who have not been caught to this day. This
year, it is even worse; the highways are full of them. To reach
the Eastern Capital from here, one can only journey by road,
not by canal or river. Thus one must pass Purple Gold Mountain,[1] Twin Dragon Mountain, Peach Blossom Hill, Umbrella
Hill, Yellow Mud Bank, White Sand Bank, Wild Cloud Ford,
and Red Pine Forest, every one of them the haunt of bandits.
Even an unladen traveller would not risk going through those
places! To blaze abroad a convoy of gold, silver and precious
ornaments would be to invite a raid with the consequent loss
of many lives over and above the treasure. No, it could not be
done, Your Excellency.'

Undeterred, the Secretary of State declared: 'In that case,
it is but a matter of sending a larger escort of officers and men.'
But Yang Chih persisted—'Excellency, even five hundred
men would not avail. At the first cry of "Bandits!" the slaves
would abandon the gifts and flee for their lives.' Secretary of
State Liang then said peevishly, 'If it really be as you say, then
there ought to be no birthday gift convoy.' At this point, Yang
Chih suddenly grew bold, shouting, 'Grant me one thing,
Your Excellency, and I undertake to deliver the presents to the
Capital.' The Regent was now reproachful—'But I have
already entrusted you with the whole business. Would I deny
any reasonable request of yours?' Yang Chih then continued:
'If Your Excellency would let me have my way, we shall
require no wagons. Let the presents be packed so as to form
ten or so loads for pole carriers, to all appearance merchants'
wares. Let ten strong militiamen be disguised as carriers,
each to shoulder a pole load. Let me have but one other companion, who, like me, shall be dressed like a merchant. Un-

[1] The geography is fanciful, and the names of these places may be regarded as descriptive. The actual route from Taming to Kaifeng lay
across the plains, and involved no detour through mountains.

noticed, we shall journey swiftly, marching day and night until we hand over the presents in the Eastern Capital. That would be the only sure way.' Secretary of State Liang was loud in his approbation of the plan: 'Rightly said indeed! And now we shall write our recommendation and so ensure that an imperial appointment be conferred on you before you return.' Yang Chih, bowing, said, 'I thank Your Excellency for the deep favour.'

That day, therefore, Yang Chih received orders to supervise the packing of the loads as well as to pick his men for the journey. The next day, he was again summoned to the main hall, from which the Secretary of State emerging, demanded: 'When do you start, Yang Chih?' Yang Chih answered: 'Informing Your Excellency, we set out early in the morning for certain. I beg for my warrant now.' Secretary of State Liang then announced casually: 'Her ladyship, who has a further load of presents for the ladies of the household, is graciously pleased to have you deliver it also. Since, however, you would be unfamiliar with the ways of the Grand Tutor's house, her ladyship has given orders for the old steward Hsieh, husband of her ladyship's wet-nurse, and, in addition, two lieutenants of our bodyguard to travel with you.' Dismayed by the new injunction, Yang Chih said with a whine, 'Your Excellency, I shall have to remain behind.' The Regent exclaimed: 'But the presents have already been wrapped up and packed! What is the matter now?' Yang Chih then explained: 'For those ten loads of gifts I alone am answerable, and the militiamen, too, are subordinate to me, their Captain. If I order an early start, we make an early start; if I decide on a late start, why, we have a late start; when I say stop, we stop; and where I deem best to put up for the night, we put up for the night. If will be as I, Yang Chih, think fit to command. But now—along comes the old major domo with, for panoply, two officers of Your Excellency's bodyguard! The man's a retainer of her ladyship's and, further- more, a trusted servant in the Grand Tutor's palace! I would not presume to order him about, and yet, in the course of the journey, we might easily disagree, as a result of which, if some- thing did go amiss, I should still be called to account.' The Secretary of State snorted: 'We see no difficulty there. It will be clearly understood that all three of them are strictly under your orders.' Upon this, Yang Chih declared: 'Since Your

Excellency has given a firm ruling on that point, I willingly accept the commission and shall hold myself responsible for even the slightest mishap.'

Much relieved, Secretary of State Liang concluded the interview—'You have anticipated every contingency! Not in vain have we promoted you!' The Regent then summoned the old steward Hsieh and the two lieutenants of the bodyguard, and spoke aloud to them in the hearing of all in the main hall: 'The Captain Yang Chih has accepted our commission to escort the birthday gift convoy comprising eleven pole loads of gold, jewellery and precious ornaments to the capital, to be delivered to the Grand Tutor's residence. For the convoy itself, his is the sole responsibility. The three of you shall travel with him and, while on your way, shall obey him in all such matters as the times for rising and setting forth, or halting, or resting for the night: on no account may you hinder or obstruct his command. Her ladyship's instructions, however, you shall carry out yourselves. You will exercise due care and caution, and return without default after completing a speedy journey.' And at each pause in the Secretary of State's speech, the old steward expressed his ready assent.

That day, therefore, Yang Chih received his warrant. On the following day, the pole loads were laid out at dawn in front of the main hall in the Regent's palace. A smaller load of silver and other objects was next brought forward by the old steward with the help of the two lieutenants, so that in all there were eleven loads. Eleven able-bodied militiamen having been chosen, they duly appeared in the guise of porters. Yang Chih himself wore a wide-brimmed bamboo hat, a green silk shirt, gaiters and hemp sandals, with a dagger tucked in his waist and a sword held in his hand.[1] The old steward being also attired like a travelling merchant, the two lieutenants of the bodyguard acted the parts of the old merchant's companions, all three of them taking swords in their hands. And they further provided themselves with canes. Secretary of State Liang now entrusted Yang Chih with the inventory and epistle, and after a hearty breakfast, the entire party proceeded to the hall to give the Regent their farewell salute.

Shouldering their pole loads, the militiamen set off, super-

[1] Yang Chih is dressed in much the same way in chapter 12 (p. 176), where he is first described.

intended by Captain Yang Chih and the old steward Hsieh and
the two lieutenants of the bodyguard, who together formed a
company of fifteen. Thus they left the Regent's palace, went
out of the Northern Capital's city gates and took the high
road for the Eastern Capital, soon passing the single archway
at the five-*li* limit and the double archway at the ten-*li* limit.
It being now the middle of the fifth month,[1] the day was glorious
but, alas, far too hot for walking. In a former age, the Seventh
Prince Wu[2] wrote eight lines of verse, which ran:

Each sun-blind is down over the vermilion balustrades;
The goldfish frisk merrily in the duckweed-shaded pond.
On a milk-white sharkskin mat reclines an illustrious lord,
His noble head supported by a blood-red amber pillow.
The Six Dragons of the Ocean are in hiding from the heat;
Around P'eng-lai Island the sea has become a seething cauldron.
Languidly my lord complains of his fan too sluggish,
While on sun-parched, dusty roads, travellers trudge their way.[3]

These eight lines of verse relate how, in the hot season, the gay
young nobleman cooling himself in some summer-house or
island pavilion, supplied with melons and plums chilled in
water from the deepest well, or slices of snowy lotus-root
dipped in ice, will still complain about the heat; whereas your
paltry merchant, for the sake of the least gain in money or
credit, will of his own accord plod along the highways in the
height of summer, without the tyrannous spur of chain and
shackles and escorting runners. On that day, however, Yang
Chih and his party, too, found themselves on the high road all
because they had to reach the capital in time for the Grand
Tutor's birthday, which fell on the fifteenth of the sixth month.

During the first five or seven days after their departure from
the Northern Capital, they indeed rose at the fifth watch,[4]
started their march in the cool of dawn, and made their stop
when it grew hot at midday. But after those first days, fewer
and fewer inhabitants were to be found along the way; travellers, too, were few and far between; and from each stage to the

[1] About the middle of June.   [2] Wu ch'i chün-wang. See Introduction.
[3] In one version of the story, the noble lord falls asleep after composing
the first six lines; a maidservant, tired of fanning him, adds the final two.
See Introduction.
[4] The hour before dawn. The Chinese time unit is two hours; in terms of
the hour, precise reference is often difficult. Thus it has not been thought
necessary to have the men get up between 3 and 5 a.m. in the first few
days, and between 7 and 9 a.m. subsequently, etc. etc.

next, the route lay through hilly country. It was then that Yang Chih made them start their day's march much later in the morning and continue until well into the afternoon. Now the eleven militiamen had loads of crushing weight, not one of them much lighter than the others. When the heat became oppressive and they found the going heavy, they would make for the nearest wood and lay down their pole loads for a few moments' rest. But Yang Chih would catch up with them and hustle them along. And if they tarried, he would curse or lash out with his cane to compel them to move forward. And though the two officers of the bodyguard had only some bundles of luggage to carry on their backs, even they were out of breath and trailed behind Yang Chih, who began to scold them: 'You laggards there, you two! As if *I* wasn't responsible for the whole convoy! Why don't you lend a hand with the cane? Well, if this isn't straggling! We're not on a picnic here.' The two lieutenants panted—'We didn't mean to hold you up; only, it is so beastly hot that we have fallen behind. A few days ago we at least marched in the cool of early morning. What are we doing now in this grilling heat? Why, Captain, your time-table's all upside down!' At this, Yang Chih flew into a rage: 'Nonsense! A few days ago we were in inhabited country. This here is the awkward part of our journey—I tell you, it's proper no man's land. If we don't travel in the middle of the day, we can't travel at all, not at dawn or midnight or any hour!'

The two lieutenants said no more. They muttered to themselves: 'He tells us! Yes, he gave us just the usual telling off!' And Yang Chih took up his sword and, swinging his cane, went after the men with their pole loads. The lieutenants of the bodyguard then sat in the shade of a willow tree until the old steward came up, when they made their complaints to him: 'That upstart Yang—what is he? Captain of the Militia through being in His Excellency's good graces. An officer of the Militia! But he plays the great lord readily enough.' The old steward sighed: 'His Excellency was explicit on the one point, that we should not cross the man's will; and for that reason I have kept silent, even though in the last day or two the fellow has become quite insufferable. Still, we shall have to put up with him.' The two lieutenants, however, said, 'It was the customary polite phraseology, and His Excellency intended no more. Master Steward, surely you can decide matters for yourself.' But the steward insisted: 'We must just put up with him.'

In the course of that afternoon, they found an inn, where they made their halt for the night. With sweat running down their faces, the eleven[1] carriers puffed and blew and, groaning piteously, complained to the old steward: 'We never asked to be of this chosen band of "able-bodied" militiamen. Nor did we expect to be sent here in this scorching weather with these heavy loads. What's more, these last two days we were not even allowed to march in the early morning! Yet the cane would crash on our backs all the same. Are we not also flesh and blood, sons of mortal parents like other men? Why, then, were we singled out for this punishment?' The old steward, however, said coaxingly: 'Don't you all begin to grumble! The day we reach the capital I shall give a reward to every one of you.' The soldiers then cried: 'If indeed we had been treated as you, Master Steward, are treating us, there would have been no grousing at all!' Thus they passed another night.

But when the men rose before daybreak to prepare for an early start, Yang Chih sprang up from his bed to shout at them: 'Where do you think you are going?—Lie down at once! You do *not* leave here until later in the day.' The soldiers muttered: 'If we miss our start at dawn, the sun will slow us down and you will want to beat us again.' Yang Chih thundered: 'Fools! Will you never see sense?' And he reached out for his cane. The men held their peace and went sullenly to sleep again. When it was broad daylight, they slowly made a fire and cooked the breakfast, after which they at last began their march. And all the way Yang Chih chased after them with his cane, forbidding them to pause and seek shelter from the sun. The eleven militiamen muttered and growled, giving vent openly to their grievances, while the two lieutenants bore endless tales, which need not here be told, to the old steward, who listened impassively but inwardly blamed the Captain.

In this manner they had journeyed for fourteen and fifteen days, and every one of Yang Chih's fourteen companions now hated him. That day, at the inn where they had spent the night, they tardily set about a late breakfast before they began marching. It was the fourth day of the sixth month and, the

[1] 'Ten' in the original, but the error is corrected in the 70-chapter edition.

morning being well advanced, the sun stood high.[1] Not a cloud
was to be seen; it was a day of intense heat, as has been
described in eight lines of verse from olden times:

From the deep south, the God of Conflagration[2] comes
                                    riding on his fiery dragon,
Waving his flaming banner, which sets high heaven ablaze.
With the glowing wheel of the sun transfixed to the noonday sky,
The nations of the world are baked in a red hot oven.
No clouds girt the Sacred Mountains,
                                    their vegetation quite withered;
The Lord of the Seas[3] now talks about extinction by evaporation.
When will fresh autumnal gusts start blowing of an evening
And sweep away the oppressive heat
                                    that plagues our good earth?[4]

The road had narrowed to a succession of mountain paths trail-
ing over rocks and ridges, despite which Yang Chih kept the
eleven with their pole loads moving for twenty-odd *li*. And
when the soldiers sought the shade of willow trees to stop and
refresh themselves, Yang Chih brandished his cane and
roared: 'Hurry along! Time enough for your rest!' The men
looked up at the sky and could not find a speck of cloud: the
heat had become unbearable. Thus it was:

A steaming hot wind blowing
Hot dust full in one's face—
The universe itself is stewing like a simmering saucepan!
Overhead hangs the sun, an umbrella of fire,
With not a cloud above all the plains.
The boiling sea stirs up cyclones of heat;
A thousand hills seem ignited,
With rocks ready to erupt and sparks flying.
The birds that drop dead from thirst in their flight
Are swallowed by the forest with its dark recesses.
Alarmed, the dragons of the deep shed their horns
As they dive into caverns on the ocean's bed.
Even the stone tiger gasps for breath.
And men of iron? They too stream with sweat.

---

[1] About the beginning of July.
[2] Chu Yung, God of Fire, reigning over the summer months (see Legge,
Li Ki, Bk.1v, 'The Yüeh Ling', ii, Part 1; vol.1, p.268, n.3); he is also
God of the South (see *Han shu*, c.87ᵃ, p.3540, n.4).
[3] Yang-hou, God of the Waves; see *Han shu*, c.87ᵃ, p.3519, n.3.
[4] The poem is Wang Ku's 'K'u je hsing' (*Yüeh-fu shih-chi*, c.65).

Thus on that day Yang Chih drove his men before him along the deserted mountain road. It was almost noon and the sun directly overhead, and the hot stones were hard on the men's aching feet. The soldiers broke out with: 'Such hot weather! That deadly sun really kills!' Yang Chih, who overheard their remarks, bore down upon the men, shouting: 'Hurry along! We have to cross that ridge in front! Time to worry about the weather afterwards.' As they advanced, a high bank heaved in sight. When they surveyed it, they saw:

Ten thousand green trees on the ridge above,

But below, one long stretch of yellow earth and dust.

The dragon-like rock, coiling and writhing,

Rises so sheer, the winds do whistle and howl.

Upon the ground where the grass grows thick,

Spears and swords from forgotten wars[1] are scattered.

The stones along their route

Seem crouching tigers and leopards lined up two deep.

Boast not of the gorges and passes of West Szechuan!

For know—this is perilous Taihang Mountain Range.[2]

With a spurt, the party of fifteen rushed up the steep bank. On attaining the brow, the eleven[3] militiamen flung down poles, loads and all, and stretched themselves at full length under the shady pine trees. Yang Chih, following upon their heels, exclaimed: 'Welladay! Do you know what this place is? How could you be actually lying down to enjoy the cool? Back on

[1] Among the battles fought over the passes and valleys of the Taihang Mountains, the least forgotten of all was the massacre in 260 B.C. of 400,000 Chao troops by the Ch'in general, Po Ch'i, at Ch'ang-p'ing (to the north west of Kaoping in Shansi Province); see *Shih chi*, c. 73 (pp. 2333–5). Near the same spot, the founder of the Sung dynasty scored a decisive victory over the last Chou general in A.D. 960; in one of the battles the Emperor himself helped to remove the stones that impeded his cavalry's progress; see *Sung shih*, c. 484 (pp. 4ᵃ–5ᵇ). Another decisive battle was the defeat in A.D. 394 of Mu-yung Yung of the Western Yen by Mu-yung Ch'ui of the Later Yen at T'ai-pi (Rock Terrace, south of Licheng in Shansi Province); see *Wei shu*, c. 95 (pp. 14ᵃ–14ᵇ).

[2] The Taihang Mountains proper are the ridge that divides the plateau of Shansi from the plains of Honan and Hopei Provinces. (As a mountain system, the hills extend all over Shansi and northwards towards Mongolia.) They were celebrated for their strange peaks and ravines, gnarled rocks, and narrow winding paths. In the T'ang, Li Po in 'Northbound' (*Pei shang hsing*) and Po Chü-i in 'On First Ascending the Taihang' (*Ch'u ju T'ai-hang lu*) complain of their horse's hooves slipping and chariot wheels cracking, as did the martial Ts'ao Ts'ao centuries before, in 'Winter Journey' (*K'u han hsing*).

[3] 'Fourteen' in the original.

your feet and away this instant!' The soldiers grunted: 'Do your worst! Chop each of us into seven or eight pieces! We will not move another step.' So Yang Chih took his cane and hit the men on the head and in the face; but when, with this beating, he had made one rise, another had lain down again. The two lieutenants and the old steward had only now struggled up the ridge, panting and puffing, and they, too, sat down under the pines to regain their breath. When they saw how Yang Chih was beating the militiamen, the old steward spoke up: 'I wouldn't come down upon them too severely, Captain. This weather's not fit to march in.' Yang Chih then said, 'My dear Master Steward, you would not know it, but this very spot is the haunt of bandits. It's none other than Yellow Mud Bank, where even in the best of times robberies are committed in full daylight. But in these troubled times we live in—would anyone venture to halt at such a place!'

When the two lieutenants of the bodyguard heard the warning, they started to jeer: 'We've listened to that one before, and, in point of fact, several times! Really, Captain, to resort to making up stories to frighten us poor innocents!' But the steward continued to plead for the men—'If you gave them until after noontide, at least they could have a rest. What do you say to that?' Yang Chih, whose patience was exhausted, cried: 'You too! Even you have lost your wits! How on earth could I allow such a thing? It will be seven or eight *li* down this slope before we find a farmstead, and I've already told you where we are! How could anyone want to remain here just to keep cool?' The old steward then declared: 'For my part, I shall sit for a while before I proceed again. If you must, you can go on before and chase your men down the slope.' Upon which, Yang Chih waved his cane and gave a roaring cry: 'Twenty strokes for each laggard!' The militiamen greeted this with a howl of protest. One of them, speaking out for the others, said in desperation: 'Captain! We each shoulder a pole load of over a hundredweight,[1] unlike yourself who walk empty-handed. This is no way to treat your men. The Regent himself, had His Excellency been here to watch over us, would have allowed a just word of complaint now and then. But with your high and mighty airs, you Captain Stickler-for-authority

---

[1] 'Hundredweight', by which no more than a rough equivalent is intended; the original has 'over a hundred and ten catties'.

are a real martinet.' Yang Chih flew into a rage and cursed the man aloud: 'The abominable beast! It's enough to drive any-one mad. Beating's the only language he'll ever understand!' And lifting up his cane, he struck the man full in the face.

The old steward now raised his voice in mounting anger: 'Hold, Captain Yang, and listen to me! When I was on the household staff of the Grand Tutor in the Eastern Capital itself, army officers came by the thousand to the gate, not one of whom but bowed his respects to me. I don't mean to be un-kind, but who were you?—a convict serving his sentence of banishment,[1] whom His Excellency taking pity on, elevated to the position of Captain of the Militia, the weight of which office is neither less than a blade of grass nor more than a mus-tard seed. And how you do lord it over us all! Supposing I had been a common village elder instead of the house steward of the Regent of the Northern Capital, even then you might have listened to me! Simply to go on beating your men—what sort of discipline do you call that?' Yang Chih then said, 'You are a townsman, Master House-steward, someone who has lived all his life in the walled residences of Ministers. You have not the least notion of the myriads of hazards on the highways.' To which the old steward rejoined: 'In my time I have been as far west as Szechuan and as far south as Kwangtung and Kwangsi, but I have never known anyone to play upon the hazards of the highway with such impudence.' Yang Chih persisted: 'But those were peaceful days, unlike the present.' The old steward, however, said sternly, 'Will you utter treason, Captain? Hold your tongue and mouth lest you lose both. Are you implying that under the present reign the Empire is not at peace?'

Before Yang Chih could explain himself, he detected a shadowy figure in the pine woods, its neck craned forward as if to spy on them. Yang Chih exclaimed: 'Did I not say bandits? There's one for you.' And he dropped his cane, grasped his sword and dashed into the woods, bellowing: 'Confound you, wretch! What do you mean by spying upon our wares?' In the dim light within, he saw, laid out in a row, seven wheel-barrows; close by, seven[2] men, stark naked, were sprawled

[1] See Introduction for a fuller account of Yang Chih's past.
[2] In the 70-chapter version, this is altered to 'six' so as to exclude the seventh, who was standing. He is Liu T'ang, who with his disfigured temple is known as the Red-haired Devil; see chapter 14, p. 203.

out under the trees, cooling themselves. One of the seven, who had a large red birthmark at his temple, a disfiguring, flaming blotch, advanced with sword in hand towards Yang Chih. The other six uttered a strange cry of 'Ho! Ho!' in unison and sprang up from the ground. Yang Chih shouted menacingly: 'What manner of men are you?' Without answering, the seven asked: 'And who are you?' Yang Chih then said, 'Am I mistaken in thinking that you are men who have taken to the road?' The seven replied: 'That should be *our* question. We are but poor pedlars, who have no money for you or anybody.' Yang Chih now faltered: 'Pedlars, are you? And you take me for a rich man?' The seven again asked: 'Who are you really?' But Yang Chih insisted: 'Tell me first where you hail from.'

The seven men said in chorus: 'We are seven brothers from Hao-chou,[1] date-sellers on our way to the Eastern Capital. Our route led us hither. Though many's the time we have been told Yellow Mud Bank was where robbers attacked travellers, yet as we pushed our wheel-barrows along, we said among ourselves, "The dates are all our riches and all our possessions; Yellow Mud Bank holds no peril for us." When we had come up the ridge, the heat quite overcame us and we repaired to these woods to rest until the cool of evening before setting out again. But then we heard noises of men making their ascent and, suspecting bandits, we told our brother to keep a look-out.' Yang Chih sighed with relief: 'So that's how it was! And you are but travelling merchants like ourselves! When some of you were out yonder peering at us just then, I too mistook you for highway robbers, and I ran in here to see what you were up to.' Thereupon the seven men said, 'Stranger, help yourself to some of our dates', but with a curt 'I have bothered you enough' Yang Chih picked up his sword and returned to his own merchandise. On seeing him re-appear, the old steward feigned alarm—'Well, if there are bandits about, hadn't we better be making a move?' Yang Chih answered shamefacedly, 'It was only some pedlars, venders of dates, but I thought at first they were outlaws.' The steward pretended to be shocked, saying, 'Surely, by your way of reckoning, they

[1] Hao-chou is near Fengyang in Anhwei Province; it is over two hundred miles to the south of Yün-ch'eng in Shantung Province where the seven really come from. Their route would not have led them to a spot north of Kaifeng, the capital.

should all be dead by now, lolling about all that time in these fearful woods.' Yang Chih, however, said: 'We won't argue. I only wanted to avoid trouble. You can all go on resting. We make our start again as soon as it is cooler.'

Smiles lit up the faces of the militiamen, and even Yang Chih, who stood a little apart, dug his sword into the earth and sat down under a tree to refresh himself. In less time than it took to finish half a bowl of rice, there had appeared at the bottom of the slope a man with two buckets hanging from his shoulder pole. The man was singing:

'The hot sun is burning like a kitchen stove!
The green shoots in the paddy fields are browned and wilting.
The farmer's insides seethe like a pot of stew,
While the prince in his tower fretfully waves his fan.'

All the way up the high bank, the man sang, but on reaching the brow, he laid down his buckets at the edge of the pine woods and sat on the ground in the shade. The militiamen, who had been following the newcomer with their eyes, now asked him: 'What's that in your buckets?' The man replied, 'It's white wine.' The soldiers again asked, 'Where are you carrying it?' The man said, 'Into the village, to be sold.' The militiamen then demanded: 'How much is a bucket?' The man named the price—'Five strings of cash, a full thousand to the string.' The militiamen were now in a buzz as they took counsel among themselves: 'We are hot and thirsty. It would be fair if we helped him off with some of his load to drown the heat.' And they began counting out money, each for his own share. Yang Chih was instantly alerted and called out threateningly: 'What is the matter with you?' The men answered, 'We are only buying a bowl of wine each.' Yang Chih swung his sword round and, hitting out with the butt, said in a rage: 'Procuring strong drink for yourselves without my permission? How dare you?' The soldiers said: 'There you go again, Captain, all for nothing! The money's our own, each of us paying for his own drink. Is it anything to do with you that you must start beating us again?' Yang Chih, however, continued fuming and cursing—'Dolts that you are, stuffing yourselves is all you are ever concerned with! I'm telling you, there's no end of snares and pitfalls on the highways. Many a stout fellow was laid by the heels with a drug.'

The man with the buckets took one look at Yang Chih and

sneered: 'What a tiresome customer! Perhaps it's as well I'm not selling anyone anything. If that wasn't a dastardly thing to say!' During their wrangle under the trees, the seven date-sellers had come out of the thick woods, all seven now armed with swords. The date-sellers asked aloud: 'What was the row?' The owner of the buckets told his story—'I was carrying this load of wine across Yellow Mud Bank into the village. It was hot and I stopped to cool myself. Those fellows wanted to buy some wine from me, but I did not sell them any. Then along comes this here traveller who tells everyone there is a drug in my wine. The sneak! If only I could help him to a drug!' The merchants said derisively, 'And that was all? We had suspected foul play. Why, we see no harm in anyone making remarks about your wine, of which we could none the less each do with a bowlful; and since they are not keen on it, you might sell us a whole bucket.' But the man now yelled: 'It's not for sale! The wine is not for sale!'

The date-sellers began to curse—'The scoundrel! Did *we* say anything about the wine? You were going into the village to sell it, and here we are ready to buy it from you now. What difference would it make? Besides, our thirst's so great you could call it a good deed, like giving free tea to the poor!' But the man continued to grumble: 'I'd have sold you a bucket, that I would. But it was their kind of talk I couldn't bear. Anyhow I have no bowl or ladle for scooping up the wine.' The seven date-sellers said, 'Why take it so hard? They couldn't have been in earnest, and we are sure they meant no offence. As for ladles, we have our own made of coconut shell.' And two of them turned back to their wheelbarrows but immediately came out again, one with two coconut shells and the other, an armful of dates.

The seven strangers stood beside one of the buckets, removed the lid and, taking turns at the coconut ladles, dipped into the white wine, which they drank with relish, chewing their dates the while. Before long, they had finished the bucket of wine and turned to ask the wine-seller: 'How much do we owe you? We forgot to ask the price.' The man declared: 'I never haggle. It's five full strings of cash to the bucket, and ten for the whole load.' The date merchants cried: 'Five strings be it—but with an extra ladleful thrown in!' But the man insisted: 'No extra ladleful! It's a fixed price!' As one of the seven proceeded to hand over the money to the wine-seller, another of them—who had the flaming blotch over one of his temples[1]—lifted the lid of the remaining bucket and scooped up a ladleful of wine, which he began to drink. The wine-seller now rushing forward to snatch the half empty ladle from him, the greedy drinker retreated with it into the woods; and as the wine-seller then ran after him, another date merchant—who had done most of the speaking[2]—rushed out of the woods with the other ladle, which he, too, dipped into the bucket. The wine-seller marking this, beat a hurried retreat, swooped upon the second greedy drinker and seized the ladle, the contents of which he poured back into the bucket. Then, firmly replacing the lid and tossing the ladle on the ground, the wine-seller swore—'Blast the unmannerly customer! And I took you for a fair-spoken gentleman too! For shame!'

The militiamen, who sat under some trees opposite, watched the scene being enacted before them. There was a curious itch in their throats and they yearned for a sip of the white wine in that bucket. One of them appealed to old Hsieh: 'Master Steward, Your Worship, use your influence on our behalf! The date-sellers bought the one bucket and drank it up. If only we could wet our throats with some of the wine in the remaining bucket to relieve the unbearable thirst brought on by the heat! There's not a drop of water to be had on Yellow Mud Bank. Help us, Your Worship!' As the old steward listened, he, too, felt a craving for that white wine. So the steward came to the Captain and said, 'The date merchants bought a bucket of that wine and finished it. Only one bucket is left. For just this once, you might relax the rules and permit them a drink to drown the heat. No water is to be obtained hereabouts.' And Yang Chih deliberated with himself: 'With my own eyes I watched them from here. Certainly the chaps gulped down the wine; and one of them had a bit from the second bucket. They seem none the worse for it. I have indeed been too ready with the cane; I might as well go easy just this once and let them each have their bowlful.' So Yang Chih said aloud to the militiamen, 'Since Master Steward himself has spoken for you fellows,

[1] 'Who had the flaming blotch over one of his temples' is the translator's addition; see below.
[2] 'Who had done most of the speaking' is the translator's addition; see below.

you may have your wine before setting out again.'

When the militiamen heard this, they at once collected their five strings of cash and went across to the wine-seller, who, however, yelled: 'It's not for sale! It's not for sale!' and added sarcastically: 'The wine is drugged.' To appease the man, the soldiers smiled and said in an abject manner, 'Brother, don't take umbrage.' But the man again shouted: 'It's not for sale! Stop bothering me!' The date-merchants now stepped in. Addressing themselves to the man they cried: 'Confound the rascal of a wine-seller! Even if our friend there had said things, you're being plain irksome yourself. Why, even we had to stand your taunts! We tell you, these fellows had nothing to do with it. Let them have the wine!' The wine-seller muttered: 'Why lay myself open to suspicion when there is so much distrust already?' But the date merchants took matters into their own hands by pushing the wine-seller to one side and carrying the bucket of wine to the militiamen, who removed the lid and found they had nothing to drink out of. The militiamen then begged the date merchants humbly for the loan of the coconut ladles, which the strangers granted, offering the men their dates also—'enough for a bite'. The soldiers swore that they were far too kind and thanked them repeatedly, while on their part the date merchants said deprecatingly, 'A hundred or so dates is nothing to us who are in the business. You are truly welcome, you who, like us, take to the road in such weather!'

Having thanked the merchants, the militiamen filled the two ladles and offered them to the old steward and the Captain. Yang Chih could not be prevailed upon to touch the wine, but the old steward drank up his and passed the coconut vessel to the two lieutenants, who each had a ladleful. The militiamen themselves, all eleven of them, now crowded round the buckets and, each taking his turn, soon finished the wine. When Yang Chih saw that all the others had had their drink with no apparent ill effects, he, too, gave way to the overpowering heat and an insistent thirst. He picked up the ladle which earlier he had spurned and left standing against the tree,[1] and drank half of the wine in it; and he even munched a few dates. It was then that the wine-seller suddenly grew accommodating; he announced: 'Seeing that my other customers had taken two ladlefuls to begin with, the wine was short of a full bucket and I will

[1] 'Ladle . . . left standing against the tree' is the translator's insertion.

let you off two and a half strings of cash.'¹ The soldiers paid
the agreed sum to the man, who took the money, shouldered
his pole with the two empty buckets and, singing the same song
as before, disappeared down the slope.

As his song died away, the seven date merchants, who had
been standing beside the pine trees, raised their right hands
and, pointing seven mesmerizing fingers at the party of fifteen,
chanted in chorus: 'Sink! Sink! Sink in heavy slumber!' Instantly the Regent's carriers felt giddy in the head and wobbly
at the knees: they stared dully at one another and sank to the
ground. The seven strange travellers now brought their wheel-
barrows out of the pine woods. Swiftly and inexorably they
emptied the dates upon the ground; then with unhurrying
assurance they transferred the eleven precious loads of gold,
silver, pearls and jewellery on to the seven wheelbarrows.
Finally, with a shout of 'By your leave, gentlemen!' they pushed
the wheelbarrows straight down Yellow Mud Bank.

Yang Chih groaned with inward rage and bitterness, but his
body seemed paralysed and he could not struggle to his feet.
With wide, staring eyes, all fifteen of the Regent's carriers
watched the seven strangers load the treasure on the wheel-
barrows, yet they could neither rise nor move nor utter a word
of protest. Let me ask you now—who were the seven men?
They were no other than: Ch'ao Kai,² squire and headman of
East Brook Village in Yün-ch'eng County;³ Wu Yung,⁴ school-

¹ Editors have thought this too much of a bargain and substituted 'let you
off half a string of cash'; the wine-seller 'suddenly grew accommodating'
is the translator's addition.
² Ch'ao Kai is first introduced in chapter 14. He is known for his strength—
single handed he lifted a small stone pagoda in the rival village west of
the brook and moved it to East Brook Village—and for his magnanimity
(p. 200). When the band of seven flee to the bandit lair of Liang-shan-po,
Ch'ao Kai is made chieftain (chapters 18–20). Since, however, he dies in
chapter 60 (p. 1010) and does not survive to the end, he is not regarded
as one of the 108 bandit-heroes of Liang Shan-po. The descriptive phrase
'squire and headman . . .' is the translator's addition, as are also the descriptions following the other names.
³ Yün-ch'eng (Yuncheng) in Shantung Province is about fifteen miles to
the south west of Liang-shan, the site of the marsh of Liang-shan-po,
where the seven robbers eventually flee; see Introduction.
⁴ Wu Yung, whose nickname Chih-tuo-hsing might be rendered 'Intelligence Unlimited', is first introduced in chapter 14 (p. 205). He is a
schoolmaster and dressed like a graduate, and the robbery of the Birthday
Gift Convoy is his first exercise in crime. When Ch'ao Kai is made bandit
chief in chapter 20, Wu Yung is chosen to be chief counsellor and second
in command (pp. 288–9), a position which he retains when Sung Chiang

master of the same village; Kung-sun sheng,[1] a wandering Taoist priest; Liu T'ang,[2] nicknamed the Red-haired Devil, tramp; and the three Yüan brothers,[3] fishermen of Stone Tablet Village near Liang-shan-po. And the wine-seller was Po Sheng,[4] nicknamed the Daylight Rat, of An-lo Village, ten *li* to the east of Yellow Mud Bank, gambler. And how was the drug administered? When the buckets were carried up the bank, they contained unadulterated wine, of which the seven themselves drank up a bucket. Next, the 'Red-haired Devil' Liu T'ang lifted the lid of the second bucket and, under the searching eyes of the militiamen, scooped up half a ladleful of the wine and drank it: the move was calculated to scatter the last grain of caution in them. Following upon this, the wily Wu Yung, who had earlier re-entered the woods to fetch the drug, which he then hid in the coconut shell, rushed forward to claim the extra drink; and when he dipped his ladle in the wine, the drug was mixed with it. He, however, filled his ladle and seemed about to drink from it, when the 'Daylight Rat' Po Sheng with one blow snatched the ladle out of his hand and poured the wine back into the bucket. It was all a pre-meditated plan, contrived by the wily schoolmaster, Wu Yung. And the story is entitled 'The Perfect Trap for the Birthday Gift Convoy.'[5]

succeeds Ch'ao Kai as chieftain (chapter 60, pp. 1011–12). Wu Yung's cunning and daring evoke a certain admiration, but his ruthlessness is repellent, as when, by murdering the Prefect's young son, he compels the Constable Chu T'ung to cast in his lot with the Liang-shan-po band (chapters 51–2; pp. 844–9, 856–7).

[1] Kung-sun sheng, first introduced in chapter 15 (pp. 220–1), is a Taoist priest possessed of magical powers, which earn him a place next to Wu Yung in the Liang-shan-po hierarchy (chapters 20, 60, etc.); his magical powers are used to good effect in certain battles, e.g. in chapters 54, 60, 79.

[2] Liu T'ang, who has the disfiguring birthmark and is therefore nicknamed the Red-Haired Devil, is first introduced in chapters 13–14 (pp. 196, 200–5), when he brings intelligence of the birthday gift convoy. Later, in chapter 79, he sets fire to the government boats in a water battle.

[3] The three Yüan brothers, first introduced in chapter 15, are fishermen of Stone Tablet Village, adjoining the marsh of Liang-shan-po. Their skill in swimming and diving makes them formidable opponents on water; see chapters 19, 40, 55, 78, 80. They are known as Yüan Second, Yüan Fifth and Yüan Seventh.

[4] Po Sheng is mentioned in chapter 16 (p. 226) immediately before the beginning of our story, in which he makes his first appearance. His home near Yellow Mud Bank is made the base for the raid; and he is also the first to be caught (chapter 18, pp. 257–9). Later, however, he makes his way to Liang-shan-po (chapter 35, p. 554).

[5] The sentence would seem to have been bodily lifted from a story-teller's version, 'The Perfect Trap...' etc. being the story-teller's title. A similar

It happened that Yang Chih had drunk but little of the wine and was the first to recover himself; he scrambled to his feet, staggering and reeling. When, however, he turned to look at his fourteen companions, he saw that their mouths were foaming and they were torpid and motionless. It was even as in the proverb:

Though you be circumspect as the devil himself,

You shall unwittingly swallow your bath water yet.

Yang Chih shrieked: 'And I have, after all, lost the birthday gift convoy to thieves! How could I go back to face my patron, the Secretary of State Liang, again? What use is this piece of paper to me now? I could never hand it up!' He paused and tore up his warrant before resuming: 'Things have come to such a pass—I have no home to return to, no State to serve. Where can I go? Would it not be best to end my life here on this mud bank?' And tucking up his clothes and striding grimly towards the edge of the ridge, he plunged down Yellow Mud Bank. Thus it was:

What is honour? What is glory?

Disaster, alas, has struck too soon.

The rains sweep away spring's early blossoms;

The hoar-frost ever bites autumn's green willow.

What eventually happened to Yang Chih, who sought death on Yellow Mud Bank, shall be resolved in our next chapter.[1]

example may be found in chapter 40 (p. 649), where towards the end of the narrative occurs the sentence: 'And the story is entitled "A Rally of Heroes at the White Dragon Temple"'. From this and other internal evidence it is clear that many such separate stories, originally all with titles of their own, were incorporated in the full-length narrative about the 108 robbers. See Introduction.

[1] The end of chapter 16 of *Shui-hu ch'üan-chuan*. Yang Chih finds a bandit lair (in chapter 17), which he shares with the terrible monk Lu Ta; in chapters 57–8, they join forces with the Liang-shan-po crowd, by which time the raid on Yellow Mud Bank has become, not only a memory, but actually a joke (p. 976).

The Clerk's Lady

'The Clerk's Lady' is taken from *Ching shih t'ung-yen* (1624), c. 13, the second of Feng Meng-lung's three collections of *hua-pen* stories,[1] its original title being *San hsien shen Pao Lung-t'u tuan yüan* ('Judge Pao decides the heinous case of the three apparitions'). It is among the earliest in the story-tellers' repertory: Lo Yeh's *Commonplace-book*[2] (thirteenth century) lists *San hsien shen* ('The Three Apparitions') under the category 'law-court stories' (*kung-an*). But the version we possess with its sly unfolding of the plot suggests considerable retouching by the practised hand of a later period, though it remains a good example of the law-court story, unmixed with other kinds. The prose, too, is tidy, the repetitive passages being treated with a fair degree of rhetorical skill. Very likely it assumed its present form in the sixteenth century, when scholars encroached on the world of colloquial fiction and literary craftmanship became a consious aim. The editor Feng Meng-lung would be responsible for the somewhat unwieldy title 'Judge Pao decides . . .', which is uniform with titles of stories in all his three collections, each title consisting of a seven- or eight-character sentence giving a summary of the events.

The idea of the two Clerks is probably derived from the celebrated story of the Magistrate's Clerk of Yün-ch'eng County, Sung Chiang, and his kept mistress, the singing girl Yen P'o-hsi, as preserved in *Shui-hu ch'üan-chuan*, chapters 21–22, especially pp. 305–7, 326–31.[3] Yen P'o-hsi barely conceals her preference for the handsome and accomplished Chang Wen-yüan, the young Under-Clerk to whom she grants her favours

---

[1] See General Introduction.

[2] *Tsui-weng t'an-lu*, c. 1; Ku-tien reprint of 1957, p. 4. See General Introduction.

[3] For Sung Chiang, *Shui-hu chuan*, *Hsüan-ho i-shih*, see Introduction to 'The Birthday Gift Convoy' *supra*. For the purpose of this discussion, *Shui-hu chuan* may be assigned to the first half of the sixteenth century.

freely, or her aversion for the stocky and dark-visaged Sung
Chiang. When, however, on discovering a letter from the
Liang-shan-po bandits to the Principal Clerk, she tries to
blackmail him, Sung Chiang beheads her. Under-Clerk Chang
now pursues his former superior and benefactor with vindictive
cunning, though without success. The story, which would be
among the earliest in *Shui-hu chuan*, is represented by a very
sketchy account in the late thirteenth century *Hsüan-ho i-shih*,
in which the rival has a different name and no stated occupation.[1] But the theme of the Sung Chiang and Yen P'o-hsi story
is not murder, merely woman's caprice and man's ingratitude,
and these only in passing, the main concern being with the
unheroic beginnings of a great bandit-hero.

Murder by an ungrateful foster-brother who had originally
been found freezing to death in the snow is shown in the Yüan
play *Ho han-shan* ('The Divided Shirt'),[2] in which the vaga-
bond Ch'en Hu (Ch'en Tiger) pushes his benefactor Chang
hsiao-yu into the river, forcibly marries Chang's wife (who was
about to give birth to a child) and takes possession of Chang's
property. Chang's faithful wife, however, remains true to her
husband's memory, and her son (reared by the villain as his
own) later avenges his real father.

The adulteress and her lover plotting to remove the husband
may be found in the story of Lu Chün-i, as preserved in *Shui-
hu ch'üan-chuan*, chapters 61–62, especially pp. 1024–8, 1046–
52, and in a dramatic version *Liang-shan ch'i-hu nao T'ung-t'ai*
('The Raid on T'ung-t'ai').[3] In the play, the guilty lover Li
Ku is sworn brother to the rich Lu Chün-i, whereas in the narrative he was discovered unconscious outside the house, nursed
back to life and eventually made steward over some fifty men
servants. In other respects, the play (probably sixteenth century) is similar to the narrative, upon which it would seem to
be based. As recounted in *Shui-hu ch'üan-chuan*, the crafty Wu
Yung, 'Star of Intelligence', is sent to lure Lu, a brave warrior,
to the Liang-shan-po marsh.[4] Disguised as a fortune-teller,

---

[1] *Hsüan-ho i-shih*, yüan chi; Ku-tien reprint of 1954, pp. 39–40.
[2] See Introduction to 'The Shrew', *supra*.
[3] In Fu Hsi-hua and Tu Ying-t'ao (ed.), *Shui-hu hsi-ch'ü chi*, vol. 1, 1957,
pp. 143–64; for the date of the play, see Yen Tun-i, *Shui-hu-chuan ti
yen-pien*, pp. 146–7.
[4] For Wu Yung, Yen Ch'ing, Liang-shan-po, see Introduction to 'The
Birthday Gift Convoy', *supra*.

Wu Yung predicts imminent disaster for Lu, to be averted only if he sets off on a journey. Lu calls his steward and other servants including the devoted Yen Ch'ing, nicknamed 'The Prodigal Son', before him to discuss the projected journey. Suddenly his wife appears from behind a screen to condemn the fortune-teller. (The good and wise Chinese woman refrains from making speeches before her husband.) Lu sets out nevertheless, and is captured by the bandits, though released after a while. The steward Li Ku, who is his mistress's secret lover, hastens home, denounces his master before the authorities as being in league with the bandits, and sets himself up as master of the house in his place, later even bribing the runners to kill the good and generous Lu, who is, however, saved by the faithful servant Yen Ch'ing and subsequently brought in safety by the bandits to Liang-shan-po.

But the parallels need hardly indicate specific indebtedness except for the theme of the two clerks, Sung Chiang, 'Protector of Justice', being the *one* great Magistrate's Clerk within the story-tellers' four seas. By drawing upon elements common to many stories about guilty lovers and adding the idea of legitimate succession to official position and marriage bed, formalized as it were by the identity of name in the two clerks, and, furthermore, the ghost crying out for vengeance, 'The Clerk's Lady' has become a Hamlet-type story with its components of fratricide, adultery-incest, right of succession, ghost and revenge.[1] To be sure, Big Sun and Little Sun are not brothers. The implication is, however, that Magistrate's Clerk Sun, having saved the unknown youth from starving to death in the cold, brought him up like a younger brother and conferred upon him the Clerk's own surname to enhance his standing in the county, eventually securing for him also a clerk's post. For the Chinese, their relation is not unlike that of two brothers and the bond between them no less sacred and binding, at least to the beneficiary. Concealment of the crime, too, by adulteress and lover has made the murder, when discovered, seem the more

---

[1] As in the version of Saxo Grammaticus (late twelfth century), translated Oliver Elton (1894), and of Belleforest (1576), English version— *The Hystorie of Hamblet* (1608), in I. Gollancz, *The Sources of Hamlet*, 1926, pp. 95–103, 179–91 (see also Gollancz's 'Essay on the Legend', pp. 1–92, and Notes); and in Shakespeare's *Hamlet*, especially act I, scene V (ed. J. Dover Wilson, 1936; see Introduction, Sections II and V, and Notes to I. V. 42–57).

monstrous. The situation is indeed summed up in the spectacle of the new cooking stove—providing food and signifying livelihood for the new husband—smothering the old well—spring of life of the old spouse—at the bottom of which lies the latter's strangled corpse.

The woefully accurate fortune-teller is found also in the sixteenth-century narrative, *Hsi yu chi*, chapter 10: by defying his prediction, the Dragon King brings about his own decapitation. The fortune-teller predicting the swooping down of the White Tiger (i.e. evil genius of the year) and the worried deliberations of husband and wife that follow are also paralleled in one of the earlier stories, *Yang Wen 'lan-lu-hu' chuan* (' "The Highway Tiger" Yang Wen'),[1] with which our story also shares a tag of two lines of verse. Another early story, *Hsi-shan i k'u kuei* ('Swarm of Ghosts in the Western Hills'),[2] may have contributed to certain features in our story: the go-betweens and their matchmaking, down to the detail of the card hidden in the corset; the newly married couple, always in each other's company; the appearance of the blood-stained and dishevelled ghost at the kitchen stove, followed by the fainting fit and the 'soul-soothing' potion; the servant girl who calls her master and mistress 'daddy' and 'mamma'. This last usage I have, with some reluctance, suppressed: it is confusing in English and endearment was not really its object. The tag 'If now your story-teller were born in the same year as the Clerk and grew up side by side with him, then I would have seized him by the waist and pulled him back by the arm' followed by 'thus was it brought about ... died a death more horrible than ... Li Ts'un-hsiao in the *Five Dynasties Chronicle* and . . . P'eng Yüeh in the *Han Dynasty Chronicle*' seems to be derived from another story of early date, *Ts'o chan Ts'ui Ning* ('The Judicial Murder of Ts'ui Ning')[3]. Some other tags in common with other stories have been indicated in the notes to the translation.

[1] Listed by Lo Yeh under the category 'cudgel fight stories' and printed by Ch'ing-p'ing shan-t'ang in the mid-sixteenth century; in T'an Cheng-pi (ed.), *Ch'ing-p'ing shan-t'ang hua-pen*, pp. 169–85, the fortune-teller being on p. 170.

[2] Found immediately after our story in *Ching shih t'ung-yen*, c. 14, pp. 185–195 (esp. pp. 188–91, 193) under the title 'Exorcism of a Swarm of Ghosts' (*I k'u kuei lai tao-jen ch'u kuai*) with this explanatory note: 'a Sung story formerly entitled *Hsi-shan i k'u kuei*'; and in *Ching-pen t'ung-su hsiao-shuo*, c. 12, Ku-tien reprint of 1954, pp. 29–42.

[3] In *Hsing shih heng-yen* (1627), c. 33, under the title 'Fifteen Strings of

Except in the one instance in which a shorter version of the explanation of the riddle is supplemented in a footnote by the full version, I have adhered to the text in the Jen-min wen-hsüeh ch'u-pan-she edition of *Ching shih t'ung-yen*, 1958, pp. 169–81.[1] The unerring Judge Pao[2] being of little real interest in the story, which professes to deal with his first 'case', I have altered the title to 'The Clerk's Lady'.

Cash' (*Shih-wu kuan hsi-yen ch'eng ch'iao-huo*) with the note: 'entitled *Ts'o chan Ts'ui Ning* in the Sung text', Jen-min reprint of 1958, p.694; and in *Ching-pen t'ung-su hsiao-shuo*, c.15, p.77. The story is translated in C.C.Wang, *Traditional Chinese Tales*, 1944, pp.127–42.
[1] I have also consulted the facsimile edition of *Ching shih t'ung-yen*, 1958, by Li T'ien-i.
[2] See 'A Dream of Butterflies' *supra*.

The Clerk's Lady

Kan Lo,[1] in his early teens, was a King's Minister;
    Chiang Tzu-ya, aged eighty, first found his royal patron.
Ancestor P'eng lived to be eight hundred years old;
              the virtuous Yen Hui died young.
Destitute Fan Tan collected dust in his rice-pot;
              Shih Ch'ung wallowed in riches.
When all is said and done,
        the lots were drawn even in their hours of birth.

The story goes that in the Yüan-yu reign[2] of the great Sung
dynasty a President of the Board of Sacrifices named Ch'en Ya,
having unsuccessfully impeached the Minister Chang Ch'un,[3]
was relegated to the post of Commissioner of Yangtze Eastern

---

[1] At the age of twelve, Kan Lo served under Lü Pu-wei at the court of
Ch'in (see *Shih chi*, c. 71, p. 2319). The wise Chiang Tzu-ya, also named
Lü Shang, first Duke of Ch'i, was a great hero of the reciters of historical
tales; it was only in his old age (historical accounts say aged seventy,
fictional accounts eighty) that, while fishing, he met his patron Wen-
wang, father of Emperor Wu-wang of Chou Dynasty (see *Shih chi*, c. 32,
pp. 1477–8). For the story-tellers' own account of this meeting, see *Wu-
wang fa Chou p'ing-hua* (1321–3), Ku-tien reprint of 1955, pp. 61–4.
Ancestor P'eng (P'eng-tsu), already cited as the example of longevity in
Chuang-tzu, chapter 1 (see Legge, *The Texts of Taoism*, ed. of 1959, p.
215), served the legendary Emperor Yao and lasted through the Shang
dynasty. Yen Hui, Confucius's most gifted disciple, died soon after the
age of thirty (see *Shih chi*, c. 67, p. 2188). Fan Jan, or Fan Tan, who was
content with his poverty, became the subject of a ballad:
  'Fan Jan's rice-pan's for collecting dust in!
  His rain-filled cooking pot serves as a fish tank!'
              See *Hou-Han shu*, c. 81, pp. 2688–9.
Shih Ch'ung indulged in lavish displays of his wealth (see *Chin shu*, c. 33,
p. 12a). A similar tag of four lines is found in the story of Lu Chün-i (see
Introduction) in *Shui-hu ch'üan-chuan*, c. 61, p. 1023; the lines form part of
Wu Yung's speech in the role of fortune-teller.
[2] A.D. 1086–93.
[3] Chang Ch'un, a member of Wang An-shih's faction, a vindictive man
who for a time enjoyed great power and was often impeached (see *Sung
shih*, c. 471, pp. 7b–10a).

Region[1] and made concurrently Prefect of Chien-k'ang.[2] One
day while he was feasting with the other officials in the River
View Pavilion, he heard someone outside the pavilion crying:

'Casting aside the five elements and the four columns of date,[3]

I can still foretell calamity or blessing, prosperity or adversity!'
The President asked: 'Who is this that has dared utter such a
claim?' Some of the officials who knew the man said in reply,
'It is the blind diviner Pien from Chin-ling'.[4] The President
then commanded: 'Have the man brought before me.' The
man was at once brought to the entrance of the pavilion, and it
was seen that:

His cap was torn, the brim missing;

His garments were tattered;

His beard was frosty, his eyes blind;

And his back was humped.

The blind Pien, a knotty stick in his hand, entered and, after
giving a deep bow with the customary greeting, groped his
way back to the top of the steps and sat down. The President,
now enraged, exclaimed, 'You are without sight and cannot
read the books of the ancient sages, and yet you dare belittle
the five elements and set yourself up in their place!' The blind
Pien answered, 'I can tell from the tapping of his bamboo tablet
whether an official is rising or falling behind, and from a man's
footsteps whether life or death awaits him.' 'But was your
divination ever put to the test?' said the President. Before he
had finished speaking, a painted boat was seen coming down
the mighty river, the scull creaking as it was propelled through
the water. The President then asked the blind Pien what fortune or misfortune the noise betokened. The reply was: 'There
is sorrow in the creaking of the scull. The boat must bear the
remains of a high official.' The President sent someone to inquire about the boat and, truly enough, it was that Senior Secretary Li had died at his post as Governor of Lin-chiang District and the coffin was being conveyed back to his native

[1] *Liu-shou-an-fu-shih* of Chiang-tung. The title seems fictitious, but *an-fu-
shih* were, in the Sung, Commissioners with special powers (see *Li-tai chih-
kuan chien-shih*, p. 58, in *Li-tai chih-kuan piao*, 1965).
[2] Chien-k'ang (i.e. Nanking) was a Sung prefecture.
[3] The five elements are metal, wood, water, fire, earth, their permutation
being governed by a person's year, month, day and hour of birth, which the
caster of horoscopes arranges in four columns of cyclical symbols, also
known as 'stems and branches'.
[4] Chin-ling is Chiang-ning, near Nanking.

village.[1] The President was astounded and cried: 'Were Tung-fang Shuo of the Han to re-live, he could not surpass you!'[2] And bestowing ten jars of wine and ten silver taels on the blind man, he dismissed him.

The blind Pien could predict weal or woe through listening to the noise made by the boat's scull. Today I will tell about a fortune-teller named Li Chieh, a man from Kaifeng Prefecture in the Eastern Capital, who set up his shop before the magistrate's court in Feng-fu County[3] of Yen-chou Prefecture. He pasted gold paper into the shape of a sword, to which he attached a streamer with the words: 'Destroyer of all sham fortune-tellers in the world.' And really this soothsayer was exact to the last degree in his reckoning of the *yin* and the *yang*:

Thoroughly learned in the Book of Changes,

Deeply skilled in the art of forecasting,

Contemplating the sky,

         he traced the motions of the heavenly bodies,

Surveying the earth,

         he discerned the magical effects of wind and water.

Acutely aware of the influences of the five planets,

He presaged good or ill with godlike prescience;

Initiated in the mysteries of the three destinies.[4]

He foretold the outcome of events like an eye witness.

That day he hung out his sign, and a man came in. How was the man dressed?

He had on a cap tied at the back with ribbons

And wore a black robe with a double collar;

A silk sash girded his waist;

On his feet were clean shoes and clean socks;

In his sleeve he carried a roll of litigation papers.

The man exchanged bows with Mr Golden Sword, and announced his year, month, day and hour of birth. And when the

[1] Lin-chiang-chün is Tsingkiang in Kiangsi Province.

[2] Tung-fang Shou, the Han emperor Wu-ti's court jester, to whom magical powers were later ascribed; see, e.g., Kuo Hsien, *Tung-fang Shuo chuan* (in Wu Tseng-ch'i, ed., *Chiu hsiao-shuo*, Reprint of 1957, vol. 1, Chia, 1, pp. 19–21), and *Han shu*, c. 65.

[3] Feng-fu, a Sung County, near Taian in Shantung Province.

[4] The three destinies, i.e. the two extremes of a possibly unmerited happy old age and of a virtuous life cut short, and the intermediary state of being rewarded or punished according to a man's deserts; see *Hsiao-ching yüan-shen-ch'i*, pp. 26^b–27^a, in *Han-hsüeh-t'ang ts'ung-shu*, edition of 1893.

cyclical symbols were arranged, the fortune-teller suddenly said, 'It can't be read.' Now the client was Principal Clerk in the Feng-fu county court; his surname was Sun, his name Wen. And he asked: 'Why won't you read my horoscope?' The fortune-teller replied: 'Begging your Worship's pardon, I am hard put to it to interpret this horoscope.'

'How so?' called out the Clerk. The fortune-teller continued: 'Your Worship, don't buy yourself any drinks. If you discover foul play, don't ask any questions.' The Clerk protested: 'I haven't been drinking, and I'm not mixed up with anything unsavoury.' 'May I then ask for the year, month, day and hour again? I could have been mistaken,' said the fortune-teller. The Clerk again announced each particular of his date of birth. The fortune-teller arranged the cyclical symbols a second time and cried, 'Your Worship, let's not read it!' But the Clerk was insistent: 'I'll hear the worst. Say on; I shall not mind.' The fortune-teller then said, 'The omens are inauspicious', and he wrote out four lines of verse:

'Today the White Tiger[1] swoops down upon you:

And where it swoops, there will be calamity.

Before dawn of the following day,

Your relatives will all be in mourning.'

The Clerk read the lines and persisted: 'What do the symbols portend?' The fortune-teller said, 'I will not conceal it. They portend your Worship's death.' And he again asked, 'They portend my death—in what year?' The fortune-teller said, 'In this year.' And he again asked, 'They portend my death—in which month of this year?' The fortune-teller said, 'In this month of this year.' And he again asked, 'They portend my death—on which day of this month of this year?' The fortune-teller said, 'On this day of this month of this year.' And he again asked, 'At what hour?' The fortune-teller said, 'At midnight, three quarters past the third watch, on this day of this month of this year, the symbols portend your death.'

The Clerk now faltered: 'If indeed I die tonight, then all's over for me. But if I do not die, we shall see about this tomorrow in the county court.' The fortune-teller replied, 'If your Worship outlives tonight, return tomorrow, take down this sword that threatens destruction to all sham fortune-tellers, and cut off my head.' When the Clerk heard this, anger rose in his

[1] Astrologer's term for the evil spirit presiding over the year.

heart; vexation burst his spleen; and, laying hands on the fortune-teller, he pulled him by main force out of the shop. How was this business to end? Alas, that fortune-teller:

> Only because he divined men's secret doings,
> He earned a bellyful of mortification and shame.

Several other officers came out of the county court to part the two and ask what the quarrel was about. The Clerk spoke: 'The impudence of this fellow! I only wanted to have my fortune told, but he says I should die tonight at three quarters past the third watch. I suffer from no disease! Would I die at three quarters past the third watch? I'm dragging him into the court to thrash out the matter before the law.' The others quoted aloud:

> 'Who trusts to divining ends by selling house and all.
> What is the fortune-teller's mouth?—A peck of lies!'

They pacified the Clerk, who then left; and they turned to the fortune-teller and reproved him, saying, 'Mr Li, now you have offended our famous Clerk, could you still peddle fortunes here? It was ever said,

> "Predict poverty; predict hardship;
> Predict not the span of a man's life."

Are you the father of Yama? Or brother to one of the judges of the underworld? How could you then prophesy life and death so precisely, to the very day and hour? You would do well to be more vague in your predictions.' The fortune-teller said, 'If I use flattery, would my prediction be true? But if I tell the truth, I only give offence. Alas,

> "Though indeed unwelcome here,
> Somewhere I shall be welcome".'[1]

He sighed, closed his shop, and moved to other parts.

To return to the Clerk Sun, though he was mollified by the others, he felt deeply ashamed. When he had dismissed the papers of that day, he left for home, perplexed and dispirited. When he entered the house, the Clerk's lady saw that her husband's brows were gloomily contracted and his face lined with sorrow. She asked: 'What is the trouble? Would it be an unresolved case?' The Clerk said, 'No. Don't you ask.' But she again asked, 'It must be the Magistrate gave you a talking-to?' He said, 'No.' And she again asked, 'Perhaps you had a quarrel with somebody?' The Clerk said, 'Nor that either. I went out-

[1] See 'The Shrew' *supra* for a parallel.

side the county court today to have my horoscope read. The fortune-teller declared that in this year, in this month, on this day, at three quarters past the third watch in the hour of midnight, I should die.'

When the Clerk's lady heard this, her willow-leaf eyebrows shot up and her starlike eyes rounded in a stare. She exclaimed, 'How! And should a man hale and hearty be dead this very night? Why didn't you drag him into the court to complain before the Magistrate?' The Clerk said, 'I was doing just that, but the others dissuaded me.' The Clerk's lady then said, 'Husband, stay you in the house. When at other times there was need, I had gone before the Magistrate to answer for you. Now I will seek out that fortune-teller for you and question him. And I will say, my husband has paid all his dues and owes no man money, and is no party to a suit, and on him has been served no writ or summons, and should he die at the third watch this night?' The Clerk replied, 'Don't you go! Let me not die tonight, and tomorrow I'll quit scores with him better than a woman like you could.'

It being then dark, the Clerk called out: 'Bring some wine. Tonight I'm not sleeping. I shall while away the night.' The wine and vessels being brought forward, he drank two or three cups at a time, and presently was blind drunk. And the Clerk Sun sat nodding in his arm-chair, the film of sleep over his eyes. His wife said, 'Husband, are you asleep already?' And she called the maid, Well-met, and asked her to rouse her master from his sleep. The maid Well-met went to her master, shook him and could not wake him; and she called him repeatedly, and he did not respond. Then the Clerk's lady said, 'Well-met. You and I will help the Clerk into his room and put him to bed.' If now your story-teller were born in the same year as the Clerk and grew up side by side with him, then I would have seized him from behind by the waist and pulled him back by the arm.[1] The Clerk Sun might have passed the night in drinking—alas and alack, why did he go to sleep in his bed? For thus was it brought about that in that year and month, on the very night of that day, the Clerk Sun died a death more horrible than the grievous dismemberment of Li Ts'un-hsiao in the *Five Dynasties Chronicle* and the gruesome chopping up of P'eng Yüeh in

[1]See Introduction.

the *Han Dynasty Chronicle*.[1] It really was:

When autumn's winds first rock the boughs,
                                             the cicadas heed the warning:
When all too silently death's harbinger beckons,
                                             the end comes unobserved.[2]

The Clerk's lady, seeing that her husband was abed, ordered Well-met to go into the kitchen to put out the fire and lights. She then confided in Well-met: 'Did you hear your master say how a fortune-teller had predicted in the day that he would die at the third watch tonight?' Well-met replied, 'I'm telling my mistress, I heard it too. It's drivel, to be sure!' The Clerk's lady continued: 'Well-met, you and I will do some sewing, and we can wait and see if he would die tonight. If he outlives the night, we must have it out with the fortune-teller tomorrow.' And she added: 'Well-met, don't fall asleep yet!' Well-met said, 'Never. How dare I?' But before she had finished speaking, Well-met was nodding. The Clerk's lady cried, 'Well-met, I told you not to fall asleep, and there you go dozing!' Well-met said, 'I'm not asleep.' But when she had spoken, she was fast asleep. The Clerk's lady again called and woke Well-met to ask her what the time was. And Well-met heard the drum sounding the watch from the county court, and it was three quarters past the third watch. And the Clerk's lady said, 'Well-met, stay awake! This was the foretold moment!' But Well-met was soon asleep and did not reply. And then the Clerk was heard to jump out of his bed, and the middle door gave a bang. The Clerk's lady hurriedly woke up Well-met and was asking her to light the lamp, when they heard the gate being opened. Well-met and the Clerk's lady lit the lamp and rushed after the sound. And they saw a figure in white, its face shrouded by one hand, leaving the house and pressing on precipitately until, with a sudden splash, it plunged into the Feng-fu River. Thus it was said:

When past anguish catches up with present pain,
A ready quietus scatters both to the winds.[3]

The Feng-fu flowed straight into the great Yellow River, and its current was headlong and swift. Could one even begin to

[1] These gruesome deaths may be found in '*Ch'ien-Han shu' p'ing-hua* (1321–3), Chung-hua reprint of 1959, pp. 31–5, and *Hsin-pien 'Wu-tai shih' p'ing-hua* (probably also Yüan), Ku-tien reprint of 1954, pp. 56–7, which were both chronicles in the repertory of the reciters of historical tales. For historical accounts of P'eng Yüeh's and Li Ts'un-hsiao's

drag for the body? The Clerk's lady and Well-met stopped beside the river and wailed: 'Dear Clerk! Why did you throw yourself into the river? Whom shall we two now depend on?' Immediately the cries woke up their neighbours, Mistress Tiao on the right, Mistress Mao on the left, and Mistresses Kao and Pao, who lived opposite them, and all these came forward. To them the Clerk's lady recounted the events which have already been told. Mistress Tiao commented: 'And such things really happen! How weird!' Mistress Mao said, 'This old one even saw the Clerk coming home today, dressed in his black gown with his papers rolled up in his sleeve. I greeted the Clerk too!' Mistress Kao said, 'Even I exchanged greetings with the Clerk!' Mistress Pao said, 'My good man went before the county court this morning on business, and he saw the Clerk pulling the fortune-teller by the sleeve, and he told me about it when he got back. Who would have thought the Clerk would really be dead!' Mistress Tiao lamented: 'Clerk, why didn't you warn us neighbours, but just walked out on us and died?' And tears streamed down from her eyes. Mistress Mao cried: 'Remembering all the good things about him, could one help feeling grief?' She too began to weep. Mistress Pao sighed; 'Oh, Clerk! Shall we never see you again?'

Forthwith the local headman reported to the authorities and, needless to relate, the Clerk's lady held services for the benefit of the soul of the deceased. In the space of a few twiddlings of the thumbs, three months had passed. That day the Clerk's lady and Well-met were sitting at home, when two women, their cheeks flushed with drink, the one on the right carrying a bottle of wine and the other holding two artificial flowers, lifted the cloth curtain and entered, saying to themselves, 'This is the house.' When the Clerk's lady took a good look, it was two matchmakers of the inevitable surnames, Chang and Li. The Clerk's lady said, 'We haven't seen you for a long time, good mothers!' And the matchmakers gushed forth: 'Poor Clerk's lady! We never knew about it at the time, or we'd have sent some incense and paper money. Please don't blame us! How long has the Clerk been dead now?' She replied: 'We had the

ending, see *Han shu*, c. 34, pp. 1880–1; *Chiu Wu-tai shih*, c. 53, p. 3[a]; *Hsin Wu-tai shih*, c. 36, p. 5[a].
[2] Two similar lines occur in *Shui-hu ch'üan-chuan*, chapter 31, p. 476.
[3] Two identical lines occur at the end of scene 15 of *P'i-p'a chi* (Ch'ien edition, Chung-hua 1960, p. 92).

hundredth day observance just the day before.' And the two: 'How time flies! And it was already the hundredth day! When the Clerk was alive, such a good man he was! He returned the bow ever so politely whenever we happened to meet and greet him! Now that he's been dead for so long, you'll find it quiet in the house. True it is, we should be arranging a match for you.' The Clerk's lady sighed: 'What conjunction of year, month and day could again produce such a man as my husband the Clerk Sun?' The matchmakers said: 'That shouldn't be beyond us. We shall find a good match for you.' But the Clerk's lady cried, 'Stop! Who could be like my late husband?' So the two of them drank their tea and went away.

A few days later they again came to talk about a match. The Clerk's lady said, 'Good mothers, leave off your matchmaking. If you can comply with my wish in three things, you may then speak. If not, do not speak of it again in my lifetime, for I would rather pass my days as a widow.' The Clerk's lady then positioned her teeth and poised her tongue in readiness to name her three conditions: thus was it brought about that lovers destined from eternity to be united, perished as a pair under the executioner's sword. A strange turn of events indeed!

Dissembling Chao Kao took a deer for a horse—

confusion worse confounded![1]

Did the butterfly dream about the dreaming Chuang-tzu?—

unknown upon unknown![2]

The matchmakers asked: 'What three things?' The Clerk's lady declared: 'First, my deceased husband bore the surname Sun; I would now only marry someone living of the surname Sun. Second, my late husband was first Clerk in the Feng-fu county court; I would now only have someone holding a similar office. Third, I would bide in my house, and he would need to

[1] Chao Kao, Prime Minister of the Second Emperor of Ch'in, Erh-shih, held his prince and the courtiers in such contempt that when, on one occasion, a deer was brought in, he deliberately called it a horse. The puzzled young Emperor turned to the courtiers, none of whom dared disagree with the Prime Minister. See *Shih chi*, c. 6, p. 273; and the historical reciters' own version in *Ch'in ping liu-kuo p'ing-hua* (1321–3), Chung-hua reprint of 1958, pp. 102–3.

[2] Chuang-tzu dreaming about being a butterfly and the disquieting thought that he might really be a butterfly dreaming about being a man conclude chapter 2 of *Chuang-tzu* (Legge, *Texts of Taoism*, p. 245). In the *hua-pen* story 'Chuang-tzu attains the way' (*Chuang-tzu-hsiu ku p'en ch'eng ta-tao*, in *Ching-shih t'ung-yen*, c. 2), Chuang-tzu becomes the re-incarnation of a huge butterfly.

hang up his hat and live with me.' The two of them heard her out and said, 'There couldn't be a better match! You say you would only marry someone of the surname Sun occupying a similar station as the late Clerk, and would have him to live in your house. If you had asked for anything else, it might have taken some picking and choosing, but in just those three things we can satisfy you. Not to keep you in the dark, dear Clerk's lady, your late husband was First Clerk in the Feng-fu county court and was known as Big Clerk Sun; your present suitor was previously Second Clerk in the Feng-fu county court, but with Big Sun Clerk dead, has filled the vacant office and is now First Clerk, and known as Little Clerk Sun. What's more, he's willing to come and live in your house. If we now propose that you, dear Clerk's lady, marry this Little Clerk Sun, would you be willing?' The Clerk's lady cried, 'Can there be such coincidence? It's not true!' Matchmaker Chang protested: 'As true as I am seventy-two this year! If an old woman like me started telling lies, may I be transformed into seventy-two scavenging bitches to scour the Clerk's lady's house!' At last, the Clerk's lady said, 'If this really be true, I would trouble you to inquire further. But was this meant by fate?'

Matchmaker Chang then said, 'Today's an auspicious day. We beg for a lucky matrimonial card with your horoscope.' The Clerk's lady said, 'I have no such card at home.' Matchmaker Li, however, shouted: 'I have one', and out of her corset she took a red card with a pattern of frolicking children — 'Five sons and two daughters'. It appeared so unexpectedly, even as

The snow hid the cormorant from view till it took wing;

The willow concealed the parrot's presence until it spoke.

And so, that day the Clerk's lady asked Well-met to bring brush and ink-slab, and she wrote out her own year, month, day and hour of birth. The matchmakers received the card and went away. A short tale to make, gifts were exchanged and messages brought to and fro. In less than two months Little Clerk Sun had moved into the house as bridegroom. Such a well-matched pair they were, Little Clerk Sun and the Clerk's lady, always cooing to each other! It was days later. The pair of them had been drinking, and they asked Well-met to make some broth as a pick-me-up. Well-met went into the kitchen and, while she re-kindled the fire, she grumbled to herself: 'When the former Clerk was alive, I'd be asleep at this time of night.

But now I'm made to prepare this pick-you-up of a broth!'
She then saw that the blow-pipe was blocked and the fire would
not light up. So she bent down and knocked the blow-pipe
against the base of the cooking-stove.

She had knocked only a few times, when the base of the cooking-stove began to rise. Soon it was a full foot from the ground
and the figure of a man emerged, his head propping up the
chamber of the stove, his neck and shoulders encased in a well-
curb, his hair dishevelled, a long tongue sticking out from his
open mouth, his eyes dripping blood, crying, 'Well-met!
Take up the cause of your master!' This threw Well-met into
such a fright that she screamed and fell flat on the ground, her
cheeks sallow, her eyes lacklustre, her lips purple, her nails
blue: the state of her five viscera was still to be ascertained,
but her four limbs were already motionless. Truly she was:

As pale as the hill-top moon by daybreak,
As feeble as the flickering lamp at midnight.

The pair of them hurried to Well-met and revived her, and
found some soul-soothing potion for her to take. They asked
her: 'What was it you saw that made you fall?' Well-met then
reported to her mistress: 'I was standing before the cooking-
stove just then to light the fire, when slowly the stove rose and
I saw the former master, the late Clerk, with a well-curb round
his neck, his eyes weeping tears of blood, his hair flung about,
calling out my name. I was quite overcome with terror.'
When the Clerk's lady heard this, she gave Well-met a smart
box on the ear, saying, 'You slave! I told you to make some
pick-me-up. You were too lazy to do it and could have said so.
Must you act the fool, conjuring up ghoulies and ghosties?
Never mind the broth. Put out the fire and go to sleep.' So Well-
met went off to sleep.

To return to the pair of them—when they returned to their
room, the Clerk's lady said softly, 'Husband! If the girl goes
about seeing apparitions, she really won't do. We'll ask her to
leave the house.' Little Clerk Sun said, 'But where will she go?'
The Clerk's lady replied: 'Just leave it to me.' When it was
dawn, they made and ate breakfast, and the Clerk went on duty
to the county court. The Clerk's lady called Well-met before
her and said, 'Well-met, you've been in my house for seven or
eight years, and I've watched you closely. You're not working
the way you did when the late Clerk was alive. In your heart

Anonymous 195

belike you long for a husband. I will arrange a match for you.'
Well-met answered: 'How dared I hope for this? Whom do
you want me to marry?' And only because the Clerk's lady
caused Well-met to marry this man, was it brought about that
Big Clerk Sun's death was avenged. For indeed:

Only when the wind falls, do we hear the cicada in the tree;
Not until the lamp grows dim,

does moonlight shine through the window.[1]
Then and there, without Well-met having any say in the
matter, she was given in marriage to a man, a fellow called
Wang Hsing, nicknamed Wang Double Drink,[2] who both
drank and gambled. Before Well-met had been married to him
for three months, her trousseau was all sold. The fellow would
come home drunk and abuse Well-met: 'You well-merited
Thwack-her! Can't you see how unhappy I am? Why don't
you go to your mistress and borrow three or five hundred cash
for our necessaries?' Unable to stand these taunts, Well-met
tied a girdle over her skirt, and walked all the way to Little
Clerk Sun's house.

When the Clerk's lady saw her, she exclaimed, 'Well-met!
you're married now. So what have you come to say?' Well-met
then spoke up: 'Mistress, I will not hide it. Well-met hasn't
hit it off with that chap. He drinks and he gambles. It's less
than three months, but he's sold all my trousseau. Now I'm
without a plan, and I've come to borrow three or five hundred
cash from my mistress for our necessaries.' The Clerk's lady
then said, 'That you didn't hit it off with your man is your own
business. I'll give you an ounce of silver.[3] But you mustn't
come again.' Well-met took the silver, thanked her mistress
and returned home.

It was no more than four or five days when the money was
spent. That day, the fellow Wang Hsing came home at dusk
after a booze and, seeing Well-met, cried, 'Well-earned
Thwack-her! Can't you see how hard up I am? Why don't you
go and borrow again from your mistress?' Well-met replied:
'The last time I went, I got an ounce of silver but only after

[1] These lines are also found in the story 'The Ape Abductor' (*Ch'en hsün-chien Mei-ling shih ch'i chi*) in *Ch'ing-p'ing shan-t'ang hua-pen*, p. 132.
[2] Wang Chiu-chiu, i.e. Wang Drink-Drink, a fairly common nickname; see, e.g., the story of Ch'iao Yen-chieh in *Ching-shih t'ung-yen*, c. 33, p. 509.
[3] The equivalent of a thousand copper cash; but the rate fluctuated.

swallowing a ten-thousand-word lecture. I couldn't go again.'
Wang Hsing continued: 'Well-earned Thwack-her! I'll break
your leg if you don't go!' Well-met could not endure these
threats. So she went that same night to the Clerk's Sun house,
and saw that the gate was shut. She could knock on the gate
but feared to be scolded again, and was exceedingly perplexed. At last, she turned back, and had passed two or three
houses, when she heard a man's voice calling after her: 'Well-
met! I have something for you.' Ah! Because of that voice, I
grow apprehensive for the Clerk's lady and Little Clerk Sun.
True it is:

The tortoise in mid-stream divides the water's green surface;

The crane on the pine tree breaks up heaven's blue profundity.[1]
Well-met turned round to see who it was that had called
her. And she saw, standing above the eaves of a neighbouring
house, a man clad in an official's dark red robe complete with
ornamental belt and a lacquered hat with two spreading horns,[2]
holding a large pile of papers, calling to her in a low voice:
'Well-met! I am your late master, the Clerk. Now I'm in a
certain place, but I may not tell you where. Stretch out your
hand. I have something for you.' Well-met reached and received something in her hand, but the hatted and robed figure
had vanished. Well-met examined what was in her hand, and
found it to be a packet of small silver pieces.

So Well-met went home and knocked on the gate. From
within came her husband's voice: 'Wife, you were at your
mistress's. What made you come home so late?' Well-met
shouted: 'So that you may know, I went to my mistress's house
to borrow rice, but her gate was shut. I didn't dare knock for
fear of their scolding me. Just as I was turning back, I saw the
late Clerk standing above the eaves of another house, and he
was wearing a lacquered hat and a dark red robe, belt and all.
He gave me this packet of silver here.' When Wang Hsing
heard this, he exclaimed: 'Well-merited Thwack-her! Will
you make a fool of me with this spooky stuff and nonsense? I
wager there's something dubious about this packet of silver of
yours. But you can come in.' When Well-met entered the

[1] i.e. the unfathomable begins to yield its secrets.
[2] The lacquered hat with spreading horns and the dark red robe and belt
were part of the Sung official's dress (see *Sung shih*, c. 153, pp. 1ᵃ, 2ᵇ);
they indicate that Big Clerk Sun had been made an official of the nether
world.

house, Wang Hsing said to her, 'Wife, what you told me
formerly about seeing the late Clerk at the cooking-stove
wasn't lost upon me. This certainly is a queer business. I was
afraid of the neighbours overhearing you just then, and so
spoke the way I did. Look after the silver. At dawn I will go into
the county court to accuse them.' Thus it was:

We grow our flowers with diligent care,
                                        yet they will not flourish:
In an idle moment one plants some willows,
                                        and soon they cast their shade.[1]

At daybreak, however, Wang Hsing thought to himself:
'Stay! Two things prevent me from making the accusation.
First, he is Principal Clerk in the county court, and I dare not
antagonize him. Second, there's no real evidence. I would need
to surrender the silver and the suit might still lead nowhere.
Better use the silver to redeem some of our pawned clothes and
buy some boxes of food as a present for them, and call on them
to spy out their secret.' Having made up his mind, he went and
paid for two boxes of delicacies to be delivered to the Clerk's
house. The two of them then dressed up and followed. When
the Clerk's lady saw that the two of them were neatly dressed
and had sent the delicacies, she asked, 'Have you come into
money?' Wang Hsing replied: 'Yesterday I was concerned in
one of the Clerk's cases, and earned two ounces of silver; so
I'm presenting you with these boxes of food. Wang Hsing
doesn't drink or gamble any more.' The Clerk's lady then
said, 'Wang Hsing, you can go back now and let your wife
stay behind for a couple of days.' And so he went away.

The Clerk's lady then said to Well-met, 'I must fulfil a vow
I once made to offer up incense to the God of the Sacred Mountain of the East.[2] You will go with me tomorrow.' That night,
there was nothing more to relate. When they had risen the
next morning and combed their hair and washed themselves,
the Clerk setting off for the county court, the Clerk's lady

[1] i.e. it is accident rather than design that leads to a successful outcome.
Two similar lines are found in the story '"The Highway Tiger" Yang
Wen' in *Ch'ing-p'ing shan-t'ang hua-pen*, p. 172.
[2] Deity in charge of life and death, officially sanctified by Qubilai in 1291
(see *Yüan shih*, c. 76, pp. 13ᵃ–13ᵇ). In '"The Highway Tiger" Yang Wen',
Yang Wen and his wife go on a pilgrimage to the Eastern Sacred Mountain (i.e. T'ai-shan), but the temple of the god was found in most cities,
often outside the city's east gate, e.g., in *Shui-hu ch'üan-chuan*, c. 46,
p. 761.

locked the gate and went together with Well-met to the Temple of the Eastern Sacred Mountain. They burned incense in the main temple and then at the altars in the two wings of the temple building. As they walked past the Hall of Retribution, Well-met's girdle, which had been loosely tied on, suddenly slipped. So the Clerk's lady went past and, while Well-met remained behind to fasten her girdle, the image of an infernal judge in the Hall of Retribution, a statue with a lacquered hat and a dark red robe and belt, called to her: 'Well-met! I am your late master, the Clerk. Redress the wrongs I suffered. I will give you this.' Well-met reached out her hand for the thing, took a quick look at it, and said: 'Of all the curious happenings! A clay image has spoken to me! Why has he given me this?' It was really an occurrence

Unheard of since the world's beginning,

Unknown even from the most ancient times.

Well-met took what was given her, hastily tucked it in her bosom, and did not dare say anything about it to the Clerk's lady. That day, when they had burnt their incense, each returned to her home. Well-met recounted to Wang Hsing what had happened, and when Wang Hsing asked to see what she had been given, it turned out to be a piece of paper on which was written:

'Older daughter's child

Younger daughter's child

Where the former sowed the latter reaped

To learn what happened at the third watch

Dig for water under fire

The second or third month in the coming year

Pu Ao shall solve the riddle.'

Wang Hsing read the words and could not explain them. So he ordered Well-met to tell no one, but to wait and see what would happen in the second and third months of the next year.

A few twiddlings of the thumbs and it was already the second month of the following year, when there was a new Magistrate. He was a man from the town of Chin-tou in Lu-chou Prefecture, of the surname Pao and the name Cheng, and was no other than the famous 'Lung-t'u' Pao in stories current today.[1] Afterwards he rose to the rank of Scholar of Lung-t'u Library and so came to be called 'Lung-t'u' Pao. But this county magis-

[1] For Pao Cheng and his titles, see 'A Dream of Butterflies' *supra*.

tracy, to which he was appointed, was still his first office. Even as a child, the worshipful Pao was wise and just, and when he became Magistrate, he was capable of

Opening up dark and obscure corners of men's hearts,
Adjudicating in all doubtful cases in the world.

It being but the third day of his assumption of the magistracy, he had not yet entered upon his duties. At night, however, he had a dream. He dreamt that he was sitting in court and found pasted on the wall two lines of verse[1] in large characters:

'To learn what happened at the third watch
Dig for water under fire.'

At the morning session the following day, his Honour the Magistrate Pao summoned all the attendant officers and demanded if they could explain the two lines; and none could do so. His Honour then asked for a white signboard, on which the two lines of verse were to be written out in a large, clear hand. And it was Little Clerk Sun who wrote them out. That done, Magistrate Pao added in red ink: 'To him who can explain these words a reward of ten ounces of silver is due.' And he had the signboard hung up by the gate of the county court. There was then a commotion all around the court. Official servants and commoners jostled one another in the hope of the reward, each wanting to be the first to read the signboard.

To return to Wang Hsing—he was at the time buying some date-cake for a snack outside the county court. When told that his Honour the Magistrate had hung up a white signboard displaying two lines of writing which no one could make out, Wang Hsing went across and found the words to be those written on the piece of paper handed out by the infernal judge of the Hall of Retribution. Secretly amazed, he thought to himself: 'If I go and make a declaration, the new Magistrate is rumoured to be an unholy disciplinarian and I'd do best not to rouse him. If I don't speak out, who else in the world could tell where these lines came from?'

He took the date-cake home and told his wife about all this. Well-met said: 'Three times the late Clerk appeared, urging me to bring about the redress of his wrongs. Undeservingly too we received a packet of silver from him. If you don't declare

[1] In the original 'an antithetical couplet', which is usually written out in large characters and hung up in two strips. The lines here do not quite form a couplet.

the matter, the spirits would surely punish us.' But Wang Hsing remained undecided. Again he went before the county court, and there he met his neighbour, Under-Clerk P'ei. Wang Hsing had always known Under-Clerk P'ei to be a man of discretion, and he pulled him by the hand into a deserted lane and sought his advice: should he, or should he not, make a declaration? Under-Clerk P'ei asked: 'Where is the piece of paper from the Hall of Retribution?' Wang Hsing replied: 'It's hidden in my wife's clothes chest.' Under-Clerk P'ei then said: 'I will go before to report the matter. You must return home to fetch the piece of paper and bring it to the court, and when his Honour calls for you, you shall produce it as evidence.' So Wang Hsing went home.

Under-Clerk P'ei waited until his Honour had dismissed court and, seeing Little Clerk Sun to be out of the way, went and knelt before the Magistrate to make his report: 'The two lines your Honour caused to be written on the white signboard—only my neighbour Wang Hsing knew where they came from. He says he once received a piece of paper at the Hall of Retribution in the Sacred Mountain Temple. More was said on the paper, but those two lines were also there.' His Honour then demanded where Wang Hsing was. Under-Clerk P'ei replied: 'He has gone home to fetch that piece of paper.' Magistrate Pao then sent men to attach Wang Hsing for questioning.

To return to Wang Hsing—he reached home, opened his wife's clothes chest, and searched out the piece of paper. But when he looked at it—oh! welladay!—it was only a blank sheet, with no trace of writing. No longer would he venture near the court, but, filled with misgiving, hid himself in the house. His Honour's runners soon arriving in burning haste to carry out their first arrest under a new Magistrate, evasion was ruled out. Wang Hsing needs must carry the blank piece of paper with him while he was escorted by the runners to the county court, straight into the inner hall. There, Magistrate Pao dismissed all his attendants, keeping only Under-Clerk P'ei by his side. Magistrate Pao then questioned Wang Hsing: 'According to P'ei, you received a piece of paper in the Sacred Mountain Temple. Can you produce it for our inspection?' Wang Hsing kowtowed again and again while he made his report: 'It was your servant's wife who was at the Sacred

Mountain Temple last year to offer up incense, and when she
went past the Hall of Retribution, the god appeared and gave
her a piece of paper. There were some verses on the paper and
they really included the two lines written on your Honour's
white signboard. Your servant took the paper and hid it in the
clothes chest. Just then, when I searched it out, however, it had
become a blank sheet. The blank piece of paper is here. Your
servant has not dared utter a lie.'

Magistrate Pao took the paper and studied it. He then asked,
'Can you remember the verses?' Wang Hsing replied, 'I can
still remember them.' At once he recited them for his Honour,
who wrote them down on paper and pondered the words a long
while before speaking again: 'Answer me, Wang Hsing.
When the piece of paper was given to your wife, was anything
said to her?' Wang Hsing replied, 'The god only asked her to
redress the wrongs he had suffered.' This sent Magistrate Pao
into a rage, and he shouted the man down: 'Nonsense! A god
to cry out for redress of his wrongs? And your wife was to be
the instrument of redress! Would a god seek your help? And
you think to deceive us with this kind of idle tale?' Thoroughly
alarmed, Wang Hsing kowtowed and exclaimed: 'Your
Honour, a hidden cause there is!' Magistrate Pao said, 'Unfold
it in each particular. If you speak with reason, you will be rewarded. But if you indulge in folly, let the rod of punishment
under this magistracy begin with you!'

Wang Hsing then reported in full: how his wife had been a
servant-girl in the house of Big Clerk Sun of the county court
and how her name was Well-met; how on a certain day of a certain month in the previous year a fortune-teller had predicted
that her master, Big Clerk Sun, would die at three quarters
past the third watch that very night and how unaccountably he
did meet his death; how the mistress then took for her husband
Little Clerk Sun but married Well-met to himself, Wang
Hsing; how, on the first occasion, his wife saw an apparition of
the late Clerk under the cooking-stove in her mistress's house,
how the Clerk's neck was encased in a well-curb, how his hair
was dishevelled, his tongue sticking out, and his eyes dripping
blood, and how he cried: 'Well-met! Take up your master's
cause!'; how, on the second occasion, she was going to her
mistress's house at night and saw the late Clerk in a lacquered
hat with spreading horns and a dark red official's robe complete

with belt, and how he gave her a packet of silver pieces; how, on the third occasion, an infernal judge from the Hall of Retribution in the Sacred Mountain Temple gave her the piece of paper and asked her to redress his wrongs and how the judge was the exact likeness of Big Clerk Sun, his wife's master of former days.

Magistrate Pao heard him out and suddenly shrieked with a terrible laughter. 'So that's how it was!' he roared, and he called out to his attendants to apprehend Little Clerk Sun and his wife forthwith. And when the couple were brought before him, he came down upon them with: 'A fine thing the pair of you have done!' Little Clerk Sun said, 'Your servant has done nothing.' Magistrate Pao then read out the verses from the Hall of Retribution, adding his own explanations:

' "Older daughter's child

Younger daughter's child"

Daughter's child is grandson or the character "Sun". By these lines are meant Big Sun and Little Sun. [1]

"Where the former sowed the latter reaped"

Undeservingly the latter has inherited the former's wife and property.

"To learn what happened at the third watch

Dig for water under fire"

Big Clerk Sun died at the third watch. To learn the cause of his death, one must "dig for water under fire". The maid-servant Well-met saw her master under the cooking-stove, his hair disordered, his tongue sticking out, his eyes dripping blood. These were signs of strangulation. A well-curb encircled his neck. A well is "water"; the stove is "fire". "Water under fire" would mean the cooking-stove is placed over the well. The dead man's body must be in the well.

"The second or third month in the coming year"

This would refer to the present.

"Pu Ao shall solve the riddle"

"Pu" and "Ao" together make Pao. The present Magistrate, arriving upon the scene, shall explain the verses and redress his wrongs.'

[1] I have shortened the explanation, but append the full version as follows: 'Daughter's child is a grandson of a different surname, or the characters "Wai Sun". But "Wai" is also "husband". "Wai Sun" would therefore be "Husband Sun". By these lines are meant Big Clerk Sun and Little Clerk Sun.'

Magistrate Pao then shouted out his orders. The runners were to keep Little Clerk Sun under guard and go with him to his house, taking Wang Hsing with them. There they were to search under the cooking-stove and by hook or by crook find a strangled corpse. Doubtfully, his attendants set about this. When they reached the house, they broke open the base of the cooking-stove and found underneath it a stone slab; this they lifted up, and there indeed was a well. So they rounded up labourers and had the well drained. Then, tying some rope to a bamboo basket, they let a dragsman down the well, and the man came up with a corpse. And when they crowded round to identify the body, the features of the face were still distinct and some recognized it to be Big Clerk Sun. Around the neck of the corpse was a tell-tale wreath of silk. Little Clerk Sun was now petrified with fright and ghastly pale. And the others too were shocked and dismayed.

It then transpired that Little Clerk Sun had his beginning as a man who lay starving in the snow; and Big Clerk Sun, finding the good-looking youth in a dead faint, brought him back to life, and later taught him to read and write. But the Clerk could not foresee that illicit intimacy was to develop between the youth and his own wife. When Big Clerk Sun returned home that day after having his fortune told, it chanced that Little Clerk Sun was hiding in the house. Hearing how it was predicted the Clerk would die at the third watch, the pair of them seized their opportunity, plied him with drink, and that same night strangled Big Clerk Sun and threw his body into the well. Little Clerk Sun then hid his face with his hand and walked out of the house, and hurled a large stone into the Feng-fu river, so that there was a loud splash. And it was thought at the time that Big Clerk Sun had flung himself into the river and drowned. Afterwards, the pair of them erected the cooking-stove over the well. Still later came the marriage proposal and its acceptance.

The attendants duly made report to his Honour. Little Clerk Sun and the Clerk's lady both confessed freely, not a stroke having been administered, and the pair of them were sentenced to death in retribution of their murder of Big Clerk Sun. Keeping his faith even with the humblest people, Magistrate Pao gave a reward of ten ounces of silver to Wang Hsing, who gave three of the ten ounces to Under-Clerk P'ei. But this forms no part of our story. Because the worshipful Pao in his first magistracy decided this case, his fame was spread all over the Empire. Even today men still say, 'Lung-t'u' Pao adjudicated human affairs by day and infernal cases by night. There is a poem to prove it:

'The verses contained a riddle which none could guess;
But Judge Pao solved it, amazing even the spirits.
A word to you evil-minded in your darkest closet—
Never say Heaven's eye sees not through the heart of man.'

Madam White

The story, which has for its full title *Pai niang-tzu yung chen Lei-feng-t'a* ('Madam White forever confined under Thunder Peak Pagoda'), forms *chüan* 28 of the collection *Ching shih t'ung-yen*, which appeared in 1624, and would at the time be of fairly recent origin. Thunder Peak is described in T'ien Ju-ch'eng's *Guide to the West Lake*, (Preface, 1547) in chapter 3, 'Noteworthy Sights among the Southern Hills':

> Thunder Peak, an offshoot of Southern Screen Hill. Shaped like a vault, it reflected the evening sun. Its former name was Centre Peak, but it was also called Reflection Peak. In Sung times, the Taoist priest Hsü Li dwelt here and styled himself Taoist of Reflection Peak. It is also said that a certain [Taoist] Lei Chiu lived here and that the hill was hence further named Lei (Thunder) Peak. The Queen consort of Wu-yüeh[1] built a pagoda here, projecting at first a thirteen-tiered structure of a thousand feet; for lack of resources, however, she resigned herself to one of seven tiers. Later, upon the advice of geomancers, the pagoda was reduced to five tiers. It was popularly known as Wang-fei-t'a (Queen's Pagoda) and, by corruption, Huang-p'i-t'a on account of the yellow-skinned fruit (huang-p'i) produced in the vicinity. According to popular tradition, two monsters from the lake, a white snake and a green fish, were imprisoned under the pagoda.[2]

In the thirteenth century, as since, Thunder Peak and its Pagoda at sunset was considered one of the ten best views of Hang-chow.[3] But the *Guide to the West Lake* seems to be the first

[1] The King of Wu-yüeh reigned 907–31.
[2] *Hsi-hu yu-lan chih*, Chung-hua edition of 1958, c.3, pp.33–4. The Queen who built the pagoda bore, in fact, the surname Huang.
[3] See *Meng liang lu* (about 1275), c.12, and Wu-lin chiu-shih (before 1290), c.5, for brief accounts of Thunder Peak and its pagoda (in Ku-tien edition of *Tung-ching meng-hua lu*, p.230; p.410).

account to link Thunder Peak Pagoda with the White Snake.[1]

The story was in fact being told to audiences in Hangchow in T'ien Ju-ch'eng's time. In his *Supplement*[2] to the *Guide* devoted to local tradition and customs, we find a reference to the then current type of story-telling known as *t'ao-chen* (refining upon the truth) in which a blind story-teller accompanied himself—or herself—on the *p'i-p'a* (lute). Four titles of stories are given, 'being all of them about unusual occurrences in Hangchow and seemingly of recent composition in imitation of Sung Dynasty stories': 'Hung-lien and Lui Ts'ui'; 'Chi, the Mad Monk'; 'Thunder Peak Pagoda'; 'Double Fish Fan Pendant'. 'Hung-lien and Liu Ts'ui' was the story of 'The Monk Bright Moon redeems the girl Liu Ts'ui' in *Ku-chin hsiao-shuo* (about 1621), c. 29; it might have been told in two parts or even as two connected stories. Stories about Chi, the Mad Monk, were collected and expanded into a lengthy narrative by a Hangchow man, Wang Meng-chi, in 1668.[3] 'Double Fish Fan Pendant' was the story of 'K'ung Shu-fang and the Double Fish Pendant' printed by Hsiung Lung-feng about 1590–1600. 'Thunder Peak Pagoda' was no doubt our story, but still in the process of 'refining' and unlikely to have attained the form it assumes in the collection of 1624.

At about the time the *Guide to the West Lake* appeared, or shortly after, an earlier story, almost certainly the ultimate source of our story but quite unconnected with Thunder Peak Pagoda, was printed by Hung Pien in the series of sixty stories in six collections of two volumes each, now known as the *Ch'ing-p'ing-shan-t'ang hua-pen* texts.[4] In this earlier tale, 'Story of the Three Pagodas on the West Lake',[5] three monsters or rather, evil spirits, one of them a white snake, are imprisoned under three small pagodas standing in the middle of

[1] I am generally indebted, and also as specified in the notes, to the following studies on the White Snake story and its derivation: Huang Shang, 'Kuan-yü Pai-she-chuan', in *Hsi-hsiang-chi yü Pai-she-chuan*, 1953, pp. 36–63; A-ying, *Lei-feng-t'a ch'uan-ch'i hsü-lu*, Revised ed. 1960, pp. 1–88; Fu Hsi-hua, Introduction, *Pai-she-chuan chi*, 1955. In the main, however, I have used my own findings and formed my own hypotheses.

[2] *Hsi-hu yu-lan chih yü*, c. 20, Chung-hua edition of 1958, p. 368; the *Supplement* and the *Guide* were published simultaneously, the Preface being common to both.

[3] Sun K'ai-ti, *Chung-kuo t'ung-su hsiao-shuo shu-mu*, Revised ed. 1957, p. 174.

[4] See General Introduction, and 'The Shrew' *supra*.

[5] *Ch'ing-p'ing-shan-t'ang hua-pen*, ed. T'an Cheng-pi 1957, pp. 22–32.

the lake. These small pagodas had been destroyed (though since restored) and, in writing about them in his *Guide*, T'ien Ju-ch'eng seems unfamiliar with the tradition represented by this earlier story:

There were formerly the three pagodas in the lake and the 'Heart of Lake' island monastery; but these no longer exist. The three pagodas stood in the Outer Lake, jutting out of the water to form a triangle. In the Hung-chih reign [1488– 1505] of our great Ming Dynasty, one Yin Tzu-shu, Senior Assistant to the Provincial Judge, discharged his duties with the utmost rigour. At that time, the monks in Heart of Lake Monastery enjoyed the patronage of the eunuch who was the local military commander; presuming upon this, they allowed no official to enter the monastery to feast and carouse. Mr Yin was so enraged that he investigated the monks' secret misdeeds, destroyed the monastery and removed the pagodas. According to tradition, there are three pools of unfathomable depth in the lake, being known as the 'Three Pools of the Moon's Reflection', one of the ten best views of the West Lake. To confine the pools [i.e. to contain their geomantic influence], the three pagodas were erected.[1]

When the *Guide to the West Lake* was reissued by Shang Wei-jui in 1619, this paragraph was revised and much amplified.[2] By then, the monastery had been converted into Heart of Lake Pavilion; the three small pagodas, too, had been restored. Reference is made to the Series of Sixty Stories, in one of which, 'three monsters in the West Lake often came out to lead sight-seers astray and a priest therefore confined them under three pagodas which he built.' Various attempts to revive the Heart of Lake island as a beauty-spot are recorded, beginning with the building of a pavilion on the site of the monastery by the Prefect Sun in 1552, only five years after T'ien Ju-ch'eng's account: thereafter, the three pagodas and their monsters were again part of Hangchow lore.

If, as I shall try to show, our story of Madam White and Thunder Peak Pagoda was derived from the story of the three monsters, it was subsequent to the destruction of Heart of Lake Monastery and its three small pagodas in the last decade or so of the fifteenth century. For the story was not so much about monsters and their metamorphoses as about the West Lake

[1] *Hsi-hu yu-lan chih*, c. 2, p. 24. [2] *Hsi-hu yu-lan chih*, p. 309.

itself with its surrounding hills and temples, its embankments
lined with peach and willow trees, its carved pavilions and
painted bridges, its pleasure boats and sightseers, its changes
of season and the festivals they brought and, not least, its adjoining city of Hangchow, bursting with talent and buzzing
with tireless activity. In that world, with its beauty and variety,
no adventure would seem too fantastic, no transformation entirely unnatural; nevertheless, order and stability prevailed.
Thus the three stone pagodas rising calmly out of the water
symbolized the 'confining'[1] of the lake's dark and evil forces.
These pagodas, which would be visible from a large part of the
West Lake, were clearly a source of wonder and mystery to
visitors and local inhabitants alike as their boats glided past the
island monastery. The too rigorous Judge's Assistant, however,
destroyed a landmark and shattered a myth. Disappointed sight-
seers turned their gaze elsewhere and perhaps perceived afresh
the strange light effects at sunset on Thunder Peak and its
Pagoda at the edge of the water to the south. That towering
octagonal pagoda, too, evoked wonder;[2] massive and enduring,
it would 'confine' any malignant spirit, and the story-tellers
got busy.

But first, the original story. The hero was a young man in his
early twenties named Hsi, a court usher (*hsüan-tsan*), son of the
late Division Commander Hsi of Golden Flood Gate. It was
Ch'ing-ming, the Clear and Bright Festival, April 5th, when
amidst sunshine and showers the world renews itself, when
men and women pent up in the city visited the graves of the
dead and rediscovered the countryside, when ghosts and spirits
too were abroad. Hsi ventured from home to see the sights of the
lake. Outside the Temple of the Four Sages he came across a
little girl, dressed in white, who had lost her way. The girl was
called Dawn,[3] her surname was White. Hsi brought her home

---

[1] The word used in all accounts is *chen*, i.e. to guard, to repress.
[2] It caught the eye of Lord Macartney as he journeyed through Hangchow
in November 1793: 'On one side of the lake is a pagoda in ruins, which
forms a remarkably fine object. It is octagonal, built of fine hewn stone,
red and yellow, of four entire stories besides the top, which was mouldering
away from age. Very large trees were growing out of the cornices. It was
about two hundred feet high.' Macartney called it (erroneously) Tower
of the Thundering Winds and made a drawing of it; see J. L. Cranmer-
Byng (ed.) *An Embassy to China*, 1962, p. 179n. Thunder Peak Pagoda
crumbled in 1924.
[3] Mao-nu, Girl of the Hour of Dawn.

with him, taking a boat to Golden Flood Gate. A fortnight later, an old woman in black called at the door to collect Dawn and invited Hsi to their home near the Temple of the Four Sages, a small gatehouse, exquisitely decorated. There Hsi met the girl's mother, a woman of startling beauty, who thanked him for looking after Dawn. They sat down to a feast, Hsi growing more and more infatuated. Suddenly the woman commanded that her former lover be 'got ready for the wine'. A young man was brought forward, tied to a pillar and swiftly disembowelled, his heart being then dished up with the wine. The woman now offered to marry the terrified Hsi, who was detained there as her husband. A fortnight later, a new lover was announced and Hsi ordered to be 'got ready'. But Dawn begged that Hsi be spared for her sake, and a heavy iron cage was then flung over him. In the night, however, Dawn carried him on her back, flew across the lake and dropped him near his home.

Hsi and his mother decided that their house was obstructing the flow of the stream at Golden Flood Gate, for which reason they had incurred the displeasure of the spirits. They moved to another part of the city. A year later, it was again Ch'ing-ming. Hsi ventured out with a crossbow and shot a crow. The crow transformed itself into the old woman in black of the year before. She put Hsi in a flying chariot and again brought him to the gatehouse. But Dawn delivered him a second time. At this point, Hsi's uncle, a Taoist priest returning from the mountains to Hangchow, was surprised to find the family in their new home, whither he had been led by the foul air rising from that quarter. The next day, the priest-uncle set up a shrine at the Temple of the Four Sages, made Hsi swallow his charmed water, and chanting his spells, caused the deities to tame the three evil spirits, who turned out to be an otter (the old woman), a black hen (Dawn), and a white snake (Dawn's mother). They were now imprisoned in an iron box and cast into the middle of the lake. The priest then had the three pagodas built in the lake to 'confine' them.

The story begins with an elaborate introductory piece (*ju-hua*), including numerous poems, about the beauty of the West Lake, leading up to the young *hsüan-tsan* Hsi in the Southern Sung reign of Ch'un-hsi (1174–89), whose only delight was sightseeing, and whose visit to the lake at Ch'ing-ming caused a great stir. The supernatural elements stem for the most part from the T'ang and Sung *ch'uan-ch'i* tales in classical prose, with an admixture of popular beliefs and practices. They are conventional, and the story falls into the category of 'spirits and monsters' (*ling-kuai*). The narrative is interrupted at short intervals by descriptive verses, upon which the story-teller depends for his effects. The simple and direct manner, too, and the total disregard for verisimilitude indicate an early text, which, as suggested above, remained in the story-tellers' repertory down to the end of the fifteenth century.

'Madam White', on the other hand, represents story-telling already in a state of sophistication: thus prose has driven out verse, which becomes merely incidental; the narrative is cleverly contrived, the characters almost convincing; and the tone, down to earth and slightly vulgar, completes the identification with its popular audience. By its time, too, story-tellers have become eclectic and follow more than one school.[1] From such categories[1] as *ling-kuai* (spirits and monsters), *yen-fen* (love stories involving female spirits), *kung-an* (crime and law courts), and from the sutra recitations, many diverse elements are blended together in a rather long love story developing on its own lines, as indeed claimed by its author (or, though it seems less likely, authors):

An ingenious writer took up his pen

And wove it all into a new love story.

(In the original, 'love story' is *feng-liu hua-pen*, not one of the established categories of story-telling.) The very reference to an author, even if anonymous, is itself something of a new departure. Even without the support of external evidence, one may conclude that the story as composed by our 'ingenious writer' dates from no earlier than the latter half of the sixteenth century.

In 'Madame White', the hero is no longer Hsi, the Court Usher (*hsüan-tsan*), but plain Hsü Hsüan, shopkeeper, part of his title *hsüan-tsan* having been transferred to his name. Of the two surnames also, Hsi and Hsü, Hsü is by far the commoner. The hero's father was no Division Commander as in the earlier story, but only a herbalist, though the military connection is maintained in a brother-in-law, an officer in the Army Treasury. Madam White herself no longer devours her lovers; still

[1] See General Introduction.

posing as a widow, she has become most proper and respectable, being suitably accompanied by a servant girl dressed in
green (a green fish). As with the earlier story, however, she
is installed every time in an attic. (Chinese snakes love an
attic.) A stretch of the embankment associated with Po Chü-i
—outside the Temple of the Four Sages near the Broken
Bridge—is still the scene of the hero's first encounter with the
evil spirits; only, Madam White appears at once and herself
takes the boat with him to Golden Flood Gate. The atmosphere of Ch'ing-ming Festival survives from the earlier story,
but the urge to re-unite himself with the fields and hills that
Spring means to the Chinese has given way to a vague religious yearning in the hero, who hearkens to the call of Festival
after Festival in monastery after monastery. This religious
theme, though present throughout, is treated no more than
perfunctorily. Faith, however, has been transferred from
Taoism to Buddhism (this, too, may bear upon the dates of
both stories), and the Taoist priest is no longer an uncle, but
yields in supernatural power to the Buddhist monk, Law
Boundless (Fa-hai, Sea of Law), Abbot of Golden Mountain
Monastery, who becomes one of the protagonists.

Golden Mountain Monastery and its abbot represent
another tradition, the averting of a flood, which could not
originally have been related to the White Snake, though in
later versions of the story they have come to occupy almost a
central position. Golden Mountain was an island in the Yangtze
river, two miles to the north-west of Chinkiang, two hundred
miles from Hangchow by boat along the Grand Canal. (Through
silting, the island is now joined to the south bank of the Yangtze.) It would appear that in 1539, in the seventh month (i.e.
August), possibly under the impact of a violent windstorm, the
Yangtze shifted its channel, receding sharply from Golden
Mountain Island and the south bank, and flooding the north
bank and, through the Grand Canal, the city of Yangchow,
drowning hundreds. Certainly Lang Ying (1487–after 1566)
records such an event in his collected notes, *Ch'i-hsiu lei-kao*,
and regards it as a repetition of the flooding of the north bank
of A.D. 726:

> In the seventh month of the 18th year of the Chia-ching
> reign [i.e. 1539], scores of salt-works in Yangchow were
> flooded, countless people died. That day also, the water of the

Yangtze receded several hundred feet, so that the foot of Golden Mountain become visible. Some days later, I learned that the flooding in Yangchow had occurred on the very day that Yangtze's bed ran dry. I only then realized that the wind had carried the water to Yangchow. To recall a previous occurrence, it is recorded in T'ang history that in the 14th year of the K'ai-yüan reign [i.e. 713] a great wind at Jun-chou [Chinkiang] swept across Golden Mountain island carrying the water of the Yangtze with it, thus flooding Kua-pu [on the north bank], but that a few days later the river regained its tranquil flow. Present events have borne out the veracity of the old account.[1]

This was the stuff of legend. As the seat of a monastery, Golden Mountain was a sanctuary invaded by the wind and waves, which conjured up—it could only be—by some angry water spirit, threatened to swallow halls of worship, monks, pilgrims and all. Suddenly, however, the waves were seen to halt and recede, beaten back—it would certainly be—by a monk of immense spiritual power. Thwarted, the evil spirit vented its wrath upon the other bank of the river, whither the receding waves rushed, drowning numberless innocent men and women, its sins thus crying out for greater retribution. For the story-tellers, the opportunity was not to be missed. Madam White strayed further, but her wicked machinations were checked by a Sea of Law: Golden Mountain now became an extension of the story of the White Snake, who rapidly assumed cosmic dimensions.

In different cities, no doubt, they told the story differently. In Yanchow or Nanking, or Chinkiang itself, the threat to Golden Mountain would seem real enough, and the White Snake all the more iniquitous for being an intruder. In Hang-chow, Golden Mountain was remote; it would be a mere episode, marking the entry of the monk, which is the beginning of the end for the White Snake. For all that, we duly find in our story of 'Madam White' the hero visiting Golden Mountain Monastery on the seventh of the seventh month and high winds and choppy waves on the Yangtze—but no flooding of the monastery nor the drowning of thousands. That these were intentional omissions we may gather from the dark hints, threats and warnings thrown out in the conversation in the

[1] *Ch'i-hsiu lei-kao*, c. 2 'Heaven and Earth', Chung-hua ed. of 1959, p. 44.

story. For our 'ingenious writer' was interested not in abstract evil but in the fortunes of a Hangchow woman, even if only a snake in disguise, and as Madam White grows tamer under his hands, so her eventual punishment—imprisonment under a pagoda 'so solid and enduring that, for thousands of years to come, the White Snake and the Green Fish would be prevented from afflicting the world'—becomes inexplicably harsh and utterly ridiculous.

Not that in other versions[1] the White Snake receives less than her due in sympathy. Two in prose, *Lei-feng kuai chi* ('Monster of Thunder Peak') in *Hsi-hu chia-hua* (1673) and *Chen yao ch'i-ts'eng chien pao-t'a* ('Building a Seven-tiered Pagoda to confine an Evil Spirit') in *Hsi-hu shih-i* (1791), simply re-tell the story of 'Madam White'.[2] A play from the first half of the seventeenth century being now lost,[3] the earliest surviving play on the subject, *Lei-feng t'a ch'uan-ch'i* ('Thunder Peak Pagoda') (1738) in 32 scenes by Huang T'u-pi, begins with a Prologue in Heaven and adds such paraphernalia as deities and a host of water spirits, but is otherwise entirely based on our story, to which it adheres very closely.[4] Two slightly later plays of the same title, similar to each other in content, one in 38 scenes in an anonymous manuscript, the other in 34 scenes by Fang Ch'eng-p'ei (1771), incorporate many changes.[5] The servant girl, Emerald, is no longer a fish, but a green snake. In a scene entitled 'Water Battle' (scene 25

[1] A large number of texts, representing various styles of singing and recitation of the north as well as the south, and also the plays by Huang and Fang are collected together in Fu Hsi-hua, *Pai-she-chuan chi*, 1955.
[2] See Huang Shang, *Hsi-hsiang-chi yü Pai-she-chuan*, 1953, pp. 38–40.
[3] The lost play, *Lei-feng* by Ch'en Liu-lung, is recorded by Ch'i Piao-chia (1602–1645) in his manuscript 'Notes on Plays'. See Huang Shang (ed.) *Yüan-shan-t'ang Ming ch'ü-p'in chü-pin chiao-lu*, 1955, p. 122.
[4] Huang's play is reprinted in *Pai-she-chuan chi*, pp. 281–338.
[5] Fang's play is reprinted in *Pai-she-chuan chi*, pp. 339–419, though without the original notes and comments, including the author's own. For the manuscript play, not so far reprinted, I have relied on the scene by scene account of all three plays on pp. 1–58 of A-ying, *Lei-feng-t'a ch'uan-ch'i hsü-lu*, revised edition 1960, in which two scenes of the manuscript play are also reprinted, one of them the 'Water Battle', with parallel texts of the songs from other versions, pp. 59–88. In his Preface, Fang states that his play is an extensive revision of an actor's text, to which he has made additions and excisions, resulting in changes in nine tenths of the songs and seven tenths of the dialogue; the alterations being noted at the end of each scene. From the information supplied by A-ying, the manuscript play seems essentially similar to (though not identical with) the 'actors' text' used by Fang.

of Fang's, scene 27 of the manuscript play) Madam White
commands her followers to raise a flood and inundate Golden
Mountain, sparing only Hsü Hsüan, and this is represented by
the water spirits storming the monastery hall. But the Abbot
covers the mountain peak with his cassock and the flood water
then recedes with its brood of lobsters, crabs, oysters and
tortoises.[1] In one text (presumably incorporating later additions),[2] the Abbot warns Madam White of the consequences of
her wantonly destroying a million lives. From these eighteenth-century plays—intended mainly for performance by
the K'un-shan school of the Southern Drama[3]—the White
Snake has passed into the repertory of the Peking opera of
today, of which the 'Flooding of Golden Mountain Monastery'
is a highlight.

But the story was being told in various styles of singing and
recitation all over China. Preserved texts, mostly from the
nineteenth century, refer to traditions not recorded in our
story, e.g. a certain Seven Star Taoist (Ch'i-hsing tao-jen) who
perished by the sword because of his part in the flooding of
Soochow.[4] Or the flood had occurred in Chinkiang;[5] or it was
in Hangchow, and caused by the Green Snake.[6] But a flood
there was, and countless innocent people died, and Madam
White and Emerald thus incurred the wrath of heaven.[7] The
demands of audiences did not stop here. The Abbot becomes
increasingly inquisitorial, and Madam White, in spite of the
devastation she causes, the tender and devoted wife. On the
fifth of the fifth month, the Dragon Boat Festival, Hsü Hsüan
(who in later versions becomes Hsü Hsien, Hsü Immortal)
offers Madam White the customary drink of orpiment dissolved
in spirit, valued for its antispetic properties and specifically as
an antidote against snake and insect poison. Overpowered by
the drink, Madam White reveals her true shape, and the shock
of this discovery sends Hsü Hsüan into a dead faint. Thereupon
Madam White makes a sally into heaven in quest of an elixir
to revive him. (The much vaunted orpiment was of no effect in
our story.) For her devotion, Madam White is rewarded with

[1] *Pai-she-chuan chi*, pp. 395–400; *Lei-feng-t'a ch'uan-ch'i hsü-lu*, pp. 59–71.
[2] *Lei-feng-t'a ch'uan-ch'i hsü-lu*, p. 70.
[3] See General Introduction, and 'The Peony Pavilion' *infra*.
[4] *Pai-she-chuan chi*, p. 14; pp. 10, 12, 15.   [5] *Pai-she-chuan chi*, pp. 3, 4.
[6] *Pai-she-chuan chi*, p. 13.   [7] *Pai-she-chuan chi*, pp. 3, 4, 11, 13, 15.

a son, who redeems her after over twenty years and releases her from confinement under Thunder Peak Pagoda.

There were further ramifications. But we have introduced our story, which must now speak for itself.

Madam White

Hill upon verdant hill, tower rising above tower—
The West Lake rings with song and dance unending.
The sightseers, intoxicated by the sweet warm breezes,
Willingly pretend Hangchow was the Empire's former capital.[1]

The story goes that the scenery of Hangchow was noted for its
clear hills and streams. In the Hsien-ho reign[2] of the Tsin
dynasty, the mountain streams were swollen and, coming
down in torrents, flooded the West Gate. In the flood was
seen a buffalo, and it was golden all over. When later the water
receded, the buffalo followed it as far as the northern hills,[3] and
was then no longer seen. This caused a commotion among the
people at the market-place of Hangchow, who looked upon it
as a miracle, which to commemorate, they built a monastery
and named it Golden Buffalo Monastery. And at the West
Gate, which is nowadays Golden Flood Gate, they erected a
temple to the Martial God of Golden Glory.[4] At that time also,
there was a foreign monk with the Buddhist name Hun-shou-
lo,[5] who arriving at this prefecture of Wu-lin[6] in his wanderings, gazed at the hills and cried: 'The little peak before Divine

[1] According to *Hsi-hu yu-lan chih yü*, c. 2, p. 14, the poem is by Lin Sheng of
the Southern Sung; elsewhere, e.g. in *Ku-chin t'u-shu chi-ch'eng*, VII. 290,
it is attributed to Lin Hung of Southern Sung. For the Empire's former
capital, i.e. Pien or Kaifeng, see General Introduction.
[2] A.D. 326–334.
[3] The Northern Hills of Hangchow, which were reached from the West
Gate, included Ling-yin (Spirit-in-hiding) Hill and Divine Vulture
Rock. See *Hsi-hu yu-lan chih*, cc. 8–11.
[4] Martial God of Golden Glory, i.e. apotheosis of the golden buffalo. The
temple was inside Golden Flood Gate, but *Hsi-hu yu-lan chih* c. 16, p. 220,
associates the gate and temple with Ts'ao Kao, who served under the King
of Wu-yüeh, in the tenth century (also c. 13, p. 171), and states that the
golden buffalo was seen in the Han dynasty (c. 1, p. 1).
[5] The monk Hui-li (Wise Reason). See *Wu-lin chiu shih* c. 5 (Ku-tien, p.
436); *Hsi-hu yu-lan chih*, cc. 10, 11 (pp. 125, 137, 139, 140).
[6] One of the ancient names of Hangchow, not in fact a prefecture.

Vulture Mountain,[1] the one that suddenly disappeared—here it is again! It could only have been borne here on wings!' Since, however, the people of the time were incredulous, the monk went on: 'I clearly remember the peak standing before Divine Vulture Mountain as Divine Vulture Rock, on which a white monkey dwelt in a cave. I can prove it, See how the monkey will come at my call.' And, indeed, the white monkey appeared in answer to his call! There was a pavilion before this hill, now called Cold Stream Pavilion.[2] There was also Solitary Hill,[3] standing in the middle of the West Lake, where the poet Lin Fu had his retreat.[4] He employed men to move mud and stones, and built a footway joining the island with the Broken Bridge[5] to its east and with Sunset Peak[6] to its west, and it was then called Solitary Hill Road. And in the T'ang dynasty, the Prefect Po Chü-i built a raised road linking Jade Screen Hill in the south and Sunset Peak in the north, and it was called the Po Causeway.[7] But the onrushing mountain streams often breached it, and on more than one occasion it had to be repaired with government funds. Then, in the Sung dynasty, Su Tung-p'o[8] became Prefect and, when he saw that both causeways had been damaged by water, he purchased wood and stones, hired labour, and had the embankments thoroughly repaired and

[1] Divine Vulture Mountain, i.e. Gridhrakuta mountain, where the Buddha preached. See, e.g., H. Kern (tr.), *The Saddharma-pundarika* or The Lotus of the True Law, 1884, p. 1. The rock in Hangchow which the monk Hui-li named after the Indian peak was near Ling-yin Hill and also known as 'Peak borne on Wings' (Fei-lai feng). The cave in which Hui-li kept a white monkey was on the west face of the rock. See *Hsu-hi yu-lan chih*, cc. 10, 11 (pp. 125, 137, 139–40).
[2] Cold Stream Pavilion and Cold Stream had associations with both Po Chü-i and Su Tung-p'o. See *Hsi-hu yu-lan chih*, c. 10, pp. 128–9.
[3] Ku-shan, a solitary rock in the lake. See *Hsi-hu yu-lan chih*, c. 2, pp. 9–20.
[4] Lin Fu (967–1028), poet and recluse of the Sung dynasty. Having spent part of his youth in travelling, he made Solitary Hill his home and, for twenty years, never set foot in the city of Hangchow. See *Sung shih*, c. 457, pp. 9a–b; *Hsi-hu yu-lan chih*, cc. 2, 8 (pp. 11–13, 139–40). Lin Fu was too poor to build a causeway and too much of a hermit to need one.
[5] The Broken Bridge acquired its name as early as T'ang times. See *Hsi-hu yu-lan chih*, c. 2, p. 9.
[6] Ch'i hsia ling, noted for its peach blossoms which gave the effect of clouds at sunset. See *Hsi-hu yu-lan chih*, c. 9, p. 110.
[7] Po Chü-i (772–846), Prefect of Hangchow 822–4; see Arthur Waley, *The Life and Times of Po Chü-i*, 1949, pp. 147–57, for an account of Hangchow in the ninth century.
[8] Su Tung-p'o (1036–1101), Prefect of Hangchow 1089–91; see Lin Yutang, *The Gay Genius. The Life and Times of Su Tung-p'o*, 1948, chapter 22, on Su and Hangchow of the 11th century.

strengthened. He had the balustrades on all the six bridges of the Solitary Hill Road [1] painted vermilion, and the embankment itself planted with peach and willow trees, so that in the warmth of springtime the view was exceedingly lovely, worthy of the brush of a landscape painter. Thus people came to call it the Su Causeway. And at each end of the causeway, they built a stone bridge to divert the current, the one at the eastern end being called the Broken Bridge and the one at the western end, Western Calm Bridge. [2] Indeed it was:

> Secretly, those hills enwrap three thousand monasteries;
> Darkly, the clouds hold their twin peaks [3] captive.

Your story-teller has told of the scenery of the West Lake and its associations with the worthies of the past. Today, however, I will tell about a handsome youth, who only because he went sightseeing on the West Lake and met two women, brought about that:

> In several provincial cities,
> Streets lined with flowering trees and willows
>   rocked with sensation:
> An ingenious writer took up his pen
> And wove it all into a new love story.

Let me tell about the young man, what his surname and name were, what sort of women he met, what sensational events ensued. For there is a poem which bears out our story:

> 'The showers at Ch'ing-ming, the showers do fall!
> Travellers forget their haste, lost in reverie.
> You and I will inquire for the nearest tavern—
> Where apricots are in blossom,
>   the buffalo boy points to a village.' [4]

The story goes that in the Shao-hsing reign [5] of the Sung

---

[1] 'of the Solitary Hill Road' is my insertion. The Six Bridges were ornate structures containing temples and memorial halls. See *Hsi-hu yu-lan chih*, c. 2, pp. 20–22.

[2] Hsi ning ch'iao. *Meng liang lu*, c. 12 (Ku-tien, p. 227) gives 'Western Woods Bridge' (Hsi lin ch'iao) and also 'Western Cold Bridge' (Hsi leng ch'iao), as does also *Hsi-hu yu-lan chih*, c. 2, p. 20.

[3] North Peak and South Peak. See *Hsi-hu yu-lan chih*, cc. 3, 10 (pp. 39–40, 131).

[4] Ch'ing-ming Festival: April 5th, when the ancestors' graves are swept. The poem, entitled 'Ch'ing-ming', is by Tu Mu (803–52); see *Hou-ts'un ch'ien-chia shih*, c. 3, pp. 7ᵃ–7ᵇ, in *Chien-t'ing ts'ang-shu shih-erh-chung*, facsimile reprint of 1921.

[5] A.D. 1131–62. The removal of the court to Hangchow is alluded to in the introductory poem.

dynasty, which was after the removal of the Emperor Kao-tsung
and his court to the south, there lived in Lin-an-fu, in Hangchow, in Black Pearl Lane by Army Bridge, an official named
Li Jen. He was a levy officer in the Treasury of the Army Administration, and was further in charge of the Grand Marshal's
land-taxes. Li had a wife, and she had a younger brother, Hsü
Hsüan, who being the oldest son, was called Little Eldest.
Their father had been a dealer in medicinal herbs, but both the
parents had died in Hsü Hsüan's childhood, and, at the age of
twenty-two, he served as overseer in the herbalist's shop of a
cousin, Squire Li. The herbalist's shop stood at the corner of
Officials Lane, and one day, as Hsü Hsüan was attending to his
customers, a monk stopped in front of the shop, held the palms
of his hands together in salute, and said: 'I am a monk from
Pao-shu Pagoda Monastery.[1] The other day I sent some
dumplings and steamed bread to your house. Ch'ing-ming
Festival is upon us, time to pray for the ancestors. We expect
you without fail, Master Little Eldest, to burn incense at the
monastery.' Hsü Hsüan replied: 'I will be there.' And the monk
took his leave.

At night, Hsü Hsüan returned to his brother-in-law's
house. For he had not yet taken a wife and was living with his
sister. That night, he said to his sister, 'A monk from Pao-shu
Pagoda Monastery came to the shop today to invite me to burn
a few straw bags of paper offerings. I will go there tomorrow
to say prayers for the ancestors.' The next day he rose early,
bought the requisite items of paper images of deities, wax
candles, paper streamers and reams of paper cash, had his
breakfast, changed into new socks and shoes and new clothes,
tied up the straw bags, paper cash, images and the rest with a
square of cloth, and went straight to the house of Squire Li at
Officials Lane Corner. Squire Li looked at Hsü Hsüan and
asked where he was going. Hsü Hsüan said, 'I have to go to
Pao-shu Pagoda today to burn paper offerings and pray for my
ancestors. I beg my uncle to allow me a day's leave.' So Squire
Li said, 'Don't tarry, but return when you have been.'

Hsü Hsüan left the shop, passed through Shou-an Lane[2] and

[1] Pao-shu Pagoda: originally known as Pao-so (Where Treasure is)
Pagoda. See *Hsi-hu yu-lan chih*, c. 8, pp. 96–7.
[2] Shou-an Lane, Flower Market Street, and Officials Lane were the same
street. *Hsi-hu yu-lan chih*, c. 13, p. 181.

Flower Market Street, crossed Pavilioned Well Bridge,[1] and made for Ch'ien-t'ang Gate[2] behind Clear River Street. Presently he crossed Stone Receptacle Bridge,[3] went past the Reprieved Creatures Tablet,[4] and reached Pao-shu Pagoda Monastery. He sought out the monk who had sent him the dumplings, did repentance by writing out a prayer on paper which he then held over the candle flames, stuffed the straw bags with his offerings, and burned them. He then went to the main hall to watch the monks chanting their sutras, partook of the refection and, bidding his friend the monk farewell, came out of the monastery. He walked with unhurried steps along Western Calm Bridge, Solitary Hill Road and the Temple of the Four Sages,[5] intending to pay a visit to the tomb of Lin Fu and linger near the Six-in-Unity Fountain.[6] But he was overtaken by the clouds that gathered in the north-west and the mists that sealed off the south-east. A drizzle came down, the drops soon thickening. It was indeed Ch'ing-ming time, and the saying rang true, to hasten the flowers the heavens sent rain ; and the rain fell unceasingly.

When Hsü Hsüan found that the ground was wet, he took off his new shoes[7] and socks, and walked barefoot from the Temple of the Four Sages to look for a boat. None was in sight. Just as he was growing anxious, he noticed an old ferryman approaching with his boat. Secretly rejoicing and recognizing the ferryman as Grandfather Chang, Hsü Hsüan shouted : 'Grandfather Chang, ferry me across!' The old man heard the shout and,

[1] Pavilioned Well Bridge stood at the west end of Shou-an Lane. *Hsi-hu yu-lan chih*, c. 13, p. 189.
[2] One of Hangchow's city gates. *Hsi-hu yu-lan chih*, c. 20, p. 252.
[3] Stone Receptacle Bridge : the 'Stone Receptacle' was part of a dam used for irrigation. *Hsi-hu yu-lan chih*, c. 8, p. 94.
[4] Reprieved Creatures Tablet : for a time in the Sung, the West Lake was a sanctuary for birds, fish and other creatures reprieved from the kitchen knife. *Hsi-hu yu-lan chih*, c. 8, p. 94.
[5] The 'Four Sages' : Li Mi (722–89), Po Chü-i, Su Tung-p'o, who were Governors, and Lin Fu. Lin Fu was buried on Solitary Hill. *Hsi-hu yu-lan chih*, c. 2, pp. 11–12.
[6] The fountain was named after Ou-yang Hsiu (1007–72), who in his old age styled himself 'Six-in-Unity Recluse'. Of the 'six', five were : his ten thousand volumes of books ; his thousand rolls of rubbings of ancient inscriptions ; his guitar ; his game of chess ; his jar of wine. Ou-yang himself formed the sixth. 'For an old man like me to end my days amidst five such things, is it not a case of Six-in-Unity ?' See his autobiographical essay *Liu-i chü-shih chuan*, in *Ou-yang Wen-chung ch'üan-chi*, Ssu-pu pei-yao edition, c. 44, pp. 4b–5a ; and *Hsi-hu yu-lan chih*, c. 2, pp. 15–16.
[7] The shoes, made of stiffened cloth, gave no protection against the rain.

taking a good look, saw that it was Hsü Little Eldest. So he brought the boat alongside the embankment and said, 'Master Little Eldest, you're caught in the rain! Where do you wish to be set ashore?' Hsü Hsüah replied, 'At Golden Flood Gate.' The old boatman then helped Hsü Hsüan on to his boat, pushed off, and started rowing towards Harvest Joy Tower.[1] They had not travelled a hundred feet on the water, when someone shouted from the embankment: 'Old uncle! Take a passenger!' Hsü Hsüan looked, and it was a woman, her raven hair curled up as in mourning and adorned by a white hairpin and comb, and wearing a jacket of plain white silk and a flax skirt. Standing beside her and reaching up to her shoulder, was a servant girl dressed in green, her hair tied up in two horn-like tufts, topped by two scarlet ribbons kept in place by two ornamental pins, and holding up a bundle in both hands as if waiting for a boat.

Old Chang said to Master Little Eldest: ' "Take one, take the lot." I might as well ferry them too.' Hsü Hsüan said, 'Ask them to come down then.' When the old man found Hsü Hsüan not averse to the arrangement, he again brought the boat alongside, and the woman and her servant girl stepped into the boat. When the woman saw Hsü Hsüan, her lips parted in a smile, revealing two rows of snow-white teeth, and she came forward and made her bow. Hsü Hsüan hurriedly got up to return the bow. The woman and her maid then sat down in the cabin. The woman kept rolling her eyes, fixing their gaze upon Hsü Hsüan. Now Hsü Hsüan was an innocent young man and when he saw this flower-like, jade-like, beautiful woman, accompanied by her equally elegant, pretty maidservant, he could not help becoming infatuated. The woman spoke. 'Dare I ask the gentleman his honoured surname and name?' Hsü Hsüan replied: 'My surname is Hsü, my name Hsüan. I am the family's oldest son.' The woman then asked: 'Where does the gentleman reside?' Hsü Hsüan said, 'I live in Black Pearl Lane by Army Bridge, and ply my trade at a herbalist's.' When the woman had asked all her questions, Hsü Hsüan thought to himself: 'It's my turn to question her.' And standing up and bowing, he said, 'Dare I ask the lady's honoured surname and residence?' The woman replied: 'I am the younger sister of Court Attendant White. I was married to Master Chang, who is—

[1] Harvest Joy Tower was at Golden Flood Gate. *Hsi-hu yu-lan chih*, c. 3, p. 25.

alas!—dead and buried on Thunder Peak.[1] It is almost Ch'ing-ming, and I brought my maid with me today to sweep the grave and give sacrifice. Coming back, we were surprised by the rain and should have been sorely distressed if the gentleman's boat had not stopped for us.'

They chatted on for a while, and soon the boat drew near the shore. The woman said, 'I left the house in a great hurry and took no money with me. Would the gentleman kindly lend me the fare? Be assured that I will repay it.' Hsü Hsüan said, 'Why worry about that, Madam? The fare is such a trifle, not worth mentioning.' The fares having been tendered and the rain still coming down heavily, Hsü Hsüan took the woman's hand and led her ashore. The woman said, 'I live at the corner of Two Tea-houses Lane by Arrow Bridge.[2] If you deign to come with me, Sir, I shall offer you some tea and refund you the fare.' Hsü Hsüan said, 'Why trouble about a little thing like that? It is getting late. I will call another day.' They stopped conversing, and the woman and her servant girl went off by themselves.

Hsü Hsüan entered the city through Golden Flood Gate and walked under the eaves of the houses as far as Three Bridges Street,[3] and there saw the herbalist's shop belonging to Squire Li's younger brother. The younger squire was standing at the door as Hsü Hsüan went past. The younger squire called out: 'It's late, Master Little Eldest. Where are you going?' Hsü Hsüan said, 'I was at Pao-shu Pagoda to burn a few bags of paper offerings, and am now caught in the rain. May I borrow an umbrella?' When the younger squire heard this, he shouted to someone within: 'Bring an umbrella for Master Little Eldest, old Ch'en!' Presently old Ch'en came out with an umbrella and, as he opened it, he said, 'Here's one made by the honest Shu family of Clear Lake Character of Eight Bridges,[4] Master Little Eldest. A good umbrella with eighty-four ribs and a stick of purple bamboo, and not a single tear! Take it now and don't break it! Be sure to handle it with great care! With

[1] Thunder Peak, to the south of the Lake, was the site of the famous pagoda. See Introduction.
[2] Arrow Bridge: Madam White's part of the city seems not to be mentioned in *Hsi-hu yu-lan chih*.
[3] Three Bridges Street: *Hsi-hu yu-lan chih*, cc. 13, 14 (pp. 188, 195).
[4] 'Clear Lake' was one of two bridges which together formed the character 'eight', the other bridge being 'Washing Bran'. See *Hsi-hu yu-lan chih*, c. 13, p. 194. Umbrellas were made of oiled-paper.

great care!' Hsü Hsüan said reassuringly, 'That goes without
saying.' He took the umbrella, thanked the younger squire, and
walked towards Sheep Quay.[1]

When he reached the corner of Rear Market Street Lane,[2]
he heard someone calling, 'Master Little Eldest!' Hsü Hsüan
turned round, and there was a woman standing under the eaves
of the little tea-house at the top of Prefect Shen's Well Lane[3]
whom he recognized as the Madam White on the boat. Hsü
Hsüan exclaimed: 'Why are you here, Madam?' Madam
White said, 'The rain would not stop and my shoes were wet
through. So I sent Emerald home to fetch an umbrella and
proper foot-gear. And now, seeing it's already dusk, would
you, Sir, allow me to share your umbrella part of the way?' So
Hsü Hsüan and Madam White walked together under his
umbrella as far as the quay, where he stopped and asked,
'Which way are you going, Madam?' Madam White replied:
'Over the bridge here, in the direction of Arrow Bridge.' Hsü
Hsüan then said, 'Madam, I am going towards Army Bridge.
It's not far. You had better take the umbrella. I will come and
fetch it tomorrow.' Madam White cried: 'But this is really too
good of you, Sir! How could I thank you enough?' So Hsü
Hsüan braved the rain and walked under the eaves of the
houses until he reached home. At the gate, he found his brother-
in-law's orderly, Wang An, who had tried without success to
meet him with an umbrella and a pair of nailed boots, turning
back into the house. Hsü Hsüan, too, entered the house and had
his supper. That night, he thought of the woman, and he
turned and tossed and could not sleep. Then he happened to
dream, and she was with him as in the day, and they were en-
amoured of each other. But the cock crowed at that moment,
and the dream was at an end. It was even:

As restless fancy soars and glides, prompted by the eager heart,
So butterflies flutter and bees buzz

                        in that precious hour before dawn.
Hsü Hsüan waited until it was dawn and then got up, combed
and washed, had his breakfast, and went to the shop. He felt
restless and confused, and could hardly keep his mind on the

[1] In *Hsi-hu yu-lan chih*, c. 13, p. 187, this is given as 'Ocean Quay'. It was
served by a canal.
[2] Rear Market Street. *Hsi-hu yu-lan chih*, c. 13, p. 187.
[3] Named after the well dug during Prefect Shen Wen-t'ung's term of office,
in the Sung. *Hs-hui yu-lan chih*, c. 13, p. 187.

day's business. When it was past the noon hour, he thought to himself: 'Unless I told a lie, I could never fetch that umbrella and give it back.' Finding old Squire Li seated at the counter, Hsü Hsüan went up and said, 'My brother-in-law wants me back early today. I am to deliver a present for him. Begging for half-a-day's leave, Uncle.' Squire Li said, 'If you have to be away, come back early tomorrow.' So Hsü Hsüan made a bow, and left at once for the corner of Two Tea-houses Lane by Arrow Bridge, where he inquired for the house of Madam White. He inquired a good long while, but no one knew her. While he paused, irresolute, he saw Madam White's servant girl, Emerald, coming towards him from the east side of the street. Hsü Hsüan hailed her. 'Miss, where is your house? I have come for my umbrella.' Emerald said simply: 'Follow me, Sir.' So Hsü Hsüan followed Emerald, who, after a short distance, announced: 'Here it is!'

Hsü Hsüan looked up. It was a two-storeyed house with a double gate overhung by a fine vermilion bamboo curtain, flanked by four narrow lattice windows, through which he could see a dozen black lacquer armchairs neatly arranged in a room, on the walls of which were four landscapes by old masters.[1] The gate faced the wall of Prince Hsiu's palace.[2] The girl went behind the bamboo curtain, saying, 'Come inside and sit down, Sir.' Hsü Hsüan followed her into the house. Emerald announced the visitor in almost a whisper: 'Madam, Master Hsü Little Eldest is here!' From within came Madam White's voice: 'Ask the gentleman to come in here to have tea.' Hsü Hsüan was full of scruples, and Emerald had to urge him three or five times to go in. At last, he followed her: a dark cloth curtain she now lifted revealed a partition, the recess dimly lit by four closely-intersticed lattice windows. A pot of 'tiger-whiskers' calamus stood on the table. On the walls were hung four pictures of ladies, two on either side, and in the centre, the picture of a deity. On another table was a flower-vase shaped like a bronze censer.

Madam White came forward and gave a deep bow. She began: 'How very kind of you, Master Little Eldest, to look

---

[1] 'through which he could see' is my addition. In English, it is difficult to be simultaneously outside and inside the house.

[2] Prince Hsiu, whose son Hsiao-tsung succeeded Kao-tsung on the Southern Sung throne, and reigned 1162–89; see *Sung shih*, c. 33, p. 1ᵃ.

after me so well yesterday evening! And it was our first meeting too! I am most grateful.' Hsü Hsüan stammered: 'It was nothing, nothing to speak of.' Madam White said, 'Do sit down and have some tea.' And when tea was done, she said, 'I have prepared a few seasonable delicacies and half a measure of thin wine—it is only a little something to show my heartfelt thanks.' Hsü Hsüan made ready to excuse himself, but Emerald was already bringing in a stream of delicacies and fruits, which she proceeded to lay out. So Hsü Hsüan said, 'I do thank you, Madam, for preparing the wine and food. I did not expect such hospitality.' After a few cups, Hsü Hsüan rose and said, 'It is growing dark, and I have a long way to go. I will take my leave now.' Madam White interrupted him. 'Oh, your umbrella, Sir —I lent it to a relative last night. Have a few more cups while I send for it.' Hsü Hsüan cried: 'It's late! I must go back.' Madam White went on: 'Have one more cup then.' Hsü Hsüan said, 'I've had my fill of food and drink. Thank you very much! Thank you very much!' And Madam White concluded: 'If you must go, Sir, please return tomorrow for the umbrella.' Hsü Hsüan could only make his bow and depart.

The next day, he was back at the shop to attend to his customers. Again he gave an excuse and hurried off to Madam White's to fetch his umbrella. Madam White received him, and again she prepared food and wine. Hsü Hsüan almost screamed: 'Let me have my umbrella, Madam. I won't put you to further trouble.' But the lady said, 'Since it's already laid out, do have a cup!' And Hsü Hsüan sat down. Madam White poured out a cup of wine and, as she handed it to him, she parted her cherry lips and showed her pomegranate-seed teeth, while her sweet tremulous voice, accompanied by the balmiest of smiles, intoned: 'Oh, my young gentleman! Before a true man like you, I will not dissemble. I have lost my husband, and it must be that I was pre-destined to be united with you. Else how could I, who am so unworthy, have won your love at first-sight? Surely 'tis a case of " two yearning hearts"! Please, my Master Little Eldest, find a go-between and we shall be wedded. Not in vain, then, shall we have been born a handsome pair. Ought it not be so?'

When Hsü Hsüan had heard her out, he thought to himself: 'Yes, indeed, what a good match! It would really be something to marry such a woman. Of course I am only too willing. But one thing is amiss. Just consider. In the day I work as overseer at Squire Li's; at night I go back to my brother-in-law's, to sleep there. I have laid by something, but it is sufficient only to provide some new clothes for myself. Where should I find the money to take a wife?' Thus, lost in thought, he made no reply. Madam White then asked: 'Why don't you speak, Sir?' Hsü Hsüan said, 'You are too kind to bestow your love upon me. But I must be frank. I am miserably poor and therefore not in a position to carry out your request.' Madam White said, 'That's no impediment! I have enough and to spare. You must not let that worry you.' And she called Emerald and commanded her: 'Go and take down a silver ingot.' Emerald rested her hand on the banisters and walked up the staircase; soon she came down again and handed a small bundle to Madam White, who then turned to Hsü Hsüan. 'Take this, Master Little Eldest,' she said, 'and spend it; and if you run short, come for more.' And with her own hands she gave the bundle to Hsü Hsüan, who undid it and found a snowy silver ingot of fifty ounces. Tucking the bundle in his sleeve, he stood up, ready to leave. Emerald now came forward with his umbrella. Hsü Hsüan took it and bade them farewell and, returning straight home, hid the silver.

That night there was nothing further to relate. The following day, as soon as he was up, Hsü Hsüan left the house and went to Three Bridges Street and restored the umbrella to the younger squire.[1] On his way back, he bought with some loose silver a fat roast goose, some fresh fish, lean pork, a chicken, fruits and the like, and carried these home with him. He next went and bought a jar of wine. He then told his sister's maid and the servant girl to dress the meats and prepare a variety of dishes. His brother-in-law happened to be at home that day and, when the dishes and wine were ready, Hsü Hsüan invited his sister and brother-in-law to dine with him. The invitation took good Levy Officer Li by surprise; he exclaimed: 'Why are you spending all that money today? You never touch wine at other times! There's some devilry afoot!' They sat down in their respective places to enjoy the repast, and when the wine had gone round several times, Levy Officer Li again said, 'My

---

[1] The original reads: 'went to Officials Lane Corner and returned the umbrella to Squire Li', which would seem a slip on the part of the story-writer or scribe. Hsü Hsüan had no reason to rush to his own shop just to deposit his employer's brother's umbrella.

dear brother-in-law! There must be a reason for your making
a splash like this!' Hsü Hsüan now spoke up. 'I do thank you,
brother-in-law, for being so concerned. To be sure, my hospitality is hardly worth mentioning and must seem ridiculous,
but I really am grateful to you both—my sister and brother-
in-law—for looking after me all this time. It is said, "A tarry-
ing guest keeps two hosts busy".[1] Now that I, Hsü Hsüan, am
of age, I foresee the eventuality of growing old with no one to
take care of me, which would never do. At this moment, there
is a lady willing to enter into a match, and I hold it best that
you, my sister and brother-in-law, should decide the matter
for me and settle my whole future.' When his sister and
brother-in-law had heard all this, they slowly chewed over his
words. They thought: 'He was always close-fisted. But today
he has spared no expense, and all so as we might get him a
wife!' So the two of them looked at each other and gave no reply.

They finished eating and drinking, and Hsü Hsüan went to
the shop to attend to his customers. Two or three days later,
he began to wonder why his sister never brought up the subject
again. When he saw her one day, he asked: 'Have you talked it
over with my brother-in-law?' She replied: 'Not yet.' He
persisted: 'Why haven't you?' His sister said, 'It's not an
everyday matter, and rushing would get you nowhere. Besides,
your brother-in-law looked worried the last few days. I didn't
want him to feel annoyed about anything at home; I couldn't
bring it up.' Hsü Hsüan cried: 'Oh, sister! Why won't you do
it for me? There is no difficulty. You ignored my request because you were afraid I would ask my brother-in-law to foot
the bill.' And he got up from his chair, ran to his bedroom,
opened a chest, took out Madam White's silver and, carrying
it to his sister and putting it in her hands, said, 'No more ex-
cuses! Let my brother-in-law act for me.' His sister exclaimed:
'So you've a tidy sum laid by from your earnings as overseer at
uncle's shop! And—who would have thought it?—just so that
you might take a wife! Be off with you! I'm staying to look after
this.' So when Levy Officer Li came back, Hsü Hsüan's sister
said to him, 'Husband, do you know that when my brother
talked about getting a wife the other day, he had a lump of
silver saved up! He's now asked me to break it up and spend it.

[1] Literally: 'One guest should not trouble two hosts', which I have slightly
altered.

We had better arrange the wedding for him.' Levy Officer Li nodded and replied: 'So that's how it was! It's at least a good thing he has some savings. Show me the silver.' His wife hurriedly produced the silver. Levy Officer Li took the silver ingot in his hand and turned it over and over again; and when he saw the hallmark, he broke into a loud wail. 'Woe! We're lost! It's death for the whole family!' His wife, greatly taken aback, cried: 'What has happened, husband?'

Levy Officer Li then gave his explanation—'It was discovered a few days ago that fifty large silver ingots were unaccountably missing from the Grand Marshal's Treasury. The Treasury seals[1] and locks were untampered with, nor was there any sign of a subterranean passage into the building. The Prefect of Lin-an was immediately instructed to take urgent steps for the arrest of the thief but, there being no clue, a great many innocent people are already implicated. Placards posted up everywhere give the hallmark and number on the missing silver, proclaiming: "A reward of fifty ounces of silver is due to whomsoever caught the thief or recovered the ingots, but any man who, having knowledge of the crime, failed to make report, or harboured the criminal, shall, irrespective of his own punishment, have his entire family banished to the frontier." The ingot here has exactly the same hallmark and number as noted on the placard, and is undoubtedly from the Grand Marshal's Treasury. A relentless search is being now made for the thief and loot, and if ever there was a case of "To hell with the relatives when your own house is on fire!"—For, if this got abroad tomorrow, we could never explain ourselves! He might have stolen it himself or, for all I know, might only have borrowed the silver, but when it comes to getting one's gruel, then rather him than us all! The only course open to me is to take the ingot along and inform against him so as to avert disaster for the family.' As his wife listened, she gaped and stared, and was dumb with astonishment. And Levy Officer Li at once took the silver ingot and went to the Prefect of Lin-an's residence to accuse Hsü Hsüan.

The Prefect listened to Levy Officer Li's story and suffered, in consequence, a sleepless night. The next morning, he despatched in burning haste Constable Ho, who took with him one

[1] Strips of paper pasted across doors, chests, etc. and then written over with characters or stamped with a seal.

or two others and a squad of quick-eyed, strong-limbed runners and set off for the Li Herbalist's shop at Officials Lane Corner to arrest the chief criminal, Hsü Hsüan.[1] They marched up to the shop counter, gave a sudden shout, and tied Hsü Hsüan up with a rope. Then, sounding their gong and drum, they escorted him to the Prefectural Court, where Prefect Han was just starting the day's proceedings. Hsü Hsüan was brought into court and told to kneel down. The Prefect commanded: 'Beat him!' Hsü Hsüan said, 'Informing your Honour, torture is uncalled for. I, Hsü Hsüan, beg to know my offence.' Now in a rage, the Prefect stormed: 'We have both the thief and the loot — what remains to be said? Will you still plead "not guilty"? Fifty first-grade large silver ingots were found missing from the Grand Marshal's Treasury, the seals and locks untampered with. You are now accused by Levy Officer Li. Can you deny that you possess the remaining forty-nine ingots? What is more — if the seals were untouched and yet the silver was removed, then — a devil, a devil you must be!' The Prefect then commanded: 'Stop beating him but draw some of his foul blood.'[2] It was only then that Hsü Hsüan understood the cause of his arrest. He shrieked: 'Not a devil! Allow me to explain!' The Prefect roared: 'Stay! — Confess how you obtained the silver.' So Hsü Hsüan recounted in detail the events told above, how he had borrowed the umbrella and then lent it to Madam White, and how on two successive days he had gone to collect the umbrella.

The Prefect asked: 'Who is Madam White? Where does she live?' Hsü Hsüan replied: 'According to herself, she is the younger sister of Court Attendant White. She lives at the corner of Two Tea-houses Lane by Arrow Bridge, in a black, two-storeyed house on a slope overlooking the wall of Prince Hsiu's palace.' The Prefect then ordered Constable Ho to escort Hsü Hsüan to the corner of Two Tea-houses Lane and there arrest the woman culprit. Constable Ho received his orders, and he and his runners went in a swarm to Two Tea-houses Lane Corner and stopped before the black, two-storeyed house opposite the wall of Prince Hsiu's palace. But what an appearance

---

[1] The prudent Levy Officer doubtless suppressed the fact that Hsü was staying with him, but referred the Prefect instead to the herbalist's shop where Hsü was to be found in the day.

[2] Presumably to unmask Hsü Hsüan as some animal-spirit or other.

it presented! To be sure, there were four windows overlooking the street and, in the centre, a steep flight of steps leading up to a double gate; but rubbish had piled up knee-deep on the slope, and the gate itself was barred by an odd-looking makeshift bamboo pole tied horizontally across it. The sight caused Constable Ho and his companions a severe shock. They therefore summoned the neighbours, who were Ch'iu First, a beggar, on the immediate left, and on the right, Old Father Sun, a cobbler; but the sudden excitement so aggravated Old Father Sun's rupture that he fell down senseless. The other neighbours now came forward. They declared that there was no Madam White. 'It would be perhaps five or six years ago that a certain Militia Commander Mao lived here. The whole family died of an epidemic, and since then, ghosts have been seen to come out of the house in broad daylight so that no one has dared live in it. Only the other day, a madman was standing at the gate, hailing passers-by.'

Constable Ho ordered the runners to untie the bamboo pole. The gate now giving way, the silence within was broken by a sudden gust of wind bearing a strong rancid smell which hit them in the face. Abashed, the crowd of them fell back several paces. Hsü Hsüan, who all this time had been struck dumb by the transformation of the scene, was utterly dazed. Among the runners was one who had the reputation of being quite fearless: surnamed Wang, he was unconscionably fond of drinking and, being the second among his brothers, was thus nicknamed Thirsty Wang Second. Wang Second now shouted 'Follow me!' and, with a loud cry, they all rushed in. Inside the house, they saw walls, a partition, tables and chairs. They reached the staircase, and Wang Second was again asked to lead. The others followed him up the stairs and found the upper floor overlaid with dust three inches thick. They came to a door; pushing it open, they saw a room complete with bed, bed-curtains, chests and boxes. On the bed sat a resplendently beautiful woman dressed in white, and the sight of her immediately checked their advance. They addressed her: 'Lady, would you be a goddess or a ghost? We have orders from his Honour the Prefect of Lin-an to summon you as a witness in the case against Hsü Hsüan.' The woman remained quite still. Thirsty Wang Second cried: 'Get a move on, chaps! Why don't you bestir yourselves? Bring a whole jar of wine for me, and when my thirst is quenched, never say I'm outdone! I'll arrest her and bring her before the Prefect.' Two or three of the runners went down the stairs and out of the house and returned with a jar of wine for Wang Second, who unsealed it, drank up the contents at one long gulp, and swearing—'Never say I'm outdone!' hurled the empty jar at the curtained bed.

It would have been well if he had never flung that jar. For no sooner had it hit the bed-curtain than was heard a loud thunder-clap. The crowd of them fell on to the floor, and when at last they scrambled up, there was no lady on the bed, only a pile of shining silver. They pressed forward, examined the silver, and shouted, 'We're saved!' Indeed a count yielded a total of forty-nine large ingots. Saying among themselves, 'At least we have the silver to take to the Prefect,' they carried the ingots on a pole and returned to Lin-an Prefectural Court, where Constable Ho reported all that had happened. The Prefect exclaimed: 'It could only be a devil! And that's as well, too. The neighbours are guiltless and may return home.' And the Prefect had all fifty ingots escorted back to the Grand Marshal with a careful re-port setting out the case in full. As for Hsü Hsüan, he was guilty of misdemeanour—'in doing what he ought to have known not to do'[1]—and accordingly given the maximum penalty of so many strokes of the rod (his face being spared the brand), to be followed by a term of corrective labour at the Prison Camp under the jurisdiction of the Prefect of Soochow. Levy Officer Li, who had been uneasy about his own role of informer, now gave the whole of his reward of fifty ounces of silver from the Grand Marshall to his brother-in-law as travelling expenses. And Squire Li wrote two letters of introduction for Hsü Hsüan, one addressed to Principal Clerk Fan of Soochow, the other to Innkeeper Wang of Lucky Bridge in that city. Hsü Hsüan cried his heart out, but at last took leave of his sister and brother-in-law, put on his cangue and, escorted by two runners, departed from Hangchow for East New Bridge, where he boarded the boat for Soochow.[2]

In a matter of days he had reached Soochow, and he first call-ed on Principal Clerk Fan and Landlord Wang with Squire Li's letters. And Landlord Wang went and offered bribes high and

---

[1] i.e. in associating with an unknown woman under suspicious circum-stances.
[2] The route lay along the Grand Canal.

low on Hsü Hsüan's behalf before allowing the runners to proceed to the Prefectural Court, where they delivered their dispatch and handed over their prisoner in exchange for a form of acknowledgement. The runners then departing for Hangchow, Principal Clerk Fan and Landlord Wang secured Hsü Hsüan's release, and Hsü Hsüan lodged in the high front attic of the inn. Feeling dejected, he wrote a poem on the wall of the attic:

Alone in a tower, my gaze directed homewards,
Sadly I watch as the evening sun bursts through my window.
A simple, trusting fool,
How chanced I to meet that bewitching charmer?
Where now is my White?
Where, too, little Emerald?
Away from kith and kin, in distant Soochow,
My spirits droop while homesickness stabs my entrails.

When events crowd upon each other, they make a story; but when nothing happens, there is nothing to relate. Time sped like an arrow: night, like a shuttle, followed day. Hsü Hsüan had stayed at the inn for over half a year, and it was now past the middle of the ninth month.[1] Innkeeper Wang was standing at the gate that day, idly watching those passing by in the street. A sedan-chair approached from a distance, a servant girl walking beside it. The servant girl stopped and asked: 'Please, Sir, is this Landlord Wang's?' The innkeeper hurriedly bowed and said, 'It is. Whom are you looking for?' The servant girl replied: 'We're looking for Master Hsü Little Eldest from Lin-an-fu.' The innkeeper then said, 'If you will wait a moment, I shall ask him to come out.' So the sedan-chair was lowered in front of the gate. Innkeeper Wang went in and called: 'Someone to see you, Master Little Eldest!' Hsü Hsüan heard the call and, coming down in great haste, joined the landlord on his way back to the gate. And there indeed was Emerald standing beside the sedan-chair, in which sat Madam White! When Hsü Hsüan saw her, he burst out with—'Accursed creature! Ever since you stole that silver from the Treasury and implicated me, what haven't I gone through! My wrongs unheard, I have come to such a pass! Why have you followed me here? Oh, the shame of it!'

Madam White began: 'Don't reproach me, Master Little Eldest! I have come specially to give you an explanation. Let's

[1] The latter half of October.

go inside the landlord's and I can then tell you everything.' And Madam White asked Emerald to take down her bundle while she herself alighted from the sedan-chair. Hsü Hsüan, however, blocked the gate, screaming: 'You're a devil! I won't let you in.' Madam White then made a deep bow to the landlord, saying, 'I have nothing to conceal from our host here. But how could I be a devil? My clothes have seams and I cast a shadow. As luck would have it, my husband died and I must endure this treatment from unkind friends. It was my poor husband who did it, while he was still alive. Though it had nothing to do with me, the thought of incurring your reproach troubled me so — I *had* to come and explain. If I have made *that* clear, I am content to go.' The landlord now said to Hsü Hsüan, 'Ask the lady to come in and sit down. You can then talk.' And Madam White proposed: 'Let's reason it out in the presence of our host's good lady.'

The crowd that had gathered outside the gate began to disperse. Inside the house, Hsü Hsüan turned to the landlord and his good lady and recounted his grievances: 'It was her theft of the Treasury silver that caused me to suffer this ignominy. And now she's even followed me here. What more has she got to say?' Madam White pleaded: 'But the silver was left behind by my husband, and for love alone I gave it to you. I had no notion where it had come from originally.' Hsü Hsüan then asked: 'Why was it, when the runners came to arrest you, the approach to the house was covered with rubbish? And why did you disappear with a loud bang from behind the bed-curtains?' Madam White rejoined: 'When I heard that you had been arrested because of the silver, I was afraid you might let out that I had given it to you, and that I should then be brought to trial, exposed to the gaze of all and sundry in the court room. So I fled to my aunt's near Hidden Glory Temple,[1] and got someone to heap up rubbish before the gate. But I left the silver behind, on the bed, and begged the neighbours to tell all the lies they could for me.' Hsü Hsüan muttered, 'You fled all right! But I was made the culprit and had to endure trial and sentence.' Madam White said, 'When I placed the silver on the bed, all I wanted was to patch up the affair. How should I know there was to be such a hullabaloo? I then learned that you'd been sent here; so I carried some funds with me and took a boat this way to look

[1] Hidden Glory Temple — Hua-ts'ang ssu; *Hsi-hu yu-lan chih*, c. 18, p. 236.

for you. And now I have explained it all, I'm off again. It would seem we were never meant for each other.' Landlord Wang intervened: 'You have come all that way, lady. Don't tell me you are leaving again. Bide here a few days. Matters will mend.' Emerald, too, chipped in: 'Since the landlord's so kind and helpful, stay a day or two, Madam. After all, you did once promise to marry Master Little Eldest.' Madam White, however, instantly rebuffed Emerald. 'For shame! It's not as if no one would have me. But I really had to come and clear up the misunderstanding.' Landlord Wang now said, 'If you have promised to marry Master Little Eldest, then you mustn't talk about going back. We'll keep the lady here.' So Landlord Wang dismissed the sedan-chair, which to be sure is no part of our story.

After a few days, Madam White having quickly gained upon her hostess, the landlady enlisted the landlord's good offices in the marriage negotiations with Hsü Hsüan. They fixed upon the eleventh of the eleventh month for the wedding. In the twinkling of an eye, it was already the lucky day. Madam White took out some silver and asked the landlord to prepare a wedding feast. The two of them then went through the ceremony at the altar and became man and wife, and when the feast was over, they together entered the curtained bed. Madam White put on her most alluring charms, in her voice and in her manner; she was at once wanton and coquettish. For Hsü Hsüan, she was like a goddess, and he regretted all his lost hours. But thrice the cock crowed and dawn appeared in the east. Thus it is:

Happy revellers complain of the night too short:
In solitary vigil, each hour is lasting torment.

From that time on, the newly wedded pair were as carefree as fish in water; they spent their days at Landlord Wang's in a state of delirious happiness.

Days turned into months, and it was nearly half a year again. Spring brought mild weather; the masses of flowers were like tapestries; carriages and horses passed to and fro; the streets were thronged. Hsü Hsüan asked the landlord: 'What is all the clamour and bustle about? Where is everyone going today?' Innkeeper Wang replied: 'It's the fifteenth of the second month, and men and women alike go and look at the Reclining Buddha.[1] You should go, too, to Pillar-of-Heaven Monastery

[1] This would seem to be a Soochow festival, though a Reclining Buddha

and see the sights.' Hsü Hsüan responded eagerly: 'I'll tell my wife that I'm going there.' So Hsü Hsüan went up the stairs and said to Madam White, 'It's the fifteenth of the second month today, and men and women from all over gather to watch the Reclining Buddha. I shall go along too. If anybody should ask for me, just say I'm not in. Don't let strangers see you.' Madam White remonstrated with him. 'What is there to see? It would be better for you to stay at home. Why go at all?' But Hsü Hsüan insisted, 'It's just for the fun of it. I shall be back at once; there is no cause for alarm.'

So Hsü Hsüan left the lodging-house and fell in with some acquaintances, with whom he went to the monastery and saw the Reclining Buddha. He then walked round the cloisters, visiting the various halls of worship. At last, leaving the monastery, Hsü Hsüan noticed a Taoist seated outside the gate in his priest's cap and robes with a yellow silk sash round his waist and hemp sandals on his feet,[1] peddling his medicine and dispensing charms and holy water to the crowd. Hsü Hsüan paused to look at the man, who was just starting his harangue: 'I am a priest from the Chung-nan Mountain. I wander all over the land giving out charms and holy water to save folk from illness and calamity. Come forward now, those of you who are in need of succour!' The priest's eye registered a jet of foul air rising from among the crowd and immediately picked out Hsü Hsüan as one haunted by an evil spirit. The priest called aloud to Hsü Hsüan: 'You there! An evil spirit has been haunting you. I warn you of the dire consequences. Let me give you two paper charms which can save your life. At the third watch tonight,[2] burn this first one and stick the other in your hair.' Hsü Hsüan received the paper charms and prostrated himself before the priest, saying the while to himself, 'I always had my doubts about that woman. So she is, after all, an evil spirit!' And he thanked the priest and returned to the inn.

That night, when Madam White and Emerald were asleep, Hsü Hsüan got up and muttered to himself, 'It should be about the third watch now.' And he rolled up one of the paper charms

is to be found in a temple in most cities. In Hangchow, the fifteenth of the second month (i.e. mid-March) was a flower festival. See *Meng liang lu*, c. 1 (Reprint, p. 145).
[1] Hemp sandals were worn by people who did much walking on the roads, and here indicate a wandering priest.
[2] Between 11 p.m. and 1 a.m.

in his hair, and was making ready to burn the other one, when
Madam White heaved a sigh and spoke. 'We've been husband
and wife all this time, my Master Little Eldest, yet you never
cherished me in your bosom. Instead you listen to the idle
chatter of others. At midnight you would even burn a charm to
exorcise me. Go on, then! Burn your charm now.' And she
snatched the paper charm from him and burned it in a trice, and
not a thing happened. Madam White continued: 'What have
you got to say? Talk of a spirit! Pooh!' Hsü Hsüan said, 'I'm
not to blame. It was that wandering Taoist priest outside the
monastery with the Reclining Buddha who thought you were a
spirit.' Madam White concluded: 'We'll go together in the
morning and see what sort of priest he is.'

The following day, Madam White rose at dawn, made her
toilet, wore her hairpins and ear-rings, and her plain white garments and, having told Emerald to mind the attic, went with
Hsü Hsüan before the monastery with the Reclining Buddha. A
crowd had already collected round the Taoist priest, who was
again dispensing charms and holy water. Madam White's bewitching eyes were now fixed in a stare. She glided up to the
priest and hissed: 'What a bore! He claims to be a holy man
and has the impudence to tell my husband that I'm an evil spirit
—even gave him a charm to exorcise me!' The priest declared,
'I am a follower of the true method of the Five Thunderbolts
from the Zenith.[1] Whenever an evil spirit swallows one of my
charms, it instantly reverts to its original shape.' Madam White
cried, 'Before this company, draw the sign of your charm and
I'll swallow it.' The priest drew the sign on paper and offered
it to Madam White, who took the charm in her hand and swallowed it with a drink of water. The crowd looked on, and not a
thing happened. Some of those present sneered: 'Fancy calling
a belle like that an evil spirit!' And everyone now abused the
priest, who grew more and more confused until at last he merely
gaped and stared in dumb astonishment.

Madam White now addressed the crowd: 'Gentlemen! With
all his spells he could not ensnare me. I learned a conjuring
trick when I was a child. I will try it out on the priest for your

[1] A form of exorcism practised by Taoist priests, as demonstrated for
instance, by the priest Ch'ien Tao-yüan in the *tsa-chü* piay *So pai-yüan*
('The Charming of the White Ape'), act 2 (in *Ku-pen Yüan Ming tsa-
chü*, vol. IV); it is also resorted to in the story about the nocturnal visitor
who posed as the god Erh-lang-shen in *Hsing shih heng-yen*, c. 13, p. 251.

benefit.' Madam White began to mumble some gibberish, and
the priest coiled himself up and was then lifted in the air, as if
seized and held by an invisible hand. The crowd was amazed.
Madam White then said, 'He could hang there for a year for
aught I care. For the sake of you gentlemen though, I let him
off.' She gave one short puff, and the priest was brought back to
earth. The priest now ran away and, but for the lack of a pair of
wings, would gladly have flown from the place. The crowd,
too, dispersed. The loving couple returned to the inn, which we
need not relate in detail, and Madam White continued to
provide for all their needs. Thus it was:

  Where wife chimes in when husband sings,
  There evening mirth follows morning joy.

Swift as an arrow the days sped. It was the eighth day of the
fourth month, the birthday of the Buddha Shakyamuni. In the
streets, people carried statues of the bathing Buddha under
canopies, making collections from every household.[1] Hsü
Hsüan remarked to Landlord Wang: 'It's like what we do in
Hangchow!' A lad from the neighbourhood nicknamed Ironhead[2] came up and said, 'Master Little Eldest, there's a festival
in honour of Buddha's birth at Pillar-of-Heaven Monastery.
You must see it.' Hsü Hsüan went into the house and told
Madam White about the festival. Madam White objected:
'What is there to see? Don't you go!' Hsü Hsüan, however,
insisted: 'It should be a nice outing.' Madam White then said,
'If you must go, the old clothes you're wearing won't do. We'll
dress you up.' And she ordered Emerald to fetch garments of
the latest fashion. When Hsü Hsüan put them on, it was as if
they had been made to fit him—they were neither too long nor
too short. He had on his head a glossy black hat with two white
jade ornamental rings sewn on at the back; he wore a loose-

[1] In Hangchow, in the thirteenth century, each of the large monasteries
held its own Festival of Buddha's Bath, commemorating the birth of
Buddha; the procession of the bathing Buddha formed the main event.
Small bronze statues of Buddha were placed in basins filled with syrup and
carried along the streets under canopies of flowers to the accompaniment
of cymbals. At the houses of the great, monks and nuns ladled out small
quantities of the syrup in exchange for gifts to the monasteries. The
syrup would be flavoured with scented herbs, as in Kaifeng in the twelfth
century. See *Wu-lin chiu-shih*, c.3, p.378, and *Tung-ching meng-hua lu*,
c.8, p.47.
[2] Ironhead is a fairly common nickname down to the present, vaguely
associated with the Buddhist's shaven head but also with pugilistic and
athletic prowess.

fitting green silk gauze robe; he was neatly shod in black boots; and in his hand he held an elegant silk folding fan with the picture of a lady painted in gold, complete with a coral pendant, all of the finest workmanship. He was now carefully dressed from top to toe, and Madam White sent him off with her sweetest singing-voice: 'Don't be long, husband! Don't keep me waiting!'

Hsü Hsüan asked Ironhead to keep him company and together they went to Pillar-of-Heaven Monastery to watch the festival. There, everyone who saw him applauded—'What a fine gentleman!' He also overheard someone telling how, only the night before, four to five thousand strings of cash together with gold, pearls and other valuables had disappeared from Squire Chou's pawnshop. An inventory had been sent to the authorities, who were even that moment searching for the thief. The account meant nothing to Hsü Hsüan, and he lingered about the place with Ironhead. Among those offering incense that day were young men from the families of officials as well as humbler men and women; they came and went but there was always a crowd. A thought struck Hsü Hsüan: 'Madam White told me not to be long. I had better return.' Turning back suddenly, he lost Ironhead in the press, and came out of the monastery by himself. At the gate were five or six men who appeared to be runners and had warrant badges hanging from their waist. One of them looked Hsü Hsüan up and down and said to the others, 'What this fellow's got on and what he's holding in his hand—they're just like so-and-so.' One of the men then recognized Hsü Hsüan and said to him, 'Master Little Eldest, may I see your fan?' It never occurred to Hsü Hsüan that this might be a trick; so he gave the fan to the runner, who exclaimed: 'Look! The pendant on the fan is the same as the one named in the inventory!' The others roared: 'Arrest him!' and tied Hsü Hsüan up with a rope. It was even as:

Vultures swoop upon the lone swallow,
And hungry tigers devour the lamb.

Hsü Hsüan protested: 'You gentlemen are surely mistaken. I'm innocent!' The runners said, 'Whether we're mistaken or not we shall soon find out at Squire Chou's near the Prefectural Court. Five thousand strings of cash disappeared from his shop together with gold, pearls and other valuables. These included white jade sash rings and delicate folding fans, one of them with a coral pendant. And you still claim to be innocent? We have both thief and loot, so there's no room for prevarication. Talk about daring raiders!—This one here treats us like a bunch of lackeys. He goes about openly parading his loot—on his head, body and feet—without the slightest scruple.' Hsü Hsüan was dumbfounded and only after a long pause did he say, 'So that's how it was! It doesn't worry me at all. Someone stole these things.' The runners cried: 'Go and confess it in Soochow Prefectural Court.' The Prefect holding court the following day, Hsü Hsüan was brought forward. The Prefect began his cross-examination. 'Where have you hidden the gold, pearls and valuables you stole from Squire Chou's repository? Answer truthfully lest, under criminal law, you bring upon yourself a beating.' Hsü Hsüan said, 'Informing Your Honour, the clothes and ornaments all belonged to my wife, Madam White, and where she had obtained them, I do not know. The case against me is unproved. I appeal to Your Honour's clear judgement.' The Prefect barked: 'Where is your wife?' Hsü Hsüan replied that she was in the attic of Landlord Wang's inn by Lucky Bridge. The Prefect then ordered Constable Yüan to proceed in all haste to the inn with Hsü Hsüan under guard, and apprehend the woman culprit.

At the inn, Landlord Wang was shocked to see Constable Yüan and his runners, and exclaimed: 'What's up?' So Hsü Hsüan asked if Madam White was upstairs. The landlord now told his story—'Yesterday, you went off early with Ironhead to Pillar-of-Heaven Monastery. Not very long afterwards, Madam White came to me and said, "My husband left early this morning for the monastery, saying he'd be back at once and telling me to mind the attic. But he's still not back, and I and Emerald had better go before the monastery to look for him. Would you keep an eye on the place for us?" With that, she went out of the gate. I waited all day but she didn't return. I thought you might all have gone to visit relatives, not finding any of you in even this morning.' The runners demanded that Innkeeper Wang make a search for Madam White, and the landlord searched high and low, all over his inn, but there was no Madam White. Thereupon Constable Yüan arrested Innkeeper Wang and brought him before the Prefect. The Prefect asked: 'Where is Madam White?' Innkeeper Wang gave a detailed account of all that had happened and declared Madam

White to be an evil spirit. After repeated cross-questioning, the Prefect shouted out his order: 'Detain Hsü Hsüan!' Innkeeper Wang, however, was allowed bail and released pending the final verdict.

To turn now to the despoiled Squire Chou—as he sat in the tea-house opposite his pawn-shop, a servant suddenly brought word that the gold, pearls and valuables had all been found again on the shop premises. They were in an empty chest on a high shelf. Squire Chou hurried back and, to be sure, the missing articles were all there—save only a hat, two jade sash rings, a fan and pendant. Squire Chou remarked: 'It's clear that Hsü Hsüan was unjustly accused; I must not ruin an innocent man.' And he spoke privately to the Clerk in charge of the case, suggesting that Hsü Hsüan be indicted on some trivial charge and then dismissed. In the meantime, Levy Officer Li had been dispatched by the Grand Marshall on official business to Soochow. He too went to stay with Landlord Wang, who related to him how Hsü Hsüan had lodged there since his arrival in Soochow the year before, and how he was now involved in criminal proceedings. And Levy Officer Li thought to himself: 'After all, he is my wife's brother; I have to see him through this.' So Levy Officer Li went about making appeals and offering bribes on Hsü Hsüan's behalf. Then, one day, the Prefect completed his examination of Hsü Hsüan, who, having signed a confession which laid all the blame upon Madam White, was found guilty of 'remissness in not reporting the presence of evil spirits etc. etc.' and sentenced to a hundred strokes of the rod, followed by banishment to the Prison Camp of Chinkiang-fu, 360 *li* away,[1] there to serve a term of corrective labour. Levy Officer Li heard the sentence and said to Hsü Hsüan, 'Could be worse! There's a man in Chinkiang who was a dear friend of my father's and whom I call "uncle". His name is also Li, and he owns a herbalist's shop at Needle Bridge. I will give you a letter. When you get there, you can throw yourself upon his mercy.' Hsü Hsüan then borrowed some money from his brother-in-law for his travelling expenses, respectfully bowed his thanks to Landlord Wang as well as his brother-in-law, treated the two escorting runners to a meal, packed his own bundles, and started on his journey. Innkeeper Wang and Levy Officer Li accompanied him a short distance and each then left for his own home.

[1] Just over a hundred miles.

To return to Hsü Hsüan—like all travellers, he rested at night and was on his way again by day, fed when hungry and drank when thirsty, and after many such days reached Chinkiang, where first he sought out old Proprietor Li. When they reached the herbalist's shop by Needle Bridge, they saw an overseer at the door attending to his customers, and the old proprietor himself emerging from behind the shop. Hsü Hsuan and the two escorting runners hurriedly bowed. Hsü Hsüan spoke. 'I belong to the family of Levy Officer Li of Hangchow. Here is his letter.' The overseer took the letter and handed it to the proprietor, who opened and read it, and then said, 'So you are Hsü Hsüan?' Hsü Hsüan affirmed that he was. Old Proprietor Li ordered that a meal be served up for the three of them, after which he sent a servant to accompany them to the Prefectural Court, where the runners delivered their dispatch and the customary bribes then secured Hsü Hsüan's release. The runners now setting off again for Soochow with the appropriate document, Hsü Hsüan returned with the servant to the house, respectfully bowed his thanks to old Mr Li, and was presented to old Mrs Li. And old Mr Li noted that in his letter Levy Officer Li had described Hsü Hsüan as a former overseer at a herbalist's; he therefore kept Hsü Hsüan in the shop to help with the business and, at night, arranged for him to stay with the bean-curd vendor Grandfather Wang of Five Lanes, who put him in the attic.

To Proprietor Li's great delight, Hsü Hsüan was always on the job and exceedingly painstaking. Now there were two overseers in the shop, Chang and Chao.[1] Overseer Chao had been a good-natured and honest man all his life, but overseer Chang was spiteful and cunning. Presuming upon his own age, he constantly found fault with younger men and greatly resented the coming of the new assistant Hsü Hsüan, which he regarded as a threat to his own position. In his jealousy, he thought up a plan. One day, when old Mr Li was passing his time in the shop, he asked: 'How's the new man getting on?' Overseer Chang heard the question and muttered to himself: 'Now, straight into my trap!' He answered aloud: 'He is doing well, but—' Proprietor Li said, 'But what?' Old Chang continued:

---

[1] An overseer (*chu-kuan*) was a steward entrusted by the family with their shop. See, e.g., the story about the overseer Chang in *Ching shih t'ung-yen*, c. 16.

'He is very attentive to the best customers, but those making small purchases are sent packing. No wonder some customers dislike him. I asked him many a time to mend his ways, but would he listen to me?' The old proprietor said, 'That is easy enough. I'll tell him myself. He shall obey me.' Overseer Chao was present during this conversation, and he said to overseer Chang when they were alone: 'Come now, we need to pull together! Hsü Hsüan is new, and we should be looking after him. Let's point it out to him if he does anything wrong. Why go behind his back and tell the proprietor? If Hsü Hsüan found out, he would think that we were jealous.' Old Chang cried: 'What do you youngsters know?' It being now late, they shut up shop and each went his own way. Overseer Chao came to Hsü Hsüan's lodgings to warn him: 'Overseer Chang has been saying things about you to the proprietor. From now on, you have to be even more attentive. Serve all your customers readily, rich and poor alike.' Hsü Hsüan said, 'I am really grateful for your kind advice. Please come for a drink with me.' The two of them then went into a wine-shop and sat facing each other across a table. The waiter laid out delicacies and fruits, and they each had a few cups of wine. Chao continued: 'The old proprietor is a proud man. Remember never to contradict him. Let him have his whims, but get on patiently with your work.' Hsü Hsüan replied: 'Thank you, Sir, for your great kindness. I am deeply indebted to you.' They each drank two more cups. It was now almost dark, and overseer Chao said, 'It's hard to find one's way about in the dark. We'll meet another time.' So Hsü Hsüan paid the reckoning and they then parted.

Hsü Hsüan felt unsteady on his feet, and being afraid of bumping against anyone, walked under the eaves of houses. As he went along, an upstair window was pushed open and ashes strewn from a box-iron landed all over his head. Steadying himself, Hsü Hsüan cursed: 'Who the deuce? Are you blind? What a thing to do!' Suddenly he heard a woman coming down the stairs and saying, 'Sir, do not curse! It's entirely my fault. My hand slipped. Do forgive my stupid mistake!' Hsü Hsüan was fuddled. He raised his head and looked. Their eyes met: it was indeed Madam White! Anger rose in Hsü Hsüan's breast; vexation burst his spleen; the flames of wrath rose sky-high and raged unchecked. He burst out: 'You thieving magpie of a witch! What troubles haven't you brought me? Two criminal sentences!'[1] For indeed—'Virulence and cruelty are part of manliness.' Thus it was:

'Search through the world, wear out your iron boots—
still she eludes you!
Spurn her, consign her to oblivion—
there, she's on your doorstep!'

Hsü Hsüan went on: 'What! Here again, and you still won't admit you're an evil spirit?' He rushed into the house and seized Madam White by the arm, shouting: 'Shall I drag you into court or will you settle this privately?'[2] Madam White smiled, and smiled again, and said, 'Husband, how goes the saying?—"Lovers for one night, memories for a hundred". What a lot of memories we have! Listen to me. The clothes I gave you belonged to my first husband. I grew so absurdly fond of you, without thinking I made you put them on. And then, alas, love turned sour and sweet friends became bitter enemies.' But Hsü Hsüan cut her short. 'When I returned to the inn that day to look for you, why had you disappeared? Why did the landlord say you had gone with Emerald before the monastery to meet me? And why are you here now?' Madam White continued: 'I did go before the monastery and it was there that I heard about your arrest. So I sent Emerald to make inquiries, but she could learn nothing and I thought that you had escaped. Then, fearing for my own safety, I got Emerald to hire a boat and we left for my aunt's in Chienk'ang-fu.[3] It was only yesterday that we came here. I knew I couldn't face you, having involved you in *two* criminal trials.[4] I deserve your reproaches only too well. And yet—since we did have so much in common and *were* man and wife, should we part again so abruptly? What about all our vows of eternal fidelity, our oaths of enduring love, our promises of everlasting affection? Husband, think of our days of happy wedlock, and take me back with you to your lodgings. We'll begin anew a life of bliss. Surely that's best!' Hsü Hsüan was again duped by her wiles. His anger slowly turning to joy, he remained a long while deep in thought. Then, desire getting the better of his judgement, he lingered by her side and instead of returning to his lodgings, spent the night

[1] Two criminal sentences, i.e. trials and sentences. See note 4, below.
[2] This was the formula for a threat, found in both the stories and the plays.
[3] Chienk'ang, near Nanking, was not in fact a *fu* or prefecture.
[4] i.e. trials and their attendant ills, which were as much abhorred as the punishment or sentence.

in Madam White's upstair room.

The next day he returned to the house in the Five Lanes by Upper River, explained carefully to Grandfather Wang how his wife and her maidservant had arrived from Soochow, and added: 'I'd like them also to move into this place.' Grandfather Wang said, 'And a good thing too! There was no need to explain.' That very day, Madam White and Emerald moved into Grandfather Wang's attic. The following day, they prepared tea and invited the neighbours. On the third day, the neighbours gave a party for Hsü Hsüan.[1] The feasting over, the neighbours returned to their homes, which forms no part of our story. On the fourth day, Hsü Hsüan rose early, combed and washed, and said to Madam White, 'I have to call on the neighbours to thank them and then go and attend to business. Just you stay in with Emerald and look after the attic! Don't leave the house!' Having said this, he left and was soon back at the shop. Thus Hsü Hsüan went early to the shop each morning and returned late each evening.

Time sped, swift as a weaver's shuttle. A month went by. One day, Hsü Hsüan suggested to Madam White that she should pay her respects to the proprietor and old Mrs Li and the other ladies. Madam White agreed. 'After all, you *are* an overseer in that family. When I have met them, I could go visiting now and then.' The next day, Hsü Hsüan called a sedan-chair and had it brought in for Madam White. Madam White mounted the sedan-chair; Grandfather Wang followed with gifts of boxes of food carried on a pole; Emerald walked behind.[2] They arrived at the proprietor's house. Madam White descended from the sedan-chair, entered the house and asked to see old Mr Li, who hurriedly came out to receive her. Madam White gave the customary greeting, bowing low twice. She then bowed low twice to Mrs Li, and afterwards met the other ladies. Now though the proprietor was no longer in his prime, his lustfulness was unabated with age; and when he saw Madam White's ravishing beauty,

Half of his awakened soul seems to have left its seat;

The other half has already entered a more attractive body.

---

[1] The party would be in Grandfather Wang's house.
[2] Like a good employee, Hsü Hsüan went to the shop as usual and took no part in this procession, the visit being one to the ladies of the family.

The proprietor's goggle eyes were fastened on Madam White. To entertain her, the family now served up dinner with wine, during which old Mrs Li remarked to her husband: 'What a clever little woman! She's unusually good-looking, and so gentle and polite, so demure and self-possessed.' The proprietor readily agreed: 'Upon my word, she's got that *something* which only the ladies of Hangchow have!' After dinner, Madam White thanked her hostess and host, and returned to Grandfather Wang's. Old Mr Li thought to himself: 'If only that woman would share my bed for a night!' He knitted his brows, and the wrinkles defined a plan for action: 'The thirteenth of the sixth month is my birthday. I can wait. She shall succumb to my trick.'

Night followed day in unending chase. The Dragon-boat Festival[1] was over, and it was now the beginning of the sixth month. Proprietor Li said to Mrs Li, 'My birthday falls on the thirteenth. We'll prepare a feast and invite our relatives and friends for a day's celebration. It will be a time for rejoicing.' That same day, they sent invitations to their relatives, neighbours, friends and the overseers in the shop. The next day, each family that had been invited sent gifts of red candles, noodles, handkerchiefs and the like.[2] On the thirteenth, the men assembled at the house to enjoy the feast, which lasted the whole day. The next day was set apart for the women, and about twenty of them came to offer their congratulations. To turn now to Madam White—she, too, came to the celebrations, and she was exceedingly stylishly dressed in a jacket of pale green silk interlaced with gold threads and a scarlet silk gauze skirt, with pearl, jade, gold and silver ornaments pinned all over her head. She took Emerald with her and, upon entering the house, they bowed their felicitations to the proprietor and paid their respects to Mrs Li. The feast was spread out in the east wing of the house. For Proprietor Li was the kind of parsimonious old man who when he ate an apple was loath even to

---

[1] The Dragon-boat Festival was the fifth day of the fifth month, i.e. early June.
[2] Red candles were used at all celebrations; noodles symbolized longevity and were served on birthdays; handkerchiefs were the appropriate birthday gift for ladies because of this ancient custom: at the birth of a child, if 'a boy, a bow was placed on the left of the door; and if a girl, a handkerchief on the right of it'. Legge, *Li Ki*, x, ii, pp. 471–2, §16.

leave the pips:[1] he had put himself to the expense of such a feast only so as to lay a snare for Madam White, with whose charms he had been deeply smitten. The cups were passed back and forth, and the company were merry with drinking. The proprietor retired from the table to change out of his ceremonial robes. Now Proprietor Li had earlier given instructions to a trusted maid: 'If Madam White should ask to retire, bring her to the secluded room at the back.' Having set the trap, the proprietor stationed himself at the back of the house, keeping well out of sight. Indeed,

With no walls to scale nor high windows to climb,

This was seduction perfected to the last degree.

Presently, Madam White really sought the closet, and the maid brought her into the quiet room at the back and left her there. The lascivious proprietor was now in a state of uncontrollable excitement; in his agitation, instead of walking boldly into the room to accomplish his design, he took a peep through a crack in the door. It would have been well with the proprietor had he never peeped through that door. For, as he peeped, the proprietor received the shock of his life; he turned tail, tottered into the servants' quarters at the far end, and there fell on his back, senseless:

His spirit might yet be hovering between life and death

But already the heavy limbs were quite motionless.

For the proprietor saw, not a flower-like, jade-like woman, but a monstrous white snake coiled in thick folds the size of a bucket, its eyes like lanterns flashing golden rays. Nearly dead with fright, the proprietor turned and fled, then stumbled and fell. The maids held him up; they found his face ghastly livid, the lips colourless. One of the overseers poured a soul-soothing potion down his throat, and only then did the old proprietor revive. Old Mrs Li now appeared with some of her guests; she asked: 'Is anything wrong? What was the row about?' Proprietor Li, however, hid the real cause. He said, 'I was up too early this morning. These celebrations can be a punishment for one of my age. I felt a sudden dizziness in the head and passed out.' And he allowed himself to be helped into his room and put to bed. The guests went back to their seats and, the feasting

---

[1] 'For Proprietor Li was the kind of . . . leave the pips.' This is my substitute for the original, which I find hard to accommodate: '. . . the kind of man who when he fed on a louse, would leave a leg for his next meal.'

coming to an end after a few more rounds of wine, they thanked their hostess and departed.

When Madam White reached home, she calculated that at the shop Proprietor Li might tell Hsü Hsüan in the morning about her apparition. She quickly decided on a plan. As she changed out of her new garments, she heaved a sigh. Hsü Hsüan exclaimed: 'You've only just returned from the birthday feast! What was the sigh for?' Madam White whimpered: 'Husband! How could I bring myself even to mention such a thing? Your Proprietor Li didn't give a party to celebrate his birthday —he was after something unspeakably wicked. When he saw me asking for the closet, he hid himself within and tried to rape me, pulling and tugging at my skirt to force me to yield. I should really have screamed, but there was all that company and I just couldn't make a scene. So I gave the old man a hard push and he fell on the floor. Afterwards he pretended that he had suddenly fainted. I suppose he was really ashamed of himself, but fortunately his guilt prevented him from taking his revenge at the time.' Hsü Hsüan said lamely: 'Well, as long as he didn't succeed! He *is* my employer and it couldn't be helped. We have to put up with it. From now on, you had best stay away from them.' 'Put up with it!' Madam White exploded, 'So that you may continue to curry favour with that vile old man?' Hsü Hsüan said, 'I came to this place with only a letter from my brother-in-law and dumped myself on him. He could have thrown me out, but instead he kept me as an overseer in the shop. What do you expect me to do?' Madam White hissed: 'And you are a man? I was insulted—it would have been worse than death!—and it's still your pleasure to be his overseer.' Hsü Hsüan cried: 'Where else can I go? How shall I make a living?' Madam White continued: 'Phui! What's an overseer? An underling! Why not set up as a herbalist on your own?' Hsü Hsüan said gloomily, 'You're telling me! But where am I to get the capital?' Madam White now concluded: 'You may be easy on that score. Tomorrow I will take out some silver and you shall go and rent a house, after which we can speak further.'

As in ages past, so too even in the present, there were those zealous in the cause of others. It happened that a next door neighbour of theirs, Chiang Ho, was the kind of person who willingly exerted himself on other people's behalf. In the morning, therefore, Hsü Hsüan asked Madam White for some silver and got Chiang Ho to rent a house close to the ferry. He then bought a set of herbalist's cabinets and started laying in a stock of medicinal herbs. By the tenth month, the preparations were complete. They chose an auspicious day and opened the new herbalist's shop. And Hsü Hsüan no longer went to serve as overseer for Proprietor Li, who, being indeed much troubled by his secret guilt, did not send for him. Hsü Hsüan set the new shop going, and his business prospered day after day, bringing in large profits. One day, while he was at the door attending to his customers, a monk stepped forward with a subscription list in his hand, saying, 'I am a monk from Golden Mountain Monastery. The seventh of the seventh month[1] is the birthday of the Illustrious and Mighty Dragon King. I hope the gentleman will come to our monastery to offer incense. I also crave contributions to the fund.' Hsü Hsüan replied: 'There's no need to write down my name, but I can give you an excellent block of lakawood incense for use at your services.' And he opened a cabinet, took out the lakawood incense and handed it to the monk. The monk received the block of incense, and saying again, 'I hope the gentleman will come himself on that day to burn incense,' gave a Buddhist salute and left.

Madam White, who had been standing by, now rounded on Hsü Hsüan: 'Blast you! Must you give your best incense to an arrant hypocrite? He'll only exchange it for meat and drink.'[2] Hsü Hsüan said, 'I offered it in simple faith. If he sold it and spent the money on himself, he would answer for his own sins.' The seventh of the seventh month came. Hsü Hsüan had no sooner opened the shop door than he found a large crowd of people in the street, some going one way, some the other. His friend Chiang Ho remarked: 'You presented a block of incense the other day, Master Little Eldest. Why don't you pay a visit to the monastery today?' Hsü Hsüan assented: 'By and by. After I have tidied the place up, we can go together.' Chiang Ho then said, 'I am at your service.' Having quickly seen to the necessary tasks, Hsü Hsüan went in to tell Madam White. 'I am going to Golden Mountain Monastery to burn incense. Will you look after the house and shop?' Madam White, how-

---

[1] The reader seems inadequately prepared for the time lag. Hsü Hsüan had run his own business for nine months.

[2] Meat and alcoholic drinks were forbidden the Buddhist monk.

ever, tried to dissuade him: 'You surely know the adage—"A temple's not for loitering in". Why do you want to go?' Hsü Hsüan replied: 'For one thing, I have never been to Golden Mountain Monastery and I should like to see it. Besides, I made a contribution a few days ago and mean to follow it up by offering incense there.' Madam White at last said, 'If you must go, I can't prevent you. Yet promise me three things.' Hsü Hsüan asked: 'Which three?' Madam White continued: 'First, do not enter the Abbot's cell. Next, do not speak to any monk. Finally, as soon as you have seen the place, come back. If you tarry, I will be there to seek you out.' Hsü Hsüan said, 'What's difficult about that? I promise you them all.'

So Hsü Hsüan changed into new clothes and new socks and shoes, tucked a box of incense in his sleeve, walked across with Chiang Ho to the wharf, boarded the ferry-boat, and landed at Golden Mountain Monastery.[1] He first offered incense at the Dragon King's Hall. He then took a stroll round the monastery and, following the crowd, found himself outside the Abbot's cell. In a flash of recollection, Hsü Hsüan shrieked: 'She made me promise not to go into the Abbot's cell!' He stopped dead and would not enter. Chiang Ho said, 'She's not here, is she? When you get home, just say you never went near it.' His qualms thus allayed, Hsü Hsüan went into the Abbot's cell, took one brief look, and came out immediately. In the middle of the cell, a monk of pre-eminent virtue was seated on the Abbot's throne—his eyebrows were well-defined, his eyes clear as light, his shaven head formed a noble crown to his holy vestments, so that his whole appearance proclaimed the true disciple. The venerable monk observed Hsü Hsüan walking past the throne and called to the cell attendant: 'Ask that youth to come here at once.' The attendant looked outside the door: there was a crowd of thousands milling about, and he could not recall what Hsü Hsüan was like. So, after a while, he reported: 'Couldn't say where the man has gone.' On hearing this, the venerable monk clutched his meditation stick,[2] descended from his throne, and himself emerged to look for Hsü Hsüan, who, however, was not to be seen anywhere in the monastery. The

[1] At the time of the story, Golden Mountain was an island in the Yangtze to the north-west of the city of Chinkiang. It is now joined to the south bank of the Yangtze. See Introduction.
[2] Originally a bamboo stick with a padded end used for prodding drowsy monks during meditation sessions.

monk now went out of the gate and found a throng of people
waiting to board the ferry-boat, which was lashed by the waves
under a rising wind.

A storm was now raging. Some began to wail: 'Oh, we'll
never get away!' As the crowd watched, a skiff appeared in the
distance, borne on the crest of the waves: swiftly and inexorably it moved upstream, as if riding on the wind. Hsü Hsüan,
who was among the waiting crowd, remarked to Chiang Ho:
'What a storm! The ferry-boat itself is held back, yet that skiff
glides effortlessly over the billows!' While thus they conversed, the skiff drew nearer and they could make out two
figures at the scull, a woman in white and a girl in green. The
skiff was now heading for shore. Hsü Hsüan looked intently:
it was indeed Madam White and Emerald, and he was suddenly filled with alarm. From the edge of the water, Madam
White called aloud to him: 'Why didn't you return? Come
aboard at once!' Hsü Hsüan made ready to join her, but a
pealing voice thundered from behind him: 'Depraved creatures!
Dare you invade these holy precincts?' Hsü Hsüan turned round
to find the crowd hailing the Great Master, Law Boundless.[1]
The venerable monk continued: 'Mean you yet again to indulge in your loathsome practices and take your toll of human
lives?[2] Know that I am here, who purpose to subjugate you.'
At the sight of the monk, Madam White brought her vessel
away with the same speed as before; in mid stream, however,
she overturned her skiff, and both Madam White and Emerald
went under the waves. Hsü Hsüan then turned to the venerable
monk and, kneeling, cried out: 'Great Master! Worm that I
am, save my life!' The monk asked: 'How did you fall in with
that woman?' And Hsü Hsüan related all that had happened,
in each particular. The monk heard him out and pronounced
judgement: 'That woman was no other than an evil spirit.
You will return to Hangchow, where, if she should again haunt
you, you could inquire for me at Cleansing Mercy Monastery,

---

[1] Fa-hai, literally, Sea of Law.
[2] In other versions of the story and in the plays, Madam White tries to
flood the monastery and drown all who were on the island. The reference
here would seem to suggest that our story-teller was familiar with this
tradition but chose not to dwell upon it. Later in the story, Madam White
threatens to drown the inhabitants of Hangchow (p.253). See Introduction.

south of the lake.[1] To sum up, here are four lines of verse:
> An evil spirit in the guise of a charming woman,
> Her wanton wiles she brought to the West Lake's shores.
> You who through ignorance became her willing dupe —
> Look to the monk in the south for deliverance.'

Hsü Hsüan knelt down and thanked the Great Master, Law Boundless. The storm had blown over,[2] and he went with Chiang Ho on board the ferry-boat, which took them across the water to Chinkiang. They stepped ashore and returned to the house, but Madam White and Emerald had vanished without trace. It was only then that Hsü Hsüan became fully convinced that they were evil spirits. Being now much afraid, he asked Chiang Ho that night to sleep in the same room with him; nevertheless his dejection kept him awake all night long. He rose early the next day and, entrusting the house and shop to Chiang Ho, came to Mr Li's house by Needle Bridge and told the old proprietor what had happened. Proprietor Li cried: 'Why, at my birthday party, she asked to retire, and I, not knowing about it, went to the same place and saw — a monster! I was nearly dead with fright, though I couldn't have told you this before. Well, since matters have taken such a turn, come and stay with me here. You can decide afterwards what to do.' So Hsü Hsüan thanked Proprietor Li and moved into his house.[3]

Soon Hsü Hsüan had stayed with Proprietor Li for over two months. One day, as he stood at the door, the local headman came and ordered every household to place burning candles and incense, lanterns, and flowers outside its gate in order to receive the Emperor's gracious Decree of Pardon. For the Emperor Kao-tsung of the Sung had appointed the prince later known as Hsiao-tsung[4] to be his heir-apparent and proclaimed an amnesty throughout the Empire. With the exception of homicides and those culpable in the extreme, all offenders were pardoned and permitted to return to their homes. Overjoyed at his own reinstatement, Hsü Hsüan composed a poem:

---

[1] Cleansing Mercy Monastery (Ching-tz'u ssu) stood behind Thunder Peak among the hills to the south of the West Lake. *Hsi-hu yu-lan chih*, c. 3, pp. 28–34.
[2] 'The storm had blown over' is my insertion.
[3] The original reads: 'as before, moved into his house'.
[4] Hsiao-tsung, the son of Prince Hsiu, whose palace is mentioned earlier in the story.

I thank my prince for the proclaimed amnesty—
The clap-net cut open, the bird now wings and sings.
No displaced ghost to be mine when I die,
But living, I shall be rooted in my native soil.
All too unhappy in my affair with a white devil,
I rejoice to find pardon and my record erased.
When I reach home, I'll burn a forest of incense
And so thank heaven and earth for my strange rebirth.

Hsü Hsüan wrote his poem and begged Proprietor Li to offer bribes high and low in the Prefectural Court on his behalf, with the result that he was personally interviewed by the Prefect and immediately granted a permit for returning to his home town. Hsü Hsüan bowed his thanks to all the neighbours and to Proprietor Li and old Mrs Li and all their family, and also bade the two overseers in the shop farewell. He then asked his friend Chiang Ho to obtain for him various items of local produce,[1] which he brought back as gifts with him to Hangchow.

On reaching home, Hsü Hsüan greeted his sister and brother-in-law and bowed four times to each of them. But when Levy Officer Li saw Hsü Hsüan, he at once blew up. 'Some people remember their relatives! Twice I wrote letters of introduction to help you out in a strange city, and yet when you got married at Proprietor Li's, you never even sent word to us. Talk about callous unconcern! All that bowing! Some people are grateful.' Hsü Hsüan cried: 'But I have no wife!' Levy Officer Li said, 'No? Two days ago a woman turned up with a servant girl and claimed to be your wife; said you had left for Golden Mountain Monastery on the seventh of the seventh month to burn incense and failed to return. She had looked for you all over the place and then learnt you were on your way back to Hangchow. So she's been here the last two days waiting for you.' And he had the woman and her servant girl brought out to meet Hsü Hsüan. Hsü Hsüan took one look, and indeed it was Madam White and Emerald. The sight of them struck him dumb. In his horror, he could not even think of giving a recital[2] of his adventures to his sister and brother-in-law; instead he submitted meekly to Madam White's nagging complaints and fond endearments. Levy Officer and Li his

---

[1] Chinkiang was noted for its vinegar among other things.
[2] In the original, the term *hua-pen* (story-teller's story) is used, i.e. Hsü Hsüan could not even think of recounting his own story.

wife now left them alone, having first told Hsü Hsüan to go with
Madam White to her room.

It being now late, Hsü Hsüan was desperate. He would not
follow Madam White, but fell on his knees before her and
howled: 'Goddess or devil—whatever you be, spare my life!'
Madam White said gravely, 'My Master Little Eldest! This
is most unseemly. We've been husband and wife all this time;
was I really such a virago? Now talk like a man.' Hsü Hsüan
cried: 'Shortly after I first met you, twice I found myself
involved in criminal proceedings. I ended up in Chinkiang-fu,
but there you were again! That day I was at Golden Mountain
Monastery to offer incense and, being a little slow in returning,
I had you and Emerald coming after in hot pursuit. Then, catch-
ing sight of the Great Master, all of a sudden you plunged into
the Yangtze, and I thought that was the end of you. But now—
here you are once more! I do entreat you to take pity on me and
spare my life.' Madam White's bulging eyes glared. She said,
'Master Little Eldest, I tried so hard to keep it going, but
you've clearly made up your mind that I was the one to blame.
Still, we are lawfully wedded, for better or worse. What loving
memories, too, we share of bed and board. Of course you
would go and listen to busy-bodies and their idle gossip, calculated to bring about our estrangement. Let's now get this
straight. If you do as I tell you, all shall be well and we may
remain the happiest of couples. But if you betray me, this city
of yours shall welter in blood-streaked water; men and women
shall grapple in vain with the waves, kicking and struggling
and clutching at straws, all and each doomed to an untimely
death.'[1] Hsü Hsüan was now trembling with fear and almost
bereft of speech, yet he would not enter her room. So Emerald
set about persuading him. 'Come, Sir, you know my mistress
just couldn't resist you, the handsome Hangchow gentleman.
She loves you, too, for all your kind favours and tender devotion. Be guided by me. Patch up your lovers' quarrel before it's
too late.' Between the grim menaces of the one and the sweet
blandishments of the other, Hsü Hsüan was left with no
escape. He set up a wail: 'Oh, misery! Misery!'

---

[1] 'this city of yours' etc.: obviously a tense moment for the story-teller's
original audience of Hangchow, for whom such a threat would seem far
more effective than the actual flooding of Golden Mountain Monastery in
other versions of the story. See Introduction.

Hsü Hsüan's sister, who was in the courtyard enjoying the cool of the evening,[1] heard his cry of 'Misery!' and hurrying into the house, found him in the midst of a deafening row outside Madam White's room. She pulled Hsü Hsüan away, upon which Madam White shut her door and retired for the night. Hsü Hsüan now told his sister in great detail all that had come to pass. Levy Officer Li, who had also been sitting outdoors in the cool, came in at that moment. His wife said to him, 'The pair of them had a squabble. I don't know if she's gone to bed. Would you go and have a peep?' Levy Officer Li went to Madam White's window. Inside, it was dark, yet there were stray gleams of light. Levy Officer Li licked the paper on the window until it showed a crack, and took a peep. It would have been well, had he not peeped. For, as Levy Officer Li peeped through the crack, he saw on the bed a python coiled up like a bucket, its head reared towards the skylight as if it, too, was enjoying the cool evening breezes. Its scales shone with a cold white light which lit the room. Aghast at the sight, Levy Officer Li flinched from the window and fled. Rejoining his wife, he made no reference to the apparition but said, 'She must be asleep—there wasn't a sound.' And Hsü Hsüan ensconced himself in his sister's room, from which he would not budge. Nor did his brother-in-law ask any more questions. Thus they passed the night.

The next morning, Levy Officer Li beckoned to Hsü Hsüan and led him to a quiet spot far from the house before coming out with: 'How did you meet your wife? Tell me the truth, and don't try to hold anything back. For, last night, with my own eyes I saw her in the shape of a white giant python. So as not to alarm your sister, however, I kept quiet.' Hsü Hsüan then recounted to his brother-in-law from the very beginning all that had happened. Levy Officer Li at last said: 'If that is your trouble, I know of a snake-charmer by the name of Tai in front of White Horse Temple. He only has to cast a spell to get his snake. We'll go together to request his services.' So the two men made their way to White Horse Temple, saw the snake-charmer standing at the gate, and saluted him. The snake-

[1] Sitting outdoors to enjoy the cool evening breezes would be a pastime of the sixth and seventh months (July and August) in Hangchow as elsewhere. Hsü Hsüan received his pardon in the ninth month (October), well after the Mid-autumn Festival, so that some modification of the time sequence would be desirable.

charmer returned their greeting, saying, 'What is your pleasure, gentlemen?' Hsü Hsüan stammered: 'There is an enormous python in our house. We would trouble you to catch it for us.' The snake-charmer then asking where the house was, Hsü Hsüan gave him directions eagerly: 'If you cross Officer's Bridge, you will find yourself in Black Pearl Lane. Ask for Levy Officer Li's house.' And taking out an ounce of silver, Hsü Hsüan continued: 'For the present, please accept this. When the snake is caught, there will be a proper reward.' The snake-charmer received the silver and said, 'If you gentlemen will go before, I shall be along immediately.' Thus Levy Officer Li and Hsü Hsüan went back by themselves.

The snake-charmer filled a jar with a solution of orpiment[1] and took the shortest way to Black Pearl Lane, where in response to his inquiry for Levy Officer Li's, a two-storeyed house was pointed out to him. The snake-charmer paused at the gate. He lifted the curtain and gave a little cough. But there was no one to answer the gate. He began to knock. After a good while, a woman came out and asked: 'Whom do you want?' The snake-charmer then said, 'Is this Levy Officer Li's?' When the woman answered in the affirmative, he went on: 'I am told that there is a large snake in the house. Two gentlemen called just now, inviting me to catch a snake.' The woman said, 'In this house? Must be a mistake. We've no snakes and things *here*.' The snake-charmer cried: 'But the gentleman left an ounce of silver with me and promised a further big reward if I caught the snake!' The woman retorted: 'Of course not. Don't you believe it! They made the story up as a joke.' The snake-charmer, however, persisted: 'But why should they have their joke at my expense?' Despite her repeated attempts, the man was not to be put off, and Madam White's patience was wearing thin. She burst out: 'A snake-catcher, are you? You won't catch this one.' Snake-charmer Tai protested: 'Since my ancestor of seven generations ago, we have been snake-charmers and snake-catchers. No snake stands a chance against me.' Madam White rejoined: 'Not stand a chance? You mean you'll escape scot-free?' The snake-charmer shouted: 'No!

---

[1] Used as a disinfectant and, when mixed with spirit, as an antidote against snake poison. In other versions of the story, Madam White drinks a mixture of orpiment and spirit on Dragon-boat Festival day (fifth of fifth month) and is then unmasked. See Introduction.

No! Certainly not! I'll wager a silver ingot that I don't run away from a snake.' Madam White gave a little laugh and said, 'Follow me.' Reaching the courtyard, she turned a corner and disappeared into the house. The snake-charmer took up his station in the middle of the courtyard and held up his jar of solution of orpiment in readiness. Presently, there was one swift gust of wind and a large python, the size of a bucket, which seemed to have sprung up from nowhere, shot out towards him. Thus indeed,

> Though the huntsman came not after the crouching tiger,
> The tiger lay in wait for the unsuspecting huntsman.

Terrified, Snake-charmer Tai fell backwards, breaking his jar and spilling the yellow mixture. The flaming mouth of the snake gaped wide, showing all its deadly white fangs, as if about to swallow him. The snake-charmer struggled breathlessly to his feet and fled, regretting only that he had not more than two legs to take to. He rushed headlong across the bridge and met Levy Officer Li and Hsü Hsüan, who were only now making their way home. Hsü Hsüan said expectantly, 'Well?' After a preamble—'So that you gentlemen may know'—the snake-charmer gave a full account of what had taken place and ended by taking out the ounce of silver and handing it back to Levy Officer Li with the words: 'I ran for dear life, and consider myself lucky to have escaped at all. Look for another man for the job, gentlemen.' The snake-charmer now departing in great haste, Hsü Hsüan turned to Levy Officer Li and said, 'Brother-in-law, what do we do now?' Levy Officer Li drawled out his reply: 'It's only too clear that she's an evil spirit. Now in Ch'ih-shan-pu[1] to the south of the city, there's a certain Chang Ch'eng, who owes me a thousand strings of cash. You might try to collect that debt for me.[2] The place is little frequented, and when you get there, you will rent a room from him and stay for some time. We must just hope that when the she-monster discovers your absence, she betakes herself elsewhere.' Hsü Hsüan agreed half-heartedly. They now returned to the house, which they found unexpectedly quiet. Levy Officer

[1] Ch'ih-shan (Red Mountain) and Ch'ih-shan-pu (Red Mountain Port) were situated among Hangchow's southern hills. *Hsi-hu yu-lan chih*, c. 4, p. 41.
[2] 'You might collect that debt for me' is my insertion; it is clearly implied by the enclosing of the borrower's receipt. It seems equally clear that Levy Officer Li did not expect immediate repayment of the loan.

Li wrote a letter for Hsü Hsüan enclosing the receipt for the loan, and told him to be on his way. But at that moment Madam White called Hsü Hsüan to her room and gave him a scolding. 'Up to your tricks again? Found a snake-catcher, have you? Be true to me, and I will be your good fairy. Play me false, and there is not a soul in this city but shall perish.'

Madam White's threats sent Hsü Hsüan into fits of shivering and quaking. He was too frightened to speak, and carrying the letter and receipt, set out for Ch'ih-shan-pu, feeling depressed and weary. Arriving there, he sought out the debtor, Chang Ch'eng, and then looked in his sleeve for the receipt. To his surprise, however, it was no longer there. He hurriedly retraced his steps, lamenting his sorry plight and searching all the way for the receipt; but it was not to be seen anywhere. In this doleful state, he found himself in front of Cleansing Mercy Monastery: the words of the Great Master Law Boundless, Abbot of Golden Mountain Monastery, reverberated in his memory—'in Hangchow if she should again haunt you, inquire for me at Cleansing Mercy Monastery south of the lake.' Hsü Hsüan exclaimed: 'It's now or never!' He ran into the monastery, rushed up to the Preceptor, and put his question: 'Pray, holy brother, is the Great Master Law Boundless on a visit to this monastery?' The Preceptor replied, 'He is not here.' The answer drove Hsü Hsüan to despair. He left in a daze and wandered off the road to the foot of the Long Bridge[1] at the edge of the lake, muttering to himself: ' "Evil spirits haunt the man deserted by fortune." What am I living for?' Then, gazing in fascination upon the clear rippling waves, he made ready to leap. Thus it was:

If Yama sent for you at the third watch,

Think you to survive until the fourth?

Hsü Hsüan was about to jump into the lake, but a voice from behind called to him: 'Let no man relinquish his own life wantonly. Detach the mind:

"If calamity should befall ten thousand,

Counting in pairs would reduce the number by half."[2]

He who is in need, let him seek help from me.' Hsü Hsüan

[1] Long Bridge, where three streams converged. *Hsi-hu yu-lan chih*, c. 3, pp. 28–9.
[2] The verses were a gag, often used by stage villains to minimize their evil deeds. In the *tsa-chü* play 'Famine Relief in Ch'en-chou' (*Ch'en-chou t'iao-mi*), act I, for instance, the young *ya-nei*, the villainous son of the

turned round and looked, and it was indeed the Great Master
Law Boundless, with his cassock and begging bowl, and a
meditation stick in his hand. For he had arrived only that
instant, and it would seem that Hsü Hsüan's hour was not yet
—had the venerable monk been delayed for even so long as one
would take over a meal, Hsü Hsüan's life would have ended.
Hsü Hsüan now prostrated himself before the Great Master,
shrieking: 'Save me!' The monk asked: 'Where is the monster?' Hsü Hsüan then recounted in detail the events told
above, concluding with 'And now that she is again here, I beg
of you, Great Master—deliver me from her!' The venerable
monk took his begging bowl from his sleeve and handed it to
Hsü Hsüan, saying, 'When you reach home, without making
a sound or letting that woman see you, put this over her head
like a hood and press it down firmly, using all your strength.
Don't panic! Now go.'

Hsü Hsüan, having again knelt and thanked the Great
Master, returned home. He found Madam White sitting by
herself, muttering and cursing. 'I wonder who's behind it all.
Someone's stirring up trouble and my husband no longer loves
me. When I find out, I shall get my own back.' It was indeed
too true :

'Deliberate cunning still awaits its innocent victim.'

From where Hsü Hsüan stood, he could see that Madam White
was off her guard. He crept up from behind, clapped the begging bowl on her head, and rammed it down with all his might.
The figure of Madam White vanished inch by inch into the
descending bowl; Hsü Hsüan dared not relax his hold but
pressed it firmly down to the ground. From within the bowl,
a muffled voice reached his ears: 'My dear husband of several
cruelly short years! No throb of pity in your heart? Leave go
but a moment!' Hsü Hsüan was once more in a quandary. At
this juncture, the excited voice of a servant announced the
arrival of a monk who 'talked about subjugating an evil spirit'.
Thereupon Hsü Hsüan shouted to Levy Officer Li, telling him
at once to invite the venerable monk in. And when the Great
Master himself entered, Hsü Hsüan cried: 'Save me, your

iniquitous nobleman Liu, says: 'What's wrong with killing a man? Even
if I killed ten, it would only be five pairs.' Such lines were no doubt familiar
and acceptable to a popular audience: they are bathos from the lips of a
holy monk. I have inserted 'Detach the mind', which is not in the original,
to give some point to the discourse.

disciple!' It was not known what spell the venerable monk used, but when he had done his chanting, he gently lifted the begging bowl. Madam White had shrunk to the size of a puppet of seven or eight inches; her eyes were shut and she was grovelling on the ground. The Great Master roared out his questions: 'What monster or spirit are you that have ventured so outrageously to haunt a mortal? Confess in full.' With her eyes still shut, Madam White answered without faltering: 'Holy monk, I was a female python who, thirsting after a higher existence, had attained a thousand years and was no longer confined to my base, scaly form.[1] In a thunderstorm I sought shelter on the West Lake, and there I came across Emerald, with whom I roamed the lake's shores. The sight of the youth, Hsü Hsüan, however, re-awakened in me a passion long dormant, and I gave in to my lustful desires. Thus a momentary aberration caused me to break heaven's law,[2] but at least I took no life. I pray you, holy monk—have mercy upon me!' The Great Master now asked: 'And what monster was Emerald?' Madam White replied: 'She was a green bleak who grew to a thousand years in a deep pool under the third bridge of the lake, and thus too attained the state of a spirit. Meeting her by chance, I made her my companion. But of fleshly lusts she was innocent, and I beg you also to show her clemency.'

The Venerable Law Boundless now pronounced judgement: 'Having regard to your thousand years' aspiration, I will spare your life. Reveal yourself now in your true shape.' Madam White shook her head, indicating unwillingness to do so, upon which the Great Master, much angered, chanted another spell and then made invocation in a thundering voice: 'Guardians of the Skies, hearken! We require the presence of the green fish-spirit. Let both creatures revert to their former shapes, to await our further pleasure.' The courtyard resounded with a terrific wind, followed by a loud crash. A huge green fish, a dozen feet in length, had dropped down from the clouds: it bounced and leaped and tossed, and shrinking before their very eyes, became a small green bleak of just over a foot. When they turned to look at Madam White, she too had reverted to her

[1] 'who, thirsting after a higher existence, had attained a thousand years and was no longer confined to my base, scaly form' is my insertion. The original is excessively bald: 'Madam White replied: "Holy monk, I was a giant python. In a thunderstorm I sought shelter on the West Lake..."'
[2] That of consorting with a mortal.

original shape, a three-foot white python with its head reared towards Hsü Hsüan and its small serpent's eyes looking askance at him.

The venerable monk picked up the two tame creatures with his hand and dropped them into the begging bowl. He then tore off a length of his robe and sealed the top of the bowl with it. Carrying the bowl with him and depositing it on the ground before Thunder Peak Monastery,[1] he ordered men to move bricks and stones so as to erect a pagoda to encase the bowl and keep it inviolate. Afterwards Hsü Hsüan went about collecting subscriptions, and the pagoda eventually became a seven-tiered structure, so solid and enduring that, for thousands of years to come, the White Snake and the Green Fish would be prevented from afflicting the world. When the venerable monk had subjugated these evil spirits and consigned them to the pagoda, he composed a chant of four lines:

When the West Lake is drained of its water
And rivers and ponds are dried up,
When Thunder Peak Pagoda crumbles,
The White Snake shall again roam the earth.

He finished his chant and wrote eight lines of verse in exhortation of men:

Of woman's beauty and charms, beware, you worldlings!
For female charm leads to enslavement by passion.
The unsullied mind is proof against evil's encroachment
And decorous behaviour wards off wicked designs.
Hsü Hsüan, who surrendered himself to woman's beauty,
Was involved in scandal and criminal proceedings;
And were it not for a monk's timely intervention
The White Snake would have swallowed him, bones and all.

When the Venerable Law Boundless had recited these verses, the crowd dispersed. Hsü Hsüan alone stayed behind and declared his intention of renouncing the world. He made the ceremonial bow to the Great Master, whom he thus acknowledged as his teacher, and duly had his head shaved and donned his cassock in Thunder Peak Monastery, where he remained as a

[1] Thunder Peak stood before Cleansing Mercy Monastery among Hang-chow's southern hills. The seven-tiered pagoda was first built in the reign of the King of Wu-yüeh (907–31), by his queen. See *Hsi-hu yu-lan chih*, c. 3, pp. 33–4, which also records: 'Legend has it that two monsters from the lake, a white snake and a green fish, were imprisoned under the pagoda.' Cf. Introduction.

monk for some years. One evening he sat with his legs crossed as in meditation and passed away.[1] The monks placed him in a coffin and cremated him, after which they erected a tower to enshrine his ashes for all time. Before his end, Hsü Hsüan also composed eight lines of verse to admonish the world[2]:

The Great Master rescued me from the cares of the world;
An iron tree put forth blossoms[3] to herald a new dawn.
The rotating wheel of life transforms as it rotates:
Birth follows mutation, which in turn follows birth.
True form is without body, is ultimately even formless—
As yet unshaped and incorporeal are the loveliest shapes.
But, though form is emptiness and emptiness still takes shape,
Beware you of well-shaped bodies in your quest for emptiness.

[1] The posture customarily adopted by monks in their last hours; their coffins were shaped accordingly. A fuller account of these rites is to be found in the story *Yüeh-ming ho-shang tu liu Ts'ui* ('The monk Bright Moon redeems the girl Liu Ts'ui') in *Ku-chin hsiao-shuo*, c. 29, pp. 431–3, 439–40.

[2] The original reads 'four lines of verse'. 'To admonish the world' (*ching shih*) is the phrase in the title of the collection from which this story is taken, *Ching shih t'ung yen* ('Stories to admonish the world'). I have translated the last four lines of the verse in such a way as to bring out the intended lesson, viz. that *se* (phenomena or the world of forms, *or* the allurement of woman's beauty) is really *k'ung* (emptiness).

[3] Metaphor for a miracle.

The Peony Pavilion

The life of T'ang Hsien-tsu (1550–1616), which is well docu-
mented,[1] bears little apparent relation to *Mou-tan t'ing* ('The
Peony Pavilion') with its story of two young lovers whose
entire existence revolved round a dream until in the end they
found each other. For he was a conscientious official much concerned with public affairs, and a bold memorial to the throne
criticizing Emperor and Ministers alike, which is quoted at
some length in his two-page biography in the official Ming
history, suggests the impetuous man of action. Born into a
scholarly family of Lin-ch'uan (i.e. Linchwan in Kiangsi Province), the home of Wang An-shih, T'ang passed his Provincial Examination at the age of twenty; but, from the start, his
advancement was blocked by the all powerful Chang Chü-
cheng, to whose patronage he had refused to submit. (The
Ming government was riddled with factions especially in its
last hundred years.) Minister Chang dying in 1582, T'ang
returned to the capital (Peking) in 1583 and passed his *chin-
shih* examination. He was appointed to an advisory post[2] in the
Bureau of Sacrifices in the Ming southern capital, Nanking,
and subsequently, in 1589, made a Second Class Secretary
(*chu shih*) in the Board of Rites in the same city, a post which
he retained for two years.

In 1591 the appearance of a comet, interpreted as a sign of
heaven's displeasure, had caused alarm and disquiet at court,
and from Nanking T'ang sent up his outspoken memorial,
lamenting His Imperial Majesty the Emperor Shen-tsung's

[1] Biography in *Ming shih*, c. 230, pp. 4a–5a; prefaces and biographies by
contemporaries and later men in the Collected Works, *T'ang Hsien-tsu
chi*, Chung-hua 1962, vol. II, pp. 1511–45; the Collected Works include a
large number of letters and dated poems. I have drawn freely upon Hsü
Shuo-fang's extended biographical study, *T'ang Hsien-tsu nien-p'u*, 1958.
[2] *T'ai-ch'ang-ssu-po-shih*, nominally Professor, but no longer a teaching
post nor of quite the standing as Professor at the Imperial Academy.

'twenty wasted years.'[1] The wrath of the Son of Heaven now descended upon him: within the month Tʿang was banished to the southernmost point of the Chinese mainland, Hsü-wen (i.e. Suwen in Kwangtung Province), facing Hainan Island, to draw his pay as the county police officer. But he obtained leave to return to his home in Lin-chʿuan the following year, and was formally recalled in 1593 and made County Magistrate of Sui-chʿang in the hills of Chekiang. The next few years were idyllic. Tʿang regarded the Magistrate's duty as to keep a benevolent eye on the people and leave them alone, to refrain from torture and reduce court cases to a minimum. Such practices were viewed askance by those in authority and in 1598, after one of the periodic checks to which all Ming officials were subjected, Tʿang sent in his resignation and returned to Lin-chʿuan, where in the part of the town known as Sha-ching (Sand Well) he bought a ramshackle old house and had it rebuilt for his retirement. Three years later, he received a curt letter of dismissal.

It was within a few months of Tʿang's homecoming that he finished 'The Peony Pavilion'. Two other plays followed: *Nan-kʿo chi* (1600) and *Han-tan chi* (1601), both dramatized versions of well-known *chʿuan-chi* tales of the Tʿang dynasty and each having for its hero a dreamer.[2] In *Nan-kʿo chi* (44 scenes), the student Chʿun-yü Fen falls asleep after drinking with his friends in the shade of a *huai* tree (*sophora japonica*). From under the tree, two robed officials come forward to invite him to the Great Kingdom of Huai Peace, where Chʿun-yü marries the Princess, presides over the Prefecture of Nan-kʿo and lives in great splendour until, suddenly falling into disgrace, he is escorted back in ignominy, and wakes up to contemplate the ants' nest that had been his dream-world. And in *Han-tan chi* (30 scenes), the student Lu of the city of Han-tan sleeps on a magic pillow while waiting for his meal to be cooked at an inn. The stoneware pillow, from a Tzʿu-chou kiln, is open at both ends, and Lu walks right through it into a garden, where he meets a rich heiress, whom he marries. Through his wife's influence, he wins honours and rises to a high position; he constructs a canal for the Emperor and destroys the invading

---

[1] In *Tʿang Hsien-tsu chi*, vol. II, c. 43, pp. 1211–14.
[2] *Nan-kʿo chi* is based on *Nan-kʿo tʿai-shou chuan* by Li Kung-tso, in Wang Pʿi-chiang (ed.) *Tʿang-jen hsiao-shuo*, Ku-tien edition of 1955, pp. 85–90; *Han-tan chi* is based on *Chen-chung chi* by Shen Chi-chi, in *Tʿang-jen hsiao-shuo*, pp. 37–9.

foreign army; and he dies at the age of eighty, a noble lord —
to find himself still in his torn sheepskin jacket, the millet
porridge not yet ready.

The plot of an earlier play *Tzu-ch'ai chi* ('The Purple Jade
Hair-pin'), finished in Nanking about 1587, also contains a
dream.[1] The presence of a dream, the feature common to the
four plays, is their most palpable link with the man's own
experience. All through his life T'ang was deeply aware of
dreams, and he recorded a number of them in the titles of his
poems as if they had been actual events. When, in 1591, friends
expressed anxiety about his safety in damp and misty Hsü-wen
in the southern wastes populated by crocodiles and apes, T'ang
replied: 'In my dreams I have visited the Lo-fou and Fou-ch'iu
Hills (near Tseng-ch'eng, i.e. Tsengshing, in Kwangtung
Province) with their peaks, Ch'ing-lei and Ta-p'eng, and in
their midst the enchanted well where the Taoist Ko Hung
attained his elixir, and also Ma Yüan's bronze pillar (near
Shang-ssu in Kwangsi Province on the border with Vietnam),
which I dared not hope to see with my eyes. By becoming the
police officer of Hsü-wen, I shall fulfil my wish.'[2] Dreaming
about Lo-fou Hill is corroborated by an earlier poem (of 1577)
addressed to his friend Ch'i Yen-tseng, who was then living
among those hills.[3]

Lin-ch'uan lay conveniently along his route to the south,
and he obtained permission to spend some time at home, where
he lay ill with malaria. During a bad attack of fever, he dreamt
of being trapped in a dilapidated building, groping his way in
the dim moonlight towards a door that continually eluded him
and suddenly realizing that he was no more than a foot high
and utterly helpless; but the re-assuring voice of his old father
woke him and he found himself bathed in sweat.[4] Later, while
in Sui-ch'ang as a Magistrate, he dreamt of becoming Prefect
of Shih-ch'ien (in distant Kweichow Province) and of his son,

[1] See Hsü Shuo-fang, *T'ang Hsien-tsu nien-p'u*, appendix c, pp. 221–2.
Tzu-ch'ai chi and the earlier draft, *Tzu-hsiao chi*, are based on another
ch'uan-chi tale, *Huo Hsiao-yü chuan* by Chiang Fang, in *T'ang-jen hsiao-shuo*, pp. 77–82.
[2] See biography by T'ang's friend, Tsou Ti-kuang, in *T'ang Hsien-tsu chi*, vol. 11, Appendices, p. 1512.
[3] *T'ang Hsien-tsu chi*, vol. 1, c. 3, p. 59. The Lo-fou hills are commemorated
in a dozen or so poems written during the actual visit, including one
lamenting Ch'i Yen-tseng, then already dead; vol. 1, c. 11, pp. 418–24.
[4] Poem of summer 1591; vol. 1, c. 11, p. 385.

a lad of sixteen, being the recipient of a jade bedstead.[1] Less reverently, in an undated poem, he records a dream in which he looks for a privy in a holy temple, but in vain.[2] Of greater interest in connection with 'The Peony Pavilion' is his poem 'On appearing to my friend Shuai in his dream', written in the twelfth month 1587, i.e. early in 1588.[3] Unknown to his Lin-ch'uan friend, Shuai Chi, T'ang had completed a trip to the capital and decided to visit home before resuming his duties in Nanking. On the night before T'ang's arrival, Shuai, who, though older by thirteen years, was a sympathetic friend, saw T'ang come to him in a dream, saying distinctly 'Surely you look thinner!' In the notes introducing the poem, T'ang goes on to observe that dreams are rooted in feeling.[4] And in the poem itself he re-affirms his friendship with Shuai, who had lent him his own cap upon T'ang calling immediately after reaching home, still wearing his robe and hat: the cap proved an exact fit, thereby showing that their heads, and therefore their minds, were alike.

Then, in the second month (i.e. about March) of 1599, when by Chinese reckoning T'ang was already fifty—at which age most Chinese counted their blessings—came the dream to end all dreams:[5] while he slept, an unusually pretty slave girl appeared before his bed-curtains. She was trying on a skirt with a plum-blossom design based on a picture. As he watched her in fascination, a servant entered with a letter from his revered monk friend Ta-kuan (from whom he had parted not many days ago). The letter turned out to be an album, on the last page of which were the words: 'Great Awakening', which prompted some reflections on semblance and reality in the poem, concluding with the thought that a man of fifty had best

[1] Poem of autumn 1594; vol. I, c. 12, p. 456. See note 3 below.

[2] Vol. II, c. 20, p. 861.

[3] Vol. I, c. 8, pp. 244–5. Shuai Chi (1537–95), who was living in temporary retirement, had served as *chu-shih* in the Sacrificial Department in the Board of Rites in Nanking and had later been Prefect of Ssu-nan (in Kweichow Province). T'ang was appointed to the same post in the Board of Rites in 1589, and no doubt proud to be following his friend's foot-steps—a Prefecture in some remote part of the empire thus seemed a reasonable aspiration.

[4] *Ch'ing*, i.e. feeling; affection; passion.

[5] *Meng chüeh p'ien* ('The Awakening from my Dreams'); vol. I, c. 14, pp. 535–6. Ta-kuan had stopped at Lin-ch'uan on his way to the Lu-shan hills; T'ang accompanied the monk as far as Nanchang before returning home, where he had the dream.

consider himself half a skeleton and wake up from his dreams, for which reminder he was grateful to Ta-kuan, his friend and teacher. In fact, he continued to dream, probably until the end of his life.[1] T'ang died in 1616, in the same year as Shakespeare.

The 'great awakening' interposed between 'The Peony Pavilion' and the two last 'dream' plays. It marks a real change of attitude, from the intense absorption in a dream that is worth all of life, being a projection of the innermost feelings, to the resignation and cynicism harboured in the age-old saying — life is a dream, an empty bubble. Thus in the author's own Preface[2] (autumn 1598) to 'The Peony Pavilion' we read:

Was ever a woman so swayed by feeling as Fair Bride, who, meeting a man in her dream, so pined for him as to fall ill and, being long ill without hope of recovery, painted her own portrait to perpetuate her memory before dying; but who, being dead three years, still sought out her dream-lover and brought about her own return to life? . . . Why,

then, deny the truth of our feelings as revealed in dreams? But in his Preface[3] (summer 1600) to *Nan-k'o chi*, feelings and passions are spoken of in terms of ensnarement:

Where the dream ends, awakening begins: when passions are spent, enlightenment follows.

Feeling is hardly touched upon, and dreams rejected as mere illusion in the Preface[4] (autumn 1601) to *Han-tan chi*. It was his last play.

Nevertheless T'ang retained his interest in the theatre and in the performance of his plays.[5] By this time he had become the mainstay of the local theatre known as the School of I-huang (i.e. Ihwang, thirty-odd miles south of Lin-ch'uan), ultimately derived from the Hai-yen School in Chekiang. Though the span of T'ang's life coincided with a great flowering of the Southern Drama centred on K'un-shan, near Soochow, and he himself had lived in Nanking and Chekiang, he remained devoted to the I-huang actors, whose art he commemorates in an essay on the dedication of their tutelary deity,

[1] See, e.g., poems in vol. I, c. 16, pp. 628, 642; vol. II, c. 18, pp. 756, 757–8.
[2] Vol. II, c. 33, pp. 1093–4; and in most editions of the play.
[3] Vol. II, c. 33, pp. 1096–7.   [4] Vol. II, c. 33, pp. 1094–5.
[5] See, e.g., the poem 'Performing the two "Dreams"', vol. II, c. 19, p. 766; T'ang's Preface (1603) to Cheng Pao-hsien's play *Ch'i-t'ing chi*, in vol. II, c. 33, p. 1091; letters to Ling Ch'u-ch'eng, vol. II, c. 47, pp. 1344–5; to Kan I-lu, c. 47, p. 1367; to the actor Lo Chang-erh, c. 49, p. 1426.

the god Ch'ing-yüan.[1] Already in 1577–9, while still a student
at home, he had written—probably in collaboration with
others—a play for performance by the local theatre, *Tzu-hsiao
chi* ('The Purple Jade Flute') in thirty-four scenes in the
Southern manner, which subsequently he recast into *Tzu-ch'ai
chi* ('The Purple Jade Hair-pin'). And it was for the I-huang
actors, too, that he wrote his later plays. 'The Peony Pavilion',
in particular, proved an immediate success[2] so that soon afterwards it was adapted, no doubt, with some concessions to the
Wu dialect and pronunciation, for performance by the then pre-
dominant K'un-shan School. T'ang was horrified,[3] and in a
letter to a leading I-huang actor,[4] warned him to have no truck
with the adapted version—'even changing a word or two for
convenience in staging would result in something false to my
intention'.

The full title of the play, which consists of fifty-five scenes
including the Prologue, is *Mou-tan t'ing huan-hun chi* ('The
Return of the Dispossessed Soul to the Peony Pavilion'). The
plot may have been derived from a story-teller's text now
lost—*Tu Li-niang chi* ('The Tale of Tu Fair Bride'), the title
being preserved in a mid-sixteenth century library catalogue.[5]
The story owes something, too, to the supernatural tales of the
centuries preceding the T'ang dynasty with their ghosts, ex-
humations and revivals after death,[6] particularly three mentioned by the author himself in his Preface: the tale of Feng
Hsiao-chiang, in which the ghost of the heroine, the daughter

[1] In 1560, when T'ang was a boy of ten, the army commander and patron
of the theatre T'an Lun (1520–77) brought back from Hai-yen (near
Hangchow) a group of actors to train the players in his home town I-
huang (in Kiangsi Province) and revive the Kiangsi theatre, then in
abeyance. The new acting school prospered, so that, by 1600 or so, the
actors and musicians—probably scattered over many towns—numbered
nearly a thousand. See T'ang's essay 'Dedication of the Temple to the
Tutelary Deity of the I-huang Actors, the God Ch'ing-yüan', in vol. II,
c. 34, pp. 1127–9.
[2] Shen Te-fu (1578–1642) notes in *Ku ch'ü tsa-yen*: 'As soon as "The
Peony Pavilion" came out, it was read and sung in every household, almost
eclipsing "The West Chamber". . .', in *Chung-kuo ku-tien hsi-ch'ü lun-chu
chi-ch'eng*, vol. IV, p. 206.
[3] Letter to Ling Ch'u-ch'eng, vol. II, c. 47, pp. 1344–5.
[4] Letter to Lo Chang-erh, c. 49, p. 1426.
[5] *Pao-wen-t'ang shu-mu*, Ku-tien edition of 1957, p. 114. See T'an Cheng-
pi, *Hua-pen yü ku-chü* (1957), p. 53; regarding Pao-wen-t'ang, see also
Introduction to 'The Birthday Gift Convoy' *supra*.
[6] See, e.g., the stories in the early Sung collection *T'ai-p'ing kuang-chi*
(A.D. 978), cc. 276–282 'Dreams'; cc. 375–386 'Revivals'.

of a Prefect, appears to the hero in a dream, followed by her unearthing, revival and marriage to him;[1] the similar tale of Li Chung-wen, in which, however, the heroine is dug up too soon and consequently lost to the hero;[2] and the somewhat different one of T'an-sheng, in which, as in our play, scene 53, the heroine's father has the hero cruelly beaten for rifling her tomb.[3]

T'ang's transmutation of this unpromising material is but inadequately conveyed by a synopsis: The story is set in the Southern Sung. The hero Willow (Liu), descended from the T'ang dynasty prose writer, Liu Tsung-yüan,[4] meets in a dream a beautiful lady standing under a plum tree; after which, longing for her, he calls himself Dreamer of the Plum (Meng-mei; scene 2). The lady turns out to be Fair Bride (Li-niang), daughter of Prefect Tu of Nan-an (in Kiangsi Province), a descendant of the poet Tu Fu (scene 3). Fair Bride is kept in almost complete seclusion by her parents; on a spring day, however, she ventures into the garden with her maid, Spring Fragrance, and succumbs to the insidious influence of spring — so that, upon returning to her room, she falls asleep and dreams of being again in the garden, where she meets the hero, a student not known to her, by the Peony Pavilion (scene 10). She loses her heart irretrievably to him, and on the following day again ventures into the garden in quest of her dream (scene 12). Fair Bride languishes and falls ill (scenes 14, 16, 18); dying, she is mourned by her well-meaning but insensible parents and buried in the garden (scene 20).

Nearly three years pass. Willow has left his home in the extreme south, where the family have settled since their ancestor Liu Tsung-yüan died at his last official post in Liu-chou (in Kwangsi Province), and is on his wanderings (scenes 13, 21; the latter, with its foreign traders from across the seas and their pearls and precious stones, recalling the author's own sojourn on the southern coast). Loaded with bundle and umbrella, he

[1] In *Sou-shen hou-chi*, c. 4 (pp. 1ᵃ–2ᵃ in *Chin-tai pi-shu*, Reprint of 1922, XI).
[2] In *Sou-shen hou-chi*, c. 4 (pp. 3ᵇ–4ᵇ).
[3] In *Sou-shen chi*, c. 16, (pp. 12ᵇ–13ᵇ in *Chin-tai pi-shu*, XI).
[4] Liu Tsung-yüan (773–819) was himself reputedly a dreamer: he dreamt of a willow tree (*liu*) falling to the ground and soon afterwards became Prefect of Liu-chou, where, however, he later died (see *T'ai-p'ing kuang-chi*, c. 279, Jen-min edition of 1959, pp. 2221–2).

finds himself in Nan-an on a winter's day, sick and weary; while trying to cross a river, he slips on the ice and is rescued by the old pedant Ch'en (scene 22), formerly tutor to Fair Bride (scenes 5, 7), who brings him to the garden, now transformed into a temple with an old nun named Stone left in charge (scene 20). The Prefect has in the meantime been transferred to the Huai valley to crush a rebellion (scenes 20, 31). Willow lodges at the temple to convalesce. Spring returns. Willow, exploring the garden, comes upon a portrait of Fair Bride (painted by herself in scene 14) in a sandalwood box hidden under the rockery (scene 24). In the night her spirit visits him (scene 28). The Judge of the Underworld, taking pity upon Fair Bride after hearing an eloquent plea on her behalf by the God of Flowers, has granted her a fresh lease of life (scene 23). Willow induces the nun, who has become suspicious (scenes 29, 30), to exhume Fair Bride, who revives (scenes 33, 35). The nun marries the pair, and all three set out for the capital, Lin-an (i.e. Hangchow; scene 36). The scandalized Tutor Ch'en hurries to Prefect Tu to report the violation of the tomb and sacrilege against the dead (scene 37), and arrives at the camp opportunely to bring about the rebel leader's surrender (scenes 45–47). The victorious Prefect Tu is elevated to the rank of Minister and returns to the capital, where Willow is accused of heinous crimes (scene 53). Fair Bride meets her mother (scene 48), but her father, firmly convinced of her being a devilish apparition, plans to exorcize her (scenes 53, 54). Willow's old gardener, a hunch-back descended from the hunch-backed tree-planter celebrated in one of Liu Tsung-yüan's essays (scene 2), goes in search of his master (scene 40) and arrives at the capital to learn of his pre-eminent examination success (scene 52). In the final scene (55), Tu and Willow, and then Fair Bride enter the Imperial presence chamber, led by the pedant Ch'en, now a palace official, and hear the Emperor's verdict that Fair Bride is quick and whole.

The impression the play leaves with any reader is one of boundless energy and imagination. Its language is at once colloquial and highly poetic, so that exquisite lyrics fit seamless into the dramatic context, and yet the gay and poignant scenes alike pulsate with life. Like strings of pearls, sparkling phrases drop from the lips of the characters, some of whom are refined but stilted, not excluding the hero Willow himself, and others children of nature, coarse and grotesque, such as the nun and the hunch-backed gardener, yet all likeable and even lovable; and their songs and dialogue are, moreover, enlivened by puns, innuendos, and the aptest and most unexpected allusions. For our author is not only gifted with fertile invention and inexhaustible wit: his essentially comic genius combines within itself the roles of dreamer and mercilessly penetrating observer of the human scene, of men and women with their passions, follies and vanities. Without a shadow of doubt, 'The Peony Pavilion' is the richest and maturest product of the Chinese stage.

It is the dreamer in T'ang that has had the widest appeal, and almost from the start the play was firmly established in the Chinese love tradition.[1] The 'dream scene' itself became one of the great love scenes of the theatre. In scene 2 of 'The Blood-stained Fan' (1699),[2] for example, the heroine Hsiang-chün, a young singer who has been trained as yet only in the one play — 'The Peony Pavilion' — goes through two songs from the 'dream scene' with her singing master. And in 'Red Chamber Dream' of the eighteenth century, the heroine Tai-yü is entranced by stray lines from this scene that reach her ear while a troupe of girls rehearse it in the garden[3] (chapter 23). For our author's bold recourse to a dream, in which the heroine's longing, freed of the restraints of correct behaviour, conjures up the hero as her ideal lover, has successfully reconciled depth and spontaneity of feeling with strict decorum. When, in scene 23, the Judge of the Underworld learns from Fair Bride that she died through despair of her dream's fulfilment, he exclaims: 'You lie! To die only because of a dream! Is such a thing possible?' But the heroine's total abandonment to the idea of romantic love, unattainable in the world she inhabits, awakened ready response in the hearts especially of women.[4] And this noble conception of love — as having an existence of its own, in feelings and in dreams, independently of outward circumstances — has come from an author who understands only too well its claims on both body and mind, who can be unreservedly and unremittingly bawdy (e.g. in the nun's soli-

[1] See Shen Te-fu's remark in n. 2 on p. 268 above.
[2] See 'The Blood-stained Fan', *infra.*
[3] See 'A Burial Mound for Flowers', *infra.*
[4] See the stories of women who pined away after reading 'The Peony Pavilion' in Hsü Shuo-fang, *T'ang Hsien-tsu nien-p'u*, appendix E, pp. 235–9.

loquy in scene 17). It was left to a Manchu aristocrat, upon whom Confucian decorum had no hold, to expound a still more idealistic—almost a metaphysical—view of love, in the 'Red Chamber Dream'.

'The Peony Pavilion' survives in a large number of Ming and Ch'ing editions, often with arbitrary changes in the text. For the translation I have followed the text in the annotated edition by Hsü Shuo-fang and Yang Hsiao-mei (Ku-tien 1958), based on the edition from the Ming publishing house, Huai-te-t'ang. The later southern Drama did not diverge greatly in form from its antecedent of the fourteenth century including 'The Lute', from which our play inherited such features as the trembling son-in-law and examinee being bullied by the irate father-in-law and Minister, the Emperor's intervention in the family quarrel, the palace scenes, etc. But the sixteenth- and seventeenth-century dramatic romance (*ch'uan-ch'i*) was addressed to a more sophisticated audience and is therefore a more polished affair. In particular, each scene of our play ends with a somewhat artificial quatrain pieced together from lines picked out of poets of the T'ang dynasty.

The I-huang school of acting for which T'ang wrote and the then and since more prevalent K'un-shan School were originally related,[1] differing chiefly in the style of singing and musical accompaniment, and individual scenes of 'The Peony Pavilion' still form part of the K'un-shan repertory (known as 'K'un-ch'ü') of today.[2] Our extract includes the 'dream scene' itself and the three preceding scenes—being scenes 7, 8, 9, 10—which hang together as an elaborate song in praise of spring's awakening. In my translation I have followed the same principles as for 'The Lute', but have omitted the type of role of each character in the notes, nor inserted cross references to earlier and later scenes.

[1] Through the Hai-yen School from which the I-huang School stemmed and also through the earlier I-yang School (of Kiangsi) which influenced the K'un-shan School; see Chou I-po, *Chung-kuo hsi-chü-shih chiang-tso*, 1958, p. 144, and Mei Lan-fang (see note 3), pp. 117–18.
[2] Especially scenes 7, 9, 10; see Mei Lan-fang, *Wu-t'ai sheng-huo ssu-shih nien* ('Forty Years on the Stage'), 1957, vol. II, pp. 112–13.

T'ang Hsien-tsu

The Peony Pavilion

Scene 7   The Schoolroom

TUTOR CH'EN[1] [*enters and declaims*]

Another quatrain composed, I polish up last spring's rhymes;
Breakfast scarce done, I already think of the morning tea.
On my desk, ants follow their trail along the wet inkslab,
While bees thread the lattice window

to suck the flowers in the vase.

I, Ch'en Tsui-liang, am installed in the Tu house as tutor to the
young Mistress Tu, whose forbears were especially versed in
the Book of Songs, Mao version,[2] and am treated with much
consideration by Lady Tu. This morning, having finished my
breakfast, I will glance over the Mao commentators. [*reads*]

Kwan, kwan cried the osprey
On the river islet;
The beautiful young lady—
A princely man well sought her.[3]

'Well' is ardently; to 'seek' is to woo. [*looks up*] It is late, and
I still do not see the pupil entering the schoolroom. How fright-
fully spoilt! I will sound the boards thrice! [*strikes the boards*]
Spring Fragrance, ask your young mistress to attend the lecture.

TU FAIR BRIDE[4] [*enters, followed by the Maid, Spring Fragrance, who is holding up with both hands a pile of books; Fair Bride*

[1] The perfect pedant.
[2] Versed in the Book of Songs: by virtue of their descent from the poet Tu
Fu. The Mao version was the only version of the Book of Songs handed
down, and the work is known for short as 'The Mao Poems' (or 'The Mao
Songs').
[3] Well sought her—the lines are here rendered according to the Tutor's
reading of them. See Legge, *The She King* (The Chinese Classics vol.IV)
Part I, I.i, and Waley, *The Book of Songs*, no. 87.
[4] The heroine, aged nearly sixteen; see Introduction.

sings]

   My morning toilet completed,

   With unhurried steps I walk across to the schoolroom,

   Languidly confronting the clean bench and the bright window;

MAID [*sings*]

   'The worthy sayings of former men'[1]

   Form one long straitjacket,

   Which worn, fits one to teach a parrot to order tea.

[*They greet the Tutor*]

FAIR BRIDE: Ten thousand blessings to the Tutor!

MAID: And pray excuse us, Tutor!

TUTOR: Young women ought at the first crowing of the cock to wash their hands and rinse their mouths, comb their hair and affix the hairpin, and go to their parents to inquire after their health. Then, after sunrise, each should attend to her daily task.[2] Now your task, my pupil, is to study. Therefore, you will need to rise early.

FAIR BRIDE: We shall not err again.

MAID: We know now. Tonight we shall not sleep. At midnight we shall ask the Tutor to start lessons.

TUTOR: Have you revised the Book of Songs, Mao version, which we read yesterday?

FAIR BRIDE: I have revised the lesson and wait for the explanation.

TUTOR: Read on, then.

FAIR BRIDE [*reads*]

   Kwan, kwan cried the osprey

   On the river islet;

   The beautiful young lady—

   A princely man well sought her.

TUTOR: Listen to the explanation. '*Kwan, kwan* cried the osprey': the osprey was a bird and '*kwan, kwan*' its call.

MAID: What was the call like?

[*Tutor makes the call of an osprey. Maid, pretending to imitate the call, adds much comic business*]

TUTOR: This bird was fond of quiet and seclusion, and so it was on an islet of the river.

---

[1] The first line of a popular collection of maxims and wise saws known as *Tseng kuang*, which the illiterate often learned by heart.

[2] See Legge, *Li Ki*, Book x, 'The Pattern of the Family', Section I, § 2–3 (vol. I, p. 450).

M A I D : That must have been it! It wasn't yesterday, but rather the day before; no, it wasn't this year, but rather last year. There was a rock pigeon in a cage in our Prefectural residence, but the young mistress set it free, and it flew to District Governor Ho's house.[1]

T U T O R : Nonsense! This is a case of the similative device.[2]

M A I D : Stimulative device? What does it stimulate?

T U T O R : A similitude leads up to its counterpart. Here, it leads up to the lines about the beautiful young lady, who was a person quiet and demure, and thus a good man came along to woo her gently.

M A I D : Why did he woo her gently?

T U T O R : Chatterbox!

F A I R B R I D E : To explain according to the notes in the book— that, your pupil can already do. Simply expound the general tenor of the Book of Songs, Tutor.

T U T O R [*sings*]

> Of the Six Classics
> The Songs are the chief ornament:
> For the young ladies
> Graceful patterns of conduct they supply—
> To cite an instance,
> The birth of the Chou race from the matriarch Chiang,[3]
> Or the selfless devotion
> Of many queens enlightened and virtuous.
> And further, as in 'The cock crows',[4]
> Or the Lament of the Swallow's Flight,[5]

---

[1] Rock pigeon, etc.: a succession of puns. The cooing osprey is also the confined osprey and, by a further twist, confined rock pigeon; District Governor Ho puns with river island.

[2] The device of *hsing*, which Legge translates as the 'allusive piece'. 'The . . . allusive piece commences with a couple of lines, which are repeated often through all the stanzas, as a sort of refrain. They are generally descriptive of something in the animal or vegetable world; and after them the writer proceeds to his proper subject. Often the allusive lines convey a meaning harmonizing with that of the lines which follow.' (*The She King, Prolegomena* chapter II. Appendix I, p.35n.) The character *hsing* may also mean elation, passion, inspiration; hence the Maid's pun.

[3] Chiang Yüan, who was with child after treading on the toe of a giant footprint, gave birth to Hou Chi (Lord Millet), the ancestor of the Chou; see Legge, Part III. II. i and Waley, no.238.

[4] 'The cock crows'—Legge, Part I. VIII. i and Waley, no.26; a poem about illicit love, it is traditionally accorded an allegorical interpretation.

[5] Swallow's Flight—Legge, Part I. III. iii and Waley, no.114.

Or the Plaint beside the Yangtze,[1]
Or Thoughts on the Broad River Han,[2]
They wash away all artificial adornment
But inculcate by force of example
Sentiments befitting the family and home.

FAIR BRIDE: How many poems are there in all?

TUTOR: The poems number three hundred, but are summed up in one phrase [*sings*]

No other than
'Without evil thought'[3]—
For handing down to posterity.

The lecture is over. Spring Fragrance, bring the four scribe's treasures for the writing lesson.

MAID [*goes off; then re-enters with writing implements*] Paper, ink, brush and slab are all here.

TUTOR: What ink-stick is this?

FAIR BRIDE: My maid has brought the wrong thing. This is a spiral jet, for painting the eyebrows.

TUTOR: What writing brush is this?

FAIR BRIDE [*laughing*] It is an extra fine brush, also for the eyebrows.

TUTOR: I have never seen such. Take them away. Take them away. What paper is this?

FAIR BRIDE: Hsüeh-t'ao's crimson note-paper.[4]

TUTOR: Take it away. Take it away. Bring the plain kind, as was invented by Ts'ai Lun.[5] What ink-slab is this? Is it one ink-slab or two?

FAIR BRIDE: A pair of entwining ink-slabs.

---

[1] Plaint beside the Yangtze—the only poem which seems to fit the rather obscure reference is about a parting followed by reconciliation and re-union, as seen in the river Yangtze parting and joining again; see Legge, Part I. II. xi and Waley, no. 79.

[2] Broad River Han—Legge, Part I. I. ix and Waley, no. 82.

[3] As succinctly expressed by Confucius himself; see Legge, *The Analects*, II. ii: 'The Master said, "In the Book of Poetry are three hundred pieces, but the design of them all may be embraced in one sentence—Having no depraved thoughts."'

[4] Hsüeh T'ao, T'ang dynasty courtesan, exchanged verses with Po Chü-i and other poets on ornamented crimson note-paper specially prepared for this purpose; see Fei Chu, *Shu ch'ien p'u* ('Notes on Szechuan paper'), *Mei-shu ts'ung-shu*, III. v. pp. 242–4.

[5] Ts'ai Lun, the eunuch who invented paper in A.D. 105 when, with the Later Han emperor Ho-ti's approval, it was universally adopted for writing; see *Hou-Han shu*, c. 68, p. 2513.

TUTOR: With all those eyes?

FAIR BRIDE: Weeping eyes.[1]

TUTOR: Why weeping? Change the lot.

MAID [*aside*] What a country bumpkin! [*aloud*] I will go and change them. [*goes off and re-enters with another set of implements*] Would these do?

TUTOR [*inspecting the implements*] They would do.

FAIR BRIDE: Your pupil can do the copying by herself, but Spring Fragrance will still need you to guide her brush.

TUTOR: I will watch while you copy the writing manual. [*Fair Bride writes with a brush. Tutor, watching her, is overcome by surprise*] I have never seen such good writing. Whose style is it?

FAIR BRIDE: It is the style handed down by Lady Wei,[2] known as 'Lovely lady's floral hairpin'.

MAID: And I shall be doing a slavishly imitative 'clumsy handmaid' style.

FAIR BRIDE: That will not be for some time yet.

MAID: Tutor, this pupil begs to be excused.   [*Goes off*

FAIR BRIDE: May I ask how old my Tutor's lady is?

TUTOR: She is just sixty.

FAIR BRIDE: I wish to embroider a pair of slippers for her birthday. I beg for a pattern.

TUTOR: How kind of you! Simply follow the pattern in *Mencius*, and make sandals without knowing the size of the feet.[3]

FAIR BRIDE: I don't see Spring Fragrance coming.

TUTOR: Do you want to call her? [*calls aloud, in all three times*] MAID [*re-entering*] You plagued with the pox!

FAIR BRIDE [*annoyed*] Where did you wretched girl go?

MAID [*laughing*] To the privy. But oh! there's a large garden,

---

[1] 'Eyes' are the variegated patterns on the inkstone; where the patterns are blurred they are known as 'weeping eyes', with which term Tutor Ch'en seems unfamiliar. See, e.g., Ts'ao Yung, *Yen lu* (Notes on Inkslabs), *Mei-shu ts'ung-shu*, I. vi, pp. 200–1.

[2] The calligrapher Wei Shuo, known as Lady Wei, who transmitted the style of Chung Yu (A.D. 151–230) and taught the great fourth-century calligrapher Wang Hsi-chih; see, e.g., *P'ei-wen-chai shu-hua p'u*, c. 23. 'Lovely lady's floral hairpin' and 'clumsy handmaid' are metaphors for natural elegance and servile imitation respectively in calligraphy.

[3] This is the very ecstasy of pedantry; see Legge, *Mencius*, VI. i. 7. 4: ". . . the scholar Lung said, 'If a man make hempen sandals without knowing the size of people's feet, yet I know that he will not make them like baskets.'"

bright with flowers and green with willow trees,[1] very pleasant to sport in.

TUTOR: Aha! Neglecting your books and wandering into the garden! Let me fetch the thornstick.

MAID: What is the thornstick for? [*sings*]

Your young ladies,
Aspire they to examination honours or magisterial eminence?
Need they do more than read,
Or write crow-like characters?

TUTOR: When the ancients applied themselves to books, some kept fireflies in a bag, others read by moonlight.[2]

MAID [*sings*]

Dazzled by the silvery light,
Poor, moonstruck Toad had giddy fits.[3]
What? They stuffed fireflies in a bag
And smothered harmless insects?

TUTOR: Were there not those who, to stay awake, tied their hair to the beam and pricked their thigh with an awl?[4]

MAID [*sings*]

Tied to the beam,
Your hair will thin;
Pricking the thigh
But adds to your scars and blotches.
And this is glory!

[*From within, the cry of some one selling flowers*]

MAID: Young mistress, [*sings*]

Hear the flower-seller's cry
Breaking in upon the sound of reading.

TUTOR: Again trying to entice your mistress from her books! I really will strike you.

[*Lifts stick to strike Maid*]

---

[1] The usual phrase is: 'bright flowers, dark willow'. 'Dark' would have jarred here. Willow the hero is young and green.

[2] Examples of the studious but impecunious who had no midnight oil for their lamps: Ch'e Yin gathered fireflies (see *Chin shu*, c. 83, p. 8ᵇ); and Chiang Pi sat on the roof reading his book by moonlight (see *Nan Ch'i shu*, c. 55, p. 5).

[3] In some versions of the moon legend, the goddess Ch'ang-o (see 'The Shrew' *supra*) was transformed into a toad; see Yüan K'o, *Shen-hua ku-shih hsin-pien*, 1963, p. 164.

[4] The somewhat hackneyed examples of Su Ch'in, who wielded the awl (see *Chan-kuo-ts'e*, c. 3) and Sun Ching, who tugged at the beam (see *Shang yu lu*, c. 4, and the biographical dictionaries).

MAID [*dodging; sings*]

    Strike? Strike this poor child,
    One of your very own disciples?
    The culprit is scared indeed!

[*Snatches stick from Tutor and throws it on the floor*]

FAIR BRIDE: Wretched girl! You have offended the Tutor.
Kneel down at once. [*Maid kneels*] Tutor, seeing that it is her
first offence, allow your pupil to punish her this time.

[*addressing Maid, sings*]

    Your hands shall not
    Touch the ropes of the swing.
    Your feet shall not
    Tread on the garden path.

MAID: But I may look on?

FAIR BRIDE: Will you retort? [*sings*]

    This incontinent mouth—
    We'll burn holes round it with a smoking incense stick.
    Those roving eyes—
    We'll stab them with embroidery needles till they go blind.

MAID: Blinded, what use should I be?

FAIR BRIDE [*sings*]

    I can then have you tied to the inkslab,
    Chained to the desk,
    Chanting after me 'The Poem says—'
    'The Master said—'
    Without default.

MAID: Default is best.

FAIR BRIDE [*pulling Maid's hair; sings*]

    We'll count the number of hairs on your head
    And give you the same number of stripes on your back!
    Some lingering fears you may have
    For my lady mother's
    Household rules.[1]

MAID: I dare not offend again.

TUTOR: It's as well to let her off this time.

[*Maid rises from kneeling*]

TUTOR [*sings*]

    Women pupils, except they seek not official advancement,

---

[1] The 'household rules' are, in the abstract, a set of disciplinary rules and,
in the concrete, a hard-hitting wooden ruler wielded by the mistress of
the household or her deputy.

Shall be taught in all respects like men students.

You may only return to the house when your lessons are done.

I will now attend upon my patron the Prefect. [*chorus*]

    We must use with diligence this bright schoolroom

                    with its new gauze curtains.

                                [*Goes off*

M A I D [*pointing her finger at Tutor's back and cursing*] The clumsy old buffalo! The dumb dog! He *would* spoil all the fun.

F A I R   B R I D E [*tugging at Maid to restrain her*] You fool!

   'He was your teacher for a day;

    Treat him as a father all your life.'

You know that he has the right to cane you.—Let me ask you now; where is that garden?

[*Maid would not speak. Fair Bride smiles to placate her and again asks the question*]

M A I D [*pointing with her finger*] Look! Isn't it there?

F A I R   B R I D E: Has it got any interesting vistas?

M A I D: Vistas? There are six or seven pavilions, a swing or two, and a gentle, winding stream in front of a T'ai-hu rockery. The place is full of the rarest herbs and flowers, and is really gorgeous.

F A I R   B R I D E: So indeed there is such a place!—However, we must return to the house. [*declaims*]

   'Willow Catkins drifting into a lady's courtyard'[1]

M A I D [*declaims*]

   'The eager chrysalis waiting to turn butterfly'[2]

F A I R   B R I D E [*declaims*]

   'Ask not about the endless sorrows of spring'[3]

B O T H [*declaim*]

   'As we walk through the green shade in a flitting moment.'[4]

                                 [*Both go off*

---

[1] The line reads in the original: 'Willow catkins drifting into the Hsieh courtyard', the allusion being to the talented Hsieh Tao-yün, who, while watching the snow with her uncle Hsieh An, compares snow flakes to willow catkins. It is taken from Li Shan-fu, 'Willow', *Wan shou T'ang jen chüeh chü*, c. 66, p. 2018; *Ch'üan T'ang shih*, c. 643, vol. x, pp. 7375–6. Willow catkins being blown about invariably evoked sadness in the Chinese poet.

[2] From Chang Mi, 'Thoughts on a Spring Evening', *Ch'üan T'ang shih*, c. 742, vol. xi, p. 8453.

[3] From Chao Ku, 'Distant Thoughts', *Wan shou T'ang jen chüeh chü*, c. 37, p. 1174; *Ch'üan T'ang shih*, c. 550, vol. ix, p. 6375.

[4] From Chang Hu, 'The Two Spruce Firs of the Fa-yün Temple at Yangchow', *Ch'üan T'ang shih*, c. 511, vol. viii, pp. 5827–8.

Scene 8   Tour of the Villages
PREFECT TU OF NAN-AN[1] [*enters, followed by his train of lictors and runners, and a porter. Prefect sings*]
  Whither the Prefect on his tour in spring,
  Collecting folk-songs[2] when the trees are again in blossom
  And the turtle-dove coos under bamboo eaves,
  His vermilion chariot trailed by the legendary deer?[3]—
  Let us linger briefly under this wild pear tree.
[*declaims*]
  That time of year
  In spring, after March and April,
  When a sudden break in the showers brings out the mists,
  Seasonably the Prefect undertakes his tour of inspection:
  For agriculture comes first;
  Taxes, conscription, litigation and trials must await their turn.
My Prefecture, Nan-an,[4] is in the region between the Yangtze and the extreme south, where spring comes early. In the seclusion of my official residence, I could never hear about those in the outlying or more distant villages who neglect their farms' and turn to idle pursuits. Thus I have instructed the country magistrate to have in store flowers and wine, that as Prefect I may encourage husbandry in person. I trust they have been prepared.
COUNTY OFFICIAL [*enters*]
  Though he brought no clerk of his to carry out instructions,
  At least I command the services of our own farmers.
Informing Your Honour, the flowers and wine for the promotion of husbandry are ready.

[1] Type of benevolent provincial governor; see Introduction for the author's own period of office as a county magistrate.
[2] Collecting folk-songs: in particular, the folk-songs of the principality of Pin, the outstanding example of which is 'The Seventh Month', which sings about the farmer's activities throughout the year. See Legge, Part I. XV. i and Waley, *The Book of Songs*, no. 159. Collecting folk-songs was part of the traditional duties of officials; see, e.g., Legge, *Li Ki, Book* III, 'The Royal Regulations', § 14, vol. I, p. 216: 'In the second month of the year [the son of Heaven] ordered the Grand Music-masters to bring him the poems [including ballads and songs] current in the different states, that he might see the manners of the people.'
[3] Cheng Hung, while Prefect of Huai-ying, went on a tour of the villages within his Prefecture and found his Chariot trailed by a white deer; see *Hou-Han shu*, c. 33, p. 1156, commentary.
[4] Nan-an (i.e. Tayu), forty miles or so south-west of Kanchow, is in the southernmost part of Kiangsi Province.

PREFECT: Give orders for the tour to continue. There must be no bawling from you when we approach a village. [*All loudly assent. The road is cleared. The procession moves on*] This is truly,

'To seize the moment of increase
                            and encourage sowing and planting,
Not to journey at leisure, contemplating the local scenery.'[1]

[*Exeunt*

TWO VILLAGE ELDERS [*enter and sing*]

As white hairs add to our years, the burden of business decreases
And we delight in the joking and shouting of the village children.
The Prefect comes on his tour of inspection
Astride his horse, exhaling an air of benevolence—
Perhaps he means to proclaim tillage as part of moral cultivation?

We are elders of Pure Delight Village in Nan-an Prefecture. We congratulate ourselves that, our good Prefect Tu having ruled for three years, his mercy and rectitude ensured that abuses were removed and manners purified. Everywhere such institutions as the village headman and tithing, the relief granary and the village school, have been established, a great blessing to our community! He is now on his way through the various villages to promote farming in person. So we must wait upon him at the Official Pavilion. But see! the attendants carrying the flowers and wine have come.

TWO ATTENDANTS FROM THE COUNTY [*enter, each shouldering one end of a pole from which is suspended a large pear-shaped earthen jar and each holding a basket of flowers in his free hand; sing*]

Fleet-foot runners we are, whom no thief outstrips—
A moment ago we were still at our district quarters,
Now we are carrying wine up the front hill-side!

[*they stumble and fall*]

Nearly cracked it!

[*each to the other*]

If the flowers are crushed, don't just accuse *me*!

VILLAGE ELDERS: So you attendants are now here.

ATTENDANTS: Only, this jar leaks and we fear there might not be enough wine left; we beg the elders to shield us from blame.

---

[1] Adapted from Wang Wei, 'Companion Piece to the Emperor's Poem "Rain in Spring on the Journey from P'eng-lai to Hsing-ch'ing Pavilion" (by command)', *Ch'üang T'ang shih*, c. 128, vol. 11, p. 1295.

VILLAGE ELDERS: No matter. Carry it to one side, and go to the village tavern for a drink.

[*Attendants go off; village headman enters*[1]]

Headman, have the chair ready in its correct place. The Prefect comes directly.

[*Village Elders retire to a far corner*]

PREFECT [*enters, followed by his train; sings*]

> The shade of the blushing almond blossom deepens;
> The sweet-flag renews its sword-like leaf;
> As the year waxes, the rice fields grow warmer. —
> Over a straw hut by the bamboo fence,
>   a wine-seller's banner flutters,
> While through the moist air a thread of smoke rises slantwise.

[*Village Elders come forward to welcome the Prefect; they join in the chorus*]

> The wood warbler cries 'Dee-woo';[2]
> The cuckoo calls 'Boo-koo'.
> We make our tour these several days,
>   suspending court proceedings,
> Without a ceremonial escort,
> And so saving the clamour and hubbub,
> Lest we frighten the scattered dwellers of these wilds.

A LICTOR [*kneeling*] Informing Your Honour, we have reached the Official Pavilion.

[*Village Elders bow down before the Prefect*]

PREFECT: Elders, which village of which division is this one?

VILLAGE ELDERS: Pure Delight Village of the First Division of Nan-an County.

PREFECT: Let me take a look around. [*looks about him*] What a goodly village! Indeed delightful through being pure and clean! [*declaims*]

> For see: the hills are clear,
> The streams are clear;
> Man responds to the call of hills and streams:
> The hand of spring is everywhere.

---

[1] Headman enters. —The direction is inserted by the translator.

[2] 'Dee-woo', as in the Wu pronunciation; in the Kiangsi pronunciation— 'Tee-foo'. *T'i-hu*, the bird named after its cry, is literally 'Carry Wine-jug' and therefore a most welcome songster; it is clearly the wood warbler. Even sweeter to the Prefect's ear must be the cuckoo's cry, *Pu-ku* being literally 'Sow Grain'.

VILLAGE ELDERS [*declaim*]

Indeed it is: the officials are clean,
The administration is clean;
Never are our villagers bothered by the law:
They sing farmers' ditties their labours between.

PREFECT: Elders, do you know the purpose of our tour?
[*sings*]

On the plains the wheat sways in pale jade ripples
And green rice fields lie clearly defined as in pictures;[1]
Rain soft as curd
Sprinkles wet mud along gaily-coloured ridges.
Remember: South of the Yangtze the soil is loose,
                               the earth's veins vigorous;
Yet I fear men's idleness and careless neglect
Or some groundless dispute or legal complication
Might spoil your proper livelihood.

VILLAGE ELDERS: Formerly, by day we had the runners, by
night thieves and robbers. But since Your Honour's coming,
[*sing*]

In a thousand villages the farmer's year has changed!
We simple elders hail you, bearing incense bowls on our heads,
While children troop merrily forth on their bamboo horses:
Warmth and springtide are where the Prefect steps
Along the homes of all his people.
Dogs no longer bark in the moonlight
                       where wild flowers cast their shadows,
But when overhead the rain stops, men still till the green fields:
Truly in every village your wise rule, like gentle rain
                       and dew, brings forth the mulberry and hemp.

[*Voices within sing 'On splashy, squashy mud' etc.*]

PREFECT: Hear the farmers singing in the next village.

FARMER [*enters and sings*]

On splashy, squashy mud
Nimble feet trip and slip;
The short rake, the long plough springily I clutch
To sow reed-grass and hemp after last night's rain;
Then under the bright sun I pour on the dung—
Oh, the odoriferous stench!

---

[1] As for example, handscrolls by Shen Chou and the more decorative painters of the fifteenth and sixteenth centuries.

PREFECT: Well sung. [*repeats Farmer's words*]

'To sow reed-grass and hemp after last night's rain;

Then under the bright sun I pour on the dung

Oh, the odoriferous stench!'

This would suggest that dung was foul. Elders, little does he know that dung can be thought sweet-smelling. There is a poem to prove it:

'Viands in tripods amid smoking incense make fit repast for a king,

Who, fed on jade-like delicacies, will yet know surfeit.

But if steaming rice is borne past you when pinched with hunger,

Then ambergris has not the sweet smell of the fruit of dung.'

Let him wear flowers and regale him with wine.

FARMER [*has flowers pinned to his hat and drinks the wine given him*] What a fine lord! What good wine! [*sings chorus*]

In the Official Pavilion I drink deep of the 'Flaming Cloud',

And grinning in the breeze, find myself decked out with flowers!

Am I not the handsomest of ploughmen?   [*Goes off*

PORTER [*announces*] A young lad comes singing.

BUFFALO-BOY [*enters, flute in hand; sings*]

Whizz cracks the whip!

Sol, lah trills the flute!

I recline on my buffalo as the slanting sun picks out

the evening crows.

[*points with his flute at Porter*]

He is even so small of girth as I,

With the same two horn-like tufts of hair,

Yet *he* may ride on a horse!

PREFECT: Well sung. But why does he point at the door-keeper and sing

'He is even so small of girth as I,

With the same two horn-like tufts of hair,

Yet *he* may ride on a horse'?

Elders, he would not know that on a buffalo one has the firmer seat. There is a poem to prove it:

'Men admire the noble and great,

And reckon the steed the finest mount:

On horseback one watches every change in the sky,[1]

But he who chooses the buffalo rides at his ease.'

Let him wear flowers and regale him with wine.

---

[1] Watches the sky for signs of a storm, i.e. the wrath of the mighty.

BUFFALO-BOY [*has flowers pinned to his bamboo rain-hat and drinks the wine given him; sings chorus*]

    In the Official Pavilion I drink deep of the 'Flaming Cloud',

    And grinning in the breeze, find myself decked out with flowers

    Am I not the handsomest village lad?   [*Goes off*

PORTER [*announces*] Two women come singing.

YOUNGER AND OLDER WOMEN [*enter as if picking mulberry leaves; sing*]

    Under the shade of the mulberry trees

    We strap our wicker baskets—

    Hand poised, shoulders bowed, cut a shoot!

Ah, what official is here?

    'I, Lo-fu, am already married.'[1]

    How could this official venture to claim me

    Alighting from his horse with his gift of gold?

PREFECT: Well sung. Tell them, it is not the amorous official of the poem or the play, but the Prefect himself on a tour to promote husbandry. Such diligence in the gathering of mulberry leaves indeed deserves our respect. There is a poem to prove it:

    'From amid peaches and plums come sounds of merry-making;

    Over a dozen *mou* here, the mulberry's shade is spread:

    Unlike the useless, unprofitable plants of this world,

    Its each leaf and each vein turn into gauze and silk.'

Give them wine and let them wear flowers.

YOUNGER AND OLDER WOMEN [*half concealed,*[2] *have flowers pinned to them and drink the wine given them; sing chorus*]

    In the Official Pavilion, we drink deep of the 'Flaming Cloud'

    And grinning in the breeze

                      find ourselves decked out with flowers—

    Are we not the handsomest gatherers of mulberry leaves?

                                     [*Go off*

PORTER [*announces*] Another pair of women come singing.

TWO OLD WOMEN[3] [*enter with baskets in their hands as if picking*

---

[1] The line is adapted from the early poem 'Mulberry along the Path' (*Mo-shang sang*, in *Yüeh-fu shih-chi*, c. 28), in which the dazzlingly beautiful Lo-fu, while gathering mulberry leaves, is wooed by a passing official. In Shih Chün-pao's *tsa-chü* play *Ch'iu-hu hsi ch'i* (*Yüan ch'ü hsüan*, pp. 542–556), Ch'iu-hu returning home as an official after an absence of ten years, finds a woman picking leaves in a mulberry-orchard. Not knowing her to be his wife, he tries to win her favours with a lump of gold.

[2] So as to avoid showing the younger woman as immodest.

[3] The two old women have different voice parts, one of them being a clown.

tea leaves; sing]

In the time of the Grain Rains [1]

We pluck the new tea —

A pennon of a gold-threaded leaf or a spear-shaped leaf-bud.

Ah, what official is here?

The Hanlin Scholar infused it in melted snow; [2]

The poor student brewed it in his dream, [3]

In a new earthen pot over smoking bamboo.

PREFECT: Well sung. Tell them, it is not Scholar T'ao of the play nor the student of Yang-hsien in the fairy-tale, but the Prefect himself come to promote husbandry; and he, seeing the women here engaged in picking mulberry and tea leaves, regards this as far worthier than the picking of flowers. There is a poem to prove it:

'Heaven's firmament lacks one luminous spirit,

Which burgeons on earth as the essence of herbs:

The dainty girls absorbed in their garden plants competition

Find all their charms eclipsed at a festival of tea.'

Give them wine and let them wear flowers.

TWO OLD WOMEN [*have flowers pinned to them and drink the wine given them; sing chorus*]

In the Official Pavilion, we drink deep of the 'Flaming Cloud'

And grinning in the breeze

find ourselves decked out with flowers —

Are we not the handsomest tea-pickers?   [*Go off*

VILLAGE ELDERS [*kneeling*] Informing Your Honour, the Elders wait upon Your Honour's pleasure at a simple repast of tea and rice.

PREFECT: They are excused. Let the Elders receive what is left of the flowers and wine, to distribute among the villagers

---

[1] Grain Rains — one of the twenty-four Solar Terms, corresponding to the period between April 20th and May 4th.

[2] The Sung Hanlin scholar T'ao Ku (903–70) taught his new concubine that the first lesson in gracious living was to make tea with melted snow (see *Ku-chin t'u-shu chi-ch'eng*, I. 93); the event is alluded to in act 2 of Tai Shan-fu's *tsa-chü* play *Feng-kuang-hao* (in *Yüan ch'ü hsüan*, Wen-hsüeh ku-chi ed., pp. 526–41), in which T'ao finds consolation in a new wife.

[3] The student of Yang-hsien, as related in one of the supernatural stories much to our author's taste, opened his mouth wide and let out a whole banquet complete with a female entertainer (see *Yang-hsien shu-sheng*, in *T'ai-p'ing kuang-chi*, c. 284, Jen-min edition 1959, pp. 2266–7); but the reference here may well be to some familiar scene in a play now lost. Yang-hsien (in Kiangsu Province) is famous for its tea.

in token of our encouragement of farming. Ask the attendants
to be ready with the horses.

VILLAGE ELDERS [*press their invitation without avail; then
stand up and call out*] Men and women of this village who were
given wine and flowers will now send off the Prefect.

FARMER, BUFFALO-BOY, MULBERRY-GATHERERS AND
TEA-PICKERS [*re-enter, wearing flowers; sing*]

The Prefect tours his province in the spring
                                    with unaffected stateliness,
Riding on his dapple-grey.
We too had at the village tavern a merry time;
The wine and flowers brought out of us a rustic grace.
Men and women,
Be ready with your Tablets of Praise along the route!
                                                    [*Go off*

PREFECT[1] [*declaims*]

'Village upon village, each winding its way up the hill—'[2]
'The new grass sprouts along thousands of green acres.'[3]
'Dusk falls to stay the Prefect's five-horsed chariot'[4]
'Near the peach blossoms by the bamboo grotto.'[5]
                                                    [*Exeunt*

Scene 9   Instructions for a Visit to the Garden

MAID [*enters and sings*]

Tiny Spring Fragrance,
No mere maidservant,
Brought up like a lady in a richly adorned suite,
Attending on my young mistress,
Applying her powder or mixing the rouge,
Fastening her jade trinkets or pinning on her flowers,

---

[1] The direction is inserted by the translator. Alternatively the lines could
be divided between the Prefect and the others in chorus.
[2] From Tu Fu, 'Song of K'uei-chou', *Tu Shao-ling chi ch'iang-chu*, c. 15,
vol. III, pp. 119–21; *Wan shou T'ang jen chüeh chü*, c. 1, pp. 120–2; *Ch'üan
T'ang shih*, c. 229, vol. IV, pp. 2507–8.
[3] From Chang Chi, 'By the Ch'ang Gate', *Wan shou T'ang jen chüeh chü*,
c. 38, p. 1193; *Ch'üan T'ang shih*, c. 242, vol. IV, p. 2721.
[4] From Yang Shih-o, 'Country Views', *Wan shou T'ang jen chüeh chü*, c. 36,
p. 1137; *Ch'üan T'ang shih*, c. 332, vol. V, p. 3696.
[5] From Hsüeh Neng, 'The Sung Family Pavilion in the Woods', *Wan
shou T'ang jen chüeh chü*, c. 48, p. 1491; *Ch'üan T'ang shih*, c. 561, vol. IX,
p. 6512.

Accustomed to my place by her dressing stand,—
Or helping her to make her ornamented bed,
Or keeping watch as she offers her evening incense—
But my slight frame shivers under the old mistress's stick!
[*declaims*]
  'A flower-bedecked little maid of not yet fourteen,
  Newly budding at spring's coming, in a sudden awakening,
  She must still wait for an emblem of love
  To guide her every step, to direct her every gaze.'[1]
I, Spring Fragrance, keep my young mistress company day
and night, and I do observe that, though she is a celebrated
beauty, she ever acts as befits dignity and honour, and is exquisitely bashful, though mature and sedate. Yet because the
master engaged a tutor to teach her and she read in the first
chapter of the *Book of Songs*,
  'The beautiful young lady—
  A princely man well sought her,'
she laid the book down and, sighing, said, 'Thus may clearly be
seen the true feelings of the sages. Then, as now, the heart remains the same. Is this not so?' And I, Spring Fragrance, thereupon spoke. 'My mistress is bored after studying her books.
How had she best amuse herself?' And the young mistress
paused a while, and then rose to her feet and said, 'Spring
Fragrance, how would you have me amuse myself?' I then
replied: 'Mistress, there's nothing else; let's go for a stroll in
the back garden.' My mistress said, 'Wretched girl! What if
my father should hear about it?' And I, Spring Fragrance, replied: 'The master has gone to the countryside. He has been
away several days already.' And the young mistress hesitated
and was silent a long while, and at last she took out an almanac
to choose a day, saying tomorrow is unpropitious, and the day
after also not favourable, and it needs must be the day after that,
ruled by the Patron of Wanderers, a lucky day. And I am to
summon in advance the garden lad to tell him to sweep the paths.
And I, without thinking, said I would do this. But what if the old
mistress should find out? Well, let that be. I will call the garden
lad and give him his orders.—Ah! From the far end of the
gallery comes Tutor Ch'en. It really is:

---

[1] The lines are adapted from Liu Yü-hsi's poem 'To Little Miss Fan',
in *Ch'üan T'ang shih*, c. 365, vol. v I, p. 4122.

Though spring's glory is present for all to see,
Your pedant will say he has never heard it quoted.

TUTOR [*enters and sings*]

An old licentiate,
I now pitch my tent as a temporary tutor.
In the warm sun the curtain hooks flap idly[1]—
Ah! against the winding gallery
Standing with her two curls,
She seems to mumble though I hear no words:
I will go near and see who it is.

It's Spring Fragrance! Let me ask you—
Where is my patron the Prefect?
Where is her ladyship?
Why does not my lady pupil attend the lecture?

MAID: I see it is Tutor Ch'en! My mistress has no time these few days for lessons.

TUTOR: How so?

MAID: Hear then, [*sings*]

This glorious time of year
To one of her acute sensibility
Brings matters that are of deep concern.

TUTOR: What concern?

MAID: You don't know it yet, Tutor, but the master is annoyed with you.

TUTOR: For what cause?

MAID: He says that in lecturing on the *Book of Songs* you showed too much zeal as a Maoist. Alas, my young mistress! [*sings*]

Because of that chapter of poetry,
Her insides were stirred.

TUTOR: But I have only lectured on '*Kwan, kwan* cried the osprey'.

MAID: That was just it. My young mistress says, even the confined osprey has its moments of exhilaration on the river island,[2] and must man's lot fall short of a bird's? Thus, [*sings*]

Though you mean to bury your head in your books,
Yet you lift your head again to admire the view.

And now she has given orders that she will visit the back gar-

[1] Spring is astir even for Tutor Ch'en, who professes never to look beyond the curtains; see note on Tung Ch'ung-shu below.
[2] This continues the punning of scene 7.

den in the next day or two.

TUTOR: Why visit the back garden?

MAID [*sings*]

> Spring has brought her inexpressible melancholy;
>
> And since spring will too soon depart
>
> In the gardens she would have spring's sorrows melt away.

TUTOR: Worse and worse. [*sings*]

> For indeed womenfolk,
>
> When they show themselves, are stared at:
>
> They should conceal their faces when they walk.

Spring Fragrance, under heaven's mercy, your Tutor is sixty years old. I have never known sorrow at spring's coming; I have never visited a garden.[1]

MAID: How is this?

TUTOR: You wouldn't know, but Mencius has said well on this point. The sage's long succession of words has for its aim man's restraining of his own vagrant mind.[2]

> So keep to the customary routine—
>
> Why be melancholy in spring?
>
> Why gad about in spring?
>
> Need sending off spring mean letting loose one's own heart?

Since the young mistress is not attending lectures, I will take a few day's leave. Spring Fragrance, [*sings*]

> When you come to the schoolroom,
>
> Have a care to the lattice window
>
> Lest the swallows under the eaves
>
>   rain mud on the guitar and books.

I go. [*declaims*]

> Noble-born young ladies may indulge in their garden pastime;
>
> The studious old man would not peep from behind his curtain.[3]

[*Goes off*

MAID [*left alone on stage*] It's a relief that at least Tutor Ch'en is gone. I will call the garden lad to find out if he is here. [*calls*] Boy!

---

[1] Pedantry carried to the extreme in imitation of some chosen example; see note 3 below.

[2] Rather, man's regaining of his original nature, temporarily led astray.

[3] Tung Chung-shu (176–104 B.C.), Han Professor of Classics, 'gave his lectures with the curtains drawn, and his senior students were able to teach the others, so that many never saw the Professor at all. He studied with such concentration that for three years he did not once look into the garden' (*Han shu*, c.56, p.2495).

GARDEN LAD [*enters, drunk and reeling; sings*]

> A budding garden attendant, I live among the flowers;
> On the sly I took some and sold them in the street.
> But the clerks, they laid hands on me!
> And the lictors, they would not let go of me!
> That burning liquor! Nearly set fire to my tender entrails!

[*salutes Maid*] I see, Miss Spring is here.

MAID: You'll get a thrashing. Stealing out of the Prefect's Residence to cadge a drink! You haven't even sent in any vegetables the last few days.

LAD: But there's the vegetable gardener.

MAID: Nor filled the water tank.

LAD: But there's the water carrier.

MAID: Nor sent in the flowers.

LAD: But I do send the flowers in every morning, a bunch for the mistress, a bunch for the young mistress.

MAID: And what about the third bunch?

LAD: I see that I deserve a beating.

MAID: What are you called?

LAD: Flower Boy.

MAID: Weave your name into a song and sing it for me. If you do well, I'll spare the beating.

LAD: Here goes! [*sings*]

> The Flower Boy has seen his fill of pretty flowers,
>   wave upon wave;
> But blooming Miss Spring is like a new blossom soaked in rain.
> Come, we'll expose you now to the quickening sun:
> La! When the blossom is dried and withered, what more's to do?

MAID: Now you get paid in your own coin. [*sings*]

> Puny Flower Boy too ready with his knavish tricks,
>   wave upon wave,—
> What! Does scrubby scallawag itch to teach his grandam?

LAD: Alas, no!

MAID [*sings*]

> When the master returns, I make my deadly report:

[*seizing Lad by the hair*]

> La! Thump-plump with a mallet on your head,
>   what more's to do?

LAD [*suppliant, prostrates himself*] Have done, Miss. Why are you in the garden?

MAID: The young mistress comes to look at the garden day

after next; so have the paths well swept.

LAD: I know, Miss.

MAID[1] [*declaims*]

'In the eastern environs the wind breathes sweet perfume';[2]

LAD [*declaims*]

'Home Hill awaits with joy its goddess's visitation'.[3]

MAID [*declaims*]

'Send not your children in search of forbidden fruit'[4]—

BOTH [*declaim*]

'All too insistently sings the amorous oriole'.[5]   [*Go off*

Scene 10   The Dream

FAIR BRIDE [*enters and sings*]

I dreamt of the oriole's reverberating song

And springtide's rioting outburst

In a small secluded courtyard where I stood.

MAID [*enters, following Fair Bride; sings*]

The incense sticks are burnt out;

A loose thread hangs from the embroidery frame.

Will this year's spring awaken the feelings of last year's?

FAIR BRIDE [*declaims*]

At dawn I gazed at the ruins of Plum Blossom Fort,[6]

Still in my last night's attire;

MAID [*declaims*]

Throwing your springtime curls all to one side

And leaning over the balustrade:

[1] For these closing lines, the parts are allotted by the translator.
[2] From Ts'ui Jih-yung, 'Companion Piece to the Emperor's Poem "A Visit in Spring to Spring View Palace" (by Command)', *Ch'üan T'ang shih*, c. 46, vol. I, p. 559.
[3] From Ch'en T'ao, 'To Governor Lo of Fukien', *Ch'üan T'ang shih*, c.746, vol. XI, p. 8480.
[4] From Wei Ying-wu, 'Detained by the Sight of New Bamboos on setting out for Ch'u', *Wan shou T'ang jen chüeh chü*, c. 4, p. 201 ; *Ch'üan T'ang shih*, c. 187, vol. III, p. 1913. The line was adapted by the dramatist and, in turn, by the translator.
[5] From Tu Fu, 'Random Thoughts (Nine Stanzas)', *Tu Shao-ling chi hsiang-chu*, c.9, vol. II, p. 136; *Wan shou T'ang jen chüeh chü*, c. 1, p. 102; *Ch'üan T'ang shih*, c. 227, vol. IV, p. 2451.
[6] Situated to the south of Nan-an on Plum Blossom Peak, which the author visited on his journey to Hsü-wen in 1591 ; see *T'ang Hsien-tsu chi*, vol. I, c. 11, p. 393.

FAIR BRIDE:

  'Too dense and glossy to yield to the scissors,

  And smoothing them but deranges'[1]—

  Endlessly confused and listless!

MAID:

  Then command your oriole and the swallows

                          to hasten the flowers of spring.

FAIR BRIDE: Spring Fragrance, have you ordered the garden paths to be swept?

MAID: I have, my mistress.

FAIR BRIDE: Bring my mirror stand and garments.

MAID [*goes off and re-enters with mirror stand and garments*]

  'Having combed her cloudlike locks,

                       she now confronts the mirror;

  Before she dons her silk robe, it shall once more be scented.'[2]

The mirror stand and clothes are here.

FAIR BRIDE [*sings*]

  Ensnaring gossamer threads wafted across an untrodden court—

  Spring itself is afloat!

  A long while I pause

  To arrange my hair ornaments;

  Who would have known?—the mirror

  Slyly peeping at my face,

  Throws all my curls again into confusion.

[*walking*]

  Yet can I conceal myself when I walk?

MAID: You are all dressed up today.

FAIR BRIDE: You would say [*sings*]

  The emerald skirt shows up the madder crimson gown,

  Matched with a glittering gem-studded floral hairpin.

Know, then:

  Love of the beautiful was ingrained in me from birth.

  But the glories of spring are here hidden from man;

  Only the birds flutter at the sight of beauty

  And the flowers in their pride grieve at their own eclipse.[3]

MAID: It will soon be breakfast time. Let us go. [*they walk into the garden*] Just look! [*declaims*]

---

[1] The lines are from Li Yü's *tz'u*-poem 'Hsiang chien huan', *Ch'üan T'ang shih*, c.889 (*tz'u* section I), vol. XII, p.10043.

[2] From Hsüeh Feng, 'In the Palace', *Ch'üan T'ang shih*, c.548, vol. VIII, p.6323.

[3] Eclipse, i.e., by the beauty of a woman.

Flecks of faded gold still dot the gallery wall;
The moss by the pond and pavilion is one thick layer of green.
Treading on the wet grass may stain new, embroidered socks,
But tug we must at the jingling bells
                                        to scare off marauding birds.
FAIR BRIDE: Away from gardens and groves, how should one
learn of spring's delights? Indeed I see—[sings]

Gay purple and exquisite red abloom everywhere,
But all abandoned to a dried up-well and crumbled walls.
That glorious moments amidst this splendid scene
                                        should enshroud despair!

In whose courtyard do hearts still rejoice in the present?
Such a fine view, though never mentioned by my father and
mother. [sings chorus]

Unfurled with daybreak till wrapped again by dusk,
Golden cloudlets over a jade-green pavilion;
Streaks of rain borne by a stray breeze;
A painted boat on the rippling waves:
The cloistered maiden holds cheap sweet springtime.
MAID: All the other flowers are out, only the peony is not yet.
FAIR BRIDE [sings]

All over the green hills are azaleas bespattered with blood;[1]
Behind the rose arbor, whiffs of smoke curl dreamily.
Spring Fragrance,
The peonies are well enough,
But they tarry even when spring is departing.
MAID: Oh, the orioles and swallows in their pairs!
BOTH [sing in chorus]

Enraptured we listen
To the swallow's unbroken, sharp-edged chatter
And the soothing trill of the oriole's roundelay.
FAIR BRIDE: Let us go.
MAID: One can never see enough of this garden.
FAIR BRIDE: Why speak about it again?
[they walk; Fair Bride sings]

We can never see enough of it—so let longing be!
Though we visit all twelve pavilions, it were still in vain;
Better to return content and while away our time within.

[1] 'Generically, the *Azalea* is called Tu Chüan in China, named after the
cuckoo. Legends say that red azalea flowers originally sprouted from
blood spit by the ever-crying cuckoo.' H.L.Li, *The Garden Flowers of
China*, p. 160.

[*They re-enter the house*]

M AID [*declaims*]

'Push open the door of the west boudoir,

Spread out my bed in the east chamber'; [1]

Fill the vase with purple azaleas;

Add lign-aloes to the smoking censer.

Mistress, rest you a while. I go to attend on your lady mother.

[*Goes off*

F AIR BRIDE [*sighs and declaims*]

Silent, I return from my springtime stroll,

Having tried out my new spring look.

Oh, spring! Could I long linger in your presence,

Then what should I do if spring did depart?

Alas, this weather! How drowsy one feels! Where is Spring Fragrance? [*looks left and right; then lowers her head and whispers*] Oh, heaven! Is the saying true—'Spring will provoke you'? I have read in poems and songs about the women of old, how the spring awakened their passion but autumn then brought sorrow, surely this is true. Now I am already sixteen, and have not come across the ideal husband; suddenly I yearn for love, but where should I find my bridegroom? In former days the maid-of-honour Han found her Master Yü and the scholar Chang met by chance Mistress Ts'ui, and their stories are celebrated in the plays *The Maple Leaf* [2] and *Miss Ts'ui*. [3] These fair ladies and talented men became lovers in secret but eventually they were married. [*gives a deep sigh*] That I who am born into the official rank, descended of a distinguished house, should be old enough to wear the hairpin [4] without finding a fitting mate! Surely I am wasting my youth while time flits past the peep-

---

[1] The lines, referring to the warrior-maiden Mu-lan's homecoming, are incorrectly quoted from the Mu-lan poem; see *Yüeh-fu shih-chi*, c.25.

[2] 'The Maple Leaf' (*T'i hung chi*, by our author's contemporary admirer Wang Chi-te), in which, unknown to each other, the maid-of-honour Han and the student Yü exchanged messages written on maple leaves floating along an open drain in the palace quarter; text in *Ku-pen hsi-ch'ü ts'ung-k'an*, Series 11.

[3] 'Miss Ts'ui'—The story alluded to is that of the student Chang and Ts'ui Ying-ying, dramatized in Wang Shih-fu's 'The West Chamber' plays (see notes to 'A Burial Mound for Flowers' *infra*) and in Southern Drama versions; but the title actually given, *Ts'ui Hui chuan*, seems not connected with Ts'ui Ying-ying and Chang.

[4] Hairpin: Legge, *Li Ki*, Book x, 'The Pattern of the Family', Section 11, § 37, vol. i, p. 479: '. . . At fifteen she assumed the hairpin; at twenty she was married . . .'

hole that is life. [*in tears*] Alas, my full-blown flower knows but
a poor leaf's cheerless lot! [*sings*]

Taken unawares, I could not resist spring's infectious warmth;
All too suddenly I am filled with longing and resentment.
Only because of my passable good looks
And the requirement of a husband of the same family standing,
Handsome, too, to make a blissful pair,
A perfect match! —
The prospect has left my prettiest years behind.
Who is there to watch over me asleep on my couch?
Primly, then, I conceal my blushes,
Indulging in secret dreams (by whose side?)
Playing hide and seek with springtime,
And so drag on
(For how might I express my true feelings? —)
In torment
This wretched existence
(Except in reproaching heaven!)

I am tired. Let me sit at the table and have a nap.
[*She sleeps. In her dream, Willow enters, holding a willow twig*]
WILLOW [*declaims*]

On a warm day the oriole's voice melts into song,
And lovers' fancies dissolve in laughter and merriment.
Guided by fallen petals along the mountain stream,
The mortal Yüan Chao now finds his goddess.[1]

I took the same path as Miss Tu, following her as she returned
to the house. Why is she not here? [*turns and sees Fair Bride*]
Ah, mistress! mistress! [*Fair Bride starts up. They bow to each
other*] Mistress, where have I not looked for you? And you are
here! [*Fair Bride looks sideways in silent embarrassment*] While
in the garden, I broke off a shoot from a drooping willow. Mistress, you who are versed in the Classics, could you favour me
with a poem to this fresh sprig of willow?[2]

FAIR BRIDE [*surprised and flattered, but restrains herself from
speaking; mutters aside*] I do not know the student. Why is he
here?

WILLOW [*smirking*] Mistress, I love you to distraction.

[1] Yüan Chao, who, having lost his way in the mountains, followed a stream
and came to the cave of a goddess, as dramatized by Wang Tzu-i in the
tsa-chü play *Wu ju t'ao-yüan* (in *Yüan-ch'ü hsüan*, pp. 1353–67).
[2] The willow and willow sprig are recurrent themes in traditional poetry.

[*sings*]

    Because of your flower-like beauty

    In the first flush of fleeting youth,

    I sought you in each nook and corner

    But find you dejected in your chamber.

Mistress, let us go over there and talk.

F A I R   B R I D E [*smiles but remains where she was; Willow pulls at her sleeve; Fair Bride, in a whisper*] Where?

W I L L O W [*sings*]

    We shall go past that enclosed bed of peonies

    And stop close by the Tʻai-hu rockery.

F A I R   B R I D E [*whispers*] Scholar, what mean you to do?

W I L L O W [*also in a whisper*] There I will [*sings*]

    Undo your collar,

    Loosen your girdle,—

    You hiding behind your sleeve

    Shall bite it for pain

    And so submit to love's brief, sweet embrace.

[*Fair Bride bashfully hides her face; Willow holds her in his arms; Fair Bride pushes him away*]

B O T H [*sing chorus*]

    Where could we have met?

    We gaze and wonder;

    What, so luckily chanced upon and yet so dumb?

[*Willow carries Fair Bride off forcibly*]

F L O W E R   G O D [*enters, clad in red, his hair tied up under a crown of flowers; declaims*]

    The Guardian of Flowers on an inviting day

    Makes annual check of spring's set task.

    A rain of red petals bespatters the lover,

    Whose sweet dream hangs among particoloured clouds.

I am a Flower God, my domain the gardens at the back of the Nan-an Prefect's residence. And inasmuch as the young mistress Tu Fair Bride and the graduate Willow Dreamer are later to be united in wedlock and, Mistress Tu being sick at heart after her first sight of spring, this has caused Master Willow to enter her dream—my office being to preserve the fair and budding, I am here to protect her. Her foretaste of love's dalliance shall be pleasing and untroubled. [*sings*]

    Touched by the great generative forces,

                        already they are transformed:

See how wormlike he writhes, fanning passion's flame,
How her limpid charms seem frozen, her soul transfixed.
This is love in the realm of shadows,
Fulfilled in the thought,
Revealed by the law of fore-ordination.
Alas, the Terrace of Flowers is now defiled.
Let me throw some petals to awaken them.
[*throws petals towards the door leading offstage*]
Must they still linger
                    when spring's dream of love is accomplished?
The fallen petals I threw are already a carpet of red.
Still dreaming, scholar? When you reach the end of your dream,
see that Mistress Tu return safely to her fair chamber. I, the
God, now depart.   [*Goes off*
WILLOW [*re-enters with Fair Bride, hand in hand; sings*]
In those lucky moments when Heaven sped man's wish,
We were sprawled out on the grass, asleep amid the flowers.
Are you well, my mistress?—[*Fair Bride lowers her head*]
Busily smoothing your locks,
Tangled with red petals, the jade ornaments awry.
Mistress, do not forget
How we clung to each other, reluctant to be untwined,
How my hands sought to knead you into snowy flakes,
How, our tremulous breaths mingling, we broke the virginal seal.
FAIR BRIDE: Scholar, you should go now.
BOTH [*sing chorus*]
Where could we have met?
We gaze and wonder;
What, so luckily chanced upon and yet so dumb?
WILLOW: Mistress, you are tired. Rest yourself. Rest your-
self. [*accompanies Fair Bride back to the house; Fair Bride sits
down at the table and sleeps as before; Willow pats Fair Bride
gently*] Mistress, I am going. [*turns back once more*] Mistress,
be sure to rest yourself well. I will come to see you again.
[*declaims*]
I came with spring's warmth in sweet, cloying rain,
And leave a speck of cloud over Dream-Lover Hill.[1]
                                                   [*Goes off*

[1] Dream-Lover Hill, i.e. Mount Wu (see note to 'The Shrew' *supra*),
associated with the clouds and rain imagery, where lovers meet in their
dreams. Willow repeatedly indicates his role as dream-lover.

FAIR BRIDE [*suddenly roused from her sleep, cries out in a low voice*] Scholar, scholar, are you gone?

[*Again falls into a deep sleep*]

LADY TU [*enters and declaims*]

'In his prefectural hall sits my noble husband;
By her window stands my darling daughter—
She muses long that on her embroidered skirt,
Perched near the flowers, the birds are shown in pairs.'

Daughter, daughter, how is it you are napping here?

FAIR BRIDE [*awakes; still calling to Willow*] Oh, there!

LADY TU: What is the matter, my child?

FAIR BRIDE [*starts up*] Ah, my lady mother is here!

LADY TU: My child, why are you not at your needlework? Or browsing on ancient history to give full scope to your feelings? Why were you asleep here in the day?

FAIR BRIDE: I was playing in the garden just now, but all the twitter and chatter on a spring day! I was suddenly vexed, and returned to my room and, finding nothing to amuse myself with, felt drowsy and had a short rest. I have been remiss in not meeting you at the door. Mother will please forgive the omission.

LADY TU: My child, the back garden is quite deserted. Stay away from it.

FAIR BRIDE: My mother has commanded.

LADY TU: My child, go and read your books in the study.

FAIR BRIDE: The tutor is not in; it is a holiday.

LADY TU [*sighs*] When a daughter grows up, she will have her moods. Let her be. Thus it is: [*declaims*]

'Deferring in turn to son or daughter,
Still diligently toils the old mother.'   [*Goes off*

FAIR BRIDE [*heaves a deep sigh as she watches her mother depart*] Oh, you heavens! What a stroke of luck for Tu Fair Bride today! By chance I went into the back garden; the flowers were all in bloom and, watching the scene, I was seized with melancholy. I returned listless and fell asleep in broad daylight in my room. Suddenly I saw a student aged twenty or so, of elegant appearance, carrying a shoot he had broken from a willow tree in the garden. Smiling to me, he said, 'Mistress, since you are versed in the Classics, why not favour me with a poem in praise of this sprig of willow?' I wanted to reply, but thought in my heart—'he is a stranger; his name is not even known to me;

how could I venture to speak with him?' While I pondered in
this way, the student came towards me and said some words
which touched my heart to the quick, and he carried me in his
arms to a spot close to the pavilion by the enclosed bed of
peonies, and there we abandoned ourselves to love's delights.
Our hearts were at one. It really was: a thousand lovings, ten
thousand tendernesses. And he sent me back to my repose,
saying repeatedly 'Rest yourself'. I was just about to see him
to the door, when suddenly my mother came and woke me. I
found myself covered with cold sweat, and it had but been a
dream! Hurriedly I curtsied to my mother, and she wearied me
with much disapproving talk. While I remained silent, in my
heart I thought of the dream, which completely occupied my
mind. And now I can neither walk nor sit still. I seem quite lost.
Mother dear, you told me to go to the schoolroom and read,
but *which* books would afford me amusement?
[*covers her face to hide her tears; sings*]

    Love's tempest dispersing,
    Re-echoed still on the horizon of my dream,
    When, alas, the voice of stern mother
    Called at the window and disturbed sweet sleep:
    Cold sweat poured down me, my wet clothes chilled the skin—
    This rude awakening leaves my mind a blank, my tread unsteady,
    My will dissolved, my curls undone!
    If now I rallied my drooping spirits
    And sat up determinedly, who would rejoice?
    Then let me sleep.

MAID [*re-enters and declaims*]

    'To array for the night, remove all traces of powder;
    For a whiff of spring, spare not the perfume-sachet.'
Mistress, I have scented the bedding. Rest now.

FAIR BRIDE [*sings*]

    The sequestered heart, tired with its ramble in spring,
    Will sleep without aid of perfume or embroidered quilt.
    Heaven above!
    Since I am so inclined, the dream cannot yet be far off.
[*declaims*]

    'In spring, in search of bliss, I left the painted hall'; [1]

[1] Taken from Chang Yüeh, 'Companion Piece to the Emperor's poem "A
Spring Excursion" (by Command)', *Ch'üan T'ang shih*, c.87, vol.II,
p. 961.

'Hedged in by the plum and willow,
                                   the scent quite overcame me'.[1]
'Where lucky mortals encountered their fairy lovers',[2]
'At each retreating step, one's very entrails are torn.'[3]

[*Exeunt*

[1] From Lo Yin, 'Peach Blossoms', *Ch'üan T'ang shih*, c. 657, vol. x, pp. 7549–50.
[2] From Hsü Hun, 'Setting out in the morning from Middle Cliff Temple in T'ien-t'ai across Pass Range for T'ien-mu Peak', *Ch'üan T'ang shih*, c. 533, vol. v iii, pp. 6090–1.
[3] Attributed in various editions to Wei Chuang, who has some similar lines, e.g. in 'Paths through the Fields in Spring', *Ch'üan T'ang shih*, c. 700, vol. x, p. 8045; but the line is really taken from the same poem, 'Peach Blossoms', by Lo Yin. See note 1 above.

The Blood-stained Fan

Of the life of K'ung Shang-jen (1648–1718), author of 'The Blood-stained Fan', a bare summary must here suffice.[1] He was born in the County of Ch'ü-fu (i.e. Kufow in Shantung Province), a lineal descendant of Confucius, and spent his childhood and youth in the hills outside the town, studying and in due course passing his licentiate's examination. In 1682, the head of the K'ung clan, who bore the title Holy Duke (Yensheng-kung), invited young K'ung to Ch'ü-fu to supervise arrangements for the Duchess's funeral. He stayed on to compile the clan history and to undertake the training of seven hundred local youths in the ancient rites and music. In the winter of 1684, the Ch'ing emperor K'ang-hsi, then in the twenty-third year of his reign, stopped at Ch'ü-fu after an Imperial progress to the south in order to sacrifice to the sage. K'ung acted as Master of the Ceremonies, and delivered a lecture on 'The Great Learning' before the Manchu emperor, who heard it with unfeigned pleasure and complimented the lecturer. It thus followed that in 1685 K'ung was appointed Professor at the Imperial Academy in Peking. A year later, however, he was posted to the Huai valley under the Vice-President of the Board of Rites, Sun Tsai-feng, to alleviate the flooding in that area. K'ung stayed in Yangchow and Taichow, but also visited Nanking, Soochow and other cities and towns along the Yangtze and the Grand Canal, seeing the sights and hunting out unrecorded traditions. In the course of his three

[1] The sources of K'ung's life are his Collected Works, *K'ung Shang-jen shih-wen chi*, 3 vols., ed. Wang Wei-lin (Chung-hua 1962), and the shorter collection *Hu-hai chi* (Ku-tien 1957) containing the poems of the significant years 1686–9; in particular, his own account of K'ang-hsi's visit to Ch'ü-fu, *Ch'u shan i-shu chi*, in the Collected Works, vol. III, c.6, pp.425–38. I have consulted the three studies of K'ung in *Yüan Ming Ch'ing hsi-ch'ü yen-chiu lun-wen chi* (Tso-chia 1957) by Fan Ning, pp.381-7; Ma Yung, pp.388–402; and Chao Li-sheng, pp.403–17.

years in the south he made many friends, particularly among the elderly, e.g. the celebrity Mao Hsiang (b. 1611) and the painters Cha Shih-piao (b. 1615) and Shih-t'ao the monk (b. 1630), whose loyalties were still with the fallen Ming dynasty (Chinese) of over forty years ago. K'ung resumed his duties as Professor in 1690, and in 1694 collaborated in a play entitled *Hsiao hu-lei* ('The Small Hu-lei'), being the name of a T'ang dynasty musical instrument he had acquired. He was now transferred to the Board of Revenue, in which he served until 1700. The following year he retired to the hills of Ch'ü-fu.

'The Blood-stained Fan',[1] projected and begun before K'ung left his home for Peking,[2] and added to intermittently and revised, was finished in 1699. It is a dramatic romance (*ch'uan-ch'i*) in the Southern manner, its forty scenes proper being divided into two narrative sequences each of twenty scenes, each sequence having additionally a Prologue and a concluding scene. This symmetry of construction is pointed out, not without pride, in the author's 'Principles of Composition'[3] (*fan-li*), which states his literary aims in sixteen short paragraphs. Thus he deplores the improvisation of actors, which debased the tone of the play itself, and declares his own prose dialogue to be full enough to preclude any interpolation.[4] He deprecates the borrowing and adaptation of earlier, often hackneyed, verse for the quatrains and couplets declaimed by characters upon their entrance and exit: his own, in contrast, were original verse and serve a dramatic function. Above all, he stresses the historical veracity of the persons and incidents in his play, and indeed 'The Blood-stained Fan' is the outstanding Chinese example of the historical drama.

For the playwrights of an earlier generation, mainly of the K'un-shan School, reflecting a change of mood in the country at large with the change of dynasty, had taken to subjects from history with a certain political flavour. Their plays are often

[1] See K'ung's three Prefaces to the play, of 1699, of 1708, and for the first printing, all included in the annotated edition by Wang Chi-ssu and Su Huan-chung (Jen-min 1959).
[2] The speaker of the Prologue states explicitly: 'This is the twenty-third year of the K'ang-hsi reign', i.e. 1684, the year of the Emperor's visit to Ch'ü-fu, which would seem to indicate the Prologue was begun in that year. (First Prologue, Jen-min edition, p. 1).
[3] In Jen-min edition.
[4] While this is generally true, some of the scenes would still seem to admit of improvisation, e.g. scene 11 and translator's note, below.

set in the Ming and sometimes deal with events within living memory, as, for example, the mid-seventeenth century *Ching-chung p'u* ('Tomb of Five Men')[1] by the professional play-wright Li Hsüan-yü probably in association with others, a play about five men from Soochow who were sacrificed to appease the wrath of the all-powerful eunuch Wei Chung-hsien in the year 1626. Thus even before K'ung had much contact with the theatre, he was afire with the idea of a historical play.[2] Being, however, a scholar, he went to great lengths to verify his history, giving even a list of his literary sources in the form of a bibliography.[3] As to actual occurrences, whether recorded or unrecorded, we learn from his marginal note to scene 26[4] that, at a meeting with the octogenarian widow of General Hsü Ting-kuo in 1693, he heard from her own lips how she had suggested to her husband the plan of laying a trap for the wilful and bad-tempered Area Commander Kao Chieh, as enacted in the scene. And, while in Nanking, K'ung called at the White Cloud Temple outside the city to pay his respects to the old and abjectly poor Taoist priest Chang Yao-hsing,[5] who in scene 40 brings the action of the play to a close. We may be certain that in the portrayal of his more important characters K'ung drew upon good evidence.

But the play's more obvious appeal—and its author's unstated intention—is patriotism rather than didactic history. Indeed, it was with much daring that K'ung, having on his one mission to the south sought out survivors from the previous dynasty—officials living in voluntary seclusion, retired army officers and others, and visited the sites of their lost battles and futile intrigues, took up his brush to paint the heroes and villains of the last sad days of the Ming. The story is set in the fateful years 1643–5, and most of the action takes place in the south, in or near the southern capital, Nanking, the main plot of the love between the student Hou Ch'ao-tsung and the young courtesan Li Hsiang-chün being interwoven with sub-plots dealing with the factions and dissensions that paralysed the tottering

[1] Text in *Ku-pen hsi-ch'ü ts'ung-k'an*, Series III; Li Hsüan-yü is Li Yü (Jade) (c. 1591–c. 1671); see Chou I-po, *Chung-kuo hsi-chü shih chiang-tso*, pp. 189–92, and *Chung-kuo wen-hsüeh shih* by members of Science Academy, vol. III, pp. 1028–34.
[2] See n. I, p. 3o4. [3] In Jen-min edition.
[4] Kuo-hsüeh chi-pen ts'ung-shu chien-pen edition, p. 124.
[5] *Hu-hai chi*, c. 7, p. 161; Collected Works, vol. I, c. 2, pp. 162–3.

Ming government and army command, faced at first with rebels who ravaged the countryside and sacked Peking, and immediately afterwards with the invading Manchus. The Manchus do not actually appear on the stage, and the references to them are shadowy and innocuous: K'ung, born at the beginning of their reign, was himself content to serve under them. But, in the play, Chinese officials who defected to the Manchus are mocked at, and the general sentiment is summed up in the words of the Taoist priest addressed to the hero and heroine:

> Worms that you are, where is your country now? Where is your home? What remains of your ruler? And your own fathers? Is your paltry love so precious that you may not yield it up now? (Scene 40.)

When, therefore, following upon the great success of 'The Blood-stained Fan', which became the talk of the capital, K'ang-hsi himself demanded one autumn evening to read the text of the play,[1] for which 'a friend's transcript' had hastily to be provided, the author's own copy being on loan, the Emperor could not have been amused. The following year, 1700, (and for many a year after) the play continued to be acted by the K'un-shan School in the capital, but K'ung was deprived of his post in the Board of Revenue. He had, however, fulfilled his early dream of a drama about the collapse of the Ming, its events revolving round the fan of a lady, whose friend's page 'first told the story to my cousin'.[1]

In the original, the play is entitled *T'ao-hua shan* ('The Peach Blossom Fan'), and the silk fan, of the sort stretched on an oval frame, is not only a connecting thread of the story but also the symbol of youth and love in the midst of bloodshed and national calamity. At the beginning the student Hou inscribes a poem on the fan and presents it as a gift of affiance to the beautiful Hsiang-chün (scene 6). Upon Hou being sent to an outpost, however, Hsiang-chün's associates compel her to become the concubine of a newly appointed Commissioner of Grain Transport; while they carry her from her room, she dashes her head against the floor, injuring herself and bespattering with blood the fan, which she has been brandishing as a weapon (scene 22). Hsiang-chün recovers and is hidden by friends, one of whom, the official Yang Wen-ts'ung, trans-

[1] See Preface to the first printing entitled 'T'ao-hua-shan pen-mo', Jenmin edition.

forms with a few brush strokes the blood stains on the fan into sprays of peach blossoms (scene 23). The fan re-appears as a message from Hsiang-chün to Hou (scene 27), who treasures it (scenes 28, 39) until their final brief reunion, at which the Taoist priest Chang, a former officer of the palace guards who had witnessed the Emperor's self-inflicted death and attended almost alone to the last rites, wrecks the fan, declaring their love to be vain in a world already lost, which forthwith hero and heroine decide to mourn by each joining a monastic order (scene 40).

Our extract is confined to scenes 10 and 11, which portray the celebrated story-teller Liu Ching-t'ing and his first encounter with his patron, the general or war-lord Tso Liang-yü,[1] then stationed in the Wuchang area (in Hupeh Province). Tso, who had risen from the ranks, had scored victories in the prolonged campaign against the rebels Li Tzu-ch'eng and Chang Hsien-chung, chiefly in the north but also in Szechuan. When, however, in 1642 he was defeated by the rebels and forced to retreat, first to Hsiang-yang (also in Hupeh Province) and then to Wuchang, he became thoroughly demoralized and let his men loose on the town, their looting and burning lasting over twenty days. In the following year, 1643, Tso came down the Yangtze as far as Anking, threatening to march to Nanking to commandeer the requisite supply of grain for his troops. It was at this juncture that a rival general, Tu Hung-yü, anxious to patch up a quarrel with Tso, sent him the resourceful story-teller Liu[2]—who had to brave a phalanx of sword-bearers and walk or crawl under their drawn swords to reach his prospective patron, a detail adopted in scene 11. Undeterred by his reception, the story-teller easily won the general's admiration and trust, and the naive and barely literate Tso—somewhat idealized in the play—would listen, evening after evening, to Liu's recitations, never tiring of their examples from history and legend of sheer heroism, of loyalty and of self-sacrifice. Of this strange friendship the versatile Liu left a record in the form of a portrait painted by himself of the two of them seated near each other discussing a sword, a picture which elicited poems from men of letters of the mid-

[1] Biography in *Ming shih*, c. 273; conveniently summarized in the notes to scene 9 in the Liang Ch'i-ch'ao edition.
[2] See notes below on Liu and especially the biography by Wu Wei-yeh.

seventeenth century.[1]

Tso's potentially treasonous move alarmed officials in Nanking. Among attempts made to halt his advance was a long and earnest plea addressed to Tso in the name of his former commander and benefactor Hou Hsün, drafted by Hou's son, Hou Ch'ao-tsung,[2] the hero of the play; and this part of the story is dramatized in scene 10, in which the story-teller Liu becomes the messenger of Hou and the Nanking officials. The young Hou, like his father and grandfather before him, was a member of the radical faction and, in addition, something of a social celebrity: later, under the Ch'ing, he attained fame as a prose stylist. In the events here outlined, Hou's friend Yang Wents'ung, an official of moderate views belonging to the government faction, had no real part. Yang was, however, a friend of both Hou and Li Hsiang-chün, an actual courtesan of Nanking and the heroine of our play; and he painted the peach blossoms on her fan: hence his presence throughout the action.

But one may hope in vain to follow the history in a short extract. Of compelling interest in the context of this book is the characterisation of the story-teller Liu Ching-t'ing[3] (c. 1587 — after 1668), no doubt based on the reminiscences, whether or not recorded, of those who had known the man. According to the poet Wu Wei-yeh[4] (1609–71) in his biography of the story-teller, Liu was born in Taichow (which formed part of Yangchow Prefecture) and bore the surname Ts'ao. Being wild and unruly as a boy, he had already at the age of fifteen been in trouble with the authorities, and had fled from the Yangchow area to Hsü-i (i.e. Chuyi in Anhwei Province),where equipped with a book of stories and relying on his native wit, he set up as a story-teller, attracting the whole town to his performances

[1] By Ch'ien Ch'ien-i (1582–1664), in *Mu-chai yu-hsüeh chi*, Ssu-pu ts'ung-k'an edition, c.6, pp. 7ᵇ–8ᵇ; and Ch'en Wei-sung (1625–82), in *Hu-hai-lou shih-chi*, c.2, pp. 4ᵃ–4ᵇ (in *Ch'en Chia-ling wen-chi*, Ssu-pu ts'ung-k'an edition).
[2] Hou Ch'ao-tsung's name was Hou Fang-yü (1618–54). The letter to Tso is in his *Chuang-hui-t'ang wen-chi*, Ssu-pu pei-yao edition, c.3, pp. 4ᵃ–5ᵃ; part of it is quoted in the notes to scene 10 in the Liang Ch'i-ch'ao edition.
[3] See Hung Shih-liang, *Liu Ching-t'ing p'ing-chuan*, 1956, and Ch'en Ju-heng, *shuo-shu shih-hua*, 1958, chapter 6, § 3. Among the sources of his play listed by the author himself, many items deal specifically with the story-teller Liu, including Wu Wei-yeh's biography.
[4] 'Life of Liu Ching-t'ing', included in *Yü-ch'u hsin-chih* (1683), c. 2 (Wen-hsüeh ku-chi reprint of 1954, pp. 21–3).

and gambling away all his earnings afterwards. In this manner
he drifted from one town to another until twenty years later,
when he became known as Liu Ching-t'ing, one of the four
great story-tellers of Nanking, patronised by high officials, at
whose table he would dine in the best company. During his
wanderings he had spent perhaps half a year at Sungkiang,
seeking at monthly intervals the advice of a local scholar Mo
Hou-kuang, under whose tutelage he had come to regard story-
telling as an art with the highest aims: he now proudly told
inquirers that, unlike his Nanking rivals, he had been bound
apprentice to no master-story-teller but had been coached by a
scholar. With the situation worsening in the north, there was
an influx of officials into Nanking, where for a time Liu numbered among his clients such figures as Ho Ju-ch'ung (d. 1641;
President of Board of Rites 1628–33; offered premiership in
1633) and Fan Ching-wen (Army Secretary 1634–8; committed suicide in 1644 when Peking was sacked by the rebels).
Then followed the glorious interlude, lasting less than three
years, of his service under General Tso, which ended when Tso
died of illness in 1644. Liu, now in his late fifties, cheerfully
resumed his profession of story-telling, continuing with unabated vigour until he was over eighty.

Popularly known as 'Pock-marked' Liu, our story-teller had
a legendary reputation even in his life-time. He seems to have
been admired most of all for his power of invention (which
meant, in practice, improvisation), and for his perfect control
of atmosphere. For he lived at a time when most stories were
already in print; and since his repertory was chiefly historical[1]
though including also the *Shui-hu chuan* narrative, he could only
invent within limits, the plot and the more familiar features of
the stories being long established. As an improvisator, Liu
followed no master and founded no school. An account of Liu
Ching-t'ing's story-telling by a contemporary admirer, Chang
Tai (1599–c. 1684), deserves translating in full:[2]

'The appearance of 'Pock-marked' Liu of Nanking was

[1] Consisting of Han, Three Kingdoms, Sui and T'ang, and Sung history
(see Hung Shih-liang, pp. 32–4), a range hardly possible to any story-
teller sticking closely to his text.
[2] 'Liu Ching-t'ing's Story-telling', in *T'ao-an meng-i* ('Reminiscences')
c. 5 (ed. T'ai Ching-nung, K'ai-ming 1957, p. 67); the work was not
printed until the eighteenth century and is not mentioned by our playwright. The passage is quoted in full in the notes to scene 1 in the Liang
Ch'i-ch'ao edition, whose reading I have followed in one or two places.

unprepossessing, his dark brown face being dotted all over
with scars and swellings. But he was good at story-telling.
He would hold one session of story-telling per day for a fee
of one silver tael, and bookings for his performances had to be
made by letter ten days in advance, and even then he was often
not available. At the time the two persons most sought after
in the world of entertainment in Nanking were the courtesan,
'Moon-child' Wang (Wang Yüeh-sheng) and 'Pock-
marked' Liu.

'I heard him tell the episode of Wu Sung killing the tigers
on Ching-yang Ridge in a plain prose text differing greatly
from the *Shui-hu chuan* account.[1] His descriptions were
minute down to the last detail, and yet the whole picture
would be clearly defined without giving the impression of
tedious repetition. His rich voice clanged like a temple bell,
and at tense moments in the story the succession of shrieks
and cries rocked the roof itself. As an instance of his use of
detail,—when Wu Sung first entered the wine-shop and
found no one in the parlour to serve him, he gave a sudden
roar, with the noise of which all the empty jars and vessels
in the place reverberated.

'When invited to perform, Liu would wait for his hosts to
be seated and to attend in silence before beginning his performance, during which if servants started to whisper to one
another or one of the seated audience yawned or showed
signs of impatience and boredom, he would stop and could not
easily be prevailed upon to resume. Or late at night, with the
table wiped afresh and the lamp-wick trimmed and cups of
tea noiselessly handed round, he would give a quietly restrained recitation, in which his delivery could vary from fast
and tripping to slow and deliberate. And the rise and fall of
his voice would seem to lead one into the very nature of
things or to penetrate to the core of men and affairs. If the
story-tellers of the world could hear him with their own ears
at such times, I doubt not but they would chew their own
tongues to bits and expire on the spot.

'Liu had an unusually ugly face and he dressed soberly; but
his eyes were expressive and his eloquence was such that he
attracted as large a clientele as the glamorous 'Moon-child'.'

[1] In *Shui-hu ch'üan-chuan* (see 'The Birthday Gift Convoy' *supra*),
chapter 23.

The text of *T'ao-hua shan* presents few problems. For the translation of scenes 10 and 11, I have used the annotated edition by Wang Chi-ssu and Su Huan-chung (Jen-min 1959), but have profited equally from the edition with copious historical notes by Liang Ch'i-ch'ao (Wen-hsüeh ku-chi reprint of 1954). I have also consulted the Kuo-hsüeh chi-pen ts'ung-shu chien-pen edition, containing the author K'ung Shang-jen's own marginal notes and comments.

The Blood-stained Fan

Scene 10   A Letter to the General

STORY-TELLER LIU[1] [*enters and declaims*]
  A wandering old story-teller, I make no boast
  Of peddling ancient traditions in exchange for present lore.
  This past year I have shunned the noble halls,
  Preferring the street-corner, where leisurely I sip cold tea.
[*laughs to himself*] I, Liu Ching-t'ing, hail from nowhere and wander all over the land; though a mere reciter of tales, I am no sponging parasite. [*makes his bow*] Gentlemen of the audience, you see me here—What do I look like? I am like Yama, King of the Underworld, with his enormous ledger with the names of countless departed souls entered in it. Or, again I am like a statue of the Laughing Buddha with his protruding belly filled with the endless sorrows and vicissitudes of this world. I rap my drum and shake my castanets, and a thunderstorm brews and the rains descend; I open my lips and flip my tongue, and there unfolds a chronicle of historical events, a veritable *Annals of Spring and Autumn*. The filial sons and loyal ministers who in their time had suffered injustice receive from my mouth redress and rehabilitation; and the wicked and depraved who had occupied positions of privilege and power now have disaster and punishment visited upon them. This is a slight case of private reinstatement, a mild exercise in the reversal of judgement. [*laughs*] I, the pock-marked Liu, say whatever comes into my mind, and enjoy myself well enough.—Yesterday young Master Hou[2] of Honan sent along money for tea and arranged

---

[1] For the story-teller Liu Ching-t'ing, see Introduction. The role is assigned to a clown (*ch'ou*). I have not thought it necessary to indicate the types of singer for the other parts.
[2] Hou Ch'ao-tsung, the hero of the play; see Introduction. The family came from Shang-ch'iu (i.e. Shangkiu in Honan Province).

to come this afternoon to listen to my recitation. I will take out
my drum and castanets and, to bait intending customers, make
a lucky preliminary offering.[1]

[*produces drum and castanets; sings*]

Being unoccupied, to while away my time, I discourse at random
On fortune's proferred crumbs both sour and sweet!
The hundred and eight thousand years

since the world's beginning,
As borne on wings, in a flash have fled.
Though whirlwinds and tempests rage in succession
And ensigns of dragons or tigers are hoisted

over tents and warships,
This sharp and strident contending for momentary fame and gain
Falls flat and silent upon the couch

of the deep-slumbering Ch'en T'uan.[2]

THE STUDENT, HOU CH'AO-TSUNG [*enters and declaims*]

Across green meadows through the thin mist

one seeks the lovely ladies;
In the evening sun, amid lengthening shadows,

one listens to the deeds of heroes.

I have come today to listen to Old Liu's recitation. From within
comes that well-known rhythmical tap. Some others must have
arrived before me. [*greets Liu, breaking into roaring laughter*]
There was no audience and you were by yourself! Whom were
you performing to?

LIU: But story-telling is my trade. If you, sir, were at leisure
in your study, playing on your guitar or chanting poetry, would
you demand an audience?

HOU: Well said.

LIU: With your permission, from which dynasty shall today's
story be?[3]

HOU: I do not care which dynasty it is. Choose a story that is
full of action and bustle, and is straightforward and brisk in its
progress, and tell it.

---

[1] Lucky preliminary offering, i.e. the 'story-teller's preamble', see
General Introduction. 'To bait intending customers' was the accepted
phrase.

[2] Ch'en T'uan, a hermit given to Taoist practices, famed for his hundred
days' sleep; see *Sung shih*, c. 457, pp. 2^b–3^b. His story is dramatized by Ma
Chih-yüan in the *tsa-chü* play *Ch'en T'uan kao wo* (*Yüan-ch'ü hsüan*, pp.
720–32).

[3] Liu's repertory was mainly historical; see Introduction.

Liu: But don't you know, Master Hou, that action and bustle bear fruits of loneliness and desolation, and that the straightforward and brisk are an offshoot of involvement and complication? Rather let me tell about an empire ravaged by invaders and about faithful ministers disgraced and disinherited sons, that all who hear me might shed a few tears.

Hou [*sighs*] Alas! So you, too, old Liu, perceive that things have come to such a pass. How very worrying it is!

THE OFFICIAL, YANG WEN-TS'UNG[1] [*enters in great haste and declaims*]

    Let not the iron chain crack that spans the wide river
    Lest again a white flag fly above the Rock Fortress![2]

I, the official Yang Wen-ts'ung, because of urgent affairs of state, am looking for my friend Hou for consultation. Inquiring all the way, I learn that he is here. I will go straight in.

[*Yang and Hou salute each other*]

Hou: Welcome indeed! Now we can listen together to old Liu's recitation.

YANG [*with impatience*] What times are these, that you should still be listening to stories?

Hou: And why is Mr Yang so agitated?

YANG: You don't know yet, my friend? General Tso[3] is sailing down the river with his troops to occupy Nanking, and has designs even on Peking itself. At his wits' end, Army Secretary Hsiung[4] has asked me to seek a plan from you.

Hou: But what plan should I have?

YANG: It is known to us all that your father was former commanding officer and patron to General Tso.[5] If a personal

---

[1] Yang Wen-ts'ung: see Introduction.

[2] Shih-t'ou-ch'eng (Rock City), a natural fortress to the west of Nanking overlooking the Yangtze, was the scene of a great river battle in the last days of the Wu kingdom (A.D. 280). The Wu defenders had an iron chain spanning the river, but the Chin army set fire to it by burning huge wooden vessels filled with sesame oil: the chain sank and the Wu surrendered. See *Chin shu*, c. 42, p. 5b.

[3] General Tso Liang-yü: see Introduction. In scene 9, Tso, stationed at Wuchang up the Yangtze, is threatened with mutiny by his troops because the grain boats coming to their relief have been held up; the men exact a promise from him to march to Nanking to requisition their supplies.

[4] Hsiung Ming-yü, Army Secretary of the time; biography in *Ming shih*, c. 257, pp. 7b–8b. Historically, it was at Hsiung's request that Hou drafted the plea to the General; see notes to scene 10 in the Liang Ch'i-chao edition.

[5] Hou Ch'ao-tsung's father, Hou Hsün, had befriended Tso and greatly advanced him in his career; see notes to scene 9 in Liang edition.

appeal to him came from your father, Tso could certainly be halted. What say you to that?

H o u: I am only too anxious to be of service. But my father has been living in retirement in our native woods, and even if he agreed to write a letter, would it really avail? Besides, it is a journey of three thousand *li* back and forth. How, then, could we avert the imminent danger?

Y a n g: My friend, you have the reputation of a man of courage and daring. Could you look on unconcernedly while matters took such a grave turn? Why not write a letter in his name to save the immediate situation? At a later time you could explain the circumstances to your father, who would hardly blame you.

H o u: In our present exigence it would indeed seem justifiable to adopt measures of expediency. I will return to my lodgings to make a draft, which we can then discuss together.

Y a n g: The matter brooks no delay. If we dispatched the letter at once, it might even be too late already. How could we wait to discuss it?

H o u: Since this is so, I will simply write the letter.[1]

[*writing, he sings*]

'The doting old man is so bold

To counsel the General to reflect again:

Be slow to advance your banners—

An army marching without orders spreads suspicion and dismay.

On the tomb of our founding Emperor[2] the trees are still green—

Who could answer for their desecration by

trampling horses' hoofs?

For the scarcity of provisions and firewood

Improved arrangements should bring ready relief.

There remains your loyal heart: let not adversity shake it.'

[*Stops writing and hands letter to Yang*]

Y a n g [*reading over letter*] Excellent! Excellent! It is rousing and yet persuasive, an indisputable case well argued and presented, making it difficult for him not to comply, causing him to be fearful of the consequences of not complying—a clear proof of your sound judgement, my young friend!

H o u: Though this may seem so to you, yet it would be best to

---

[1] The letter itself, which is included in Hou's collected works, corresponds to Yang's description of it in the next speech; see Introduction.
[2] The tomb of the founding emperor of Ming, T'ai-tsu, is outside Nanking.

send the letter to Army Secretary Hsiung for a detailed revision.
YANG: There is no need for that. I will tell him about the
contents. [*suddenly showing anxiety*] Just one thing. We have
the letter; we must send a trusty servant of yours to deliver it.
HOU: But I am here on my travels and am attended only by two
pages, who certainly could not be dispatched on such an
errand.
YANG: Could a letter of this nature be entrusted with a total
stranger?[1]
HOU: I really cannot help there.
LIU: Don't panic! Supposing I, old Liu, did the trip?
YANG: If Mr Liu is willing to go, that is indeed excellent. —
But there will be the cross-questioning at all the sentry posts
along the way, and it is no joke.
LIU: Let me explain myself. I, pock-marked Liu, originally
had the surname Ts'ao,[2] and like my namesake in *Mencius*, am
nine cubits in stature but shame to be merely feeding on millet.[3]
As for possessing enough verbal dexterity to suit my words to
circumstance and enough strength in my limbs for the odd
scuffle or two, I shall not be found wanting.
HOU: I am told that at General Tso's camp the gates are
guarded with the utmost vigilance; neither the local villagers
nor any passing travellers are ever allowed through them. And
a weather-beaten old man like you hopes to gain entry?
LIU: There you go, Master Hou, trying to rouse me to action!
It's a well-worn trick of us story-tellers. But old as I am, I do
as I please, staying or going. I am not to be roused in this way.
[*sings*]

While over there, brush in hand,

you carefully composed your epistle,

Here, too, I harboured uncommon schemes in my breast:

To engage in a battle of the tongue

You must still trust to me.

[1] I am taking this to mean: 'Would the employing of a total stranger as
messenger not arouse the General's suspicion?' The implication that
Yang and the Army Secretary could not between them find a trustworthy
messenger seems ludicrous.
[2] See Introduction.
[3] Passing one's days in inactivity. Ts'ao Chiao, who wished to emulate the
sages, lamented: 'I have heard that King Wen was ten cubits high, and
T'ang nine. Now I am nine cubits four inches in height. But I can do
nothing but eat my millet.' (See Legge, *The Works of Mencius*, VI, ii. 11.
1–2.)

So as to convey a letter to the Dragon King
Liu I did not shirk descending the depths;[1]
I will cast aside my fool's disguise
But so employ my bantering wit
That, though leaving in darkness and secrecy,
                                        I return in broad daylight
To the applause of a gazing multitude.

YANG: Truly a man of parts! But you will need to expound fully the meaning of the letter before it can be of avail.

LIU [*sings*]

Need one explain in detail the purport of the letter
Or further clarify its meaning?
Armed with these untiring lips and this cheek,
Even unprovided with a missive,
I still will act the messenger
And seize upon his least vacillation:
In a fit of scolding my tongue shall lash at the General,
                                        men, horses and all,
And beat them back a good eight hundred *li*.

HOU: You will scold him! How?

LIU: I will just ask him—[*sings*]

To guard against the rebels, you yourself turn rebel—
Guilty or not guilty?

HOU: Well done! Well done! Indeed more effectual than my written message.

YANG: Go in now and pack up your things. I will send along money for your expenses. You must try to leave the city to-night.

LIU: I know. I know. [*makes his bow*] You gentlemen must now excuse me.   [*Goes off at once*

YANG: I never realized that old Liu was a man of such ingenuity and courage.

HOU: I have often praised him as being really one of ourselves. Story-telling is the least of his gifts. [*sings*]

Under pressure of circumstance I wrote the letter
                                        in my father's name,

---

[1] Liu I carried a message from the daughter of the Dragon King to her father under the Tung-t'ing Lake; see Li Ch'ao-wei's *ch'uan-ch'i* tale *Liu I* (in *T'ang-jen hsiao-shuo*, pp. 62–8). The story is dramatized by Shang Chung-hsien in the *tsa-chü* play *Liu I ch'uan shu* (in *Yüan-ch'ü hsüan*, pp. 1625–38). The identity of surname adds point to the allusion.

And rely upon Mr Liu's sharp tongue and ready wit
To ward off the dreaded sight some frosty dawn
                             of the rash General's ten thousand horse
And to save the twilight glow on these hills
                                         by our river stronghold.

YANG [*declaims*]

With a missive mightier than the cavalry's charge

HOU [*declaims*]

Warships heading downstream were halted at Ching-chou.[1]

YANG [*declaims*]

From of old, Yangtze's lower reaches have boasted of talent;

HOU [*declaims*]

Today a fly-whisk-waving dilettante turns staff officer.

[*Both go off*

Scene 11   The Tongue mightier than the Sword[2]

[*Two soldiers enter*]

FIRST SOLDIER [*sings*][3]

Kill off your rebel and claim his loot;
Rescue the people and requisition their houses;
Be an official and control the granary,
And each soldier shall have three men's rations!

SECOND SOLDIER: That's not how it goes these days.

FIRST SOLDIER: You sing it, then.

SECOND SOLDIER [*sings*][3]

The rebel is ferocious, he leaves behind no loot;
Fled are the people, their houses stripped;
The officials are poor, the granary doors are locked,
And a thousand men receive not one man's rations!

FIRST SOLDIER: If it is as you say, then we poor soldiers may really starve to death.

SECOND SOLDIER: Like enough.

FIRST SOLDIER: The other day when we were in an uproar,[4]

[1] Ching-chou: the Prefecture coinciding with the area then under General Tso's command, and scene of numerous land and river battles in the Three Kingdoms period.
[2] The title of the scene is the translator's; the original title being 'Admittance to the General's Camp'.
[3] The song is not part of the theatre's repertory of tunes and the verses do not conform to a 'song' pattern. The soldiers therefore sing to any folk tune without musical accompaniment.
[4] See note to General Tso in scene 10 above.

we had the General really worried. He said that he would allow
us to march to Nanking to seek provisions. But nothing has
happened in the last few days. He must have changed his mind
again.

SECOND SOLDIER: He changes his mind; we start an uproar
as before. There's no difficulty about that.

FIRST SOLDIER: Stop this idle talk. Let us go to the gates of
the main camp to answer the roll-call. We can confer again
later. Indeed it is:

  'But for the fear of starvation,

  Who would break the law?'   [*Both go off*

STORY-TELLER LIU [*enters, disguised as a fisherman and shouldering a bundle; sings*]

  Leaving the lonely woods with their plaintively rustling leaves,

  I am greeted by clusters of flowering rush and smartweed.—

  With my cormorant plume hat worn all askew

  And my trusty sword hanging sidelong,

  And my white beard fluttering in the wind,

  Who would know me for a madcap latter-day court jester?[1]

I, Liu Ching-t'ing, braving the wind and rain, walked all the way
up the river, but never saw any mutinous troops plundering the
grain. Perhaps it was only a rumour. However, I am glad that
I have arrived at Wuchang's city wall. I must now sit on the
grass, open my bundle, change into hat and boots, so as to
deliver the letter. [*sits on the ground and changes out of his fisherman's headgear and shoes*]

FIRST AND SECOND SOLDIERS [*re-enter and sing*]

  By the city wall, hungry crows caw at a wet dawn,

  As we pace the misty highway

  Half a *li* from the main camp.

[*they point with their fingers*]

  Flags and banners are streaming in the wind

  Though the drums and horns barely show through the haze.

Yonder lies the camp gate. Let us hurry!

  The unfilled belly brooks no discipline:

  But the army will have its roll-call each fifth morn.[2]

LIU: Officers, begging your pardon, where is the General's

---

[1] Liu prided himself on the hidden moral purpose behind his banter and his
story-telling; and his service under General Tso confirmed him in the role
of wise court jester in the mould of Tung-fang Shuo, jester and counsellor
to the Han emperor Wu-ti.

[2] On the third, the eighth, the thirteenth, etc. of the month.

main camp?

FIRST SOLDIER [*aside to Second Soldier*] The old fellow has a north-of-the-river accent.[1] He would be either a deserter or a rebel.

SECOND SOLDIER: Why not trip him up, cheat him out of a few coppers and buy ourselves a meal?

FIRST SOLDIER: Capital!

SECOND SOLDIER [*to Story-teller Liu*] Are you looking for the General's headquarters?

LIU: Quite so.

FIRST SOLDIER: I will accompany you there.

[*throws noose round Liu*]

LIU: Alas! Why are you arresting me?

SECOND SOLDIER: We are bowmen on patrol from the Wuchang Command. If we didn't arrest you, whom would we arrest?

LIU [*gives the soldiers a sudden push; they both fall; Liu points at them and laughs*] Just a couple of blind beggars! No wonder you were so faint with hunger you went tumbling one after the other.

FIRST SOLDIER: How did you know we were suffering from hunger?

LIU: If you weren't suffering from hunger, why should I be here?

SECOND SOLDIER: You don't mean to say you had actually come with the convoy of grain!

LIU: If I wasn't convoying the grain, what should I be doing?

FIRST SOLDIER: Confound it! So we *were* blind. Let's get a move on with the luggage; we'll send you, brother, to the gates of the main camp.

[*Second and First Soldiers walk on with Liu*]

LIU [*sings*]

See how the city[2] reclines on the river's billowing waves,
Which buoy up broad Parrot Island,

[1] Liu was in fact from Taichow just north of the Yangtze, where the author himself was stationed for some time; see Introduction.
[2] The ancient city of Wuchang (part of the modern triple city of Wuhan) on the south bank of the Yangtze. Yellow Crane Tower on Snake Hill in Wuchang itself is frequently alluded to in T'ang and later poetry. The mid-stream Parrot Island, situated nearer Hanyang on the other bank, is named after the parrot celebrated in 'Ying wu fu' (in *Wen hsüan*, c. 13) by the irascible Mi Heng (A.D. 173–198), whose grave may still be seen on the island.

While tall Yellow Crane Tower rises sheer!
The crowing cock, the barking dog are alike silent;
Where is the smoke of habitation,
Where the market throng?
The wolf and jackal are surfeited with predatory feeding,[1]
Having torn to shreds the glowing map of city and river.
Hark! Shrill voices now cram my ears
Rising above the loud beat of the war-drum
And the proud neighing of mail-clad horses.

SECOND SOLDIER [*points with fingers*] We are before the gates of the general's camp. [*to Liu*] Wait here, brother, while I sound the drum. [*beats drum*]

CAMP COMMANDANT [*enters above gates and declaims*]
    Foremost in rank comes the General,
    Whose authority in battle rivals the Emperor's.
You there, beating on the drum outside the gates. What intelligence have you? Report at once.

FIRST SOLDIER: As we made our rounds just then, we caught a suspicious character who claimed to be escorting the grain convoy. We didn't know whether to believe him, and have brought him to headquarters for questioning.

COMMANDANT [*to Liu*] You claim to be escorting the provisions. Show me the official dispatch.

LIU: There is no official dispatch, only a private letter.

COMMANDANT: This seems doubtful.[2] [*sings*]
    Your intention in coming this way calls for careful investigation:
    A letter you brought along, yet would reveal no name.
    Surely this wild talk rests upon false pretences;
    Do army provisions, then, spring from nowhere?—
    He prevaricates right and left, making claims without foundation;
    To judge by his facial expression,
    He is likely to be either a deserter or a despoiler.

LIU: You are clearly mistaken. If I had been a deserting plunderer, would I have sought out the army camp?

COMMANDANT: This seems not unreasonable. Since you have a letter, I will send it in for you.

---

[1] Wolf and jackal and, later in the scene, fox and tiger: cruel and predatory men, whether rebels or the Emperor's soldiers; see note on the rebel Chang Hsien-chung below.
[2] From the lines that follow, some further exchanges between the Commandant and the story-teller left to the actor's own devices may be presumed.

L I U : It is a confidential letter, to be handed over to the general in person.

C O M M A N D A N T : This sounds even more doubtful! Wait outside. I will report to the general and then summon you.

[*First and Second Soldiers and Story-teller Liu go off. To the sound of pipes and drums, the centre gate opens.*[1] *Six guards holding spears and other weapons enter ; they stand, three on either side of the gate, facing one another*]

G E N E R A L T S O [*enters in military dress and declaims*]
    Keeping watch on the great river at its confluence with the Han[2]—
    The security of the empire may pivot upon one man,
    Much burdened with the cares of military supplies:
    For glib talk and laughter spoil victory's plan.

[*takes his seat ; aloud, as in giving command*] The other day the men being in a ferment for want of food, seeing no other means of alleviation, we said that we would allow them to march to Nanking to seek provisions. But upon reflection, it would seem far better that the provisions should come to the troops than the troops to the provisions. We hear that the relief grain from Kiukiang is due any day. This morning, therefore, we will omit the roll-call so that all may return to their posts and wait patiently for the arrival of the provisions.

C O M M A N D A N T : The general has commanded. [*retires to far corner of stage ; then again steps forward*] The command has been carried out. The 'No roll-call' signs are up and the troops returning to their various posts.

T S O : What is the latest intelligence ? Report now.

C O M M A N D A N T : We have no fresh intelligence, but there's a courier arrived who claims to have brought the provisions and asks to see the general.

T S O [*much relieved*] So the grain boats are here at last! This certainly is cause for rejoicing. But from which department came the official dispatch ?

C O M M A N D A N T : There was no official dispatch. He only had a private letter, which he said he would deliver in person to the general.

T S O : Strange indeed ! He could be a spy sent by the rebels.

[1] The scene has shifted to within the camp. As the pipes and drums sound, a chair and table are placed on the stage. Another chair is later brought for Story-teller Liu.
[2] The Han river flows into the Yangtze at Hankow and Hanyang, on the opposite shore from Wuchang.

[*raises voice to give command*] Guards, take special precautions.
Order him to advance on his knees.

ALL: Yes, general.

[*Camp commandant calls 'the courier'. Guards lower their spears.
Story-teller Liu enters by crawling under the crossed spears*[1]]

LIU [*rises and salutes General Tso by merely making a low bow
with the hands held together in front*[2]] Saluting the General.
Your servant makes his bow.

TSO: Hey? Who are you to be playing the great lord here?

LIU: Your servant, a mere commoner, play the great lord?
How dare I? [*sings*]

An old fisherman and woodcutter I am,
                                        a mountain village dweller;
What should I know of great princes and lords
                                        or the lesser nobles?
From afar I saw the spears and swords,
                                        and the rows of banners waving,
And took them to be one dense forest,
                                        thick with trees and spreading weeds.
Let the fox snarl and steal, and the tiger bellow its wrath—
Pray, is all this display of might really necessary?
It terrorized a poor old man who, finding no exit,
Made his deep bow, but more through fright than effrontery.

[*gives his usual story-teller's bow*]

Begging pardon,
With the army's etiquette I am not conversant.

[*laughs*]

Let anger now die down;
There is a letter for the General's perusal.

TSO: From whom comes the letter?

LIU: Old Mr Hou of Kuei-te[3] sends it with his compliments.

TSO: Minister of Instruction Hou was my commanding officer
and great patron. How came you to know him?

LIU: Your servant is now a retainer of the Hou family.

TSO [*bowing*] I have been remiss indeed. Where is the letter?

[*Liu hands up the letter*] Give orders for the gate to be shut.[4]

[*To the sound of pipes and drums, the gate is shut. Camp Comman-*

---

[1] See Introduction. [2] A salute as between equals.
[3] Kuei-te, i.e. Shang-ch'iu (in Honan Province); see note on the student
Hou in scene 10 above.
[4] To indicate that the General's morning session is at an end.

dant and Guards go off]

Tso: My honoured guest, please be seated.

[*Story-teller Liu takes a side chair*]

Tso [*reading letter, sings*]

  See how his great sincerity overflows!

  He admonishes me as though I were his own son.

In a rapid reading I cannot fathom the full implication of this. He exhorts me to remain stationed in these border regions and not to move my men to the interior.[1] [*sighs*] Alas, my former chief, you little know your Tso Liang-yü!—[*sings*]

  Would I could show him my loyal heart!

  How indeed could I betray his high trust

  And dishonour one who promoted my official career?

[*turns to Liu*] What is your honoured surname and style?

Liu: The General honours me too much. You servant is called Liu Ching-t'ing.

[*servant enters with tea*]

Tso: Have some tea, Ching-t'ing. [*Liu takes the teacup*] Do you know that ever since its sack by the rebel Chang Hsien-chung,[2] nine houses out of ten in this city of Wuchang have stood empty? Though I am the commanding officer here, there is such a dearth of hay and provisions, that the men clamour and riot every day and I am no longer in complete control.

Liu [*flushes*] What is the General saying? From of old it was remarked, 'The men followed where the leader went'. Was it ever said, 'The general came after while the rank and file led'? [*sings*]

  Seated in your great military camp,

  Supreme power and grand strategy within your iron grasp,

  You rule an army of thousands so that,

                        though earth itself might quake,

  Orders do not give way:

  Some hunger-bitten soldiers turn restive,

                        defy the Imperial throne;

  The General flounders, utterly at a loss,

---

[1] Nanking, being the Southern Capital, was thought of as the centre, and Wuchang, in contrast, as of the border regions.

[2] Between Tso's first moving into Wuchang in the autumn of 1642 and his return from Anking further up the river in autumn 1643, the rebel Chang Hsien-chung had occupied Wuchang and butchered the inhabitants (in the spring of 1643); the events being here telescoped. See *Ming shih*, c. 309, pp. 16b–17a; c. 273, pp. 5b–6a.

Lets them go scot-free, following their own giddy inclinations!
The shame and ignominy of it—how may you hope to escape?
The shame and ignominy of it—how may you hope to escape?
Never be it said,
           the General failed to wield his sword of authority.
[*flings his teacup aside, dashing it*]
T s o [*angered*] Hey! How dare you? Throwing the teacup on
the floor!
L i u [*laughing*] Would your servant have dared to offend? I
was excited with talking and, gesticulating with my hand, I
tossed it away.
T s o : 'Gesticulating with your hand, you tossed it away.'
Come, come, you surely admit that your head holds sway over
your hand.
L i u : If the head had held sway and been the true captain, would
restlessness have got so out of hand?
T s o [*laughing*] Rightly said, Ching-t'ing. It was because of
the exceeding hunger of my men that I promised them to go
after the provisions and march into the interior. I was desperate; I could not help it.
L i u : As for that, your servant has come a long way and is also
exceedingly hungry, but the General seems not much concerned.
T s o : Oh, I had forgotten. I am sorry. [*shouts*] Give orders for
dinner to be served.
L i u [*folding his hands over his belly and rubbing it*] Oh! Oh! I'm
hungry! I'm hungry!
T s o [*in a loud voice*] The wretches! Have dinner served at once.
L i u [*rising*] I can't wait any longer. I'll go within to look for
some food.
[*strides towards the inside of the General's residence*]
T s o [*angrily*] Where do you think you're going?
L i u [*turns and faces General, appealing pitifully*] But I am exceedingly hungry.
T s o : Just because you're exceedingly hungry, would I allow
you to march freely into the interior of my camp?
L i u [*bursts into laughter*] Hear that? Though you may be exceedingly hungry, yet you shall not be allowed to march freely
into the interior: I see that even the General understands the
rules.
T s o [*laughing loudly*] Again you score! Each time you open

your mouth, you mock my failings. What a tongue! There's room in my camp for someone like you.

[*sings*]

> Among the numberless of my acquaintance,
> I perceive that you alone wear the mantle of the jester
>   Tung-fang-Shuo: [1]
> What resourcefulness is encompassed within his breast,
> Who with a straight face reproves one
> And the next moment laughs one to scorn!

LIU: Not at all. I am only a loafer, just earning my keep as I wander along the rivers and lakes.

TSO: Ching-t'ing, it seems to me that if you move in official circles, you must be possessed of some unusual gift. I should like to know more.

LIU: As a boy I had but little schooling, and I learnt none of the arts. It was only because by chance, I knew snatches of various tales and chronicles [2] and recited these as fancy led me that I won the acclaim of former Army Secretary Fan of Wuch'iao and former Prime Minister Ho of T'ung-ch'eng. [3] It was thus that I became acquainted with many officials. But indeed I hardly merited it all. [*sings*]

> In my time I had read many fictitious chronicles,
> Repository of other men's bottled-up grievances.
> Oh, those fictitious chronicles,
> Repository of my own bottled-up grievances!
> Contemplating the river and the hills, [4]
>   I quaff a full peck of bitter pine lees. [5]

---

[1] Tung-fang Shuo: see note on court jester above, and *Han shu*, c. 65.

[2] Liu followed no master and, therefore, depended on printed texts in the first instance for his stock of stories; see Introduction.

[3] Fan Ching-wen (biography in *Ming shih*, c. 265, pp. 1ᵇ–2ᵃ) and Ho Juch'ung (in *Ming shih*, c. 251, pp. 7ᵇ–8ᵃ) were among Liu's patrons; see Introduction.

[4] The river and the hills, symbol of the empire: hence all good patriots took to landscape painting when the empire was lost to the Mongols (Yüan) or the Manchus (Ch'ing), the activity according well with retirement to the countryside.

[5] A drink concocted by Su Tung-p'o, who, camping out with the soldiers under his command, deplored their felling of pine trees for firewood. Coming upon a branch with streaming resin, he had the bark boiled and fermented, finding the beverage sweet yet slightly bitter: the drinking of this essence of a noble tree day after day so inspired him that he felt at one with the elements. See '*Fu*-poem to the Pine Lees of Chung Mountain', *Ching chin Tung-p'o wen-chi shih-lüeh* (Wen-hsüeh ku-chi edition 1957), c. 2, p. 21.

On my small drum I lightly tap with a nervous stick;
With adroit fingers I rattle my castanets.
With each uttered syllable, loyal men and filial sons take shape;
With each throbbing sound, the dragon puffs and the tiger howls.
At the tip of my nimble tongue,

steel blades leap flashing out of sheaths;
From the reed-pipe that is my throat,

thunder cracks and the cannon roars.
Alack! As for this teasing
And blowing hot and cold,
I need not resort to stories transcribed with the brush
And recorded in ink,
But I do counsel the brave warrior
To cancel with a single stroke his muddled accounts.

Tso: Brisk and to the point! I did not know that you, Ching-t'ing, possessed such an outstanding talent. I will provide a bed for you in the study at my headquarters, so that I may hear you from time to time.[1]

[*sings*]

From now on, range through past and present,

holding forth, to my daily admiration,
On stirring events that fire the imagination.
With the eloquence of your volatile tongue.
And the swift arrows from my unerring bow,
More's the pity we may not allay

the tumult and dust enwrapping this world!

Liu: After this long, rambling talk, — to conclude, what has the general decided about moving his troops to the interior?

Tso: My upright and loyal heart, ever open to heaven's inspection, required no persuading by word of mouth and deserved no rebuke by letter.

[*declaims*]

My faithful allegiance, pure as a stream that mirrors the clear skies,

Liu [*declaims*]

Craved a vision of the Emperor's visage,[2]

forgetting the gulf of distance.

---

[1] See Introduction.

[2] i.e. contemplated a visit to the capital. At the time (1643) the Emperor (Ch'ung-chen) was still in Peking; in 1644, following the Emperor's death, Ministers rallied round Prince Fu in Nanking.

Tso [*declaims*]

But, so as to prop up the wall of defence
for the immense south-west,[1]

Liu [*declaims*]

He forwent the sight of the precipitous bore at Yangtze's estuary.[2]

[*Exeunt*

[1] i.e. defence against the rebels; the south-west was being marauded by Chang Hsien-chung, but Tso's defence had been but half-hearted.
[2] i.e. he did not sail down the Yangtze with his men.

Young Master Bountiful

'Young Master Bountiful' is the translator's title for chapters 31 and 32 of the satirical novel *Ju-lin wai-shih* ('An Unofficial History of the World of Learning') and is—under poetic licence—a self-portrait of the author Wu Ching-tzu (1701–1754) at the age of twenty-seven or twenty-eight. Of Wu's actual life much is now known[1] and at least one anecdote from his later years is preserved which would have been fit for inclusion in the novel itself. For a dozen or so generations the family had been physicians in the county of Ch'üan-chiao (Chuantsiao) in Anhwei Province, when towards the end of the Ming and early in the Ch'ing dynasty, within a span of sixteen years, four brothers distinguished themselves in the examinations and the Wus rose from secure respectability to unchallenged eminence. Among the brothers was Wu Kuo-tui, the author's great grandfather, who was third top candidate in the Palace Examination of 1658 and subsequently held the post of Reader in the Hanlin Academy. Thus the illustrious ancestor's Presentation Library, which housed a collection presented by the Emperor, duly appears in our story. The next generation, too, attained renown as scholars and held official posts of varying importance, though the author's grandfather, Wu Tan, had died early and was noted for his filial piety alone, which earned him a place in the local history.[2]

Distaste for the conventional official's career would seem to have begun with the author's father, Wu Lin-ch'i, who was content to be, rather late in his life, a mere Education Officer

---

[1] The relevant material is to be found in Hu Shih, *Wu Ching-tzu nien-p'u* (1922), in *Hu Shih wen-ts'un* (edition of 1953), vol. II, pp. 320–53; supplemented by Ho Tse-han, *Ju-lin wai-shih jen-wu pen-shih k'ao-lüeh* (1957), section III, 'Materials concerning the Author', pp. 164–200. Much may still be gleaned from Wu's collected essays and poems, *Wen-mu shan-fang chi* (reprint of 1957).

[2] *Ch'üan-chiao hsien-chih*, edition of 1920, c. 11, p. 12[b].

(*chiao-yü*) in the poor and somewhat remote county of Kanyu on the coast of the northernmost part of Kiangsu Province, where he fulfilled his duties by giving away part of his patrimony for the re-building of the County College. It was at the age of eighteen[1] that Wu accompanied his father to Kanyu, where he probably gained his first insight into the workings of officialdom. Certainly, in view of his father's position,[2] he would be in close contact with members of the local College, Senior Students with stipend (*lin-sheng*) and mere Licentiates (*sheng-yuan* or *hsiu-ts'ai*), and in those four or five years he probably formed indelible impressions of the pedantry of scholars, still aspiring or already approved, trembling examinees and ruthless examiners. (The common run of officials he would earlier have met at home, when they came to pay their respects to his father, still basking in the reflected glory of the ancestors.) Wu venerated his father's memory to excess and aggrandized him in the novel. Thus the insignificant Education Officer of Kanyu County becomes in our story Prefect Tu of Kan-chou, who has showered benefits upon his home county of Tienchang (which is over fifty miles from Ch'üan-chiao, the family's actual home), where his benevolence is a byword. In the interest of good story-telling also, the great grandfather topped the list of Palace candidates of his year. And for the benefit of the actor Pao, the family's genealogy is traced with unconcealed pride by the hero's cousin.

The shafts of satire Wu reserves for himself and his cousin, Wu Ch'ing. With the death of his father (whose post had terminated the year before, in 1722) Wu came into his inheritance

[1] On the evidence of the poem by his cousin Wu Ch'ing addressed to the author on his thirtieth birthday (in Ho Tse-han, p. 164), — i.e. in the year 1718. Wu's own poem addressed to the monk Hung-ming speaks of accompanying his father to a post at the age of fourteen, which could conceivably be a reference to some earlier appointment or to an examination or interview that led eventually to Kanyu, which is referred to in the next line—'On the sea a thousand *li* away'. *Wen-mu shan-fang chi*, c. 3, p. 7a.)

[2] The *chiao-yü* was in effect Senior Tutor of the County College, of which the County Magistrate was nominally head. Local students who held the first degree, i.e. licentiates (*sheng-yüan* or *hsiu-ts'ai*) were admitted to the College, and a fixed number of them would be made Senior Students with stipend (*lin-sheng*). The students prepared themselves for the higher degree examinations, in which process they were subjected to regular tests. See, e.g. P. T. Ho, *The Ladder of Success in Imperial China*, 1962, pp. 171–83; T. T. Ch'ü, *Local Government in China under the Ch'ing*, 1962, pp. 9–10; p. 317 n. 21.

at the age of twenty-three. He seems to have been embroiled at
once with rapacious clansmen in disputes over property, as
hinted darkly in his essay 'Moving House'[1] and in his cousin's
poem addressed to him on his thirtieth birthday:[2]

Others then entered your house
                              and sounded your bells and drums,
The strange hooting kite-owl, the greedy wolf;
But old Mr Liu in his kind heart
Commiserated with you in your weariness and sorrow.

The kind old Mr Liu was very likely the original of Old Lou
the cashier and estate overseer in our story, who enjoyed
Prefect Tu's absolute trust. The poem continues:

Your enemies placated, your estate already diminished,
The riff-raff of the town now sought you out—
You who are free from the habits of the vulgar rich,
Who know nought of the weight and beam of the steelyard.

In our story, the hero, Tu Shao-ch'ing, did not know his scales
and could not be bothered with the steelyard, on which silver
was weighed. According to the same poem, much of the author's
time was taken up with singers and actors, which led to a life
of dissipation and a swift drain on his diminished fortune. Wu,
however, remained impenitent, shutting his door on the un-
welcome, laughing and singing away in a perpetual state of
mild intoxication, unaffected by the jeers of clansmen and local
worthies:

Last year you sold your land, this year your house, too.
Grumbling and taunting, your elders remonstrate with you;
With hands folded in salute, you express yourself much obliged,
Your upstanding eyebrows like lances,
                              your voice a roaring tiger's.

The detail about the eyebrows comes out in our story, with the
actor Pao's swift survey of his prospective patron.

In chapter 34 of the novel itself, old Mr Kao from the next
town, Liuho, himself a Hanlin scholar, condemns the hero in
no uncertain terms:

'. . . And how indeed should I not know about him? Forgive

---

[1] 'Moving House', a *fu* composition written on the occasion of his removal
from his home town to Nanking in 1733, in *Wen-mu shan-fang chi*, c. 1,
pp. 4b–10a; hints of disputes with relatives and clansmen are to be found
on p. 8a. The essay is of great interest, but its details are obscure.
[2] In Ho Tse-han, pp. 164–6; see also p. 172.

my plain speaking, gentlemen: that fellow Shao-ch'ing is
the black sheep of the Tu family. For countless generations
his ancestors were doctors, piling up merit in heaven while
adding also to the family estate. The great grandfather
reaped the harvest of all this, attained his examination success and was an official for thirty or forty years without
bringing a cent home. And the father at least had it in him
to take a *chin-shih* degree and land a Prefect's post—but the
man was a fool! While at his post, he was never at pains to
show deference to the great; he coveted the good opinion of
the people and really took to heart precepts like 'enforcing
filial piety and subordination to elder brothers' or 'promot-
ing agriculture and sericulture', mistaking time-honoured
essay subjects for the art of government. Thus he ended by
displeasing his superiors, who had him summarily dismissed.
But that son of his is the height of absurdity! The fellow idles
away his days in drinking and foppery, and fraternizes with
Buddhist monks and Taoist priests, artisans and beggars,
not caring to cultivate the friendship of a single respectable
person. He squandered his entire fortune of sixty or seventy
thousand taels of silver in under ten years and then, no longer
able to hold his own in Tienchang, moved to Nanking, where
he would actually take his wife day after day to the common
taverns! Clutching his own bronze wine bowl too, like a
common beggar, wherever he goes! And to think that such
a ne'er-do-well should spring from such lineage! Therefore,
at home, when I supervise my sons and nephews at their
studies, I invariably cite him as a warning. In fact, I had a
slip of paper pasted on the desk of each member of the
younger generation: 'Take heed of the evil example of Tu
Shao-Ch'ing of Tienchang.'[1]

When at the age of thirty, as we learn from the cousin's
poem, Wu was compelled to sell his house, he left for Nanking
with the intention of making a fresh start. But already at the end
of that year, 1730, we find him penniless and cheerless in that
gay city, and the series of eight *tz'u* poems he wrote on New
Year's Eve[2] (i.e. early in 1731) tell a sad tale:

[1] Chapter 34, Tso-chia edition, pp. 335–6. Tu had pawned his gold goblet
for thirty taels in chapter 33 (p. 329).
[2] 'Mu-lan-hua' (abbreviated form), in *Wen-mu shan-fang chi*, c. 4, pp.
2ª–3ᵇ.

New Year's Eve!

A lone traveller against a windswept sky darkened with snow—
    These past thirty years

My storm-beaten brows were but too seldom unknit.

In the same poem, reference is made to a Mr Pao, apparently
a familiar,—the actor in our story?—who shares a jar of wine
with him, huddled over a stove. The second poem recalls his
visit to the city in a previous year, which had been a succession
of revels on the Ch'in-huai river, by day and by night. More
recently, some songs that he composed had been popular with
the singing girls and had won him acclaim. But now that the
silver which he kept at the top of his bed is spent, he could no
longer hold his head high.

In the third poem, the sight of a man about town, young and
wealthy, makes him realize with a pang all that he has thrown
away. It confirms the story of old Mr Kao's admonition to his
sons and nephews:

My fields and ancestral home forever gone,

I yet remain—the latest cautionary tale for the local sons!
    That fur-clad youth

Astride his sleek horse—he sneers too soon at my tattered robes.
The fifth poem laments his father, dead nearly nine years, and
his mother (dead almost twice as long), both not yet buried.
And we learn from the sixth poem that his wife, too, had died.
In his bereavement, he took a kitchen-maid as his concubine,
not having found a lady willing to marry him. (The first poem
speaks of 'neither marrying nor becoming an official'.) Wu
subsequently remarried[1] and, if we go by the account in his
novel, went sightseeing with his second wife, a physician's
daughter, all over Nanking. The eighth and last poem begins:

A lackey absconded, the other servants dispersed,

Leaving my lone shadow to console poor sleepyhead me.

In our story, Shaggy-beard Wang the steward runs off with a
sum of money at the end. The poem continues with Wu's plan to
establish a home in Nanking, which he was able to carry out
two years later, early in 1733.[2]

---

[1] See Ho Tse-han, pp. 199–200.
[2] In the second month of 1733, when he wrote 'Moving House'. In chapter
33 of the novel, the family and their effects arrive at their house on the
river bank in four boats (p. 326).

For in the eighteenth century Nanking was rich and populous and a city of great splendour, as Wu himself describes it in chapter 24 of the novel:

The city was built by the First Emperor of the Ming, who made it his capital. With its inner wall of thirteen gates and its outer wall of eighteen gates, it measures lengthwise forty *li* and its perimeter is a hundred and twenty *li*.[1] Its scores of wide streets and hundreds of narrow lanes are crowded with busy inhabitants and crowned by resplendent towers. The Ch'in-huai runs through the city, its length from the East Barrier to the West Barrier being ten *li*. When the river is high, painted barges glide along it with musicians playing their flutes and drums day and night. Already in the earlier city of the Six Dynasties[2] the temples and monasteries with their jade green tiles and vermilion ridge tiles numbered four hundred and eighty; such is their profusion now both inside and outside Nanking that there could scarcely be less than four thousand eight hundred. Scattered over the city are six or seven hundred eating-houses and over a thousand tea shops; even in a secluded lane one would still find a lantern or tea-shop's sign, where, in a parlour decorated with flowers in vases, one waited for one's turn—the place being usually full—to be served tea freshly brewed with rain water. At night, thousands of lamps in the eating-houses shine upon the streets; thus passers-by need have no use for lanterns but walk about as in daylight. On the moonlit river, the thrilling notes of music and singing would rise from some passing boat; the later the hour, the more melancholy the song. In the houses on the river's banks, girls dressed in light garments with jasmine flowers pinned to their hair would roll up their bamboo curtains and, leaning out of their balconies, listen in rapt silence to the singer. Thus,

At the sound of a drum from each illumined boat,
On either side the river, curtains roll up, windows are flung open.

[1] Forty *li* is over ten miles; a hundred and twenty *li*, over thirty miles. Only portions of the walls remain, most of the city having been destroyed in the 1850s and 1860s during the Taiping Rebellion.
[2] The Six Dynasties (Wu, Eastern Tsin, and the Southern Dynasties: Sung, Ch'i, Liang and Ch'en) all had their capital at Nanking, then known as Chien-k'ang. From the time of Chien-wen-ti (enthroned 371 A.D.) of Eastern Tsin, successive rulers in the next two centuries erected magnificent monasteries in the capital. See, e.g., T'ang Yung-t'ung, *Han Wei liang-Chin Nan-Pei-ch'ao fo-chiao shih*, pp. 443–4.

From the opened windows, fumes of ambergris and sandalwood would burst upon the river like so many fragrant jets,
which, mingling with the mist in the moonlight, give the
impression of clouds that half-conceal godlike figures in
celestial barks as well as goddesses looking down from
heaven.[1]

Needless to say, the banks of the Ch'in-huai river were the
fashionable quarter, where singing girls, but also men of
learning and distinction, congregated. Each of the houses had
a back door (known as a 'water door') which opened on to the
river.[2] The rent, however, was dear, especially during Examination year; it might easily be eight taels of silver per month,
payable in advance, with for 'key money' an additional eight
taels.[3] It was in such a house — 'a pavilion on the Ch'in-huai'[4]
— that Wu settled with his family, meeting with new friends
among the talented and erudite, and doubtless still maintaining
a certain style, but professing no aim or ambition in life.[5] The
city and its environs he seems to have looked upon as one large
pleasure ground.[6] There were the two lakes: Mo-ch'ou, outside the West Gate, planted with lotus flowers, scene of the
dramatic festival in chapter 30 of the novel; and immediately
north of the city, the unexpectedly wide expanse of Hsüan-wu,
surrounded by hills, with its five little islands, four of them
housing maps and records, the fifth one in the centre with a
garden and bamboo grove being used for an official residence
— where, in chapter 35, the unworldly Chuang Shao-kuang is
installed by the Emperor. And among the hills, Wu's favour-
ites were: Ch'ing-liang (Airy and Cool), to the west of the

---

[1] Chapter 24, p. 242. See also chapter 41, pp. 400–403, for further descriptions of the Ch'in-huai by night and during the religious festival of the
seventh month.

[2] Chapter 41, p. 400.

[3] Chapter 33, p. 325. Nanking was an expensive place, 'where a stranger
could starve to death' (chapter 28, p. 278: Chi Wei-hsiao's conversation
with the actor Pao about a friend newly arrived in Nanking.)

[4] See the *tz'u* poems 'Mai p'o-t'ang' and Wu's own note (*Wen-mu shan-
fang chi*, c. 4, pp. 4ᵃ–4ᵇ), quoted in part in Hu Shih, p. 330.

[5] See the 'Mai p'o-t'ang' poems and the final section of 'Moving House'
beginning with 'Beautiful Nanking . . .' (*Wen-mu shan-fang chi*, c. 1, pp.
9ᵃ–10ᵃ).

[6] In chapter 34 of the novel, Tu Shao-ch'ing says to his wife: '. . . But
there's so much fun to be had in Nanking, where we are! If I stay at home
with you here, we can go and look at the flowers any day in spring or
autumn, not forgetting the wine. What a happy life! Why ask me to seek
office in Peking?' (p. 333).

city, where in chapter 33 Tu Shao-ch'ing and his wife walk
hand in hand, thus becoming the talk of the town;[1] and to the
south, Yü-hua-t'ai (Rain Flower Terrace), a high mound of
multi-coloured pebbles which, according to legend, were the
flowers that rained from heaven during a sermon by the monk
Yün-kuang in the reign of Liang Wu-ti (6th century A.D.),
with its commanding view of the city and the Yangtze—'a
white silk band'—in the distance.[2]

On the Rain Flower Terrace was a temple dedicated to the
memory of the sages of the entire region, foremost among them
and the most ancient, Wu T'ai-po, founder of the Wu kingdom
and a member of the Chou royal house, who brought civilization
to an area inhabited by barbarous tribesmen.[3] The temple was
in ruins, the rites neglected. There had been a move to restore
the temple and hold regular sacrifices, notably by the father of
our author's friend Ch'eng T'ing-tso,[4] and no doubt kept up by
Ch'eng himself, a dedicated scholar portrayed in the novel as
Chuang Shao-kuang, exceedingly learned in the *Book of
Changes*.[5] The idea of sacrificing to the first Wu in history must
have been irresistible to Wu Ching-tzu, who was more than
ordinarily proud of his name and ancestry: he collected funds
from others and spent the remainder of his own fortune in re-
building the temple, at the completion of which an elaborate
sacrifice was performed according to notions of ancient ceremony then prevailing—the proceedings being described at
length and in punctilious detail in chapter 37 of the novel. It
was the event of his life and merited two lines of mention in the
local history of Ch'üan-chiao, which records even the sale of his
house for the cause.[6]

The venture reduced him to stark poverty and debarred him

---

[1] Chapter 33, pp. 327–8. See also chapter 55, p. 539, for a description of old
Yü's garden on Ch'ing-liang Hill, where the musical tailor Ching Yüan
would repair in order to play on his guitar.
[2] For descriptions of Yü-hua-t'ai, see chapter 29, p. 291; chapter 55,
p. 538.
[3] T'ai-po was heir to the Chou throne, but fled with his second brother
Chung-yung to the south to make way for their youngest brother Chi-li,
whose son became the great Wen-wang. The brothers lived with tribesmen in the Wusih-Soochow area, where T'ai-po founded the Wu kingdom.
See *Shih chi*, c. 31.
[4] See Ho Tse-han, section I, 'Identification of the More Important
Characters in the Novel', pp. 71–2.
[5] Chapters 34 and 35, esp. pp. 338–9, 350; chapter 49, p. 481.
[6] *Ch'üan-chiao hsien-chih*, c. 10, p. 47ᵇ; quoted in Hu Shih, p. 338.

from further acts of patronage. Indeed, extravagance and generosity appear to have been equally strong motives in Wu's dealings with others. The former he readily admits in 'Moving House':

> My progenitors lived on the fat of the land, and I indulged in reckless spending.[1]

And his friends have testified to the latter:

> Of a generous turn of mind, he gave freely to the poor and feasted his literary associates day and night.[2]

But in the society of Wu's day, a landed gentleman or an official back in his home town was expected to provide for the poor and help the deserving: his hospitality could be counted upon, and friends and relations who had travelled from afar waited to be sent off with considerable sums of money. The system was open to abuse with its attendant perils. In chapter 44 of the novel, for example, we find the admirable Yü Eldest expecting to collect a gift of a hundred taels or less from a visit to his friend, the newly appointed District Magistrate of Wu-wei-chou, who promptly allows him a share in the four hundred tael bribe offered in a case of manslaughter.[3] Since, however, patronage hung upon means and influence, by taking his social obligations seriously but not his property or official career, Wu doomed himself to bankruptcy from the start. In this he differed from his more astute cousin, Wu Ch'ing.[4]

The main facts about the cousin also are known.[5] His great grandfather and Wu's were twin brothers, and he himself was five years older than Wu. (In our story, the cousin is only two years older than the hero.) Their intelligence set them apart from the scores of others of their generation, and they were constant companions and had the same circle of friends. (Among the friends was Chang Ch'ing-ch'uan[6] — referred to as Chang

---

[1] *Wen-mu shan-fang chi*, c. 1, p. 4b.

[2] Biography of Wu by Ch'eng Chin-fang, in Ho Tse-han, p. 182.

[3] The case was investigated and the District Magistrate impeached, but Yü, who had in the meantime left Wu-wei-chou without returning home was saved through his family's repeated pleas of mistaken identity, his name not appearing correctly on the warrant of arrest (chapter 45).

[4] Wu Ch'ing was descended from Wu Kuo-lung, the twin brother of the illustrious Wu Kuo-tui; see Ho Tse-han, p. 38.

[5] See Ho Tse-han, section I, pp. 35–44; section III, pp. 164–6.

[6] References to 'Chang Third' occur in Wu Ch'ing's poem on the author's thirtieth birthday; and Chin Chü's poem addressed to Wu Ch'ing (Ho Tse-han, p. 166; p. 39). Chang does not figure in the honours lists in the local history of Ch'üan-chiao (*Ch'üan-chiao hsien-chih*, c. 12).

Third—possibly portrayed in the obsequious Tsang Third in our story.) The two cousins were alike in their connoisseurship of acting and singing, and were themselves somewhat theatrical and fond of ostentation. In appearance, apart from the chilling eyebrows, Wu was not striking, but his older cousin's grace and elegance (*feng-ya*) were the envy of contemporaries,[1] and in the novel the contrast between the two is drawn with a good deal of mischief. Much, too, is made of Wu's nonchalance and unconcern,[2] and his cousin's fastidiousness and finesse. Thus, according to the Venerable Wei Fourth, who had known both from childhood, Tu Shao-ch'ing is the 'manly one' and Shen-ch'ing, 'a cultivated man but too much of a cissy'. Also in our story, the dying old Lou sums Shen-ch'ing up as rich in accomplishments but poor in kindness. For all its caricature, the portrait of the cousin is not unflattering,—though in our story he hardly comes to life, doing no more than 'engineer' a profitable visit for the actor Pao. In chapter 29, however, where Tu Shen-Ch'ing is first introduced after an initial glimpse of him in a sedan chair, we find him dressed with consummate care like any dandy yet possessing something of the charm of an immortal. And in the ensuing incidents the man is shown to have a devastating wit; a faultless, uncompromising taste in all civilized matters; and a weak stomach, for food or fools.[3] Indeed, in their disdain of the common crowd as well as in their predilection for unorthodox views,[4] the cousins are at one in the novel.

In the year 1736, having become licentiates some years before,[5] they were both chosen to take part in the resuscitated Great Literary Scholarship examination (*po-hsüeh hung-tz'u k'o*), aimed at those of unusual ability who scorned the normal

---

[1] See Ho Tse-han, pp. 39–42; specifically, Wu Ch'ing's *feng-ya* is praised in an essay by Chin Chao-yen (p. 39) and a poem by Liu Ming-ho (p. 42).
[2] See poem by Chin Chü in Ho Tse-han, p. 39, and Wu Ch'ing's poem quoted above, p. 331. Chin describes our author as flushed with drink and shouting like a madman with utter unconcern for decorum at a gathering in the height of summer in Wu Ch'ing's home.
[3] Chapter 29, pp. 287–90.
[4] e.g. Shen-ch'ing's views on Fang Hsiao-ju and the Emperor Yung-lo in chapter 29 (p. 291) and Shao-ch'ing's interpretation of the love poems in *Shih ching* (the Poetry Classic) in chapter 34 (pp. 337–8). The latter is clearly based on Wu's treatise on *Shih ching*, now lost; see Ho Tse-han, pp. 174–6.
[5] Wu seems to have obtained his licentiate when he was about twenty-three, i.e. in about 1723; see Ho Tse-han, p. 199.

channels of advancement. The cousin proceeded to Peking but returned without success, and his burning hopes and subsequent disappointment and chagrin are mentioned in a poem by Wu.[1] Wu himself had pleaded illness and declined the honour, of which he nevertheless remained proud all of his life.[2] In chapter 37 of the novel, Kuo, the paragon of filial piety, openly declared his admiration for 'the great man of Tienchang who would not answer the summons to the Emperor's court.'[3] As to the illness, it could have been feigned, and had caused some speculation in official circles.[4] Certainly in the novel Tu Shao-ch'ing had merely put on an act. When, in chapter 34, the Magistrate calls on Tu with the Provincial Governor's personal invitation to attend at the capital, Tu, who had a handkerchief tied round his head and wore his oldest clothes, totters out on the arms of two servants, grovels to the ground in salute and is unable to rise again, upon which the discomfited Magistrate agrees to accept his letter of withdrawal.[5] Of the two other candidates from Anhwei Province who had answered the summons along with Wu's cousin, one actually died in Peking after finishing the examination.[6] Thus the hardship and hazards of the journey (as described in Chuang Shao-kuang's eventful trip in chapters 34 and 35), reluctance to leave his home and new-found delights in Nanking, the uncertain issue of all examinations, and aversion to the business and pomp of office could have weighed equally with our author. From then on, Wu took no more

[1] Poem addressed to his cousin, in *Wen-mu shan-fang chi*, c. 3, p. 1[b].

[2] The title-page of a manuscript, dating from the last year or two of Wu's life (1753–4), of some poems about Nanking scenes by Wu proudly announces that he had been recommended for the Great Literary Scholarship Examination of 1736. The poems were transcribed by a friend, Fan Ming-cheng, in a variety of calligraphic styles, but the title-page, which bears Wu's seals, including one with the words 'Presentation Library', was possibly in Wu's own hand. See the photograph of the title-page printed with the poems, and Fan Ning, 'Concerning the Poems about Nanking scenes by Wu Ching-tzu', in *Wen-hsüeh yen-chiu chi-k'an*, vol. IV (1950), pp. 272–87; pp. 288–93.

[3] Chapter 37, p. 370.

[4] T'ang Shih-lin, who was Director of the Prefectural Academy at Nanking and who had recommended Wu in the first place, thought it necessary to explain, in his Preface to Wu's Collected Works, that the man had looked sickly two months after the event, and could not therefore have *feigned* his illness. See *Wen-mu shan-fang chi*, Prefatory Matter, p. 1[a]; Hu Shih, p. 333.

[5] Chapter 34, pp. 333–4.

[6] See Hu Shih, p. 336; and Wu's poem lamenting Licentiate Li in *Wen-mu shan-fang chi*, c. 3, p. 2[a].

examinations and turned his back on the only career open to him. His cousin, however, made further repeated attempts and attained his second degree (*chü-jen*) in 1741 at the age of forty-six. (In our story, Tu Shen-ch'ing boasts somewhat too soon about his impending success in the Provincial Examination to the actor Pao.) Eventually, in 1745, Wu Ch'ing attained his final degree (*chin-shih*), which earned him the position of Second Class Secretary (*chu-shih*) in the Board of Punishments, and this, too, is alluded to in the novel.[1]

The rest of our author's own story may easily be told. From the expensive Ch'in-huai quarter he moved to a less favoured part of the city, from which, on bitterly cold winter nights, being without fuel, he and his impecunious friends would set out by moonlight on long walks outside Nanking's city wall, leaving by the South Gate and re-entering at dawn by the West Gate, having chatted and joked and whistled and sung all night, which activity they termed 'warming cold feet'.[2] The writing of congratulatory poems and addresses and other such compositions on behalf of the busy and affluent brought in fees of varying amounts,[3] and now and then he parted with one of the prized volumes retained from his inherited library to procure rice for the family. His oldest son — Master Eldest in our story — Wu Lang, later a noted mathematician, was compelled to leave home at an early age to earn his living, perhaps, like old Lou, as a cashier and estate overseer.[4] Wu himself wandered

[1] In the conversation between Brigade General T'ang and Tu Shao-ch'ing in chapter 46, p.452. For Wu Ch'ing's examination successes, see Ho Tse-han, p.43.

[2] See Ch'eng Chin-fang's biography of Wu in Ho Tse-han, pp. 182–4.

[3] This may be inferred from Tu Shao-ch'ing's literary activities in the novel. In chapter 36, Professor Yü passes on a request for a eulogy of a militantly chaste woman in Prince Chung-shan's household, to be carved on a stone tablet; the fee offered was a hundred taels, of which Yü himself keeps twenty, giving Tu the rest (p.358). But in chapter 44, some years later, Tu is described as dependent for his livelihood entirely on hack writing (pp.435–6).

[4] See Wu's poem 'To My Son, Lang, on New Year's Eve as I languish in the Inn at Ning-kuo' (*Wen-mu shan-fang chi*, c. 3, p. 12ᵃ) and his own note: 'At a tender age, my son is already providing for himself; his employers are kind people ...'; also Hu Shih, p. 337. In Wu Lang's poem, 'Thoughts in a Village', the young man is seen as tired and hungry in a poor, deserted village away from home, lamenting his plight as well as the plight of the tenant farmers (in *Ch'un-hua hsiao-ts'ao*, p. 2ᵇ, which is included with *Wen-mu shan-fang chi*). Wu Lang returned to a scholar's career and obtained his *chin-shih* degree in 1754, the year of his father's death. Earlier, his appointment as a Clerk in the Grand Secretariat (*nei-ko chung-shu she-*

from place to place, staying for periods with friends north of the Yangtze, at Icheng and at Yangchow, where he died, aged fifty-four, a pauper.[1]

Early editions of *Ju-lin wai-shih* contain a curious Preface by a certain 'Old Man of Leisure',[2] who in a tone of authority pronounces it a better work than all previous novels, in particular the four up to then acknowledged as the greatest, *San-kuo yen-i* ('The Three Kingdoms'), *Hsi-yu-chi* ('The Quest of Tripitaka'), *Shui-hu-chuan* and *Chin P'in Mei*. For 'its title *Unofficial History* distinguishes it from history proper', a distinction not observed by the writer of the fictional 'Three Kingdoms'; and '*World of Learning* indicates its concern with the actual, as opposed to the world of fantasy', preoccupation with which constitutes the real objection to the Tripitaka narrative. Men's attitudes towards honours and rank are declared to be the framework of the book, which sets out to delineate such varied types as those who pursue these goods with servile and sedulous attention; and those who, being elevated to position and privilege, show themselves proud and overbearing to their sometime equals; and those whose overt lack of interest disguises deep-seated desires for gain and promotion; and finally those truly disinterested, who reject honours and rank without regrets. Thus the novel is recommended as a mirror to the reader, of whatever type he might consider himself. The Preface is dated the second month, 1736, and its mixture of effrontery and sense of achievement suggest the hand of a young man in a hurry: it would seem to be a statement of aims by the author himself, then aged thirty-six. For in March 1736 — the year of the Great Literary Scholarship examination — much of the 'history' had not yet been enacted, and the writing could not have proceeded beyond chapter 33.

The novel survives in two versions: a fifty-six chapter version dating from 1803, from which most later editions are derived; and a sixty chapter version dating from as late as

---

jen) had led to the same rank being conferred on his father in 1753, as emblazoned on the title-page of Wu's manuscript poems about Nanking. Wu Lang's Commentary on the ancient mathematical treatise *Chou-pi suan-ching* was printed in 1768. For the manuscript poems, see n.2, p. 339.

[1] For Wu's death, see Wang Yu-tseng's colophon to Wu's collected poems, in Ho Tse-han, pp. 186–7. Wang obtained his *chü-jen* degree in the same year as Wu Lang, 1751, on the occasion of the Emperor Ch'ienlung's visit to the south.

[2] The Preface is reprinted in the Ya-tung edition of 1922.

1888.[1] The latter has no authority and includes in its added
chapters a number of incidents of doubtful taste and relevance.[2]
The fifty-six chapter version is itself not beyond suspicion. The
1803 edition may not have been the first,[3] and the final chapter,
a canonization of all the characters in the story, sedulous and
disinterested alike, is a manifest forgery.[4] We are thus left
with fifty-five chapters of the work, as reprinted, for example,
in the Tso-chia ch'u-pan-she edition of 1954. Yet contemporary
references to *Ju-lin wai-shih* speak of only fifty chapters.[5]
Whether the novel consisted originally of fifty or fifty-five
chapters, it is to be presumed from the afore mentioned Preface
that a substantial portion of *Ju-lin wai-shih* — long and complete
enough to justify such a discourse — had already taken shape
by 1736. Wu must thus have begun writing his novel soon after
settling in Nanking, in the early 1730's, when he was already
a wit and, being still above want, could call his time his own.
He must also have continued from 1736 onwards — in spite of
increasing hardship after the great Sacrifice recorded in chapter
37 — to add to the completed portion. Indeed, as will presently
be shown, the novel as a whole could not have been finished
before 1748–9.

The first independent reference to *Ju-lin wai-shih* occurs in
a poem about our author by Ch'eng Chin-fang (1718–84), the
closest friend of Wu's later days, written about 1749:[6]

In his Unofficial History he chronicles the World of Learning:
    With what incisive lines are its figures engraved!
I grieve for this man of outstanding gifts,
    Who shall be known to posterity by a mere work of fiction.
Ch'eng further states in the biography of Wu he composed after

---

[1] See Sun K'ai-ti's *Catalogue*, pp. 198–200; and Editors' Note to the Tso-
chia ch'u-pan she edition of *Ju-lin wai-shih* (1954), pp. 1–4.
[2] The only edition of the sixty-chapter version available to me is that
published by Shih-hsüeh shu-tien, Hong Kong, in 1958; apart from the
added chapters, it is an abridgement of the fifty-six chapter version.
[3] No earlier edition has been found, but according to Chin Ho (1818–
1885), a descendant of the author's cousin Wu Ch'ing, the work was first
printed in Yangchow in the 1770s. See Chin Ho's colophon to one of the
editions of 1869, in Ho Tse-han, pp. 202–5; also Sun's *Catalogue*, p. 198;
and Hu Shih, pp. 351–2.
[4] Chapter 56 was first rejected by Chin Ho, who endorses the other fifty-
five chapters in his colophon of 1869.
[5] See discussion below.
[6] See Hu Shih, pp. 341–2. For the friendship between Wu and Ch'eng
Chin-fang, see Ho Tse-han, pp. 182–4, 188, 189–90, 191–2.

Wu's death: '... He also wrote a novel in the style of the T'ang writers, *An Unofficial History of the World of Learning* in fifty chapters, portraying to the full the manners and behaviour of men of letters, of which readers vied with one another in making copies.'[1] In the local history of Ch'üan-chiao, the number of chapters of *Ju-lin wai-shih* is also given as fifty.[2] Thus external evidence points to a work of fifty chapters completed about 1749. In the novel itself, allusions to events involving Wu's friends and relations continue until the years 1745–8. The cousin Wu Ch'ing's appointment to his Board Secretaryship, Second Class, which took place in 1745,[3] is duly noted in chapter 46 (p.452). Chin Chü, a relative as well as friend to Wu, was made Assistant Director of Studies at the Hsiu-ning County College in Hui-chou-fu in 1745,[4] and in chapter 48 (p.469) we find Yü Eldest, who is based on Chin, suddenly elevated to the position of Assistant Director of Studies in the Prefectural Academy of Hui-chou-fu. Chapter 48, in fact, contains the last dateable references to Wu's circle of friends in the book. In 1748, the much admired Wu P'ei-yüan, who had for some years been an Education Officer in Nanking, was appointed to a Magistracy in Chekiang Province,[5] and in the novel (chapters 48, p. 475) Professor Yü (i.e. Education Officer Wu) is mentioned as having taken up his post in Chekiang, where he is followed by Tu Shao-ch'ing.

When, therefore, towards the end of chapter 48, the old licentiate Wang of Hui-chou-fu, while mourning his daughter, sets off for Nanking armed with letters of introduction from Yü Eldest to Tu, Chuang Shao-kuang, and other notables, but finds them all gone, the 'history' seems rapidly drawing to a close. It is nevertheless drawn out for another seven chapters, the last of which (chapter 55) begins:

The story goes that in the twenty-third year of Wan-li,[6]

[1] Ho Tse-han, p.183.
[2] *Ch'üan-chiao hsien-chih*, c. 15, p. 5[b].
[3] See Ho Tse-han, pp.43–4; also above, p.340.
[4] See Ho Tse-han, p.110; and for Chin Chü generally, pp.102–14.
[5] See Ho Tse-han, p.60; and for Wu P'ei-yüan generally, pp. 51–61. His appointment as Education Officer in 1737 is represented in the novel as Professor Yü's assumption of office (chapter 36).
[6] The story is set in the Ming dynasty. Twenty-third year of the Wan-li reign is 1595. Earlier, in chapter 35, the year was mentioned as the thirty-fifth of the Chia-ching reign, i.e. 1556. For a discussion of the time sequence in *Ju-lin wai-shih*, see General Introduction.

there were no celebrities left in Nanking. Of Professor Yü's generation, some were too old, others had died. Literary men had departed for the provinces; and those who had remained had shut their doors upon the world . . .

After this preamble, we are introduced to four charming characters with a claim to honourable mention in a not quite official history of learning, the temperamental calligrapher, the chess-playing hawker, the prodigal artist and the musical tailor, with whom the novel ends. The six intervening chapters (49–54) with a whole succession of incidents seem disproportionately long. Chapter 49 follows chapter 48 neatly and its episode of the unmasking of the fraudulent Clerk of the Secretariat Wan is in the spirit of the book; but the redoubtable boxer Feng Fourth, who appears towards its end and whose tedious intervention in the Clerk's case—told in tiresome detail as, according to the story-tellers' tag, no story should be—leads to some further crude adventures in Hangchow, Kashing and elsewhere that fill chapters 50, 51 and 52, would seem an interpolation, added by a later hand. Thereafter chapters 53 and 54 take up the story again in Nanking and lead up to chapter 55. It would seem, therefore, that Wu's original work *was* only fifty chapters, that some of the final chapters in current fifty-five editions—in particular, chapters 50–52, which read like an offshoot of chapter 49, probably originally self-contained—are suspect, and that some at least of the earlier chapters (1–48) have been tampered with, and the chapter divisions redistributed.[1]

Thus the book draws freely upon events and persons known to the author and is deeply rooted in his own experience.[2] It asks the searching question: whether learning, so devoutly professed by all members of the scholar class, is to be pursued for its own sake or as the royal road to advancement—'honours and rank'. It exposes the hollowness and self-seeking of the

[1] My own re-allocation of the fifty-five chapters in current editions would be: chapters 1–48 in current editions formed the original chapters 1–46, chapters 49–52 formed chapter 47, and chapters 53–55 formed chapters 48–50. Doubts are expressed about parts of chapters 38, 39, 40 and 43 in Wu Tsu-hsiang, 'Ideology and Art in *Ju-lin wai-shih*', pp. 29–30, in *Ju-lin wai-shih yen-chiu lun-wen chi*, 1955, pp. 1–38.

[2] A key to the persons who figure in Wu's 'history' was first supplied by Chin Ho in his colophon of 1869. Most of the clues supplied by Chin Ho and others have been followed up by Ho Tse-han in his section I; see also section IV, p. 204.

pseudo-learned and ridicules the treadmill of their examination-orientated lives. It further vindicates, and in a few cases glorifies, those who, prizing leisure and peace of mind and friendship and conjugal affection above the manifold rewards of office, are content to remain obscure and often poor while they devote themselves—for love only—to books and scholarship with or without ultimate achievement. Clearly, then, the novel was also meant as Wu Ching-tzu's apology for his own life. He himself was author of a treatise on the Poetry Classic (*Shih ching*), to judge by the highlights featured in chapter 34 of *Ju-lin wai-shih* a work of considerable originality, which was never printed and is now lost;[1] but it was his mode of living with all its folly and recklessness that he sought to justify, and our extract 'Young Master Bountiful' may in that way be regarded as characteristic of the man and his book.

Wu's satire, which I have made the most of in the translation, is not at its best here; nor does the extract do justice to his ideal of the true scholar. These topics must, however, be left to some other occasion.[2] The setting of our story is the typical large town house of a prominent old family, with its secluded garden of peonies and cassia trees surrounded by pavilions used as libraries and guest rooms. The novel as a whole is notable for its pictures of houses and gardens. As examples may be cited the ornate Yangchow dwelling of the (newly) rich salt merchant Sung in chapter 40, with its succession of courtyards and galleries, curiously shaped gateways and gilt doors, and its elaborate rockery and balustraded fish pond (pp. 397–8); and the tiny hut of the happy-go-lucky Yang Chih-chung in chapter 11, its walls filled with poems and pictures, its papered window lit up like a painted screen with the shadows of plum blossoms under brilliant moonlight (p. 118). But the descriptions of outdoor scenes, especially river views, are equally delightful. They are scenes in colour or monochrome caught by the eye in passing and sketched in simple, spontaneous phrases without allusion or artifice, as, for example, the influential Lou brothers travelling incognito at night, their small boat picking its way under the dim wintry moon through the large rice boats crowding the river (chapter

[1] See Hu Shih, pp. 345–6; Ho Tse-han, pp. 174–6; *Ju-lin wai-shih*, chapter 34, pp. 337–8.
[2] See also General Introduction.

9, pp. 96–7); or the river seen in rain and mist, and a single sampan with a rush awning braving the downpour in its search for shelter (chapter 2, p. 19); or strong headwinds on the Yangtze (chapter 43, p. 422) and crossings, rough and smooth, from Nanking to Icheng and back (chapter 27, p. 272; chapter 35, p. 348; etc.).

It is on a stormy trip on the Yangtze that Tu Shao-ch'ing steps ashore at Wuhu in chapter 33 and comes across the Venerable Wei Fourth again. From Wei's upstair room in a Taoist temple, the wind having dropped, they together watch the sunset and the thousands of masts of anchored vessels against a flaming sky (pp. 330–1). The occasion is commemorated in a poem by Wu[1] which identifies the Venerable Wei Fourth as Chu Nai-wu, undoubtedly a gourmet but not otherwise of note. Of the other characters in our story, the actor Pao was the adopted son of Pao Wen-ch'ing, whose family had for generations led one of Nanking's leading theatrical companies. But Pao Senior having died, old Mrs Pao disinherits the adopted son, Pao T'ing-hsi, who is by now saddled with an epileptic scold for a wife and has to make his way in the world without any capital (chapters 25–27). Hence his search for a patron and his meeting at first with Tu Shen-ch'ing and finally with our Young Master Bountiful.

The translation of *Ju-lin wai-shih* by Gladys and Hsien-yi Yang entitled *The Scholars* (1957) is full and accurate, and generally reliable. It also contains a valuable Appendix about the examination system and the various official ranks. The present translation, undertaken independently, focuses attention on Tu Shao-ch'ing as a character sketch. Confined as it is to two chapters, it gives prominence to details in a way not perhaps feasible in a translation of the whole book. It seeks to reproduce something of the *tone* of the original, and a certain amount of interpretation—resulting sometimes in an intensification of effects—is superimposed on the translation. The Tso-chia ch'u-pan-she edition of *Ju-lin wai-shih* is used throughout, but its punctuation is not always followed.

[1] 'Mu-lan-hua' (abbreviated form), in *Wen-mu shan-fang chi*, c. 4, p. 9a.

Young Master Bountiful

The story goes that[1] when Tu Shen-ch'ing had held the drama-tic festival,[2] the actor Pao, who had managed the entire under-taking,[3] was startled as he secretly added up the amount of silver expended. Pao deliberated with himself: 'This is as open-handed a patron as I shall ever meet! I should seize my opportunity, borrow a few hundred taels of silver from him and set up as a company again.' Being thus determined, he came day after day to Master Tu's house on the bank of the Ch'in-huai river[4] and made himself useful in countless little ways so that Tu began to feel that he was under a real obliga-tion to the man. One day, they conversed until late at night; Tu noticed that the servants had retired and said: 'Pao, what do you do for a living? You ought to take up a trade and provide for your family.' Pao, according to his cue, fell on both knees before his chosen benefactor, who, however, jumped in surprise and, pulling him up by the arm, asked: 'What is the meaning of this?'

Pao then delivered a little speech: 'As I serve your Worship faithfully, I do declare that such a question from your worship is an instance of the highest favour. Wretched as I am, I began

---

[1] This is the beginning of chapter 31, which has the heading:
'Two chance acquaintances together call on the hero of Tienchang;
The august Presentation Library is the scene of a drinking bout.'
[2] The dramatic festival was held on Mo-ch'ou Lake (named after the courtesan Mo Ch'ou, 'Never grieve') in Nanking. The performers sang in an island pavilion approached by a causeway. From all over the city people gathered round the pavilion in hired fishing boats to listen to the music on the water. Nearly seventy singers took part, each being rewarded with half a tael as well as gifts; a gold cup was awarded to the best per-former. The performances began in the day and lasted all night, it being then early summer. See chapter 30.
[3] Pao T'ing-hsi suggested the locality, assembled the performers, and officiated during the performances. See chapter 30.
[4] The most favoured quarter in Nanking. The back doors of the houses opened on to the river.

by leading an acting troupe and was bred to no other trade. Since your Worship now deigns to be concerned for me, I can but entreat the favour of a loan of several hundred taels so that I might resume the theatrical profession—which kind favour I shall not fail to requite by re-imbursement the moment I come into money.' To which Tu Shen-ch'ing replied with studied composure: 'That is easy enough! But pray be seated, and let us discuss the matter. Several hundred taels would not suffice; to assemble a troupe complete with wardrobe you need at least a thousand. Since you are no stranger to my house, I shall not conceal the fact that I have several thousand taels laid by in ready silver. There are compelling reasons, however, for my not touching this money; for in the next year or two I expect to pass my higher degree examination,[1] and when I have passed that one, the call on these funds would be incessant.[2] As to your leading your own company, I will tell you about someone else who could further your plans, and it would be the same as my helping you personally. Only, you will remember not to mention that it was I who first thought of him.'

Upon this, Pao cried in dismay: 'Someone else! Who other than your Worship would befriend a poor actor?' Tu Shen-ch'ing, however, went on: 'Stay! Hear what I have to say. There are seven branches to our family.[3] My late great-grand-father, who was President of the Board of Rites, belonged to the fifth branch. My great-grand-uncle of the seventh branch was the top candidate in the Palace Examination of his year; one of his grandsons, whom I call 'uncle', was Prefect of Kan-chou in Kiangsi,[4] and the son of the Prefect is my twenty-fifth

---

[1] i.e. Provincial Examination leading to the *chü-jen* degree. The author's cousin, Wu Ch'ing, upon whom Tu Shen-ch'ing is based, actually passed his *chü-jen* examination at the age of forty-six (in 1741). See Introduction.

[2] The chief items of expenditure would be a journey to the capital and a sojourn of several months there while one took part in the *chin-shih* examination and waited for the outcome and, if successful, for an appointment to a post.

[3] The genealogy here is not in exact accordance with that of the Wu family, which had only five branches: the author's great-grandfather, Wu Kuo-tui, ranked fourth among his brothers, and was the third top candidate (*t'an-hua*) in the Palace Examination of 1658; Wu Ch'ing's great-grandfather, who was Wu Kuo's-tui twin brother and ranked fifth among the brothers, was a Supervisory Censor (*chi-shih-chung*) assigned to the Rites Section. See Hu Shih, pp. 321–2; Ho Tse-han, pp. 37–8; and Introduction.

[4] The author's father, Wu Lin-ch'i, was in fact only Education Officer of Kanyu County in Kiangsu Province. See Introduction.

cousin. His name is Yi, his style Shao-ch'ing; he is my junior by two years[1] and, like me, a mere licentiate. That uncle of mine was a scrupulously honest official so that all they had at home was the estate handed down by the ancestors, and when my uncle died, my cousin inherited something less than ten thousand taels. But like the fool he is, he has been behaving as if he was worth over a hundred thousand. To start with, he can't even tell sterling silver from the inferior sort. Besides he must always be the grand seigneur, the unfailing patron from whose inexhaustible silver chest anyone with a hard-up story may help himself to a handful. If you will remain with me for a little longer, when it is cool again at the beginning of autumn, I shall naturally provide your travelling expenses and you can then throw yourself upon his mercy. I warrant you—a thousand silver taels or so would be yours for the asking!'

Pao interposed: 'When the time comes, I do beg that your Worship would at least favour me with a letter of introduction.' Tu, however, protested: 'No, I don't come in at all, and such a letter must on no account be written! My cousin wants the stage to himself, and when he gives succour, it will be of his own accord, not at the prompting of others. If I wrote a letter for you, he would then say that you had already secured my assistance and, if only to spite me, would have nothing to do with you. But, of course, when you go, you will look up one other person first.' Pao said, thoroughly bewildered: 'Whom again?' Tu then resumed: 'In former days they had an old steward named Shao in the house, who was the husband of the wet-nurse. Did you ever know this person?' Pao recalled—'It was through him that in my father's time the family sent for our company to take part one year in the birthday celebrations of the old lady.[2] On that occasion I even met the late Prefect of Kan-chou.'

[1] Wu Ch'ing was five years older than the author; see Introduction. To have a difference of only two years between the cousins, Master Seventeenth and Master Twenty-fifth, makes their close companionship more convincing; at the same time it postulates, less convincingly, the birth of seven other male cousins bearing the surname Tu within that interval.

[2] In chapter 25, Shao went to Nanking and engaged the company of Pao's father, Pao Wen-ch'ing, for the seventieth birthday celebrations of the mother of the Prefect. The company brought along a repertory of twenty plays and performed for over forty days, for which they were paid well over a hundred taels. There were a dozen or more actors in the company beside Pao and his father; Pao was then seventeen (p. 252) or eighteen (p. 249). The grandmother's seventieth birthday celebrations would

Master Tu cried: 'Capital! Couldn't be better! Shao, the
husband of the wet-nurse, is now dead, and his place as steward
has been taken by a fellow with a shaggy beard, one Wang, a
scoundrel through and through, but my cousin *would* listen to
all he says. My cousin has a weakness. He holds in esteem who-
ever is said to have once known my uncle, his father, even if it be
only a dog. You will first call on that fellow Wang with the
beard when you get there. The rascal loves drinking; ply him
with wine and ask him to report to my cousin that you were a
favourite of the late master's—your pockets would then be
filled with spending money time and again. One more thing.
My cousin hates being addressed as 'the master' and you will
take care to call him only 'young master'.[1] He has a further
weakness. He positively detests any talk within his hearing
about other people making a success of their official career or
rolling in wealth. What you once told me about the Magistrate
Hsiang conferring benefits on your father and yourself,[2] for
instance, is certainly a topic to be avoided in conversation with
him. You must pretend that he is the sole benefactor in the
world, the only one who readily and willingly extends his
helping hand to the poor and struggling. It thus follows that
you should deny we ever met if he asked whether you knew me.'

Tu Shen-ch'ing's talk left Pao in a happy frame of mind, and
he hung about the house cheerfully for another two months.

precede Wu's father's Kanyu appointment: Wu Lin-ch'i was devoted to
his mother and would not accept office until after her death. See 'Moving
House', *Wen-mu shan-fang chi*, c. 1, pp. 7ᵃ–7ᵇ.
[1] In order to keep alive the memory of the old master.
[2] The friendship between the Magistrate Hsiang and Pao, Senior, is one of
the most affecting episodes in the whole of *Ju-lin wai-shih*. Hsiang had
enjoyed a considerable reputation as playwright and song-writer before
being belatedly appointed Magistrate of Antung, but the casual dismissal
of a case of mistaken identity had led to an order for his impeachment. Pao
Wen-ch'ing, an actor in the employ of Provincial Judge Ts'ui and an
admirer of Hsiang's, pleaded with the Judge, who thereupon revoked the
order but despatched Pao with a letter to Hsiang informing him of the
actor's secret intervention. In gratitude, Hsiang ever afterwards treated
the actor Pao as a personal friend, and when he himself rose to be Prefect
of Anking, had Pao and his son stay with him throughout his period of
office, eventually sending them home with a gift of 1000 taels. At Pao
Wen-ch'ing's funeral, Hsiang, who happened to be passing through Nanking on his way to a governor's post, tendered public tribute to his actor
friend in a short inscription on the flag to be borne in the procession
(chapters 24 and 25). A series of mishaps after his father's death reduced
young Pao to the state of a pauper (chapters 25, 26, 27 and 28). See also
Introduction.

When, towards the end of the seventh month, the weather
turned cool, Pao borrowed a few taels from Master Tu Seventeenth,[1] packed his clothes into a bundle, and set out for Tienchang[2] across the river. On the first day, he crossed the
Yangtze and stayed the night in Liuho.[3] Rising early the next
day, he covered a few dozen *li* on foot until he reached a little
place called Szu-hao-tun, where he went into the inn and sat
down on a chair. Before he could call for hot water to wash his
face, a sedan-chair was brought to the gate and a venerable-
looking personage set down. The new arrival was clad in a
graduate's square cap, a white silk clerical robe and crimson
silk shoes; and he had a drinker's jolly red nose and a large,
silvery beard. The gentleman now entering through the gate,
the innkeeper rushed forward to receive his luggage and greeted him aloud: 'Why, it's Old Master Wei Fourth![4] Step inside
and take a seat.'

The Venerable Wei Fourth proceeded to the parlour, where
Pao stood up to make his bow, which that worthy guest returned. Pao then made Wei take the seat of honour, himself
moving to a chair lower down, after which he accosted the distinguished old man: 'Your esteemed surname is Wei. Dare I
ask your illustrious home district?' The other replied: 'Wei is
my name; I come from the market town of Wuyi in Ch'u-
chou.[5] And you, Sir? I beg to inquire your honourable name and
place of origin, and your destination.' Pao declared: 'The name
is Pao; I am your Worship's humble servant. I belong to
Nanking, but am now travelling to Tienchang to visit young
master Tu of the top Palace graduate's house.' Wei said:
'Which one? Is it Shen-ch'ing or Shao-ch'ing?' Pao answered:
'It is Master Shao-ch'ing.' Old Master Wei Fourth then said:
'Though there are sixty or seventy of that generation in their
family, it is only those two who entertain visitors from all over

[1] See n. 1, p. 349.
[2] Tienchang (Pinghui) is forty miles or so north of Nanking, and is in
Anhwei Province. It is a transparent disguise for Ch'üan-chiao (Chuantsiao), the author's home town, which is also in Anhwei Province and about
thirty miles to the west of Nanking, but also north of the Yangtze.
[3] Liuho, about twenty miles from Nanking, is on the way to Tienchang.
[4] Wei Fourth seems to have been based on one of the author's father's
friends, Chu Nai-wu. See Introduction. He appears only in chapters 31–33.
[5] Wuyi (in Anhwei Province), the home of Wei Fourth, is only a dozen or
more miles from the author's home in Ch'üan-chiao, though over forty
miles from Tienchang.

the land. The rest are content to keep within their houses with the gates tightly shut, jealously guarding their estates and preparing themselves for the examinations. That was why I asked straight off whether it was one of those two. They are of course both widely known north and south of the Yangtze. Shen-ch'ing is a cultivated man, but too much of a cissy for my liking. Shao-ch'ing is the manly one. I am also calling on him, and we might travel together after our meal.' Pao then asked: 'Is your Worship related to the Tu family?' Wei said: 'The late Prefect of Kan-chou and I were at school together and looked upon each other as brothers.[1] We were the best of friends.' Pao made a note of this in his mind and became even more deferential in his manner.

Having eaten their midday meal in each other's company, the Venerable Wei Fourth mounted his sedan-chair, while Pao hired a donkey, which he then rode so as to keep up with his important new acquaintance. When they reached the gate of the county town of Tienchang, Wei stepped off his sedan and said, 'Mr Pao, we can walk to the house together.' Pao, however, excused himself, saying: 'Your Worship will please use the chair and go before. I have to call on his steward first, and will then attend on the young master.' Dismissing Pao with a brief 'As you please', Wei swept into the chair and was carried straight to the Tu residence. The porter having announced the visitor, Tu Shao-ch'ing[2] came hurriedly to the gate and invited his father's friend into the parlour, where they exchanged bows. Tu Shao-ch'ing began: 'Uncle, it's half a year since we last met, yet I've not had a chance of coming to Wuyi to pay my respects to yourself and my good aunt. I trust you have been well all this time.'

Wei replied: 'Tolerably well, and all the better because of your concern. It being autumn, with nothing to do at home, I remembered your garden, where the cassia trees would certainly be in bloom. And with that thought I found myself on my

[1] Entered voluntarily into a bond of brotherhood, as friends and fellow examination candidates frequently did. It is one custom not satirized in *Ju-lin wai-shih*, though ridiculed again and again in the much later *Erh-shih nien mu tu chih kuai hsien-chuang* (1907–9), by Wu Wo-yao, e.g. in the Shanghai Wen-hua ch'u-pan-she edition of 1957: chapter 8, p. 41; chapter 23, p. 132; chapter 24, pp. 135–6; etc.

[2] Tu Shao-ch'ing—intended as the author's self-portrait. See Introduction.

way here, my purpose being, first, to see how you are, my nephew, and, secondly, to crave a drink from your cellar.' Tu Shao-ch'ing thereupon said: 'When tea has been served, my uncle will please go to the library, where we can sit at greater ease.' The page-boys now brought the tea, and Tu commanded them: 'Fetch Old Master Wei's luggage from the gate and take it into the library. Pay the chair-bearers and send them away.' He himself then conducted Wei from the back of the parlour into a passage which led, after a number of turnings and twistings, into a garden.

On one side of the garden was a light structure consisting of three rooms facing the east. At the far end of this, rose a two-storied building, in which the collection of books presented by the Emperor[1] was kept; this Presentation Library had a fore-court flanked by two raised beds of peonies, one of *moutan* tree peonies, the other of the herbal *shao-yao*, and two enormous cassia trees in full bloom. On the opposite side, facing these buildings, was a summer-house partitioned into three rooms. And on the far side of the garden, there was another structure consisting of three rooms facing the south, which actually served as the library. Behind these rooms was a large lotus pond, spanned by a foot-bridge, which led to a house screened by some trees and containing a suite of three rooms used by Tu Shao-ch'ing as his study.

The Venerable Wei Fourth was invited to sit in the library with the southern aspect, near the window and in full view of the cassia trees. When he had sat down, he asked casually: 'Is old Mr Lou[2] still with the family?' Tu Shao-ch'ing replied: 'Uncle Lou has been ill lately and I have invited him to stay in my study at the back.' Wei then said: 'If the old man is in a bad way, why don't you send him home?' Tu explained: 'I had his son and grandson fetched, and they are both here to attend to his medicine. It is some consolation to me to be able to ask after his health every morning and evening.' Old Master Wei then remarked: 'After keeping the family's purse for over thirty years, the cashier himself ought at least to have some savings. Has he bought some property at home?'

Tu rejoined: 'It is true that when my late father left for

[1] The books were presented to the author's great-grandfather, Wu Kuo-tui.
[2] Regarding the identity of old Mr Lou, see Introduction.

Kan-chou to take up his office,[1] he entrusted the whole of our estate accounts to Uncle Lou, who from then on had complete control over receipts and payments without my father ever raising the slightest query; but Uncle Lou never took a copper for himself beyond his annual salary of forty taels. At harvest time, he would call at the houses of the tenant farmers himself to collect the rent, and if the tenants laid two dishes of food before him, he would eat only one dish, insisting that the other be kept for themselves.[2] And when his own sons and grandsons came to visit him here, Uncle Lou allowed them a stay of only two days, after which he packed them home, giving them their fare but not a single cash more. He would even search them before their departure lest the stewards offered them any bribes. But with the rent and interest collected at harvest, he would help our poorer friends and relatives unstintingly, and that, too, was something which, though my father would have known about it, he certainly never looked into. For whenever it became clear to Uncle Lou that some debtors were really in no position to repay us, without more ado he burnt the bond there and then, and cancelled the debt.[3] Yet such has been his own scrupulosity that even in his old age, with a family of two sons and four grandsons, he is still as poor as when he first came to us, and indeed I feel extremely uneasy about it all.'

The Venerable Wei Fourth heaved a sigh in tribute and murmured: 'Truly a living example of the uncorrupt probity of the ancients!' Then, changing the subject, he asked: 'How is Shen-ch'ing?' Is he well at home?' His host replied: 'Since your last visit, my cousin has gone to Nanking.' While they were thus talking, Wang, the steward with the shaggy beard, appeared noiselessly outside the window with a red visiting

[1] In our story, the Prefect's departure for Kan-chou took place just under ten years ago. For Wu's father's term of office, see Introduction.
[2] The object of Lou's rigorous rules was to minimize expenses for all concerned and to prevent any abuses. His severe economy made possible his acts of generosity on behalf of the family.
[3] Thus relieving the debtors and creating goodwill towards the family. This somewhat high-handed practice has its precedent in the exploits of Feng Huan, a retainer of Meng-ch'ang-chün (T'ien Wen), a nobleman of the State of Ch'i. When despatched to Hsüeh to collect his master's debts, Feng Huan gave a feast to all the debtors, whom he divided into two groups: those ready to pay their interest and willing to re-pay their loans by a mutually agreed date; and those unable to pay even the interest. The bonds of the latter group he consigned to the flames. See *Shih chi*, 75, 'Life of Meng-ch'ang-chün' (pp. 2359–61).

card[1] held up in his hand, waiting to enter. Tu Shao-ch'ing caught sight of him and called out—'Wang, have you something to tell me? What's that in your hand?' The bearded steward sidled into the library and, handing up the card, reported: 'It is a man named Pao from Nanking, who started off by leading an acting troupe but spent the last few years in business in outer parts. Being newly returned there, he has journeyed across to pay his respects to the young master.' Tu Shao-ch'ing said with some impatience: 'If he is an actor, tell him that I have a visitor and cannot see him. You will keep the visiting card[1] and ask him to leave.' Wang, however, went on: 'But the man insists on thanking the young master for numerous favours which the late master had bestowed on him.' Tu asked: 'Did this man enjoy the patronage of my father?' The steward then said: 'In former days, old Shao summoned his company from across the Yangtze, and the late master expressed a real liking for this fellow Pao and promised to look after him.' Visibly touched, Tu Shao-ch'ing cried: 'I was not aware of this. Bring him in.' And Wei added: 'It's the Mr Pao from Nanking whom I met just then on the way.'

Shaggy-beard Wang made his retreat and before long was leading the actor in from the gate, moving with his silent, furtive tread. Pao's eyes wandered over the spacious garden with its unobstructed view until the steward paused outside the library door. When Pao looked within, he saw, seated with the distinguished guest of his acquaintance, Master Tu Twenty-fifth in a graduate's square cap, a turquoise silk clerical robe lined also with silk, and shoes adorned with pearls. He had a sallow complexion and bushy eyebrows that shot up like two hanging swords, as the eyebrows of Kuan-kung, God of War, on pictures.[2] Wang entered and beckoned to Pao—'Come this way and greet our young master.' Pao crossed the threshold and knelt down to perform the kowtow, but Tu Shao-ch'ing

---

[1] For visiting cards, see p.363, n.1. To keep the card would mean: the visit has been noted. Unlike the author, Tu Shao-ch'ing takes little interest in the theatre; this is also in contrast to his cousin Shen-ch'ing.
[2] This would seem to be the only actual description of the author, Wu Ching-tzu, we possess. The near vertical eyebrows are corroborated by a poem written by his cousin Wu Ch'ing (the original of Tu Shen-ch'ing), which speaks of the author's 'upstanding eyebrows like lances, your voice a roaring tiger's,' when under provocation. For the most part, however, contemporary notices are confined to the author's wit and learning, and his unconventional ways. See Introduction.

held him by the arm and said, 'Between old friends, this ceremony is uncalled for.' Thereupon Pao rose and made his bow
instead, and when this was over, and he had also bowed to Old
Master Wei, Tu Shao-ch'ing motioned him to take a seat
lower down.

Pao began: 'At the hands of the late master I received such
condescending favours that, were I to risk a thousand deaths in
service of the family, I could not hope to repay the kindness.
In the last few years, however, my livelihood took me to outlying places, where, being continually in want, I was wretchedly busy and could not call to pay my respects to the young
master. While I now rejoice to be in the young master's
presence, I must also crave the young master's indulgence for
my past remissness.'[1] Tu said: 'Our steward Wang informs
us that the late master had a good opinion of you and intended
your advancement. Since you are here, you may remain with
us for the present. As to the future, we shall so devise matters
as to satisfy you.' The steward Wang, who had earlier with-
drawn, now reappeared to announce that dinner was ready and
to ask the young master where it was to be served. Wei Fourth
cried with undisguised eagerness: 'This is as good a place as
any!' Tu Shao-ch'ing hesitated for a moment and then remarked, 'There is room for one more at table.' And he ordered
the library page, Rank Plus,[2] to go through the back gate and
invite Master Chang to dinner.

Rank Plus hurried off and soon returned with the guest, a
big, burly fellow[3] with large, round eyes and a thin, yellowish
beard, in a tile-shaped cap[4] and loose-fitting cotton garments,

[1] Pao uses 'young master' three times at the end of his speech in the
original: the same number is retained in the translation.

[2] Chia-chüeh (Nobility increases), a common name among servants.

[3] Physician Chang turns out to be a real charlatan. Posing under the name
of Iron-armed Chang as a warrior and redresser of wrongs, he cheated the
hospitable Lou family of five hundred taels in chapter 12: he claimed to
have the head of his mortal enemy in a leather bag which he deposited with
them, but it was a pig's head that they later found in it. The story is taken
from 'The Counterfeit Knights Errant' in Feng I's *Kuei-yüan ts'ung-t'an*
(Ts'ung-shu chi-ch'eng ed., pp. 2–3), itself a parody of the bona-fide
warrior in Tu Kuang-t'ing's *ch'uan-ch'i* tale, *The Curly Bearded Stranger*
(in Wang P'i-chiang, ed., *T'ang jen hsiao-shuo*, pp. 178–81). The author
connives at Chang's present disguise by not alluding to his stature, so that
the description 'big, burly fellow' has had to be supplied here, but the
large eyes and yellowish beard, suggesting foreign blood, identify him as
the imposter of chapter 12.

[4] A close-fitting cap worn by artisans and others, the Chinese tile being

fidgeting and swaying, clumsily aping the manners of the learned. The man having entered and made his bow, sat down and inquired his name of Old Master Wei, who introduced himself and asked in turn: 'Your honourable name, my dear Sir?' The man replied: 'My surname is Chang, my name Chün-min; I have been a follower of Young Master Tu for some time. Being acquainted in some slight measure with physic, I have, at the young master's command, been attending old Mr Lou, for the past few days.' Then, addressing himself to the young master, he asked: 'How is old Mr Lou today? Has he taken his medicine?' Tu Shao-ch'ing sent Rank Plus to find out, who presently returned to report: 'Old Mr Lou took his medicine and slept for some time, but is now awake again and feeling clearer in the head.' Chang then turned to the actor and asked: 'Your esteemed name, Sir?' Tu Shao-ch'ing replied on his visitor's behalf: 'It is Mr Pao, a friend from Nanking.'

The dinner being then laid out, they sat down after some further bowing, the Venerable Wei Fourth taking the seat of honour, the physician the place opposite, Tu the host's customary place, and Pao the lowest seat. Wine was poured out, and the meal began. The viands were choice, having all been prepared in the house:[1] among the delicacies was ham that had been seasoned for over three years, and crabs half a catty each in weight which had been shelled to make broth. While the others ate and drank, Wei Fourth paused momentarily to speak to Chang—'I presume, Sir, that you are indeed accomplished in the art of healing.' Chang said, still fidgeting in his chair, 'It is as the saying goes:

"The Treatise of the Pulse[2] well conned is only theoretical;

Administering drugs to many patients is better being practical."

To be quite open with your erudite Worship, I misspent my youth in drifting from place to place and hardly ever read a medical book, *but* the number of cases I have attended is by no manner of means small or insignificant. Lately, however, under

shaped like a shell. In chapter 27 of *Ju-lin wai-shih*, Pao T'ing-hsi's bride, the former Widow Wang, finds him wearing a tile-shaped cap day after day and concludes that her new husband was no graduate, as had been claimed by the go-between, but only a commoner. When, however, he then proceeds to tell her he is only an actor, she throws a fit, remaining an invalid for two years (pp. 267–8).

[1] Not purchased ready cooked from a market stall or food shop.

[2] By Wang Hsi of Tsin dynasty, better known as Wang Shu-ho, author of several works on the pulse.

the young master's guidance, I came to realize the importance of studying. I have a son, and instead of putting him straight on to medicine, I have sent him to study the classics with a tutor, and when the boy has penned an essay, I bring it to show the young master, who would favour it with a few written comments, which I myself then learn by heart as a guide to the rules of composition. It is my plan of course to enter the boy for the local examinations in the next year or two: in that way he would get his share of rice dumplings for candidates,[1] and when later he hangs up his plate, no one could dispute it if he called himself a "learned physician".' Wei Fourth heard the practical healer to the end and burst into hilarious laughter.

The steward Wang now re-entered with a card and reported: 'Tomorrow Wang the salt merchants of the North Gate are holding a birthday celebration in their house and are inviting his Worship the County Magistrate. This invitation is for the young master, whom the Wang family are counting on as a guest to keep his Worship the Magistrate company.' Tu Shao-ch'ing answered aloud: 'Tell their messenger that we are occupied at home with our own visitor and are unable to attend.' He then continued with a sneer—'Is not the man ridiculous? If you must do the honours of the house to your betters, there are plenty of newly rich higher graduates and doctors in the county to keep the Magistrate company. Have I got time to entertain a bigwig on behalf of a salt merchant[2] not even known to me?' Wang waited for his master to stop; he then shouted his assent and made his silent departure.

Tu Shao-ch'ing then turned to Wei Fourth and said: 'Uncle, it is no secret that you can outdrink anyone in this neighbourhood. In former days, you and my father had bouts that lasted half the night. For my sake, therefore, you must drink your fill this evening.' Wei replied: 'As to that, I am never one for false modesty. But, my boy, I do regard it as my duty to tell you that, though your dishes are indeed select, the wine was

[1] Rice dumplings were distributed to candidates in the examination hall and became associated in the popular mind with examinations. See, e.g., the scene of an examination in progress in chapter 26 of *Ju-lin wai-shih* (p. 256).
[2] Though the salt merchant was among the richest in the land, he was often also among the most despised. For descriptions of the homes of rich salt merchants, see *Ju-lin wai-shih*, chapter 22 (pp. 223–5); chapter 40 (pp. 397–8). For the social status of merchants, see P. T. Ho, *The Ladder of Success in Imperial China*, pp. 41–52 and *passim*.

bought at the market and is, to say the least, somewhat commonplace. There was a jar in your cellar about eight or nine years ago; I dare say it is still intact.' Tu Shao-ch'ing looked dumb and finally confessed: 'I know of no jar nor cellar, Uncle.' Undaunted, Wei continued: 'Of course you would not know. It was the year in which your father assumed his office in Kiangsi, taking you with him.[1] I accompanied him to the boat and he said to me, "I have a jar of wine buried in my cellar. When I return from my post, we shall open it and drink to our hearts' content!" That's how I remembered. You might ask your folk inside.' The physician laughed, saying, 'The young master really could not be expected to know about it, then.'

Thereupon Tu Shao-ch'ing left the table to hunt for the missing jar. Wei Fourth declared in his host's absence—'The present Master Tu may be young in years, but he is undoubtedly already the leading figure in our several counties.' Chang, too, said: 'An exceedingly kind gentleman, though much too open-handed! No matter who came to him for help, he would hold out silver by the handful!' Pao then added: 'I have certainly not come across anyone who bears himself with such easy dignity as Young Master Tu.'

In the inner courtyard, Tu Shao-ch'ing asked his wife about the jar of wine, but she could tell him nothing; he then questioned the older servants, men and women, who all denied knowledge of it. Finally he sought out old Shao, his own wet-nurse, who recalled—'There was such a thing. It was in the year the master left for his post that he had a jar of wine buried in the tiny room way behind in the seventh court, saying it was to be kept until he could drink it with Master Wei Fourth. The wine was brewed from two pecks of glutinous rice and twenty catties of yeast mixed with twenty catties of spirit, with not a drop of water added, and the jar has been underground these nine years and seven months. Talk of potency! That wine had the power to kill. If you dig it out, don't you drink it, my young master!'

Young Master Tu nodded and said, 'I know, nurse; I know.' He then asked the beldam to fetch the key and, the cellar door being opened, he entered with two serving lads, who located the spot, unearthed the jar and carried it bodily into the library. Tu Shao-ch'ing himself preceding them, announced in

[1] 'Taking you with him' is the translator's insertion. See Introduction.

triumph: 'The wine has been found, Uncle!' Wei rose from the table with the two other guests, took one look at the jar, and cried: 'The very thing!' The lid was now removed and some of the wine scooped up with a cup, but the drink was thick as paste and stood in a heap in the wine-cup, only an unusually pungent fragrance betraying its hidden strength. The Venerable Wei Fourth took measured sniffs and declared: 'This is very interesting! Now there's only one way of drinking the stuff. My dear nephew, get some more wine from the shops — ten catties, to be exact — and mix it with this one, after which it will be fit for drinking. It is late tonight, and the jar can remain where it is: we have all day tomorrow to enjoy it. The two gentlemen will of course join us here.' Chang responded — 'I am always ready to keep the young master and his learned guest company.' Pao said in a pious tone of voice: 'I thank my stars that one of such lowly condition as I should partake of the excellent wine handed down by the late master!' The meal being at an end, Rank Plus was ordered to take a lantern and send Master Chang home. Since Wei Fourth was staying in the library, Pao was asked to sleep there also, so as to keep Old Master Wei company; and Tu Shao-ch'ing waited until his father's friend had been tucked up in bed before returning to his own apartments.

The next morning, Pao rose early and found his way to the Steward Wang's room, where Rank Plus and another page-boy were seated together. Wang presently asked Rank Plus: 'Is Old Master Wei out of bed?' Rank Plus answered: 'He is up and washing his face.' Wang then asked the other page-boy: 'Has the young master got up yet?' The page-boy said, 'Young master's been up a long time and is now in old Mr Lou's sick-chamber, watching the preparation of the medicine.' Wang snarled, his beard bristling: 'An example of singular benevolence — *that's* our young master! Who, after all, is Old Grandfather Lou? One of the late master's retainers! Why, the man is now an invalid, waiting only to be dismissed and sent home with a few taels of silver! But our young master must keep him in the house, make obeisance to him like an ancestor, and attend at his sick-bed every morning and every evening!' The page-boy exclaimed: 'What are you saying, Uncle Wang? You know very well how every day the vegetables and rice porridge we prepare for Mr Lou have first to be inspected by his son and grandson and then by the young master himself before they are served to the sick old gentleman; and how in administering the ginseng, the stew-pot for which is kept in the young mistress's own room—and I need hardly tell you the young mistress prepares it all herself, ginseng, medicine and what not—it is the young master himself who twice daily, morning and night, brings it to Mr Lou, or else has the young mistress bring it on his behalf. If the young master had heard you, you would be in for a scolding . . .' A porter from the gate came abruptly in and said, 'Uncle Wang, will you announce Master Tsang Third? He is in the parlour waiting to see the young master.' Shaggy-beard Wang now rounded upon the page-boy: 'Why aren't you on your feet? Get back to the sick-room and ask the young master to come out and welcome his guest.—Don't expect me to go there to inquire after some people's health.' Pao, however, concluded: 'Such kind actions, though, do show up Young Master Tu's good nature and generosity.'

The page-boy hurried across to the secluded building behind the lotus pond and announced the caller, and Tu Shao-ch'ing soon emerged and met Tsang Third[1] in the reception hall. After they had exchanged bows and sat down, Tu said, 'I have hardly seen you lately. Have you been busy with the activities of your essay club?' Tsang began uncertainly, fishing for news: 'Yes, quite—but, er, I hear that you have a visitor from afar— your gate-keeper told me—oh, and how is Shen-ch'ing? Enjoying himself as usual in Nanking with no intention of returning to us?' Tu Shao-ch'ing came straight to the point: 'The visitor is Uncle Wei from Wuyi, for whom I've laid on a dinner party, very special. Look, old chap, join us, will you? Let's go to the library now.' Tsang protested—'No, remain seated. I want to talk to you. Er, his Worship the County Magistrate Wang, whom in his capacity of head of the local College I call "Master", has spoken to me several times about his admiration for your great talents. Supposing you and I called on him at some future date,—what do you say to that?'

Tu said bitingly: 'Really, my dear fellow! That kind of thing I must leave to you, kowtowing to the Magistrate and acknow-ledging yourself as his disciple. My great-grandfather's and

---

[1] For the identity of Tsang Third, see Introduction.

my grandfather's time I, of course, never knew,[1] but even in my father's day how many such Magistrates came to pay homage! He admires me, does he? Why, then, does he not call on me first but instead must have me dance attendance on him? As a mere licentiate, too, worse luck!, I am at the mercy of every local Magistrate, who could always claim to be my "Master". As for your learned Doctor Wang, who for all I know sprouted from some refuse heap, though he should offer himself as *my* disciple, I wouldn't have him. Why indeed should I meet the man? By the way, the salt merchant Wang of the North Gate sent an invitation for today "requesting the presence of Master Tu to keep His Worship the County Magistrate company", which I had much pleasure in declining.'

Tsang broke in: 'That's just what I was coming to! Now the mercantile Wang family had expressly stated that you would be present as second principal guest, and it was on that understanding that the Master accepted the invitation at all, in order to meet you. The Master would be severely disappointed if you failed to turn up! Besides, since your visitor is staying with you, you could easily spend tomorrow with him and feel free to go today; or I could remain here and look after him while you attended Wang's birthday celebrations.' Tu cried: 'Enough, my friend! No more of that nonsense! I will not be convinced that your honourable and worshipful Master really takes an interest in talent or worth; more likely his interest is kept alive by a shower of presents, presents obligatory to new disciples. Me, his disciple? Ask him to wake up! Anyhow, it's no ordinary fare we're having today: there's a seven-catty duck on the simmer, and wine matured for nine and a half years, newly discovered and unearthed. The Wang family couldn't possibly offer you anything like it. You are staying?—I won't take "No" for an answer. We'll now go to the library.' And he dragged his visitor after him. Tsang stopped short and said: 'Stay! Why the rush? Never having met this old Mr Wei, I shall need to write a card first.' Tu agreed—'Oh, *that* I would allow'; and he ordered the page-boy to bring brush, inkslab and a folded sheet of red paper. Tsang took the sheet and wrote on it:

---

[1] The author's grandfather, Wu Tan, had died at an early age. See Introduction.

'Compliments of Tsang T'u, who is your junior in years yet presumes to call himself a fellow student, being kinsman to one who passed his higher degree examination in the same year as yourself.'[1]

He then asked the page-boy to hand the card up to Old Master Wei in the library, he himself following with Tu Shao-ch'ing.

The Venerable Wei Fourth was at the library door to welcome Tsang, with whom he exchanged bows. They sat down, Tu motioning to the two others, who had stood aside at their entry, to join them. Old Master Wei said to Tsang: 'I beg to know your illustrious style.'[2] Tu replied for his friend: 'My schoolfellow is known as Liao-chai; he is quite the star of our College,[3] and a friend and colleague of Shen-ch'ing's in the essay club.' Wei mumbled: 'Much honoured!' Tsang said effusively: 'I have long heard about you, Sir. Most delighted to make your acquaintance!' Tsang, who knew the physician, now turned to Pao—'Your esteemed name, Sir?' The actor replied: 'Your humble servant Pao, newly returned from Nanking.'[4] Tsang asked: 'Come from Nanking? Perhaps you would know Master Shen-ch'ing, the young master's cousin?' With but a moment's delay, Pao answered: 'I have indeed met the seventeenth master.'

Breakfast, which was but a simple affair, having been despatched, the Venerable Wei Fourth took over for the day by giving orders that the jar of spirit paste be brought forward; ten catties of new wine were next poured into the jar; finally, red-hot charcoal fetched from the kitchen was heaped up on the ground beside one of the cassia trees, with the wine jar positioned vertically on top. It was some considerable time before the jar and its contents were thoroughly warmed. Chang the physician had meanwhile joined the company from the sick-chamber, and he bustled about directing the servants in re-

[1] The wording, a masterpiece of pseudo-etiquette, was in fact one of the set forms in such greetings. The visiting card was a folded sheet of red paper on which one wrote one's name and the relationship in which one stood to the person being called on.

[2] Style, i.e. *tzu*, by which one is addressed in polite conversation, in correspondence, etc.; the 'style' did not appear on the visiting cards of our author's day.

[3] 'Star of our College': coming from Tu Shao-ch'ing, the compliment is double-edged.

[4] After a night's stay, Pao regards himself now as an inmate of the house; he has therefore 'returned from Nanking'.

moving all the six window frames that overlooked the garden
and in shifting the table to the side thus opened, under the very
eaves. They sat down at the table, on which a banquet of dishes
in season was spread. Tu, as befitted the occasion, ordered a
page-boy to bring a gold goblet and four jade drinking cups.
The warm drink was ladled from the jar on the charcoal into the
wine-pot before it was poured out: the Venerable Wei Fourth
holding the gold goblet in both hands, emptied it, at intervals
interjecting — 'A great wine!'

They had feasted in this manner a long time, when the
steward Wang tiptoed in, followed by four page-boys carrying
a chest. Tu Shao-ch'ing turned to ask what the matter was.
Wang with the shaggy beard reported: 'The chest contains
new clothes for the autumn made on the young master's orders
for the mistress and Master Eldest,[1] just completed and await-
ing inspection. The tailor's wages have been paid.' Young
Master Tu then dismissed Wang and the others, saying,
'Leave the chest on one side. I shall examine the clothes after
dinner.' No sooner was the chest laid down, however, than the
tailor himself was seen coming towards the library, so that the
steward Wang stepped forward once more to announce:
'Tailor Yang himself is coming to report to the young master.'
Tu asked with mounting irritation: 'What more has he got to
say?' And he left the table to attend to the sartorial business.
But when the tailor saw Young Master Tu coming towards
him, he knelt down on both knees in the courtyard, performed
the kowtow, and burst out weeping and wailing. Much surprised, Tu called out: 'What's wrong, Yang?'

The tailor said between gasps: 'I am but a poor tailor who
has been working these many days in the young master's house.
This morning I collected my wages and went home, but, alas,
I had been home only a short while when my mother had a fit
and suddenly died. Not being prepared for such a misfortune,
I had already paid the firewood and rice shops with my wages
on the way home, and now my mother's coffin and funeral
clothes have still to be provided for. And I am a poor man
with no other means but my own hands, so that I had to come
back and beg the young master for the loan of a few taels,
which I shall repay through deduction of my future wages.' Tu

[1] Master Eldest, i.e. Tu Shao-ch'ing's own son.

asked with concern: 'How much silver will you need?' The
tailor answered: ' A humble family like us have no pretensions
to ceremony. If the young master be willing, six taels at the
most—but I should be satisfied with four. It is in terms of my
wages that I must fix the amount; more I cannot hope to repay.'

Tu Shao-ch'ing was deeply affected and said, 'How could we
demand repayment from you? You may only be a tradesman,
but the rites of filial devotion are common to all and must not
be neglected, lest present remissness become a cause of reproach the rest of your life. A few taels would get you nowhere.
You will need sixteen taels for a coffin, and the clothes and
other items add up to twenty. But now we ourselves have run
short of cash. — Well, my chest of clothes over there would
fetch over twenty taels at the pawn-broker's. — Wang, take it
away to be pawned and give the proceeds to our friend here.'
And turning again to the tailor, he went on: 'Yang, the money
is but a trifle, not worth remembering about, and we would ask
you now to forget the matter. It wasn't as if you went about
gambling with our money and having a good time. Since you
have to perform the last rites for your mother—and who that
is born of woman has no mother?—it is clearly our duty to
help you.' Wang and the tailor now carried the chest between
them and, as they retreated, the tailor began again to weep and
sob.

Tu then returning to his guests, Wei Fourth burst into
applause—'A good deed that, my dear nephew! quite excep-
tional!' Pao stuck his tongue out in silent wonder and then
chanted: 'Amitabha! Mine eyes have this day beheld a truly
generous giver!' They continued to imbibe the wine for the
rest of that day. By the afternoon, Tsang, who never could
hold his drink, was sick and tottered away, leaning on the arms
of a servant. The Venerable Wei Fourth and the others, however, lingered at the table until almost midnight, when, having
finished every drop of the priceless wine in the jar, they at last
dispersed for the night.[1]

[1] This is the end of chapter 31, which has the formal conclusion:
'Thus was it brought about that,
    Prizing friends more than his patrimony,
    All over the district he helped the poor and needy;
    At banquets and gatherings throughout the land,
    Men sang the praises of a magnanimous man.
As to what happened next, it shall be resolved in our next chapter.'

The story goes[1] that following the banquet the Venerable
Wei Fourth slept until late in the morning and when finally he
rose, he went to take his leave of Tu Shao-ch'ing, declaring:
'I had at first intended to do a round of visits to your uncles
and cousins, but after yesterday's glorious feast, I am filled to
my heart's content. What the others have to offer would at
best be a dilution of that quintessential drink, for which reason
I shall now depart. By the by, there was your friend Tsang,
whose visit I shall not be able to return. You will remember
to give him my regards, nephew.' His host, however, prevailed
upon him to remain for one more day. On the third morning,
Tu ordered a sedan-chair to be hired and, taking out a jade
drinking cup and two of the late Prefect's resplendent robes,
he brought these himself to Wei's room in the library, saying,
'Of my late father's bosom friends,[2] you alone remain, uncle.
I beg that from now on you will visit me regularly; I, too, shall
come more often to Wuyi to ask after your health. Pray accept
this cup, which my father drank out of, and use it yourself for
drinking, and these two robes of his also, that when wearing
them, you might be reminded of him.' And Wei accepted the
gifts with unfeigned delight. A jug of wine was now brought,
the actor Pao proving useful once more as a drinking companion. An early dinner followed. Old Master Wei then setting out
for his home, Tu Shao-ch'ing accompanied the sedan on foot—
with Pao following at the young master's insistence—beyond
the city gate, where the hosts made their final bows to the guest
in his sedan-chair. Thus the Venerable Wei Fourth made his
exit.[3]

Tu Shao-ch'ing returned to the house with Pao, and went
across to the study to inquire after old Mr Lou, who, sitting up
on his bed, declared that he was feeling better and required
only the assistance of his son, so that his grandson could be sent
home. To this Tu gave his assent. As he left old Lou's bedside,

[1] The beginning of chapter 32, which has for its title:
    'Tu Shao-ch'ing in his home carries out acts of reckless generosity:
    The old cashier Lou on his sick-bed tenders his parting advice.'
[2] Those with whom he had entered a fraternal bond.
[3] A formula peculiar to *Ju-lin wai-shih*, in which most characters appear in
only a few chapters and then play no further part in the story. Apart from
being a convenient narrative device, the phrase suggests succinctly the
transience of human existence and the utter insignificance of any individual,
good, bad or indifferent. In fact, however, Wei Fourth appears again
briefly in chapter 33; see Introduction.

however, he realized that there was no money in the house for any extra outlay, and he summoned the steward Wang for counsel. Young Master Tu began: 'It's about that rice-field enclosed by the dike—I am now ready to part with it. Will you arrange for its sale to the fellow who was interested?' Shaggy-beard Wang recalled with a wry face—'That villager, he wanted it cheap. It was a thousand five hundred the young master asked for, but the yokel offered only thirteen hundred. It was at that point that I broke off, fearing to exceed my authority.' Tu nodded: 'I shall accept thirteen hundred, then.' Wang said, clinching the deal in his head: 'You will, young master? For I cannot go without making the position absolutely clear. If I got what might appear a poor bargain, I should only earn a scolding.' Tu shouted with vexation: 'A scolding? Who's scolding you? Go and sell it now. I need some money immediately.'

Wang, however, persisted: 'There is another matter which I might as well bring up too. When the rice-field is converted to silver, the young master ought really to attend to one or two proper tasks. A pity to part with any piece of land if all that happens is, hundreds of taels are given without good cause to other people.' Tu exclaimed: 'Without good cause! Who the deuce did you see me give money to without cause? It's more likely a bit of squeeze you're after yourself—Confound your insolence! I order you to leave at once for the country.' Wang with the shaggy beard then repeated: 'So long as I have made the position quite clear to the young master!' But when he withdrew from the young master's presence, he took Pao aside and said with conspiratorial glee: 'Fortune smiles! Your affairs now look like prospering. I set out for the dike today to sell a rice-field, and when I return, I shall get busy on your behalf.'

Wang the steward was away for a few days and, having completed the transaction, returned with a thousand and some several hundred silver taels, which he carried in a bag. Reporting to the young master, he gave full particulars as follows— 'The price, one thousand three hundred, was as had been agreed upon, but with these qualifications: instead of sterling silver of ninety-seven per cent, their silver was only ninety-five per cent pure; and for the actual weighing, a pair of market scales were used instead of currency scales, entailing a loss of .135 per ounce. Furthermore, these deductions were made:

brokerage on their side, 23.4 taels; and notary fees, about twenty or thirty taels, which went to the young master's own clansmen. The silver is in this bag, and I shall now fetch the scales in order that the young master may weigh the pieces and check the amount.'[1] Tu snapped: 'Scales? Who's got the time and patience to work out the conversion with all the percentages and decimals? Since you have collected the money for me, I shall now put it away, and the matter is at an end.' And Wang with the shaggy beard again insisted: 'As long as I have explained it to the young master's satisfaction.'

Tu Shao-ch'ing laid the silver aside and summoned old Lou's grandson to the library. He said to the lad, 'I hear you may be going back tomorrow.' Young Lou answered: 'Yes. Grandfather has ordered me to return home.' Tu then handed him a pile of silver, explaining: 'There's a hundred taels for you — but you are not to tell your grandfather about it! You have a widowed mother to look after, and with this money you might start a small business at home so as to provide for her. If your grandfather recovers, I shall send your uncle home with another hundred taels.' The lad received the silver and carefully hid it in his clothes; he then offered his thanks to the young master. The next day, young Lou took leave of his grandfather, who ordered that a tiny piece to the value of three tenths of a tael be given for his fare, and dismissed him.

Tu Shao-ch'ing saw the lad off at the gate. Upon turning back, he noticed a peasant who had been standing in the hall, waiting. As the man knelt down and did the kowtow, Tu recognized him and said: 'Surely you are Huang, the caretaker of the clan ancestral temple! What are you doing here?' The man, who indeed was Huang, told his story — 'Ever since, as caretaker, I was given a hut beside the ancestral temple by the late master, who had specially bought the hut for me, I have always lived in it. But, with the passing of time, the little house fell into disrepair and part of the roof caved in. I then did a rash thing. I removed some dead trees from the tombs and used them as props for the roof, not thinking that when the gentlemen of the clan heard about this, they would accuse me of steal-

[1] Had Tu Shao-ch'ing bothered to check the amount and do the conversion — the use of the market scales alone had cost him $13\frac{1}{2}\%$ of the total! — he would have found just over 1000 taels in the bag. 'A thousand and some several hundred taels' would seem to suggest that Wang received considerably more than 1300 taels from the sale.

ing the trees. They not only gave me a thrashing but also sent a dozen or so stewards to the hut to take away the wood, with the result that even the part that had previously been standing was also pulled down, and I am now left with no shelter. So I have come to beg the young master to intercede with the gentlemen of the clan for me, that money might be paid out of the clan chest for repairing the hut, and I be allowed to live in it as before.'

Tu said contemptuously: '*Which* gentleman of the clan? Since it was the late master who bought the hut for you, we hold ourselves responsible for its repair and upkeep. You say it has been completely pulled down. How much will it cost to have the hut rebuilt?' Huang replied: 'One would need fully a hundred taels to rebuild it, something I cannot hope for; but with repairing and some patching up, the place would be habitable again, and even that would come to forty or fifty taels.' Tu concluded: 'It's perhaps as well, then. We haven't a great deal in the way of funds. For the present, take fifty taels, but in the event of more being needed, you may again approach us.' And he handed fifty taels to Huang, who took the money, offered his thanks and departed.

The gate-keeper now came in with two cards and reported: 'Master Tsang Third is inviting the young master to a banquet tomorrow. The other card is for Mr Pao, who is also invited.' Young Master Tu replied: 'Give my compliments to Master Third and say I shall be present tomorrow.' The next day, therefore, he went with Pao to Tsang's house, where a splendid and costly repast awaited them. Tsang bowed his two guests to their seats with unaccustomed punctilio and offered the wine with extreme deference. The conversation was desultory, but when the last course had been served, with sudden animation Tsang poured out a cup of wine, held it high with both hands, danced across the table and offered it to Tu with a histrionic bow. Then, promptly kneeling down, he declaimed shrilly: 'Best and noblest of friends, I beg a favour of thee.' Tu gave a start, hurriedly laid down the cup and fell on his knees himself so as to help Tsang up; he exclaimed: 'Are you mad, old chap? What is the meaning of all this?' Tsang screeched: 'Drink up and promise you will grant me the favour! Else I shall remain thus all day.' Tu cried in protest: 'You have not told me what it is about! Get up like a man and speak your mind.' Rallying to the young master, Pao also extended a hand to his host who, however, continued to employ his knees to the best advantage while pressing for an answer: 'You have promised, then?' Tu gave in with a shrug—'Well, I suppose I could promise anything.' Tsang again insisted: 'Drink up the wine.' Tu raised the cup and said, 'I *am* drinking.' Tsang shrieked: 'Drain it! You must drain it!' At last, Tu finished the wine, and Tsang rose to his feet and returned to the host's seat.

Tu Shao-ch'ing again demanding to be told, Tsang specified the favour he sought: 'The Chief Examiner[1] is currently at Lu-chou, conducting the degree examination[2] there, and our locality is next on his schedule. A little while ago, I took it upon myself to purchase a "Pass" on behalf of a local candidate —an agent sent in advance by the Chief Examiner had claimed that he could look after that sort of thing, and I paid out the three hundred taels to him. But the man now swears that the proceedings at degree examinations are watched over with such vigilance that no guaranteed "Pass" could possibly be arranged; instead he could secure the nomination of a licentiate for the vacant position of College Stipendiary.[3] I thereupon put forward my own name—for I would dearly love to be made a Stipendiary, the senior student of the year!—not thinking that the family who had wanted the degree for their son would immediately demand the three hundred taels back! My noble friend, the silver has been paid out and may no longer be recovered—yet if I failed to return the sum, the whole wretched business would come to light, and the disclosure would be my

[1] Chief Examiner (*tsung-shih*) i.e. the Provincial Director of Studies (*t'i-tu hsüeh-cheng*). It seems unnecessary here to explain the intricacies of the examination system; only the earlier stages are relevant to our story, and these are described in detail in Shang Yen-liu, *Ch'ing-tai k'o-chü k'ao-shih shu-lu*, 1958, chapter i, and summarized in C.L.Chang, *The Chinese Gentry*, 1955, pp. 10–20.

[2] *Yüan-k'ao*, the final in a series of three examinations leading to the Licentiate; it was conducted by the Provincial Director of Studies. See Shang Yen-liu, pp. 1–13; C.L.Chang, pp. 10–12. The degree examination was relatively free from corrupt practices; see P.T.Ho, *The Ladder of Success in Imperial China*, pp. 190–4.

[3] *Lin-sheng* (Senior Student with stipend), chosen from among the Licentiates of the College normally on the results of regular tests presided over also by the Provincial Director of Studies. The stipend was no more than an annual rice allowance of four taels, but the Stipendiary enjoyed the privilege of sponsoring candidates for the licentiate; the number of Stipendiaries in a given College was fixed. See Shang Yen-liu, pp. 18–20, 22; C.L.Chang, pp. 17–18.

ruin and the ruin of my family! I beg of you, therefore—for you can well afford it, having sold some of your surplus land only the day before—let me have a loan of three hundred to hush up the matter. I shall of course repay you in due course,—in due course. Do not say "no"! You promised just then!'

Tu gave a puff in amused contempt: 'Pff! And is it but this? I thought with all that agitation and fuss the world was coming to an end! And the bowing and kowtowing, too!—You shall have the silver on the morrow, delivered to your door.' Pao now clapped his hands in loud applause, shouting: 'What alacrity! What generosity! Let us have large cups and drink to all generous givers!' Large cups being now brought, they drank copiously out of them. Tu, now intoxicated, turned to his host—'I insist though, Brother Tsang, on knowing why you should pay good money for a worthless stipendiary's position.' Tsang suddenly assumed the exalted rank of a Senior Student and said with a swagger: 'The advantages of the position are not, of course, obvious to the uninitiated. In the first place, the Stipendiary—Ha! Ha!—stands a far greater chance of passing the higher examinations, which lead to the devoutly wished consummation of office! And even if he succeeds nevertheless in not passing them, after a mere fifteen years or so he is sent up to the capital as a Presentation Candidate[1] and given a specially devised test at the Palace, after which he is appointed Magistrate or Prefect's judicial officer. And then—the glory of it!—he wears boots with spiral-knotted heels, sits in state in the great hall, shakes out his order slips and has every prisoner beaten. And if you with your high and mighty airs came to bother me, I could have you locked up in a private cell with nothing for food but bean-curd for a whole month. That would teach you a lesson!' Tu exclaimed, roaring with laughter: 'What, man! Already in the racket? Shed every stitch of

[1] As a *kung-sheng*, a student chosen on merit or seniority for presentation at the capital: Stipendiaries stood a fair chance of qualifying through seniority for the honour. See C.L.Chang, p.5 and n.9, pp.27–9, where the term is translated as 'Imperial Student'; Shang Yen-liu, pp.26–32. In the Ming, Presentation Candidates were sometimes appointed 'Magistrate or Prefect's judicial officer'; see *Ming hui-yao*, c.48 (Edition of 1956, p.893). In the Ch'ing, they were given a number of minor posts, mostly educational; see *Ch'in-ting ta-Ch'ing hui-tien shih-li*, 1818, c.57, pp.2bff.

shame to slip all the more easily into your Magistrate's robes?'
Pao also joined in the laughter but prevented further squabbles
by shouting 'Mere jesting! Ribald jesting! My masters! For
penalty, a refilled goblet for each of you!' Thus the banquet
continued until night.

Early the next morning, the steward Wang was despatched
to Master Tsang's with a casket containing the silver, and for
this service he received a tip of six taels. Stopping for breakfast
on his way back at a fish and noodle shop, he saw Chang the
physician, who was already seated at breakfast there. Chang
called out to him—'Master Steward Shaggy-beard, come and
sit by me!' Wang went across and sat at the same table, and as
he gulped down the bowl of noodles placed before him, the
physician began: 'I crave your mighty assistance in a humble
matter.' Wang paused and asked guardedly: 'What is it? You
would like a reward when you have cured old grandfather
Lou?' Chang said: 'Not at all! Old Grandfather Lou's a goner.'
Wang quickened with interest and asked again: 'How long will
he last?' Chang replied: 'Not more than a hundred days. However, there is no need to tell anyone. It is quite another matter
about which I seek your advice.' Wang grunted: 'Go on.'
Chang then explained: 'The Chief Examiner is coming this
way, and I want to enter my son for the examinations, but the
College could debar him on the ground that we were not
originally of this district.[1] So I wondered if I might ask your
young master to have a word with the gentlemen in the College.'

Wang dismissed the proposal with a wave of the hand,
saying, 'That wouldn't do at all. The young master will have
nothing to do with the gentlemen in the College, and the mere
mention of anyone wishing to take the examinations infuriates
him. If you approached him in that way, he would try to dis-
courage your son from the attempt altogether.' Chang cried in
dismay: 'How then?' Wang went on calmly: 'There is a way,
though. I shall report to the young master that as a family you
are debarred from the examinations on the ground of residence,

[1] In the Ch'ing statutes may be found detailed regulations governing the
residence of candidates: a candidate discovered entering under a false
name or residence was disqualified and the sponsoring Stipendiary
punished. See *Ch'in-ting ta-Ch'ing hui-tien shih-li*, c. 313; Shang Yen-liu,
p. 22.

but that since the examination hall at Fengyangfu[1] was built with money given by the late master, it would seem a pity if the young master did not sponsor a candidate, thus overruling the objection of the local College. Once he is roused in this way, he would do his utmost for you, nor—spare the expense.' Chang sighed with relief: 'Master Conjurer! I leave the matter entirely in your hands. But be assured, if you succeed, I shall offer my T H-A N-X[2] in an appropriate manner.' Shaggy-beard Wang, however, replied with an air of disdain: 'Thanks, eh? What do I want of thanks? Your son is but my nephew and when he passes that examination and wears for the first time his licentiate's cap and gown, he will perform a ceremonial kowtow to me, his uncle. A graduate in his new cap and gown kowtow to me! That would be something!' Thus their conference came to a close. Chang paid for the noodles and together they left the shop.

As soon as Shaggy-beard Wang returned to the house, he asked the page-boys where the young master was. Upon learning from them that the young master was in the library, he went straight there and reported on his errand. 'The silver was delivered to Master Tsang Third in person, who dwelt at length on his deep indebtedness to the young master and declared that the young master had averted a scandal for him, Master Tsang, and, moreover, ensured the success of his official career. — If Wang might be permitted the observation, it is the sort of kind deed that nobody else would think of doing.' Tu Shao-ch'ing said irritably: 'Have I got to listen to that all over again? The thing was of no importance.' But the bearded steward continued: 'There is a further matter to which I should draw the young master's attention. Now that Master Tsang's stipendiary has been bought and paid for and the rebuilding of the caretaker's hut by the ancestral temple settled, it will not be many days before the gentlemen of the College come forward with a request to the young master for the repair of the examination hall, which the late master erected at a cost of several thousand taels, all to the good of the community. And really, to my way of thinking, if the young master

---

[1] An allusion to the re-building of the College at Kanyu by Wu's father; see Introduction.
[2] The three components of the character *hsieh* (thanks) are given in the original: *yen* (speech), *shen* (body), *ts'un* (inch).

entered a candidate for the coming examinations, surely the
College would not dare oppose it.'

Tu remarked: 'Candidates always make their own applica-
tions. Why should I enter anyone?' The sly domestic then
rambled on: 'It was only my way of putting it. But I did think
—supposing I myself had a son, and the young master wished
to enter him for the examinations, still no one could debar him.'
Tu laughed derisively and said: 'But that goes without saying!
Anyhow, are the licentiates of the local College any better than
lackeys?' Wang seemed suddenly to recall—'The son of
Master Chang now, who lives outside the back gate—he is a
young scholar! Might not the young master enter *him* for the
examinations?' Tu asked in surprise: 'Does young Chang
want to take the examinations?' Wang replied: 'The Changs
are not of this district, and whether the boy was inclined to or
not, he would not be allowed to offer himself as a candidate.'
Tu gave a snort—'That indeed so? Then tell him from me
that he should enter for the examinations. And if any of the
Stipendiaries at the College question his right to do so, he is
to inform *that* Stipendiary it was I who sent him.' Wang
shouted his assent and departed to carry out his orders.

In the meantime, old Mr Lou's illness took a turn for the
worse. Another physician was sent for, and Tu Shao-ch'ing,
being full of anxiety about the old cashier's health, seldom left
the house. One day Tsang called and announced with great
excitement even before he had sat down: 'Wang the County
Magistrate is ruined! You haven't heard the news? Last night
he was deprived of his seal and his successor ordered his ejec-
tion from the official residence. The people of this town now
call him rogue and villain, and no one would let a house to him.
He was worried to death there!' Tu asked: 'What does he
propose to do?' Tsang continued scathingly: 'He stayed on
brazenly at the residence last night, but if by tomorrow he was
still found there, he would be evicted by force, and that would
be a frightful loss of face. But why should anyone want to take
him in? The old people's home's the place for someone like
him!' Tu muttered: 'You don't say so!' and told the page-boy
to summon the steward Wang, whom he thus commanded:
'Go before the County Court at once and ask the porter to send
this message within to His Worship Magistrate Wang—"In
lieu of a suitable house elsewhere, His Worship would be very

welcome to use one of my summer-houses as a temporary residence." The Magistrate is desperately in need of rooms. Hurry!'

As the steward retreated in haste, Tsang broke out in loud protest: 'There was a time when you could not be persuaded even to meet him. But now—dare I ask for what reason?—of your own accord you invite him to stay in your house! This affair of his could implicate you, and if the rabble should rise against him, they might easily lay waste your garden!' Tu said quietly: 'The numerous and not inconsiderable benefits conferred by my late father are remembered with real gratitude by all in this county. No one would molest us even if I harboured a highwayman in my house. You need therefore have no uneasiness on my account. As for the learned Doctor Wang, if indeed he admired me, it showed a glimmering of sense—so much the better for him! But for me to have called on him earlier, while he held sway, would have looked like fawning on the reigning Magistrate. Now that he is relieved of his post and has nowhere to live, I consider it my duty to look after him. He will doubtless avail himself of the invitation, and you, my friend, will wait for him here and entertain him properly.'

Their conversation was interrupted by the gate-keeper coming into the reception hall to announce Master Chang.[1] The physician himself followed but, to their surprise, he suddenly knelt down and performed the kowtow. Tu Shao-ch'ing asked: 'What do you want now?' Chang replied hesitantly: 'It is about entering my son for the examinations. I shall never forget the young master's extraordinary kindness.' Tu made a gesture of impatience, saying. 'I have already given my word.' Chang, however, continued: 'When the worshipful Stipendiaries heard the young master's instructions, they raised no objection but exacted a sum of a hundred and twenty taels for the repair of the College. A poor physician like me could ill afford such a donation, and I have thus come to seek the young master's help!' Tu now asked: 'You are certain that a hundred and twenty taels is all they demand? Was there mention of other payments?' The proud parent answered: 'No other payment is required.' Young Master Tu then declared: 'That can be managed. We shall pay the sum for you. You will write a

[1] Having stopped attending old Lou, Physician Chang no longer had the freedom of the house.

petition in which you offer to donate the said amount for the repair of the College building in return for the privilege of registering as residents of the county. —Brother Tsang, please hand in the petition for him at the College. I shall provide the silver.'

Tsang turned to the candidate's father and said: 'We have pressing business today, but tomorrow I am at your service.' Physician Chang again thanked the young master and Tsang, and as he left, he met the steward Wang flying through the door in a tearing hurry, bawling out—'Magistrate Wang is at the gate, alighting from the sedan!' Tu and Tsang came out to welcome the Magistrate, who still wore his silk hat but had discarded his official robes in favour of ordinary dress. Inside the gate, the Magistrate made his host a ceremonial bow and began: 'I have long looked up to you, Sir, without the chance of a meeting. And now, in my extremity, all unexpectedly you have generously lent me the use of your study, putting me to great shame. I have, therefore, called to give my thanks before attending on you at your leisure. Ah, quite a coincidence that Licentiate Tsang is also here!' Tu replied: 'Honoured Magistrate, it is the merest trifle, to be dismissed without delay from your mind. My rooms were originally vacant. Pray move over at once.' And Tsang turned right-about and gushed: 'My friend and I were about to wait on you, Master. To have thus put you to the trouble of calling was an inexcusable omission on our part.' Magistrate Wang muttered: 'Not at all! Not at all!' Then bowing once more, he re-mounted the sedan and made his departure.

Tu Shao-ch'ing went back into the house with Tsang, took out a hundred and twenty taels, and handed the money to Tsang with the repeated request that he arrange on the morrow for young Chang's candidature. Tsang received the silver and left. The next day, Magistrate Wang moved into his suite of rooms in the garden. The day after, Physician Chang ordered a dinner to be sent to the Tu residence and invited Master Tsang Third and Mr Pao to keep the young master company. Shaggy-beard Wang now said to the actor when they were by themselves: 'The scene is laid. "Enter Master Pao." You know the burden of your own speech. I have been figuring it out; that matter of a certain sum is approaching an end, and if one more should come along to beg for his share, you would draw a blank. This evening, therefore, you shall speak.'

Host and guests duly appeared. Dinner was served in the front study adjoining the reception hall,[1] and while Tu Shao-ch'ing and the two others took their seats, Chang the physician held up with both hands a cup of wine which he offered to the young master in expression of his thanks; he then poured out the wine for Master Tsang and bowed his thanks before sitting down in the host's place. The meal progressed, and the conversation revolved round the affairs of the latest beneficiaries from the young master's magnanimity. Suddenly the actor Pao burst into tears, sighing and wailing: 'Alas, it is all too clear to me, who have served the young master for the past half year and more, that silver flows through the young master's hands like water! Even a tailor could lay claim to a large handful. But I alone, who have been kept in the house these seven or eight months,[2] am accorded the honour of a place at table with a goodly share of the meat and drink but not the benefit of a single hard cash! I can no longer sustain the role of honorary retainer. Let me dry my tears and carry my tale of woe elsewhere! I beg leave to depart tomorrow.'

Tu Shao-ch'ing exclaimed: 'But, my friend, I am still in the dark! Without being told, how should we know about your concerns? If you have something on your mind, tell us now.' Pao poured out a cup of wine and offered it to the young master before resuming: 'Like my father before me, I was leader of a troupe of actors. But our venture failed when—oh, greatest of misfortunes!—my father died; I lost all our capital and disgraced my father's memory. What was more, my aged mother was left destitute.[3] Unworthy as I am—indeed unfit to live— I must yet somehow provide for my mother, and unless the young master bestows a sum upon me to be used as capital, all my hopes are vain.' Tu Shao-ch'ing commented approvingly: 'A member of the theatrical profession who remains a votary to filial piety, who honours the memory of his father and serves his mother with care and devotion![4] We bow to you, friend,

[1] The gravity of old Lou's illness and Magistrate Wang's occupation of a suite of rooms necessitate revised domestic arrangements.

[2] Time passes imperceptibly in *Ju-lin wai-shih*, though events seem to be recorded from day to day.

[3] For Pao's sad story, see n. 2 on p. 350, and Introduction. Old Mrs Pao was in tolerable circumstances, Pao himself really destitute.

[4] Actors were classed, as in many countries, with rogues and vagabonds and thought to be without morals.

and are yours to command.'

As befitted one who was about to receive a favour, Pao rose from his seat, declaiming rapturously: 'Oh, kindness rare in such times!' Tu, however, cut him short—'Pray be seated and tell us how much you need.' Pao turned his gaze sideways and his eyes rested upon the steward Wang, who was standing at the lower end of the room. Shaggy-beard Wang now came forward and said gruffly: 'Mr Pao, to start a company you will need silver in plenty, what with assembling your players and picking and choosing the costume, props and what not, easily five or six hundred taels! Our young master is in no position to supply you. At the most he could dismiss you with two or three score, but that should enable you to return home, round up a few monkeys and start a street circus, before you look higher.' Young Master Tu paused a moment and declared: 'Two or three score would not avail. You shall have a hundred taels to begin with. Take the money and get the company started, and come back again when it is spent.' Pao knelt down to express his thanks, but Tu pulled him up, saying: 'I would have given you more, had more been at our disposal; but our old Mr Lou is gravely ill, and I must make arrangements for a certain event. Be satisfied, therefore, for the present and return to your home.' And the rest of the evening Tsang and Chang kept up a chorus of praise for the young master's generosity until they dispersed for the night.

From that time on, old Lou's illness grew worse with each day that passed. One day, while Tu Shao-ch'ing sat by the sick-bed, old Lou suddenly said: 'Good young master, I have waited until this moment before speaking. I had hoped to recover but fear that I shall soon succumb. You will need to send me home!' Tu cried: 'Not before I have done my duty by you, Uncle Lou, and made recompense in some measure for your loyal services —and that will be a long time yet! How could you talk about leaving us now?' Lou sighed: 'There you go again! I have my sons and grandsons, but the greater part of my life was spent away from my family; and now I wish to die at home. No one could ever suggest you did not want to keep me here.' With tears in his eyes, Tu said solemnly: 'If that is how you feel, Uncle, I will not try to detain you. I did of course have your coffin prepared, but since it is not required, it had best not be sent along; instead I shall provide a few score taels for a substitute. Your funeral garments and sheets had been made some time ago, and I shall see that they are packed and travel with you.'

Faithful to the last, Lou replied: 'The coffin and shroud I gratefully accept; but do not give any more silver to my son or grandson! Within three days I must leave for home and, being no longer able to sit up, I shall have to be carried in my bed. Tomorrow morning, go before the altar of your father and say in your prayer to him that old Lou, long in his service, now bids his spirit farewell. For over thirty years I served, first, your father, who came to regard me as one of his most trusted friends, and then, after his decease, yourself, who have treated me with such deference and respect that I could never complain on my own account. As for yourself, good young master, in your conduct and literary attainments, you are indeed without a peer. How you must rejoice, too, in your young son, a truly remarkable boy,[1] whom you will exercise great care in teaching that, as he grows up, he may be confirmed in the ways of virtue! But you have not learned how to run the household or to make friends with the right sort, and your inheritance will surely be squandered! Pleased as I am to find you acting generously in the cause of others, for your part you must temper munificence with judiciousness. You are so free in giving that you have been cheated right and left, and no one will repay you. Though it is said—"The bestowing of the gift is its own reward", you ought nevertheless to distinguish between the deserving and the unworthy.

'Master Tsang Third and that fellow Chang, with whom you associate, are the type who will never requite your favours to them. There has lately been added to their number a certain Pao, a good-for-nought strolling player, and yet you *would* befriend him. And your steward, Shaggy-beard Wang, is of course the worst of the lot! However, money is but a secondary consideration. When I am gone, remember, you and your son must model yourselves upon the upright conduct of your late father; for upright conduct comes even before a man's liveli-hood. All your life you have been on the best of terms with

[1] The author's son, Wu Lang, was a precocious boy. Some verses he wrote at the age of fifteen are preserved in his collected poems, which are included with his father's collected works. In later life, he became an accomplished mathematician. See Introduction.

your cousin, Master Shen-ch'ing, who, though rich in accomplishments, is but poor in kindness and graciousness. No, you
should only follow the example of your late father: you will
never regret it.

'You have shown scant respect for local officialdom, and
your clansmen you hold in contempt—here in your home
town life could soon become insupportable for you.[1] Nanking is
a capital city. With your talents, if you settle there, you may
hope to meet others of a like mind, and establish yourself in a
career. For what is left of your inheritance, alas, will soon be
reduced to nothing! Good young master, hearken to what I
say, that my eyelids may drop in peace when I die!'

With tears streaming down his cheeks, Tu cried: 'Your
words of admonition are engraved in my heart!' He retreated
from the room in confusion and gave orders for two teams of
porters to be hired, to carry old Lou on his sick-bed by way of
Nanking to Lou's native town, T'ao-hung-chen.[2] He then took
out a hundred and ten taels and gave the money to old Lou's
son for the funeral. And on the third day he saw Lou off at the
start of the old man's journey home. . . .[3]

[1] The author finally left his home town in 1733 to live in Nanking. See
note 3 and Introduction.
[2] T'ao-hung-chen is probably T'ao-wu-chen, to the south of Nanking.
[3] This is the end of chapter 32, which has the formal conclusion:
'Thus was it brought about that,
    The halls and gardens in the capital
    Were again frequented by a man of fashion;
    But his native district north of the Yangtze
    No longer witnessed deeds of like munificence.
As to what happened next, it shall be resolved in the next chapter.'
The story is, however, not quite complete without the beginning of
chapter 33, which runs—
'The story goes that when Tu Shao-ch'ing had sent old Lou on his way,
there was no one in the house to remonstrate with him, and he made no
scruple to spend whatever silver he could lay hands on. When the
proceeds from the sale of the field in the dike were exhausted, he
despatched Shaggy-beard Wang to sell another field, which brought
in over two thousand taels so that he was able to indulge even more
freely in spending. And he dismissed the actor Pao with the promised
gift of a hundred taels, with which Pao crossed the Yangtze and returned
home. In the meantime, Magistrate Wang's affairs had been wound up
and the Magistrate vacated his suite of rooms and took his leave. Tu
Shao-ch'ing stayed on in the house for over half a year, by which time
the silver was nearly all spent; and he thought of making over his house
to a clansman and moving to Nanking to live, to which proposal his
wife agreed when he discussed it with her. But when the others advised
him against adopting such a course, he was deaf to all their entreaties.
After a further six months of arguing and wrangling, the transfer was

effected, and what with settling his debts and redeeming his pledges, he was left with a thousand taels or so. And he said to his wife: 'I shall leave for Nanking by myself, to call on my mother's relations, the Lu cousins, but when I find a house, I will send for you.' He then packed his luggage and set off for the great city, taking the steward Wang and the page-boy Rank Plus with him. At the ferry, however, the bearded steward decided that the game was up and absconded with twenty taels. When told about Wang's desertion, Tu Shao-ch'ing gave a laugh and thought no further of the matter; and he crossed the Yangtze, accompanied only by his page-boy.'

The author himself set out for Nanking in 1730, aged thirty, and the 'Mu-lan-hua' *tz'u* poems were written at the end of that year (i.e. early in 1731): the eighth poem opens with—

'A lackey absconded, the other servants dispersed,'

Eventually, early in 1733, he moved his family to Nanking. See Introduction.

A Burial Mound for Flowers

'A Burial Mound for Flowers' is taken from chapter 23 of *Hung-lou meng* (first printed in 120 chapters in 1791), a long narrative in the Chinese manner written by a Manchu, Ts'ao Chan, better known as Ts'ao Hsüeh-ch'in, in the language that he naturally spoke, Mandarin Chinese; Ts'ao, however, who died early in 1764 while still in his forties, completed only eighty-odd chapters of it, the remainder being by another hand but also written in Mandarin. It is a story about the decay of an aristocratic Manchu family and gives an intimate picture of high life—admittedly only of its period, the reign of Ch'ien-lung—as in no other Chinese work. The external world, however, is seen as reflected in the hero's heart, and the book has a symbolic scheme. Thus its original title is *Shih-t'ou chi* ('The Story of a Stone'), a stone as old as the world itself which for one brief life's span was transformed—with the help of a Buddhist monk and a Taoist priest—into a young man and lover, and tasted the joys and sorrows of the human lot before reverting to its stone-hearted rock's existence. The young man, who is the hero, was born with a piece of jade in his mouth and named Pao-yü, i.e. Precious Jade, jade being stone carved, polished and rendered artificial. His family, among the noblest in the land, bears the surname Chia, i.e. unreal; and the un-reality of the world with all its vanities is indicated by the novel's later and better known title *Hung-lou meng* ('Dream in a Red Chamber').

Even apart from its symbolism, it is the only work in Chinese colloquial fiction in which the feelings are of paramount im-portance. The reader is made aware of the slightest emotion, the least change of mood, each vagary and caprice, every blush, flutter and palpitation of the hero and his cousin Tai-yü, the heroine, which outweigh all other circumstances affecting the household and the family's fortune. In this respect, *Hung-lou meng* pertains to the Chinese tradition in drama rather than in fiction,[1] and it should cause no surprise that the author's original intention was to cast his story in a dramatic mode.[2] Certainly, as we have it, much of the story is told in terms of the hero's feelings. Pao-yü—descended from the Duke Jung, who, together with his brother the Duke Ning, was raised to the highest station by an earlier Emperor—is utterly indifferent to the *a priori* claims of filial piety, family honour and duty, but is swayed by tenderness, graciousness, kindness and all appeals to his generosity and good nature. He has not a notion of the obligation of rank, the power of money, the necessity of decorum, the achievement of scholarship, the exhilaration of success; instead he is completely naive and, being witty and gifted and knowing his books without great application, idles away hours and days allotted to study. Pao-yü is subject to the most wayward fancies, each fancy being bred in the heart, of which he is unashamedly the slave.

Under the tutelage of his heart, then, Pao-yü, protected from a stern and almost hostile father, Board Secretary Chia Cheng, by his mother and his over-indulgent grandmother, the Dowager Duchess, and surrounded by adoring maids and fastidious female cousins, who could bear the company of no other male cousin, decides at the age of seven that the world is populated by two distinct species: woman, whose substance is 'water', clear, liquid, pure; and man, whose substance is 'earth', gross, solid, dense.[3] And indeed it is the female cousins in the story who possess both talent and worth; the male cousins, uncles, their friends and associates are, on the contrary, shown as coarse or vulgar or dull. For the hero's attitude would seem a reflection of the author's own. At the beginning of the novel, the author professes, in the words of the Stone, to be recording the lives of a few women he had known all his life:

> ... As to the run of the mill love story about the cleverest of men and the fairest of women, a thousand of them are fashioned from the same mould. They are seldom completely free from lewd descriptions and their pages are covered with the names of famous lovers of the past, all so as to lend occasion to a few low verses of their author's own composi-

---

[1] See General Introduction.
[2] See S. C. Wu, *On the Red Chamber Dream*, pp. 84–5.
[3] Chapter 2, Yü edition, p. 19.

tion, around which a hero and a heroine (stereotypes with new names) would be placed with a villain to stir up trouble between them like some scheming stage clown. In such stories, the very servant girls declaim in classical prose! Not one of them bears even a cursory examination: their endings belie the beginning and the stories themselves are often impossible or absurd. Far better, therefore, to write about the few women I have known all my life, who are, to be sure, not superior to heroines in books of former ages, but whose story, traced from beginning to end, is at least entertaining, and supported, too, by some verses for the interested reader. As to the joys and sorrows of meeting and parting, and fortune's vicissitudes, these are recorded with scrupulous fidelity, no attempt being made to touch up or falsify merely to impress the reader: thus the portraits are true likenesses.[1]

The conventions of fiction, as indicated in the hero's surname Chia (unreal, i.e. fictitious), only conceal but do not erase the autobiographical element; and as a statement of the aims of a novelist, the passage is unique. To do justice to *Hung-lou meng* or its author,[2] however, would require an extended study, going far beyond the confines of this book. Our extract is intended, in the first place, to bring out the setting of the story, the ducal residence and the magnificent garden with its archways and rockeries, its lake and streams, its halls, pavilions and villas, known as Ta-kuan-yüan, which is rendered 'Garden of Pomp and State', being for the use of the Queen Yüan-ch'un, who is also the eldest daughter of the family and the hero's sister. Against this setting are further shown the hero and heroine, aged respectively thirteen and twelve but both precocious, in a charming scene in which their love for each other is awakened. The scene—chapter 23—is symbolic in that the beautiful and flower-like Tai-yü who laments the fallen petals and prepares a burial mound for them may seem to be tending her own grave. Tai-yü re-appears at the spot in chapters 27–28,

---

[1] Chapter 1, Yü edition, p. 4. The translation is for the particular purpose of this discussion; it is free but not deliberately unfaithful. An adequate but not quite complete rendering of the passage may be found in C. C. Wang's translation, edition of 1959, pp. 5–6.

[2] See General Introduction. S. C. Wu, *On the Red Chamber Dream*, 1961, gives a very thorough account of manuscript and printed versions known up to then, and discusses the author in great detail.

but by then she is already filled with a deep foreboding, to which she gives expression in a string of verses that chill Pao-yü to the bones.

The passage also shows something of the love tradition under which novelists and romancers laboured. Upon looking into 'The West Chamber', Pao-yü is suddenly emboldened in his love prattle; and the stray lines from 'The Peony Pavilion', overheard by Tai-yü while the tunes were being rehearsed on the other side of the garden wall, define and give shape to her own feelings. In the context of this book, the passage also reveals the reading habits of the young in rich households and the insidious influence—so greatly dreaded by their elders—of novels and plays.

I have used *Hung-lou-meng pa-shih hui chiao-pen*[1] (Jen-min wen-hsüeh ch'u-pan-she, 1958) edited from the manuscripts with full collation by Yü P'ing-po as being the closest to the author's own version, the early printed editions having undergone revision by the first editor, Kao O. The episode here entitled 'A Burial Mound for Flowers' is translated fully in H. Bencraft Joly's literal version of the first fifty-six chapters, *Hung Lou Meng or The Dream of the Red Chamber*, 1892–3, pp. 351–61; it may also be found in Chi-chen Wang's abridged version, *Dream of the Red Chamber*, revised edition, 1959, chapter 20, pp. 187–94; and in Florence and Isabel McHugh's translation of the abridged German version by Franz Kuhn, *The Dream of the Red Chamber*, 1958, chapter 18, pp. 171–7.

[1] Referred to in the notes as the Yü edition.

A Burial Mound for Flowers

To return now to Queen Yüan-ch'un in the Palace,[1] when she had read over the poems written on the occasion of her visit to the Garden of Pomp and State[2] and rearranged them as a collection with her own comments on their respective merits, it occurred to her that the Garden with its arbours and rockeries would be utterly desolate if, after her own visit, her father, Secretary of the Board of Works Chia Cheng,[3] as he was in duty bound, had the gates locked and sealed, thus hiding it from the view of all. Besides, there were all her literary female cousins at home, and who better than they to inhabit a place so delightful? They need never feel their inspiration dry up; nor could the flowers and willows languish in such lovely company. She then thought of her own younger brother, Pao-yü,[4] who— unlike her male cousins—had been brought up with the girls, —how that, if he should be left out, he would certainly feel

[1] This part of the story begins in chapter 23 (Yü edition, p. 229). Yüan-ch'un, i.e. Prime of Spring, was born on New Year's Day; hence her name. She is the daughter of Chia Cheng, and is one of the Emperor's Queens. To enable her to visit her parents in comfort and seclusion, the family built for her sole use the Garden of Pomp and State adjoining their residence. The visit itself is described in chapter 18. Yüan-ch'un is a dozen or more years older than her brother Pao-yü, whom as a child she taught to read (chapter 18, p. 177).

[2] Ta-kuan-yüan, by which is meant 'world in a nutshell', including, as it does, buildings in various styles, an artificial village and a temple in a varied landscape setting; see chapters 17 and 18, especially p. 180, where the name Ta-kuan is explained in a poem by Queen Yüan-ch'un as 'embracing all the glorious scenes on earth and in heaven'. The immediate associations of the phrase *ta kuan* are, however, pomp and grandeur.

[3] Chia Cheng, grandson of Duke Jung and son of the Dowager Duchess, is only Junior Secretary (*yüan-wai-lang*) in chapter 2, but in chapter 85 is made Senior Secretary (*lang-chung*), of the Board of Works.

[4] Pao-yü, i.e. Precious Jade, the hero of the novel, was born with a piece of jade in his mouth. In this part of the story (in chapter 23) he is about thirteen years of age; in chapter 25, which deals with events of a month or so later, the Buddhist monk and Taoist priest of chapter 1 reappear and speak of having been separated from Pao-yü (i.e. the Stone) for thirteen years (p. 260). See Introduction.

lonely and neglected, which in turn might affect the spirits of her own mother and grandmother, the Dowager Duchess: she therefore considered it best to allow Pao-yü to move into the Garden with the female cousins.

Having thus decided, Yüan-ch'un sent the Steward of the Palace, the eunuch Hsia Chung,[1] to the Jung Residence[2] with the order that Pao-ch'ai and the other female cousins[3] should take up their abode in the Garden, which was on no account to be locked up with entry debarred to all, and that Pao-yü was also to move in, to pursue his studies along with the cousins. Secretary Chia and his lady respectfully received the Queen's command and, when the eunuch had made his departure, reported the matter to the Dowager Duchess before ordering the servants to enter the Garden and sweep and tidy up each corner of it, and fit up the various buildings with curtains, screens, beds and hangings.

While all who heard the news rejoiced, Pao-yü alone was in raptures: he began at once to demand this or that piece of her furniture from the Dowager. But his animated conference with his grandmother was interrupted by a servant girl entering to announce: 'The master wants Pao-yü.' The effect of this upon Pao-yü was like a thunderbolt[4]—his countenance fell, almost as if his face was charred; all his newly raised hopes seemed dashed; and like a stick of gum he attached himself to the Dowager, turning and twisting in every direction and refusing to come unstuck. The Dowager, however, said soothingly: 'My precious! Go to your father, who won't eat you! Remember, there's always grandmamma behind you. Besides, you've just written that good essay for him! Since the Queen would have

---

[1] The eunuch's title 'Steward of the Palace' is taken from chapter 16, p. 150.

[2] Residence of the Duke Jung, now inhabited by his descendants. The residence of Jung's brother, Duke Ning, is similarly referred to as the Ning residence.

[3] Pao-ch'ai (Precious Hair-pin) is the daughter of Aunt Hsüeh, sister of Mrs Secretary Chia; she is aged fifteen (chapter 22, p. 217) and a rival to the heroine, Tai-yü, who is mentioned below with the other female cousins. As a relative rather than one of the Dowager Duchess's grand-daughters, Pao-ch'ai is given precedence over the others.

[4] The strange antipathy between Pao-yü and his father is a recurrent theme in the novel; see, e.g., the irate parent's heavy sarcasm in chapter 9 (p. 94) on the subject of Pao-yü going to school—'I shall die of shame if you ever mention school again! I say, isn't fooling around your proper activity? And mind where you're standing—that spot is now contaminated! Mind what you're leaning against—that door's now befouled!'

you and the girls housed in the Garden, I suppose your father will have a few things to say to you, only so as to keep you out of mischief. Be a good boy now and agree with whatever he might say.' And even as she calmed Pao-yü, she called two of her own serving women and told them to accompany Pao-yü and not let the master scare him.

Pao-yü was now obliged to obey his father's summons and came away with the old women, though advancing no more than a few inches with each step he took. Eventually, however, he reached his mother's apartments[1] where, a family council being in progress, the servant girls Gold Bangle, Rainbow Cloud, Sunset, Bird of Paradise, and Embroidered Phoenix[2] stood waiting outside, under the eaves. At the sight of Pao-yü crawling along, they puckered up their mouths and sniggered. Suddenly Gold Bangle pulled Pao-yü towards her and announced with a chuckle: 'I've just smeared my lips with rouge soaked in fragrant oil. Lick me! Now's best!'[3] Rainbow Cloud hurriedly pushed Gold Bangle aside and, herself giggling, said below her breath: 'We aren't in the mood. No teasing!' And turning to Pao-yü, she continued: 'You'll find the master in a good temper—better go in at once!'

Pao-yü dragged himself into the room, only to learn that his parents were in the inner room. Madam Chao, the concubine,[4] who had remained in the outer room, now lifted the door curtain for Pao-yü, who entered the bed-room and made his bow. Secretary Chia and his lady were seated opposite each other on

[1] As the lady of the house, Mrs Secretary Chia occupies the centre court-yard with a main suite of five stately rooms, but lives for the most part in three smaller rooms constituting the east wing. See chapter 3, pp. 29-31; also Chou Ju-ch'ang, *Hung-lou-meng hsin-cheng*, 1953, pp. 151-4. The seating arrangement on the brick-bed (*k'ang*) and the row of three or four chairs identify the room as the one in which Mrs Chia received Tai-yü in chapter 3 (p. 30). The centre courtyard is connected by a rear passage to the Dowager Duchess's courtyard, situated to its west.

[2] Gold Bangle (Chin-ch'uan); Rainbow Cloud (Ts'ai-yün); Sunset (Ts'ai-hsia); Bird of Paradise (Hsiu-luan), the name being rendered somewhat freely—since *luan* is usually translated as 'phoenix'—to avoid confusion with Embroidered Phoenix (Hsiu-feng). Embroidered Phoenix, the servant girl, is not to be confused with Cousin Phoenix (Feng chieh), one of the chief characters in the novel, though not mentioned in this excerpt.

[3] It is Pao-yü's habit to lick the rouge off the lips of the servant girls, for which he is reprimanded by his personal maid, Bombarding Scent (chapter 19, p. 195), but to no effect (chapter 24, pp. 237-8).

[4] Secretary Chia's concubine, being regarded as an inferior, is kept out of the family council, though her two children are not.

the heated brick-bed, talking. A row of chairs facing the brick-bed was occupied by the girls, Ying-ch'un, T'an-ch'un and Hsi-ch'un,[1] and Pao-yü's half-brother Huan,[2] and the three last, being all younger than Pao-yü, stood up upon his entering. Secretary Chia raising his head, saw before him Pao-yü with his lofty and graceful air and his strikingly handsome appearance, which showed up all the more the drooping hangdog look and ill-bred, clownish manners of the son of the concubine—Huan, who stood beside him. Secretary Chia then remembered his eldest boy,[3] Chu, now dead, and realized with a twinge of remorse how deeply his wife loved and cherished her sole surviving son. He himself, too, was ageing, his beard already turned grey. All these considerations combined to militate against his aversion for his son and his inclination to chastise him. After indulging for some time in this musing, which left him nine tenths mollified, Secretary Chia said, not unkindly: 'It is the Queen's wish that you, who are in the habit of following your idle whims day after day outside the house, should now be confined to the Garden, where you will carry out your reading and writing in the company of your sister and cousins. Ply well at your books, my lad. If you persist in your dawdling, rest assured that you will hear about this.'

Pao-yü responded with a whole string of yesses, and his mother pulled him on to the brick-bed beside her. The others, too, sat down again. Gently rubbing her hand against Pao-yü's neck,[4] Mrs Secretary Chia asked: 'Have you finished the pills, my boy?' Pao-yü said, 'There is one left still.' His mother continued: 'I'll send for another ten tomorrow, and remind Bombarding Scent[5] to make you take it at bedtime.' Pao-yü protested: 'Why, Bombarding Scent does give it to me every

[1] Ying-ch'un (Welcome Spring) is the daughter of Pao-yü's uncle, the Duke, noted below; Hsi-ch'un (Pity Spring) is descended from Duke Ning and not one of the Dowager's grand-daughters; T'an-ch'un (Seek Spring) is Pao-yü's half-sister, i.e. the daughter of the concubine, but unlike her brother, Huan, she is in no way handicapped by her birth.
[2] Huan, Pao-yü's half-brother, is the son of the concubine.
[3] Chu, Pao-yü's older brother, does not appear in the story but leaves a widow, Li Wan, mentioned below, and a son.
[4] To detect any glandular swellings the pills were expected to cure.
[5] The name gives a false impression of this demure and level-headed girl, who was one of the Dowager's own maids before she is assigned to Pao-yü, whom she jealously guards and protects. Her surname is Hua (Flower). Pao-yü alters her own name, Pearl, to Bombarding Scent in chapters 3 (p. 34). She is a few years older than Pao-yü.

night! She has not once forgotten ever since you, mother, told her to.' At this point, Secretary Chia broke in with some impatience—'Who is this Bombarding Scent?' Mrs Chia replied blandly: 'Oh, one of the maids.' The head of the family went on contemptuously: 'A servant girl might of course be called anything. But why such a name? Whose far-fetched conceit was this?' His manner alarmed his lady, who, to shield Pao-yü, declared: 'It was our gracious mother who gave the girl the name.' Secretary Chia sneered: 'Mother? Would mother even dream of such an expression? It could only be Pao-yü.' Pao-yü saw that concealment no longer availed; slipping off the brickbed, he justified himself thus before his father: 'In reading the old poets, I chanced upon the line—"The flowers' bombarding scent proclaims a sultry morn"[1] which came pat when I learned that the girl's surname was Flower; so I gave her that name.' Mrs Chia hurriedly added: 'You had better hunt out another name for her, Pao-yü, as soon as you get back to grandmamma';[2] then turning to Secretary Chia, she said: 'I should not have thought it necessary, my lord, to lose one's temper over a thing like that.' Secretary Chia conceded: 'There is no real harm in that name and certainly no need to change it now. But it does serve to show that Pao-yü wastes all his time on precious verse compositions to the detriment of his proper studies.' And suddenly rounding upon his son, he barked: 'Wretch! Be off with you!' Mrs Chia, anxious for Pao-yü to be gone, also said: 'Go now. Don't let grandmamma wait dinner for you.'

Pao-yü assented gravely and slowly withdrew from his father's presence. But when he found himself among the servant girls outside, he remembered their joke and stuck his tongue out at Gold Bangle before scurrying off, followed by the two old women. At the end of the corridor leading to the Dowager's courtyard, he noticed Bombarding Scent herself leaning against the door, waiting for him. When Bombarding Scent saw Pao-yü return, safe and unscathed, she asked, beaming: 'What was it about?' Pao-yü said: 'Oh, hardly anything at all. Merely that

[1] The line is derived from Lu Yu, 'Joys of Village Life', *Chien-nan shih-kao*, Ssu-pu pei-yao ed., c. 50, p. 7b.

[2] Pao-yü, being the Dowager Duchess's favourite grandchild, lives in his grandmother's courtyard, as does also Tai-yü, who, at least in the earlier part of the story, enjoys a position of privilege (chapter 3, p. 34; chapter 5, p. 45).

I was to keep out of scrapes in the Garden, the usual words to that effect.' As he spoke, he started for the room of his grand-mother, to whom he reported the interview with his father. His cousin Tai-yü[1] happening also to be there, he now asked her: 'Which house would you rather have?' Tai-yü, whose mind had been engaged on the same subject, responded to his question with a smile; she said, 'I was thinking of Hsiao-Hsiang Hermitage. I love those bamboos screening the curved railing—it's so much quieter there than anywhere else.' Upon hearing this, Pao-yü grinned and clapped his hands in glee, crying, 'Just as I thought! And it's just where I wanted you to stay! I'll live in Crab Red Court, where we shall be near each other and both in secluded spots.'

As the two of them went on planning in this fashion, a woman servant entered with a message from the head of the household to the Dowager: 'The cousins are to move on the twenty-second of the second month, an auspicious day, into the Garden, which is being swept. The houses will be got ready in the few intervening days.' Pao-ch'ai chose for her abode Aromatic Herb Rockery; Tai-yü, Hsiao-Hsiang Hermitage; Ying-ch'un, Tapestry Tower; T'an-ch'un, Autumn's Breath Studio; Hsi-ch'un, Smartweed Bank Loggia; Li Wan,[2] Sweet Paddy Village; and Pao-yü himself, Crab Red Court. At each of the dwellings, two older women and four girls were to be in attendance, not counting the wet-nurse and the personal maid; cleaners and gardeners being additionally provided. Thus on the twenty-second, the entire company took posses-sion of the Garden of Pomp and State: embroidered waist-bands now brushed against the flowers, and perfumed breezes intoxi-cated the willows, so that the place was no longer desolate.[3]

Pao-yü dwelt in the Garden and found everything to his heart's content and longed for no other happiness than that of

---

[1] Tai-yü (Lustrous Jade) is the daughter of Aunt Lin, the Dowager's daughter. Aunt Lin dying, Tai-yü is taken, at the age of six, from her father's official residence in Yangchow to live with her grandmother in the capital (chapter 2, p. 16; chapter 3, pp. 23–4). In chapter 3 (p. 30) Tai-yü describes herself as being a year younger than Pao-yü, whose favourite cousin she fast becomes.

[2] Li Wan, the widow of Chu, Pao-yü's older brother. She is the only adult among the seven, her son Lan being only two or three years younger than Pao-yü. (Lan was five when Pao-yü was seven or eight years of age in chapter 4).

[3] See translator's note on the cousins' dwellings, pp. 402–3.

spending each day in the company of the female cousins in reading or practising calligraphy, in playing the guitar or games of chess, in painting or composing verse. And in such pastimes of theirs as the tracing of embroidery patterns, perhaps of some phoenix or bird of paradise, and the embroidery itself, or the hunting out of rare plants[1] and the arranging of flowers as part of their head-dress, or singing and humming tunes, or word-games and riddles, he too joined with zest. And Pao-yü wrote some poems in which he described scenes in the Gardens at various times of year, of which four are quoted below, not, to be sure, for their excellence, but because they were based on his actual experience:

Night in Spring

Shut in by rainbow-coloured silk bed-curtains,

I fancy I hear frogs croaking beyond the wall.

A chill creeps up my pillow; rain taps at the window.

Before my eyes, lo, she whom I wooed in my dream—

'The candle drips tears—tears shed for whom?

The flowers in the vase seem a cluster of griefs—my griefs!'

'Let alone a simple nurse-maid, poor sleepyhead me!

When lying abed, I can't abide jesting and teasing.'[2]

Night in Summer

The girl has fallen asleep at her embroidery;

The parrot in its golden cage[3] renews its call for 'tea';

The full moon shines through the open window—

a rounded mirror;

Sandalwood fumes from rival censers circle about the room.

Amber cups overflow with sparkling 'Dew on Lotus';

Breezes rustling the willows

spread cool through the glass verandah.

Silk fans now wave all over the water pavilion:

Roll up the curtain—my lady's evening toilet is done.

---

[1] *Tou ts'ao*, a competitive game in which each participant produces an unusual plant or flower, or a branch or shoot notable for its shape or colour, and sets forth the claims of his particular specimen in poetical or horticultural terms. The game is described in chapter 62, pp. 691–2.

[2] Personalities are deliberately vague in Chinese verse, and the apportioning of the lines to two speakers is the translator's own. The more favoured servant girls slept in the same beds as the children, often even when they ceased to be children.

[3] Chapter 26, p. 266, supplies the detail that the cloistered part of Crab Red Court is filled with exotic birds in cages of various colours, thus further adding to the 'maze' and 'trap' symbolism; and Tai-yü has a parrot that recites verses (chapter 35, p. 362).

Night in Autumn

A breathless hush reigns within the Crimson Library,[1]
But shimmering moonlight *will* peep through gauze curtains.
Sheltered by the moss-grown rockery,
                               the cranes curl up in sleep;[2]
Crows perch on the well-curb wet with dew.
A drowsy maid brings a quilt, unrolling a golden phoenix;[3]
The beloved one returns from the window, her hairpin undone.
Awake in the still night, athirst with too much wine,
I poke at the smouldering embers and infuse fresh tea.[4]

Night in Winter

Flowering plums[5] and bamboos
                     engulf each other's dreams at the third watch:
But embroidered coverlet and kingfisher-down
                           would still induce no sleep.
Amidst shadows of pines in the courtyard, a lonely crane flaps;
Frost, like pear blossoms, bestrews the ground,
                             though no oriole sings.
The girl with the green sleeves tosses off verses about the cold;
His golden sable pledged for wine,[6]
                        the gay young lord declares it insipid.
Luckily my lord's page is thoroughly adept in blending tea —
Sweeping up the new snow, he makes an instant brew.[7]

[1] Crimson Library (Chiang Red Court (Chiang yün hsien) is used as an alternative name for Crab Red Court, as in the titles to chapters 36 and 59. It is to be regarded as the name of Pao-yü's study rather than any specific part of Crab Red Court, since it also figures in the title to chapter 8 in the sixteen-chapter MS version, before the Garden is built.

[2] Cranes are described as preening themselves under a pine tree in Crab Red Court in chapter 26, p. 266; and as sleeping under the palms in chapter 36, p. 377.

[3] A golden phoenix embroidered on the quilt.

[4] For Pao-yü's unquenchable thirst, see, e.g. chapter 8, pp. 86–8; chapter 28, p. 292; and chapter 41, p. 438, where he is ready to swallow a huge bowl of tea. Mr Chou Ju-ch'ang relates this to accounts of the author's own unquenchable thirst (*Hung-lou-meng hsin-cheng*, p. 493).

[5] The Chinese plum (*mei-hua*) with its five-petalled flower blooms in winter and early spring. The plum, the bamboo and the pine were designated the 'Three Friends of Winter', symbolizing hardiness and purity. See H. L. Li, *The Garden Flowers of China*, pp. 48–56.

[6] Yüan Fu (279–327) exchanged his official cap of golden sable for wine, for which he was impeached, though later pardoned. See *Chin shu*, c. 49, p. 4ᵃ.

[7] In chapter 41, the nun Miao-yü makes a special brew of tea with snow gathered from plum blossoms five winters previously and sealed in a jar buried in the ground (pp. 437–8). For tea made with new snow, see note to 'The Peony Pavilion', *supra* (p. 287, n. 2).

It being then known that these verses were by a scion of the Jung branch of the Chia ducal house, aged but twelve or thirteen, the crowd of sycophants made copies of them and took every opportunity of reading them aloud and praising them. Flippant young men, attracted by the showy, amatory diction, wrote them on their fans and on the walls of their rooms, reciting them repeatedly with undiminished pleasure. It thus came about that, through intermediaries, strangers would approach Pao-yü with requests for a poem or a piece of calligraphy or an inscription on some picture, which he, being much flattered, willingly obliged, spending days on end upon such extra-mural activities.

Nevertheless, the very tranquillity of the Garden became a source of vexation. One day, Pao-yü suddenly felt out of sorts and declared himself dissatisfied with one thing after another, and wandered in and out of the place, moody and dispirited. For the Garden was inhabited mostly by young ladies in a state of primordial innocence, given over to childish candour and oblivious as yet of the proprieties, neither shunning one another while sitting or lying down nor intending by a smile or laugh more than the spontaneous expression of gladness or merriment. How indeed could they divine what went on in Pao-yü's mind? For his part, being continually in an ill humour, he would no longer remain within the Garden but loafed away his time outside its precinct, looking all the while blank and abstracted.

When the library page, Tea-Tobacco,[1] saw his young master thus pre-occupied, he took it upon himself to devise some means of diverting him. Tea-Tobacco considered one expedient after another, but Pao-yü seemed already familiar with them all, and tired of them all, and unlikely to be amused by any of them. There remained, however, a source of delight not yet known to Pao-yü, which having at last hit upon, Tea-Tobacco went straight to the booksellers and bought many

[1] Tea-Tobacco (Ming-yen), whose duty it is to accompany Pao-yü to school during the fitful periods of the latter's attendance, and generally to wait upon his young master in and about the library; see chapter 9, p. 98. He would be a few years older than Pao-yü. Tea-Tobacco is later named Firing Tea, i.e. Pei-ming (chapter 24, p. 244), for which the printed edition of 1792 adds the explanation that the change is made on account of Pao-yü's distaste for tobacco; see Tso-chia ch'u-pan-she edition, 1957, p. 242 and the relevant textual note.

volumes of stories old and new,[1] and the Intimate and Revealing Histories of Chao Fei-yen and her sister Ho-te,[2] and of the Empress Wu,[3] and of the beauteous Yang *kuei-fei*,[4] and the texts of numerous plays,[5] and showed them to Pao-yü, who never having read such books before, rejoiced exceedingly in the new discovery. Tea-Tobacco then warned Pao-yü not to take the books into the Garden;[6] for if they should be seen, the wrath that would descend upon him, Tea-Tobacco, would be great and terrible. Pao-yü, however, would not now hear of being deprived of their company. After prolonged debate with himself, he picked out a few sets of elegant diction and refined sentiment, and these he brought with him into Crab Red Court, where he hid them above his bed[7] and read them when no one was about. But the ones that were low and coarse he kept in the library outside.

It being now the middle of the third month,[8] Pao-yü took with him after breakfast one day a copy of *The Meeting with a Fay*, otherwise known as *The West Chamber*,[9] and sat on a stone

---

[1] Light reading was anathema to Confucian orthodoxy and regarded as a source of corruption, which it often was. *Ku-chin hsiao-chuo* ('Stories Old and New') was the title of Feng Meng-lung's first collection of colloquial stories of about 1621, and a general title to all his three collections (see General Introduction); but the reference here would seem to be to stories generally rather than specifically Feng's collections.

[2] *Chao Fei-yen wai-chuan*, in *Shuo-fu*, Commercial Press reprint of 1930, pp. 20ᵇ–25ᵇ. Chao Fei-yen and her equally beautiful sister Ho-te were ladies in the harem of Emperor Ch'eng-ti of Han Dynasty. In such 'intimate histories' (*wai-chuan*), the secrets of the harem are recounted with undisguised relish.

[3] A fictional narrative bearing the title *Tse-t'ien wai-shih* ('Intimate History of Wu Tse-t'ien') seems not to have survived; see Sun K'ai-ti's *Catalogue*, edition of 1957, p. 46. But the intrigues of the Empress Wu are part of traditional lore; see, e.g., Lin Yutang, *Lady Wu*, 1957.

[4] The celebrated favourite of Emperor Hsüan-tsung of T'ang Dynasty. *Yang T'ai-chen wai-chuan* ('Intimate History of Yang *kuei-fei*') is included in Lu Hsün, ed., *T'ang Sung ch'uan-ch'i chi*, 1956, c. 7, pp. 252–74.

[5] The mid-eighteenth century reader had access to almost the entire range of Chinese poetic drama.

[6] In spite of the fourth poem, 'Night in Winter', Tea-Tobacco is not allowed into the Garden.

[7] i.e. above his four-poster bed, concealed by the bed-curtains. Pao-yü reading a book while reclining on his lacquer bed with its crimson curtains is described in chapter 26, p. 266.

[8] About the middle of April.

[9] 'The West Chamber' (*Hsi-hsiang chi*), a series of five plays about two lovers, is based on Yüan Chen's *ch'uan-ch'i* tale, *Ying-ying chuan*, also known as *Hui chen chi* ('The Meeting with a Fay'), under which last title the plays are also known. Their author, Wang Shih-fu (active in the Ta-te reign, 1297–1307), is supposed to have written only four of the

under the peach tree by the bridge above Soaking Fragrance
Weir.[1] Opening the book, he read slowly from the beginning,
drinking in each line. When he reached the lines

'A fresh shower of red petals descending,
Ten thousand flakes of melancholy!'[2]

a sudden gust shook the boughs and robbed the peach tree of a
good half of its blossoms, the falling petals alighting all over
Pao-yü and the pages of his open book and the surrounding
earth. Pao-yü was on the point of dusting himself but, at the
thought of the flowers being scattered and trodden upon, he
desisted; instead he lifted the skirt of his robe and, moving
forward a few steps, emptied the blossoms into the pond. The
red petals floated and whirled on the water until, drifting with
the current, they disappeared down the weir. Returning to the
spot where he had sat before, he now noticed the blossoms on
the ground, and when he paused to consider what to do with
them, a voice from behind called to him—'And what business
brings *you* here?'

Pao-yü turned round: it was Tai-yü, who came up, shouldering a small hoe, from which hung a dainty silk bag, and holding
a besom in her hand. Pao-yü shouted with joy: 'Well met! The
very thing I wanted! Come and sweep up the blossoms so that
we may throw them into the pond! I have already thrown a
whole lot in.' Tai-yü, however, said, 'It would be a pity to do
that! The water is clear enough here, but once it leaves the
Garden and flows through the crowded part of the town, it will
be polluted and the poor blossoms themselves outraged. Over
there, in that corner, I have prepared a tomb for the flowers.
I shall sweep up these petals and put them in my silk bag and
consign the whole to earth so that the flowers may return to
dust, a clean and proper end for them.' Struck by the idea,[3]
Pao-yü was in transports; he agreed eagerly and then added:

plays, the fifth being attributed to Kuan Han-ch'ing (see *supra* 'A Dream
of Butterflies'). Thus Tai-yü is said to have finished the book when she
reaches the end of the sixteenth act, i.e. the end of the fourth play.
[1] The bridge is directly above Soaking Fragrance Weir, below which the
stream flows into a river outside the garden; see chapter 17, p. 170.
[2] *Hsi-hsiang chi*, II, i, 'Hun chiang lung' (ed. Wang Chi-ssu, 1954, p.
50). Only the first line is quoted in the original, but the full force of the
allusion is lost without the second line (itself taken from a poem by Tu
Fu), which has therefore been supplied in the translation.
[3] The sanctity of earth does not readily occur to Pao-yü, who places his
trust in the purity of water. For the symbolism of earth and water, see
Introduction.

'Let me put down my book first. I can then help you to gather them up.' Tai-yü asked: 'What book?' At the recollection of which, Pao-yü tried hastily to conceal the book he had been reading and stammered: 'Ah, well, only *The Doctrine of the Mean* and *The Great Learning*.[1] Why, what else could it be?' Tai-yü laughed, saying, 'I know your tricks! Now surrender that book at once!' Pao-yü then said sheepishly, 'Dearest cousin! It's not that I am afraid of your seeing the book, but don't—for heaven's sake!—tell anyone. In truth, its style is inimitable! I wager you'll be forgetting your meals when you're reading it.' And with that he handed over the text of the plays.

Tai-yü laid down her gardening tools and took the book. Reading from the beginning, she became more and more absorbed in it as she went on, so that within a short while she had read through all the sixteen scenes.[2] Being herself enthralled by its arresting tropes and frothy eloquence, she laid the book aside and, looking vacant and pensive, repeated in her mind many of its lines and phrases. Pao-yü ventured to smile; he asked, 'Did you like it, cousin?' And when Tai-yü returned his smile and said, 'Yes, I really have enjoyed it', Pao-yü suddenly giggled and started to quote from the plays:[3] ' "The melancholy and sickly lover"—*that* I am assuredly! And yours —yours, "the face that overthrew cities and kingdoms"!' Tai-yü instantly flushed, her cheeks, neck and ears turning a furious crimson; she frowned, then half raised her eyebrows;[4] her sparkling eyes narrowed to two slits, then opened wide again in a disdainful stare: her exquisite features were now the picture of anger and reproach. Pointing her finger accusingly at Pao-yü, she exclaimed: 'How dare you! It's death that you deserve for this! Foisting lewd verses upon me and using such

[1] Forming, with *The Analects* and *The Book of Mencius*, the 'Four Books' studied by every schoolboy.
[2] Strictly speaking, sixteen acts (*che*). The term 'scene' (*ch'ü*) is taken over from the Southern drama, and the four plays regarded as one long play. See also note above.
[3] *Hsi-hsiang chi*, I. iv. 'Yen-erh lo' (Wang edition, p. 41). The lines read:
  'How could I, the melancholy and sickly lover,
    Match up to her face that overthrew cities and kingdoms?'
[4] Tai-yü is noted for her frown, which is regarded as a sign of her poor health and for which she is nicknamed 'Miss Eyebrows' (P'in-erh; P'in-ch'ing; etc.). See chapter 3, pp. 32–3; also chapter 8, p. 88; chapter 26, p. 273; title of chapter 67; and *passim*. Here Pao-yü has already had more than his share of her smiles and laughter.

rude language too! What an affront! I'll tell my uncle and aunt.'

At the word 'affront' two red rings showed round her eyes, and she turned abruptly to go. Pao-yü started up in a panic and barred her way, pleading: 'Forgive me this once, dearest cousin! I was at fault in giving utterance to such absurdities, but if I really had intended any affront, then let me fall into the pond tomorrow and be swallowed by a monstrous turtle, and so be re-born as a large turtle myself that I might bear the stone tablet on your tomb[1] when one day you die, the lady of some great Minister or other!' This grotesque protestation caused Tai-yü to burst out laughing again. Hurriedly rubbing her eyes, she cried triumphantly: 'That scared the daylight out of you, didn't it? I won't stand any more nonsense from you :

    "Tut! A weak sapling—

    A spearhead of tinfoil—that you are!" '[2]

The allusion did not escape Pao-yü, who broke into hilarious laughter, saying, 'What about yourself then? I'll go and tell on you too!' Tai-yü, however, refused to be put out. She answered playfully: 'But it did come out of *your* book. If—like the prodigy you are—you can memorize and recite whole essays after a single reading, will you not allow that I may be able to take in ten lines at a glance?'

Pao-yü now put away the book and, with a happy grin, declared: 'To our task! Let us bury the flowers and forget the other part.' So the two of them swept up the fallen petals, which[1] they placed in the silk bag and solemnly deposited in a hollow in the earth. When finally they had covered up the hollow with a tiny mound,[3] Bombarding Scent rushed up and

---

[1] Stone steles often had for their pedestal the figure of a tortoise; 'turtle' and 'tortoise' are words of abuse which readily occur in oaths. Pao-yü's momentary fancy of himself as a stone tortoise at Tai-yü's tomb is, however, the foreboding of an unhappy end for both.

[2] *Hsi-hsiang chi*, IV. ii. 'Hsiao t'ao hung' (Wang edition, p. 153), where the maidservant Hung-niang taunts the scholar Chang with his cowardice, the reference in the first line being to *The Analects*, IX. 21: '... the blade springs, but the plant does not go on to flower' (Legge). In teasing Pao-yü, who stands in terror of his father, Tai-yü slightly misquotes the lines, which occur in the fourth play, i.e. towards the end of the book: hence her claim to great speed in reading, to make clear that she was not previously acquainted with 'The West Chamber' but has only just read the lines.

[3] 'Which they placed ... tiny mound' is the translator's own version. The original merely reads: 'So the two swept up the fallen petals, and just when they had buried them, Bombarding Scent . . .'.

said reproachfully to Pao-yü: 'Here of all places! As if I haven't looked all over the Garden for you! The cousins have gone across to ask after your uncle, the Duke,[1] who is indisposed, and the old mistress has ordered you to go, too. Come back now for a change of clothes.' Pao-yü thereupon picked up his book and, having excused himself to Tai-yü, returned with Bombarding Scent to Crab Red Court to dress for the visit to his uncle, which forms no part of our story.

Being now left alone and having heard that the female cousins were all away, Tai-yü turned her steps sadly towards the Hermitage. As she reached the corner of Pear Courtyard, from across the wall came the sweet notes of pipes, now loud, now muted, blending with the melodious voices of singers, and it occurred to her that the troupe of twelve girls from Soochow were rehearsing the airs of their Southern repertory.[2] Only, Tai-yü had never cared much for the Southern drama and, paying no regard to the music, she walked on.[3] But borne by the breezes, two lines of a song assailed her ears, each word falling clear and distinct:

'Gay purple and exquisite red abloom everywhere,

But all abandoned to a dried-up well and crumbled walls.'[4]

The words filled Tai-yü with a deep melancholy and longing. She stopped and, inclining her head, listened intently. The song now went:

'That glorious moments amidst this splendid scene

should enshroud despair!

In whose courtyard do hearts still rejoice in the present?'

These last two lines caused her to sigh and nod inadvertently in agreement. She thought to herself: 'It is true, then, that one may come across fine verse even in the theatre, but I suppose

[1] The Duke is Chia She, elder brother to Secretary Chia, who lives in a separate part of the Jung residence, entered through its own street gate (chapter 3, p. 28). Being neither learned nor a man of affairs, he is content with a role secondary to his more ambitious younger brother.

[2] The twelve girls were brought to the capital from Soochow to give musical and dramatic performances on the occasion of the Queen's visit. They are appropriately housed in Pear Courtyard adjoining the Garden, Emperor Hsüan-tsung of T'ang having trained his three hundred musicians in a pear orchard (chapter 16, p. 157; chapter 17, p. 174).

[3] Tai-yü's native place is Soochow (chapter 2, p. 15) and, in spite of her lack of interest, her ear would be attuned to Southern melodies. For Southern drama, see General Introduction.

[4] The song is from *Mou-tan t'ing*, scene 10; it is sung by the heroine, Fair Bride; see 'The Peony Pavilion', *supra*, p. 295.

most people simply follow the action and do not pause to savour the language.'

The next moment, however, she blamed herself for letting her mind wander instead of attending to the song. And when she listened again, she heard:

'Because of your flower-like beauty
    And tender years like a rushing stream,'[1]

and almost trembled with excitement. She then heard the lines that followed:

'I sought you in each nook and corner
    But find you dejected in your chamber.'

Being now quite overcome with emotion, she could hardly remain on her feet but sank on to a rock to brood over the words,

'Because of your flower-like beauty
    And tender years like a rushing stream,'

alert to their each nuance and suggestion. Suddenly she recalled a line she had read in the T'ang poets only the other day:

'Faded blossoms borne on a plaintive stream: lovelorn both';[2]

and also from among the *tz'u* compositions:

'The water rushing, the blossoms falling: Spring is gone forever!
    Alas, heaven above and man's despair!'[3]

and the lines, too, she had just read in *The West Chamber*:

'The stream speckled with red petals falling,
    Each speck a grain of sorrow.'[4]

Buoyed up from the depths of memory, all these lines floated in her mind, juxtaposed as in some conspiracy. She pondered over each passage and her heart was touched to the quick; her crowding fancies raced one another; and tears dropped from her eyes. While Tai-yü was thus enveloped in her thoughts, she felt a sudden pat on her back, and when she turned to look . . .

---

[1] *Mou-tan t'ing*, scene 10; sung by the hero, Willow. The lines are here rendered literally to suit the context (cf. 'The Peony Pavilion', p. 298).
[2] From Ts'ui T'u (late ninth century), 'Ch'un hsi' ('Evening in Spring'), *Ch'üan T'ang shih*, c. 679; vol. x, p. 7783.
[3] Being the last two lines of Li Yü, 'Lang t'ao sha', *Ch'üan T'ang shih*, c. 889, Tz'u Section 1; vol. xii, p. 10046. Li Yü (937–78) was the last ruler of the Southern T'ang kingdom and the poem, written after he was deposed by the Sung in 976, contrasts his state of captivity with his regal past. The two concluding lines, which point the contrast, lend themselves to a variety of interpretations. An alternative version reads:
    'The water rushing, the blossoms falling—gone for ever!
    Alas, heaven above and man's despair!'
See, e.g., 'Lang t'ao sha ling', *Nan-T'ang erh-chu tz'u*, Ssu-pu pei-yao ed., p. 6b.   [4] *Hsi-hsiang chi*, I. Introductory scene (Wang edition, p. 2).

This is followed by: 'but as to who it was that she saw, it shall be told in the next chapter' and two lines of verse which end chapter 23.

Translator's Note on the Cousins' Dwellings

The style of each house or bungalow with its courtyard and interior decoration is a clue to the character of the inhabitant, whose name (itself an indication of personality in this subtle work) and distinctive traits are suggested in numerous details. Thus Tai-yü, whose surname is Lin (Forest or Grove), resides in a bamboo grove; and the house of Pao-ch'ai, surnamed Hsüeh, of which Snow is a homophone, is compared to a snow cave. Pao-yü, whose unashamed addiction to rouge and predilection for all things red (see chapter 19, p. 195) are symbols of his attachment to the mundane world with all its cares (i.e. *hung-ch'en*, red dust), is housed in Crab Red Court. Of the seven different dwellings, the more distinctive are described twice, as they impress themselves upon the unpoetic, though by no means obtuse, Secretary Chia during his tour of inspection in chapter 17 (supplemented by some further information in the account of Queen Yüan-ch'un's visit in chapter 18), and as seen through the staring eyes of the old peasant woman, Liu Lao-lao, in chapter 40 and 41:

Hsiao-Hsiang Hermitage, i.e. Hsiao-Hsiang kuan. The Hsiao and the Hsiang, two rivers in Hunan Province, are the subject of numerous misty landscapes by painters. The bamboo grown along the Hsiang belongs to a speckled variety known as the *Hsiang-fei* (Hsiang Queens) bamboo, the speckles being the stains of tears shed by the two Queens of Hsiang, who later became goddesses, upon the death of the Emperor Shun; on account of which allusion, Tai-yü is much teased by the others (chapter 37, p. 385). Her cottage consists of three small, neatly furnished rooms with a verandah, shaded by hundreds of bamboos. It is approached by a winding pebble path over ground covered with moss. A stream runs through the back courtyard into the bamboo grove in front. As clues to her personality, we may note: the name Hsiao-Hsiang with its pictorial and mythological associations, suggestive of an ethereal inhabitant but also tears of grief; bamboo grove with its atmosphere of seclusion and other-worldliness; narrow, winding path, reflecting a narrow introverted outlook; gushing stream, sign of a lively mind (see, e.g., *The Analects*, VI. 21: 'The wise find pleasure in water; the virtuous find pleasure in hills'). See chapter 17, p. 164; chapter 18, p. 180; chapter 40, p. 421; also chapter 26, p. 268.

Crab Red Court, i.e. I hung yüan (Delightful Red Court), is entered through a moon-shaped rose trellis leading into a courtyard with some palms, a small rockery, and a large crab-apple tree, 'transplanted from the Women's Kingdom'!! (pp. 170–1). The courtyard is enclosed on three sides by covered walks, Pao-yü's apartments forming the remaining side. The five rooms are a maze of exquisitely carved wooden shelves and partitions, all of which are filled with antiques and curios. A mirror-door, 'an imported contraption' (p. 441), which opens into Pao-yü's bedroom but also leads to the back courtyard, is calculated to mislead the casual visitor and utterly confuses Secretary Chia himself as well as the beldam, Liu Lao-lao. As clues to Pao-yü's personality may be noted: name of courtyard, deriving from red crab-apple blossoms and echoing title of the novel; ornate elegance; labyrinthian interior, reflecting tortuousness of thought and tangled feelings, the whole dwelling suggesting an artfully contrived trap for the Stone's original nature; mirror on door with spring, i.e. illusion leading to sudden final release. (Chapter 17, pp. 170–

172; chapter 41, pp. 440–2; also chapter 26, pp. 265–6).

Aromatic Herb Rockery, i.e. Heng wu yüan. Pao-ch'ai's suite of five rooms with awnings and a verandah is hidden behind a tall rockery overgrown with aromatic creeping herbs and vines, which scent the air. (In chapter 8, pp. 85–6, prior to the building of the Garden, Pao-yü detects an unusual fragrance about Pao-ch'ai, caused by a 'fragrance pill' which she has been taking.) The rooms are excessively bare, with for decoration only a vase of the coarser Ting ware holding a few chrysanthemums. The fragrance denotes purity of character; the unadorned interior, thrift and the plainer feminine virtues. But the over-all plainness and whiteness, which the Dowager comments unfavourably upon (pp. 428–9), forebode a sad ending, the rocks and cave-like apartments being further reminiscent of a tomb. (Chapter 17, p. 168; chapter 40, pp. 428–9).

Autumn's Breath Studio, i.e. Ch'iu shuang chai, where T'an-ch'un lives, is probably a wing of Morning Green Hall (Hsiao ts'ui t'ang), one of several small banqueting halls in the Garden. The usual three-roomed division having been dispensed with, the entire wing is made into a studio and bedroom combined, in the middle of which stands a large marble-topped table with 'a forest of writing and painting brushes'. The decorations include a large bronze cauldron (*ting*) and a turquoise vase of Ju ware of prodigious size, and also an ink landscape by the Sung artist Mi Fei in the blotchy manner, flanked by a couplet written bold and clear by the T'ang calligrapher, Yen Chen-ch'ing. Thus the impressions conveyed are: spaciousness; candour; force of character. (Chapter 40, pp. 424–7).

Tapestry Tower, i.e. Chui chin ko, forms the east flank of the Hall of Pomp and State (Ta kuan lou). The tower itself is used as a storehouse for tables, chairs, lanterns, screens, boats, oars, etc., the rooms below being presumably occupied by Ying-ch'un but later serving as a banqueting hall. (Chapter 18, p. 180; chapter 40, pp. 429–30). In chapter 37, p. 386, Ying-ch'un is mentioned as staying at Water-chestnut Island (Tzu ling chou), which would be near the pond but is not described.

Sweet Paddy Village, i.e. Tao hsiang ts'un, inhabited by the widowed sister-in-law, Li Wan, consists of some straw huts surrounded by a low mud wall (upon which, during the Queen's visit, rice stalks were laid to suggest paddy fields in the distance) and complete with apricot and mulberry trees, a village well, hedges, and rows of vegetables, the whole situated in an artificial valley. Within the huts, the beds are wooden and the windows covered by paper instead of silk gauze as in all the other buildings. It is thus a dwelling for someone truly homely and contrite, untouched by the surrounding pomp and state. (Chapter 17, pp. 165–7).

Smartweed Bank Loggia, i.e. Liao feng hsien (Smartweed Breeze Porch) is presumably near Smartweed Bank, which is below a waterfall (Chapter 17, pp. 167–8; chapter 18, p. 180). It is not described; nor is Lotus Root Pavilion (Ou hsiang hsieh), which Hsi-ch'un later inhabits (chapter 37, p. 386).

Li Ju-chen

The Women's Kingdom

'The Women's Kingdom' is taken from chapters 32–37 of *Ching hua yüan*[1] ('Romance of the Flowers in the Mirror'), an inimitable blend of mythology and adventure story, fantasy and allegory, satire and straight instruction, throughout informed with learning and sustained by wit, with an admixture of games and puzzles for the unhurried reader. The book opens with a quotation from the Grand Instructess Ts'ao[2] about the four aspects of feminine conduct—virtue, speech, appearance and accomplishment—in justification of its professed aim, the praise of womanhood (chapter 1, p. 1). But its three chief characters are, in fact, men: the inspired and resourceful T'ang Ao (Wandering Chinese), scholar; the ingenuous and down-to-earth Lin Chih-yang (Ocean-faring Lin), merchant; and the wise and experienced Tuo Chiu-kung (Old Man long at the Helm), mariner. It is the merchant Lin who, in his sales talk, provides us with an alternative title, as well as a summary, of the book. In chapter 23, while hawking his wares in the Nation of Pedants, the unstudious Lin so far forgets himself as to brag of his wide reading to a group of earnest students; he mentions *Lao Tzu* ('The Old Philosopher') and, without thinking, adds—*Shao Tzu* ('The Young Philosopher'). Being then pressed for exact information about the origin, period, authorship and contents of this hitherto unknown text, Lin resorts to fabrication:

'The book *Shao Tzu* was born in a peaceful reign of our

[1] References are to the Tso-chia ch'u-pan she edition of *Ching hua yüan* of 1955, which has been used for the translation, though I have not felt myself bound by the punctuation or annotation of the editors. The book is in 100 chapters.

[2] Pan Chao, sister of the historian Pan Ku (A.D. 32–92) and wife of Ts'ao Shou. She was summoned to the palace to teach the Empress and other court ladies; hence her title. Her treatise *Nü chieh* ('Instruction for Women') contains a section on feminine conduct with great emphasis on domesticity. See *Hou Han shu*, c. 84, pp. 2784–92.

present Dynasty; it came from the pen of a graduate in our Celestial Land descended of the same Lao Tzu,[1] the old philosopher, who in his *Tao te ching* had written of the ineffable wonders of the void. But this *Shao Tzu*, or The Young Philosopher, while setting out to provide entertainment, has for its hidden purpose exhortation of men to reform, even through many veiled hints and suggestions.

'For in this book are to be found the teachings of the Hundred Schools; a gallery of men and women; a whole collection of flowers and birds; the arts of calligraphy and painting, of music, and of chess; the sciences of medicine, of divination and astrology, of phonology and phonetics, of arithmetic and computation. It further contains all manners of riddles, an extended drinking game,[2] the Double Six,[3] cards, archery, football, a plant competition,[4] 'arrows and pot',[5] and a hundred other pastimes, so diverting as to chase away the languor of sleep even on the hottest afternoon and so mirthful as to cause much spurting out of rice if recounted at the dinner table. . . .' (p. 165).

The story is set in the twenty-one years' reign (684–705) of the usurping Empress Wu which interrupted the continuity

[1] According to tradition, Lao Tzu was Li Erh (*Shih chi*, c. 63) and, therefore, of the same clan as our author, Li Ju-chen.

[2] *Chiu-ling*, in which each participant makes up a rhyme or quotes an apt saying, in accordance with rules devised by a leader, before drinking himself or proposing a toast; the tardy or poor speaker is also made to drink, but as a penalty. As played in *Ching hua yüan*, the game requires of each player that he name an object or specialized term in some specified category (horticulture, ornithology, entomology, astronomy, etc. etc.) in two syllables showing either alliteration or assonance, and to follow it up with a relevant quotation from an ancient text. Upon this game, which lasts from chapter 82 to chapter 94, the author lavished so much attention that, when his book was first completed, he held back the manuscript to revise the quotations used and eventually had each of the hundred players quoting from a different ancient text; see Sun Chia-hsün, 'More about the Origin of *Ching hua yüan*', in *Hsüeh-shu*, vol. 3 (1940), pp. 157–64, in which a letter from the author Li Ju-chen to Hsü Ch'iao-lin is quoted on p. 162. (The letter is also quoted in K'ung Ling-ching, *Chung-kuo hsiao-shuo shih-liao*, revised edition, 1957, pp. 216–17).

[3] See note to 'The Shrew', *supra*; some of the rules of the game are discussed in *Ching hua yüan*, chapter 74.

[4] See note to 'A Burial Mound for Flowers', *supra*. In *Ching hua yüan*, chapter 77, this game becomes a purely verbal contest, the participants citing the aptest plant names in repartee without actually producing the plant or flower.

[5] Part of an ancient drinking ceremony (see Legge, *Li Ki*, Book xxxvii, 'Thau Hu, or the Game of Pitch-pot'); the game—pitching arrows into a pot—is played in *Ching hua yüan*, chapter 74.

of the great T'ang dynasty—an era of the ascendancy of women, or rather of one woman.[1] Being of indomitable will, the Empress commanded the hundred flowers in the Imperial Shang-lin Park to blossom on a winter's day:[2] they obeyed, thus disrupting the harmony of the seasons, and for their pains the hundred fairies in charge of the flowers were banished from heaven, to be born as girls in families all over the empire and even in lands across the seas (chapters 3–6; chapters 1 and 2 take place in heaven). T'ang Ao, a graduate recently deprived of his hard won title of *t'an-hua* (literally, Seeker of Flowers) because of his earlier association with the Empress's political enemies, decides to join his brother-in-law, Lin Chih-yang, on a voyage; being advised by a temple god in a dream to search for twelve famous flowers and transplant them back to China, T'ang Ao sets off armed with flower pots, and for merchandise tons of cast iron 'useful as ballast should they prove unsaleable', to the amusement and disgust of the commercially astute Lin (chapters 7–8).

The missing flowers turn out to be young ladies[3] in distress (Lien Chin-feng, caught in a net while diving for sea slugs, chapter 13; Ssu-t'u Wu-erh, being sold at the market, chapter 24; Yao Chih-hsing, who kept silkworms and was waylaid by a murderous cotton merchant, and her companion Hsüeh Heng-hsiang, chapter 28; the 'Crown Prince' of the Women's Kingdom, chapters 37–8), or living in exile (the huntresses Lo Hung-ch'ü and Wei Tzu-ying, chapters 10 and 21; Hsü Li-yung, of unerring marksmanship, chapter 26; Yin Hung-yü, whose father, the former Censor Yin and patron to T'ang Ao, had taken to the ways of the Black Legged Country and become a fisherman, chapter 15), or ill (Chih Lan-yin, Orchid Voice, daughter of the interpreter of the Forked Tongue Country, chapter 30), or afire with scholastic ambition (Hung-

[1] For a summary of the story with a slightly different emphasis, see my *Allegory and Courtesy in Spenser*, 1955, part I 'The Storming of the Passes of the Four Vices'. Lin Tai-yi's translation, *Flowers in the Mirror*, 1965, is in the nature of a 'digest'.

[2] The blossoming of the flowers by command is derived from *Ch'üan T'ang shih-hua* (attributed to Yu Mou), c. 1, 'Empress Wu', pp. 10ᵃ–10ᵇ, in Ho Wen-huan (ed.) *Li-tai shih-hua*, 1770. The event is supposed to have occurred in the winter of 691–2.

[3] As young women they have names taken from flowers and trees, but these show no correspondence to their former functions as fairies of the flowers. A full list of the reincarnated flowers is given in chapter 48.

hung and T'ing-t'ing of the Black Teeth Country, chapters 18–19, 51–3), who seek sanctuary or kinsfolk or cure or examination success in the Middle Kingdom, and who board their ship at various stages.

In the meantime the Empress has instituted a special examination for women (chapters 41–2), and the reunion of the hundred flowers at the examination and subsequent celebrations is the occasion of endless disputations, learned notes and queries, anecdotes and jokes, as well as many riddles, quizzes and games (chapter 41–95). The book ends with a sustained allegory: the heroines and their brothers and husbands take by storm four perilous passes—of Wine, Lust, Covetousness and Anger—and their overcoming of the Vices leads to the dethronement of the usurping Empress (chapters 96–100).

While on their voyage (chapters 8–40), T'ang Ao and Lin and their coxswain Tuo visit many strange kingdoms, in various degrees also allegorical. Thus the travellers find complaisance to be the first rule of conduct in the Gentlemen's Country (chapters 11–12); and in the Country of Noble Presence, they see men walking on coloured clouds, the colour indicating the state of each man's moral health (chapters 13–14). In the Land of the Busy, all bustle and fidget whether going about their business or even sitting down: no time may be spared for tilling the soil or reaping the harvest or cooking—for nourishment there is an abundance of fruit (chapter 14). In the inhabitants of the Country of the Entrail-less, the digestive tract is missing, and consequently they re-use excrement for food (chapter 14); but the neighbouring Nation of Gluttons are shown to have dogs' heads (chapters 14–15). And in the Hairy Country, inhabited by misers, no man parts with so much as a single hair of his own to benefit the community (chapter 15).

The Heirless Nation are without sex: instead of procreating, they die and re-live in cycles, so that 'dying was merely sleeping, and living came to be thought of as dreaming' (p. 107, chapter 16). And in the Land of Ranging Vision, each man has but a single eye—located on one of his hands, which he holds out in all directions (chapter 16). In the Black Teeth Country, the women neglect their appearance to cultivate the mind and the merchant Lin finds no demand for his cosmetics (chapters 16–18). The travellers also visit the Lands of Pygmies, a foot in height and comparably mean (chapter 19), and Giants, eighty feet tall (chapter 20), and Cube-shaped Men, absolute 'squares' (chapter 20). And in the White Country, they find the soil limy, the hills chalky, the fields white with the flowers of buckwheat, and the inhabitants white-skinned and clad in white (chapters 21–2).

While approaching the Nation of Pedants, T'ang Ao detects a sourness in the air even on the high seas (p. 158): arriving there, they mistake the local wine for vinegar (p. 166; chapters 22–3). In the Double-faced Country, each person has a hidden face, evil and bestial in expression, with a foul mouth and a knife-like tongue (chapters 25–6). In the Land of Flames, ape-men spout flames at the travellers: Lin's beard catches fire and he escapes smooth-chinned (p. 185, chapter 26). The Long-armed are a nation of grabbers (chapter 27), and the Swollen-headed feed on flattery and have heads the same length as the rest of the body (chapter 27). Next come the Country of Snouts and the Nation of Worriers (chapter 27). In the Forked Tongue Country, the inhabitants are highly musical and speak a language more difficult than any other: they excel in phonetics, which knowledge they withhold from foreign visitors (chapters 28–31). And in the Country of Surpassing Intelligence, men are hoary-headed before they reach the age of thirty (chapters 31–2).

After their adventures in the Women's Kingdom (chapters 32–7), the travellers reach the Land of the Yellow Emperor's Descendants (Hsien-yüan kuo) in time to attend the Snake-emperor's thousandth birthday celebrations: they find him seated on his throne in a robe of Imperial yellow, his snake tail coiled round his golden crown (chapters 38–9). Finally, a sudden gale carries them to an enchanted island in the furthest part of the southern seas, Little P'eng-lai, where T'ang Ao, realizing that his was no accidental intrusion into this domain of the gods, leaves his companions and disappears into the mountains to attain an immortal existence (chapters 39–40). When his daughter, Kuei-ch'en, the reincarnation of the fairy in charge of *all* the flowers, learns of this, she sets out on a later voyage with her uncle Lin in search of him; but she, too, soon grows aware of her own divine nature and dutifully turns back to assemble her hundred flowers (chapters 43–50): only after fulfilling her earthly obligations does she return to the island to join her father among the immortals (chapters 94–5).

The names of the kingdoms and of the curious animals and birds seen by the travellers are derived from *Shan-hai ching* and other mythological works[1] as well as early geographical accounts, e.g. in the Dynastic Histories. For the author Li Ju-chen[2] (c. 1763–1830) was not only versed in mythology, but also in most branches of traditional lore. His native place was Ta-hsing, near Peking, but he spent the greater part of his life in Kiangsu Province, living mostly with his older brother, Li Ju-huang, who was Salt Receiver at Pan-p'u (Kwanyun) from 1783 to 1799. In Pan-p'u, which was administratively part of Hai-chou, the young Li found a teacher in Ling T'ing-k'an (1757–1809), an outstanding scholar noted for his studies in ritual, musicology and phonology, and friends in the Hsü brothers, Hsü Ch'iao-lin and Hsü Kuei-lin, both phonologists, whose sister he married. Li himself became accomplished in phonology and, being conversant with the living speech in both the north and the south, wrote in 1805 *Yin chien*, a pioneering work in phonetics, which was printed in 1810. In 1803, Li's brother was appointed Salt Receiver at Ts'ao-yen-ch'ang, fifty miles or so north-east of Yangchow, and there, too, Li visited him (certainly in 1804), probably spending considerable periods also in Yangchow, where our author would have access to one of the Imperial Collections of Books (*Ssu-k'u ch'üan-shu*). (In the concluding chapter of *Ching hua yüan*, he claims to have read abstruse treatises in the Imperial Library, p. 771.)

Li's protracted stay in Pan-p'u—from 1782 to 1801, almost twenty of his best years, and later also[3]—probably contributed

---

[1] See, e.g., Ch'ien Ching-fang, *Hsiao-shuo ts'ung-k'ao*, 1912, section on *Ching hua yüan* (Ku-tien reprint, pp. 53–6), where the various sources are traced, but not exhaustively. *Shan hai ching*, a collection of myths ranging from perhaps the fifth to the second century B.C. edited by Kuo P'u (A.D. 276–324), gives only a brief entry of each name or place.

[2] The materials for a study of Li Ju-chen are scanty and have not so far been collected together, as have the materials for the authors of *Ju-lin wai-shih* and *Hung-lou meng*. I have used Hu Shih's *Introduction* to *Ching hua yüan* (*Hu Shih wen-ts'un*, edition of 1953, vol. 2, pp. 400–33), supplemented by the valuable corrections of Sun Chia-hsün (*Hu Shih wen-ts'un*, vol. 3, pp. 580–8) and the additional information in Mr Sun's 'More about the Origin of *Ching hua yüan*', *Hsüeh-shu*, vol. 3 (1940), pp. 157–64. The biography by Tu Lien-che in A. W. Hummel, *Eminent Chinese of the Ch'ing Period*, 1944, pp. 472–3, and the *Introduction* to the Tso-chia edition of 1955 are reasonably accurate summaries of Li's life.

[3] In the Introduction to *Ch'ü-hai shih ts'un* (1831), a collection of poems by local poets no longer living, Hsü Ch'iao-lin felt it incumbent on him to explain that Li Ju-chen and three others mentioned by name, though long

as much to the plan of *Ching hua yüan* as his agglomerate learn-ing. The town is served by a Salt Transport Canal, which leads southward to the Grand Canal itself; northward, after a dozen or so miles, the Salt Canal joins the Ch'iang-wei (Rosa Multi-flora) River at its mouth and flows into the Yellow Sea. It was the centre of a flourishing salt industry, and the Salt Receiver's brother would be in daily contact with salt merchants and other traders, ship-owners and sailors, divers and fishermen. The proximity of the sea,[1] the sight of vessels, large and small, laden with merchandise, and, not least, sailors' yarns—all lent sub-stance to the accounts of fantastic lands and peoples in his read-ing in old books, thus giving rise to the idea of a new kind of story, about a journey by sea to strange countries with out-landish customs.[2] From models among those of his acquaint-ance in the town, it was easy enough to portray an old helms-man (Tuo) or an enterprising trader (Lin). As for the lofty scholar, there was no need to look beyond his own circle; in-deed he could have looked within himself: for T'ang Ao is shown as no ordinary mortal and his commanding stature, in-creasing with each divine herb he gathers from some deserted shore and swallows (chapter 9), is something remarkable, at times awesome. It is Li's interest in feminine welfare that remains a mystery.

In 1801, Li was himself appointed to a post in Honan Pro-vince, as Assistant Magistrate of one of the Counties where the Yellow River had flooded its banks. He seems to have felt elated, regarding the call as a challenge, and we find his brother-in-law, Hsü Ch'iao-lin, gently reminding him of his

resident in the Ch'ü-hai (i.e. Hai-chou) region, were not really local men and, on that ground, excluded. (The reference to Li as among the dead in 1831 has made it possible to date the year of his death as 1830.)

[1] The amount of sea traffic to and from Hai-chou and Pan-p'u in the early nineteenth century was probably small, being limited to private traders, but Hai-chou was already on the sea route for government ships carrying grain to the north in the Yüan and at different times in the Ming dynasty; see Wu Ch'i-hua, *Ming-tai hai-yün chi yün-ho ti yen-chiu*, 1961, p. 7 and map facing p. 348.

[2] Our author is anticipated to some extent by the Ming writer Lo Mou-teng (active 1598), whose narrative *San-pao t'ai-chien hsi-yang chi* ('Voyages of the Admiral Cheng Ho') is, however, devoted almost ex-clusively to the supernatural and the marvellous; the *hua-pen* story about the down-on-luck trader who eventually sold his mandarin oranges at an unheard-of profit and found on a deserted island a gigantic tortoise shell stuffed with large pearls in *P'ai-an ching-ch'i* (1628), c. 1, is also a clear precedent.

grave responsibilities, technological and magisterial, in a poem[1] that begins:

> No perfect scheme exists for taming the waters;
> Even Chia Jang[2] of Han knew only half the answers.
> With the Yellow River repeatedly changing its course,
> New methods must still be devised for flood control.

Such causes of flooding as silting and the rising of the river bed are spoken of, and the examples of P'an Chi-hsün (1521–95) and Chin Fu (1633–92), who had achieved signal success in water conservancy, are cited for Li's encouragement. It is further hinted that the problem of discipline among the men at work on the river, labourers numbering several hundred thousand who had lost their homes through successive inundations, could lead to trouble for an Assistant Magistrate as for higher authorities.

It emerges also from the poem that Li's father, Li Chieh-t'ing,[3] had worked for twenty years as a river engineer in the Huai basin, often wading knee-deep in mud; specifically, he had been engaged on the series of stone embankments, dikes and locks at Kao-chia-yen on Hungtse Lake in the year 1781, when they were inspected by the Manchu viceroy, A-kuei.[4] Li, Senior, had moreover written a treatise on water conservancy, *Ho-fang pi-yao*, not now preserved but doubtless treasured by the sons. Our author, therefore, may be presumed to have left for his post, well-equipped with advice and burning with ambition. For flood control is a symbol of good government to the Chinese scholar-official,[5] for whom the mythical Yü, tamer of floods, ranks as one of the sage-kings. The actual outbreaks of

---

[1] 'To Li Ju-chen on his appointment to an Assistant Magistracy in Honan', quoted by Sun Chia-hsün (*Hu Shih wen-ts'un*, vol. 3, pp. 583–4).
[2] Chia Jang, who at the end of the first century B.C. advocated dredging instead of building higher dikes; see *Han shu*, c. 29, pp. 1691–6. For P'an Chi-hsün, see *Ming shih*, c. 223; and Chin Fu, *Ch'ing shih*, Kuo-fang yen-chiu-yüan 1961, c. 280.
[3] Li Chieh-t'ing is not otherwise known, nor is his treatise elsewhere recorded.
[4] See *Ch'ing shih*, 1961, c. 319. Both P'an Chi-hsün and Chin Fu had worked on the dikes at Kao-chia-yen, where flooding frequently occurred as a result of the Yellow River overflowing into the Grand Canal; see Chu Hsieh, *Chung-kuo yüng-ho shih-liao hsüan-chi*, 1962, p. 148.
[5] The full implications of this are traced in an illuminating chapter (28f (4)), 'Engineering and Its Social Aspects in the Corpus of Legends', and in the conclusion to an ensuing chapter (f(6)) in Dr Joseph Needham's *Science and Civilisation in China*, vol. IV, part 3, to which I am indebted for orientation as well as specific points about water conservancy.

the Yellow River in Honan Province during Li's tenure of office seem not to have been serious, except in the autumn of 1803, when the collapse of the dike at Feng-ch'iu led to extensive flooding in the neighbouring provinces.[1] But by 1804 we already find Li on a visit to his brother at Ts'ao-yen-ch'ang in Kiangsu Province: after three years, his official career was terminated—he had seen, at first hand, something of river engineering and the legions of refugees at their toil on dike and embankment, but not had the chance of carrying out any 'new methods' he could devise. A year later, his book on phonetics was written.

In our story, the river causing widespread havoc year after year in the Women's Kingdom is a transparent reference to the Yellow River (Hwang-ho):

> Chinese history records more than 1,500 inundations in the last 3,000 years and twenty-six changes in course, nine of which were of a major nature. . . . The cost in human loss of life and suffering through the centuries has been enormous. The cost in material loss each year—loss of harvest, ruined fields, and so on—is staggering. Flood spells famine and disease. The river richly deserves the stigma attaching to its name 'China's Sorrow'.[2]

The tens of thousands of the homeless who surrounded the Palace on the wedding night, shouting and roaring in a state of revolutionary frenzy, are almost certainly drawn from his experience of mutinous crowds in the flooded areas. And T'ang Ao's plan for bringing the river under control—the more technical part of which has been omitted in the translation—is the remedy Li himself would have proposed for the afflictions of the Hwang-ho. The conversations between the Royal Brother-in-Law, Lord She, and T'ang Ao are reminiscent of the dialogue between the Director of River Administration, Chin Fu, and his counsellor, Ch'en Huang, as recorded (or reconstructed) by Chang Ai-sheng in *Ho-fang shu-yen*.[3] But, unlike the engineers of Li's time, who favoured the building of dikes as the chief measure, T'ang Ao is shown to be an adherent

---

[1] See *Ch'ing shih*, c. 127, p. 1551; Cheng Chao-ching, *Chung-kuo shui-li shih*, 1939, pp. 84–5.
[2] T. R. Tregear, *A Geography of China*, 1965, pp. 218–19.
[3] I have used the extracts from *Ho-fang shu-yen* in Chang Han-ying, *Li-tai chih-ho fang-lüeh shu-yao*, 1945, chapter 6, pp. 43–70. The life of Ch'en Huang is included with that of Chin Fu in *Ch'ing shih*, c. 280.

of the 'dredging' school, derived from the great Yü himself;[1] the strange spectacle of the ever rising river enclosed by dikes constantly being raised until they were almost like hills he describes as 'a bath tub placed on the ridge tiles'. And the key-word 'dredge' so impresses the nobleman She, that he becomes an immediate convert.

There was talk of a further post in Honan Province for Li in 1805, but this somehow failed to materialize, and it would be soon after the appearance of his treatise on phonetics in 1810 that Li, disappointed in his hopes of official advancement, began writing *Ching hua yüan*, in which the disillusioned T'ang Ao goes on a journey in quest of some better world. There seems little reason to doubt that much of it was written in Pan-p'u. The Hsü brothers followed the progress of the book with interest, occasionally contributing a riddle or perhaps a mathematical puzzle;[2] the younger brother, Hsü Kuei-lin, states explicitly in the Preface to one of his own literary compositions, that he is indebted for its main idea to Li's 'Four Passes' in *Ching hua yüan*[2] (being chapters 96–100). In a marginal note[3] in the opening chapter in early editions of *Ching hua yüan*, one of the commentators mentions that Hsü Ch'iao-lin was one of several responsible for the highlighting of subtleties in the text by the use of certain punctuation marks, viz. circles and dots, analogous to underlining or italicizing. Since the younger Hsü died in 1821,[2] it may be inferred that by 1820 the book was substantially in its present form. Li is likely to have continued revising and altering details until the actual printing in 1828:[4] a long Prefatory Poem[5] appearing in that edition describes the

---

[1] See 'Engineering and Its Social Aspects in the Corpus of Legends' in Needham, vol. IV, part 3, cited above.

[2] See Sun Chia-hsün's article, 'More about the Origin of *Ching hua yüan*', cited on p. 410, which unfortunately contains a number of inaccuracies. The Hsü brothers were both versatile men; Hsü Kuei-lin's *Hsi t'an ch'iao*, seemingly allegorical, also has the 'Four Passes'.

[3] In the edition of 1832 in Cambridge University Library, errors have crept into the names in this note, found on c. 1, p. 1[b]; misprints of the worst kind are usually found in marginal notes in Ming and Ch'ing editions of stories and novels.

[4] A certain letter about earlier arrangements for printing the book and even about a pirated edition, reported by Sun, is not quoted in full and not valid as evidence.

[5] The Prefatory Poem is by Sun Chi-ch'ang, a professed admirer of Li, who, in Sun's opinion, could have achieved outstanding success in any field but chose to spill out his life's blood in the writing of a novel, to which he devoted ten odd years.

author as in abject poverty and failing health, having laboured unceasingly at the book to the exclusion of all else. And congratulatory poems dating from 1829–30 speak of the man's 'twenty years' effort'. A brief spell of fame followed the publication. According to two other congratulatory poems,[1] Li won the acclaim of lords and princes in the capital, where, encouraged by the reception of his book, he must have returned, being originally from Peking. In the editions of 1832,[2] the congratulatory poems accompany a Preface by the publisher Mai Tap'eng dated the middle of the twelfth month of 1829, i.e. January 1830; but in 1831, the elder Hsü refers to our author as among the deceased.[3] Li would seem to have died in Peking, in 1830.

'The Women's Kingdom' has for its immediate precedent the 'Women's Country' visited by the monk Tripitaka and his disciples in the Ming (sixteenth century) narrative work, *Hsi yu chi*, chapter 54, in which the Queen, never having seen a man before, tries to detain the monk and make him her consort. In our story, allusion is made to this episode on the pretext that the historical Tripitaka pre-dates the Empress Wu by half a century, and indeed a number of features seems to have been borrowed from it: the stay at the government hostel, the lucky omen, the too ardent queen, and the male visitor's bashfulness and dread of the impending wedding. The episode occurs even in the earliest known version of the story of Tripitaka's quest, *Ta T'ang San-tsang fa-shih ch'ü-ching chi*,[4] dating from the thirteenth century, and is ultimately derived from the T'ang monk's own account in the record of his travels, *Ta T'ang hsi-yü chi* (seventh century):

[1] One of the two congratulatory poems is also by Sun Chi-ch'ang, who after dwelling in his Prefatory Poem upon the poverty and neglect suffered by Li, now rejoices in his sudden renown.
[2] In the Chi-ch'eng-t'ang edition in Cambridge University Library, the Congratulatory Poems precede Mai's and the illustrator's Prefaces and the illustrations; in the Chieh-tzu-yüan edition in the British Museum, the Poems follow the Prefaces and illustrations. Both editions bear the date 1832; their illustrations—by the same artist—are printed from different blocks.
[3] See p. 410, n. 3.
[4] Also known as *Ta T'ang San-tsang ch'ü-ching shih-hua*, under which title a much fuller fragment is preserved, reprinted by Ku-tien 1954; see episode 10, pp. 20–4. For information on the date of this work and the relation between the two printed fragments, see G. Dudbridge, *The Hsi-yu chi: A Study of Antecedents to the Sixteenth Century Chinese Novel*, 1970, pp. 25–9.

To the south-west of Fo-lin [generally supposed to be Byzantium], in an island of the sea, is the kingdom of the western women: here there are only women, with no men; they possess a large quantity of gems and precious stones, which they exchange in Fo-lin. Therefore the king of Fo-lin sends certain men to live with them for a time. If they should have male children, they are not allowed to bring them up.[1]

But in our story, the 'Women's Kingdom' is of a different sort, as the old coxswain points out (p. 421) ; it is more akin to the Country of Eastern Women, as reported by the T'ang monk:

> . . . in the midst of [the great Snowy Mountains] is the country called Su-fa-la-na-kiu-ta-lo (Suvarnagôtra). From this country comes a superior sort of gold, and hence the name. It is extended from east to west, and contracted from north to south. It is the same as the country of the 'eastern women'. For ages a woman has been the ruler, and so it is called the *kingdom of the women*. The husband of the reigning woman is called king, but he knows nothing about the affairs of the state. The men manage the wars and sow the land, and that is all.[2]

Similar, but somewhat fuller, accounts of the 'Eastern Women' may be found in both the official T'ang histories,[3] which describe a kingdom of eighty cities and towns with multi-storied houses, ruled by a female king, aided by a female chief minister and holding court every five days; the palace attendants, who numbered several hundred, were female, and female officials transmitted orders from the nine-storied buildings in the palace to male officials, who attended to business outside. By custom, men were held inferior, women being the superior sex: children took their surname from the mother. Women of rank had male concubines, who wore their hair long and painted their faces green and who only tilled the land and fought in wars.

Our author could have found a hint also in the story 'Four Wise Men of Liang Dynasty' included in the tenth century

---

[1] S. Beal, *Si-yu-ki*. Buddhist Records of the Western World, translated from the Chinese by Hiuen Tsiang (A.D. 629), 1884, vol. 2, p. 279; *Ta T'ang hsi-yü chi*, c. 11. The earliest mention of a Women's Country is in *Shan hai ching*, 'Hai-wai hsi ching', where the women bathe in the Yellow Stream and become pregnant.

[2] Beal, vol. 1, p. 199; *Ta T'ang hsi-yü chi*, c. 4.

[3] *T'ang shu*, c. 221ᵃ, and *Chiu T'ang shu*, c. 197 ; similar accounts are given in *Wen-hsien t'ung-k'ao*, c. 339, and *T'ai-p'ing kuang-chi*, c. 481 : all use the name 'Country of Eastern Women'.

compilation, *T'ai-p'ing kuang-chi*, c.81,[1] in which the much
travelled Chieh-kung, when questioned about a certain Women's Country, gave the reply that there were, in all, *six*
Women's Countries; in the second of these:

> ... the women were fierce and the men tame; a woman was
> the ruler, and had a nobleman for her consort, and male con-
> cubines as many sometimes as a hundred ...

The noblewoman's male concubines were not unknown in
China itself. During his eighteen months' reign in A.D. 464–5,
the young Emperor, the former Fei-ti of Sung of the Southern
Dynasties, presented his sister, the Princess Shan-yin, who had
complained about the unequal licence permitted to the sexes,
with thirty good-looking youths, whose appellation was 'Pleasing Faces'.[2] In *Ching hua yüan*, chapter 51, this historical precedent is alluded to by the irate wife of the bandit chief, who
held four of the 'Flowers' captive and intended to make them
his concubines:

> 'How would *you* like it if I had a male concubine and you were
> left out in the cold? ... Therefore, I say, if you take no con-
> cubine, well and good! But if you must have a concubine, then
> you will first find me a male concubine, whom the ancients
> called "Pleasing Face".'

Concubinage is, however, only one of many evils satirized in
Ching hua yüan. In chapter 12, the Wu brothers, Ministers of
the Crown in the Gentlemen's Country, expatiate on the folly
of certain customs prevailing in the Celestial Land. These included such superstitious practices as blind faith in geomancy,
resulting in the postponement for years or even decades of the
burial of one's parents while one searched for the right site; or
foolish reliance on the matching of horoscopes rather than potential compatibility in the choice of marriage partners; or the
irresponsible surrendering of one's own children (for a mixture
of selfish and superstitious reasons) to Buddhist monasteries
and nunneries, to be reared as monks and nuns, thus swelling an
unproductive, and often immoral, section of society: and such
wasteful practices as the wholly unwarranted succession of celebrations following the birth of a son or daughter, usually on the

[1] 'Four Wise Men of Liang Dynasty', *Liang ssu-kung chi*, is set in the
T'ien-chien reign of Liang, early in the sixth century A.D.
[2] *Mien-shou*, literally, face and head. See *Sung shu*, c.7; the reign ended
disastrously, the vicious Emperor himself dying as the result of a plot.

third day, and again at the end of a full month, and again on the first birthday; or the lavish displays at feasts and on ceremonial occasions, especially weddings and funerals, entailing vast expenditure and the throwing away of much good food; or indeed showiness and extravagance generally: and, moreover, such malpractices as the careless and unconcerned slaughter of oxen, the ox as the beast of the plough being man's best friend; or all forms of litigation, and the proliferation of unscrupulous pettifoggers; or the free access to the inner apartments granted to nuns, priestesses, female fortune-tellers, healers, match-makers and the like, resulting in theft, confidence trick, scandal, intrigue, and the ruin of a wife or daughter; or the callous ways of stepmothers;

> At which point, the elder Wu took up the argument: 'We have heard reports about the practice of footbinding in your esteemed land, how that, when a young girl was first subjected to it, she would howl through the night with pain, her small hands nursing her wrapped feet, which drip blood and putrefy—thus she would forego sleep and even food, laying herself open to the attack of all manner of disease. For some considerable time, I had laboured under the impression that such a child had been guilty of unspeakable filial disobedience, punishable by death, but that the poor mother could not be prevailed upon to carry out a measure so extreme and devised instead this form of perpetual torture. I then learned, to my horror, that the stunted foot was a votive offering at the shrine of beauty, it being held that no woman that had not bound feet could be considered beautiful. I ask you, gentlemen: Does one resort to knife or chisel to flatten a too prominent nose or to smooth down a protruding forehead? *That* would be mutilation, you say; and yet feet that are maimed and render their owner a cripple are thought beautiful. Should one demand of the loveliest women of all time, Hsi Shih and Wang Ch'iang, that they cut off their toes for our benefit? But a moment's reflection would convince anyone that the custom is no more than a shameless pandering to perversion and depravity.'[1]

In our story, the merchant Lin steps ashore at the Women's Kingdom, his inventory complete with every cosmetic item,

[1] Chapter 12, p. 78. Hsi Shih and Wang Ch'iang, beauties of the ancient world, lived over a thousand years before footbinding became prevalent.

expecting exorbitant profits from sales to the vain local house-wives and their adoring husbands; but, being himself taken for a woman, he receives in his turn the full treatment—pearls and jade for my lady's hair coiled in the latest fashion, a powder mask for her face, rouge for her cheeks, a stout needle for piercing her ear-lobes, and a whole roll of silk gauze for binding her feet. Thus the waiting women double up his toes, crush the arch of his foot, wrap it in tight layers of silk and sew up the bandage to his howls and groans and cries of 'Mortification and shame!' So much for the ordeals of womanhood. To complete the picture, the masculine point of view ought perhaps also to be represented:

> The small feet of Chinese women are not only pleasing in men's eyes but in a strange and subtle way they influence the whole carriage and walking gait of the women, throwing the hips backwards, somewhat like the modern high-heeled shoes, and effecting an extremely gingerly gait, the body "shimmying" all over and ready to fall at the slightest touch. Looking at a woman with bound feet walking is like looking at a rope-dancer, tantalizing to the highest degree. The bound foot is indeed the highest sophistication of the Chinese sensual imagination.[1]

Li's championship of the cause of women is strange for his age, and remarkable by any standards,[2] but in his portrayal of feminine life, he had before him the recent example of the 'Red Chamber Dream', published in 1791–2. In *Ching hua yüan* the heroines' hearts are not probed as in the earlier, and greater, work; yet its world of rational and purposeful living, of diligence about one's tasks and uncomplaining acceptance of duty and circumstance, of civilized—if at times too learned—conversation and repartee, is equally attractive and comes closest, among works of fiction, to the ideal Chinese life as seen from hearth and home. What is more, its sanity and cheerfulness are downright infectious.[3] That feminine readers were at once de-

[1] Lin Yutang, *My Country and My People*, 1936, 'Footbinding', pp. 158–161, to which the reader is referred for further information on this topic, the translator sharing our author's distaste for bound feet.
[2] Li's feminism is rightly stressed in Hu Shih's article in *Hu Shih wen-ts'un*, vol. 2, cited above.
[3] This is also claimed by the author himself in the conclusion to his book: a friend of his, suffering from deep melancholy, read the manuscript and broke into fits of laughter and so regained his high spirits (chapter 100, p. 772).

lighted with *Ching hua yüan* is clear from the poems of several literary ladies among the congratulatory verses in the early editions.[1] One of them declares that she loves nothing better than to read *Ching hua yüan* under the lamp late at night, when she would commune with the spirits of its talented women; another, for ten years an addict of the 'Red Chamber Dream', confesses herself now deeply involved also in the Romance of the Flowers in the Mirror. A third, who styles herself 'Lotus in the Karma' (Lien-yin), pretends to have been a flower in her last existence and entreats our author to chronicle also *her* story.

[1] For the congratulatory poems, see discussion above. The three ladies here referred to are: Hsü Yü-ju, Chu Mei, and Ch'ien Shou-p'u (Lien-yin).

The Women's Kingdom

After several days, they reached the Women's Kingdom. Having anchored the ship, the coxswain, old Tuo,[1] came within and invited T'ang Ao[2] to go ashore with him to see the sights. Now T'ang Ao had heard about the monk Tripitaka's sojourn in the Women's Country[3] during his journey to the Western Paradise to fetch sutras at the command of the Emperor T'ai-tsung, how that the monk had there been detained by the queen, from whose enticements he had with difficulty extricated himself; T'ang Ao, therefore, was wary of disembarking. The old helmsman, however, laughed hilariously, saying, 'You are, of course, right to be circumspect, Master T'ang, but this Women's Kingdom is quite unlike the other! If this had been the same Women's Country that Tripitaka journeyed through, then not only had you to remain on board; for all the profit his merchandise could bring him, even Master Lin[4] durst not venture forth. This Women's Kingdom is another sort. There was never any lack of males among them, and men and women mate as we do, but with this difference, that the men wear skirts and tunics and call themselves women and run the household, whereas the women wear boots and tall hats, call themselves men, and preside over public affairs. Thus though men and women are connubial partners as in other places, the roles of domestic and external affairs are reversed.'

Upon this, T'ang Ao cried: 'If their men call themselves women and look after the house, must they daub their faces with

[1] Tuo Chiu-kung, i.e. old man long at the rudder.
[2] T'ang Ao, i.e. the Chinese on a journey.
[3] Tripitaka in the Women's Country; see *Hsi yu chi*, chapter 54. The story being set in the T'ang dynasty, Tripitaka's journey is alluded to as a recent event. See Introduction.
[4] Lin Chih-yang, i.e. Lin who traversed the ocean. Lim, i.e. Lin, is probably the commonest surname among the Chinese inhabitants of Malaya and Singapore.

powder and rouge? Do they bind their feet?' His brother-in-law, the merchant Lin Chih-yang, now joining them, said, 'Bound feet are a fetish[1] among these people—so I have been told—and the small foot is prized in families great and humble alike. As for powder and rouge, they could never do without those. I congratulate myself that I was born in the Celestial Country.[2] Had I been born here, I too should have had to bind my feet, and what mortification and shame that would have been!' Then, producing from his bosom an inventory, he unfolded it and continued: 'Look, brother-in-law. The goods listed are all intended for this place.' T'ang Ao took the paper and saw that the items consisted entirely of powder, rouge, comb, fine-toothed comb, etc., every one of them some toilet or cosmetic article. Handing it back to Lin, he said, 'I remember, when the freight was being checked just before our departure from Ling-nan,[3] I did wonder at the large quantity of these things, but I now see why you brought them along. Having so carefully listed the goods, why have you not included the prices?'

The merchant Lin replied: 'When you engage in trade abroad, you never fix the price beforehand; instead you try to discover what they are short of, and raise the price of that commodity accordingly. For us who traverse the seas, the very secret of success is readiness to clench a deal on the spur of the moment.' T'ang Ao then asked: 'If, in spite of its name "Women's Kingdom", the country is not in fact inhabited only by women, why should there be such a demand for cosmetics?' The old coxswain said in reply: 'It is the custom of the land. They are otherwise thrifty enough, from the ruler down to the populace; but their sole indulgence is the adorning and beautifying of their women. When they speak of female attire and ornaments, rich and poor alike start raving, and even those who could ill afford them would try to purchase powder and rouge and trinkets from abroad. Being acquainted with their customs, Master Lin deliberately chose his merchandise; once his inventory has gone round the richer households, the whole lot will be

[1] See Introduction.
[2] The exact translation is 'Celestial Court', to which lesser nations send bearers of tribute. I have used 'Celestial Country' and 'Celestial Land' indiscriminately as the name for China recognized by the travellers and the foreign countries alike.
[3] Ling-nan, where they started on their journey (chapters 7–8), is roughly Kwangtung Province.

bought up within two or three days, and when the goods are delivered and the silver collected, his profit could easily be two or threefold or more, even if not quite the windfall of his transactions in the Lands of Giants and Pygmies.'[1]

T'ang Ao now observed: ' I had always regarded the words of the ancients—"Men's place was in the home, but women's in the sphere of public affairs"[2] read in my youth, as pure invention, little imagining I should really be visiting such a land today. An unusual country, to say the least, one that I must go ashore and see for myself! But my brother-in-law's flushed cheeks seem to augur some event of great felicity. Very likely he now goes to meet his best customer yet, and their brisk commerce would be the occasion of feasting and merry-making.' Lin himself also said, 'Two magpies kept up a loud chatter before me this morning, and a pair of black spiders landed upon my feet. Perhaps there will be a stroke of luck—as when those birds' nests came to me unsought!'[3] And grinning all over, he started out with his inventory.

T'ang Ao then went ashore with Tuo, the coxswain, and they entered the city, determined to take a close look at the inhabitants. They found old and young alike to be beardless and, though dressed like men, speaking with high-pitched feminine voices; and, furthermore, not only slight in build, but possessing a certain elegance and charm. T'ang Ao remarked: 'Have you noticed, Tuo, my friend?—They are really women, but perversely disguised as men. Is not this the height of affectation?' The mariner said, laughing, 'That is what *you* maintain, Master T'ang. But if *they* saw us, would they not regard us as women dissatisfied with our natural lot and, in our folly and affectation, masquerading as men?' T'ang Ao nodded in agreement and continued: 'You are right! There was the saying—"Habit

[1] In the Land of Giants, the inhabitants were eighty feet tall; in the Land of Pygmies, they were under a foot in height (chapters 19–20). The profitable transactions are touched upon only in passing, in chapter 20 (p. 139).

[2] See Introduction for the early accounts of a Women's Kingdom.

[3] The magpie (*hsi ch'iao*) and black spider (*hsi chu*) both have the character *hsi* (i.e. joy) and were omens of joyful occasions, especially of weddings. In chapter 12, at the end of their visit to the Gentlemen's Country, the crew received ten piculs (roughly, hundredweights) of edible birds' nests as a present from the Wu brothers. Finding the birds' nests tasteless, the sailors sold them to Lin for a few strings of cash. On that occasion, too, the magpies made a chatter (p. 80).

is nature's strongest propensity". We may find them extraordinary, but since this is how they always ordered their affairs,
we too must seem odd to them. If the "men" here are like this,
what about the "women"?'

Slyly the old helmsman pointed to one side and whispered:
'Look! There's a middle-aged person with needle and thread in
hand, making a pair of slippers. If that is not a woman—' T'ang
Ao turned and saw a humble dwelling, in the doorway of which
a middle-aged woman was seated. Her hair was jet black and,
being liberally sprinkled with some fragrant oil, presented a
surface so smooth and glossy as a passing fly might have slid
on; it was carefully braided and coiled in the shape of an elaborate crown. At her temples, pearls and jade hair-pins dazzled in
their profusion, and from her ears hung golden ear-rings. She
wore a purple rose tunic over an onion green skirt, from under
which protruded the tiniest feet encased in scarlet embroidered
slippers just three inches in length. Her white hands were held
up before her, their ten dainty fingers busy at a piece of embroidery. Her almond-shaped eyes were clear and sparkling, matched by eyebrows coquettishly arched, and her face was heavily
painted with powder and rouge. Agreeably surprised, T'ang Ao
slowly directed his gaze towards her mouth, and it was then
that he noticed thick bristles, in truth, bushy side-whiskers, at
which sight he could no longer contain himself and burst into a
titter. The woman laid aside her embroidery, gave T'ang Ao
one look, and said imperiously: 'Young woman! How dare you
snigger at me?' Her voice boomed and twanged like a cracked
gong, hearing which T'ang Ao beat a hasty retreat, dragging
Tuo after him.

From where she sat, however, the woman railed at them in a
loud voice: 'Don't tell me, with that beard on you, you are not
a woman! And yet you go about in a long robe and a high hat and
pass yourself off for a man! Have you never heard of such a thing
as the segregation of the sexes? Now while you pretend to be
spying upon women, your real purpose is of course to peep at
the men. Take a good look at yourself in the mirror, trollop,
and see if you remember what you are! Have you no sense of
shame?—The minx! She should be thankful, too, it was I who
caught her out. —Hey, you could really have been mistaken for
a man peeping at the women! And the blows that might have
rained upon you!' T'ang Ao heard it all but, being now safely

distant, he turned to the old helmsman, saying, 'Well, at least their speech is readily intelligible! Judging from the way she spoke, she really took us for women. Minx and trollop indeed! Was ever a man called such names? I wager it is the strangest insult on record. My poor brother-in-law! Let us hope that in his dealings in this place he is at least treated like a man.'

The coxswain wondering at his words, T'ang Ao explained: 'With his fair complexion my brother-in-law always gave the impression of having painted his face.[1] Besides, during our recent visit to the Land of Flames, his beard caught fire, with the loss of which he seems younger than ever.[2] If these people should look upon him as a woman, surely there is cause for alarm.' Old Tuo then said, 'They have always been on the most amicable terms with their neighbouring states. Coming, moreover, from the Celestial Country, we shall be treated with the utmost respect. You need scarcely worry on that score, Master T'ang.' Observing a crowd gathered round a roadside placard, reading aloud, T'ang Ao suggested finding out what was happening. As they drew near, however, they could hear, from what was being said, that a certain river channel was blocked. T'ang Ao was suddenly impelled to break through the crowd and read the placard for himself. But Tuo protested: 'Must you read it? What have the rivers here to do with us? Surely you do not mean to dredge their rivers and claim a reward, Master T'ang.'

T'ang Ao said: 'Do not tease me, Master Coxswain. What do I know about river channels? But I *am* interested in the vulgar forms of characters, of which this placard reminds me, such as certain local forms in the southern provinces: "$\frac{\text{LARGE}}{\text{SEAT}}$" for "secure"; and $\frac{\text{NO}}{\text{LIFE}}$ for "end"; and others with equally obvious meanings.[3] And that is sufficient reason for my wanting to read any proclamation, to discover the language of the country. To

[1] Ho Yen (190–249) was so fair that many suspected him of painting his face. On the hottest day in summer, the Emperor Wei Ming-ti offered Ho Yen hot dumplings, watched the beads of perspiration on his forehead and cheeks, and was at last satisfied to find that, after Ho Yen had wiped his face with the sleeve of his red robes, his skin remained fair as before; see *Shih shuo hsin-yü*, XIV, Wen-hsüeh ku-chi ed., pp. 389–90.

[2] In chapter 26 (pp. 184–7). Lin Chih-yang having nearly lost his beard in the flames, Tuo the coxwain himself thus describes him: 'Master Lin is a man of forty years and over, but with his beard perished in the fire and his fair complexion, he would seem no more than twenty.'

[3] Local forms of characters, mainly coinages, such as are still common in Cantonese and Hokkien.

be sure, it would not qualify as scholarship, but the odd character picked up here and there comes in useful at times.' Thus pushing his way through the crowd, he studied the placard and re-emerged, saying 'The style is clear enough and the calligraphy passable; moreover, I did find a character, $_{HIGH}^{NOT}$, which was new to me.' Old Tuo said: 'It is read "low", as far as I remember, in the southern provinces and refers to height.' T'ang Ao cried: 'It occurred in the phrase "high and $_{HIGH}^{NOT}$ dikes" and "low" would certainly be correct! So from my visit to the Women's Kingdom I have actually learned a new word!'

As they went on, they saw some women walking about, who seemed no different from women elsewhere: their skirt tails revealed the tiniest feet and their slender waists swayed sinuously and, where there was a crowd, they shunned the public gaze and sought to hide themselves, the bashfulness itself awakening much admiration. Some carried infants in their arms; others held on to their children. Some were middle-aged women with beards of varying thickness; others, also in their middle years, had no beard at all. Upon closer inspection, however, the beardless ones turned out to be those unwilling to grow old, who had removed the evidence of their age by plucking every hair off their chin. T'ang Ao remarked: 'Look, my friend! There are pores where the stubs were, and the cheeks seem indeed somewhat improved, but to pluck the hair from the chin and upper lip and denude the whole surface like a mower rooting out every blade of grass would seem too drastic an alteration of the contours, and the face should consequently acquire a new name.' The old helmsman, too, quipped —'I recall that phrase in *The Analects*, "hides of tigers and leopards".[1] Since the chin and upper lip of these persons have been plucked clean, why not call their faces "dressed human hides"?'[2]

Thus joking and punning, they moved on to other parts of the city, where after lingering for some time, they went back on board the ship, to learn that Lin Chih-yang had not yet returned. After supper, they sat up waiting for him till the second watch, when Mistress Lin expressing much anxiety about the

---

[1] *The Analects*, XII. viii. 3 (Legge): 'Ornament is as substance; substance is as ornament. The hide of a tiger or a leopard stripped of its hair, is like the hide of a dog or a goat stripped of its hair.' Prejudice against the razor has tended to persist.

[2] Some more facetious exchanges that follow have been omitted in the translation.

merchant's safety, T'ang Ao and the old coxswain set off again with lanterns to look for him; but the city gates were shut and they had to turn back. The next day, the search was resumed, but there was not a shadow of the man. On the third day, they took some of the crew with them and made a thorough search in several directions without success. They continued their inquiries in the ensuing days: the man seemed, however, to have vanished, like a millstone dropped into the ocean. Mistress Lin and her daughter Wan-ju[1] now spent their days in weeping and wailing, while T'ang Ao and the coxswain combed the city's streets and environs.

They could hardly have known that—when, on that first day Lin Chih-yang ventured into the city and called at various warehouses with his inventory, he found that, though there was a scarcity of the commodities he had to offer, the prices were well below his expectations: which led him to try a rich household, where, an order having been placed, he was further directed to —'the residence of the Royal Brother-in-law, with a very large domestic establishment taking up vast supplies, where, if you ask, you shall secure abundant profit.' Lin inquired the way and came to an imposing mansion with a high gate and an air of unusual splendour.[2] Taking out his inventory, he begged the gatekeeper to hand it up for inspection. Presently a reply came from within—'The articles listed are required for use at the Royal Palace, where His Majesty the King has for the past twelvemonth[3] been exercised in the choice of a royal consort as well as ladies of the Inner Palace. The inventory is being forwarded to the Palace, whither the trader should hasten in the company of our messenger, there to await further instructions.' Shortly afterwards, the house-steward appeared with the inventory and conducted Lin through a succession of golden gates into the Palace grounds, where, walking along jade-paved paths, Lin was chilled by the sight of armed guards stationed at every turning.

When they reached the gate leading to the Inner Palace, the

[1] Wan-ju, see note on p. 460.
[2] This is the end of chapter 32, and the narrative is followed by the formula—'As to what happened next, it shall be told in the following chapter', here omitted. Chapter 33 begins with: 'The story goes that when Lin Chih-yang came to the Royal Brother-in-law's residence', which is also omitted in the translation.
[3] In the original, 'the past few years'; since, however, the Queen died only the year before (p. 458), I have thought the change desirable.

house-steward stopped and said to Lin, 'Wait here, my good woman. I must now attend upon His Majesty and will let you know presently the requirements of the Palace.' The steward then went through the gate but soon came out to say, 'My good woman, how may one figure out the prices, which are not listed with the goods?' Lin replied: 'I carry them in my head. When you have made up your order, I will quote you the prices of those goods required.' The steward went in again, but was back before long to ask: 'What is the price in silver of a hundred-weight[1] of rouge, my good woman? And of a hundredweight of fragrant powder? And of hair oil? And of hair cord?' Lin gave his answer, and the steward returned within. A little while later the steward again appeared and said: 'My good woman, how much for a box of flowers worked with kingfisher's feathers? How much for a box of silk embroidered flowers? And for a box of sandalwood beads? And of combs, ordinary and fine-toothed?' Lin gave his answer, and the steward went in, but came out yet once more, and this time he said, 'His Majesty is graciously pleased to place an order for every available item on your list, though in varying quantities. As regards price, my running back and forth can but lead to error, and the commerce must be between yourself and His Majesty. My good woman, since you are from the Celestial Country, a land acknowledged as our superior, His Majesty commands you to enter the Inner Palace. But I warn you—take heed lest you incur royal displeasure.'

Lin Chih-yang replied, 'I shall be discretion itself.' And he followed the steward into the Inner Audience Chamber, where, after making his obeisance to the King, he stood to one side. Now though the King was already over thirty, his pale cheeks and blood-red lips presented an appearance of youth and beauty which was highly attractive. His Majesty, who was surrounded by a great many maids of honour, held up the inventory with the tips of ten delicate royal fingers and demanded in a melodious voice the price of each article. During question and answer, however, His Majesty's piercing eyes scanned the merchant from top to toe, at which, Lin growing uneasy, said to himself: 'What does this King want of me that he should look me over in this fashion? I suppose he has never met a Chinese trader.' A maid of honour then entering to announce dinner, His Majesty dismissed the house-steward with compliments to the Royal

[1] A picul (*tan*), which is a hundred catties.

Brother-in-law, intimating that the inventory was to be left at the Palace. And commanding the maids of honour [1] to entertain 'the woman from the Celestial Court' at dinner, the King retired to the Royal Apartments.

There was but a moment's delay before several maids of honour brought Lin Chih-yang up the staircase of another building, where a sumptuous meal with wine was spread in an upper storey room. [2] Before they had risen from table, a clamour broke out below and court ladies swarmed up the stairs hailing Lin as their Queen and sovereign, kowtowing to him and offering him their congratulations. More maids of honour followed, and these held in their hands the phoenix bridal crown and ceremonial collar, the jade girdle and ceremonial dragon robes, as well as skirt and undergarments, hairpins and ear-rings, and other ornaments. Despite his protests, their several pairs of hands now fell upon Lin, undoing all his garments and underclothing; for these maids of honour were of prodigious strength and they laid hold of him as a hawk might pounce upon a swallow, without the least fuss. When Lin had been unclad and his shoes removed, they deposited him in a perfumed bath and, having washed and scrubbed him, dressed him in blouse and underpants, over which he was made to wear a skirt and the dragon robes. His large feet were afforded the protection of stiff silk socks; his hair was carefully braided and copiously sprinkled with hair-oil, after which they laid the phoenix crown on his head; scented powder was daubed all over his face; his lips were painted scarlet; and rings were placed on his fingers, and a gold bangle on each wrist.

A curtained bed was now set up, which Lin was invited to sit on. Poor Lin Chih-yang! He thought of himself as being in a dream or in a drunken stupor. Staring about him in blank astonishment, he at last resolved to ask one of the maids of honour, who explained that His Majesty had chosen him, Lin Chih-yang, as a Royal Concubine and that they awaited only an auspicious day for his installation in the Royal Apartments. Though now in a state of extreme agitation, Lin noticed more waiting

[1] I have used 'maid of honour', 'waiting woman', etc. indiscriminately, the distinction not being made in the original.
[2] In the 'Country of Eastern Women', according to the accounts in the official T'ang histories, the inhabitants lived in multi-storied houses, buildings in the Palace rising to nine storeys; see *T'ang shu*, c. 221[a]; *Chiu T'ang shu*, c. 197; also Introduction.

women enter: these were middle-aged and fully bearded, tall and thickset. One of them, whose beard was turned steel grey, came up with needle and thread in her hand and knelt before the bed, saying, 'By my lady's leave. His Majesty commands the piercing of my lady's ears.' Upon this, four waiting women sprang forward, their arms gripping Lin like so many clamps. The grey-bearded one herself then rising, pinched and twirled Lin's right ear-lobe with her practised fingers and suddenly sent her needle through the flesh. Lin gave a loud shriek: 'That stab! It's the death of me!' And he threw his head back, but the waiting women held him tightly, and the grey-bearded one then pinched and twirled the left ear-lobe and, with one thrust of the needle, pierced it too. Lin howled with the pain.

The ears having been pierced, the wounds were smeared with powder, the ear-lobes gently massaged, and a pair of gold ear-rings affixed. Her task dispatched, the grey-bearded waiting woman retired. Immediately afterwards, however, a black-bearded waiting woman came up with a roll of white silk gauze in her hand and knelt before the bed, saying, 'By my lady's leave. His Majesty commands the binding of my lady's feet.' Two others also came forward and, kneeling down, grasped Lin's legs, removing the stiff silk socks. The black-bearded waiting woman then placed a low stool near the bed, sat down on it and tore off a good length of the silk gauze. Then, pulling Lin's right foot onto her knees, she sprayed the chinks between the toes with alum; next, she doubled up the toes and pressed them down by main force so as to accentuate the curvature of the arch; finally, she wrapped the crushed foot in tight layers of silk gauze. Another waiting woman came up with needle and thread and, as soon as the second layer of bandage was done, sewed up the hem in close stitches; and even as the cruel band-aging progressed, so the relentless stitching followed. All this while, Lin had been wedged in by the four waiting women; the two others kept his legs firmly in place so that he could not move them an inch. When at last the binding came to an end, his feet were in searing pain as if he was treading on red-hot charcoal. He felt suddenly sick at heart and burst out sobbing—'Oh, mortification and shame!'

Both feet having been bound, a pair of soft scarlet slippers were quickly sewn and put on for him. Lin Chih-yang now stopped crying and, having racked his brains in vain for a better plan, proceeded to implore the mercy of those present, saying: 'Gentlemen, intercede on my behalf, I beg of you, with His Majesty. I am a *man*, with a wife of my own. How, then, could I be turned into a Royal Concubine? As for my man-sized feet, they never knew restraint till this moment; they are like reluctant students who, having played truant from the beginning, would not now submit to the tyranny of the examinations.[1] I only beg for my early release. Be assured that my wife, too, would be grateful to you.' But the waiting women only said: 'His Majesty has commanded that my lady be installed in the Palace as soon as her feet are properly bound. Who are we to say otherwise?'

Before long, lamps were brought and supper laid out. Though it was a veritable feast, Lin had lost all desire for food, and left it to the maids of honour and waiting women to enjoy the splendid repast. Presently, however, feeling the need to discharge water, he spoke to one of the waiting women: 'My dear fellow, kindly help me downstairs. I must make water.' The waiting women nodded and soon brought out a night-commode, at the sight of which Lin squirmed. But struggle was useless; for his feet had been so tightly bound that he could not walk. He resigned himself to leaning on the arms of the waiting women, with whose help he climbed down from the bed and sat on the commode. Then, when his hands had been washed, a further basin of hot water was brought by a waiting woman, who said: 'Water for my lady's ablutions.' Lin exclaimed: 'But I have already washed my hands! Why should I wash again?' The woman replied demurely: 'Not the hands, my lady; the privates.' Lin cried in exasperation: 'The privates? Where? I have never heard of such a thing.' The waiting woman persisted—'Whence the water issued, my lady, there wash with water. But if my lady is not accustomed to doing so, we will carry out our duty.' Instantly two other fat waiting women came forward; one of them undid Lin's underpants, and the other soaked a red silk handkerchief in the water and began wiping and cleansing. Lin Chih-yang screamed: 'Stop, gentlemen! The

---

[1] This is topical and the exact translation should be: 'like licentiates who had wandered far from their home districts and had taken no revision examinations for many years, and who, having been left alone, would not submit to such restraints again.' See notes to 'Young Master Bountiful', *supra.*

joke is getting out of hand. I am a *man*, and this will give me a terrible itch. Stop it, I say. The more you wipe, the itchier it gets.' The waiting woman, however, only muttered: 'That may well be. You say, the more I wipe, the itchier you are; but, of course, the itchier you get, the more I'll wipe!'

These ablutions being over, he was again placed on the bed. His feet were now in excruciating pain and, being unable to sit up any longer, he lay down in his clothes. The foot-binder came forward once more and said, 'Since my lady is tired, we beg to commence the bedtime toilet.' The others now crowded round the bed, bustling confusedly, one of them holding a candlestick, another a hand spittoon, a third a basin, still others a dressing case, jars of oil and cream, face cloth, silk handkerchiefs, to all whose attentions he politely submitted. His face having been washed and carefully dried, a maid of honour offered to apply the face powder, which Lin resolutely refused. Thereupon the grey-bearded waiting woman who had pierced his ears came forward to deliver a grave discourse: 'The preparation of a powder mask at bedtime is a practice conferring inestimable benefit. Being mixed in the right proportion with unctuous musk, powder renders the skin smooth and white. To be sure, my lady has an excellently fair complexion, but her skin is at present not deeply imbued with sweet fragrance, and she must therefore invoke the aid of powder, with prolonged application of which not only will her face seem carved out of white jade, but a warm, delicious fragrance will ooze from the very pores. In short, the whiter the skin, the more sweet-smelling; and the more sweet-smelling, the more spotlessly white. Its effect upon the beholder is indeed irresistible — a single sniff leads to enslavement and, being thus enslaved, one longs to touch and smell again. But the full benefit is felt only with regular application over an extended period.' And she went on earnestly, though unheeded by Lin.[1] The others now cried: 'What a contrary new Concubine! We shall have to memorialize the throne without omission or concealment, and request the presence of the Mother of Correction!' Thus they dispersed for the night.

Fits of pain caused Lin Chih-yang to start from his sleep. He tugged and tore at the silk bandage and succeeded, after endless exertion, in unripping the gauze and removing the wrapping.

---

[1] Lin being himself a dealer in cosmetics.

Freed from their bondage, his ten toes were again spread out, each delighting in its new won freedom—like licentiates exempted from their revision examinations![1] With this feeling of release, he sank into a deep sleep. Sitting up in bed the next morning, having washed his face and rinsed his mouth, he was confronted by the black-bearded waiting woman, whose province was his feet. Discovering, all of a sudden, both her charges shorn of their elaborate covering, she at once reported to the King, who straightway commanded the Mother of Correction to administer twenty heavy strokes to the new Concubine and, furthermore, to station herself within the courtyard for strict enforcement of the household regulations. The Mother of Correction received the command and, leading her four attendants who carried the bamboo for her, marched up the stairs and knelt before the bed, saying, 'The Concubine has flouted the household regulations. His Majesty commands the use of the bamboo of correction.' Lin stared. The Mother of Correction, a long-bearded woman, then rose and took the bamboo, a heavy rod eight feet in length and three inches wide at the thick end, at which sight Lin trembled, protesting feebly: 'The bamboo! What do you mean?' The four attendants, strapping women with small beards and brawny arms, rushed up and, ignoring his protests, laid him prostrate on the bed and removed his lower garments; and the Mother of Correction, herself briskly wielding the bamboo, smote hip and thigh. Lin set up a howl, finding the pain more than he could endure; for, by the end of the fifth stroke, the flesh was lacerated and blood came gushing out on to the bed. The Mother of Correction paused and, turning to the foot-binder, said: 'Talk of a bath of blood! And it's only five strokes, too! The new Concubine has indeed a delicate behind, and to administer the full twenty might inflict real injury. Besides, her wound taking too long to heal would delay the wedding. Before I start again, go, my good sister, and report to His Majesty on my behalf, and beg for fresh instructions.' The foot-binder assented and left immediately.

The Mother of Correction, still clutching her heavy bamboo, began muttering to herself: 'It is skin and flesh same as anybody has got, but so soft and white! And such a shape too! One would have to admit that this precious bottom is worth every bit of the

[1] See notes to 'Young Master Bountiful', *supra.*

handsome faces of P'an An and Sung Yü.'[1] But correcting herself, she added hastily—'P'an An and Sung Yü—theirs were,
of course, faces. A bottom's only a bottom, not to be spoken of
in the same breath.' The foot-binder now returning, announced: 'His Majesty has sent to ask if the Concubine will from this
moment abide by the household regulations, and has commanded that, if the Concubine repents of her past misdeed, further
punishment be waived.' Being in dread of more beating, Lin
hastily cried: 'I have thoroughly reformed!' The Mother of
Correction and her attendants then desisting, the maids of
honour wiped away the blood with silk handkerchiefs. The
King presently sent a dressing for the wound and a potion com-
pounded of the ginseng root and various soothing herbs. The
dressing being then applied and the potion taken, Lin fell back
on the bed and found the pain suddenly eased.

The foot-binder now re-asserted her authority and bandaged
the feet anew with great care. She insisted that Lin descend from
his bed and walk about the room, and he took a few steps, leaning on the arms of the waiting women; though the hip wounds
no longer bothered him, the feet were still in pain, and he longed
to rest. The foot-binder, however, was bent on keeping to her
schedule and became implacably strict, so that, whenever he
made as if to sit down, she threatened to report to the King.
Thus Lin remained on his feet as best he could, and continued
walking back and forth as if his life depended on it. And night
brought no remission: for pain interrupted his sleep and kept
him in a state of vigil, and waiting women sat by his bed day and
night, watching him by turns and noting his every movement.
Having reached such a pass, Lin Chih-yang, he who traversed
the ocean, felt his manly courage and resolution ebb and dissolve in womanly sighs and tears.[2]

The story goes that Lin's 'lily feet' having daily been first
dipped in a solution of alum and then even more tightly bandaged by the waiting women, within a fortnight the arch of each

---

[1] Sung Yü (about 3rd century B.C.), the *fu* writer, was noted for his
beauty; see 'Master Teng-t'u' in Arthur Waley, *One Hundred and Seventy
Chinese Poems*, 1918 and reprints, pp. 26–7. P'an An is P'an Yo (247–
300), much admired by women, who pelted him with fruit as he drove
along in his cart so that he would return loaded with provisions; see
Chin shu, c. 55.

[2] The end of chapter 33, the concluding formula: 'As to what happened
next, it shall be told in the following chapter' being omitted in the
translation.

foot was crushed into two halves; and all the ten toes had turned septic and were dripping blood. One day as, in his agony, he was being walked by the maids of honour, he felt anger and vexation mounting within him. He said to himself: 'I, Lin Chih-yang, have held my temper in check until this moment, submitting to a hundred tortures and indignities in the hope of my brother-in-law and the coxswain coming to my rescue. Yet there has not been one word from them and I am clearly abandoned! Rather than go on suffering piecemeal in this fashion, far better die at once and so get it over and done with!' Still leaning on the arms of the others, he took a few more steps, but his aggrieved feet now smarted with the slightest motion. He made a dash for the bed, where he planted himself and, to the pleas of all present, gave one reply only, which he addressed repeatedly to the Mother of Correction: Would the good gentleman inform the King that he, Lin Chih-yang, preferred instant death to the binding of his feet, which he would resist to the bitter end. And as he spoke, he kicked off his embroidered slippers and tore at the white silk bandages. The waiting women all rushing up to restrain him and repair the damage, the ensuing struggle resulted in endless confusion. The Mother of Correction having sized up the situation for herself, left forthwith to report to the King, but returned before long, fortified by a fresh mandate, which she announced without kneeling: 'His Majesty has ruled that, in refusing to comply with custom in the binding of the feet, the Concubine did violate the household regulations. His Majesty commands that the Concubine's feet be tied to the beam, her body to hang upside down.'

Lin, who looked to death for his release, heard the word 'hang' and appealed aloud to the maids of honour: 'Make haste —I beg of you, gentlemen! The sooner I die, the better! And the more grateful I shall be. Therefore, hurry!' And he co-operated eagerly in their latest manoeuvres. But as soon as they had tied his feet together with a rope, a new pain brought out the old again; and when they had actually hung him from the beam, feet up, body suspended in mid air, stars seemed to pop out of his eyes as his head swung round in a dizzy spin. Cold sweat flowed all the way up his spine, and his two legs were, in turn, sore and numb. With manly fortitude, Lin clenched his teeth, bit his lip and shut his eyes, expecting at any moment to expire and thus contract out of the unending instalments of punishment. A long while he held out, but death failed to come to his relief. Instead a heightened consciousness descended upon him, intensifying every sensation of pain and discomfort. One moment he felt his feet pricked by hundreds of needles; the next, a knife blade seemed to be cleaving bone and tendon. As a last resort, he set his jaw, but this no more warded off the pain, which soon getting the better of him, all of a sudden Lin squealed like a pig in the slaughter-house and entreated the King's mercy.

The Mother of Correction again reporting to the King, His Majesty commanded that the Concubine be set down. From then on, Lin endured all his troubles uncomplainingly, not daring to show the least intransigence. Knowing that he had been thoroughly cowed, the waiting women now sought the quickest returns from his feet, which, dead or alive, they would bind and constrict in their desire to please the King. Though, time and again, Lin looked for some opportunity to do away with himself, yet, since he was under constant watch day and night, even as liberty was denied him, so death, too, was beyond his reach. Imperceptibly the flesh on his feet and toes putrefied and decomposed; the wounds dried up and healed; only the bare bones remained. His feet had shrunk beyond recognition. Moreover, his raven locks, having been rubbed with every variety of hair-oil, shone with a new gloss; and daily immersion in a fragrant bath had rendered his skin smooth and soft; and plucking and trimming had transformed his thick eyebrows into two crescents. In addition, his lips were coated with a blood-red rouge, which set off his powder-masked face, topped by pearl and jade ornaments all over his head—a splendiferous sight!

Several times a day the King sent to inquire about the progress of the ticklish business. When, at last, the Mother of Correction reported one day that the feet had been bound, His Majesty ascended the stairs to inspect the new Concubine. And the King found a face as fair as the peach blossoms; and a waist that swayed like the weeping willow; and a pair of eyes clear as autumn rivers; and eyebrows arched like distant hills.[1] Each gaze awakened yet greater admiration in His Majesty, who could not help musing: 'Quite a gem! And to think she was actually disguised as a man! Had not our observant eyes picked her out, such a rose would have been left to blush on the high

[1] A parody of the stereotyped Chinese heroine, especially in novels.

seas!' And the King took out a bracelet, which was a string of
real pearls, and with his own delicate fingers slipped it on Lin's
wrist. The maids of honour having made him bow low to give
thanks to His Majesty, the King pulled him up and, still holding
him by the hand, bade him sit down, so that they sat shoulder to
shoulder. The King then contemplated the newly bound feet
with unconcealed delight, after which His Majesty sniffed and
kissed and stroked and cuddled him all over, displaying a love
full to overflowing.

On his part, Lin was already flushed with shame upon the
King's arrival, and he found it mortifying to sit like a concubine
shoulder to shoulder with that obviously female King ; but when
his feet were then subjected to the monarch's amorous scrutiny,
and his hands to fond caressing, and his forehead and cheeks
and neck and arms to rapturous kissing, he blushed scarlet and
was covered with confusion. The doting King returned to the
Royal Apartments, all the better pleased with the new favourite. On the instant His Majesty fixed upon the morrow as the
happy day on which the Concubine was to be installed ; and, to
mark the joyful occasion, the warders of the King's prisons were
commanded to set their inmates free. Lin Chih-yang, who until
that moment had still retained hope of T'ang Ao and Tuo the
coxswain coming to rescue him, was now resigned to the certainty of his removal on the next day to the Royal Apartments.
With sharp pangs he remembered his wife, and tears all but
drenched him. What was worse, the binding of his 'lily feet'—
the bones weakened, the muscles tender—had so emasculated
him that he was too weak to stand nor capable of moving about
without the support of the waiting women. Ruminating on his
present distress, he recalled happy days of the past and concluded ruefully that one could live in two different worlds. Thus
assailed by a thousand bitter sorrows, he felt every inch of his
entrails crack, and he wept all through that night.

The next morning—it being the day appointed for the wedding—the maids of honour and waiting women rose at an un-
earthly hour. Some of them came to 'pluck the bride's face',[1]
others to comb the new Concubine's hair, still others to apply

---

[1] To remove the fine hair on a girl's face on her wedding day and thus
declare her a woman. The ceremony should precede the plucking and
trimming of the eyebrows, but Lin's beauticians had already transformed
his eyebrows into crescent-shaped curves many days before.

the powder and rouge, all with redoubled solicitude. The 'lily feet' were indeed still somewhat long; yet, being well arched under their bandage and cushioned by a high in-sole, they appeared suitably tiny in their scarlet phoenix slippers. Lin was now arrayed in his ceremonial dragon robes with the phoenix bridal crown firmly placed on his head; for ornament, he wore a dozen or more tinkling jade pendants; and his sweetly scented face perfumed the air:

Though, in truth, not of transcendent beauty,

This bride was, at least, comely and charming.

Breakfast being over, the other Royal Concubines called to offer their congratulations. All morning, the staircase was lined with visitors; and in the afternoon, the maids of honour bustled about in great excitement, re-arranging each detail of Lin's dress and adornments in preparation for the grand event, which was heralded by the ceremonial entry of a number of court attendants holding lanterns in their hands. The new arrivals knelt in a row before Lin and announced: 'The lucky hour has struck. My lady will now proceed to the main audience chamber, where, His Majesty having dismissed court, the nuptial rites will be celebrated, to be followed by installation in the Royal Apartments. The sedan waits below.'

The announcement descended upon Lin Chih-yang like a thunderbolt. There was a confused buzzing in his ears, and his soul was temporarily dislodged from its seat. His protests went unheard: the women in attendance rushed up and kept him supported all the way down the stairs until they deposited him in the phoenix sedan, which was then carried to the main audience chamber, followed by hundreds of maids and women in waiting. His Majesty had already dismissed court, and the audience hall was resplendent with hundreds of candles and lanterns. Leaning on the arms of the maids of honour, Lin advanced, swaying and trembling like a full-blown flower, until he reached the King's presence, when, guided by firm, controlling fingers, he bent with a jerk and, pulling his sleeves over his hands, made a bride's low bow. The other Royal Concubines, too, came forward to bow to the King and offer their felicitations. The bowing over, it was time to retire to the Royal Apartments, but a sudden commotion was heard from outside the Palace: men were shouting and screaming, and their shrill cries startled the King, whose composure soon gave way to fear and doubt.

It turned out that the shouting in the street was a ruse of T'ang Ao's. For ever since that first evening, he had continued to search with the old coxswain high and low for his missing brother-in-law, though without the least result. One day, the two men had gone ashore as usual to look for Lin Chih-yang, each taking a separate route. After a fruitless morning's search, T'ang Ao had returned to the ship, where, sitting down to his mid-day meal, he found Mistress Lin and her daughter both weeping. While he was trying to comfort them, old Tuo rushed on board, his forehead covered in sweat, shouting: 'There's news of Master Lin! It was worth all my efforts—at last I have got news of him!' Mistress Lin asked anxiously: 'Where is my husband? Is he dead or alive?' The old helmsman, however, went on: 'As I made my inquiries, by chance I came across a steward of the Royal Brother-in-law's household, from whom I learned that Master Lin had been detained at the Royal Palace. It would seem that the King of this land of women had expressed an interest in Master Lin's commodities, then taken a great liking to Master Lin himself, and eventually decided to make him, Master Lin, a Royal Concubine. Master Lin's large feet proved an impediment and, at the King's command, the wedding was postponed until the feet could be bound. According to the steward, the foot-binding is now completed and the King has chosen tomorrow as the day for the installation of the new Concubine.'

Before he could proceed further, Mistress Lin, who had been crying piteously, swooned in her grief. Her daughter Wan-ju, herself bitterly weeping, revived her, whereupon that afflicted lady went on her knees before T'ang Ao and the coxswain, solemnly invoking their help in saving her husband. T'ang Ao having ordered Wan-ju and her companion to help Mistress Lin up, old Tuo finally resumed: 'I then persuaded the steward to request his master to intercede on our behalf with the throne, offering our entire cargo as ransom for Master Lin. The steward most obligingly transmitted my message, but the Royal Brother-in-law, regarding intercession at this late stage to be futile, the wedding being imminent, would have nothing to do with the matter, and I could make no headway. Thus I have returned in the hope that Master T'ang might know of a better plan.' Being, however, struck dumb by the intelligence, T'ang Ao was slow to answer. At last, he said, 'Since it is already the eve of the wedding, our hope is but slender. Under these circumstances, we should draw up a petition for clemency, pleading extreme hardship, and hand up copies at the various ministries and departments, trusting that some upright minister of the King's would take up our cause and argue the case before the throne so as to secure my brother-in-law's release. No other course remains to us.'

Mistress Lin thereupon cried: 'My brother-in-law has certainly thought up a good plan! They are a great kingdom; there must be no end of ministers, among whom some doubtless will be upright. An eloquent petition, placed in the hands of one such minister, will surely restore me my husband! Please, then, good brother-in-law, have as many copies transcribed as you can, and see that they are handed up soon!' T'ang Ao at once drafted the petition, of which the coxswain approving, the two each made several copies and, leaving their dinner untouched, departed in great haste for the city. At every government department or office they could find, they presented a copy of the petition: invariably the paper was taken within, studied, and thrown out again with a cheerless—'It is no concern of ours. Try another department.' By the end of the day, they had called at several score government offices, all with the same result. At dusk, famished and exhausted, they returned to the ship, and when Mistress Lin learned what had happened, she broke into a loud wailing. And she and her daughter lay awake all through that night, sobbing.

The next morning, T'ang Ao and the coxswain again went into the city for news.[1]. . . There was a crowd in the distance, and men were walking in procession towards them. As they hurried forward, they found the procession to be formed by scores of porters, shouldering pole loads of splendid gifts. Old Tuo observed in a whisper: 'The courier bringing up the rear is the house-steward of the King's brother-in-law I was telling

---

[1] Snatches of conversation between T'ang Ao and Tuo, in the leisurely manner of Chinese novels, forming the last page or so of chapter 34, have here been omitted. The two overhear reports of a new Concubine being installed in the Palace, of an amnesty, and of government offices being closed for the day to enable officials to attend at the Palace and offer their congratulations to the King. At noon, T'ang Ao and Tuo stop for tea and dumplings at a tea-house and, at the beginning of chapter 35, they consult a fortune-teller, whose cryptic reply—that a wedding will lead to but a brittle union and that a certain person now in trouble will be freed after ten days—buoys them up for the moment.

you about. — What would he be doing with all those gifts?'
T'ang Ao said, 'Just look at their embroidered wrapping! They
are certainly gifts for the King.' The coxswain now approaching the steward for news, returned presently, looking even
more downcast; jesting bitterly, he cried: 'Gifts for the King,
did you say, Master T'ang? They are for our good Master Lin!'
To T'ang Ao's question — 'What do you mean?' — Tuo replied: 'The courier tells me that the gifts have been prepared
by the Royal Brother-in-law for distribution among the ladies
at court by the new Concubine on the occasion of her installation.
And you maintain they are not for Master Lin?'

T'ang Ao scratched his ears in sullen silence. Overhead, the
afternoon sun was slowly sinking. The officials who had converged upon the Palace to offer the King their congratulations
now began to disperse, seated in their sedans or riding on horseback. The released prisoners, too, were trooping past, smiling
happily as they made their way home. Before long, the porters
re-appeared, their loads now empty. It was almost dusk, and
there was nothing left that the two of them could still try; so
they hung their heads and took the road back....[1] As they walked on, they again reached the spot where they had read the
proclamation. T'ang Ao sighed: 'On the day we sailed into this
port, while my brother-in-law went about his business, you and
I came ashore and stood before this placard. But we never fore-
saw our long stay nor the grievous misfortune. My poor
brother-in-law! I wonder how he has fared and what strange
torments have been his! What longings, too, for our rescue, all
in vain!' As he spoke, tears rolled down T'ang Ao's cheeks. In
a flash, however, a thought struck him; it took him but a few
more moments, with his head lowered pensively, to follow it
through. Striding up to the notice-board, he carefully detached
the placard and lifted it up.[2]

The guards stationed by the placard rushed forward to cross-
question T'ang Ao: 'Where are you from, woman? Do you
realize what you are doing? You are absolutely certain you
have understood the King's proclamation?' A large crowd had
meanwhile gathered. For when word went round that a stranger
had intimated acceptance of the King's commission by lifting
the placard, the sensation it created was electric. From the city

[1] A further short exchange between T'ang Ao and Tuo has been omitted.
[2] Thus indicating his acceptance of the undertaking advertised.

and its environs, old and young trooped in great numbers to the notice-board. When T'ang Ao saw that there was a crowd, he addressed those present in a loud voice, declaring: 'My name is T'ang. I have journeyed across the seas from the Celestial Land, where every man or woman knows the art of taming floods. Passing through your esteemed country, I find this placard containing your King's proclamation, from which I quote: "The floods have devastated our land for years in succession and caused our people extreme hardship, in view of which we solemnly proclaim that, in the event of the sovereign of a neighbouring kingdom succeeding in confining our rivers and averting disaster for our people, we would willingly acknowledge ourselves a vassal state and tender tribute. If the subject of a neighbouring state effected the same, we would freely offer in reward riches, rank and honours . . ." The desire, thus expressed, of bringing this great evil to an end seems to me most sincere and admirable and I have therefore come forward to offer you my services in the assuaging of the floods, in which cause I shall not spare myself . . .'

The beginning of this speech found a number of people in the crowd kneeling confusedly and chanting aloud: 'We beg the distinguished visitor from the Celestial Land to be compassionate and save us and our homes now.' T'ang Ao now went on: 'Pray, rise, my friends, and let me resume. Though I am able to regulate your rivers, I am unmoved by the proffered reward of riches and high rank, which our Celestial Country offers in abundance. No, my friends, grant me but one thing, and I commence my labours without delay.' Those who were kneeling rose and cried: 'What would our distinguished visitor have us do?' T'ang Ao then said: 'I have a brother-in-law, who, on being admitted to the Royal Palace to sell his goods, was against his will detained there and made a Concubine elect. The wedding, I now learn, takes place this very evening. If you wish me to assuage your floods, then go before the Palace and, with weeping and wailing, plead with your King for this person to be released, so that I may start work on the rivers. But if your King should spurn your lives and welfare by refusing to restore my relative, then not for the greatest treasure in the world would I tame your floods, but must instead return to my homeland.'

As he spoke, the crowd grew ever thicker until a great multi-

tude was assembled. And when the people heard T'ang Ao
threaten to leave for home, they made a thunderous outcry, and
all rushed headlong towards the Palace gates. The guards having earlier marched off to report to their superiors the stranger's
answering of the Proclamation, T'ang Ao and the coxswain
found themselves alone. Tuo broke into an urgent whisper:
'Master T'ang, you do, of course, know something about river
conservancy?' T'ang Ao said: 'Was I ever an officer in the River
Conservancy? No, my dear sir, never. Frankly I know nothing
about inundations and flood control.' The mariner cried: 'You
know nothing about them! I hope you knew what you were doing when you took down that placard. If you bungle the job and
spend their public funds to no purpose, why, we all exchange
rudder and sail for the distaff!' T'ang Ao persisted: 'It was rash
of me, I admit, to remove that placard, but my brother-in-law's
plight is desperate; he has to be saved somehow and, there being no alternative, I took a leap in the dark. However, now that
we have set the people on to worry their rulers, it seems not
unlikely that the King might give in to public opinion and post-
pone the wedding. As for that river, something must be done,
but not until I have examined the flooded area in the next day
or so. Let us hope that my brother-in-law's ruling planet is now
in the ascendant; for there is no telling what luck may do, even
to a river channel! But if the situation really got out of hand,
Master Coxswain, I entreat you: depart for some neighbouring
kingdom, offer them our shipload and beg for their intervention. We could do worse than follow such a course.'

Old Tuo shook his head, frowning hard at T'ang Ao's sudden eloquence. The guards now returned with a sedan-chair
and a horse, and T'ang Ao was escorted like a great personage
to the Government Guest House; Tuo, adopting perforce the
role of servant, trailed behind on foot. The Warden of the Guest
House had dinner and wine laid out for T'ang Ao, Tuo being
served separately at a lower table, but since both were hungry,
the seating arrangements did not prevent either of them from
enjoying a hearty meal. After dinner, the coxswain returned to
the ship to give Mistress Lin the news and what cheer he could,
before rejoining T'ang Ao at the Government Guest House,
where they calmly awaited an official summons.

In its noisy progress towards the Royal Palace, the crowd
that had heard T'ang Ao's harangue attracted a host of others,

so that eventually tens of thousands were gathered outside the Palace gates, where shouting and holla-ing, they made a great clamour. In the audience chamber within, the King was receiving the final ceremonial bows from the Royal Concubines, when shattering cries reached the royal ears, causing surprise and consternation. An usher presently entered to announce that the Royal Brother-in-law craved leave to confer with His Majesty on urgent affairs of state. The King now dismissed the Concubines and others, and summoned the Brother-in-law, who, having made his salute, reported at length how a woman from the Celestial Country had answered the Proclamation, claiming to be able to confine the rivers but stipulating, as prior condition, the freeing and restoration of her relative, a female vender of cosmetics from that same country upon whom His Majesty had been graciously pleased to confer the rank of Royal Concubine; and how tens of thousands were assembled at that moment outside the gates, crying out for a clear sign of their King's solicitous regard for their welfare and the welfare of half a million others, all His Majesty's loyal subjects, whose homes were all threatened by the rising floods,—even the immediate release of the said person in order that work on the flooded areas might begin and their dwellings and means of livelihood be preserved.

The King replied shrilly but regally: 'The custom of our land has ever been that no wife, even among the humblest, is ever cast out or permitted re-marriage. Shall we then, the country's sovereign, so far forget ourselves as to act against age-old custom in regard to a Royal Concubine?' The Royal Brother-in-law persisted nevertheless: 'The point was indeed made perfectly plain in a carefully worded statement, which Your Majesty's servant himself read out repeatedly to the people—"Let all hear and comprehend: inasmuch as among the subjects of this land a wife is never granted a dispensation from the marriage bond, so His Majesty the King would under no circumstances deign to forgo a Royal Concubine." The people, however, argue thus: that this being the day fixed for the wedding, the Concubine is not yet installed in the Royal Apartments and the Royal marriage therefore not yet consummated; that the case is thus to be differentiated from that of a Royal Concubine already so installed, on which ground they beg Your Majesty to take pity on them and grant their plea.' The King was a long while silent. At last, making as if to rise from the throne, His

Majesty snorted: 'Is this what they say? Then tell the people: "The King has retired and is not to be disturbed until the morning audience." In the morning, we confront them with a *fait accompli*: our action thus legitimized, their demand falls to the ground.'

The King proving adamant to all further entreaties, the Royal Brother-in-law returned to the gate-tower, where, as commanded, he made the announcement. When the people heard it, they feared that by morning their battle would have been lost: there was instant uproar, with thousands of voices simultaneously raised in protest. Their piercing cries reverberated through the audience chambers and the King was stricken with horror, being conscious of his own blame in the matter; yet, as to relinquishing his new favourite, he was no more willing than before. While thus he debated with himself, the cries came nearer and nearer, and men seemed to have broken through the Palace gates. Suddenly roused, the King exclaimed: 'My craven scruples! It's neck or nothing now!' At once His Majesty called the Colonel of the Guards on duty and placed a hundred thousand troops under his command with orders to march immediately on the rabble and crush the revolt. The Colonel of the Guards having received his command and mustered his men, reports of cannon and musket fire soon rocked the Palace walls.

The besiegers, however, would not be dislodged. They shouted: 'Kill us! We would sooner be blown up by the King's gunpowder than swept away by the floods and devoured by fish and sea monsters!' Thus the swarming multitude howled and wailed, their thunderous roar seeming to shake the heavens. The Royal Brother-in-law, sensing the reckless mood of the crowd and fearing a full-scale rebellion,[1] had earlier instructed the guards on no account to aim their guns at His Majesty's good subjects. He now stepped forward once more to pacify them, and addressed them thus: 'Good people, return to your homes. Be assured that I will transmit your request to the throne and secure the services of the person who answered the King's Proclamation in the relieving of the floods. You may safely entrust this matter to me. Tomorrow, at my home, I shall have further news for you all.' His speech, repeated a number of times, by degrees took effect. The crowd dispersed, and the Colonel of the Guards also recalled his men.

[1] See Introduction.

It being then reported that the mob had scattered, the King retired to the Royal Apartments, where Lin Chih-yang was commanded to sit shoulder to shoulder with His Majesty. Under the lamplight, the royal eyes flashed and twinkled as they renewed their measured survey of the new Concubine. What a slim figure—undoubtedly supple and lithe! Bashful, too, every bit the blushing bride! Eyebrows knit in an enticing melancholy! Perfect, indeed, in each particular! Having revelled in so vital a scrutiny, the King took a swift glance at the chiming clock[1] and declared in a shrilly musical voice: 'You are now our consort. Such melancholy does not become this gay occasion. It is of course a misfortune to be born female; that conceded, you have risen as high as any in the world. Just think! You are now a First Lady of our realm. What more could a woman ask for? For the future, if you bring forth children, your days of happiness will be lasting.—Rather than go about pretending to be a man and so contravene the laws of nature, is it not far better thus to resume the feminine role and share our throne like a queen? Let us drink on that thought!' And the King commanded that the banquet be spread and that gifts of jewellery, gold and silver be bestowed upon the new Concubine.

The banquet being presently ready, the maids of honour filled a goblet for Lin to offer to the King. Now Lin, who at the mere thought of his wife and daughter felt his heart pierced by a thousand wounding arrows, was left without the least spark of animation; besides, he was faint with hunger, having tasted neither tea nor rice for the few preceding days, so that he could find no strength in his limbs. When, therefore, he reached for the goblet, he was trembling all over, and his unsteady hand found the drinking-cup the weight of a millstone; his knees grew cold, his fingers lost their grip, and the goblet fell on the

---

[1] 'During the reign of Ch'ien-lung [1736–96] a large number of European clocks and watches were brought into China through the Canton trade. The Emperor and members of his Court seemed to have delighted in possessing them, and elaborate clocks and automata ('sing-songs') which played tunes were sent by the officials at Canton as gifts in order to obtain favour at Court.' (J. L. Cranmer-Byng, ed., *An Embassy to China*, p. 355, n. 1). Being of foreign origin and associated with exotic palaces, the chiming clock has found its way into the Royal Palace of the Women's Kingdom, as has also the pocket watch. In *Hung-lou meng*, chapter 92 (Yü edition, IV, pp. 122–3) an elaborate chiming clock of over three feet is mentioned as suitable for presentation to the Emperor; the price demanded for the clock together with an intricate inlaid screen was five thousand silver taels.

table with a loud clink. A maid of honour picked it up and filled another goblet, at the touch of which Lin was affected with a worse panic than before, and he again spilled the wine. The nuptial cup had, therefore, to be presented to the King by the others. And the King commanded that a goblet also be filled for Lin and held up to his lips. This, with an effort, he drank, and a second cup was immediately poured out, it being deemed lucky to have two of everything, two denoting a happy couple. At other times Lin Chih-yang held his liquor as well as any man but, his inside having been many days empty, he was caught unawares, after his second cup, by the floor and ceiling slowly gyrating, and barely managed to keep his seat. The King drank a few more cups and asked for the time. His Majesty's pocket watch having been brought, after one glance the King declared the feast at an end.

A smile now lit up the King's flushed cheeks; his misty eyes leered; he said merrily, 'It is late, my love. Time for bed.' Servants of the bedchamber came forward to undress the bridal pair; they removed Lin's jewellery and ceremonial garments, and the King, too, divested himself of his outer robes. Then stretching out both hands with their jade-like fingers, the King firmly held Lin's wrists and dragged the new Concubine after him into the bedchamber, where they ascended the royal couch and, the sharkskin bed-curtains[1] having been lowered, reposed for the night.

Thus did the King celebrate the royal wedding. In the Government Guest House, T'ang Ao gave rein to his imagination, reckoning a postponement of the happy event as a certainty. As the evening wore on, however, and he waited anxiously for news, some old men returning from the Palace called at the Guest House and told how the army had been called out to crush the revolt. Their story sent a shock through T'ang Ao, who turned ashen pale. Tuo the coxswain, on the contrary, now found his tongue. 'The wedding deferred in deference to the people's wishes? What has happened to your confident prediction, Master T'ang? Eh, quite the opposite, do you now say? Mind you, the guards actually opened fire, and the King's army

[1] *Chiao-hsiao chang*. As described in *Hung-lou meng*, chapter 92, (Yü edition, IV, p. 123), Chiao-hsiao was a fabulously thin and light fabric manufactured from the skin of the shark and used as curtains or netting in the Palace. It was of foreign origin and a large piece of it was priced at five thousand silver taels.

is to stamp out any further revolt. From what we have just heard, the King is a real lecher, utterly indifferent to the welfare of his people.—So from tomorrow we draw our pay as river dredgers and clean out their river channels for them? A sailor must try his fortune, but we deceive ourselves if we expect Master Lin back.' To hide his confusion, T'ang Ao resorted to scratching his head. In the meantime, the Royal Brother-in-law had sent his steward with bedding for T'ang Ao and Tuo, together with a team of servants, who were placed at the disposal of the two visitors. The steward made a speech: 'My master, the Royal Brother-in-law, sends his best compliments. It being late tonight, my master is unable to call, but will himself attend upon our honoured guests after the morning audience, to discuss the repairing of the river channel. Our guests will kindly overlook any unintended negligence, for which my master will apologize in person.' With this, the steward departed, followed by the old men who had brought the news.

The next day, T'ang Ao and his companion waited in the Guest House for the Royal Brother-in-law, who failed, however, to appear. Late at night, the old helmsman set out to make inquiries and only then learnt that the Royal Brother-in-law's residence was completely hemmed in by the people, who had swarmed there, impatient for news. The report caused T'ang Ao a sleepless night. When they rose at dawn on the third day, Tuo remarked, 'Well, Master T'ang, one more day in the land of women! Don't take it amiss, but at this rate we shan't sail for home until they've presented us with red eggs.'[1] T'ang Ao cried: 'What do you mean?' The helmsman then said: 'It's two days they've been married, good Master Lin and the female King. Let a few more days elapse and we may expect to hear of an heir on the way. Next comes the birth of the infant prince, at which red eggs are certain to be distributed, a large share falling to yourself as brother-in-law to the King's concubine.' Annoyed and perplexed, T'ang Ao did not answer but continued to wait for the Royal Brother-in-law.

The latter, after pacifying the crowd on the evening of the wedding, duly attended at the Palace in the morning. His Majesty was, however, now reported to be indisposed: no

[1] Hen's eggs with shells dyed red, distributed among relations and friends after the birth of a child.

audiences were to be held that day. Debarred from the King's presence, the Royal Brother-in-law paced the audience chamber and courtyards, tormented by anxiety yet powerless to act. Word was meanwhile brought that his own house had been surrounded many times over by the people, who were clamouring for the King's reply, and not being ready with the promised reply, he could not face them. He was afraid, too, of T'ang Ao escaping and ordered a strong guard to be posted at the city gates; and he sent men at intervals with food and wine to the Government Guest House, and others with pole loads of fish and meat, and chickens and ducks, to T'ang Ao's ship as a gesture of goodwill, while he himself watched his time. And that night he slept in the main audience chamber in the Palace.

On the third day, the King rose before dawn, highly displeased. The Royal Brother-in-law having been summoned, His Majesty asked abruptly: 'Where is the woman now who answered our Proclamation?' The Royal Brother-in-law replied: 'That person is lodged in the Government Guest House but, having waited in vain for Your Majesty's commission, is understood to be on the point of leaving for her homeland.' The King then said: 'We must have some assurance that the woman knows what she is about. If she proves indeed capable of regulating our rivers and watercourses, considerations for the lives of our people are naturally nearest our heart, and we shall be prepared even to relinquish our Royal Concubine. To be sure, so momentous a sacrifice is contingent upon the woman successfully carrying our her task. Our plan, therefore, is to keep the new Concubine in the Palace until such time as the flooding has been relieved. Thus in the event of the repairs not proceeding according to plan or yielding no results and our treasury depleted to no purpose, we would hold the Concubine hostage and the woman may redeem her — if need be, at some later date — with silver to the amount wasted in the venture. What does our Brother-in-law say to the plan?' Overjoyed, the courtier cried eagerly: 'An excellent one, Your Majesty! With the guaranty for any potential losses to Your Majesty's treasury, it would curb extravagant spending. It would calm and comfort the people. And if the regulating of the rivers should indeed succeed, a great evil would have been removed from our land. A master-stroke of statecraft, Your Majesty!' Upon which, the King dismissed him, saying, 'Then act upon it, good

Brother-in-law!'

The Royal Brother-in-law now went straight to the Government Guest House, where he met T'ang Ao, with whom he exchanged civilities. For the King's relative was a nobleman with the surname She,[1] under fifty years of age, with a smooth chin and a high-pitched voice reminiscent of a eunuch. When tea had been served, the courtier began in earnest: 'The people of our land congregated yesterday outside the gates of the Royal Palace and gave a full and moving account of how our honoured guest, deeply affected by reports of persistent flooding of our fields and valleys, has come forward to deliver them from danger and destruction. Being at the time engaged with other business at court, I was unable to attend upon our guest, for which omission I crave our guest's indulgence. In regard, Sir, to your honourable relative, who was suddenly taken ill while displaying her wares and has since lain on a sick-bed in the Palace, be assured that, as soon as she regains her health, she will be safely escorted back to the ship. As for the preposterous story of her having been made a Royal Concubine, we rely on our guest's good sense for his lending no credence to such idle rumours. Now to the relief of the floods—I stand ready to be instructed in the subject.'

T'ang Ao then held forth: 'The exact cause of the inundation in this most remarkable country is, of course, still to be ascertained. Not having inspected the flooded areas, I would not hazard an opinion. But, in general, the mitigation of floods may be traced back to the great Yü,[2] who, we learn, dredged the

---

[1] *K'un*, the female, as opposed to *Ch'ien*, the male.

[1] Yü, who according to the legendary account in the Book of History (*Shu ching*), brought the floods under control in the reign of the Emperor Shun and, himself succeeding to the throne, founded the Hsia dynasty. 'From beyond the western bounds of the present China proper, Yü is represented as tracking the great rivers, here burning the woods, hewing the rocks, and cutting through the mountains that obstructed their progress, and there deepening their channels until their waters flow peacefully into the eastern seas . . .' (Legge, *The Shu King* or Book of Historical Documents, 1879, Introduction, p. 16). 'Yü the Great controlled the waters . . . Probably no other people in the world have preserved a mass of legendary material into which it is so clearly possible to trace back the engineering problems of remote times. The essentials of the story are that two culture-heroes of civil engineering were successively put in charge of regulating and controlling the floods and rivers by legendary emperors; the first, Kun, failed, but the second, Yü, succeeded,' Kun being the patron and inventor of dikes, embankments and walls, whereas Yü 'opened the courses of the nine rivers, conducting

nine great rivers. Now 'dredge' is the keyword in river engineering:[1] so to dredge the various streams as to cause them all to flow freely, each leading to some other stream or, alternatively, to a lake or the sea. Thus the water should be traced to its source and conducted to its outlet. Once the source is kept clear of sand and gravel, and the middle section unobstructed, the river can no longer cause devastation. These, however, are but ill-considered views, rashly expressed. The Royal Brother-in-law must instruct me further when we have examined the river itself.' And the nobleman repeatedly nodded his head in assent.[2]

The story goes that when the Royal Brother-in-law had heard T'ang Ao's learned exposition, he nodded with approval and cried: 'My honoured guest, you have suddenly made it all clear to me with that one word "dredge"! And I bow before your superior wisdom. It would seem, then, that we might expect a speedy end to all flooding in our land. For the present, I must take my leave in order to report to the throne, but tomorrow I will accompany you on a tour of the inundated region.' And having ordered the servants to prepare a sumptuous dinner for their distinguished guest and to serve him with the utmost care and diligence, the Royal Brother-in-law mounted his sedan-chair and departed with his train of attendants.

The old coxswain now remarked: 'It is curious how Master Lin, who appeared irrevocably lost to us when the army was called out night before last, would seem now to be on the point of joining us again. Perhaps the wedding ceremony never took place — I wonder!' T'ang Ao, too, said thoughtfully, 'It would certainly be the influence of the populace then. For fear of the people breaking out in revolt, the King might have postponed the whole affair.' Tuo continued: 'Time enough to find that out. But to come back to that river, I hope you will agree it requires careful handling. The slightest mishap and not only must Master Lin remain forever in the harem, but we ourselves would be doomed to perpetual servitude to these women. It is not as if a sailor worries easily either. What plan are you putting forward

them to the four seas and deepening the canals. The motive of dredging the beds of waterways is always connected with the work of Yü' (Needham, vol. IV, part 3, chapter 28f(4)).
[1] See Introduction.
[2] The end of chapter 35, the formula: 'As to what happened next, it shall be told in the following chapter' being omitted in the translation.

when we have looked over the floods tomorrow?' T'ang Ao
replied: 'The inspection need only be a formality: my plan has
been ready for some time. After all, when a river overflows its
banks, either its channel is choked or it has no proper outlet or
it is turbid at the source. When we have actually seen where
the flooding occurs, I shall start by deepening the channel
there,[1] then widen the river's surface along the whole of that
stretch, and finally check the flow of the stream into its outlet.
Once the river has been both deepened and widened, its capacity is greatly increased; and with the increased capacity and
unobstructed current, there would be no flooding.'

The helmsman exclaimed with barely concealed impatience:
'Nothing could be simpler! Would they not have thought of
these expedients before?' T'ang Ao said, 'When you went
back on board the ship yesterday to give them the news, I
called two of the servants before me, and it became clear in the
course of my conversation with them that little in the way of
copper and iron is produced in this land. Furthermore, to prevent crime and armed uprisings, the possession of weapons and
even edge-tools is prohibited, most families possessing only
bamboo knives; only the rich occasionally use silver knives,
which are considered a rarity. As for digging and dredging, the
very implements are unknown to them. But, as luck would have
it, we have tons of cast iron laid up in the hold![2] Tomorrow,
therefore, I will prepare sketches of the implements needed,
and teach them how to make them. The situation, my friend, is
by no means irretrievable.'[3]

The following day, the Royal Brother-in-law took T'ang Ao
outside the city to inspect the offending river, and again on the
day after. Upon their return, T'ang Ao said: 'It is clear from
our careful inspection of the past two days that the flooding is
due precisely to the omission of dredging, the subject of my
previous discourse. To take the level of the river in relation to
its banks—the dikes on either side are as high as hillocks,[4] and

[1] See notes on last two pages and Introduction, there being no mention of
dikes in T'ang Ao's plan.
[2] The tons of cast iron were brought along as merchandise by T'ang Ao
and accepted with great reluctance by Lin; see chapter 8, p. 45 and Introduction.
[3] Some facetious comments by Tuo that follow are here omitted.
[4] An unmistakable reference to the Yellow River: '. . . reliance has been
placed exclusively on dyke building. These dykes have not been built as
one concerted scheme but piecemeal, locality by locality. Generally their

the river, too, is almost as high; yet its channel is of no great
depth so that it holds no more water than a shallow dish of that
size and is ready to overspill at any moment. Such a state of
affairs first came about through the setting up of dikes and embankments at a time when the river was already rising and
threatening to overflow its banks. But once the danger was
averted and the water had receded, no further thought was
given to the preventive measure of deepening the channel
through dredging; instead, more and higher dikes were built
whenever the river rose again. The depositing of silt year after
year, however, kept on raising the river bed until now it is as
if you had a bath tub placed on the ridge tiles: if the tub overflows, the water rushes down a slope to drench a whole area
and turn it into a lake. To protect the surrounding area, you
must sink the tub in the earth so that its bottom is much lower
than the level of the ground, thus reducing the risk of violent
outbreaks, and this may be accomplished by thorough digging
and dredging. Your shallow dish would then be transformed
into a cauldron with ample capacity for the current even at its
greatest, and you need have no fear of any inundation.'

The Royal Brother-in-law readily agreeing with the diagnosis, proceeded to ask about tools for dredging. T'ang Ao
gave a further discourse on the need for labour and the futility
of half-hearted measures such as reliance on the force of the
current itself for the removal of silt, finally offering the iron in
the hold of their vessel for the making of dredging tools. The
noble courtier, having repeatedly nodded his head in approval,

constructors have favoured building the dykes 5 to 8 miles (8 to 12km.)
apart, thus allowing the river plenty of room with the idea that when it
was in spate it would be accommodated. The trouble has been that . . .
the river is very slow and consequently deposits much of its load of silt on
the bed. As time has gone on the bed has been continually raised in this
way and this, in its turn, has necessitated constant raising of the dykes,
with a result that today the bed of the river stands higher than the
surrounding country. As one approaches the river, it looks like an endless,
uniform range of low hills.' (Tregear, *A Geography of China*, p.218).
See also Needham, vol.IV, part 3, chapter 28f(2): '. . . for two thousand
years the Yellow River has been enclosed with dykes, constantly in-
creasing in dimensions. Every few years the river would rise to levels
which threatened to overflow them, or else the meanders of the low-water
channel would carry the river against an embankment and cause its
collapse . . .'; '. . . the bed of the Yellow River has risen by about three
feet per century. In some places it has been necessary to build dykes up
6ft. per annum for stretches of 20 or 30 miles to combat the huge silt
deposits.'

promised the entire national labour force;[1] he also gave orders for craftsmen from all over the city to be in attendance early the next day, and large numbers of labourers also, to carry out whatever tasks were required of them. The Royal Brother-in-law then taking his leave, T'ang Ao drew sketches of various dredging tools,[2] while Tuo was entrusted with the unloading of the iron. In the morning, the craftsmen having been assembled, T'ang Ao showed them the designs and, after giving detailed instructions, made them light their furnaces and forge the metal parts of the implements. Now, though these artisans were dressed like men, they were really women and, therefore, clever and adroit, unlike your clumsy louts who looked blank even when you had talked yourself hoarse; these, on the contrary, needed but the merest hint to see what was expected of them, so that within two or three days they had all the tools ready, whereupon an auspicious day was chosen for work on the river itself to begin.

On the appointed day, the Royal Brother-in-law went to the flooded area with T'ang Ao, who directed that a series of mud embankments be erected across the river, thus breaking it up into many sections. Next, through the use of chain-pumps worked by water-wheels,[2] every other section was drained and the water emptied into its adjoining section. The drained section having then been dug and the channel much deepened, the embankment dividing it from its adjoining section was removed and the water allowed to flow back into the first section with its vastly increased capacity; the adjoining section itself was now dug and a deeper channel formed. All along the inundated part of the river, men were digging with might and main. It was at first found difficult to remove the mud scooped up from the river-bed; large baskets were then lowered into the pits and, when they were filled, hoisted up by means of a windlass[2] with unstinted exertion. For the people of that land had for years

[1] 'The Royal Brother-in-law readily agreeing with the diagnosis . . . promised the entire national labour force' being the translator's summary of the rest of the conversation between the nobleman and T'ang Ao (pp. 254–5). Removal of silt by the force of the current itself was a method first tried out with success by P'an Chi-hsün; see *Ming shih*, c. 84, 'Yellow River' B. As regards labour — 'One cannot too much emphasize the role of man-power in the ancient and mediaeval achievements of Chinese civil engineering' (Needham, vol. IV, part 3, chapter 28f(5)).

[2] The interested reader is referred to Needham, vol. IV, part 2, pp. 330–362 (chapters 27g(1–6)), esp. figures 574 and 582.

been harassed by the floods, so that directly work on the river was begun, the whole country joined in, digging and dredging and building dikes. Thus within ten days the task set by T'ang Ao was completed. And they further checked the flow of the current, continuing to dig and dredge as they went along. And the people observed that T'ang Ao was at the river from dawn to dusk,[1] utterly unsparing of himself as he superintended the progress of the work, and their gratitude and admiration knew no bounds. The elders of the land made a collection, commissioned his portrait, and set up a shrine with huge characters inscribed in gold on an overhanging horizontal tablet: 'Overflowing Benevolence.'[2]

Reports of T'ang Ao's success in subjugating the river reached the Palace and, before long, were conveyed to Lin Chih-yang by one of the royal princes. For when, after the wedding, Lin ascended the royal couch hand in hand with the monarch of the Women's Kingdom, he suddenly recalled how, after their visit to the Black Teeth Country with its learned women,[3] T'ang Ao had teased him about having to be rescued from the hordes of females in the Women's Kingdom. And he thought to himself: 'Why, this has indeed come to pass! What a strange premonition on my brother-in-law's part! At the time, old Tuo had actually said, "And supposing you really were detained in the Women's Country, what would you do?" And without a moment's hesitation I had replied: "Why, if they did detain me feigning ignorance would be my best defence."[4] That, too, having been spoken in jest, might be an omen! Yes, since this female king is determined to have me, why don't I act the insensate statue and, like a clay figure or block of wood, feign ignorance of warmth and animation? Precious time could be

[1] T'ang Ao's tireless exertion is true to the type of the Chinese 'tamer of waters' beginning with the great Yü, the latest example being the author's own father, Li Chieh-t'ing; see Introduction.
[2] More prosaically, 'His benevolence shall last for as long as the river itself'. See, e.g., the description of the temples dedicated to the great river engineer, Li Ping, and his son, Li Erh-lang, builders of the immense irrigation system on the Chengtu plain in Szechuan in the third century B.C., in Needham, vol. IV, part 3, chapter 28f(7).
[3] The Black Teeth Country was a country of bluestockings, whose learning so overawed T'ang Ao and his companions that they trembled at the prospect of further disputations in the Women's Kingdom (chapter 19; the jokes about the Women's Kingdom are on p. 134). In the translation, the sentence has been expanded to allow room for the allusions.
[4] Defence from being drawn into learned arguments.

with this news I have hurried here.'

Jubilant with relief, Lin cried: 'What have I not owed to you, my dear prince, ever since His Majesty consigned me to these upstair rooms? But if I leave tomorrow, shall I ever see you again? At least I hope to return your great kindness at some future date.' Observing no one to be near them, the prince suddenly knelt before Lin and, bursting into tears, confided: 'Royal mother! I am in extreme danger. Help me! Remember what little filial piety I have shown you and throw open the gates of mercy in your heart, that I might yet be saved!' Lin helped the young prince to his feet and asked: 'What is this danger that you speak of, prince? Tell me at once!' The prince then told his story—'It was six years ago that, at the age of eight, I was chosen heir to the throne. Such, however, was my misfortune that my own mother, the Queen, died last year; and now, another—whom I must also call "royal mother"—has become the favourite, whose sole purpose is for her own son to supplant me, in furtherance of which she sought on numerous occasions to destroy me, though without success. Lately her calumny has so wrought upon my father, the King, that he, too, has turned against me and appears eager to have me removed. Now, therefore, is the time to betake myself to flight; for if I remain, I should never escape her deadly clutches. My father sets out in ten days[1] to attend the birthday celebrations of the King of the Yellow Emperor's Descendants.[2] The vicegerent and other ministers who shall be left in charge, the palace servants, the government officials, all are of her faction. Being young and inexperienced and having, moreover, pored too long over my books, I am without even a confidant, far less a party of followers to keep a constant watch over my safety. One careless step and my life could be forfeit! Royal mother, have pity on me and, when you return to the ship tomorrow, take me with you! If I am delivered from this den of perils, believe me, even to my dying day I shall be grateful to you.'

Lin Chih-yang almost screamed: 'But you will have to dress

---

[1] 'Ten days' is taken from the Prince's speech in the next chapter.

[2] The Hsien-yüan, a long-lived nation, whose King was celebrating his thousandth birthday. Hsien-yüan happens to be T'ang Ao and Lin's next port of call; the Palace there being thrown open to all for the royal birthday celebrations, Lin Chih-yang finds himself, for a few embarrassing moments, face to face again with the monarch of the Women's Kingdom. See *Ching hua yüan*, chapters 38, 39; also Introduction.

like a woman if you go with me to the Celestial Country — so much do our customs at home differ from those of your Women's Kingdom! My prince, you have always been accustomed to the freedom of a man's life. How could you possibly endure the ways of women? And don't forget the rigours of hairdressing and foot-binding!' The crown prince, however, declared: 'I must just adopt your ways, then. For if I escape with my life, I should be content with even the humblest lot in the company of my royal mother.' Lin then said: 'But what if the maids of honour should discover us leaving the Palace together? Would it not be better if I went on board first and you, my prince, then joined me secretly?' The Crown Prince shook his head[1] and replied: 'I may not leave the Palace without good cause, and even then only under escort. There is not the least chance of my boarding the ship by myself! Since, however, the waiting women are seldom in attendance now, I shall hide in the sedan tomorrow before you are seated and, unnoticed, be carried to the ship with you. Do allow me to come with you, royal mother.' To which Lin replied: 'If you can contrive this in secret, my prince, I shall naturally be at your service.'

The next day, however, His Majesty sent a sedan-chair with bearers for Lin's return to the ship and commanded that the maids of honour all attend on him as he changed into male garments and mounted the sedan. The crown prince stood apart from the crowd and, being almost in despair, shed many secret tears. As Lin was entering the sedan, the prince rushed up and whispered urgently in his ear: 'Our movements are watched and I cannot now leave with you; but my life is in your hands, good royal mother. Rescue me within ten days, or we may never see each other again. Remember, I live in the Peony Tower.[2] Remember!' And he followed the sedan a few steps until, suddenly breaking into sobs, he returned to his own apartments.

Thus Lin Chih-yang found himself once more on board his ship, where T'ang Ao and Tuo the coxswain had preceded him, having at the King's command been escorted there the previous day by a procession of courtiers and a band. When Lin saw

[1] The end of chapter 36, the formula 'As to what happened next . . .' being here omitted.
[2] See note on p. 456. The Crown Prince is the reincarnation of the Fairy of the Peony.

T'ang Ao and Tuo, he thanked them again and again for his deliverance. Joy and grief intermingled in his reunion with his wife and his daughter, Wan-ju,[1] whose companion, Lan-yin,[2] he also rejoiced to see again. Then turning to T'ang Ao, he said: 'When I took you, brother-in-law, as a passenger, all you wanted was to see the lands across the seas. But now you have saved my life and become my benefactor! I was often tempted in my state of captivity to do away with myself, but a dream about an immortal coming to my aid[3] made me endure it all in patience. It was surely no immortal that delivered me, but my own brother-in-law!' The coxswain, too, said: 'It was no co-incidence you had Master T'ang with you on this journey—it was Providence! I remember now that, after our visit to the Black Teeth Country, Master T'ang said that he would repay your kindness by rescuing you from all the women,[4] which has indeed come to pass. It would seem that, unknown to us, this strange mishap was presaged even then.'

Suddenly T'ang Ao cried out: 'My dear brother-in-law! Why are you shuffling along with such mincing steps? Don't tell me the King really had your feet bound!' Laughter getting the better of his shame and embarrassment, Lin said in a tone of disgust: 'He might have contented himself with treating me like a woman and his concubine. But no! it had to be authentic down to the last detail—piercing the ears, footbinding and all. My poor feet felt as hedged in as a new bride and as sorely pressed as a new teacher taking his first class, so smothered they were all day and night! To cap it all, the waiting women boiled monkey's bones and bathed my feet in the broth to hasten their contraction. A strange concoction indeed for one's foot-bath! So heady and potent it was that, though my feet have since been loosened, I am still like a man half-drunk, unsteady and weak-kneed. And to think that on the day I set off with my inventory of goods, a black spider actually landed on my feet! To judge by the amount of attention they received, my feet enjoyed

[1] Wan-ju, Lin Chih-yang's daughter, reincarnation of the fairy of the *jasminum grandiflorum* (*su-hsing*).
[2] Lan-yin, Orchid Voice, daughter of the interpreter in the Forked Tongue Country; see Introduction. She joins the ship in search of a cure for her illness (chapter 30, pp. 212–21).
[3] An immortal, etc., being a hint of the immortal existence T'ang Ao was later to attain.
[4] See p. 455, n. 3 above. Here, too, the sentence has been padded to bring out the point of the allusion.

more luck than was good for them!'

His daughter, Wan-ju, then exclaimed: 'You've still got gold ear-rings on, father! Let me remove them for you.' Thus reminded, Lin went on: 'And the waiting woman who pierced my ear-lobes — I do believe she would have had her will of me, dead or alive! For she seized one ear at a time and gave a fierce stab, at the recollection of which my ear-lobes know the excruciating pain again. And it was all because those wretched apes in the Land of Flames had burnt my beard,[1] so that, with my smooth chin, I appeared a far younger man to the King, which led to disaster! — But I hear that, besides sending my brother-in-law back to the ship in state, the King also offered a reward of ten thousand ounces of silver. Has this money been paid?'

T'ang Ao replied: 'It has been paid, but how did *you* know about it?' Lin then recounted in each particular how the crown prince had continually brought him news and looked after him throughout, and at the very last solemnly invoked his help in effecting his, the Prince's, own escape. When he had heard the story, T'ang Ao declared: 'If the prince is in danger, it is incumbent on us to rescue him; all the more so, since he has befriended you. Let us repay his kindness, too, by saving *him* from all those women![2] His plight must truly be desperate who would throw away a kingdom's inheritance to adopt a female disguise in a strange land, and we really cannot set sail without him. What says my friend Tuo?' The helmsman replied: 'Repay his kindness and rescue him, too, from all the women — by all means! But how shall we do it? Without careful planning, such a venture could never succeed. You were a good many days in the Palace, Master Lin, and would be familiar with its layout; you might know of some means of effecting this.' T'ang Ao then asked: 'Is the Crown Prince at all like the Prince of the Forked Tongue Country?[3] If he is a good horseman and ready with his bows and arrows, we should soon have him with us.' Lin replied: 'The Prince is of course a girl in her teens, though dressed like a man — she is unlikely to be much of an archer or

[1] See p. 425, n. 2; and Introduction.
[2] 'Repay his kindness,' etc. takes up the joke on the preceding page.
[3] Forked Tongue Country, a land of phoneticians; see *Ching hua yüan*, chapters 28–31, and Introduction. The Prince of the Forked Tongue Country fell off his horse while hunting, but was brought back to life by Tuo the coxswain (pp. 205–7).

horsewoman. But, good brother-in-law, if you really mean to save the Prince, help from you alone will suffice; no others would avail.' T'ang Ao cried: 'Talk of taking up arms in a good cause! I am never among the tardiest. What is your plan then?'

Lin said: 'It is simply this. Tonight, when it is dark, you will carry me on your back and, with me as guide, scale the Palace walls,[1] find the Prince and rescue him.' T'ang Ao demurred: 'The Palace is enormous. Do you know where the Crown Prince lives?' Lin replied: 'At our parting this morning, the Prince whispered in my ear that he was staying in the Peony Tower. —Their peonies grow to such a height that, to see them properly, you have to lean from a tower.[2]—Once within the Palace, we shall look out for peonies: where they grow thick, we should find our Tower and Prince.' T'ang Ao now expressed agreement, saying 'Let us at least sally forth tonight, make reconnaissance and decide on further action.' But the old helmsman broke out in loud protest—'Hold, gentlemen! Master Lin is, to be sure, under a real obligation to the Crown Prince and Master T'ang zealous in a worthy cause, and in your selfless devotion you think to defy the sanctity of the Palace precincts. Pray consider. Are there no guards outside the walls? No watchmen patrolling the grounds? Supposing you gentlemen did enter the Palace and were then caught—have you allowed for that in your plan? Listen to me, an old man, and deliberate further. Rashness makes a poor beginning to so dangerous an enterprise.' T'ang Ao, however, protested—'Not rashness, Master Coxswain! On the contrary, we shall exercise great caution, my brother-in-law and I, and watch our every step when we are near the Palace. Set your mind at rest, Master Tuo.'

Having supped by late afternoon, T'ang Ao changed out of his scholar's robe into short garments. Lin Chih-yang also girded himself for the expedition; his old shoes being much too large for him, a sailor went ashore and obtained a pair—

[1] After swallowing a divine herb on East Mouth Mountain early in their voyage, T'ang Ao finds that he could leap to a height of fifty or sixty feet (chapter 9, pp. 51–3).
[2] 'The choicest kinds of moutan were grafted by inserting buds in stocks transplanted from the wild. Many varieties were also developed by grafting on the herbaceous peony. One fanciful kind of moutan, over 10 feet in height, was said to have been grafted on the Chinese mahogany tree (*Cedrela sinensis*) so that the flowers could be viewed from an upstairs window.' H.L.Li, *The Garden Flowers of China*, pp. 26–7.

'men's size', Women's Kingdom—that fitted him. By the time their preparations were complete, it was already dusk, but Mistress Lin, fearful of further enterprise, began to remonstrate with her husband, who however was not to be dissuaded. Thus with a hurried 'Adieu!' to the coxswain, Lin departed with Tʻang Ao for the city, eventually reaching the Palace wall. There being no one about, Tʻang Ao bore Lin on his back as planned, and leapt with ease on to the wall, where they paused to find their bearings. Within, the watchman's bell and rattle sounded from court after court. They passed over several more high walls, when at last the bell and rattle grew faint and distant. Tʻang Ao said in a hushed voice: 'Hark, brother-in-law! Not even the cawing of a crow or magpie! The stillness itself is forbidding. We must now be in the inner courts.' Pointing with his finger, Lin said: 'See where the high shrubs are? That structure should be the Peony Tower. Let us alight there.'

As directed, Tʻang Ao descended into the court. Lin slid down from his back, but no sooner were their feet upon the ground than two huge dogs swooped upon them from behind a grotto, barking furiously and biting their clothes. The watchmen being now alerted, converged swiftly upon the scene of the noise, lanterns in hand. Thus taken by surprise, Tʻang Ao frantically shook off the dog and, with a sudden leap, regained the high wall. The watchmen rushed up to Lin, shone their lanterns upon him, and shouted: 'Ah, a woman thief!' But a court attendant who had also appeared, cried: 'Hush, you fools! It's the new Royal Concubine—yet dressed so queerly and alone in this court late at night! Still, it is not for us to ask questions. The King is at the Palace banquet, and I shall at once report to His Majesty.' Forthwith Lin was escorted to Sunshine Pavilion, where the banquet was in progress. When the King's eyes once more alighted upon Lin's face, that former ardour, though for some little while cooled, revived in full blaze in the royal bosom. His Majesty spoke. 'We did of course send you back to the ship, woman. Why, then, are you here again? Explain yourself.' Lin could find no ready answer and remained dumb.

The King was pleased to be amused and said with a smirk: 'We have understood you. When it came to the point, you were not prepared to forsake the splendour of these halls and have returned in the hope of gaining our favour anew. Since, then, you express yourself willing, for our part, we never dwell on past errors. Only, from tonight you really must have your feet bound properly, and we shall in due course instal you in the Royal Apartments. Behave yourself, woman, and mend your stubborn ways: you shall be amply recompensed.' The King then commanded that Lin be sent to his former upstair apartment and dressed in feminine attire as before, and that the same maids of honour and women wait upon him; and further, that the successful completion of the footbinding be immediately reported, to be followed by preparations for the installation.

The maids of honour and waiting women received their commands, helped Lin up the stairs and, having dipped him in a perfumed bath, arrayed him once more in embroidered garments. Before they could proceed to combing his hair and binding his feet, however, Lin thought to himself: 'I am, alas, again trapped, but at least my brother-in-law is moving about freely on the high walls; he will know where I am and is certain to rescue me. At all costs, therefore, I must ward off these women from my regenerate feet!' So he said aloud to the waiting women: 'I re-entered the Palace of my own accord, and this time am fully as anxious as you to accomplish the footbinding in order to hasten the blissful event. On no account would I allow any of you to tamper with my feet and delay the process of contraction. Besides, if I am kindly treated, when I am installed in the Royal Apartments yonder, I shall remember you all kindly; and if harshly treated? — I, too, shall remember the harshness and requite you accordingly! Tra-la-la, the King, my sun, will shine upon me! Heads will start rolling and the Royal Concubines themselves shall implore my mercy!'

The maids of honour and waiting women now recalled the occasion on which, following upon their complaints, Lin had been beaten; quaking at the thought of his revenge, they grovelled and kowtowed, begging the new Concubine to forgive their past misdeeds and spare them for the future. Lin went on: 'It is of the future that I speak, not the past. Rise now and banish all fear. If you will obey me in three things, I shall gladly be merciful.' The women got up and shouted: 'We shall obey you in a hundred, gracious lady. Tell us *which* three!' Lin then said, 'First, I will look after the business of footbinding and powder application and every detail of the toilet myself. It shall be none of your concern. Do you hear?' The women replied, 'We hear and obey.' Lin continued: 'Next, when the Crown

Prince and I are at conference, you will remove yourselves from our presence. Do you hear?' The women cried: 'We shall obey you in this, too. What is the third thing?' Lin said, 'There are many rooms on this upper floor; instead of crowding into my bedroom, you shall all sleep in another room. Do you hear?' The women heard but remained silent. Lin went on: 'I suppose you are worried about my escaping if left alone in the night. Very well, I shall take the inner room and you can all stay in the outer one, adjoining the staircase; and you can have the windows of my room locked up every night and the keys removed. Not satisfied yet with these precautions? Would I have come back had I wished to escape?' The women, hearing this, cried in unison: 'We shall obey you in all three!' And they busily set up beds while Lin made a show of binding his own feet with great vehemence, which soon allayed their suspicions. It being then the second watch, the maids of honour locked the windows, removed the keys, and went to sleep; before long, loud snoring[1] broke out from every corner of the room.

Towards the third watch, Lin Chih-yang, who lay awake expectantly, heard a tap at the window. Hurrying to it from his bed, he asked softly: 'Are you there, brother-in-law?' T'ang Ao's answer came through clearly—'I had to shake off that dog, but from above the walls I followed your movements and remained up there when I saw them escorting you to this room. The others are sound asleep. Open the window now and come with me.' Lin, however, replied: 'The windows are fast and the keys hidden. Our plan would miscarry if we woke up the women. Go back now but return tomorrow evening, when I shall have seen the Prince again. We shall have a red lantern hanging outside the window: at the sign of a red lantern, come at once to our rescue. Leave me now!' T'ang Ao assenting, Lin then heard a whiz and knew he was gone.

The next day, the Crown Prince came to visit the new Concubine, having heard about her return. When Lin explained his presence in the Palace, the Prince was overcome with gratitude; but recovering himself, though still with tears in his eyes, he said: 'This is the eve of my birthday. Good royal mother, command your women to prepare a feast in my honour and have it sent to the Tower. I will attend to the rest.' Lin nodded and presently gave orders to this effect. When it was almost dark,

[1]The waiting women were really men.

the Prince sent one of his own servants to invite the ladies from the upper storey to join in the birthday eve feast. The Prince's invitation started a flutter; the maids of honour were impatient to be gone, and Lin readily granted permission to one and all.

Now when the Prince saw the maids of honour and waiting women all gathered at the Tower and seated, he himself went across to Lin's apartments, opened the window and hung out a red lantern in the dark. From high above, a figure suddenly descended and entered. Realizing it could only be T'ang Ao, the Prince knelt down, but T'ang Ao pulled him up, saying, 'Do I see the Crown Prince?' Upon Lin nodding repeatedly in confirmation of this, T'ang Ao declared: 'There's not a moment to lose. Let us go!' And he carried Lin, as before, on his back, but held the young prince in his arms; then, with a bound, he regained the nearest wall. They crossed several more high walls before alighting outside the Palace, where the Prince was gently laid down and Lin also dismounted from T'ang Ao's shoulders. A faint moon having risen to guide their steps, the three walked towards the city wall, which they scaled in the same fashion. When at last they reached the ship, Tuo the coxswain welcomed them on board and immediately weighed anchor. Thus they sailed in the dark from the Women's Kingdom.

The Crown Prince changed out of his royal robes into the dress of a Chinese young woman and, kneeling before the merchant Lin Chih-yang, called him 'father', and again before Mistress Lin, called her 'mother'; the girls, Wan-ju and Lan-yin, being then introduced, they took to one another at once. But it was old Tuo, who, joining them later, asked the name of the Crown Prince, which turned out to be: Woman Like Flower.[1] When T'ang Ao heard the name 'Flower', the dream that had appeared to him before he set out on the voyage flashed through his mind again . . .[2]

[1] Yin Jo-hua, i.e. Female Like Flower.

[2] This is the end of chapter 37. The dream occurs in chapter 7: a temple god, who turns out to be the God of Dreams, tells T'ang Ao to seek out the twelve lost flowers across the seas and bring them back to China (pp. 39–40). At the beginning of chapter 38 (p. 266), T'ang Ao goes over the names of the young women they had met on the voyage and finds that each contains the name of a flower, e.g. Lan-yin (Orchid Voice). The Prince, Yin Jo-hua, being the twelfth, completes the list of 'lost flowers'. See Introduction.